Always Merry and Bright

By JAY MARTIN

Conrad Aiken: A Life of His Art
Harvests of Change: American Literature 1865-1914
Twentieth Century Interpretations of "The Waste Land" (editor)
Nathanael West: The Art of His Life
Robert Lowell
Twentieth Century Views of Nathanael West (editor)
A Singer in The Dawn (editor)
The Paul Laurence Dunbar Reader (editor)
Always Merry and Bright: The Life of Henry Miller

Always Merry and Bright

THE LIFE OF HENRY MILLER

An Unauthorized Biography

Jay Martin

CAPRA PRESS

Santa Barbara

1978

SHELDON PRESS
London
1979

All photographs not otherwise credited are from Henry Miller's collection through the courtesy of the Miller family, Henry, Valentine and Tony.

First grouping: 173 (top) by Brassai, ca. 1933; 174 (bottom) by Mary Willis; 175 (bottom) by Arthur Knight; 176 (middle) by Pat Pence; 176 (bottom) by Yukichi Watabe. *Second grouping:* 341 (top) by Hal Baird; 341 (bottom) by Wynn Bullock; 345 (top) by Edgar W. D. Holcomb; 345 (bottom) by Jose Alemany; 346 (top) UCLA Special Collections; 346 (bottom) by Geoffrey Palmer; 348 (top) by Alfredo Valente; 348 (bottom) by Tony Miller; 349 (top) by Christian de bois Larson; 349 (bottom) by Wynn Bullock; 350 (bottom) by Bishop; 351 (top r.) by William Webb; 351 (bottom) by Pat Pence. *Third grouping:* 495 by William Webb; 498 by Emil White; 499 (top l. & r.) by William Webb; 499 (bottom r.) by Georgia Longini; 500 (top) by William Webb; 500 (bottom) by Tony Miller; 501 (top) by Tony Miller; 501 (bottom) by Robert Young, Jr.; 503 (bottom) by Michel Paretiako; 504 (top) by Edgard W. D. Holcomb; 504 (bottom) by Johan Hagemeyer; 505 by Arthur Knight.

First published in 1978 by Capra Press, 631 State Street, Santa Barbara, California 93101.

Published in Great Britain in 1979 by Sheldon Press, Marylebone Road, London NW1 4DU.

Printed in the United States of America by R.R. Donnelley & Sons.

Library of Congress Cataloging in Publication Data

Martin, Jay.
    Always merry & bright : the life of Henry Miller.

    Bibliography: p.
    1. Miller, Henry, 1891-   —Biography. 2. Authors,
American—20th century—Biography. I. Title.
PS3525.I5454Z716   818'.5'209 [B]   78-6912
ISBN 0-88496-802-X (Capra Press)
ISBN 0-85969-166-7 (Sheldon Press)

To Helen

Of love we may expect anything. . . . Our inner wealth or poverty is in proportion to our vision. Love wipes the mirror clean. There can be no broadening of one's vision without a corresponding leap of love.

—HENRY MILLER
"Love and How It Gets That Way"

A Programmatic Preface

Henry Miller has always been a mystery—even to himself. Once, when he was trying to understand the nature of the special kind of fiction he was trying to write, he concluded that his work was the creation of his "legend." And that "legend," he continued, applying Miguel de Unamuno's words to himself,

we have written together, the others, and me, my friends and my enemies, and my friendly-me and my enemy-me . . . . . Can I be as I believe myself or as others believe me to be? Here is where these lines become a confession in the presence of my unknown and unknowable me, unknown and unknowable for myself. *Here is where I create the legend where I must bury myself.*

This appeared in an early draft of *Tropic of Capricorn*. But all of Miller's work constitutes the autobiography of his legend, not of his life. His art is metamorphic, a creation of a self based on an obliteration or at least a masking of self. "I see everything as metamorphosis," he once confessed to Claude Houghton.

Most of the studies of Miller have assumed, however, that his works accurately present facts from which his personal history may be inferred. Thus, his critics have naively attempted to reverse the creative process and to resolve the invented legend back into the experienced life. Certainly, Miller's books themselves encourage this approach; for a strong aroma of personality hovers about them and impresses them with an assurance of authenticity.

But there are three fundamental limitations to the biographical approach which discerns the figure in the fictions. First, even could one assume that Miller's "revelations" in his books are true to his life, he has never pretended to have given the complete truth about his life. Quite the reverse. "I have by no means told the whole story in my books—and never will," he once explained to the German editor of a biographical sketch derived from this method. Second, Miller's account of his life is self-evidently misleading on innumerable points. Lawrence Durrell tells the story of walking into Miller's apartment in the Villa Seurat to find him "scribbling madly," his breakfast uneaten. Miller explained his urgency:

"This morning . . . as I took the first mouthful of food the thought came to me: 'Whatever happens, death will come, sooner or later.' I pushed aside my plate and feverishly, madly, started to make some notes about my life which will be of use to my biographers. Just the names of places and people and influences—a sort of synoptic history of my life. I have got so little of the truth on paper as yet. It makes me wild with impatience. . . . . And do you know what?" he said in a low conspiratorial tone. "Here and there I'm deliberately putting down a lie—just to throw the bastards off the track, like."

Finally and more generally, any attempt to derive Miller's life from his writing involves dubious assumptions about the information-giving capacities of fiction as well as elaborate webs of guesswork and sheer invention.

Several of his friends have written about Miller in volumes of personal recollection. At first glance these promise to be more accurate. But none of the acquaintances who have written about Miller knew him intimately for more than a few years or from more than one particular angle. As Miller once remarked to me, even his "closest" friends "know or knew only a fragment of my life, and that *with them*." His celebrated association with Lawrence Durrell provides a salient example of the truth of this observation. Though these two writers have had a rich, extensive correspondence, their personal associations, taken all together, amount to little more than a few months' time. Moreover, authors of memoirs invariably will be found to defend some special, highly censored version of themselves through describing their relation to Miller.

Certainly I have read all of Miller's books and all the critical works and reminiscences written about him. I have gone further and interviewed several of Miller's acquaintances, bringing personal recollection under the control of the biographer's probing, and, even then, not so much for information about Miller as to achieve a sense of certain personalities critically important to him.

But in this book I have derived Miller's life through a very different procedure, a manner at once more immediate and more objective than printed works or interviews can offer. I have tried to write almost as if no previous printed work concerning Miller existed. Indeed, my biography is based almost exclusively upon the vast collections of manuscript material residing in twenty-three libraries and also in private hands. In all, during a three-year period I read over a hundred thousand pages of manuscript material for this biography. Wherever possible, I read the printed works—including those by and about Miller, even collections of letters—in their original manuscript versions, an exercise which demonstrates conclusively how misleading the final printed version can be. No other American writer, apparently, has left such a compendious record of his life in public depositories. Assembling letters, notes, diary and journal entries, marginalia, correspondence from others, contracts, financial records, outlines for books, clippings and jottings, drafts of fiction and essays, wall charts, photographs of different periods, and a varied miscellany of other material, I began to see the shape of Miller's life emerging.

To write my account of Miller's history was quite a different matter, however, from gathering the materials for it. From the manuscripts I made about two hundred thousand separate notes, a vast paper mosaic of Miller's life and mind. But I never intended to compose a "Miller log," a "Works and Days" documentary of his life. The biographer, too, must be metamorphic; and I wanted to create a style which could drive beneath and beyond the façade of Miller's career into the chambers of his heart and corridors of his imaginaton. I wanted to know where he lived and how, what he ate and what he wore, whom he spoke to and where, and what he said. But I also wanted to follow him just a little into his legend, since the "facts" of his life become the most interesting—and perhaps the most true—just at the edge of mystery.

Certainly, then, this biography does not propose to *be* Miller's life: no work of a few hundred pages could recreate a life in its entirety. Even though there are long stretches of time when my materials allow me to follow Miller's life with great exactitude, my biography is, as it must be, a symbolic rehearsal of the facts of Miller's life. I must partly agree with the cautionary advice which Miller once gave to me: "I am," he wrote, "highly suspicious of well-documented biographies, just as I am skeptical about historical records and events. If, on the other hand, the biographer would write about his subject purely from his imagination, from what he *thinks* the subject was or is, that is another matter. It's this business of writing *as if* he knew all about the subject that bothers me."

But I must partly disagree as well. I have traveled both of the paths which Miller outlines, enmeshing my book in the infinite details of Miller's life, yet of necessity acknowledging that at best I must rely upon my own perspective on the facts in order to create the truth they possess. I submit not to what I think, but what the materials make me think. After my struggle to assemble the facts, they struggled against me to express their life. Imagination did not create the details which I drew from the documentary record, but I have tried to interpret and express their significances imaginatively and to draw the Miller of my imagination through the sieve of my sources.

I would wish, then, to claim that this book is parallel to Miller's life: it exhibits the process of Miller's life. Instead of beginning with Miller's completed work and extrapolating his life from it, in this biography I cling to the moment, the mundane trifle, rooms, streets, houses, and especially to all those instances of the tentative groping toward self-understanding which would eventually lead to the creative work. I try to stay as close as possible to the life as it was lived, and to catch Miller at the point just before his imagination buries its origins.

I must confess that I have satisfied neither myself nor Henry Miller. I do not suppose that this book contains all the truth about Miller, and I know that there are other kinds of truth to be sought. Miller has devoted a lifetime to creating the myth of himself and at the end it proves impossible—perhaps, however, it may also be undesirable—to separate him from his myth. "I had a thousand faces, all of them genuine," he once told a friend. I have drawn only a dozen or so of his portraits.

Miller's dissatisfactions with the biographical process are deep and, like mine, irremovable. They are of several sorts. "As one who has lived a 'complicated' life," he once revealed, "I should certainly never want my motives examined into with a cold, worldly eye." Every man has a right to be tender about his life. More generally, he has argued in print that "one author does not even know how another author's mind works," and therefore "biographers are mistaken when they think they know an author by reading his letters, meeting his friends, [and] picking up scraps of one sort or another here, there, everywhere." This sort of solipsistic argument, of course, would put an end to all kinds of writing except that concerning one's personal mental processes, and so, even though it cannot be convincingly denied, it may be speedily dismissed.

On another occasion Miller wrote me that a biography such as I contemplated was impossible: "I frankly don't believe any one could write the kind of biography I would like to see. Not that I think I am such a complicated being, though I am too, but because I feel the biographer should have known his subject from the start and not seventy years later." I qualify poorly as a lifelong friend, and on these grounds the only qualification I can muster is that I grew up in his section of Brooklyn, among the same buildings and the same kind of people, and though this was forty years after Miller, my Brooklyn had not changed drastically from his.

Yet I *have* written as if I could satisfy my own and Miller's objections. Several of his metamorphic faces are, I think, clearly sketched in this book. I have tried not merely to look at his life with a worldly eye, but also with a tender glance from what D.H. Lawrence called the pineal eye. I have assumed—correctly, I believe—that any author, particularly one like Miller, who has put his mind and being on display so often and so fully, must at last allow the careful reader to discern the way his mind works—or else his books would be meaningless.

And finally, in a certain limited and artificial sense, by following the quotidian record of Miller's life through more than eighty years of his history, I have done what a friend who knew him from the start might ideally do, I have participated in his history without preconceived theories, mixing dismay with affection.

"My book is the man that I am," Henry Miller says in one of the films about him, "the confused man, the negligent man, the reckless man, the lusty, obscene, boisterous, thoughtful, scrupulous, lying, diabolically truthful man that I am." During the years that I spent studying Miller's life and writing his biography, I have learned that his books—and he—possessed all of these qualities.

Henry Miller never wavered in his belief that no one could write his biography. But he gave me permission to read the mountain of restricted personal material in the Library of Congress, in the Special Collections Division of the University of California, Los Angeles, and in a dozen other libraries. And so, though he always counselled despair, he gave me the means and the courage to write this book.

Contents

BOOK TWO: PARIS

BOOK THREE: PASSAGE TO AMERICA

Illustrations appear following pages 168, 340, *and* 494

NEW YORK

One

Little Henry and His Horse Dexter

"**I** was born under a lucky star," Henry Miller has always been fond of saying. Mystery and power seemed to be in his cards from the beginning. He was born at about 12:17 p.m. on the day after Christmas 1891 under the conjunction of Pluto and Neptune. These, the farthest planets from the earth, the latest to be discovered by science, were astral influences pregnant with meaning, he liked to boast. Besides, though Capricorns are "born old," as one astrologer would tell him, they are capable of any act of will or perseverance in their quest for success: they endure.

"I was born happy," Henry Miller would say much later. ". . . For me it was the natural state." Perhaps he would have to endure so much suffering because he was doomed to happiness.

Born at the tag end of the nineteenth century on the top floor above a saloon at 450 East Eighty-fifth Street, near York Avenue in Manhattan, he would need the quality of endurance, the ability to make good and bad fortune serve him equally.

The stars were only one influence at his birth. Another was the whole constellation of his ancestry. Though both were of German descent, his parents had very different backgrounds. Heinrich Müller, his paternal grandfather, was born in Minden, Hanover, near the Weser River; and Barbara Kropf, his grandfather's wife, came from Bavaria. His mother's father, Valentin Nieting, came from Hesse-Darmstadt and her mother, whose maiden name was Insel, was born in Bremen. His father's side consisted of jovial, sunny folk, while his mother's family lived lives of austere regularity. His father's family was easy-going, adaptable and adjustable, falling into the spirit of things wherever they went. Many of the men in the Nieting family were sea-captains, who restlessly traveled all around the world and settled in places as far away as the Marquesas. But even the Pacific breezes never blew away their Teutonic frigidity.

Both of Henry's grandfathers came to America to escape military service and settled in the Yorkville section of New York City. Like many other German immigrants, Heinrich Müller soon Americanized his name. His son, born in 1865, he named Heinrich Miller, after himself. In 1870 a daughter was born to the Nieting family and named Louise Marie. Eventually in 1890, these two, Heinrich and Louise, would unite in marriage. But they always remained quite dissimilar people; for each inherited and carried the marks of a different background and family temperament.

So far as anyone knew, Henry Miller's father had read few books in his life and remembered only one of these—written by "a fellow named Ruskin"—but he was, nevertheless, an excellent storyteller. He was easy-going and affable, he loved to talk and had a retentive, inventive memory. He drew people out by listening sympathetically to their tales of woe or enthusiastically to their adventures. Marooned though he may have been in his tailor shop, he listened to the tales of all the varied customers whom the waves of commerce swept in, and he could reel off episodes and details about the most remote places on earth, elaborating and embellishing the stories for the sake of the sheer imaginative pleasure of identification with these exotic travelers. Heinrich liked working on his tailor's bench in his own father's house in Yorkville, he liked to drink and to eat, he enjoyed singing. He spent or loaned his money freely, taking it for granted that when he needed help it would appear.

Louise Marie Nieting loved order, a comfortable, well-regulated bourgeois life. She was strong just where Heinrich was weak and sometimes gave the impression of being proud and critical, intolerant, and scornful of waywardness. She seemed to possess, above everything else, an instinctive flair for detecting the flaws in people or situations. She viewed human frailty with the same distaste that she had for bad odors in kitchens or disorders in dress.

The son to whom Louise gave birth in December 1891, a little over a year after her marriage to Heinrich Miller, was endowed with his own temperament. Still, he was, as it turned out, stamped by his divided heritage and so it was fitting that he was named "Henry" after one grandfather and "Valentine" after the other: Henry Valentine Miller.

Before Henry was a year old, his parents moved from Yorkville just across the East River to 662 Driggs Avenue, Williamsburg, Brooklyn. In 1892 this was not yet a borough of New York City. Forever after, Henry thought of himself as "a Brooklyn boy." Yorkville meant the mysterious, inaccessible place of his origin, the place where German was insistently spoken, where he could visit his adored cousin Henry Baumann in the summertime. But Williamsburg was the arena for his growth and it gave him his earliest memories.

Until he went to school, Henry spoke only German and remained insulated in the thoroughly German atmosphere of his family. The birth of a sister, Lauretta Anna, on July 11 of 1895, seemed to make little difference in his settled routine; his life circulated around two fixed points, his house and his parents.

Red brick and three stories high, with a store on the ground floor, the Miller house was a notch up from the flats which lined the side streets. Little Henry, dressed in a Lord Fauntleroy suit with lace collar, hardly dared to venture outside his door. Of streets and stores and buildings, Henry knew only what he could see from his own house; he lived almost entirely inside the neat, clean, well-ordered rooms. His life was guarded and sheltered as suited the darling of his mama and papa, but it was a rich life; for what he could see from the windows and what he possessed inside the house constituted a world complete enough for any child, however inquisitive he might be. In the garden he could see his mother's beloved lilacs and chrysanthemums and snowball bushes. On one side of the garden was the smoked fish house, and on the other, Goeller's summer house, through whose intricate lattice work Henry tried to glimpse the ineffable social mysteries of the people flickering about within, like hazy figures in an Edison film.

From the second story windows he could see the tin factory, which caught on fire with fearsome regularity: it caused the fish house to burn down one winter when the temperature fell so low that the firehoses froze. Henry looked with wonder at the charred walls and heavy beams with massive iron hooks still dangling from them. Alarms were so frequent that though each sent a tingle of terror through Henry, other members of his family grew blasé, and once, grandfather Nieting refused to get out of bed until the firemen actually broke in upon him and started to spray his room.

Inside the house, each room held a special interest. The best was grandfather's. There he worked on a massive bench, laying out his paper patterns and cutting and sewing or running his big iron over wet seams. His eyes had a queer, faraway look, particularly when he washed at the sink in preparation for a spree at Paul Kerl's tavern, singing strange songs or murmuring to himself and the little boy about the old times, telling tales of a strange fellow named Buxtehude. In this room Henry shined his grandfather's shoes for a penny and cut out paper patterns for make-believe suits for the old man. He tried to read newspapers, not understanding the words. Grandfather had a beautiful Chinese-like face and nearly the same name, Valentin, as Henry himself. And he spoke lovely English—like an Englishman—because he had been an apprentice-tailor for ten years or more in a shop in a wonderful place called Savile Row in London.

The parlor was much more grand, with its antimacassars and overstuffed, stiff furniture. Its walls were lined with sentimental engravings and family photographs. One was a photograph of Henry himself taken at the age of three in a little dress with a white bib, standing beside his wooden horse Dexter. He had curly hair and a hurt, half-frightened look in his eyes.

Nearby was the kitchen, chiefly associated with the heavy, steamy odors of German cooking, soups, meaty joints, spinach with egg, potatoes, puffy dumplings with thick gravies, liver-balls, seven-layer torte, puddings, and pastry. When relatives from Yorkville in Manhattan or acquaintances from Ridgewood in Queens arrived for dinner, the feasts were preceded by whiskey and schnapps and washed down with beer or Rhine wines or cider for the children. When the sea people, the wandering relatives, arrived from distant parts of the world—Germany, California, Alaska, the Carolines—the odors that came from the kitchen were so rich and so varied that the air itself seemed edible.

In the center of the house was Henry's own alcove room. Here, when he was very little, his mother took him to the sink and said, "Henry, you don't want to drink from a bottle any more, do you?" And when he said "No," she broke the bottle in the sink. Here he suffered through the childhood ailments which stretched the hours out agonizingly, but which also brought his father to his room, to rub special soap on him to take away his itching, or to amuse him with a magic lantern show. Sometimes he had sore eyes and had to wear dark glasses. He feared being left alone in the dark room and dreamed that a big bear was trying to break through the bars over his window.

But troubles came soon into his life. Many of his relatives lived abroad, as if they were aristocrats, and their visits humiliated him. His first rebuff from the outside world came from them—just because he made noise eating his soup. A little German cousin dressed in a velvet suit rebuked him: "*Schleuse nicht so!* Why does he *slurp* so?" inquired the pompous, well-bred monkey. Henry could have murdered him. And yet his mother and aunts kowtowed to these uppish, over-refined relatives, just as if the Millers of the Fourteenth Ward, Brooklyn, were *dreck*. Henry felt that he must get to those distant places whence his superior relatives came in order to become as good as they were. Real life, he began dimly to feel, was not at home—but somewhere else. He plagued one of his father's friends, a ferryboat captain, with questions about sea voyages. He yearned to visit his cousins in Yorkville or Glendale, Long Island, for when he did his cousin Henry Baumann ceremoniously introduced him to each of his own friends, "This is Henry, Henry Miller from Brooklyn," as if he were a traveling dignitary.

However, at home he felt that his mother was classing him with his father's family. None of their photographs hung on the parlor walls; as mother made patently clear, they were "too common" for such notice. This insult came to trouble Henry. Perhaps his mother also thought him "too common." Perhaps that was why he never got the bicycle or the real horse that he craved, the mythical bronco from Texas his father promised him. He had to be content with his rocking horse, Dexter. Perhaps that was why his mother always ordered him about and forced him to attend Dr. Roberts's Sunday School and dolled him up like a sissy in a velvet Eton jacket and a cream-white Tam O'Shanter with a pom-pom, and thus attired, made him parade down Bedford Avenue with his class. She made a slave of him; he had to wash the windows every Saturday, where all the kids on the street could

see him. Mother humiliated him by telling others that little Henry loved to
help his mama. Why was she always complaining, then, that he dragged
behind in everything, just "like a cow's tail."

She humiliated him terribly when he was attending kindergarten in a
tiny wooden building on Fillmore Place. At Christmas, the teacher handed
out practical gifts—stockings, mittens, handkerchiefs. His mother became furious when he returned home emptyhanded and demanded to know
where his presents were. Henry explained that he had done a good deed,
giving the gifts back to his teacher with the suggestion that she offer them
to someone who really needed them: he knew he would receive all these and
more from Santa Claus for his birthday. Outraged, his mother dragged him
to the school by the ear and forced him to beg for the return of his presents.
That pained him unbearably and told him that his mother really classed
him with the trashy Müllers.

So, more and more, even as he sat on the sill washing the windows, he felt
a need to escape the house. The street, almost audibly, called out to him:
walk me, touch me, smell me, hear me, taste me, live in me. The streets
were vivid and elastic, alive with the intermingling of alien people and
places, flecked all over with brightness and mystery.

All the streets were marvellous. Driggs Avenue, of course, was the best
of all; for this was his own street, the street on which he, Henry Miller,
lived. North First Street, between Driggs and Bedford, was the place for
summer games—marbles, potsy, prisoner's base, leapfrog, Red Rover, and
tops. It was a street for running, the street where all of the older boys of the
neighborhood, young Henry's heroes, gathered. Loitering and leaning
against light poles, or teasing the girls, these fellows seemed like Vagabond
Kings to the timid little boy. Down this same thoroughfare, scattering
sunlight all over Brooklyn, the cyclists whizzed Indianfile along the narrow
strip of asphalt between the curb and the cup-shaped cobbles.

Streets changed with the seasons. In the winter, after school, he'd drag
his sled to Fillmore Place to go belly-whopping. Sometimes the boys had
battles with snowballs that became really savage. Once Henry got chased all
over the neighborhood by Billy Ayres, the victim of a deliberately thrown
ice-ball. Billy would have smacked him good, had he caught him, but
Henry ran for his life. (He remembered then the rock-fight he had gotten
into once in Yorkville. He was haunted by the belief that he had actually
killed a boy with a hard thrown rock: the kid dropped as if poleaxed, and

Henry hadn't waited around to inspect the damage. "Val Miller: Murderer," he whispered to himself to hear how it sounded.)

From Fillmore Place radiated games of capture and release, cops and robbers, war, and tag. Henry and his pals raced through tangles of streets, leaped fences, darted into yards or hallways, and cut dangerously through backyards. The widening orbit of his adventures began to give Henry a sense of neighborhood, which replaced his house as the center of his life. At the corner of Driggs and Grand Street was Pat McCarren's saloon. Reynolds' Bakery was on Grand. Not far from it was Vossler's Drug Store with its tessellated floor, and Daly's fish market, where strange submarine creatures lay on glistening ice. At the very end of Grand Street was the East River, the ferries, and Paul Kerl's beer hall where grandfather went to listen to the syncopated German songs as well as the speeches of the Socialists. Nearby, along Kent Avenue, was the great basin of the Navy Yard where the battleships tied up. Derricks and hoists loaded and unloaded enormous carts. Off Navy Street between the waterfront and Myrtle Avenue, was a street called United States Street. Henry called it a dream street—and it haunted his dreams for years—because though he could describe it down to its last detail, he could only occasionally locate it; the street seemed to appear or disappear of its own accord. Other streets induced other dreams: Myrtle Avenue, Berry Street, Metropolitan Avenue, Havermeyer Street, and North Fourth. He walked these avenues dreaming of running away, as if these flowing arteries would lead him into the big world.

He was growing up, growing away from his family. Part of him wanted to remain little Henry, to stay where he was, to remain a child, to ride his rocking horse in wild excitement but never to go forward. Young as he was, however, he began to feel pulled in directions for which his protected childhood had not prepared him. He was aware, dimly and uncomfortably, that another kind of education awaited him.

The theater gave him intimations of an outer world. His mother took him to the Novelty Theatre to see his first play, *Uncle Tom's Cabin,* and later *Way Down East,* and *The Old Homestead* with Denman Thompson. (Later came blood-curdling thrillers at Corse Payton's Theatre and such dubious theatrical offerings as *Alias Jimmy Valentine*.) What a thrill of sophistication he felt when he himself took his cousins, Joey and Tony Imhof, to the Novelty—and the simple country boys began to blubber because the gallery was so high up.

Even more than the theater, books introduced him to a wider life. Among his first books were: *Robinson Crusoe,* the dark, Germanic tales of the Grimms and Andersen, *Pinocchio,* the books of Henty (which arrived five or six at a time on Christmas mornings), the story of the young genius Paul Morphy, the romances of Rider Haggard, *Alice in Wonderland,* the novels of Dickens, the *Arabian Nights,* Ellis' *A Boy's History of England,* and *Knicker-bocker's History of New York.* Once, his father secured a whole bookcase full of beautifully bound boys' books from another merchant tailor, an Englishman named Isaac Walker. Because his father read to him when Henry was ill or at the delicious hour before sleep, Henry early on associated books with lassitude, or with fabulous beings like King Arthur or Saladin, who drifted into his dreams. Books gave him an entirely new geography to explore. Sometimes he tried to read to his grandfather as the old man worked at his bench. On one particularly frustrating occasion, he pestered grandfather by insisting on reading aloud about the fate of Admiral Farragut during the Battle of Mobile. Grandfather complained to Henry's parents that the boy read too much. Perhaps his grandfather was right. The stories made his imagination race. Sometimes when he awoke in the middle of the night, it seemed that the mythical, angelic personages of fiction were all about him, that their wings brushed his face.

But nonetheless he remained a Brooklyn boy, a city boy. A visit to Joey and Tony Imhof in Glendale was fine, but Henry could never acquire their passion for birds or flowers. Sojourns to Glen Island, Far Rockaway, or Sheepshead Bay might gleam in his memory like an illuminated Japanese print, but they remained discernibly irrelevant to the life of his neighborhood. Williamsburg was engraved, as if by acid, upon his youth. More than anything else, city life gave him an education that marked, when he was about nine, a dividing line between his childhood and his youth.

Around this time Henry also began to realize that there was something wrong with his sister Lauretta, that she was half-witted, if not "cracked," as the kids called her. And Henry himself was in trouble because he said he wanted to be a river pilot rather than a tailor like his father. This was his first rebellion. The idea lodged in his head—the harder teachers and parents oppposed it, the more passionately did he cling to it. In a fine vision he saw himself on the bridge, steaming down into Mobile Bay like Farragut or into Havana like Dewey, or bound for the Carolines, as imperturbable and lordly as any Nieting. Henry was pleased to have discovered his vocation, and he pestered his parents for their acquiescence. But instead of ignoring him they opposed him and gave him reasons why it was a bad choice—an irresponsible, almost criminal choice. Open war broke out over it. They flatly said "No" to his life's choice, the only one he could imagine.

Two

The New Neighborhood

One day Henry's father and mother announced that they had bought a house in the Bushwick section of Brooklyn, at 1063 Decatur Street. Although Henry had certainly begun to feel that Williamsburg was in decline, at this news he suddenly became a defender of Williamsburg, about to become his "old neighborhood." He announced, to no avail, that he did not want to move. He felt betrayed by his parents. If only they had let him alone he would have been all right. Trouble came when others pushed and prodded him, according to their own desires, in ways he did not wish to go.

And now in the early winter of 1900, they were moving him away from the river, miles further inland, sinking him more deeply into the Brooklyn mudflats, marooning him in a "better," more respectable, Germanic neighborhood. And dull—thoroughly bourgeois—the name of the street itself gave the key to it: Van Voorhees Street! It sounded like the grunt of a fat Dutchman, but his parents explained to him that the street name was being changed, Americanized. It was soon to be renamed Decatur Street.

Leaving behind the empty rooms at Driggs Avenue and carrying only the packages too precious to entrust to the movers, the Millers walked to Broadway, under the shadow of the new bridge. In front of a savings bank which looked to Henry as solid and imposing as the Capitol at Washington, they waited for the Broadway trolley traveling in a direction he had never taken. All the way he turned his head backward, his eyes fixed on what he was losing but sneaking glances at the new streets they were passing. They were all named for the heroes of the Revolutionary War: Greene, Gates, Kosciusko, and DeKalb. And the houses, newer than those in Williamsburg, were not bad.

When they finally stepped off the trolley, instead of crossing Broadway to the street lined with wealthy-looking brownstones, father led them to the seedier side of the street, where the exteriors were made of brick on the first floor and clapboard on the top two stories. Designed as a connected block-long unit, house after house was built identically: steps led up to the gingerbread doorway on the second floor; and there was a little grassplot in front. On alternate houses bay windows bulged. But 1063 had a plain flat façade. Even renamed, Decatur Street looked shabby to Henry.

The new neighborhood did actually turn out to have certain attractions. In empty lots children's bonfires glowed cheerily on gray winter days. Near his house was a wonderful ice-house and near that a railroad line. The windows of the stores that lined Broadway were swell to look into. German street bands and gypsy jugglers, tambourine dancers, mustached Italians playing hurdy-gurdies, and men with parrots that picked out one's fortune for a penny, vegetable vendors with carts piled high with produce, scissors grinders ringing bells, and horse drawn fire engines, all rattled down Decatur Street. He found new friends, like Joe Mauer. Another, a fat boy of sixteen, talked to Henry about Eugene Sue's *Mysteries of Paris*. A traveler named Dr. Brown came to the grammar school and told the boys about Asia and Africa.

But Henry never really forgave the neighborhood his first, bad impressions. For him it was always doomed, declassé, *fin de siecle.* Everything around there was nipped in the bud or seemed blighted—like the stunted patch of grass where the Millers sat on summer evenings in front of their house—like Lauretta, who had to bear the torment of the insults hurled at her—like Henry, who had to suffer shame for his sister's sickness and sorrow for all he had lost in having been plucked out of the old neighborhood.

Henry was nine, ten, eleven. He seemed to sink into acceptance; he forgot about being a riverboat pilot. He helped his mother with the chores, the neighbors said he was a model boy, his teachers thought him a prize pupil—his classmates found him obnoxious, a know-it-all and a tease. In outward appearance he was well dressed, blond, and very Germanic looking. At first shy, he soon became eager for friendship, particularly with older boys.

He followed the lead of older boys because he was accustomed to obeying his parents' directions. One fine day, after his mother chatted with Mrs. Tisch, whose husband was in the music business, she became convinced that Henry should begin piano lessons. Henry said yes to anything she wanted. Accordingly, an instrument was purchased at a discount price from Mr. Tisch. Henry started right in, actually showing a real musical talent, and he made astonishing progress. Soon he was playing "Two Little Brown Eyes" for his Tante Melia—for dear Aunt Emilie, before she went mad. His father also made suggestions. Wouldn't Henry like to help by delivering packages of clothes? Although Henry agreed, he winced every time he had to come to a side door or back entrance and hand his goods over to an insolent servant, just as if he were a nonentity.

Henry obeyed, but he was "spoiled." Perhaps because Lauretta was retarded, his parents petted him all the more. They unwittingly taught him to think himself better than they thought him, to wish for more and expect more than they anticipated for him. So, though all appeared placid, everything was going wrong. Strange streaks of wildness exploded from him. In October of 1902, at the age of 10, he was suspended from grammar school for being incorrigible, a loafer, and a wild Indian. Even though he was the best student in the class, his teachers could not stand his antics. The cold-blooded thrashing his mother administered to him on this occasion was calculated to put him back on the right track, and it seemed to work for the rest of the school year.

At P.S. 85, his intermediate school, he made friends with a boy—Emil Schnellock was his name—who could make pictures appear on the blackboard with a few quick strokes. Henry himself couldn't draw anything that anyone could recognize, and he admired Emil's talent without reserve. A pattern was slowly emerging, of identification with boys who were "different," even queer in some way. Perhaps he suspected that he himself was not quite "right." Perhaps he did not want to be right.

Henry was not rebelling outwardly yet, but he was getting ready to do so. When he graduated from P.S. 85 in February of 1905 and announced his intention to attend McCaddin Hall (Eastern Distrct High School on Wythe Avenue in Williamsburg), anyone should have recognized something curious in this choice. Built in 1841, it was one of the oldest schools in Brooklyn; and it was not distinguished academically, having been used in the early 1890s as an "attendance school" for juvenile delinquents. Why should he have wanted to attend a high school so far from home? Why wouldn't he have wanted to go to the same school as all his friends? The reason was simple. He seized the first opportunity to return to the old neighborhood and break out of the life designed by his parents.

Henry chose McCaddin Hall for its associations with his past. But during his absence the beloved neighborhood had been propelled into the future. The Williamsburg Bridge from Delancey Street had opened and the trickle of immigrants had become a steady flow. Henry found himself in a newborn ghetto when all he was searching for was his youth's revival. He was astonished that eight of every ten of his classmates were Jewish and most of the rest were Italian. Only a favored few of the students—the old settlers, as it were—had names like the streets, with the ring of an earlier America to them—George Wright, Frank Carroll, Steve Hill, William Dewar. The teachers, of course, were mostly Anglo-Saxon relics from the older Williamsburg. Between these teachers and the handful of Anglo-Saxon students there existed a silent compact to set standards and lick the newcomers into shape as bears do their cubs, while letting them know their place.

Yet, before long, Henry went over to the enemy. He found he liked the newcomers: they stood with him against the unalterable law of his mother's Teutonic domain. The newcomers were easy-going, noisy, dirty, and disorderly—but this suited Henry. His parents had moved to Bushwick to get away from the anarchic, sensuous mob of immigrants. Very well: he would be their ally, revolting against the teachers openly, as the newcomers themselves could not dare do.

The formidable principal, Henry openly averred, was really just a blunderbuss and dunderhead. He satirized his composition class by reading aloud a wacky theme which began: "Give a man more taffy when alive and less epitaphy when he's dead," and he had the temerity to ask: "Why study geometry?" (An immigrant child would not have dared throw out such a taunt.)

Henry was always ready for a prank; he was becoming a wild Indian again, and now he was too old to spank. He like to poke a ruler into the big glass aquarium and make the crayfish and seaweed and fish spin together in a dizzy whirlpool. Once, when a guest was visiting the physical education class, he slipped out of line behind the teacher and commenced to jump back and forth over the gymnastic horse until he set the whole class tittering. Finally he caught his foot and slammed face first into the floor, breaking a tooth and shoving it through his lower lip. He leaped up and stuck his tongue through the hole for the amusement of the girls. No wonder he told the school's French teacher that what he *really* wanted to be was a clown. He got away with all this because he was German and, despite everything, a bright student.

When he graduated in 1909 he placed second in his class. By the age of seventeen, however, he had lost the desire to be educated by his parents or school, and he was no longer keen enough to learn from the streets. Only reading adventure books restored his capacity for wonder. *Ivanhoe, Idylls of the King, The Lay of the Last Minstrel, The Rime of the Ancient Mariner,* books which he read in high school, stood out in the dreary curriculum. The books went further than any other source of education in helping him to answer the crucial questions about his life. "What did he want to be?" his teachers were always asking. Why, David Copperfield, Hiawatha, the hero of "The Pit and the Pendulum," or William Tell, Quasimodo, Henry the Fourth, Richard the Lion-Hearted, Hamlet—anyone, so long as it was out of the world of parents and school. Books filled his dreams. One dream recurred—of a secret library of books all his own, a ten-foot shelf, like President Eliot's Harvard Classics. Individually, each book made sense. But how did they all fit together? He dreamed that one book in the set held the key to the knowledge contained in all; each dream ended with his groping about for that one magical book, the begin-all, end-all volume that would make everything crystal clear. He never found the dream key.

But he did have the set of Harvard Classics which his parents had bought him during his second year of high school. Henry sat in the upstairs parlor and raced like an unwearied six-day bike rider through the Greeks and the Elizabethans and the Restoration, then into the plays of Goethe, Schiller, Shelley, and other nineteenth-century dramatists. In New York's lively theater life Henry actually was seeing many of these plays performed and so getting a genuine sense of the real power and palpability of literature. This started one day when Henry's father asked him if he would he like to see a play called *The Gentleman From Mississippi,* starring Douglas Fairbanks, a young actor who was attracting some notice? Once Henry had had a taste of Douglas Fairbanks, he went to the theater as often as possible. Not long afterwards his high school German teacher was to take him to the Irving Place Theatre to see *Alt Heidelberg.* With a high school buddy, he began to go to the Broadway Theatre in Brooklyn, to which stock companies brought the touring hits and the stars that had fallen from Manhattan's empyrean. Ordinary fare though most of the plays were, Henry swallowed them whole, for they possessed both the aroma of life and the splendid reality of romance.

The romanticism of late adolescence bound him to his high school chums in the fellowship of improvised fraternities formed after their graduation.

The chief of these were called the "Deep Thinkers" and the "Xerxes Society." These groups were bridges in the life of Henry and his friends between youth and early adulthood. Many young men around 1910 were finding the transition to adulthood particularly difficult. American life was changing very rapidly and young American boys tried to find ways of banding together in comforting fellowship—to talk of the jobs they might have, their troubles with parents, and the girls who terrified them. They had left school and parents behind, but they secretly dreaded the jobs and wives that lay in their futures. Sophisticated, scornful, and jesting, telling each other "there's nothing to anything, everything is fake," Henry and his friends hid each other's doubts. Their fraternities provided them with a sunny romance of male conviviality: being "with the boys" brought brief respite from the conditions which hedged their future. The Xerxes Society, in particular, had a lasting effect on Henry's conception of the world, the last hope that youth might go on.

The fellows in the society all liked to sing. They were all "such fine musicians, they practiced every day," as their song said. Whenever they got together, there was music. Henry was wild about singing: the day began when he raised his voice in solo song. By the time he was a senior in high school he was giving piano lessons for twenty-five cents an hour to eke out a little spare change, which usually went towards the purchase of sheet music or records at five, six, or even seven and a half dollars a throw. He felt that a good recording of the "Egmont Overture," Caruso, Cantor Sirota, or Mme. Schumann-Heink was worth almost any amount.

So when the boys gathered at the Old Triangle Hofbrau in Richmond Hill, Henry was ready to plunk himself in front of the piano and race through Chopin's "Revolutionary Etude," or Percy Grainger's arrangement of the "Londonderry Air", to render a Hungarian Rhapsody, or to wow his chums with a jazzy rendition of "The Maple Leaf Rag." Nearly all of the fellows in the group played an instrument, and sometimes three of them would slaughter the piano at once while the rest crowded behind, and George Gifford and Al Burger led them in songs like "I Wonder Who's Kissing Her Now" or "Meet Me Tonight in Dreamland." Then they *were* in dreamland, and everyone would cry: "Always merry and bright!"

Big cold spreads at midnight, prepared by mothers and grandmothers, added to the general atmosphere of careless abundance and increased the hilarity of the Xerxes Boys. Sometimes they went out to a big event—a new play, the debut of a female performer, boxing or wrestling matches, or six-day bicycle races. They went to Webster Hall or the Arcadia to dance, to the hockey games, ice-skating. Afterwards, they'd repair to one of their favorite eateries, get tipsy on dago red, and argue the relative merits of various athletes as if they knew as much as their favorite sports commentator. Sometimes, in the summer, they sauntered out to Brighton Beach or Coney Island and took in the music hall shows and the dizzying rides, and they downed high-piled seafood platters and foaming mugs of beer. Those jolly adolescent days were as bright and breezy as the polka dot bands on their straw hats. But they were singing because they were afraid. Like Tom Sawyer's gang, the Xerxes Society had a constitution, rules, a secret grip, a button with an insigne; and even a password. Perhaps it was organized so tightly because the boys knew that it was destined to fall apart. It lasted a year. The boys divided over trifles. They lost faith that fellowship could save their youth. The workaday world was catching at Henry and his friends from every side; the dull, drab daytime world was casting odd shadows on the make-believe adventurous world of the theater or stadium; life was beginning to look like Coney Island in the winter. Henry was having trouble with his eyes (undergoing a quack cure too), almost as if he could not bear to see how gray his future looked.

The tailor shop threatened to snare him. In 1908, after years of delay, while other tailors grabbed off the best pigeons, and just as the economy took one of its periodic plunges into depression and new customers for a gentleman's tailor became as rare as a dodo, Henry's father had belatedly taken the step of opening up his own tailor shop. The shop began as a mistake and soon slid toward disaster. No sooner had Heinrich invested his money in this shop than he had to economize to keep it going. There was no time for dallying: Heinrich needed help from his son and demanded he learn the trade. Henry, who had seen his father wear himself out, wanted nothing to do with the grind of paper patterns and welted seams, cutting and fitting and then refitting, or dealing with customers who seemed always ready to rebuff him.

Henry wanted to be a Yale man—that was his dream. But with economy necessary, the dream of Yale was changed to Cornell, where his German teacher believed Henry could get a scholarship. He failed to get it; but still resisting the tailoring trade, he became a freshman at City College in 1909. Soon, disgusted with the curriculum and the intolerable atmosphere of City College, he left in the midst of a hopeless encounter with *The Faerie Queen*. Yet he avoided the tailor shop and began working as a clerk for the Atlas Portland Cement Company at 30 Broad Street in the financial district of downtown Manhattan, for twenty-five dollars a month, with an additional fifty cents on days that he worked overtime.

Nickels and dimes—was that the meaning of life? With such a prospect, who could sing? During his first days at the cement company, whenever the office manager left the room, Henry would lead the boys in Irish melodies. But after a few weary months, when the manager left, the only noise was the hiss of pencils pushing down columns of figures. Day after blank day, Henry, the sleepiest clerk in the office, vacantly perused the itineraries of the salesmen, checking their expenses, and spinning fantasies about the distant places to which they brought the fair name of Portland Cement. The maps were right, with their towns and rivers and mountains; but for him, chained to his desk, things were wrong.

Full of vague yearnings and all too sharp regrets, he shuttled to and from work each day on the "el" across Brooklyn Bridge. He had resumed his childhood friendship with Stanley Borowski, who felt much as Henry did, and in voluminous letters to each other the two young men spilled their melancholy views. Stanley opened up Henry's eyes about European literature and loaned him books by Pierre Louys, Pierre Loti, Anatole France, and Joseph Conrad, the Pole who was Stanley's favorite writer. Once Henry's father caught him reading Balzac's *The Wild Ass's Skin* and confiscated it abruptly. But Henry kept on, bought books on his own, purchased German magazines, and borrowed numerous volumes from the Brooklyn Public Library, where Emerson had once delivered a lecture on "Natural Religion." If Henry had a religion at all, it was in his reading. Emerson would have approved of Henry's request for *Esoteric Buddhism* ("Yes, we have it," the librarian remarked, "but do you know what you are asking for?"). He borrowed Madam Blavatsky's *The Letters from the Mahatmas, Walt Whitman in Camden,* and the books of Tagore. By 1910 or 1911 Henry was also reading Jack London, Sudermann, Petronius, Rabelais, Maeterlinck, and an assortment of other authors.

Particularly in the letters he wrote Stanley, Henry tried to say how this varied reading fare related to his experience, but mostly he made a confusing mess of it. Stanley complained that Henry had no style, no sense of tradition, and no form. But each day, as he rode the elevated to and from work, swinging from a strap in the crowded car, Henry kept reading, storing up material.

By 1911 he was convinced that what he really wanted to do in life was write, write stories. He read so much because he was afraid to write, convinced that he would reveal only how little he had to say. He had read so much it seemed there was nothing left to write. How dispiriting to confess one's personal doubts and to have them sound like the windy broodings of young Werther. In high school, Henry recalled, one of his teachers had always been urging the class: "Make it your own!" At that time Henry scorned the teacher. But now Henry feared that like a sausage-maker he too could grind out only what had been fed into him, and even then thoroughly mangle it. He cringed under Stanley's attacks. Before he took up his pen he saw himself speaking impassioned monologues, constructing dramatic scenes, devising rich characters, offering original philosophical disquisitions, and making sharp exposures of social hypocrisy. But these vanished when he started to write. The best he could do was emit sporadic bursts of the electric currents always running through him. He dared not attempt a real story. Stanley would slaughter it. But, he told himself, who at the age of twenty knew enough to write?

But even this self-defense was dashed. Occasionally, on the el, he met a boyhood acquaintance, Billy Ayres. Billy looked pale and unhappy. (Had that iceball made the poor guy daffy?) Finally Ayres confessed that he was a writer of fantastic tales. Now Billy—even Billy Ayres—was an author. Henry dared not claim so much. Henry's dilemma was that he wanted to be known as a writer much more than to write. Though he certainly wanted others to feel that he was a very talented guy, he couldn't conceal from himself that he was a fake. People thought he was witty and insightful and inventive. Better, then, not to expose himself.

So, in the end, he spun tales only in his imagination, monstrous scraps that blew this way and that with the day's influence. And he consoled himself: "Some day I will write an enormous, ultimate book in which everything will be recorded: the street, the crowded cars, the Grand Street markets, the Xerxes banquet at the Astor House, the six-day bike races, Bergen Beach, Stanley Borowski, Glen Island—all, all of life."

With such an overbearing goal, he kept on yearning and wrote nothing.

Three

Wine, Women and Song

"Wine, Women and Song"—that was the title of the first play that made a lasting impression upon young Henry. But as he approached adulthood, the songs seemed off-key and the wine of life soured. As for women—sex affected his life in many different, but mostly unhappy, ways.

There is no doubt that Henry's experience with sex had been maimed from the start by his mother, who alternated between treating him with coldness and overattention. Unless he obeyed her to the letter she would withhold her praise; but when he behaved like his mother's darling little boy she praised him to the skies. She was a perfectionist, extremely difficult to please; and when she thrust the small boy from her even after his best efforts to please her she made him suspicious of himself and evasive of her. He could not easily turn to his father for affection, nor look to him for a model, for Henry adopted his mother's low opinion of her husband. So far as Henry could see, neither his father nor he could satisfy her. Early in his life, then, he became wary of women, sure that he was likely to suffer defeat at their hands, uncertain of his own masculine powers.

Of course, he had had the usual childhood experiences with sex. Once, when Henry was nine, he and his cousin Henry Baumann cajoled a little girl named Weesie into the basement and persuaded her to lift her skirt and let them feel her drawers. Another time he and his pals paid crazy Willie Maine's sister Jenny a cent to let them rub against her. That didn't give him any more pleasure than sliding down the lamp posts on Grand Avenue, but he was scared as hell that he'd get caught doing such a dirty thing.

The next year he *was* caught—well, almost. He was staying with his cousins Joey and Tony Imhof. One night after they had become weary of roughhousing Henry got an idea—where it came from remained a mystery to him. In the next room Tony and Joey's older sister, Minnie, lay sound asleep. Henry led the boys into her room. She was sleeping under a crucifix. Stealing over to the bed he carefully lifted back the sheets. To his astonishment she was completely nude. He had never seen a woman's body exposed before. Almost as if hypnotized, he began to stroke her thighs. With his forefinger he lightly touched the stiff black hairs on the edge of her amazing bush. Suddenly Minnie awoke, furious and embarrassed, and threatened to tell. He was caught at his dirty game. But Joey and Tony, who must have regarded Henry's antics and their sister's excitement as ridiculous, roared with laughter until Minnie chased them all out of the room.

A few years' lull in his experience with sex followed. He was entering adolescence—dangerous ground, especially with his self-doubts and anxieties. It was better, he must have thought, to look on sex from a distance—as he had in pulling back Minnie's sheets—to keep women at arm's length. Certainly that's the way he treated the girls in the new neighborhood around Decatur Street—he knew they were there, he watched them run by the house, tossing their curls, but he made no move. It was bad enough to be twelve or thirteen and forced to live in a drab new neighborhood without having to face the threat posed by the opposite sex.

Until he was in high school, Henry did not even kiss a girl except in fun. Then Frances Glanty, a pretty Jewish girl in his class, left a love note in his desk, and after she saw that he had read it, she cornered him in the wardrobe and kissed him shamelessly before all her girl friends. He learned something from that. But perhaps he was learning even more from one of his cousins, Marguerite. Every week he went for a hot dinner to his Aunt Annie Heller's house in the old neighborhood. After dinner his cousin's girl friend always came over and the three of them would go to a stable owned by Henry's uncle. In the odorous dark they played hide and seek, groping about and wrestling and pulling at each other. There was a lot of heavy breathing and fleshly exploration, but it never proceeded any further, and after a while they broke it off.

Whether he wanted to or not Henry was being pushed toward girls. He went to boarding hotels with his parents for summer vacations, and boys were expected to chase girls at such places. Custom made this a little easier. There was a certain Miss Green that he had his eye on in the Catskills; and later, there was Edna Booth in Sparta, New York. But sex was still a game to him and after the ice was broken he didn't know how to proceed.

While he was still completely unprepared for it, he had a painful sexual experience when he was sixteen, just before entering his senior year in high school. Henry and his pal Grimmy were strolling around the old German Village area behind the Metropolitan Opera House when they got the high sign from two old whores, genuine bloodsucking bimbos. They lifted the boys' wallets and one left Henry with a dose of gonorrhea. In pain, Henry went to a pharmacist who took him to the back room. "Let's have a look at it," he said, and then he whistled, "That's a beauty!"—meaning the infection. On the sly, Henry had to begin regular treatments— accompanied by lectures—with the family doctor. "What do you think that thing is for?" the old geezer demanded upon examining his dripping tool. "Why, to pee with, I suppose," Henry replied, flustered. "Yes, but it is also to have children with, or by," he grunted with sententious superiority. Henry had to suffer this in silence, fearful that the smug bastard might take it into his head to tell mother what had happened to her darling Henry.

Eventually, Henry lost his fears. The next summer he visited a French whorehouse near the Herald Square Theatre and came out with another infection. Now he joked and boasted about this male dilemma with the fellows in the Atlas Cement office.

The burlesque theater embodied the attitudes toward women formed during his adolescence. From his youngest days he had been peeking at his uncle's *Police Gazette* and collecting the portraits of coquettish soubrettes from packages of Sweet Caporal. But he didn't actually get inside a burlesque house until he was a high school student and accompanied an older boy to the Empire. Henry loved the burlesque stew of humor and obscenity. Whether burlesque taught Henry his view of sex or whether he was so fascinated with burlesque because his own attitudes were so similar, Henry ended up treating women in a burlesque way—as objects for rough jokes and naughty desires.

Typically, during the years that Henry was catching the clap and learning about women from burlesque, he also built up an intense idealism about love and was always looking for a woman to worship. His mother always told him how much he had adored her, and he seemed to be seeking another woman to serve. Cora Seward, a schoolmate at Eastern District High, seemed to meet this need fully. He was thoroughly intimidated at first glance by the physical Cora—with her firm upstanding breasts, full mouth, and apple blossom cheeks—but he was completely annihilated by the image of her which his yearnings created. She seemed too perfect ever to be possessed. Everything about her appeared radiant, romantic and distant; her porcelain blue eyes shimmered like icebergs, mirrors of her Arctic soul; her hair was perfectly blonde, like Guinevere's in *The Idylls of the King.* He was as helpless as Galahad. His chums loved to drag him before Cora and urge him to make a declaration of love. But whenever she gazed at him with disconcerting shyness he was absolutely tongue-tied.

All he wanted to do was adore her from afar, to walk through the Greenpoint streets she trod. Every step he took resounded with the echo: Cora walked here. In his anguish, he was almost ready to kiss the flagstones of the dirty, oppressive streets. Several of his high school pals lived in Cora's neighborhood. One took pity on Henry's mooning and advised him to hang around till eight o'clock when she was sometimes sent out for a scuttle of suds, to hide in the telephone booth and just pop out on her. So, after dinner Henry would occasionally trek back to Greenpoint and watch her from a dark corner. But, though the other boys thought it easy to jump in front of her and give her a squeeze in the dark before she could resist, Henry could never treat Cora in that common way. He made no progress in his love affair : he really didn't want to make any. After all, for sex there were plenty of beery old sluts slinking around Herald Square—Henry needed a woman to worship.

During the winter and spring of 1909, after he had graduated, once or twice he made bold to ask Cora for a date. He took her to the theater and sometimes saw her at dances. But the few times they danced together his legs felt like stiff joints of mutton. At parties she never came and stood behind him, as other girls did, when he played the piano. Clearly, they were awkward with each other. In the summer of that year, Cora went to Asbury Park with her family while Henry began his drudgery at Atlas Cement. With Cora physically removed, he liked her all the better, and he wrote long, serious letters to her. She answered him only a few times during this bitter season, but whether or not a letter waited on the mantlepiece for him, he experienced a lot of romantic anguish. Often, he would down his dinner and take solitary, distraught promenades on the sacred Greenpoint streets, or all over Brooklyn, from the East River to the Highland Park reservoir. Several times he had the same dream. He and Cora, a perfect Cora, were at a party together. As usual, Henry played hard to get, ignored her and even treated her disdainfully, until George Wright announced that Cora, disgusted with his behavior, had fled the house. Wild with grief, Henry rushed out to bring her back. But it was too late! Repeated, the dream became wearisome. Worse, the dream was true—Henry was driving her away. He said that he wanted Cora, but he wanted a divine ideal; he could not accept the fleshly Cora and he rejected her by his reverence.

By 1910 Henry's life was fragmented and incongruous, and it was not surprising that he attempted to find guidance through an intensely sexual relationship with a woman who was almost old enough to be his mother. He felt that he couldn't have Cora, and so he settled for another, more easily available woman. But the truth was surely that he was afraid to win Cora, and wanted a woman that he could have for the asking. He thought he wanted a cold romantic ideal, but he really wanted a passionate mother. He longed for his childhood, a return to the womb. When sex was so mysterious, perhaps he thought that it would release him from the mundane world to which he felt doomed. In Pauline Chouteau he found a mother and lover in one. She was ready to take him into her womb anytime he knocked, quite unlike his own mother who could never, he felt, accept him outright, for himself alone, he had to be doing something for her.

Pauline had good taste and lovely manners and a face modeled by fine bones. Once, her hair had been red, she said, but now she had turned it blonde with peroxide. Her taste in clothes suited Henry to a tee—especially one plum colored outfit trimmed with fur and with a low square neck which showed her white, high bosom to advantage. Her arms were strong and firm without being muscular; when she rolled up her sleeves and took a broom to the house, she made everything fly, and she was always whistling and singing cheerily in a frail light voice as she worked. But she was always humble and quiet and kind with him: she did need him and she let him know it. She told him the kind of secrets young men rarely hear. She confessed, for instance, that she had been treated badly; while her husband lay dead drunk, she gave birth to her baby in an outhouse. Now that same son, George, a boy only a year younger than Henry, was dying of consumption and lay helplessly weak in his bed, eating up every cent of Pauline's, and eventually of Henry's, money. Masochistically perhaps, Henry was fully prepared to sacrifice himself for a woman, to gratify her slightest need and meet her every whim. In truth, for the first time in his life he was giving love, even if his friends thought he was pissing his future away; and, strangely, he was nourished even as he was devoured by his sacrifices for Pauline.

Besides, he was swimming in a sea of sperm, in a storm that was raging almost out of control. Pauline was a delicate but fully passionate woman who knew how to please a man, and herself. Every time she and Henry got

near her house, the drums of love started throbbing, increasing as he
followed her up the stairs. She would giggle with pleasure and anticipation
as he ran his hand up her dress. The pulsations receded for a moment as she
made sure that George, dying in the next room, was thoroughly tucked in.
They undressed in the steaming kitchen. Carefully, deliberately, Pauline
hung her clothes on a nail in the door, in an unintended striptease. First she
slid out of her dress. Then came the corset and stays. Her breasts swung
heavily as she bent over to step out of her stiffly starched pantaloons. Finally
she removed her stockings: often these had different colored tops sewn to
them from discarded hose. It excited Henry to see the colored silk pulled
tight against her transparently white skin just below her big bush, its hairs
already so moist they were plastered on her belly and legs. This was the
burlesque of his dreams. He'd become so absorbed in watching, he'd almost
forget to undress himself. But the fucking began almost immediately—in
the tubs, on the tables and floor, with her straddling him on a kitchen chair,
or him picking her up and walking around the room carrying her while she
squirmed around on him. It was an explosion.

When they finished such a bout, Henry always experienced self-doubts.
Such screwing, he was certain, could only weaken him mentally and
morally. He recollected that the men of the utopian Oneida Community
believed they could preserve their strength by holding back ejaculation.
Yet, here he was, spending his seed as if he were Hercules! He made
resolutions, but all his efforts failed. When he tried to read, Pauline would
cuddle next to him and put his books aside. She had a fine mind, but she did
not care at all to discuss Nietzsche, Westermarck's *History of Human
Marriage,* or Lecky's *History of European Morals,* Henry's favorites at the
time. He rented a piano, but after a few minutes of practice he didn't need
to look around to know that Pauline was standing behind him, quietly
removing her corsets and colored stockings, ready to pounce upon him
where he sat, spinning the stool until they fell off onto the floor. So he ended
up devoting his life to fucking.

Worse still, everybody knew about the widow, even Henry's father.
Every morning the old man gave his haggard son a blasting, mournful
glance which seemed to say: "You'll drive yourself dippy if you keep this
up." Whether in fact this was what father meant or not, it was exactly what
Henry was telling himself. But he had no intention of leaving Pauline. He
was successful with her just where he was a complete failure with Cora, and
it was no easy thing to give up a triumph over a woman, particularly when
mastery included unsurpassable sex. Besides, he had moral scruples about

tossing Pauline aside; by having made love to her he had assumed an obligation, an eternal duty, to care for her. In romantic and sexual matters Henry felt inferior and all-powerful at one and the same time. When Pauline made the mistake of falling for him, he couldn't deny her the benefit of his company.

But he was ashamed to be seen with her: he trembled all through one cement company dance for fear someone would remark on her age; and perhaps he would have broken with her long before if his friends had not taken exactly the wrong approach by advising him to ditch the old dame with no further ado. But he couldn't accept such advice and he clung to Pauline, giving up seeing his Xerxes friends who unanimously opposed this relationship.

Privately, he was sure that his friends were right and was convinced that all this dissolute screwing was ruining his health. During the winter of 1910-11, he started on a Spartan regimen of exercise. Each morning before 5:30 he would ride to Coney Island and back on the Bohemian racing wheel which he'd bought from a six-day bike rider at Madison Square Garden. As he sped over the cracking ice, he cursed himself for clinging to Pauline. Sometimes he'd don his running togs and race three miles or more. Finally, he started a memorandum book to record the dates on which he did not screw Pauline, hoping thereby to cure himself of sex, just as Benjamin Franklin had intended to rid himself of sin. He rejoiced whenever a little blank space appeared on his calendar.

At this time he was learning muscular eye exercises from a Dr. Cassius in order to cure his myopia. Each morning, when he examined Henry's eyes, the doctor gave him a look as baleful as his father's. By spring, Henry was defeated all along the line; he discontinued the eye exercises, stopped running, and let his bike stand idle—but he kept right on fucking his head off. At last, one morning, leafing through the recent pages of his memorandum book, he noticed that all of them were filled: there was not a single, simple white space. He gave up all hope of being cured of anything.

By the summer of 1911 Henry had been in love with Cora for nearly four years—from a considerable distance. He had also been intimate with Pauline for over a year. His life seemed to be going nowhere. Like the national economy, he seemed sunk in a depression.

His family fortunes took an upward swing, however, when the country showed signs of emerging from the recession of 1909-10 and the demand for custom-made clothes picked. Suddenly Henry's father had plenty of money and offered to send Henry to Cornell University in the fall. Henry was delighted at this unexpected resurrection. He began to think of this as an opportunity to break decisively with Pauline, make a future for himself through college, and—best of all—become worthy of Cora. His self-esteem took a leap upward: he thought he was a pretty big bug, a man of the world, attractive to women, magnetic—even the divine Cora must see that.

And lo and behold one night he found himself at a party with her. This was no dream. Everything worked out in a perfect way. She seemed to have eyes for no one else. At nineteen, they were still playing post office. The game got going. Henry waited in feverish anticipation for the time when he might get up the courage to call Cora out into the hall to receive a few letters. He never anticipated that she would call him to "come outside," but she did so, suddenly. They were in the hall, she was in his arms. Even in his dreams they had never been so close. Yet she made no resistance. Somehow, in desperation, she wanted to make it clear that she liked him too; silently, he felt, she was pleading with him to declare himself. This goddess clung to him—pressed against him—allowed him to push her against the wall, to kiss her eyes and moan her name; and she returned pressure for pressure. His hands roved all over her body. Then, to his horror, she broke away, confused and shocked, and ran back into the parlor. Wave after wave of shame swept over him. He had behaved like a gross beast, treating his ideal as one would a whore, as if he were a moral moron who didn't know the difference.

He felt like a dog, the way he treated Cora. But he was still determined to break with Pauline and go off to college, to drag himself away to the shores of Lake Cayuga. The evening before he was to leave for Ithaca, he said goodnight to his father and mother, and in hopeless despair crept out of the house to say goodbye to Pauline. He stayed all night and, as unable to leave her as to explain anything to his parents, he remained hidden in her house all fall, utterly miserable, watching his money slip away like snow swallowed by water. Shortly before, he had felt he was looking through binoculars at a widened future. Now the glasses were turned the other way, and he looked down a narrowing tunnel which came to nothing at the end—only himself, immobilized, friendless and loveless.

It was obvious to everyone that he had made a dismal mess of his life. He had lost Cora, he was hiding out from his parents and avoiding his friends, he had quit his wearisome job at Atlas Cement. In October, without conviction, he looked for work; then he applied himself seriously to the search for a job—but he was unable to find any work. Finally, he just drifted, reading Herbert Spencer or Henri Fabre, toying aimlessly with the piano, or spending hours fumigating the rooms and airing the bedding on the roof, living with the fear (and possibly the hope) that he would contract George's consumption.

Only abject flight seemed possible. After four and a half months, he returned to Decatur Street. He didn't fool himself that his parents believed he had been in college since September. Pauline's flat on Macon Street was hardly more than a mile from his parents' house, after all. His mother and father looked ruefully at him and said they knew all about it. They were good about it, his parents, and wanted to aid him, restore him, to help him find a purpose in life. Through his recent experience some connection between morality and physical conditioning had lodged in his mind. So he now announced his intention to become a gymnasium instructor, and he enrolled in a four-year night course at the Savage School of Arms on Columbus Circle at Fifty-ninth Street.

Living at home again, Henry soon realized that his father had been ruined by drunkenness. He saw the flash of fear and the shudder of disgust that passed over his mother whenever father rolled home in an alcoholic frenzy, and he felt her hurt, wounded, uncomprehending anguish as she caught a whiff of Heinrich's breath and heard him begin his silly, boozy jabber. Somehow he wished to make up to mother for his own and his father's lapses; he took her side against his father. He hated his mother's scornful attitude toward his own person, but he had adopted her exasperation toward his father; and no doubt he secretly hoped that by siding with her he would win her approval, at least her acknowledgment that he was better, in her eyes, than his father. Henry became her champion and covered the old man with contempt and mockery, wounding him for his mother's sake.

Henry had disgraced himself so completely that now he was ready to do anything asked of him. After all his resistance, finally, he agreed to join his father in the tailor shop. His mother argued that if Henry would show an interest in the business, it would buck the old man up. He could give his father a hand with the customers, collect on some of the accounts that were long overdue through his father's easy indolence, and drag him away from his cronies at the Wolcott Bar. She pleaded with Henry to undertake these little tasks for her sake.

The door to the tailor shop had closed upon him. But he was bitter and expressed his contempt with silence, not communicating with his father except in grunts and in sharp, quick remarks. The old man couldn't last

long under such scorn and by noontime each day, racked with the need for a
drink, he rushed out to find his boon companions. Perhaps Heinrich would
have been perked up had his son taken an interest in tailoring. But Henry
mocked that too. Holding out all too obviously from learning the business,
he taught himself to type and occupied his time banging out philosophical
rambles on the machine or chatting with the cutters about the mysteries of
the cosmos. Mostly, though, he sulked in the shop, writing letters to his
friends. Sometimes he knocked off work altogether and walked the crowded
streets of lower Broadway, taking in a penny arcade or a movie, or he simply
sat on a bench in the sunshine at South Ferry. If some pretty skirt took his
fancy he might close his book and follow her right to her door. He was
simply dreaming and drifting because he had nowhere, really, to go. At the
end of every day Henry would drag his shamefaced father from the bar and
hustle him home. Every day was bitter, opening a fresh wound. Henry was
doing no good in the tailor shop and although he dreamed of Cora, he
drifted back to Pauline.

In the spring of 1912 Pauline became pregnant and her belly swelled up
like a watermelon. Henry hated to be seen with her. One night in late
summer, though, with Pauline bitching about the stifling warmth in the
house, he agreed to take her to Coney Island where they could be lost in the
crowds. Despite his anguish, the night seemed wonderful. He sat with
Pauline in the Luna Park bandstand where they listened to a concert. Above
them, on a slack wire, a woman with a parasol swayed, as if able to walk
upon the music itself. The appeals of the pitchmen; the way the chute-the-
chutes sprayed the night with silver as they hit the artificial lake; the daring
dives of the coasters; the whistles and clangs and calliope music—all the
sights and sounds filled him to bursting. He wanted to dance. The exercise
would do Pauline good, he said. Miserable over Henry's recent unkindness,
Pauline beamed at his little attentions. He led her cavalierly from the
bandstand, just like a husband who is ministering to the comforts of his
pregnant wife. Together they meandered through the crowds toward the
dance floor whence the sounds of razzmatazz and summer waltzes drifted.

But just as he arrived at the pavilion, arm in arm with Pauline, he looked
up straight into the face of Cora. Her blue eyes were fastened upon him. She
was standing alone, at the very entrance to the pavilion. She had taken in
everything, everything, and he, in his shame, would have to pass right
beside her. His feet plodded on. When he and Pauline came up next to
Cora, who had not moved, he could not say a word; he only bowed
awkwardly and touched his hat, so slightly that Pauline almost failed to
notice. Cora said nothing, gave no sign.

After a few paces more, Pauline asked in a casual voice, "Who was that?" "Oh, some girl I knew once," Henry said in an agony which showed. He stumbled spiritlessly through a few dances trying to deny the defeat he felt, then scurried home, like a whipped dog. "Oh God, Harry," Pauline cried when they lay in bed, big round tears rolling down her face, "why don't you tell me the truth? I know you don't love me any more. I know I'm too old for you." She was a worn, used thing, a soft hurt creature, with a kid inside her that neither of them wanted, and she was desperate about the loveless futility of her life. In his own desperation Henry lied and comforted her, and made love to her until they fell asleep. He had tried to stay away from her but Pauline needed him, she really needed him. That night and for months afterward, he stayed with her and they talked and echoed each other's complaints about fate and made love like two squirrels, all without satisfaction.

It was hopeless. He was utterly tied to Pauline. That was what he kept insisting to Frances Hunter every time she called him on the phone. He could always tell Frances' voice at once. She had a throaty, vibrating voice and when he said "Hello?" she always began by saying, "Henry, darling!"—with Frances Hunter it was always "Henry, darling." During the summer he met Frances at a vacation resort in Pine Bush, New York. Mother and Lauretta had gone up there for the summer, while Heinrich and Henry continued to work in the tailor shop. Henry was obliged to get the old man up to Pine Bush on the weekends, and he welcomed the chance to get away from Pauline.

He was ready to have fun in a hearty, open, natural way. He liked Frances' marvellous sense of humor, and he found himself released, joking and clowning. He didn't chase her at all. He simply liked her warm laugh, he liked her naturalness, and he liked to hear her insert into her talk the slightly quizzical, very warm phrase, "But *Henry darling. . . .*" They got along famously and she fell for him hard.

Henry wanted to fall for her too—he wanted to tell himself that he was in love with someone else so that he could ditch Pauline, unborn kid and all, and not feel guilty. When they got back to the city he took Frances on a double date up to Coogan's Bluff above her Lenox Avenue apartment. Things turned a little serious there. Frances was stuck on him, and in the dark she sat on his lap and lifted her dress for him to enter her. After that they fucked wherever they could, sometimes even in her own parlor while her deaf mother sat sewing in the next room, but mostly in the grimy halls of her Harlem tenement. Everytime he got ready to leave she would whisper: "Henry, darling, when am I going to see you again?" Whenever he called her up or went out walking with her, before the fucking got going, he was always explaining to her that it was useless—he couldn't escape. And she would always begin her argument against his reasons: "But, Henry darling." But he was telling Frances the absolute truth. He *was* chained to Pauline. He and Pauline both were miserable, but neither seemed to have any plan for escape.

Then, one night in the fall of 1912 when he came to Pauline's apartment after work, the rooms were full of the stench of sweat and alcohol and blood. Pauline lay weakly in bed, dark circles around her eyes, and a broken, mutilated fetus lay in a drawer of her dresser.

Four

Slave Days and Schizophrenia

In the winter of 1912 Henry sat on a bench in Union Square feeling that if his destiny was to be a complete failure he had fulfilled his role in life completely. He checked off his failures: Cora, Yale, Cornell, Atlas Portland Cement, writing, concert piano, Frances, Pauline, Brooklyn, America, existence.

Here and there in the park little groups had gathered about political speakers, evangelists, or con artists. People walked to and fro, hurrying on their missions or strolling at ease, scattering chicken feed to the pigeons and peanuts to the squirrels. Everyone else, Henry moaned to himself, had some direction or purpose; but for him life had dwindled to absolute zero. The cosmos was arranged to suit him: his planets—Mars, the Moon, and Uranus—were disastrously conjunct in Scorpio, the House of sex and death. But Henry couldn't even get up the courage to do away with himself. Listlessly, he looked about him, casting a fishy eye on the entire scene. His gaze fell upon a phrenologist's shingle: *Fortunes Told.* He had only a few dollars left and no future prospects. The idea of tossing his few bucks to the fakir to hear his non-existent future told appealed to him; then he'd be completely flat. What could a phrenologist make out of the bumps on his head when he himself could make nothing out of the bumps inside it? Even the most meager action seemed to demand enormous resolution. Gazing at the sign, he made the gigantic effort of raising himself from the bench and starting his shoes shuffling in the right direction. At least he was doing something, imagining the fiction of a future, and to that extent he was still alive.

The phrenologist jabbered foolishly. *He's flattering the shit out of me,* Henry told himself as he recognized a good salesman's technique, but he found that he really agreed with what the fellow said: "You have great potential. You are a man of many talents. Why, you could be anything you set your mind to, even a corporation lawyer or an architect." Though he didn't take all the particulars seriously, Henry leaped at the assurance that he might be more than a blundering misfit. Almost literally, he was dying for praise, and even a stranger's paid-for praise was welcome.

Henry's trouble was that he was a cynical perfectionist. He wanted to be perfect. If he could not achieve his ideals, he declared himself lower than a worm, but he also mocked the idea that anyone could be perfect. He was nearly twenty-one, but he was experiencing very intensely all the feelings of personal inadequacy and idealistic aspirations characteristic of early adolescence. He was at an age when, in the period before World War I, most young men had embarked upon their life choices, but he was still drifting. He had proved to everyone's satisfaction, especially his own, that he was an abysmal failure. Like his mother, he nosed out the defect in anything; he would not rest until all the flaws in existence were revealed and life withered. And yet he clung to a grandiose vision of his own spectacular potentialities, convinced that when he bloomed, he would be the central flower of perfection. His idealization of Cora, his readiness to make real sacrifices for Pauline, and the high regard in which he held literature, were all evidences of an idealism so overblown that it became paralyzing. He tied himself to unrealizable goals: perfect love, total sacrifice, unmatched books, the final word in everything. Wanting to do so much prevented him from doing anything and wholly concealed his real capacities for achievement. Dimly he sensed that he had blunted his own potential; and his friends and acquaintances often encouraged him. Stanley admitted the power of his mind, and Fred Plate had sincerely urged him to publish an essay on Nietzsche which he wrote in the tailor shop. Even the German salesman from Fisher & Company called Henry *ein echter Philosoph von Geburt* and begged Heinrich to free him for the serious study of philosophy.

The cynical side of Henry's character had developed through the influence of his best friend, William Dewar. Destined to be a lawyer, Dewar was scornful about everything, regarding ideals as delusions and man as an assemblage of portable plumbing. For a year or so Henry had regarded himself as a disciple of Dewar's. But by the end of 1912, when his cynicism extended to his own being, he was ready, and secretly yearning, for a new mentor who would reject his skepticism and accept and encourage his idealism. By a series of ironic coincidences, at the end of 1912, a few days after Henry went to the Union Square phrenologist in complete despair, Dewar introduced Henry to his half-brother, Robert Hamilton Challacombe, a guy whom Dewar openly regarded as a crackpot. Challacombe was a successful inventor, having made a great fortune with his rotary oil drill, but he was also, to Dewar's disgust, a member of the Theosophical Society at Point Loma, California. Challacombe believed openly in the existence of a mysterious, spiritual, inner world. The notions of Theosophy, New Thought, Ethical Culture, and Bahá'í filled his conversation. Phrases like "the way," "God," a "purpose in life," "universal religion," and "mental power" fell easily from his lips. He struck Henry with just the force to arouse his idealism. What was more, Challacombe seemed to see something in the desperate young man. He didn't have to chart the bumps on Henry's head, he needed hardly a look at him to tell him his verdict: Henry had a vast reservoir of spirituality in his nature which he had been afraid to release—that was the chief reason for his suffering. What Henry saw as failures, Challacombe regarded as positive signs. True, Henry had no career, the theosophist admitted, but this was really evidence that his nature was resisting the spirit-strangling aspects of American life. His inability to adjust proved the existence of a spiritual nature which was seeking liberation, the road to awareness.

Henry was stunned at these revelations, so closely did they match his own suppressed dreams, and he became Challacombe's disciple. He attended a series of lectures which Challacombe's friend, the former evangelist Benjamin Fay Mills, offered in New York in the late winter. Particularly stressing New Thought, Mills assembled a *mélange* of spiritist ideas—telepathy, hypnotism, mental suggestion, the "divinity within," and the "transmigration of mental powers"—tied loosely to Christian Science and expressed in a tone of moral earnestness. Certainly, he was a popularizer, but Henry was ready for a total conversion to idealism, even at the simplest level. At the very first of Mills's public lectures he was ecstatic. Afterwards, he rushed down to catch Mills on the platform. "Dear sir," he pleaded, "I believe that I am one who should hear your private lectures; for your ideas seem directed expressly at me. Couldn't you let me work for you in order to pay for those lectures?" Henry exhibited the sort of earnestness preached by the lecturer. From the stage Mills looked down piercingly at the young man—almost, Henry felt, as if he were reading his very soul—(possibly he was weighing the hundred-dollar fee he was about to toss away)—then he broke into a smile: "Of course, you *are* the man, you *shall* hear the lectures." For weeks after, Henry passed the salver at the public lectures in return for the exhilarating private consultations.

Challacombe and Mills undertook to resurrect the self that Henry had seemed intent on burying. "Follow your highest, strongest, best impulses, no matter what the cost," both kept urging him. He confessed his personal dilemmas to them, he told them all his fears. They said, as his friends had, that he must break with Pauline; but unlike his friends, whose verdict against Pauline was due to her age, Challacombe and Mills struck a much higher note. His sacrifices for her, his fidelity to her, were evidences of his fineness of character, but it was false pride for him to believe himself responsible for Pauline's destiny. He was on his own path.

Challacombe and Mills set his steps in the direction of Point Loma. Challacombe was convinced that, in the East, men's inner lives were stunted, but in California were encouraged to grow. When he talked, Henry could almost see the sun crash into the sea and the Point Loma light begin to blink. After a few months this Brooklyn boy, who knew nothing more about the rural life than summer vacations could teach him, determined that he must make his way to California, lead the outdoor life, Teddy Roosevelt's "Strenuous Life," rid himself of his self-doubts and Pauline, cure his eyesight, reject the dismal philosophy of his favorite books, and discover who he was and what he was. If Bill Dewar had cynically told his half-brother: "Look, I'm going to introduce you to a poor sap whose life is being ruined by an old bitch; find some way of packing the goof off," Challacombe could not have done a better job.

Pauline was alarmed. He persuaded her that he would find a job and send for her, but both knew this was a lie: he wanted to break with Pauline and was thinking about Cora again. He wrote to her suggesting a talk before he departed. But Cora's patience with him had run out: she was nearly twenty-two and anxious to be married. When he arrived, instead of inviting him into the house, she closed the door behind her and led him outside to the gate for a short interview. Was she afraid that once inside the house he might have forced himself upon her? he wondered. He had dreamed that she would avow her intention to wait for him, and he pictured taking her in his arms and kissing her passionately. But both were ill at ease; he muttered a few platitudes, shook hands politely, and left.

In March 1913 he left New York, afraid of the future and once more looking backward as he moved forward. He despaired of his past, but mixed with his regrets was a holiday feeling. As he sat in the train he remembered a dream he had had the night before, a vast and fantastic vision of all the places he was to see, a world fit for monsters of an antediluvian age. It was an incredible and grotesque dream, but somehow it left a happy feeling that ahead lay a primitive realm of the spirit. Wintry winds were still buffeting New York—but they were blowing west, and he was blowing with them.

He watched the scenery but had no interest in the continent: his eyes were fixed on the California border. When at last the train pulled into Barstow, everything seemed new. He threw open the car window and breathed the fragrance of orange trees. His first job was on a cattle ranch near San Pedro. Never finding the world he had seen in his dream, he soon concluded that California was a place like any other, and he drifted from one job to another. For some time he worked as a ranch hand at a lemon grove in Otay, near Chula Vista. All day long he burned in the broiling sun, toiling like a slave, perceiving definite inconsistencies between Theosophy and the routine of a cowboy. He was drifting again, losing grip on the identity he had traveled west to find. Why had he come? he kept asking himself. He wondered whether he had really understood Mills, Challacombe, and Madame Blavatsky. His disappointment was bitter.

He didn't know how precariously balanced his psyche had become until he completely lost grip on himself one day when, off work, he was rambling aimlessly in the streets of National City. His mind went blank. Around him people moved back and forth, strangely unreal and without purpose, like weird Chinamen walking across the Brooklyn Bridge. He didn't know where he was or who he was. It was as if his mind had committed suicide, leaving only a dazzling blank. This vacancy lasted only a minute but left him petrified. Back in the bunkhouse, he studied his face in a mirror to find lines of insanity in it. Was he cracked, and in a far worse way than feeble-minded Lauretta, who merely prattled on innocently? Had he inherited the family dementia that Tante Melia and other aunts and uncles and cousins exhibited? Was all his suffering only because he was nuts? Was he about to have a total breakdown? He gazed in that black-flecked bunkhouse mirror, but only his own familiar sun-browned oriental face looked back, quizzically, at his inspection.

Slave days and schizophrenia! Grubby toil and madness were not what he had expected to find in California. The gods thumbed their noses at his dreams and showed him they could crush his mind; but what they took with one hand they gave with the other. Henry had become pals with a cowboy from Montana named Bill Parr, a guy who bummed around a lot and liked

to talk books and "Wobbly" politics in a sort of Jack London vein. He
introduced Henry to the tradition of protest in America through talking
about such figures as W.E.B. DuBois, Hubert Harrison, Big Bill Hayward,
Eugene Debs, Jim Larkin, Elizabeth Gurley Flynn, Carlos Tresca, and
Arturo Giovannitti. But they hardly spent all their time exchanging
philosophies. Saturday nights they reserved exclusively for visits to a San
Diego whorehouse. On one such Saturday, they were deflected by a
billboard announcing a lecture series by Emma Goldman on "The Social
Significance of Modern Drama" and decided to postpone the whorehouse.
Actually, Goldman, a well-known anarchist, was not allowed to speak but
was soon hustled out of town by the guardians of public morals. In the
interim, Henry managed to exchange a few words with her. More
important, he purchased two books from her consort, Ben Reitman: Max
Stirner's *The Ego and His Own* and Nietzsche's *The Anti-Christ*.

This encounter with Goldman and Reitman gave Henry's previous
experience a new turn and helped him to put the spiritualism promoted by
Mills and Challacombe into perspective. He was not by any means ready to
reject propositions concerning "inner dynamics," "positive thinking," or
"spiritual energy," but he decided that his own experience did not exactly
confirm such notions. He didn't conclude that Mills and Challacombe were
wrong, but he had no reason to insist that they were right. The same with
Goldman. He paid little attention to her politics, but as a philosophy of life
her anarchism matched the value he himself placed on personal freedom and
paralleled his earlier reading of Whitman and Jack London. She was an
idealist who believed that, although at present history had taken a brutal
turn toward war, in the future man would be transfigured. Nietzsche's *The
Anti-Christ* put a cap on these ideas. Finally, in Stirner's flaccid book he
found summaries of the leading ideas of other major anarchists such as
Kropotkin, Bakunin, Tolstoy, and Johann Most.

Important new influences entered Henry's life through this encounter.
But to all outward appearances little had changed: bedbugs still lay in wait
in the bunkhouse, brush still needed to be cleared away, tired whores still
loitered in San Diego. He had come to the Golden West, meaning to give
up literature and lead a healthy, outdoor life; but it was no more nourishing
than a vacant lot. Escape was the only solution Henry had ever been able to
devise for anything, and for a time he thought of following the Jack London
trail to Juneau, Alaska, to work as a placer miner in the gold fields.
However, a siege of fever left him weakened and convinced that Alaska was
too risky. Finally, he wrote to Pauline saying that he was ready to return to

her, and asking that she send him a telegram saying: "Return immediately. Mother Dying"—so that his boss would let him depart. In December, 1913, after nine months in California, he arrived back in New York, back in Pauline's arms, back in the tailor shop.

By the time Henry got settled again in New York, Emma Goldman's book on the European theater appeared. Henry used it as the guide to a course of study in the works of Hauptmann, Strindberg, Ibsen, Wedekind, Schnitzler, and Gorki, writers in whom Goldman saw a spirit of protest. More generally, these dramatists represented a very different kind of European literature than that to which Stanley Borowski had introduced him, with less emphasis upon the agonized sensibility and more on the representation of tragic human relations. These writers seemed more Henry's type. Goldman's book helped him to pass well beyond the plays he had liked earlier (such as *The Yellow Ticket, The Merry Widow,* and *The Red Mill*) and sent him toward the Portmanteau, the Cherry Lane, and the Provincetown theaters, where he swallowed large doses of the new experimental drama. This formed only a part of the literature he consumed in the beginning of 1914 when nothing else but literature seemed to matter to him. He read everything he could get by Nietzsche, Dreiser, Knut Hamsun, George Moore, and Bergson. He also dipped into classical philosophy and found Heraclitus and Marcus Aurelius particularly appealing. As always, he apparently needed to integrate his knowledge and experience. He was attracted to all kinds of universalizing ideas—world literature, the "one religion" concept, the *Spiritus Mundi,* universal history—and he was always trying to make everything hang together, as if his life would become harmonious when his ideas cohered. Sitting in a café with Bill Dewar, George Wright, or Stanley, he could endlessly discuss the possible relations existing between Herbert Spencer and Friedrich Nietzsche; Edward Bellamy and Lewis Carroll; Paul Eltzbacher's *Anarchism* and Rider Haggard's romances; *The Secret Doctrine* and the figure of Saladin. How did his recent favorites "fit" with his earlier ones? How could he accept Hamsun without rejecting Goethe, Heine, and Schiller, from whom he had once memorized lengthy passages? He was really still seeking the single golden key which, in that old dream of his, promised to unlock the secret of all knowledge.

He never found that key. But his compulsion made synthetic scholars especially attractive to him. One of his great favorites was John Cowper Powys, the Welsh man-of-letters whom Henry would meet later, in 1917, when Powys toured the United States with the series of talks on the appreciation of literature on which his book *Visions and Revisions* was to be based. Powys was engaged in exactly the study of self, society, and the cosmos that attracted Henry. Henry, attending his lectures in downtown New York, believed that Powys might give him the key to life. So, as he had once approached Mills for aid, at the close of a lecture he also approached Powys to ask if he had ever read Knut Hamsun. No, Powys confessed, because Norwegian was one of the few languages he did not know. More than from any writer, however, Henry got intimations from Powys of the high calling of authorship.

His meeting with Powys, however, was still some years off when Henry returned from the West. Before his trip to California, Henry had been a provincial Brooklyn boy, but on his return he entered the varied intellectual life of Manhattan. One of his favorite haunts was the Café Royale on Second Avenue where James Gibbon Huneker wrote his cultural column, newspapers in many languages hung on the wall, and recordings of Scriabin might be heard. Henry went occasionally to the Yiddish Theater to see the great actor Jacob Ben Ami performing. And he ate in the Roumanian, Viennese, and Russian restaurants where the music of cymbalon, zither, balalaika, and violin would be heard. Perhaps the best place of all for literary discussion was the back room at Lüchow's. Lectures and readings were offered at the Rand School and the Henry Street Cultural Center. At the Armory show, modern painting, including Duchamp's "Nude Descending a Staircase," was sensationally on exhibit.

Henry reached the age of twenty-two on December 26, 1913, shortly after his return from the west. With Christmas, his birthday, and the New Year all coinciding, this time of the year always put special stress on a review of the past and made the holidays a period of bitterness and regret as the family sat around the creaking dinner table making a gloomy reckoning; Mother would mention the promise he had shown and lament the folly and emptiness of his more recent actions.

Perhaps it was not altogether bad that he and his parents sang a litany of his misdeeds. At least they still remembered the time when he promised great things. As a result of this stress on time past, Henry began to be obsessed by the image of his childhood, the time when his life still seemed whole—life hardly outside the womb, before the conventionalizing intrusions of school, the awareness of Lauretta's affliction, the move to Decatur Street, the rift brought about by sex—life anytime, anywhere, before his personality was broken apart. Once, he felt, he walked on two feet; but he had been turned into a crab with a hundred legs, all moving in different directions. Persistently he inquired of anyone who knew him in his earliest youth what he had been like then. He was generally dissatisfied with the answers he received, particularly those from his mother, who liked to sentimentalize her memories of his youth, to tell him how cute and bright he was. She wanted to tell him what his boyhood meant to *her.* Annoyed, he demanded that she give him only facts and details. Where did they go? What did he do? What did he say? How old was he on this occasion or that? He wore her out with questions. Whenever she would mention certain items he had owned as a youth, he would ask where these were now. He wanted to see them, have them again. And her answer was always the same: she had "long ago" given these things away—to the Goodwill Society or the Society of Saint Vincent de Paul, to some neighborhood brats who had moved away. She seemed to want to deprive him of his youth itself, by letting him have only what she herself retained of it. He wanted to see himself on his own terms, not as others saw him, and to this extent his obsession with his childhood was a healthy sign that he was fumbling toward an identity suitable for the future. Once he had led an integrated life; he was determined to do so again. By taking his own childhood as a standard, he was also questioning the value of "civilization" and the conventional grooves into which family and society seemed to be driving him.

He took long walks to all the scenes of his earliest youth, as if trying to recapture his image in the visitable things of the past. One evening, for instance, he boarded a trolley for Bergen Beach to revive the glow that the place once had; all that remained in his memory was the feeling that on a holiday outing there he had been really happy. But after an interminable ride across swamps and dump heaps he arrived at a barren beach resort, populated by toughs and factory girls. He could have his childhood, then, only in his memory of it; but holding on to the image of his sacred childhood allowed him to hold off painful acquiescence to the adult world in which he had failed in so many ways.

Certainly, he had to recognize, finally, what a colossal failure he had been with Cora. Not long after he came back from California he was riding on a Brooklyn streetcar with an old pal when Cora stepped on. She seemed paler and thinner, a little worn. Henry wanted to tell her about everything that had happened to him, to begin on new friendly terms with her. But the first thing she said cut him short: she had married—to someone he didn't know—a writer, a reporter. After a few minutes she mumbled that she had reached her stop. To his horror it was his stop too: she was obviously living close to Pauline's house. Diabolically teasing Henry, his friend suggested she invite them up to her flat. Henry was in a daze as she led them through her rooms, ending with the bedroom. "This," she remarked awkwardly as she pointed to the double bed, "is where we sleep." The idiotic remark tore into him like a dull, crude blade. When he came outside, he realized for the first time that he had only to walk around the corner, from Monroe to Macon Street, to arrive at Pauline's apartment. So, without having known it, whenever he had sat in the kitchen and looked across the backyards he had been looking at Cora's house. Perhaps Cora looked, as he did, listlessly and hopelessly, into the cold, scabby Brooklyn backyards, while her husband, like Pauline, moaned: "Please come to bed!"

Henry worked at a great variety of jobs, at anything and everything. Some lasted for only a day because he did not want to commit himself to any job at all. He moved back into Pauline's flat and became unofficial janitor of the three story house. Downstairs lived a man named Lou Jacobs with whom Henry became friends. Lou laughed at everything in a good, kind-hearted way and taught Henry not to take life so seriously. The tailor shop was always beckoning him to "save" it: business continued to dwindle alarmingly, and the overhead was draining away the money which mother had put aside through much scrimping and saving. Finally, to please her and to make her cease accusing him of heartless irresponsibility, Henry went back to the tailor shop. This time, he took his surrender more lightly: he relished the belief that he would not be in the business for long, and once he got over the resentment he felt at being forced into the shop, he found he rather liked doing things for his father. Sometimes he'd fling a collection of samples together, rush out to a nearby office building, burst in on strangers with his wares and make long, elaborate speeches about the fine clothes made by the one and only firm of Henry Miller & Son. (He invariably began with the query, "Are you interested in clothes?" And once, when a fat man interrupted his rhetoric with "Why yes, seeing as how I'm obliged to wear them," he didn't know how to continue.) He was ironical, partly obsequi-ous and partly insulting, and he seldom received any orders except from established clients.

At other times he attempted to collect on overdue accounts, a large cause of his father's economic woes. Henry wrote letters reminding these clients of their obligations, in the same ironical tone used in his sales pitches. Father always made a point of saying: "Ask so-and-so for a little on account, but don't insult him!" But once Henry got started, there was no telling where his letter might take him. Everybody told Henry that he had the wrong attitude toward life. The Hendricks Brothers, associates of his father who specialized in fancy vests, were always advising him, "Henry, be a little more civil to the customers, can't you?" But he whispered to himself: *Fuck them! Why should I kiss the ass of a rich customer who complained that a sleeve was wrong when it was right? Look what that had gotten my father.* Henry resolved that rather than get to this state himself, he would offend potential customers.

For years, Henry's resistance had been closely connected to his yearning to be a writer. But his resistance itself consumed the energy he might have devoted to composition. He "worked" only on an imaginary "book." Every day, when he rode the elevated line to work he picked up the threads of his imaginative work; its subject changed with his moods. In the spring of 1914, there was such tension in his house—with mother attacking Henry and father, Henry striking out at both, and Heinrich taking his lumps with a killing meekness—that Henry's imaginary book came to center upon a murderous family situation. He gave it an imaginary title too—"The House of Incest." He had resisted tailoring because he wanted to write; but ironically, now, the tailor shop stimulated Henry's interest in writing. Some of Heinrich's customers were men of literary distinction, such as Frank Harris, the first writer Henry met. This occurred in the most ordinary way in 1914. When Henry was twenty-two years old, he had the honor of helping Harris on with his trousers while the great man discoursed on Shakespeare, Jesus, and Oscar Wilde. Once, when the Millers made him a loud blazer, he quipped: "I'm not a minstrel, I'm just a writer." And though Henry laughed with him at this, it was precisely the claim he himself would have wished to make. Walter Pach, the art critic and translator of Elie Faure's *History of Art,* also came in; Henry was too shy to mention that he had read Pach's translation. Boardman Robinson was another client who could make the claim of being a writer, for he conducted a newspaper column in addition to being a well-known painter and illustrator. Henry found him less intimidating than the redoubtable Harris and made a special visit to his studio once to ask him just how one goes about becoming a writer. The artist rubbed his brow. "Why, as far as I know," Robinson said, "you just write." Promptly, Henry began to keep a little notebook which he titled "The Intellectual Tailor's Son," but he jotted only a few pallid ideas into it. Often, he walked to the shop by way of the Bowery looking for materials for fiction, assuming that his material must come from outside himself. Walking through flop-house row he would improvise books in his head: "I, the Embryo," "The Palace of Amusements," "From Brooklyn Bridge to Cooper Union."

He wanted to write. Even more, he wanted to *be* a writer and to have a reputation like Jack London's as a romantic personage. The news of London's death in 1916 "really pained him," he wrote to a California poet named Charles Keeler. Then he went on to express his own sense of desolation:

To tell the truth, I am getting more disgusted and pessimistic every day over the situation here in America. It may be that I am living in a narrow sphere, being only a tailor, but from using my powers of observation, I am able to form some judgment of the masses that surround me and I can truthfully say that I loathe them thoroughly. Their own sheer stupidity will be the death of them. I am no longer capable of railing against the capitalists and politicians as I did several years ago. What bothers me now is the fact that there is no material from which to make men nowadays. As materialistic as I am, I am not foolish enough to believe that the system is responsible for everything. That seems to me now to be on a par with the old outworn theology that attributed everything to the will of God.

Do you know where I have had to turn for any satisfaction for my disgust? To the Russian authors. There is a grim reality about their writings that appeases me.

He wanted to be a writer himself, he added, and he had had "the devil's own torments lately from imagining that I have something in me to give the world. I can't quite believe that I am capable of writing anything worth while and yet, for the life of me, I can't repress the desire to put my thoughts on paper. Have had some notions of writing a play, but I have such outlandish stuff to dole out that I am almost afraid to begin. If there is one thing worse than having an artistic temperament, it is thinking you have."

One evening, while Henry and two pals, a down-and-out correspondent named Raymond Gram Swing and Karl Karsten, a statistician, rode back from Bear Mountain in the excursion boat, they discussed Herbert Spencer, Rabindranath Tagore, and Bergson. Then they set up a ouija board on their knees and called on Nietzsche and Jack London. Swing got Nietzsche. "Is there any Zarathustra beyond?" "Can you explain the doctrine of eternal recurrence a little more precisely?" Henry made contact with London, who was still warm in his grave. "What about the coming revolution?" "How is the grub up there?" "Or are you in Hell?" Exactly the answers that they expected came back. Henry was obviously interested in serious questions at this time, but he lacked the energy and will and certitude to look for serious answers. He worked fitfully, he lingered in Pauline's kitchen, he read voraciously, and he planned to write. But most of all, following a sure life-giving instinct, instead of adjusting himself to his dreary circumstances, he drifted.

Five

The Love Songs of Henry Val Miller

One of the customers of Henry Miller & Son—old man Pack they called him—was the photographer who took studio shots for the Metropolitan Opera and Carnegie Hall performers. In partial payment for tailoring he supplied Henry with tickets to Carnegie Hall musical performances several times each week all during 1914 and 1915. As a result, Henry further extended his musical education. He began to study and practice piano really seriously and to entertain the prospect of a career as a concert pianist. He was particularly encouraged to pursue this goal after October 1915, when he met a young and pretty Brooklyn pianist named Beatrice Sylvas Wickens who lived on Ninth Street, on the edge of the old neighborhood. Beatrice was good looking in a conventional way and had a nice slender figure. Her face was rather small, with high cheekbones, large dark eyes, a small mouth, and rather pointed chin. Her hair was dark and bobbed. She had studied piano in a convent while under the protection of a maiden aunt— her mother having remarried—and had become a very accomplished performer. Henry catalogued her qualities at once: technique: perfect; presentation: flawless; wrist movement: excellent; pauses, legato, arpeggio: fine. If she lacked musical originality—if she played the same pieces over and over again and preferred Liszt's "Fourteenth Rhapsody" to anything by Stravinsky or Schönberg, Henry didn't care: he had his eye on her evident good qualities. He began to take lessons from her.

One day, he introduced Pauline to Beatrice. Pauline immediately had her guard up, seeing a rival in this young woman. She always could read Henry well and she was right to be alarmed. Henry liked Beatrice, he liked to try to slip his arm around her waist, he liked the challenge of courting her. In the old days, when he was first chasing Pauline, he had often knocked off early at the tailor shop to visit her, giving his father all kinds of excuses. Now it was Pauline's turn to hear Henry's inventions: he had to work late at the shop cutting patterns, the old man needed to be sobered up, a pal was in trouble, and so on. He was ducking Pauline, of course, in order to drop by Beatrice's house to hear her play or to take her to the matinee at B.F Keith's vaudeville theater not far from her house, where they could mush it up during the dark acts. Though she was naturally passionate and impulsive, she had been made puritanical concerning sex by her religious upbringing, and so he had to proceed delicately, circuitously: he had to be patient, commenting on her technique in certain difficult passages or speaking of anything else under the sun. This chase was enormously exciting to him, and Beatrice never irrevocably surrendered. The further they went, the worse Beatrice felt. "I feel so ashamed," she'd moan after the heat had cooled. "You don't really care for me," she kept telling Henry, "the only reason you want me is for 'that.' " Yet, the word *marriage* often dropped from her lips as she lay back in her green dressing-sack among crumpled pillows. "Miss Wickens and I are progressing rapidly toward mutual conquest," was Miller's terse summary of his love affair.

Whenever the subject of marriage came up, Henry was likely to drift. He thought of escape again; and circumstances, for once, abetted him. Pauline's son George, who had been sent to a sanitarium, died. Curiously, this made Henry feel that he was no longer tied to Pauline. Good, he thought to himself, *Now she'll leave me alone!* Coincidentally, a clerk's job in the mail division of the War Department in Washington, D.C., was offered to him in the spring of 1917. In preparation for war the government was hiring lots of office workers. It was just the chance he wanted. He deserted Pauline and moved to the capital. Washington was buzzing and the news stories were burning up the wires. After a couple of weeks in the War Department, by some fast talking, he also managed to convince the day editor of the *Washington Post* to take him on, without salary, as a cub reporter. This was a bust. The newspaper freelancing lasted about ten days, and the work in the mail room hardly more than a month. Then, when he was required to register for the Selective Service, he didn't hesitate a moment in deciding what to do. Like his grandfathers, he knew that he did not want to go to war. He applied for deferment because of impending marriage, and the hardship need of his mother and ill father. Lots of soldiers marched to war. But Henry returned to New York, re-entered the tailor shop and made Beatrice his wife. His wife's wedding present to him on the hurried wedding day was the price of a shave and a haircut; she paid the marriage fees. It was a day neither of them would ever forget.

It wasn't long before the trench warfare began at 244 Sixth Avenue, the new address of the couple. Beatrice's attitudes proved to be as sharp and angular as her face. Her breath, which once seemed sweet as cinammon to him, soon seemed as bitter as tansy and spiked with complaints. Before marriage, he had been in the position of pursuer; she had been passive. Now, however, her domineering and aggressive nature came to the fore. She was either after him not to sit around, to get out and hunt up a better job, to make something of himself; or she assumed a grim, pathetic, long-suffering look. She openly told visitors that he was a "vulgar, coarse fool," a "lunatic." For his part, he resented her slovenliness, her lack of taste in clothes, her complaints about his lack of ambition. What did she do but sit on her backside all day playing Liszt, that charlatan, with an open box of bonbons beside her, always in the same puke-green chemise? Why didn't *she* go out to work? Why should he have to piss his time away at stupid jobs when she was perfectly able to support them both while he wrote? He never saw any of the money which she earned from lessons, yet she expected him to fork over whatever dough he brought home so that it could go into *her* budget. Why should he receive a meager five dollars a week—so much for carfare, so much for lunch, so much for cigarettes—but nothing extra to jingle in his pockets, nothing for a little spree, a burlesque show or a ride out to Luna Park? Besides, Beatrice hated his idea of being a writer. One evening, when he said to her, "Let's not go out. Perhaps I'll stay home and do some writing," she snapped back: "Remember that you have a job. Don't go starting a book again." Now he blamed his inability to write upon her: he moaned to his friends that she robbed him of his energies. Just like his mother, she spit out her disapproval on everything he did, every prospect he cherished.

For all practical purposes, Beatrice might just as well have let him write, because even though work was plentiful during the war, he had difficulty finding it and even greater difficulty remaining on a job. By 1920 he had held so many positions that employment managers gave him a fishy eye. When he was not working he hung around the tailor shop, which was on Fifty-third Street just east of Fifth Avenue; from there he would walk over to Sixth Avenue to check the blackboards outside employment agencies where vacancies in hotels and restaurants were chalked up. It became a nightmarish experience for him to enter one of these dingy buildings to apply for a posted lead. The jobs themselves were even more nightmarish—some he held for less than a day. During the war years for brief times he was: dishwasher, newsboy, garbage-collector, street-car conductor, hotel bellhop, typist, bartender, adding machine operator, dock-worker, gymnasium instructor, advertising copy-writer, editor, librarian, statistician, mechanic, charity worker, insurance collector, and gas man. A few jobs lasted longer. For some time he did successfully struggle with the Belgian system of indexing in the Bureau of Economic Research. He also spent a considerable stretch grappling with preparing the forthcoming edition of the catalogue of the Charles Williams Mail Order House, but this job ended when his boss discovered him reading German philosophy and doing his own writing on company time.

To make matters worse, Beatrice was far from merely obeying premarital conventions in her sexual restraint. Her hesitations and prohibitions were deeply ingrained in her character. Henry's casual treatment of sex horrified and amazed her. Whenever Henry seemed to step over the borders of refinement by treating sex as comic or experimental or matter-of-fact, she pulled back. He had to maintain a serious and romantic attitude with her. Naturally, this made Henry all the more casual. They began to humiliate each other by using sex as a weapon in their domestic contests. She fought him over sex because he was not a conventionally good spouse to her; and he fought her, with promises or lies if necessary, for the pleasure of surprising her into sex or breaking down her resistance. Her attempt to bring him into line by withholding sex only made him concentrate all his energies and expend all his efforts to possess her without being brought to net. Far from emasculating him, she challenged and concentrated his sexuality; he planned his conquests as General Pershing did his strategies. Perhaps she might eventually win the war of attrition, but he could still dominate her with surprise assaults and guerrilla tactics.

Sex, unfortunately, lost the war for him. He made a strategic blunder. About a year after they were married, in the summer of 1918 Beatrice proposed that they go on a belated honeymoon to visit her mother in an out-of-the-way Delaware town. She hardly knew her mother and step-father, having been placed in boarding schools most of her life, but she gave Henry to believe that they were a bubbly, typical small-town couple. Complications started as soon as they arrived. Beatrice's mother resembled Pauline amazingly; she was the same age, had the same accepting disposition and the same easygoing, sensual twinkle in her gay eyes and in her greeting. Besides, Henry was not slow in sizing up the domestic arrangement: obviously, this man and woman had long ago come to a friendly agreement which left each to his separate devices. And from the looks of it they obviously had made cozy arrangements. Right away, in fact, the mother seemed to be giving him the eye! Under such circumstances, it was not long before Henry and Beatrice's mother were left alone in the house. One morning, while he was sitting in the sunny parlor reading his paper and listening to the birds chirping wildly in a chinaberry tree, he heard Beatrice's mother humming, almost purring, in a soft, Southern, moist, and throaty voice while she soaked in the tub. He almost held his breath to hear the valved hum of her voice. Then she called: "Val, are you there? Bring me a towel, dear, will you?" He stepped into the bathroom in his loose pajamas and never remembered whether he picked up a towel or not before he slipped into the tub with her.

Only after Beatrice gave birth to a daughter, Barbara Sylvas, on September 30, 1919, did she indignantly face him with the fact that she had known all along that the previous summer each morning, at the same hour, he had been screwing her mother. Any man who would lay his mother-in-law, she seemed to imply, must be totally corrupt; and so, by some strange logic, since his amorality had been so thoroughly exposed, he should now be a good boy and do whatever she required of him. *Shit on that,* Henry thought, and the war expanded. They fought bitterly and steadily. They slept in separate rooms; but even so, sometimes they would sit up in bed to hurl insults and abuse at each other, striking out in the dark, from one room to another. Sometimes their rage would reach such a maniacal pitch they would jump out of bed ready to go for each other's throats. It was no wonder that Henry grumbled in public that she was a puritanical monster. Who could blame him if he stayed out at night?

And yet, despite their constant, running skirmishes, it could not be fairly said that he ceased to love Beatrice. She tantalized him as much as ever, challenging him when she triumphed over him and appealing to his quick sympathies when she lost. And without question, he was wild about his daughter Barbara. He hovered over her, daydreaming about what he would do for her in the future, trying to observe each of her reactions as if through her he could have all his questions about his own childhood answered. Like him she would grow up in the old neighborhood and be allowed, always, to run wild in the streets. As if watching an old movie remade with new actors, he saw Barbara as himself and himself as Barbara.

As for his adult self, that bumbled on. After experiencing so many frustrations of his desire to be a writer, he was timid about asserting himself. Only to a close friend like Bill Dewar would he speak of his admiration for Waldo Frank and his secret desires to emulate him. He took a masochistic pleasure in tallying up the equipment or talents that he would need to acquire were he to become a writer—to travel, to have big thoughts, to be fluent in numerous languages, to possess a grand style, to speak well in public—and he condemned his existence for the few opportunities it offered him to realize his dreams. But he hadn't given up the dream. In January 1919 his eye fell on an editorial in *The Black Cat: Clever Short Stories* magazine, published in Salem, Massachusetts. The editor reminded his readers that around 1900, when Jack London had almost despaired of publication and was ready to go back to coal-heaving, *The Black Cat* had accepted one of his tales. Ever since, the editor continued, the magazine "held to the policy of encouraging young writers." Henry pricked up his ears at this and at the following advice: "The editors of *The Black Cat* are constantly receiving manuscripts that are apparently the first, last, and only efforts of writers who look with longing eyes upon authorship as a profession, but haven't the courage to keep eternally at it. It never occurs to many of them that in the writing game, as in any other profession, it is necessary to serve an apprenticeship. They are a long time in finding out the first rule—that only by steeping themselves in technique can they master the art of short-story writer." How, any reader would have wondered, was one to acquire mastery in technique then? The editor had the answer. To any subscriber he offered the opportunity to study technique through writing critiques on any story appearing in the magazine. *The Black Cat* would publish intelligent criticisms and compensate critics at the rate of a penny a word. Some of those who had started as critics had later published stories in *The Black Cat*—and one, the editor noted, had even earned enough money to buy a Liberty Bond. Here was a chance indeed.

Of course, this was a device to raise the number of subscriptions to the magazine. But Henry had been looking for the education in writing which *The Black Cat* editor seemed to offer and did not hesitate to subscribe his $1.50. Promptly, by return mail, he received his "handsome club emblem" and a copy of the February issue of *The Black Cat*. The lead story was Carl Clausen's "The Unbidden Guest," and Henry sweated and squeezed and prayed until he finally turned out a few hundred words of a critique. It was accepted! This was Henry Miller's first publication. The lead piece in the reviews section of the May 1919 issue, it revealed a good deal about the direction of his literary talents and preferences at this time.

The longer a man lives the more convinced he becomes that the essential thing is not what a man says or does but how he says it or does it. Men like Lincoln, Walt Whitman or Ralph Waldo Emerson may prove the rule by being the exceptions, but on the other hand we have innumerable others like Shaw, Wilde, Kipling, Rabelais and Arthur Brisbane who keep the theory within the realm of pragmatic truth.

When one has not the endowments of a Balzac or a Zola, that is to say, when one has not the infinite patience and exactitude of these artists, then a good imagination is a very fine substitute. I should like to pay the author the compliment of saying that certain of his descriptive passages recall vividly to my mind one of Pierre Loti's works, "An Iceland Fisherman," which I consider to be a gem for word-painting.

He also saw "suggestions" of Joseph Conrad, Jack London, and Lord Dunsany in the story, and then he concluded his critique with a statement of aesthetic principle: "A Burton Holmes Travelogue may be scientific, entertaining and photographic, but a vivid canvas done by an artist is ever so much more interesting and stimulating." This piece was signed: "Henry V. Miller."

When Henry received notice in early May that this critique had been accepted, as well as payment for it in a check for $4.86, he was bowled over. He was made, he told himself. Now he could fairly claim that he was an author, even if he never again published a word. He got so worked up that he ran outside waving his letter of acceptance and skimmed his Borsalino slouch hat into the air. It descended in the gutter, where it was immediately crushed by a passing truck. No matter!—the dough rolled in: in the next few months, he had four more essays published and earned a total of $9.50. Occasionally in these pieces, he made general observations which revealed something about his aesthetic views around 1919. American writing, he remarked, was characterized by "glittering sterility," which placed it below that of "the Russian and French productions." His most consistent response as a critic seemed to be associated with the representation in fiction of modern marriage and relations between the sexes. (Clearly, the failure of his marriage had shattered certain romantic, idealistic expectations which he had held secret—perhaps even from himself. His critiques dealt with conflicts in marriage because he had so many conflicts over it himself.) His third critique, of a story involving the unhappiness of a married woman, began: "The single truth about marriage is that it is a disillusion. The author . . . has shown us the one side of the medal, wherein marriage has disillusioned the woman. We men, of course, do not need any story to depict the other side of the medal. It takes only about three days of matrimony to open a man's eyes. As an old philosopher I once knew described it: 'Man naturally places woman on a pedestal, but she always insists on stepping down from it.'"

The story which was the subject of his fourth essay gave him a "complete surprise" by containing a "faint suspicion of the risqué," a hint, he thought, which added "eighty per cent" to the interest. The "risqué" in "Propriety and a Pullman" derived from the efforts of a young man to share a lady's Pullman bed; only at the end do we discover that the lady is his wife. "At bottom," Miller wrote, "all women are actresses. Added to that, all jealous women, such as our heroine is, derive pleasure in a little display of cruelty, especially toward those whom they love." His final critique, appearing in the October 1919 issue, admitted that "men neglect their wives even though the latter are occasionally talented or gifted," but he couldn't accept the story's premise that a woman could speak out impressively with short notice on a recondite matter.

Henry was becoming the star critic of the Black Cat Club. Apparently, however, the idea had not brought in as many new subscriptions as anticipated, and the October 1919 issue was the last to print critical essays. Henry's outlet for writing was abruptly cut off. If he had expected to learn the techniques of short fiction from writing about others' stories, he was apparently disappointed, for he never submitted a story to the "all-new" *Black Cat.* Still, on the basis of the criticisms that he did write, it is fairly easy to see what kind of stories he admired and probably would have liked to have written. Obviously, he was taking the side of whatever was regarded as "modern" and up-to-date. As yet he did not show that the European dramatists and novelists that he had been reading had influenced him except superficially, but he had nurtured an easy, somewhat facile, philosophical turn of mind.

Henry earned a lot of self-esteem for his published articles, but Beatrice merely counted the fifteen dollars (at a penny a word) and pointed out that he didn't have a permanent position. In the matter of employment he seemed to have reached a dead end. Even the tailor shop offered no solution: it had virtually gone into receivership. Not long after his marriage to Beatrice, Henry also gave up all dreams of becoming a concert pianist; temporarily at least, his irritation with her disgusted him with the instrument, and he practiced only sporadically. But everytime he crossed his hands and attempted the opening measures of Stojowski's "Love Song" or uncrossed them to make a stab at Czerny's studies in velocity, he realized how rusty he had become and concluded it was too late for him to be a serious musician. The first gift he gave Beatrice was a two-hundred and fifty dollar victrola—an extravagant symbol of the music which had brought them together. But he never paid for it and finally had to sell it. His marriage, his possible future as a concert pianist, and the victrola all seemed to go about the same time.

Of course, there must be other jobs to be had. Beatrice kept telling him to get out and hunt one up.

Six

The Cosmodemonic Telegraph Company

Henry had held so many other jobs that it was surprising that he had never been a messenger for the Western Union Telegraph Company. *Anyone* who could walk, could be a messenger—it was the last job possible. Finally, he felt so low that at the age of twenty-eight he seemed to be ready for the lowest possible job. Early in 1920, he applied at the Western Union office in the famous Flatiron Building at Fifth Avenue and Twenty-second Street. The switchboard operator glanced at his application and to his complete astonishment informed him that there was no place for him on the staff, even though it was apparent that the turnover was enormous and messengers were being replaced hourly. The worst job in the world—one which he wanted chiefly to provide him an excuse for wandering around New York—and he was told that he did not qualify for it. It was humiliating to explain to Beatrice that he had applied for a job as messenger and been rejected. A sharp glance from her added salt to his wounds, for she obviously refused to believe that if he had applied for the job at all, which she doubted, he had done so seriously. She well knew the obsequious, ironical, half-insulting tone he used with employment managers. Almost outright, she accused him of low deceit. The more Henry thought about it the worse he felt. By nightfall he got so worked up that he decided to lodge a complaint with the company president. Imagine the nerve—Henry V. Miller, author and respectable citizen, refused such a measly job.

The next morning, shaved and neatly dressed, Henry set out in a fine frenzy for the main offices of the company at 33 Park Place. The president, whom he asked to see, appeared to be out of town. All the vice-presidents were deeply engaged, it seemed. By the time he agreed to file his complaint about the company's employment practices with the first vice-president's male secretary, he was fuming and ready to deliver a real blast. Though he usually felt tongue-tied in the presence of others, occasionally he would break into a verbal explosion. (This had happened, for instance, one night after a literary lecture at the Rand School when Henry stood up and delivered a long, impromptu speech which began with Waldo Frank and ended with Knut Hamsun and was so impressive that afterwards a group of people there approached him and asked him to direct a literary society.) Now, the fit was on him again when he saw the secretary face-to-face. "So you think I am not in earnest in making an application for the job of messenger," he began and swept into a speech whose theme was his human right to be given a job for which he was in every way suited. Look at how he had been treated. What if he did qualify for far better jobs? If he qualified for this job, why should he not be given it? As he spoke, he regarded the question from every side, dispassionately, judicially. He tossed the subject up as a juggler does his Indian clubs and looked at it from various angles—ideal, practical, economic, personal, industrial.

It was clear, the secretary said smoothly when Henry's tirade ran down, that something was indeed amiss. He certainly wanted to thank Henry for pointing out the inefficiencies in the hiring policies of the company. He intimated to Henry that he was aghast to see things had come to such a state that a crumby little switchboard operator, virtually the lowest paid Western Union employee, was in a position to reject the application of a man whose qualities were so obvious. The general manager, he said, would be only too glad to hear about this. By this time Henry had cooled down enough to realize that this was probably the first step in the old runaround. But when the secretary got on the telephone with the general manager and repeated Henry's story to him with certain unmistakable omissions and emphases in it, Henry began to understand that they were actually taking the matter seriously. The secretary sent him to the general offices uptown, and there the general manager ushered him into a big chair and popped a cigar into his mouth. Obviously, Henry saw that he had hit upon a special sore spot. The problem of the messenger crew, it soon began to emerge, had perplexed all the executives, though messengers were really the heart of the whole company. Efficient business methods had been introduced everywhere else in the organization, but the messengers still gummed up the whole works. In order to keep the work force of a thousand or so messengers going, the company had to interview about ten thousand applicants a year. It appeared that Mr. Willever, a vice-president, had recently been sharply critical of the general manager's inability to solve the delivery problem. Having spent a fortune in capital improvements in order to reduce the transmission time between San Francisco and New York to forty-five minutes, Willever saw no reason to have a message sit in the office for hours with a sticker on it pompously announcing the rapidity with which the transmission had occurred. Then, when the message was finally picked up it might remain in the pocket of some half-wit while he took in a ballgame, or be stuffed down a sewer by a new recruit who despaired his first day on the job. The machinery was fine, but the human system was going absolutely crazy.

Henry's story seemed to expose all the worms in the apple, and he sized up the situation quickly. The general manager liked Henry's complaints so well that he called in his assistant to hear them all over again. An old hand at job-hunting and adept at manipulating others when he wanted to, Henry let them draw out of him the story they wished to hear; he allowed them to tip him off. They obviously had it in for the "little kike" at the switchboard, Sam Sattenstein, but their real target was the employment manager. The general manager proposed a plan: Henry would be hired to serve as a company spy. Under cover of employment as a messenger, he would be transferred around to the company's local offices (there were over a hundred in New York alone) and by going from place to place, in a matter of months he'd be able to make a thorough survey of the irregularities and problems of the messenger service. Eventually, Henry would be made employment manager himself. In the meantime, out of a special fund he would receive an equivalent salary.

In the space of two days Henry had been rejected as a messenger at about $17 a week and been offered a job as spy and future messenger employment manager at $240 a month. Always merry and bright! He accepted at once. Subsequent events seemed to follow the manager's impromptu plan. After a few months, the personnel manager was sacked and Henry took possession of a new employment office at Park Place. He retained Sam Sattenstein, who was willing to solve the problems that could be solved or to muck things up as much as possible, whichever Henry wished. Long before he took over, Henry had logically concluded that there was really no solution to the messenger problem. In fact, it was apparent that the worst source of trouble was the idiot on the thirteenth floor, Willever himself. He believed that the only solutions of any value were those of his own making or those which his "efficiency experts" presented him. But even though he had been a messenger in his youth, he was as distant now from the problems of the messenger service as his time control men were. Any half-assed employment manager who worked steadily could eventually assemble a semi-permanent work force of reliable messengers. After all, the newspaper ads which announced that messengers could earn twenty-five dollars a week kept pretty high-level applicants streaming in. But whenever the messengers reached full force, the personnel manager would receive a call from the thirteenth floor: the laws of supply and demand meant *Cut Wages! Increase Hours! Speed Up Delivery!* Soon, the whole thing would begin to fall apart. The best messengers would quit. Some others found their wages diminishing and the pace killing; others simply despaired and slowly tore their messages into the wind. Others would lose their sense of direction and be found sitting in a trance on a bench at the last subway stop in Canarsie. No manager could hold an experienced crew together under these circumstances. Eventually, when things got so bad that the employment manager couldn't get any applicants but mental defectives, the company would again allow wages to increase. And Willever couldn't figure out why the messenger service was so screwed up.

No one could solve the problems in this situation. But for virtually the first time in his life Henry was challenged. The job brought out the almost fanatical missionary idealism which his failures had repressed but not destroyed. His romantic idealism had surfaced in relation to Cora and even Pauline, but his social perfectionism had never had any worthy object to work on before, and it blossomed fully, so fully, perhaps, because it could not be fulfilled in Western Union. In short, he couldn't quite understand what was happening to him. He felt like a little tin god whom a world of poor saps were looking to for aid. But this was good for him: his pity was shifting from himself to others. When he couldn't give a deserving man a job, he tried to help him find a position elsewhere, through his friends or other employment managers. Sometimes he brought him home to his house for board and bed, or let him sleep on the office floor, or loaned him money. When he couldn't give anything else, he tried to give him courage. Henry became absorbed by the notion that he could solve the insoluble. And in an oblique way, he really had prepared for this job. His seven-year period of athleticism had left him in excellent physical shape, his many jobs had given him abundant experience with employment procedures, and his dormant sympathies were ready to be provoked by the human suffering he found waiting for him. If he did not have the Ph.D. from Columbia University which he had listed on his Western Union application, he did have some curious qualifications which he could not list.

He sat at his desk at Park Place and the applicants came streaming in, debasing themselves before him, begging for jobs. They wrote him grotesque notes like the one sent him by one supplicant, Rosario Dimiceli, in 1921: "When I was up to the main office at 33 Park Place I recognized to your looks and the way you used your language that you would give a boy in my case another chance to work for Western Union." They were all, it seemed, dippy. But they told him life stories that were heartbreaking in their misery or grotesquely humorous in their imbecility. Some wept whether hired or not. Others were ready to kiss his hand, to kneel at his feet, to grovel on the floor, to send up prayers to the Almighty or offer novenas on his behalf, to beg, plead, offer him bribes, offer him their wives—or children, or mothers!—anything!—for a job, the mere chance of a job. Their lugubrious dog-like gratitude affected him as terribly as their despairing entreaties. He wanted to hire everyone, but he also wanted to perfect the messenger service and he couldn't do both. Somehow, Henry had to sort things out; for almost the first time in his life he had to use his mind and confront his foggy ideals with the demands of social necessity. Many applicants had special and not entirely respectable reasons for wanting to become messengers: second-story men or blackmailers who found a chance to get inside offices or buildings to which admission would otherwise be denied them; prostitutes who used the job as a cover; aging male homosexuals who found employment a way of mixing with the young boys. These had to be spotted and weeded out, along with a gang of other unreliables.

Those he did hire had to be shuffled around as if they were chess pieces in order to keep the offices supplied and stave off checkmate for the company. In his spare time Henry had to arrange for the tailoring of uniforms to fit the messengers' weird shapes. He had to keep account of the state of the current force and also to interview new recruits continuously. To keep his army up, he sent his assistants out to beat the bushes, in school-lots, playgrounds, pool parlors, parks, and movie houses—anywhere an eligible boy was likely to be buttonholed. He made contact with an ex-warden of Sing Sing and against company orders hired quite a few men recently out of prison. He had an Indian friend in the theater and, through him, became a clearinghouse for Indian students looking for work; Buddhists, Mohammedans, and Hindus made the office into a congress of religions. The heads of the

Salvation Army and the Bowery Y.M.C.A. sent him fellows who were down
and out. It almost looked as if he were running a flop house mission himself.
And, every time he got the staff at full-strength through all these sources,
Willever would conclude that the wages were too high and order them cut.
After all his efforts, Henry would be back where he began, hiring and firing
like a whirlwind.

So, the flotsam of New York passed through the various offices that he
occupied as employment manager, at Park Place, the Flatiron Building,
and 195 Broadway. The messenger employment office seemed to be the last
stop before oblivion for most of the applicants. As each new candidate
appeared at his desk it was as if Henry had to note and file him before he
dropped off the edge of the world. There were Gupte, the flute player, who
was murdered in Greenwich Village; Waldman, the mathematician, a
gentleman *par excellence*; Murkland, the old fat tub who read Dante and
Cervantes in the original; Schiller, the prison rat and dope pusher; To-
bachnikev, the Bolshevik and Hebrew scholar; Eugene Sullivan, who wrote
poetry in the elevator; Hugh Russell Fraser, the son of a country minister;
Anderson of Yale, who had also spent fifteen years in jail; Joe Schriber, the
messenger with a sweet voice, known along Broadway as "Al Jolson";
Muriel Silber, the 17 year old *violiniste*; Jac Dun, the globetrotter; and
Johnny Murry, the ex-boxer. These were only a few among many of the
characters he encountered. He could pluck their files up out of his cabinet as
one would lift exotic fish from a tropical aquarium.

This miserable job saved Henry by crushing his false attitude of superiority and his excessive preoccupation with himself. All his attitudes were
turned around by his new experience. To say that his personality was
transformed by the job would hardly be an exaggeration. Now that he
appeared to be a successful executive, a man of affairs, he came to feel that he
was as low as the lowest of his messengers. He began by thinking that he
might save *them,* save them by offering them jobs, but after some months he
had the uneasy feeling that they might be saving him. The Hindu messengers who politely called him Meester Hendie Millar explained Ramakrishna
and Tagore's "Shantinikefan" to him and took him to hear Tagore lecture at
Carnegie Hall. They were winged messengers, bright messengers, to him.
The criminals and the hoboes spilled out tales of suffering. All the messengers opened his eyes to the fact that his own suffering was only a tiny part of
the misery in America. From the experience of collective misery into which
he was thrown, he began to make a decisive repudiation of American
institutions. He himself had been buffeted by the system. Now, for the first

time, he was in a position to declare his failure America's rather than his own and to question the social system not for reasons of personal failure but on behalf of others. Like a man raised from the dead, Henry had accidentally been elevated into a position of social authority and economic power. He was allowed by this bird's-eye view to see how hollow was the successful life which he thought he wanted. Now he knew that along with his messengers he too was standing on the edge of oblivion. They were all doomed. But this experience also constituted a spiritual reawakening for him and, in an eerie way he began to think that he and even the lowliest messengers were all on the same mysterious path to ordination. If he could have known in the winter of 1920 what he was getting into, he would probably have blanched and sunk back into the ooze of his defeats; but to his surprise he found himself responding wonderfully to all these changes in his life.

In truth, just when existence seemed to have narrowed to a needle's point, the job reopened him to life itself. He had a vague purpose, a day-to-day occupation, an army of new friends, an end to his vacant days. His life once more filled with laughter. As his assistant he hired a kind of soldier-of-fortune, adventurer type named Joe O'Regan. Henry's secretary, a good looking seventeen-year-old named Muriel Mauer, was promoted out of the file room when Joe spotted her reading *Crime and Punishment* on company time. Just the secretary for Henry—what did it matter if she couldn't type? The company detective, Richard Carey, hung around, exhibiting a sure eye for deadbeats, perverts, and dope pushers, and in a fine, casual way he told astonishing stories about his experiences as a flatfoot. The imbeciles among the applicants were shuffled off to Seymour Emil Cohen, a young psychiatrist. Joe Ramos and Mike Rivise and Sam Sattenstein waybilled the messengers all about town; and Dave Kasevoi generally loitered about, waiting to follow Henry's bidding.

Henry formed this group into a later Xerxes Society—with rules entirely of his own devising. Their adventures began after five o'clock. If he needed dough, Henry dipped into the petty cash drawer, telegraphed himself a tidy sum, or put the touch on one of the messengers. What was in store for the evening depended on who showed up: he was ready to move with any wind (so long as he could manage to stay out until Beatrice and Barbara, lying in a crib in the corner of the bedroom, were fast alseep). If Joe O'Regan and Muriel, sometimes accompanied by a young architect named Herbert Sleaco, showed up to lead him off to Child's for a cheap meal, he'd gladly sit at the table swapping stories in his funny, ironic, engaging way, wagging his head and roaring with laughter to press home his points.

When things got dull, he'd collar the diner at the next table and soon elicit the fellow's life story. Or, they'd cut the chatter and hustle off to the Labor Temple on East Fourteenth Street and Second Avenue; there they attended lectures on literature by Powys and on psychology by André Tridon. Cohen sometimes took them to lower Second Avenue for inspection of patients at Dr. Schlapp's Clinic for Mental Defectives. If the whim took them, they'd attend the Irving Place or the Houston Street burlesque theaters. If instead of his other friends, Joe Ramos and Sam picked him up at the office, then he'd be whisked off to Broadway, to the dancehall dives, the Diana Dance Hall or Wilson's, or the chop suey joints.

Sometimes, with plans of his own, Henry waved his friends away. After hours he'd grill one of the eccentrics among the messengers, interpreting his dreams, advising him on his marital problems, regulating his sex life, giving hygienic advice, studying his mannerisms and above all analyzing his phobias and obsessions. Henry would go on for hours. Perhaps the session would end with his accompanying the messenger home for a meal, particularly if he could guess that the wife might be attractive and possible to make later. Often, he wrapped the session up with a loan. Besides, some of the messengers were girls, usually young ones, between fourteen and seventeen, and Henry gave them particular attention. He kept the addresses of the good looking ones in a memorandum book, and when things got dull he started to call them up—first those whose names he had starred. If things went right, the evening might conclude cosily on his consulting table in the back room. Sometimes, to Beatrice's dismay, he'd arrive home accompanied by an assortment of his chums. Beatrice would give them all a withering, miserable look, as if believing that Henry had assembled the group for her special punishment (sometimes she was not far wrong). In front of his friends he mocked her ideas and discussed their domestic differences. Even more than this she detested being expected to cook for the mob and then to have Henry ask the guests to shell out for the food, which violated her meager sense of hospitality.

Henry also arranged to take in boarders, and though this looked like another insult, it actually turned out, for once, in a way that pleased Beatrice. Their ad in the *Times* was answered by a gifted musician from Osage, Minnesota, named Harolde Orvis Ross, who had come to study music theory and keyboard at Julliard. The three of them hit it off from the very beginning, Ross and Beatrice through the piano and Ross and Henry through literary discussions. Orvis was a fountain of literary observation and knowledge, with enormous energy, and for Henry's files he made copies of such literary works as "I am the People, the Mob" from Carl Sandburg's *Chicago Poems*. Indeed, he even translated the entire novel *Batouala,* by René Maran, at Henry's request. For a while, by liking them both, Ross brought Beatrice and Henry closer together. Sometimes, in a scene of domestic harmony unlike any Henry had experienced in a long time, the three of them together would bang out musical selections on the piano or else sit after dinner and talk about books. But after three months, Ross went back to Minnesota and left them where he found them, stranded on the mud-flats of an unhappy marriage. Ross was a letter writer, however, and big fat envelopes began arriving at the Miller house. Not since Stanley Borowski had been stationed at Fort Oglethorpe during the tail-end of the war had Henry had so gargantuan a correspondent. A measly ten pages or so on the subject of *Jennie Gerhardt* would simply wet Ross's whistle. Once he got started, he'd follow up with, say, a full-blown thirty or forty page critique of *The Bomb;* then he'd be in fine fettle and compose a little book on *The Idiot* accompanied by reams more about Dostoievski in general. This was good for Henry. He was so preoccupied by his Western Union adventures that he might have neglected books otherwise. Ross kept his literary interests alive.

Big as were the letters which Henry received, Beatrice always seemed to get letters just as big. Henry was convinced that these epistles weren't solely about Bach's organ music. Indeed, even before Ross left, Henry had been half convinced that he had fallen in love with Beatrice. Certainly, Ross appealed to Beatrice. Whenever they had an argument, Orvis always was dragged out to serve as a contrast to Henry: *he,* Beatrice wailed, was kind and attentive and considerate. Well, if she would have preferred to be married to him, Henry thought, why didn't Ross come and take her? That would be an excellent solution to the difficulties of their domestic life. There would be no hard feelings. He'd even be able to keep Ross's friendship, which he valued a good deal more than Beatrice's affections.

Henry was beginning to understand his own situation through parallels found in his favorite novels. Reality was confused and dismal, but literature seemed to expose the secrets of things. Characters in fiction led lives that were intelligible. He looked to books in order to make some sense out of his life. Before 1920, the writers he savored and those who influenced him most had been, in the most general sense, philosophers, thinkers. Now he ceased to believe that ideas would explain his life; rather, things and actions, life-accounts, promised to do so much more coherently, and for this reason novels gained a hold over his imagination.

But fiction didn't change the bitterness of his relation to Beatrice. Their marriage reached a stage of such open misery that in the fall of 1921 Beatrice suddenly threw up her hands and moved herself and Barbara to Rochester, New York. This sudden and unexpected action brought Henry up short. He didn't feel grief exactly, though he missed Barbara a little; but he did begin to feel a self-analytical curiosity about how he would take this abandonment, and he also began to try to imagine the feelings Beatrice was experiencing. He felt so little personal emotion of any kind that he was obliged to wonder how he should feel. In a roundabout way, he was beginning to see himself as an object for contemplation and his experience as a subject for fiction. Already, he was becoming a fiction, almost a myth, to himself.

Ten days after her departure, Beatrice wrote to him. She and the child, she said, were well and would like to hear from him. She seemed quiet and easy, a little dreamy, like a convalescent after a serious illness. There was a merest hint at the end of the letter about running short of funds, though not an outright request for aid. By this time he had worked himself up into an emotional sweat. His strongest impulse was defensive and egotistical: to behave in such a way that she would fall in love with him all over again so that he could take revenge upon her. Immediately he telegraphed money to her and sent a ten-page letter special delivery. "Look after yourself," he wrote. "Enjoy yourself. Perhaps I've been a big fool." Three days later he received a letter thanking him for his kindness and urging him to continue writing. Perfect. He wrote longer and longer letters. At last he became, though he had tortured Beatrice relentlessly ever since their marriage, spellbound by his own tenderness and by the nostalgia he had manufactured in his letters designed to woo Beatrice back. Now he told himself he had been a fool: he adored Beatrice. And Barbara—her budding consciousness had just begun to interest him. At lunchtime he wandered about, peering in store windows, looking for presents that would appeal to the two of them. More than once, he telegraphed Beatrice flowers and mailed her books and candy and clippings from the New York papers which he thought would amuse her. He asked her forgiveness and confessed himself a wretch.

This all worked to perfection. Before long, she urged him to come to her for a visit. Henry took a train up to Rochester. She was in his arms almost from the moment she met him at the door. For three days they coiled together like a pair of eels. But then Henry realized that he didn't love her at all: what he really loved was to manipulate Beatrice's reactions: he had fallen in love with his own letters, not with his wife. He loved his own supreme ability to win her even against her will. When they dragged themselves from bed like fagged-out swimmers, nothing had changed. When it was time to leave, he could certainly feel that she was silently entreating him to be a good husband. But even as she drew him from the door back into the hallway for one final word of affection before his departure, he was so bored that he blushed for shame.

As he sat on the city bound train, Henry was feeling that a chasm had irrevocably opened between them. Absently, he opened his bag to look for a trifle. There, on the top, was a surprise gift from Beatrice of Knut Hamsum's novel *Victoria*. Obviously, Henry reflected, Beatrice must have seen in the book an emblem of her own frustrated love. She had even inscribed Victoria's words on the fly-leaf: "I am a grotesque written upon an old oak leaf vomited by a storm in late winter." Before the train reached the city, he had read through the entire novel, and with tears in his eyes, reread the closing pages, Victoria's last letter. The novel hit him hard, and he did apply the lessons of Victoria and Johannes to his own situation, but not in the way probably anticipated by Beatrice. *You must break out from this mundane existence,* he kept telling himself. When he reached his room, he scribbled out a letter to Beatrice which began: "Dear Victoria . . ." and told her of his need to run free, to expand. "I must do something, dear Beatrice, dear Victoria . . . Yes, I read your inscription on the fly-leaf . . . I prefer, however, to think of page 39, on which it is written: 'Ah, love turns the heart of man into a garden of fungus, a luxuriant and shameless garden wherein mysterious and immodest toadstools raise their heads.' " True, he was deeply anguished—but he was weeping for the fictive Victoria whom he felt he was destined to meet. He did not even bother to send the letter to the real Beatrice. But he did determine that he must free himself utterly from the manacles of bourgeois existence, so that he could be ready to welcome the real Victoria when she appeared.

Victoria wasn't likely to be found in the studio of his Western Union assistant, Joe O'Regan, but Henry moved in with Joe after Beatrice ran off to Rochester. Together, he and Joe made the studio into a kind of whorehouse, where they invited and exchanged women, combined with a psychiatric laboratory, where they mercilessly examined the strangest job applicants. Henry treated these characters cruelly, as objects, as if they were animated case histories from books he was reading. Until they spilled all their secrets and revealed their hearts' desires, he'd be elaborately polite. Then he'd analyze their motives until they were ready to admit to anything—from leprosy to body odor—and perhaps he'd turn vicious and mock their most sacred dreams. One of these victims whom he had cheated out of his pay, wrote to him: "You and your man 'Friday' O'Regan are as dirty a pair of crooks as could be found in the worst prisons of the country . . . In your dealings with the messengers you use the same despicable tactics as the Germans did with the 'Belgian' children." *Fuck him,* Henry thought and put the letter into his "Humorous File."

The beginning of the "Humorous File" was a signal that Henry's attitude toward the job had changed. After a year and a half his original enthusiasm had dwindled and his idealism had disappeared. In a sense, he had become heartless. Though he was still as kind and attentive to most of his friends as he had been in the balmy days of the Xerxes Society, his position toward them had subtly altered. Very clearly, he shied away from intimate relations and looked upon people from a distance. Instead of giving himself to experience, as he had tended to do before, he began to cannibalize the experience of others for his own benefit. When he could absorb no more from a particular person, he showed no regrets at terminating their relations or drifting away. Henry had been unstable as an adolescent because he was so self-effacing, so ready to sacrifice his own interests for the sake of others. The Henry of 1922 had made a rapid about-face and was unstable because he was so completely self-interested.

He was in danger of losing his job; for now the messenger corps had returned to the level of sodden inefficiency in which he had found it. It did not help that he and Joe would often go off on three or four day sprees. Fatigued, they'd sleep by turns during the day in the back room on the zinc table.

Henry was simply wearing himself out, fraying the edges off his good disposition and natural friendliness. He was short-tempered with the messengers and grumpy with the staff. One day, he flared up over a minor disagreement and fired Joe O'Regan. Not only did he have to move back to his own apartment, what was worse he was left without an effective assistant. He had, he now realized, depended upon Joe for a great deal. The Western Union job was hard enough for two men to handle—but for one (when that one was worn out), impossible. Naturally, conditions worsened. His bosses began to show their displeasure. Now and then they called him onto the carpet. But he had become indifferent about being fired and his casual tone helped him: the general manager even began to tell him to take things easy, not do anything hasty. He could tell himself that he had the bosses bamboozled—so instead of seeing that they were biding time until he could be replaced, he did nothing to restore sanity in the office.

In the meantime, he had rediscovered a long-lost acquaintance named Emil Schnellock and made him a friend. Henry had first met him at P.S. 85 when he found the young boy magically covering the blackboard with colored chalk pictures of Santa Claus and his reindeers. By the time they met again by chance in 1921, Emil had recently returned from art studies in Europe, and his conversation was filled with talk about the European masters, in particular Botticelli, Cimabue, Giotto, and Uccello. Emil had a fine academic and human acquaintance with the history of painting and painters and gave Henry many a lecture. He was then beginning a career, though very hesitantly, as an advertising artist, convinced, like many of his friends, that he was selling out, yet also wanting to sell out because he secretly feared that he did not have the spark of a great painter. In any event, Henry came to his studio on Bedford Avenue many an evening, and they'd stroll down to Prospect Park, walking around the lake and talking about Europe, painting, D.H. Lawrence (a favorite of Emil's), problems of the artist in modern society. Those nights with Schnellock had such a glow for Henry that when he made his way home alone, the streets of Flatbush seemed horrible and empty. The Fifth Avenue-Sea Beach El, under which he ducked on his way to Sixth Street, loomed like an obscene crab crouching above the pedestrians; the brownstone stoops looked like ugly gashes in the houses. When at last he approached his own flat, he would be so overcome with melancholy, he would have to stop off at the house of his old friend Stanley, by now a hopeless drunkard, and get drunk with him. By the time that Beatrice moved to Rochester, Schnellock had moved his studio to 60 West Fiftieth Street in Manhattan. Henry often showed up here. In his curious, impulsive, yet hesitant way, Henry would gallop up the three flights of stairs, knock and say tentatively, "Is it all right?" It was always all right. At Emil's he could always have fun, laugh easily. Days with Emil were jolly. If Emil had a model posing, Henry would grab a pencil and pretend he was drawing her in order to take a good look and decide whether to give her a try. Otherwise, he might try to write while Emil finished his own work, then off they might go to the galleries or a museum. Occasionally, Emil practiced by sketching Henry looking like a saint or a satyr. Many times they played chess, though Henry hadn't the patience for the game. (In this, his impatience with life, the fact that he was living on the ragged edge of rebellion showed clearly. One night, after Emil had captured a number of pieces Henry shouted: "Damn it all, it's a war of attrition!" The steady wear of the game was too much like his life with Beatrice.) Grimly, Henry was inclined to sacrifice all his pieces so as to get the contest down to the barest essentials, when he had only one last piece to deal with.

The only piece he had to play was himself. But existence, as he well knew, was never as simplified as a chess game. First of all, Beatrice returned after a two months' absence, with nothing resolved. In the end, the only lasting result of her departure had been to convince Henry that he was better off without her. This persuasion, to be sure, never prevented him from knocking off a quick piece whenever the opportunity presented itself. Unfortunately, Beatrice was soon pregnant again. She hid the bulge in her figure from Henry as long as she could, and then she locked herself in the house away from everyone else's gaze. Henry told her flatly that he would have nothing to do with her or her child. (*Why hadn't she stayed in Rochester?*) He simply washed his hands of the whole matter. Someone else would have to settle the problem somehow. By this time Henry's former secretary Muriel had become a buyer for a New York department store, and Henry had replaced her with a mulatta named Camilla Fedrant. Camilla was always good for a touch. She had enough money of her own to make it unnecessary for her to earn a living; she worked because she was neurotic, a little ashamed of her drop of Negro blood, and she was afraid of going to pieces. Soon after hiring her Henry told one and all that he was in love with Camilla. No one really believed him of course, but when he was inspired by her to write the very first poem of his life, concerning a subject as thoroughly unlikely as that of the Metropolitan Life Insurance Tower, his friends began to blink in surprise. Even Camilla began to swallow his line and became completely devoted to him. So, when Beatrice learned she was pregnant again, he simply turned the matter over to his secretary. Camilla consulted with Beatrice and raised the cash for an abortion. What was more, she offered to nurse Beatrice afterwards. (Who was going to tell the bleeding wife that while she was having her womb scraped, Camilla and Henry were making love on the dining room table, and that while she recuperated Henry and Camilla were making out everywhere else in the house? Henry appreciated such fine ironies and in between screws wrote out some notes about them for his "Humorous File.") For several weeks after her recovery Beatrice insisted on total abstinence. But, as usual, he was stirred by the challenge and set his mind to breaking down her resistance, with the result that in 1923 Beatrice wound up pregnant again. This time, heartlessly, Henry wouldn't lift a finger for her. Without great concern he gathered from her complaints that she had visited a baby butcher on Henry Street to perform the sanguinary affair. But he almost completely shut his mind to everything.

Everything but his image of himself as a writer, an American Hamsun. In imitation of the Norwegian, he developed the habit of keeping a loose-leaf journal to record his experiences and reflections. More and more began to go into this journal—newspaper clippings, long excerpts from passages he admired in his favorite books, lists of words, copies of his own letters, reminders of books he intended to read someday: in short, everything connected with literature. The journal became, for him, an alchemical device by which mundane existence was transfigured into fiction. Once he had dreamed of a magical book that would unlock the secrets of all knowledge. Whatever that book might be, he was making a start on it in his loose-leaf journal, whose maw opened so wide that it could swallow any part of his experience. What monsters it might regurgitate—remained to be seen. At least, he knew, the journal gave him an intimation that he had some kind of meaning in his life and that he might regain the sense of the wholeness of personality which he had lost during his adolescence. His wholeness was his work: it consisted in the daily reinvention of his being. It didn't matter if the work was bad—that was for the moment irrelevant. In the work—there he was free: "But when I took the newspaper along with me tonight, to glance at during my repast," he wrote to Emil, ". . . I didn't look at the newspaper. Do I want to know what the rest of the world is doing? There's nothing the matter with my imagination. I know they're buggering one another, bitching up the works, fighting, scrapping, bedeviling themselves and making of this vale of tears a bed of thorns." Granted that existence was botched and bitched. What, he wanted to know, was the daily news of the imagination?

Seven

"Clipped Wings" and Other Angels

With a three weeks' vacation scheduled to begin in late March 1922, Henry planned a test of his imaginative powers. Dreiser's *Twelve Men,* a series of sketches about real men whom Dreiser had known, struck him as a model for the kind of book he could write about the messengers who had passed through his hands. He wrote to Orvis Ross that he was confident his human material was far superior to Dreiser's. He riffled through his Humorous File and his loose-leaf journal, and from the hundreds of "cases" he had recorded, he selected an even dozen. Willever had once dropped a sappy remark lamenting that Horatio Alger had not had the opportunity to write about Western Union messengers. Miller selected his specimens with premeditation to mock the Alger success story. The book would be called *Clipped Wings* since it was about murdered angels.

Anderson would be one of his cases, surely: Anderson who had graduated from Yale, become a drunkard, then cured himself as a messenger, only to become jealous of his wife, kill her, and hang himself. Anderson had all the American virtues—and he had gone haywire. Gupte, the Hindu saint, was another instance of a deluded one. The poor doomed sap made fuckee with one too many females and was found one morning, after some husband finished with him, with his throat cut from ear to ear in a red smile. Dave Kasevoi, Henry's helper, and Tawde, a Hindu student, were two further exhibitions of the last turning of the Alger screw. Somewhere, also, he would have to get in the story of Charles Candles, the moron who at last blackjacked his children to death—not precisely a Horatio Alger story.

One more influence, a recent one, affected his attitudes and approach as he planned *Clipped Wings.* One luminous evening, in a moment so important that it was stamped upon his consciousness—five minutes past seven at the corner of Broadway and Kosciusko Street beside a haberdashery shop window in which empty shoe boxes were banked beside half-dressed manikins—his friend Benny Epstein told him the story of Raskolnikoff in *Crime and Punishment,* and to Henry the parallels to his own life seemed so numerous that he felt that the Russian had read his own heart. When he read Dostoievski he realized that the lack of tight form in the Russian novelist's attack on chaos was not a serious defect—this encouraged him. So, Stanley was wrong: despite Pierre Loti and the rest of his precious crew, it was *not* necessary for a great writer to perfect his form.

On March 20, 1922, Henry sat down for his first day as a writer of books. Anything that was serious he always did methodically. His bond paper, typewriter, carbons, and erasers had been laid out neatly the night before. In advance of writing a word, he decided the number of pages his book would be, calculated the number of words, and divided these by days at his disposal. He made himself a mental promise that he would write no less than 5,000 words a day. As soon as he sat down he discovered that this would be no easy matter. His mind was blank. Even for this eventuality Henry was prepared. He had taken eight volumes of modern poetry out of the library in order to stimulate a possibly wilting inspiration. Emil Schnellock had put him on to Ezra Pound; and next to *Lustra* on his desk he stacked books by Carl Sandburg, Vachel Lindsay, Maxwell Bodenheim, and Edgar Lee Masters. He spent the morning reading in these volumes before he could get a word down. Finally he started, beginning his book with a sketch of his erstwhile messenger Charlie Candles.

As he slaved away on *Clipped Wings* the influence of the volumes of modern poetry mingled in curious and unpremeditated ways with the spirit of Dreiser and the philosophical reading to which Miller had devoted himself. Unfortunately, the combination was a disaster: he hit the wrong tone right away in "Charles Candles, the Moral Moron." His desire to satirize the dream of success forced him to present himself, the speaker, as a supercilious spectator on human misery; and his philosophical habits moved him toward proposing reforms in the arrangements of civilization. He describes a visit to the public baths on Henry Street, which are "used every now and then (mostly then) by the inhabitants of that vicinage

because of the lack of sanitary conveniences in their tenement dwellings."
In Candles' rooms on the East Side, "Laziness, torpor, indifference, apathy
[were] plainly indicated by the physical aspect of the place." Next, to his
horror, he spies roaches: "One of them had been bold enough to inhabit my
person in desecrating fashion. I . . . shuddered and flicked him neatly to the
floor, careless of his fate but secretly longing to squash him under foot." He
regards Candles with nearly equivalent horror and wraps up his sketch with
"a few pages of a more serious turn" in a little lecture on eugenical reform:
"We need . . . more children of the better sort and fewer of the worse
variety." All this is finally topped by a quotation from Nietzsche: "The
weak and defective must go to the wall; that is the first principle of
dionysian charity. And we must help them to go."

Clearly, the book was being produced by the will, not the imagination.
It has a cardboard flavor, as if Miller were following a recipe and using
prepackaged ingredients: into a mixing bowl by Dreiser, he dropped his
own journal and sprinkled it liberally with spice from Bodenheim's
bohemia; despair in the mode of Dostoievski; reform à la Mike Gold; and
colloquial speech in the style of *The Triumph of the Egg;* he let it marinate in a
brew of Galton, Darwin, and Nietzsche; and he decorated the product with
images in the manner of Pound. Hardly a pinch of himself could be
detected.

The best evidence that the book gave of his possible talent was that he
was able to work steadily on it. In the beginning he worked at home. But he
soon shifted over to Emil's studio in order to avoid Beatrice's woeful
glances—these always froze him and set him back. Hour after hour he sat
stiffly pounding away at the typewriter, forcing the words out one by one,
feeling self-conscious, a novice, almost paralyzed by his fear that through
writing he would reveal he was not a writer. And because of this, he sought
refuge in his education, his knowledge, his learning; he was always moving
away from the lives of the messengers who were ostensibly his subjects, to
the extracts he had copied out from other writers. Yet, though his style was
evasive, arch, and even artificial, he was learning that he could put words
together. However contrived the book may have been, it *was* a book, the
words did mount up, 75,000 of them. For years, walking the Bowery or
Brooklyn Bridge, he had told himself, *Get it down.* But he could never do so
until now. At the end of his first day's writing, he wrote gleefully to Emil:
"I almost believed I was a business man, one of them there efficient guys,
with his welfare didoes and amorous pecadillos with the gay stenographer.
Ho, ho, and a bottle of rum. Man alive, I am on an intellectual bat. I feel

like a gayly caparisoned cacique among cormorants, like a bashaw among bastinados—a bat out of hell! Let's sing Goddam and to hell with the Western Union that feeds my brat and all the other stinking mit-glaumers that help the W.U. to do it." By the end of his three weeks vacation he was convinced that he was a writer.

Miller recognized the defects of *Clipped Wings*. It was "literary" in just the wrong way. Uncertain of himself, sure that he never knew enough, he had kept reading until he knew too much; contradictory influences pulled him this way and that until any effort he made seemed wrong somehow. He could never be true to all his influences at once, and he didn't know yet how to be true to himself. But he didn't give up. First of all, he tried to get *Clipped Wings* published. Macmillan promptly rejected the manuscript. Morosely, Henry repackaged it for Boni and Liveright, but before it was mailed he lost heart and let the package lie on his desk. However, he did extract a section dealing with Tawde, combined this with a commentary on Tagore, titled it "Black and White," and sent it off to W.E.B. DuBois's magazine, *The Crisis,* where it was published in May 1924. Besides, all through 1922 and 1923 he worked incessantly on other short pieces, sketches, essays, diatribes, and lyrical prose improvisations. Few of these satisfied him. The best were "Auctioneer," a dramatic monologue by the huckster; a long prose poem called "Wrestlers," deriving from his admiration for Jim Londos; a brief set-piece, "Make Beer for Man," in which he argued against Prohibition and for the civilizing influence of lager; a sketch called "Asphodel;" and a comic essay on chewing gum. All of these were returned, rejected, by magazine editors. A friend of his, Eugene V. Brewster, promised to show his sketches to Alfred Knopf and Horace Liveright, but if he did these publishers showed no interest. One of Henry's friends tried to cheer him up by saying that his work was caviar for the few. But there was never any doubt in Miller's mind on this score: his aim was definitely to be a big writer, a popular one.

Outwardly, his life had not changed much since he began to work for Western Union; nonetheless, his understanding of the world and of his relation to it had altered substantially. He was full of contradictions. He was beginning to see the "successful" man as a failure, and he believed a man's state of being, not his status, indicated his value. Yet he himself was not content with merely being: he wanted to write and he assumed that he could measure literary achievement by success. At the same time, it went without saying that he scorned most of the books of the day and found the stuff in mass circulation magazines beneath contempt. He still believed with all his heart that Bob Challacombe was right: spirit was the fundamental ingredient in existence—but he saw few people whose spiritual life was much in evidence. He agreed with Emma Goldman that the writer's mission was to attack social decadence, but he didn't want a thing to do with politics. His experience was decisively divided between the hustle and bustle of his work at Park Place and his increasing conviction that this life was unreal. Certainly, though he dreamed of liberation, each day his obligations shoved his vision of release to the side. There were a thousand messengers to waybill, Beatrice and Barbara to support, as well as the habits he had developed of going to eat in certain restaurants, having escapades, going to lectures and shows regularly.

Naturally, he imagined that the main problem of his life was that he was shackled to Beatrice—as he had been to Pauline, and, before that, to his own mother. Whenever life went sour he looked for a new woman to replace the one of whom he had tired. Early in 1923 he decided to leave Beatrice for a young woman named Gladys Miller. She was a waitress in a restaurant, had trim legs, and was studying Greek. He found her attractive. And so one night after a quarrel with his wife, he got up, dressed, and left a note on the kitchen table telling Beatrice that he was going for good. "I am through," he wrote in pencil. "Don't expect to see me ever again. Will look after you and the kid all right." But when he arrived at Gladys', he had to get her out of bed. She looked frumpy and a little greasy. He could only say over and over to himself, "She's not the same—it's not her!" As he stood in her doorway before the wondering woman he was sure that Gladys offered no solution. He explained that he had merely dropped in to say hello. He went home mechanically. In the kitchen again, he switched on the light and looked at the little white note in his own familiar hand staring pathetically up at him from the red tablecloth. Methodically, he ripped it into minute squares and threw them into the fire. Some weeks afterward he received a telegram from Gladys asking him to meet her at Grand Central Station, where she was arriving from Poughkeepsie with her mother's body. True, she had trim legs, and she was studying Greek and Latin—but she worked in a restaurant and her hands smelled of grease. So he left her waiting at the station, with the stiff on her greasy hands. He couldn't remember why Gladys had ever appealed to him.

Women were his central contradiction: for him woman sometimes meant loss of freedom, sometimes the promise of liberation. His childhood had centered about this paradox; and his adult life still orbited around it. He was always swinging from freedom into bondage—from mother to Cora,

Cora to Pauline, Pauline to Beatrice, Beatrice to Camilla, and Camilla to Gladys. A woman who promised release, he felt, was laying a trap. Yet he was asked not for love but for obedience, conformity, control. Love, it seemed, required him to diminish rather than expand his life. He felt he was asked to become more and more helpless, not to grow up but to become smaller each day until he could at last be tucked back into the womb—of mother, of Pauline, of Beatrice—utterly defeated by them.

Henry resisted this, and, as usual, he rebelled passively, by drifting, by becoming inert. By 1923 even his recent pleasures had become merely mechanical. The burlesque queens had wrinkled stomachs, the comedians were cracked, the dramas and the lectures were uniformly dreary, the chop suey tasted of glue. Even the dames that dumbly spread their legs for him on the zinc table were flea-bitten. The dead weight of habit oppressed him. He felt the urge to shatter the complacency of his routine.

Seven years, he thought. Perhaps there was something magical about it. Seven years with Pauline, now nearly seven with Beatrice. Perhaps he was preparing to shed his old life, like a withered skin. He was yearning for an entirely new adventure. And he saw no cause whatsoever for alarm in the fact that every vision of a new life included the dazzling and mysterious image of some wonderful, new, completely satisfying woman.

Eight

June, Julia, Juliette, Henriette, She, Her

One Thursday evening, late in the summer of 1923, Henry stood in his office alone. It was payday: he could feel the weight of the money in his pocket, and he kept saying to himself hypnotically, feverishly: *Adventure—at all cost!* He resolved to squander every cent of his pay that very night entirely on himself. He strolled up Broadway until he neared the Palace Theater; for him this whole area was rich with associations of pleasure, and this night he was bent on doing something exciting. His steps led him toward Wilson's Dance Hall, with its red lanterns hanging in the windows just below the ventilators. The year before, he often went there after finishing a day's work on *Clipped Wings*. Recently, the literary impulse seemed to be drying up, and in the back of his mind was the notion that he might buck up his flagging inspiration by taking a little flyer at Wilson's. At the entrance to the dime-a-dance he bought his string of tickets. He dragged a sodden partner around the floor, chatting away for the pleasure of talking, rhapsodizing to himself really, about his favorite writers. After a time he sat down—the dance tickets which the Greek sold at the door disappeared like snow, like childhood, too fast. But he didn't care on this night. He figured he'd try out another jane—he was just getting warmed up. He'd let the evening take him with it.

Then She came sailing toward him, one of the taxi-dancers. She was attractive, but in a dark, heavy way, with a too-full face like one blocked

76

out by Renoir but completed by Rouault. Somehow she seemed to move *in* her body, with a sort of drugged, sleepy, dreamy animal aura about her. Central European with a touch of the gypsy. She told him at once in a hasty, hectic way that she wanted to meet him, she had her eye on him in particular. It was Strindberg she wanted to talk to him about—she had heard him mention Strindberg out on the floor. And in the meantime, she said, why not dance? He was flustered a little and stammered, "Yes, yes, oh yes. I'll be right back." He bought a fist full of tickets. So the tickets flew, while she spun out a long ramble about Strindberg's Henriette, who she believed to be the personification of evil. And, she said, "Henriette is me, myself!" Her talk was just his style, with just the pitch he himself liked to strike in his own improvisations. Her conversation began and ended with Henriette, but in between it ranged all over the cosmos, from gods to perversions to her friends—whores and addicts and drunkards—to her British background, her education in a New England girls' school, to gangsters and assorted gorillas. Merely listening to her was like being bathed half-asleep in a warm milky tub. Henry felt he had nothing to say to her in return—to listen to her was enough. And yet the listening got him nowhere. What was she? June Edith Mansfield was her name—of only that much was he sure. But wherever else he probed her talk, it shifted like a wall of fog, dancing magically in another direction. Always the desire to know had driven him into relentless inquisitions of friends, his messengers, even his parents. But June seemed to have no being of her own because her talk was made entirely of quotations.

After midnight, he stood on the street outside looking up at the strings of red lanterns which were never extinguished. What he wanted was not to possess her, but to penetrate to her secret, to satisfy his curiosity. Yet his head was in a whirl, and when she came out of the entrance toward him, holding her chin high and moving with such strength and poise that for a minute he believed she was taller than he, he experienced an agonizing twisting inside, a trembling, an absolute desire to take her then and there right on Broadway. "She is magnificent," he whispered to himself. But she was already talking before she got beside him and swept him up with her as she moved carelessly, recklessly, through the traffic. There was no sensation of fear, hardly an awareness that anyone else was about, only the urgent need to talk, to flow with the words. Henry had all he could do to maneuver her up to the Chinese Garden.

There was an orchestra but they didn't dance. In a booth he gathered his wits about him and began to talk to her. It suddenly struck him, and he told her so, that there was a character, a woman named Victoria, in a novel by Knut Hamsun that she resembled in many interesting ways. Strange to find Victoria in a dance hall. He told her all about the book, omitting any mention of how he had first become acquainted with the novel himself. Then there was his own book, *Clipped Wings,* which reminded him of another book about a strange collection of characters, *Winesburg, Ohio.* The mention of Sherwood Anderson made him think of Ben Hecht. Wouldn't she allow him to lend her some of these books? She also talked—their talk was like a fugue. She finished off Strindberg and then moved on to spiritualism and New Thought—his ears perked up at this—then jumped to accounts of her past loves, stews of sexual mystery. A man had insulted her on her stoop at home by suddenly pulling up her dress; she had once been in love with a man who never knew of her love; a rich lawyer had loved her; another lover had committed suicide over her. These tales stirred a furnace of desire in Henry. But she was already moving on to observations about Dostoievski's *Eternal Husband,* her own belief in the double, her strange birth, her gypsy blood, and a tale of a missing Stradivarius. Each story was covered by another more mysterious or erotic than the first.

All the way to Bensonhurst in the taxi her words clicked out in time with the meter. She talked in a frenzy. It didn't take long, either, for June to throw her arms about him, almost straddling him right there in the taxi. He was paddling for his life to keep up with her, stunned by her passionate kisses, by the absolutely demoniac fury of her every move. It was nearly dawn before he stepped out of the taxi in front of his own home. He crept into the room where Beatrice and Barbara were still sleeping, the same room where he had struggled to write. All this was finished, he thought; nothing could deter him from entering upon a new life, a life with June. Standing silently over the peaceful bodies like a murderer in the darkened room, his whole life seemed to blaze up in an ecstasy of promise.

Feeling surprisingly fresh, Henry began the next day by playing a recording of "Liebestraum" on the loud needle, had the same old fight with Beatrice, and left to resume work in the seething chaos of the Park Place office. Camilla was in a sentimental mood and presented him with a copy of Ernest Dowson's poem—*I have been faithful to thee Cynara! in my fashion*—and whether she meant the verses as a confession of the fact that *she* was keeping a white mistress herself, or as an accusation of him, didn't matter. She was saying, Camilla, that she wanted to go on a boat ride that evening, but first she invited him to dinner in a Syrian restaurant. He hardly heard—but he did manage to borrow a sizeable sum from her. She talked on while the applicants lined up and the office went crazy. And all he thought about was the letter he intended to write to June.

Always looking backwards, counting his losses, he had never been good at planning his future. He went into the future sideways, like a crab. He liked June instantly because in a curious way she incarnated the vital and crude, even brutal, atmosphere that he associated with the old neighborhood and his youth. She was a creature of mystery—but she also seemed *real*. Her friends at Wilson's were lax, easy-going, and good natured, like Dreiser's women, and could talk about their whorish experiences with men as freely as one would talk about Sunday's picnic. June was a real woman with all her organs intact and her heart unrusted by the conventions of the unsexed Village girls—who all wanted to be writers or thought they were intellectuals. But when Henry started to spout his artsy stuff to June, she stopped him with: "Say, listen, what kind of dope do *you* take?" Yes, she had seen *Miss Julie* and she was bright and quick and had picked up a sophisticated lingo, and even a slightly British accent, but what was important was that behind this phony façade she really was passionate about life and felt genuine emotions when she began to speak of literature. She talked as if characters in books were real people in whose fate she was absorbed. In a wholly unpremeditated way, she showed Henry the bridge between life and imagination. He had teetered from one to another for years. It was June he must win if he was ever to possess himself.

But to win June—to possess himself—these achievements might have sinister consequences. June was angelic—but so was Lucifer; June was engaged in raw life—but such an existence had its sordid side. In choosing June, Henry hardly knew what he was choosing. But an incident which occurred on the third time he took June out gave him an intimation concerning the contradictions he was letting himself in for. They had had a fine, passionate evening, which ended thrillingly when June led him into a dark vacant lot opposite her home to make love on the grass. As they finished and he was about to rise, June seized him with astonishing force and pulled him down to her. "You're wonderful. I love you, I love you," she whispered in a broken voice.

She paused. They rose together.

Then her voice hardened, and she said in an offhand, nonchalant, vulgar tone, *"And now for the dirt."* And then: "Lend me fifty dollars. My mother has to meet a mortgage on the house." She asked this just like a hard girl of the streets. It sent a shudder through him. And had he been more blasé, he

might have given her a whore's price, a few dollars. But he said "Yes,"
rapidly, without hesitation.

She pulled him back to the grass and held him to thank him, and when at
last he pushed himself up, she threw her arms around his legs and kissed
him repeatedly, as if in a delirium: "You're my god! You're my god!" What
could he make of these changes, this succession of emotions? In truth, he
never made much of it, but it was a foretaste—he saw later, when he was
miserable with her—of the torments she would put him through with her
wanton cruelty and the ecstasy she would give him with her adoration.

For the moment all it taught him was that he needed money to pursue
June. Money became his constant preoccupation. He managed to hit up his
pals Garvey and Carey for moderate sums. He borrowed on his life insurance. He was willing to allow June to gather from his well-tailored clothes
that he was rich. Of course, he could not keep up that pretense for long. On
Saturday night, two days after they met, he had to confess when the bill
arrived at Jimmy Kelley's speakeasy that he didn't have enough to pay it.
He saved himself the possibility of being roughed up by thinking fast and
telephoning the Western Union night manager to slip fifty dollars from the
till and send it over by messenger. Then he borrowed another twenty-five
from the old boy who delivered the money. So new debts began to pile on
old ones. But then, to his astonishment, the bonus which the company had
been promising for a long time did actually come through, to the tune of
$350. Yet, instead of hoarding this up to make his break, he blew it all in
paying back all his debts—even to Sam who served him like a dog and never
expected to see those loans again. Not only did he pay off all his creditors,
he also took them all for a grand spread and drinks at the Crow's Nest.
Later, he dragged the boys over to Wilson's. He was drunk himself and he
almost fell off the balcony. Though he dimly felt he had humiliated
himself, June grandly took a deep red rose she was wearing and put it in his
buttonhole. "You must be a great writer—for me!" she whispered. That
struck him piercingly. *I have been faithful to thee, Cynara! in my fashion,* he
whispered to himself in a dizzy whirl.

These days, he saw June as often as possible and wrote her in between. He
had been ignoring Beatrice's complaints for a long time, and he was ready to
desert her, but he felt pangs of sentiment where Barbara was concerned. On
Sunday, only three days after meeting June, he took the little one for a long
walk, until she became exhausted. Then he picked her up and carried her
home, holding her close and planning unrealistically what he would do for
her when she grew up. When he felt the little arms around his neck and

heard the murmurs of the singular quavering voice, so like his own, he felt deep bitterness toward the hatchet-faced Beatrice, who was driving him away, mixed with tenderness for the little girl. But he couldn't go on without June. One Sunday after wandering desolately about Ulmer Park alone, he resolved to confess the truth to Bea. He sat down at the kitchen table, where she was busy feeding the child, and gently whispered, "Bea, I want to be free." He so obviously meant it that her eyes became large with tears and sudden fear. She moaned and wept bitterly and the child became hysterical to see her mother carrying on so. But he continued to the end and told her about June; he went further and mentioned his numerous women friends.

He didn't move out of the house, but he saw June more openly now. Often, when he changed clothes to go out after dinner Beatrice would ask caustically: "Getting ready to meet your sweetheart?" And he'd respond: "Yes, I'm going to meet my little whore." He'd even make Bea give him the carfare, which she methodically chalked upon the slate, weeping that she had to give him money for other women. Sometimes he'd pat her or pinch her rear, that made her so angry now—now he had no right to her, she said. Sometimes he'd keep after her until she gave in to him. Her resistance was a spice that still excited him.

Things were entirely bad with Beatrice—but not entirely good with June. She stood him up one night when he had two tickets to the Palace to hear Thomas Burke sing "Roses of Picardy." She often pulled back from him in such unexpected ways. She claimed she couldn't figure out what kind of game he was playing. What did he want with her? She had even taken Henry's love letters over to her aunt's and asked the woman to figure out what his motives were. Was he experimenting with her, she wanted to know, only for the sake of a story, as he had done with the messengers he wrote about in *Clipped Wings*? He wrote such strange, exotic things—was it possible he was a dope fiend?

For his part, Henry began to recognize that the tales she told about her life were too fantastic to be actually true, though the narratives tumbled out as smoothly as musical silk. Life for June almost entirely lay in the past or the future: she never employed the present tense except when she was hungry. Was she trying to attract him by casting mysterious webs or fan his sexual ardor by speaking of her innumerable lovers? Or to give herself an allure of adventure by detailing her close scrapes? Had there really been a car following their cab as they drove toward Bensonhurst after their night in Jimmy Kelley's? Was it true that June had been in Chicago and associated with gangsters? Amours, alarums, escapades, wanderings, flights, risks were common ingredients in all her stories. It seemed as if she had a dozen different lives. She seemed to have given herself up to terrible commitments, to the worst individuals, and yet to have kept a sacred attitude toward herself, as if she were never soiled. Drenched in sex though she was, she made herself out as virginal and inviolable, as if her cunt were a billiard ball, and as if sex were poisonous. She kept repeating that she had never really given herself to anyone, though lovers hovered about like bees. Henry was supposed to appreciate that because so many others had loved her, in loving him she had bestowed a signal honor upon him, but he really felt pangs of jealousy whenever one of her lovers was mentioned. Names fell easily from her lips—old man Marder and Baker the millionaire shoe manufacturer, both were chasing her. Baker offered her $200 for her favors every time he came to town, but she had no intention of accepting his proposition. She could always gold-dig a couple of hundred from the octogenarian owner of a laundry or a clerk in the Imperial Hotel. She was always entering the flames yet always rising from the ashes, clothed in an asbestos robe. She complained: "People come, and they suck the life out of me to bring life into themselves." But this was absurd. In her stiffly starched dotted swiss dress, her figure full and her throat columnar, she was magnificent—as if she herself had dined on the lives of others.

Perhaps she thrived upon Henry's wounds, for certainly she was slashing him with revelations, particularly those concerning her lovers. The lovers were invariably sandwiched in for spice between other tales. She had been born illegitimately, she said, in Sherwood Forest. Her mother was a Roumanian gypsy who had died in childbirth. (June offered to prove her blood by singing "Ochi Chornia" in Russian in her deep, throaty voice with the very soul of a gypsy.) She had subsequently grown up in Vermont and gone to Wellesley, played the violin and worked as a proofreader. She had never become a citizen. Her father, an Englishman, had had a fabulous youth, made a fortune as an engineer, and kept a string of racing stables, and he had later been an intimate friend of Caruso. But he had since lost his fortune. Now he was lying in a sanitarium in Canada, riddled with cancer. She worshipped him, even though he had beaten her; but she hated her aunt, who was her guardian. June held this woman in such contempt, she told Henry, that she would shame the old hag by supporting herself and her brothers and, yes, even her aunt, in any way that she could, even by terrible perversions. She had, in fact, already earned enough money to save their house when the aunt could not otherwise prevent them from being dispossessed. Old man Harris, she said, had offered her $1,000 to deflower her, and to save the house she had accepted the offer, as one would sign a contract, and gone through with it the whole way, even though it took the old geezer ten days to break her hymen. She harbored no grudges against him. But later, for Russell Hughes, a man who had merely tried to lift her dress after bringing her home, she held a merciless spite. She had made him her helpless slave—he had been obliged to desert his wife and children and lie and steal for her, and she made him beg on his knees to marry her; she treated him with scorn. Nor was she finished yet with the poor devil, she confessed. She firmly intended to drive him to suicide, and she had no doubt she could do so. (Not long afterwards, the young man actually did kill himself, as she promised she would make him do. Later she was at least partially to blame for the suicides of two other men who admired her.) Almost all of June's tales were based on one theme: how, by her great courage and cunning, she had evaded the clutches of some vicious male. After talking about her lovers, she'd switch to the subjects of drugs, perversion, necrophilia, thievery, incest, sadism, rape, and amnesia. She was no addict, she insisted, though she had certainly had experiences. One of her stories stuck in Henry's mind like an icepick. She said that once when she had appendicitis her doctor (who, like everyone else was in love with her) administered drugs to her through the rectum—this last grotesque and bizarre anatomical detail she especially emphasized.

June's mind was a swamp. Henry could never tell how one sentence was connected to the next. It was like hearing a familiar language spoken in accordance with an entirely new and incomprehensible grammar. Her talk was feverish and compulsive. But after she made herself seem almost a Lamia—always harping on her resemblance to Henriette—she might let drop some comments which seemed to reveal that she knew hardly anything at all of the world, that she was a good, wholesome, kind, innocent girl whose mind had been filled with decadent or sensational literature, from Strindberg to Bernarr MacFadden, and that her natural talent for acting impelled her to play a role that was almost too convincing. One moment he'd want to persuade himself that she was a complete fake. The next moment, he'd be split wide open by her suffering, utterly convinced of the truth of her tales.

Henry had never before met such a fabulist as June. His own weak sense of the division between fiction and reality left him without a guide by which to judge her truth-telling. Though it gave him pain to hear her stories, he needed knowledge more than tranquility. Thus, for hours on end he would question her minutely about the most intimate details of her emotional life, her physical sensations, her relations with other men. How had she felt at this or that occasion? What had pleased her more? Excited her more? Tales that made him wince in horror only drove him on to question her more closely, particularly when the narration was shameful and humiliating. "Wait," he would say, "go back." Then he would savor the cruel tale over again in all of its specific horror. It seemed as if his analyses of the messengers had been allowed him by fate in order to prepare him to dissect the impulses and reactions of this woman, to uncover and expose shamelessly every one of her responses, even if he tore out his own guts in doing so.

Certainly, her tales of her lovers were an aphrodisiac for him; even her deceits increased his passion. The masochist had found or created his sadist. Henry's divided attitude toward women, whom he regarded as either sacred or sluttish, found its exact equivalent in the way June presented herself. He found a painful, joyful consolation in saying to himself: *She is a whore,* and then correcting it to *a cheat,* and then to *a liar. What am I to do?* he would moan inwardly—and almost immediately concluded: *Whatever she is, I love her: and for the moment she is mine.* And at last: *She is a saint, inviolable.* And then for suspecting her, condemning her, he would accuse himself of defects in love, of faithlessness, frailty, and attribute an enduring and noble love or extraordinary generosity to June. Lashing himself, defaming himself, he'd build her up as high as he made himself low. He'd tell himself then that this perfect woman pitied, not loved, him. And so he'd wind up wallowing in the strange thrills of self-abasement.

June learned to fulfill his need for the fabulous. Besides, she really excited herself by her imagination of her own disaster. Bill Dewar was wrong in calling her once a "filthy crawling liar," and so was Henry in supporting him at that moment; for her truth lay in her violent creation of herself. It gave her almost a sexual pleasure, this invention of her life of pain and exploitation. Telling Henry of her fabulous lovers aroused her desire to become the perfect lover for him. This was why she took so readily to the books he loaned her—because they filled her—each one was a new readymade life for her. Now she was Ayesha, now Henriette, now Trilby, now the Fillipovna woman, now Stavrogin, now the Duse. Each one, too, had the appeal of having appealed to Henry. If she could remake herself in terms of the fictions which possessed him, then, as they did, she too could hold on to him. Before long, she was acting out his favorite books before his eyes.

But when they reversed positions and she began to question him about his life, he became awkward and unsure of himself. His narratives became so convoluted and involved that they made no sense at all.

Henry still had not discerned the nature and meaning of his own experience; the most he could do was create himself through his response to her fictions. He was being sucked into a thoroughly fictive, mythical life.

He wanted to understand everything; and he was willing, even anxious, to destroy the other truths of his life for this one all absorbing goal. He began talking about setting the date with June. It might be sensible enought to cut loose from Beatrice, his friends said, but certainly he should not be thinking of marriage again. Schnellock, Cohen, Muriel, Dewar, and the others were unanimous in pointing to his eternal inconstancy. No, he argued forcefully, he had simply not yet, not until June, met a woman for whom he could pull the stars down from the sky. Calm in defending himself against the arguments of his friends, he harbored secret doubts about June: everytime he asserted his trust in her another head of doubt hissed at him. Once June had knelt before him on the street in Bensonhurst and told him he was everything to her. She clung to him passionately and cried out: "O Val, you're wonderful. You're like a god to me. I could do anything for you!" This mutual worship was life's wildest moment. *(But why had she stayed, more than once, all night with Marder and, even in Henry's presence, perched on his lap, kissing and petting him while she sang German songs?)* June had written him from Massachusetts: "I want to be your wife." *(But why had she gone to Massachusetts as the guest of a backwoodsman, along with a pair of trollops? And what, for Christ's sake, had the three guys and three girls been doing in that cabin?)* Upon her return he had met her at Rockaway Beach. Certainly, she was passionate and begged him to sleep with her; and so he had taken her to a hotel. *(But why hadn't she been able to have a climax with him? And if the reason was, as she said, that she was sore and that he hurt her, what was the meaning of that?)*

So he made no break with Beatrice—he just drifted toward June. Beatrice was sullen, monumentally cold and immovable. One night he dreamed that he was hurtling in a dizzying tumble from a precipice, falling, falling until he slipped into the warm waters of the Caribbean; then he kept swirling downward in great spiral curves that had no beginning and promised to end in eternity. When he awoke he felt worn and used, sore at Beatrice because she dumbly took all his insults and refused to break with him. On his own, he was no more able to pull himself away from her than he had been from Pauline. He tried everything he could think of to force her to reject him. One evening he took her to the Palace Theatre. She was pitifully grateful to be taken out, pulled herself from the slovenly habits into which she had fallen, and dressed up to please him. All evening she kept shooting pathetic glances at him to see if he was in a good mood, if he was happy, if he was enjoying the show. After the variety acts were concluded, Henry proposed that they go across the street to Wilson's Dance Hall. He made the suggestion as casually as possible, but Beatrice noticed the edge in his voice. She knew that his doxy was a taxi-dancer and probably understood that he had arranged the whole evening just to make her angry enough to break with him—but her tears had turned to stone and she was determined to give him no excuse.

Stanley Borowski remarked one day that if Henry wished, he would solve his problem. Henry readily agreed, but Stanley seemed to do nothing. Henry looked about for other solutions, and happily, one seemed to be in the offing: Orvis Ross wrote that he was planning to visit New York in connection with his studies of Wagnerian opera. Perhaps he would take Beatrice back to Minnesota (*just the frigid climate for her,* Henry thought). Henry knew that despite her puckered, holier-than-thou face Beatrice had been writing to Ross and that they were really very fond of each other. If only they could get over their scruples and cuckold the poor husband and run away, then (Henry ruminated) everything would be find and dandy. Not long after Ross arrived, Henry steered the conversation around to his own domestic situation. Things, he intimated, were not as happy in his household as might be hoped. The fault was his own, Henry professed, he was not as good a husband as Beatrice deserved. Now, had Beatrice had the good fortune to be Mrs. Harolde Orvis Ross—then things would have been different . . . The next thing Henry knew Harolde was on his way back to Minnesota, *sans* Beatrice, with the score of *Parsifal* to cuddle up to in his Pullman. *Well, fuck a duck!* Henry thought.

Henry could be heartless, but he also had a vast repository of sympathy and sentiment, and even as he saw the end with Beatrice coming, he felt a revival of tenderness for his wife and an increase in affection for his child. He was even a little sorry to learn, when he arrived home from a two-day absence with June, that Beatrice was herself intending to take a vacation in the country with a former convent friend. She said cooly that she knew he wouldn't care if she went off for a good long visit. True, Henry immediately began to make mental plans for June to move in, but he also behaved sweetly, just like a good husband sending his wife off to the country; he even rode on the train with them for a few stations, just as his father had once done when he sent his son—Henry—and his wife to the country. "Tell Daddy goodbye," Beatrice said, "you won't be seeing him for several weeks." The little arms twined around his neck, and he and Bea said a friendly goodbye. As he rode back toward the city, he felt that he was riding back toward Victoria, without having to bother with evasions and excuses—for several weeks. Nothing could be better—unless Beatrice meant to stay away for good.

An excruciatingly painful earache tarnished the romance of Henry's first day of liberation, but on the next day he met June. They ate first, then walked over to Prospect Park and strolled casually in the warm fragrant dark of the late summer. Feeling mellow, Henry wanted to rent a rowboat and go out on the lake, but the boats were locked up for the night. The two lovers went dreamily toward a little pergola built out over the water. June had on the little stiff dotted swiss dress which he liked so well. The trees were dark against the sky, bushes on the shore were like a woven wall, the water lapped against the piles. Dreamily, they made love, June straddling him as he sat on a rough grained bench. They were quiet and he moved inside her gently as she shifted and groaned with pleasure. June's stiff dress rustled in the air, already filled to overflowing with night sounds.

But just as they were washing themselves with a little water from the lake an angry policeman surprised them by stepping out from the bushes. They were both scared silly but managed to convince the policeman that they had only recently been married. At last he let them go, after following them to the very door of Henry's house to be sure that they were really wedded. They bid the Irish cop goodnight and prepared to play at man and wife. June inspected his and Beatrice's things as if she were remaking herself as his wife. The whole house interested her. He showed her their bedroom upstairs, suddenly remembering what Cora had said years before: "This is where we sleep." By unspoken agreement they decided not to use that room and went to bed downstairs in the parlor, discretely closing the rolling doors behind them. Though fatigued, they made love again and talked and held each other until they fell to sleep.

Around seven a.m. Henry arose and started to prepare a breakfast of bacon and eggs—a romantic breakfast for two. He went back into the room, shut the doors and lay down, stark naked, with June. The bacon was just beginning to sizzle when suddenly, the doors rolled apart with a great clatter, and Beatrice burst in with two witnesses, the landlord and his daughter. They all seemed ready to go into hysterics. June pulled the sheet up to her chin, but Henry jumped up in surprise. In the back of his mind

were only two thoughts, that Stanley had worked his trap to perfection, and
that unless he could get the unwelcome visitors out soon the bacon would be
burned—the fragrance of the meat was vivid. Beatrice was curt and cold as
ice, ordering him and his trollop to clear out at once. *And in my own house,* he
kept thinking, as he took the offensive and said he'd depart when he was
good and ready. And that is just what he did. After all, the only satisfactory
answer to Bea's imperious demand was for him, incongruously, to hustle
Beatrice and her witnesses out, finish cooking, and sit down with June to a
breakfast of eggs and bacon (by now very crisp).

Trapped into freedom. Stanley had devised a plan for Beatrice to catch
Henry—and Beatrice had fallen into it. Now that she had caught him,
with witnesses, she would have to go ahead and divorce him. Soon, Henry
packed a small valise and took June over to Emil Schnellock's. Stanley, who
had begun to celebrate the success of his trap even before it was sprung, was
drunk as a lord by the time he joined them, and he promptly fell asleep in
the bath tub. Stanley's fate seemed to prove to Henry that he had been
right. Stanley was washed up already, ruined by the army, married to a
drudge and saddled by a brood of children, a more and more confirmed
drunk every year. Indeed, all of his friends—from Emil Cohen to Emil
Schnellock—seemed to be crumbling. Looking at the quietly sleeping
drunk, Henry congratulated himself that he had been brave enough to leave
his friends to their weak compromises and start a new pure life, a life with
June.

Nine

A New Life

Almost as soon as Henry made the leap forward into a new life, he started to look backward. By his own choice he had cut himself off from his child. He couldn't do so at once, but he hoped someday to get custody of Barbara and raise her as he wished he had been raised. In the meantime he and June rented a single room in a house in the Bronx owned by one of Cohen's friends, a Dr. Luttinger, whose specialty was the disposal of unwanted embryos. They called this dump "Cockroach Hall" in honor of the insects which marched in columns up and down the walls. Henry thought of himself as only camping at Cockroach Hall until he could get his life straightened out and claim his daughter. Every Sunday he went back to Sixth Avenue to visit her. Once, when they were sitting on a green knoll in the park she whimpered in her quavering voice, "Daddy, why don't you come home with us? Why don't you sleep with Mommy again?" He turned his back and wept in blank despair. Another week she begged for some pennies to buy peanuts for the bunnies, but though Daddy searched his pockets, he knew there was nothing for the little bunnies or the little girl. One time, he allowed June to see them together. "She's the image of you, Val," June cried out as they wept together. Perhaps June thought that Henry's love for Barbara might have driven him back home, and she indicated her willingness to have the child with them by sending presents to Barbara and always taking a great interest in her welfare. In fact, astonishing as this was, Henry *was* thinking of returning home within a week after leaving it. With June working in Wilson's at night, they were together for only an hour or so after he got off and then for another hour when she got home. Alone all night, Henry found himself drifting into Brooklyn. Just as he had once passed Cora's house, he now walked furtively by Beatrice's, hoping to catch a glimpse of his past life. Even reconciliation seemed possible. One Sunday they sent Barbara out to play, and as Henry began telling Beatrice a long humorous tale about one of his recent escapades, they edged together until they were touching. He liked the fragrance of her body and her slightly revealing dressing gown, and soon they were lovers again. June was capable of imagining anything, but even she never guessed that on Sunday afternoons while she sat and waited for him in Cockroach Hall, he was in his old living room screwing his wife on the couch.

June did know that she was desperately unhappy. One Sunday, while Henry was visiting his family, she made a half-hearted attempt at suicide. It was soon apparent that June was in no real danger, but Henry was fearful and confused. He moved them from Cockroach Hall at once, and camped first in Emil's studio and then with one of his intellectual and musical friends, Harold Hickerson. But the tension was terrific. Finally June decided to leave Henry. They all treated her like a child, she complained. And like a child running away, she tied up all her belongings in a parcel wrapped with paper and twine. And though she was soon back, this was a sign of trouble—present and future.

On top of all this the divorce proceedings came on quickly. One of the last things Beatrice said to him was: "I feel truly sorry for you. You don't know what you are walking into," but when he didn't beg her to allow him back, she hardened against him. In early December of 1923 he went to the civil and supreme court buildings in Brooklyn for the hearing on his divorce and legal obligations. Toward the conclusion of the legal fol-de-rol there was a whispered consultation between the judge and Beatrice's attorney. The judge gave Henry a disgusted look, and then a short but withering lecture. By his immoral behavior Henry had forfeited the rights of parent-hood: Beatrice was given sole custody of Barbara. The alimony would be set at $25 a week. At this point Henry had reached such a stage of adolescent embarrassment that he wanted to make some rejoinder to the judge, and he cried out: "Twenty-five dollars? It is not enough. *Make it thirty.*" He made the suggestion as if it were a card game in which he was raising the ante. Soon he was lamenting to his friends about having to pay thirty dollars a week—*for life*. There had certainly been a portion of masochism in his protest; this was proved, if proof were needed, shortly after the trial when Henry wrote Bea's lawyer a letter congratulating him on a masterful presentation of the case.

Early in 1924 he took part of his vacation time to put the messenger book in shape. Though Dreiser and Anderson's influences were still most evident, Somerset Maugham's *On a Chinese Screen* affected the book formally. Trying to make the book more popular, he lessened its bleakness. For instance, he added a long section on Jacobus Dun, a young man who had come to America hoping to sell paintings he had brought from the estate of a Hungarian nobleman. When all else failed he took a messenger's job. An old acquaintance spotted him on the street one day and offered him a job which brought him into contact with the crowned heads of Europe. In this section of *Clipped Wings* Henry inserted some of the letters Dun wrote him from Europe, and the book actually seemed to be proving that Horatio Alger, after all, might be right. He imagined that Willever might be impressed by a book about Western Union and he handed a copy to him. The Vice-President didn't have time to read it immediately.

Certainly, Henry's own Horatio Alger story was turning bleak at this point. Willever brought a team of efficiency experts from Des Moines to look over the company. In short order, they began to focus on the office of the Messenger Employment Manager. Their computations seemed to indicate that the trouble was not in the messengers or in the delivery system or in the wage scale or company benefits. All their graphs seemed to point in the same direction—at Henry V. Miller. They suggested that in order to see to the proper dispatching of messengers as well as to the needs of each office, the Employment Manager should move his office from place to place. As a result, Henry's headquarters was shifted to offices all about town. Moreover, the experts concluded, the messenger staff was in such bad shape because Henry had hired so many undesirables. What might be an interesting worm in the apple for him, would hardly be in the best interests of the company, they pointed out. He had filled the ranks not only with criminals, but even worse, with foreigners—Egyptians, Hindus, East Indians, West Indians, even American Indians—and these clearly did not measure up to the Western Union standard and had to go. Finally the experts from Iowa wondered about the manager himself. He didn't appear to give his Western Union job proper respect. They didn't like the way that Henry put a sign on his desk at about 2 p.m. saying "Closed for the Day" when he felt he had solved enough problems. They felt that he resented regulation, he dressed like a Greenwich Village bohemian, and he was suspected of being a

Bolshevik. Finally, they appointed an assistant for him, Mike Rivise, whom Henry regarded as a company spy. It looked as if the same trick was being played on the employment manager as the one Henry had participated in four years earlier—only now he was on the receiving end. The job was becoming hell for him, especially since after all his sweat most of the money went to Beatrice. It irked him to see Beatrice better off than ever, buying new furniture and geegaws with his dough.

Ludicrously complicating Henry's efforts to cling to his job, were the phone calls from June who pestered him at the office continually. She reminded him of nothing so much as Frances Hunter, with her pleading; it was "Henry darling" all over again. He had no inclination and certainly no time to be lovey-dovey—yet she'd go on all day, unless he gave Sam the high-sign to disconnect them. He had already started to see through June's mysteries. Almost none of the stories she told him about herself turned out to be true—the real truth, when it came out, was pretty mundane. June acknowledged that her real name was June Edith Smith—but even that was not quite true, for her family called her Julia, and once she admitted to having been named Juliette. As to Smith, the original Polish family name was Smerth, meaning death, but it had been anglicized to Smith in 1911 when the family had immigrated to the United States from Czernowitz in northern Roumania. Her family was one of those that had flowed over the bridges from the lower East side of Manhattan around the time that Henry's parents were moving to Decatur Street in order to avoid the foreign tide. Her father was a farmer and lumberman who, like many other Polish Jews, had emigrated because of persecution and poverty. When he came to the United States the only work he could find was in the garment trades; eventually he settled down to the profession of used clothes dealer. If he had ever known Caruso it was backstage, when he provided used clothes for the extras' costumes at the opera. In all his life he had never been in England. The father whom she purported to adore had beaten her brutally and at last drove her out of the house, calling her a worthless slut. The only relation he had to horses was in his passion for betting on slow ones. The woman whom she spoke of as her aunt or stepmother turned out to be her natural mother—hardly a gypsy, unless at some very remote remove. June admitted that though she had been to high school, she had not graduated, and certainly she had never been to Wellesley, hardly even to Massachusetts, having spent almost every day of her whole American life in Bensonhurst, Brooklyn. But she certainly did know the ropes, having been a taxi-dancer at Roseland before Wilson's, and she understood the value of a good line—one that would make her stand out from the common trash. Tales of her romances proved almost as false as the account of her background. When she allowed herself to be deflowered by old man Harris, for instance, it was hardly for money to save the house—she had squandered the money, whatever tiny sum it was, on a Macy's stenographer named Maureen.

Henry simply didn't know what to believe. Was it true when she announced that her father had died? She did purchase a black dress—and then she disappeared for ten days. When she suddenly appeared in his office at 395 Broadway she looked pale and noble, with her skin stretched tightly across her fine cheekbones, almost like an Italian countess. What had made for the transformation? Once she admitted that she had not worked at the dance-hall for several weeks. Where, then, had she gotten the money she continued to bring home? Well, from old men, she explained, nice old rich men she'd become acquainted with in the dance-hall, men who were willing to pay for the mere company of a beautiful young girl at dinner and a show. Whenever he tried now to pin her down, she only laughed as if she couldn't stop, complained of headaches or the pain which came from trying to recollect details of the past that she had long ago forgotten; or she retreated entirely into multiplied mystery. One evening June arrived home to announce that she had quit Wilson's and had been accepted into the Theatre Guild company. As evidence she showed him a script of a Schnitzler play. In Wilson's, she said, she had met a man named Ian MacLaren, who was connected with the Guild, gave him a line about her college dramatic courses, got a tryout, and was allowed to become an understudy in *Saint Joan*. Thereafter, Henry never knew when to expect her home. She could always say that rehearsals went late, even when she didn't get home before he had to go to work.

She was torturing Henry with jealousy and yet continuously urging him to marry her. In fact, she was surprisingly upset by his talking of remarriage with such reluctance. Finally they did set a definite date. On Saturday, June 1, 1924, Henry and June took the Hudson Tubes to New Jersey. Cele and Emil Conason (Seymour Cohen's new name) were to meet them in Hoboken to witness the marriage ceremony. On the way over, June was querulous and kept telling him that he didn't really want to marry her. He had heard that wail so many times that he was sick of it and said she was right. The stop before Hoboken, June got off the subway, resolved to go home. He followed her and put his arms around her, saying he was sorry. But when they did arrive at the office of the civil magistrate, A.G. Carsten, the Conasons were not there: most likely, they hadn't really believed that

Henry and June themselves would show up. Just before the magistrate's office was to close at noon, Henry had to go out on the street and pick up two drifters. For a few bucks the bums agreed to swear that they had known the happy couple for the required time. The ceremony itself was as romantic as a sewing machine. After it the newlyweds felt sick and disappointed. They couldn't think of anything else to do, and so they telephoned friends until they found Ned Schnellock, Emil's brother. Restless and anxious to celebrate, yet listless and not knowing where they wanted to go or how to celebrate, they had a few drinks with Ned and his girl and then they all went to the Houston Street Burlesk. And so they passed their wedding night.

Now the troubles came in bunches. Willever finally read *Clipped Wings* and didn't like it at all: at best he regarded the book as a low blow at the company, at worst as a subtle form of blackmail, and he was fuming. The bosses were watching Henry closely, and this was sheer torment. Beatrice was annoyed that he had remarried and she gave him trouble about visiting Barbara. June, on the other hand, was jealous of these Sunday visits. His alimony payments were placing him deep in debt. Tensions with the Hickersons built to such an extreme that they had to make a move before someone was murdered. But in his haste to find a new place to please June, he got over his head in rental payments for an apartment at 91 Remsen Street in Columbia Heights, Brooklyn. This was an elegant place, with a red brick front and brownstone steps. At that time the Heights was the last aristocratic section left in Brooklyn. The apartment, which had once belonged to Judge Manton, rented for $90 a month, far more than he and June could afford; it had floors of inlaid wood, wooden panelled walls, stained-glass windows, and beautiful velvet portières. Henry put the daybed in the middle of the big open room. Everything seemed so clean, polished and simple, he thought of it as a Japanese Buddhist's room, but June insisted that he should have a special, far too costly, desk as well as a typewriter of his own. And they had to decorate, too, buying prints like "The Opium Smoker" and "The Wailing Wall." She was sinking them into hopeless debt. No wonder they called it their "Nip-and-tuck Apartment."

With so many pressures bombarding him he had to make a decisive break. He looked to his favorite writers to find a fictive situation similar to his own and find guidance. Sherwood Anderson came to his aid. In more than one place Anderson told how he had walked out of his managerial position in an Ohio factory after years as a businessman—determined to write and never again to hold a job. It was a grand story, even if not strictly true to the actual facts of Anderson's life; and for many would-be writers in the twenties it was vibrant with rich symbolic appeal. It certainly appealed to Henry. He conjured up a little tableau of himself and June together all day long. Between bouts of love-making he would turn out a steady stream of saleable yet superb essays, sketches, and stories.

On a Monday morning in November of 1924, he locked the hiring slate in his desk and walked off the job without a word of notice, vowing he would never work in an office again. Walt Whitman had proclaimed himself his "own master absolute." Really surprised at his own action, Henry repeated this phrase to himself as he walked down the street away from the office.

June rejoiced. Now, she said, he could devote himself entirely to writing. Whatever was needed she would provide, not only for him and herself, but also for Bea and Barbara—with silk robes, moroccan slippers, cashmere sweaters, and a tin of paté thrown in. She was serious: she wanted to do everything possible to make him happy. If he merely mentioned something he desired, June was likely to turn up with it. She urged him not to bother about jobs—he was to write. He needn't worry about meeting her after the theater. Flatly and decisively, all he was to do was write.

It was a new—and a rather intimidating—experience to be encouraged to do nothing but write, when his parents had always discouraged him so absolutely in this ambition. In their opinion it was bad enough that he had made such a mockery of work at the tailor shop; it was a shame that he had frittered away a good job at the Western Union; it was almost unforgivable that he had stopped paying alimony to his wife and child and almost got Heinrich's slim profits attached. On top of all this, to be a writer, they believed, was so deeply to wrong society and betray their trust that it was beyond not only discussion but even acknowledgment. He never showed his parents anything he had written for the simple reason that they didn't want to see anything. They always referred to his writing as—*scribbling*.

When Henry took June to meet his parents for the first time, his mother asked her if they were really married. When June answered, "Yes," Louise blurted out: "Too bad, he's no good, he's a murderer!" She meant that his irresponsibility had murdered her. To think that little Henry, who had loved to please her and for whom she had such exaggerated hopes, should turn out to murder his fond mother's dreams. At another dinner mother told Henry witheringly: "I hope you're doing something now to earn money." Getting no response, she turned to June: "You poor girl, are you still working at that miserable job? Why don't you make him give up that nonsense? We all have to work for a living." June defended him splendidly, saying that his books would one day earn money, but mother wouldn't give in: "You're daffy, both of you," she said. "There are plenty of writers around already, and most of them are starving. You ought to be working. It's a disgrace for her to slave for you all the time. You were doing so well once, you had a job. Now you're leading a loafer's life. You drift from one thing to another, you have no money, nothing. And what of your Barbara—who do you think's going to take care of her?" It was a castigation of the worst kind because he was afraid that everything she said might be true.

Henry enjoyed playing at being a writer, sitting at his desk, riffling through books, consulting dictionaries, spinning plots, designing charts and making notes. But June's proposition too thoroughly tested him; it made him feel that he was incapable of doing anything at all. Probably his parents were right and June wrong. During a whole month, he wrote only one sketch, called "Rhapsody in Blue." He found that he had nothing about which he really burned to write. He diddled around, revised old manuscripts, visited Emil, or gabbed with Joe O'Regan (who had turned up again and moved into Remsen Street with them). Mostly Henry wondered what June was doing. Though June simply breezed along, exulting in her sacrifices, for his part he was rapidly coming to regard them as a refined sort of torture, and he ended up blaming his creative sterility upon her irresponsible behavior.

But when June, with the greatest nonchalance in the world, reported to him that she had picked a quarrel with the director of the theater and had quit, he was frantic, even though she soon got another job, as a proofreader on Orloff's *PM*. Instantly Henry dropped his writing and started to look for a job. But he, who had hired thousands of messengers, couldn't get a job himself. He was rejected everywhere, just as if FAILURE had been branded on his brow. His nerve cracked and he could seldom even go through with the interviews. He couldn't, as the advertising slogans of the day had it, "sell himself" at any price. Whenever he returned home defeated, June would clap hands and sing. "Let me manage things," she'd plead. Henry had a bloodless Germanic way of adding up their debts and liabilities and would reply: "Is *this* how you manage things?" "I have no heart to do anything when you show no confidence in me," she'd wail, begging him on her knees just to leave things up to her. He'd agree, but the next day he'd be out, frantic as ever, searching for a new position, frittering his time away. Self-defensively, he kept blaming June: she was wrong in telling him to relax: he *should* worry, he *should* struggle, he should *strive*—she was robbing him of the very experiences a writer needed.

Even had he wanted to stay home and write, he couldn't have done so. If he did briefly emerge from the slough of despond and actually begin to pound away on his machine, then June would soon be at him, picking up his manuscript, gloating over it, making him subtly feel the sacrifices which she had endured to make this moment possible for him. Now and again she interrupted him briefly since she wanted him to know how good it was for her to see him at work. This was usually enough to stop him. But if he did persist at work, if he wasn't distracted by the sight of her flesh as she went by with only an unfastened silk bathrobe on, if he asked her to leave him entirely alone for an hour or two, if he fell into a reverie and failed to answer her remarks, or if he wanted to take a walk alone on the Heights to think an idea through—then she would fly into a rage of desperation. He didn't notice her any more, he was a fanatic for work, a misanthrope interested only in himself, certainly more interested in his work than in her despite all her sacrifices. He had ceased to love her, he wanted only to use her—accusations tumbled out of June. Sooner or later he'd have to take her in his arms and more than likely they'd end up in bed. Then, when she was thoroughly pacified, if he jumped out of bed, she would be more furious than ever. She couldn't tolerate the notion that at such a moment, a sacred moment, anything else could attract him more than she did, and she pouted. What was she—just a little piece of tail to be knocked off quickly? Was that all he thought of her? Doubtless the work was more urgent. After an hour or so of accusation and denial, when he was feeling thoroughly beaten and ready to admit that he had been wrong, then she would forgive him grandly and pull him to his desk. "Go to work," she'd tell him, "I won't bother you any more today."

Exhausted and dispirited, he would sit there under her watchful eyes, his mind as blank as a block of wood, and try to squeeze out one thought, even one sentence, to prove that her sacrifices were not in vain. She was destroying him with her liberality. He called himself a pimp, a slacker, a spendthrift, a failure. Her sacrifices were too great, too unselfish. It wasn't long before he felt that had he been able to write the Bible and the Upanishads rolled together with the works of Shakespeare, he could still not compensate her for all she was doing. Naturally, therefore, he wrote nothing. Literature almost became an object of hatred for him: it reminded him that he hated himself.

If she went out, he would not be far behind her, escaping his desk and typewriter with the same relief he had experienced only a short time before in walking out of the Western Union office.

Ten

Candy, and Other Rackets

Whatwith the rent, the alimony, the expensive gifts June lavished upon him, and the help that June's mother now required, they were spending over a hundred dollars a week, yet June always managed to keep the whole shebang afloat. She started hostessing at Raymo's, a kind of nightclub and speakeasy, and she moved around to other similar clubs in the Village; now, as Miller's friends remarked, she was "gold-digging with a vengeance." The idea was to dance only enough to raise the thirst of the customers, since her pay came from a percentage of the drinks she sold. Her job at each club lasted only a short time, but the suckers were innumerable everywhere. For obvious reasons, she and Henry also kept on the move. During 1924 and 1925, their string of apartments matched the sequence of clubs at which she worked. June had always been erratic and her narratives broken and disconnected; but now they took on a thoroughly unbelievable character.

June stayed home all day, almost like a beast in hiding. She hated the sunlight. She did not go out until dusk. Often she did not return until dawn from a night of pushing drinks, cadging loans, and getting her percentage from the bartender. Some of the old marks from the dance-hall followed her to the clubs, still surprisingly devoted to her. Some of them even trailed her home and could be found knocking on the door in the cold, gray dawn of New York. And a whole new group of admirers gathered around her as she went from Raymo's to the Peroquet, the Roman Tavern, and the Pepper Pot. The wealthy young Mori; Nat Pendleton, the wrestler;

Hans Stengel, the artist who drew illustrations for *Snappy Stories;* millionaires like Neuberger and Johnson; Young, the editor of *Young's Magazine,* a cheap pulp; the Cuban chess champion Roberto de Silvor . . . these and a dozen more hovered around June in the taverns and tea-rooms and returned her to her door at about the hour that Henry was rising.

Henry's main creative activity was inventing fresh swindles. They needed plenty of rackets since it was difficult to hostess successfully for very long without begging or whoring, and even more difficult to keep up a single swindle for long without getting stung. They started off with simple con games. When June met the banker Howell P. French, for example, she maneuvered and put him off whenever he became too ardent, until they were ready to stage an "artists'" party for him at Remsen Street. Cele Conason posed as Henry's wife, Henry played the bohemian writer, Emil Schnellock the starving artist, Conason the cracked analyst, and June (of course) the grisette; the whole gave the appearance of a cross between Puccini and Maxim Gorki. They concocted the kind of bizarre talk which artists were supposed to speak; Emil described his futurist paintings, and Henry read him imagist "cockroach poems." Then they sprang a story on French about their friend, dying in the hospital for lack of funds. The only fly in the ointment was that Henry got drunk and (quite naturally) fell asleep in his own bed, and Schnellock had to pull him out in the morning when French demanded to know why that writer fellow stayed all night. (But what was it, the masquerading husband might have wondered, that June and French were doing in the next room until dawn? He didn't dare ask.) And to top it all off, June discovered a few days later that French's supposed fortune had already melted away to practically nothing. Somehow, this seemed to suggest that perhaps the two hucksters were dupes themselves, a suggestion that echoed hollowly through almost all the swindles that Henry and June tried.

The imported candy racket promised better success than the sick-friend-swindle—at first, anyway. In the winter of 1924-25 a candy store dealer on Second Avenue persuaded Henry to introduce a line of imported candies to restaurants in New York. The candy, he assured them, would sell itself, and when it was established they could live off the commissions on repeat sales.

The candy racket lasted for three months. All during this time Henry was completely absorbed by the business: he dropped his writing altogether and walked around Manhattan for sixteen hours a day with nothing on his mind but the need of the American public to consume all the sweets that the importers could produce.

But he was unable to do the selling himself. He hated to walk into his old haunts like the Café Royale as a beggar; he hated the insults; he was ashamed to come down to the position of a suppliant. Soon he had June doing the peddling inside the restaurants while he waited outside in the cold and snow, dreaming of sumptuous dinners—talking only to occasional cops, hall-men, and taxi-drivers. Wearing his overcoat with boxes of candy stuffed into every pocket, June went right into the very places where she had once been a hostess, impervious to the insults, and got her admirers to buy candy at a dollar a box; she went into office buildings around Borough Ball and the East Side and sold from office to office. Henry waited outside like a pimp while June ducked down into cellar cafés. When she came out he usually growled at her, grabbed her by the arm, and dragged her along the street, cruelly, silently, to the next place he wanted to try. He could have tolerated the walks, the loneliness, the cold, and the failure: but he hated himself for letting June go on with this, and he focussed his self-hatred on the woman he idolized.

Finally, Henry stood the candy dealer up for $50 of merchandise they had taken on account. Then they persuaded Beatrice that she could get on easy street by making homemade candy which they, with their contacts, could sell easily. Characteristically, Bea haggled over the percentage they would pay, the trademark and patent rights, and so on, but she was really licking her lips at the thought of easy money. Henry was mindful of the ironical fact that his present wife was selling his former wife's candy, and that the alimony he was still struggling to pay Bea came from the profits June made on Beatrice's work. But when the candy trade eventually went bust altogether, he never paid Beatrice for her work anyway, and he stopped paying alimony too.

In the spring of 1925 June thought up a variation on the candy business, one that might make a hit with the Village tourists. She laid out their dilemma clearly: Henry had become thoroughly disgusted with the candy selling. He couldn't do it himself and he hated to see her do it. On the other hand, he did want to write and she agreed with him in this. Yet, they had to make money. So far this was obvious. "Fine," June said, "the problem is its answer. If you simply do what you wish to do—write—I will sell your writing."

It was an appealing idea. Even Whitman, after all, had printed his own work and sold it from door to door. In April of 1925, as Henry decided to write up a series of prose sketches short enough to be printed on a single card which June could sell, he had Whitman's career in mind. He drew the parallel by typing out copies of Whitman's poem "Native Moments" for his friends and noting: "For a complete and unequivocal understanding of the undersigned the rendition below is absolutely prerequisite":

Native moments—when you come upon me—when you come upon
   me—ah you are here now,
Give me libidinous joys only,
Give me the drench of my passions, give me life coarse and rank,
To-day I go consort with Nature's darlings, to-night too,
I am for those who believe in loose delights, I share the midnight orgies of
   young men, . . .

* * *

I will play a part no longer, why should I exile myself from my companions?
O you shunn'd persons, I at least do not shun you,
I come forthwith in your midst, I will be your poet,
I will be more to you than any of the rest.

Henry saw himself as having shed his civilized, conforming role in society and as living, instead, a life devoted to the "loose delights" of "libidinous joys" and self-understanding. But perhaps the most crucial line is: "I will play a part no longer."

In accordance with June's proposal, he wrote a series of philosophic, lyrical, or descriptive sketches, each 350 words in length, and had them printed up on various colored six by nine inch papers, in editions of 100. With the impressionist technique of Whistler in mind, he called these sketches "Mezzotints"; each mezzotint would give a single impression as it had been received by the author's mind.

However, because these mezzotints were products which June intended to peddle, they agreed to have them signed "June E. Mansfield/91 Remsen Street/Brooklyn." Henry began to crank his sketches out—at first with grim resolution and then with increasing pleasure. Eventually, he wrote about thirty-five mezzos, though not all were finally printed. Starting was laborious. But Henry's methodical habits paid off. He had kept scrap books and note books of experiences, he saved copies of his letters, and he never threw away a literary effort. So, in 1925 he began to dip into his files. For the first mezzotint he reached back two or three years to one of the earliest pieces he had written—an effort praised by Orvis Ross—"Make Beer for Man (Apologies to Horace Traubel)," written at least partially under the influence of the brew it celebrated. Its theme was: "Keep your libraries.

Keep your penal institutions. Keep your insane asylums . . . GIVE ME
BEER." It was a howl for freedom from convention, symbolized by the
restrictions imposed by Prohibition: "You think man needs rule. He needs
beer. The world does not need your morals. It needs beer. It does not need
your lectures or your charity. The souls of men have been fed with
indigestibles. But the soul could make use of beer." Henry was ready to be a
spiritual teacher like Emerson: he had found Emerson's style, but he could
not yet express an Emersonian theme seriously.

A letter which Henry had written to Emil Schnellock in August 1924,
was the basis for another mezzo, titled "A Bowery Phoenix." This same
sketch also appeared under June's name in the February 1925 issue of
Pearson's Monthly Review, a journal previously edited by Frank Harris, but
now run by Alexander Markey. In this piece, Henry shows how much he
had profited from his talks with Schnellock about the Italian Renaissance.
Rhapsodizing sarcastically about a luxurious Renaissance-style bank which
has sprung "out of the squalor and poverty of the Bowery," he concludes:

As a depositor I should crave just one privilege. To surrender my shekels
and dream: of Michael Angelo's tomb for the Pope Julius, of Leonardo's
wasted efforts in "The Last Supper," of the superb cruelty in Donatello's
"Judith and Holofernes," of the perverse, sadistic mien of Lorenzo the
Magnificent, and of Savonarola's bon-fire "de luxe" in that splendorous
Florentine city of the Renaissance.

Squat little monsters poke their ugly visages at the populace from out the
huge bronze portals. Misshapen, bowlegged, sinister little devils. But
beautiful when raised in lacquered bronze on a hammered door.

This bank of the Bowery Medicis is a luminous Dantesque vision in a
crowded thoroughfare, a shimmer of frozen music in a seething mart of
commerce. Truly, a Bowery phoenix.

Another, titled "Christianity at the Sink" was a panegyric upon the
performance of Emil Jannings in *The Last Laugh,* a film in which Henry saw
an apt parallel to the story of his own degradation. "This expressionistic
photoplay has the everlasting bite of a Daumier print," he somewhat lamely
wrote of the film. Another mezzotint was a satire on modern funeral
practices and particularly on "the latest thing," mausoleum burial. This
was called: "If You're Dying, Choose a Mausoleum." "First we had the
rubber tire epidemic, then a chewing gum splurge and now the undertaker
is having his orgy of publicity," Henry writes. Miller mocks the preoccupation with death in modern America. Three other mezzotints derived
directly from his experience as candy vendor between December 1924 and

February 1925. "The Art of Peddling" was about the difficulties of door-to-door direct sales. "Papa Moskowitz," portrayed the owner of one of Henry's favorite restaurants. "June the Peripatetic" concerned the strange wanderings of his wife. Others, like "The Prince" and "Bernard Shaw," gave his impressions of people. "Cynara" had originally been sent to June as a letter during their earliest days of courtship. "Bike Race" was based on a six-day event he saw from the press box a year before in the company of his Western Union pals. "The Awakening" sketched out the story of the night when Henry had intended to run away with Gladys Miller, only to return home in disgust. "Circe," an exhibition of the baleful influence of Edgar Saltus on Miller, was the portrait of a New York streetwalker, some of whose features were drawn from those of Camilla Fedrant. Circe is "a crepuscular odalisque with a torso like a groundswell. Suggesting Whistlerian nocturnes . . . Not the baleful, iniquitous curves of an Utamaro. Something begun by Praxiteles, rather, and left for the moderns to complete." Another mezzotint was called "Nigger" and dealt with the brutal treatment shown by a cop to a Negro. This sketch got Henry into temporary trouble with the police when a copy fell into the hands of the lieutenant of his precinct. He called Henry in and read him the riot act.

"Dance Hall," was clearly a meditation on some of June's mysterious evenings at Wilson's:

AMERICA'S nocturnal pasturage of innocuous iniquity.

Invites the weary business man to enter. Entices the shop girl, the Ford mechanic, the swivel-chair nincompoop.

Religiously interpreted the electric lights read: "Come on, you mincing satyrs, you four-square strumpets, you lovely tangerines, you Broadway beldames. Step in. Shake a wicked hip."

On a low dias, with heavy drapes, five perspiring automatons belabor their instruments, producing jazz. Led by a 'nigger' in shirt sleeves, glued to a fiddle. A black Satan whimpering crazy tunes. And ecstasy beating a blanket of smoke.

Price: a nickel a dance. Hire an instructress. She will put you through the ropes. Will walk you through a hundred dances on a piece-work basis. And tell you her family troubles.

Music crashes, hammers, moans piteously. Glistening fiends in patent-leather slippers assume eccentric poses, leer at the on-lookers, press hot bodies together until they fuse into one shameless, molten quadruped. No one gets weary. Jazz babies with haggard eyes keep up a fierce, relentless pace under signs reading:

"No improper dancing"

Can a girl retain her virtue? At a nickel a dance? Ask me whether it was ethical of Socrates to drink his cup of hemlock. I know some respectable people who come here twice a week for recreation. Ask them.

All the mezzotints but one were signed by June. The exception was "Dawn Travellers," signed "Henry V. Miller." This is an account of the workers who people the city at dawntime—people whose activities Henry had had plenty of chances to see since he had started waiting up for June. These are those "who clean and sweep out places, who open and close shops, who sweep the streets and deliver coal, who drive trucks, hawk wares and push carts." This "subway world," he writes, could only be portrayed by a masterful painter, a Rembrandt, Goya, or Zuloaga. "But they were never in the subway when the rabbit hutches unloose their breed. No, these monsters of despair, fashioned out of our industrial civilization, have yet to be portrayed. We need another Gustave Doré for this modern Inferno."

These mezzotints were hardly demonstrations of special artistic talent. Here and there a spark of wit, a sharp insight, or an illuminating detail flashes out of the schist of prose in which it is encrusted. They were as good as Henry hoped they would be. And June was right—they did sell! June hawked the mezzotints as she had the candy, and far more easily and comfortably. They sold not only surprisingly well, but at astonishing prices—chiefly to June's customers at the Pepper Pot. Who could refuse to purchase the artistic efforts of the young waitress who was serving tea and smiling so sweetly?

By the spring of 1925, the time that the first of the mezzotints were appearing, Henry and June had made a thoroughgoing mess of their Remsen Street apartment and were evicted. For a while they stayed with Stanley, sleeping on the floor. Dispirited as he was with his own life, even Stanley was quickly fed up with them and he ejected them brutally. Broke, they sought a place with Henry's old pal Karl Karsten, a successful statistician. He allowed them to camp there only until they found a place of their own. Finally they temporarily rented a flat on Clinton Street. The candy and mezzotint rackets had both run out—and both for about the same reason: Henry simply could not persist in either one. He was quickly worn out, fast to see the defect in anything, early to despair. He really could not respect the mezzotints, and soon after using up ideas drawn from his letters to June (as in "Free Fantasia," "Pursuit," and "Suicide Letter") he ran completely out of ideas.

He saw at once the blight in the project which next blossomed in June's fertile mind. But she was getting inured to his hesitancies and fears and went rushing on. For her the question was pure—or not so pure—and simple: they needed money, always money, and they would do whatever they must to get it. In order to make a start on her new project, however, they needed initial capital for supplies.

June's idea was a speakeasy. After Henry cadged a loan out of his mother, he sank into a stupor and left the rest of the arrangements to June. He had become almost completely numb, withdrawn, and ineffectual; all he wanted to do now was lounge around with Ned and Emil Schnellock, Joe O'Regan, or Harold Hickerson, discussing the war, art, modernism, or burlesque, and playing chess or pingpong. No matter how she tried, June could not rouse him from his lethargy. Well, she decided, she could get along without him, and she went ahead to get things ready. This was one more humiliation for Henry to suffer—but he almost ceased to notice how often he had been shamed. With the aid of her admirers, June rented a basement apartment on Perry Street and fixed it up to entertain drinking customers; she arranged with some bootleggers to provide a stock; and she bought sacramental wine from the Orthodox Jewish shops on Allen Street. Then she was ready for business. The Perry Street place was a dive with only three rooms. In the living room they placed a chess board, a pingpong table, and some comfortable chairs. In the other room June could privately entertain her special friends. This meant that she and Henry had to live in the kitchen.

Almost at once they were behind in the rent, and she had to gold-dig as fast as possible to keep from being evicted. Henry served as bartender and short-order cook. Under these circumstances a husband was not an asset and he had to pretend to be her employee, which griped him. When June shot him an order he'd sometimes sullenly pretend not to have heard. What was worse, when some of the very special customers arrived he was occasionally obliged to duck out the back window. And of course, new swains *were* always showing up.

He sulked. Once he flew into an uncontrollable rage and smashed things in the apartment. He had always experienced fits of anger, but recently these seemed to be getting worse. He felt that he might become insane. Anyone who wished to make a case for his insanity could certainly have adduced many proofs in addition to the strain of mental weakness in his family, Lauretta's illness, and his own momentary imbalance in National City, California. One day after he had returned, for instance, he was standing on a Brooklyn elevated platform and decided to buy a penny stick of Wrigley's chewing gum from a machine. As he inserted his penny he looked in the mirror—but he saw a face he did not recognize and he realized again that he couldn't remember his identity. *What is your name?* he asked the face in the mirror. *Who are you?* The rails glistened, the billboards embroidered the air with color, other people moved about—but for a minute it was all a tableau and he was frozen at its center, without existence. Now June looked right through him—as if he did not exist— and hardly talked to him at all. Her friends and customers treated him contemptuously and humiliated him. This low life itself shamed him, and he secretly longed to disengage himself from it, from June, from their bickerings and their financial woes. Morose, he began to make serious inroads on the liquor stock and kept himself pickled.

Again, he hatched a plan for escape. The next "new life" always looked better. He decided to go to Florida with Joe O'Regan and Ned Schnellock to clean up a little dough quickly in the real estate boom. The three of them planned to get jobs, make a little money, pool it, and then quickly multiply it in the spiraling real estate speculation. June paid attention to him now: she screamed and stamped her feet. She wailed accusingly that she was working her heart out and all he wanted to do was go off on larks. He probably wouldn't have gone otherwise, but June's fierce opposition set his mind on striking it big in Florida to prove to her how serious he was. He kept after her until she gave in to him and tackled one of her old lovers to get up a stake for him, not because she believed he would be successful there, but simply to get rid of him.

Yet she softened at the last moment. Just as Henry was about to take off, on Thanksgiving Day 1925, she threw her arms around him saying that she knew he could do anything, that he was a great man. She would join them as soon as they made a success. Now that June was nice to him again, Henry wanted to stay. He walked away hesitantly, promising to call frequently (reversing the charges: by the time the bill was due June would skip South). They started to hitchhike in a blazing snowstorm, and at every step Henry moaned that he was deserting June to the wolves of New York who'd pick her bones clean in the Perry Street basement. Only Joe's soldier-of-fortune spirit pulled him, weakly, along. As soon as they hit Wilmington, the first night, he called June, thrilled just to hear her voice.

The hitchhiking was a horror. Once, Henry and Joe were given a ride by a young man who confessed as they sped along that he had committed an accidental murder and was fleeing the sheriff, whom he supposed was on his trail. All through the Carolinas and Georgia and into Florida they sped.

One night they stayed in a bawdy house. The driver slept dressed, his gun on the pillow. But he paid all the way, even giving Henry money to telegraph June.

Straight into Jacksonville they went, and there they were met by the wave of fortune seekers who were returning north following the bust of the Florida bubble. Already the country was feeling an economic pinch, though prosperity was still the watchword, and the Florida boom had attracted far more adventurers than it could possibly support. They were hanging around the streets and parks, begging meals and bed until some driver who still had money for gas might pick up a few riders for the trek back to New York. It was hopeless before they started.

Of course, they were out of money. June had been expected to hustle some up and telegraph it, but he lost touch with her. Henry begged enough money to buy a stack of newspapers and he tried to hawk them. But no one seemed interested in the daily news or had a nickel to purchase it. When it came time to sleep, they thought they could rely upon the Salvation Army, but they couldn't come up with the quarter it cost to sleep on the floor in the barracks. Finally, they went to the park. It was early December and chilly and wet, but they stretched out on benches, hoping to sleep. Henry dozed off; he hadn't been alseep for more than a half hour when, without a word of warning, a cop smacked him with a paddle just as if he were a naughtly child, rousting them out. The night was long, and he felt miserable and worried about June; but most of all his rear burned from that gratuitous whack. The next morning he noticed that the park he had been routed out of was situated between June and Mansfield streets.

One night, he passed a synagogue and heard music which cut at him like a razor. He thought back to a summer night more than a year earlier when he and June were eating at the Scotch Bakery. From a radio shop the voice of Cantor Sirota drifted to them. That was the night when June had first confessed that she was Jewish. She was wearing a marvellous deep red dress, and he felt he had never been so much in love with her. She seemed like a rich legendary character, a Rebecca from *Ivanhoe*. What had happened to those days? And where was June now? Henry became so wrought up with self-pity that he attempted to make a touch on the Rabbi and did get a note to the Salvation Army requesting he be given a free bed. But by the time he got over there, every bed was filled. Everything was filled in Jacksonville. One man suggested he go west. But he had tried that almost a decade ago.

A week of this suffering and he was completely dejected. Desperate to get back to June and unable to bear the thought of the slow, uncertain process of hitchhiking back, he turned to his parents. His father sent the full fare, and Henry was on the first train back to New York, still smarting from his hurt pride and his bruised backside, in December of 1925.

Unable to locate June, like a prodigal child he took the subway over the Williamsburg Bridge to Decatur Street and dragged himself ignominiously to number 1063. Only a few days after he returned home the year's two most sullen reminders of his failure came, as always, one after the other—Christmas and his birthday. As usual he could not buy presents for his parents or sister. What his birthday said to him now was: *too late*. He was beginning his thirty-fifth year—too late, too late for any expectation of achievement when he had so obviously made such a thorough mess of the first half of his life.

Henry had left home thirteen years earlier. In the meantime, he had kept one mistress, been married twice, traveled to California and Florida, and become a parent himself. If he looked back on his earlier trip to the West or his more recent one to the South it seemed to him that he had not really moved at all: he was simply back where he had started, still going down a tunnel which narrowed to a pinpoint at the end, so that at last it seemed altogether to shut out any possibility of emergence and escape.

Eleven

Visions and Revisions

Henry was worried about not locating June, but he felt even worse when he actually did locate her living at her mother's. She said she saw no hope that they would be able to live together again; her desperation increased his. She was nervous and suffering terribly with earaches. They couldn't get a place to sleep together, they only met at noontimes. And June's talk was always the same: she was going to go away, there was no hope. Beatrice was giving him trouble from another angle by complaining loudly about his arrears in alimony payments. He felt as if a wall were being raised around him.

Authorship, which had so often sunk him, this time began to save him. He knew nothing about the Dada movement in Europe, but to him, as to his European contemporaries, all life did appear senseless, random, and absurd. He did not develop a theory about it, as the dadaists did, but he certainly had what in his own slang he might have called his "Ga-ga period." On his own he discovered automatic composition. One day, after he had been looking up words in the dictionary for some time, he went out for a walk, his mind blank. Suddenly, of their own volition the words themselves began to seethe and form sentences and paragraphs. The words came like a tornado. He dashed home and, still wearing his hat and overcoat, he pounced on the typewriter and took down the dictation. When it was finished, he called it "The Diary of a Futurist." He had made a momentous discovery. As a writer he had always planned and plotted his work carefully, relying upon common-sense to guide his choice of situations or characters. But now he suddenly saw that what was most true about common-sense was that it was *common*. Now he discerned the uncommon sense possessed by words arranged according to their own logic. That his "Diary of a Futurist" didn't possess common sense, but instead a sense of its own, seemed decidedly to be in its favor. Henry made no claim to understand the logic or the origin of his work—he rejoiced in its mysteriousness. Once, in a joking mood, he explained the origin of his creativity to Emil Schnellock: "Well may you ask on what meat doth Caesar feed that he can spew such vile vomitings. Well then, here you have it: an article on Henry James in the Yale Review, long and intimate association of a purely involuntary sort with insectivora, a charcoal acquisition of a Red Indian-like Dante, three pipefuls too many of Prince Albert tobacco, a too eager anticipation over the possession of a noiseless typewriter, plus an hereditary love of ease displayed in the use and abuse of an unexpected amanuensis, and—a dirty bed-spread, a mania for alliteration, a very splendid bowel movement, and the thought that Emil would go Schnellocking thru this jabberwocky chortling chic chuckles." His literary genius, Henry hinted, lay in a purposeful literary buffoonery and "The Diary of a Futurist," he thought, was valuable for its jabberwocky sense.

Along with some of his best sketches, Henry sent "The Diary of a Futurist" to a well-known advertising man named Bruce Barton, who had just recently published what was to be one of the best selling non-fiction works of the decade, *The Man Nobody Knows*. (The title referred to Christ and in the book Barton attempted to apply business principles to the understanding of Christianity.) A brilliant publicist with his finger on the pulse of the masses, Barton, Henry felt, might give him some really helpful advice. But he hardly got the advice he expected. Barton returned the manuscript with a letter that concluded: "It is obvious, young man, that you will never be a writer. Writing is clearly not your forte." He advised Henry to discover his real talents. A more eminent critic agreed. H.L. Mencken, the distinguished editor of the *American Mercury* to which Henry consigned the same manuscript, returned the work with a polite note of refusal addressed to "Miss Miller." Henry was hurt but not crushed. He felt he was discovering his own unique role as a writer. He recalled the remark of Walter Pater in *The Renaissance,* a book he first read in Remsen Street: "Besides those great men there is a certain number of artists who have a distinct faculty of their own by which they convey to us a peculiar quality of pleasure which one cannot get elsewhere." He used this quotation in

"Houston Street Burlesque" (printed in *The Menorah Journal*) and vowed to live by it. He didn't presume that he was a great one, but he supposed he might possess a distinctive talent. He began to sense that he might be a special kind of artist if only he could give clear expression to his personal faculties.

In the meantime, Ronald Millar, the editor of *Liberty Magazine,* liked some of Henry's sketches in manuscript and commissioned him to write a simple article on "Words" based on an interview with Dr. Vizetelly, editor of Funk and Wagnalls, the beloved dictionary which Henry himself used. Everything went swimmingly: Dr. Vizetelly cooperated and spent an hour with him, giving him a thorough lecture on words, from which Henry carried away the gratifying fact that his own vocabulary was greater than Shakespeare's. Vizetelly not only offered to read a draft of Henry's essay, he even wrote to Henry's father to say that his son was a genius.

The article didn't fare quite so well. Asked to produce 5,000 words for a general audience, he wrote 15,000; and even when he pared this in half, it was still judged "too good" for the magazine. The article was canned but Henry did receive his $250 fee. At least he could show his mother that writing did pay off. (This backfired; thereafter his parents kept asking about his "latest sale" and his mother was always urging him to emulate each new bestseller.) Best of all, the $250 check allowed him to rent a cheap furnished room on Hancock Street in Brooklyn in which he and June could live together again.

But they were on different paths. Almost at once, Henry began to speak of the possibility of his renting a separate room in which he could work without interruption on saleable articles, while June kept saying he was to remain at her side for good now. He was talking about earning enough to see them through, while she was bursting with monumental schemes. Each went in his own direction, thinking they were going together. The aged editor of *Young's* magazine gave her a commission for a few stories. She also got a commission for a dozen tales from *Snappy Stories,* a magazine for which her friend Hans Stengel did illustrations. Henry, of course, wrote up the tales, but they were printed under the name June E. Mansfield. The first two tales he saw accepted were original, but when Henry learned that anything sent in under the name of June E. Mansfield would be accepted, he lifted the remainder of the stories from the magazine's back files, and cut up and rearranged them. The editors loved the tales. Even so, Miller, who was never able to persevere for long in any swindle, became disgusted with the whole idea. Early in 1926 he got a job at $50 a month on a Long Island newspaper. That infuriated June. She spewed out a violent tirade: "You'll be sorry for having left my side. If you are so ungrateful as to leave me to go off to work, I can't be responsible for what I might do!" When he returned from his first day, June was missing. When he hunted her up at last she calmly explained that if he must know, the moment after he walked out the door she accepted a date from a charming young Spanish singer whom she had recently met. Henry capitulated and gave up his job at once.

He was ready for any scheme that promised to keep them together without obliging him to live wholly on June's terms, and a solution appeared. Like a cork, Joe O'Regan surfaced in Asheville, North Carolina. Here, he reported by mail, was an authentic real estate boom. If Henry would hurry to Asheville, he could knock off a tidy sum by serving in the capacity of public relations man for the real estate interests.

Henry reasoned—none too sensibly—that if they could just get away from June's dance-hall and Pepper Pot cronies, things would go more smoothly, June would be forced to depend upon him. Instinctively, however, June knew that her freedom derived from familiarity with New York and her association with a group of friends. Whatever wrecks she might have, in New York she would walk away unhurt. Thus, when Henry urged Joe's Asheville scheme upon her, June resisted. He wouldn't let up on her, though, and finally she faltered and was swept along by the force of his arguments. By the end of July 1926, combining the checks which June collected from *Young's* and *Snappy Stories* with her usual percentages from hostessing, they managed to scrape $145 together. Henry did not intend to undergo the suffering that he experienced in Florida. Even though he still had two stories pending at *Young's* and one at the Putnam Syndicate, this time he hoarded his money. Though he dreamed of great wealth, he was learning to discount Joe's rosy estimations by fifty per cent.

Twelve

By the Shores of Junaluska

Henry should have discounted Joe O'Regan's enticements entirely. True, he made prudent preparations for hard times, but no one could have asked him to prepare for complete and utter disillusion. June disappointed him first. While he was being bowled over by the beauty of the American scene, she bitched all the way South. Scenes of pioneering, the Revolution, the Civil War, or of natural beauty stirred his feelings of awe, while June couldn't get beyond her scornful *New Yorker*, Greenwich Village views concerning the stupidity of the people and the generally pedestrian character of the scene. He didn't realize that she was this completely attached to New York, and he nursed a secret hurt that his unspoken plan, by which they would leave New York for good and settle down in the D.H. Lawrence territory of New Mexico, was not feasible.

As events unfolded, none of his dreams was realized. Joe's projects were all wisps of the imagination. When Joe himself didn't even seem capable of collecting the $1000 in back pay already owed him, what chance was there for Henry to fill his wallet? No sooner had Henry and June arrived in late July of 1926 than Joe announced that the boom in Asheville had burst and declared himself ready to go to Miami, where he would make a fortune—"if conditions are right."

Joe did not depart before he clouded Henry and June's eyes with gold dust. With her style, June could make a fortune in Asheville, he said. All she needed to do was dress up in a classy rig and dazzle the local businessmen. June spent most of their $145 on an outfit of clothes to make an impression on the businessmen, but Joe didn't really know any influential businessmen and June sauntered around the dusty Carolina streets all dressed up and feeling foolish. However, she soon came up with a grand scheme of her own—to put in a fancy stock of ladies' silk hosiery and sell stockings to the local rich society women and *nouveau riches,* then afterwards tour the South, from the Carolinas through Florida and as far west as New Orleans, drumming up a desire for silk hose in the hearts of Southern belles. Everything seemed ridiculously simple. All she would need was a little expense money, a dealer to give her hosiery on consignment, contacts, a car, a permanent center of operations, and a campaign—the rest would be easy.

There was the matter of money. A dozen begging telegrams brought $100 from friends. Henry ground out a few more stories intended for the pulps. George T. Bye, the editor of the Putnam Syndicate, seemed to believe in him, and though he rejected articles on "Vocabularies" and "Stamps," he encouraged Henry to model a story on one of the well-tried formulas in *Liberty;* he went so far as to say that if Henry didn't know a good plot, he would tell him one that couldn't fail to hit the mark. June located a hosiery distributor. Everything was going swimmingly. They scouted around for a home base, and first had their eye on a cottage on the shores of Lake Junaluska; but then they located a cosily and artistically furnished little cottage 32 miles away in Hazelwood, which they could rent from a female writer for $20 a month. Henry dropped this when he received an even better proposition from the Chamber of Commerce in Waynesville, offering him a house for the winter rent-free in exchange for maintaining it. He also talked to a fellow who had "a damned good" year-old Oldsmobile coupe for sale and offered to pay him $50 down and the remainder over a year.

Then, as usual, Henry and June began to see the blight, the tarnish. Their hundred dollars meant for the down payment on an auto and on stock disappeared. Twenty more telegrams brought no response. The chance that June might be hired by a local theater company fell through. By the end of August, they already owed a month's rent; at a local restaurant they had arranged to pay $18 a week for meals, and were behind by almost three weeks. Henry's new creditors were polite and hospitable but very firm: credit didn't extend as far in Asheville as in New York. The local citizenry didn't trust this strange couple.

The literary lights in the town were about as alive as O. Henry and Bill Nye, writers who were planted in the local graveyard, and Henry himself was utterly occupied by the formula plot and the tastes of the editors of popular magazines. His hopes were almost hysterically fixed upon a popular success, and everything—his reading, his literary plans, his critical judgment—was dragooned into the service of this aim. He kept saying to himself: *Do something that the editors will like. Write pieces that will sell. For god's sake, earn some money, pull yourself out of this hole.* He had trapped himself in the pulp field and realized that after all his flailings and struggles, he was grubbing for pennies just as he had done in Western Union or in Atlas Cement—just as in the hated tailor shop. The only difference was that Henry was expected to lick the boots of editors instead of customers; he was still essentially in the tailoring business—making stories cut to someone else's pattern and taste. He wrote to Conason from Asheville: "the only means of subsistence for yours truly seems to be the cheap magazines. God knows whether I have talent enough to make them or not . . . Hell, I'm not sure that I can do anything any more." He told Conason to take over the books and magazines he had left behind, including not merely *Masses* and *Two Worlds,* but a number that were "good for reference, in case you want to dabble in the dirty story field." By mid August, 1926, he was depressed enough to be signing his letters "Dostoievski, Jr." But this did not mean that he was ready, Dostoievski-like, to explore misery in America. "Say, I am just about finished with the 'Possessed'," he told Conason in another letter, "—supposedly the best of the mad Russian's stuff. . . . Reads like a dime novel, for the most part. Would have made good serial stuff for *Liberty* or *Collier's,* barring an occasional nasty scene. . . ." He analyzed Upton Sinclair's *100%,* a wooden novel, from the same point of view: "What difference there is between it and a dime novel is hard to detect. . . . He can tell a corking story, I'll say—with all the hokumlocutions of plot that are required by the average editor. No wonder he's a howling success." He read now only in order to learn the formulas for popularity. Caught in an economic trap, he had almost completely abandoned his standards. He even found himself defending Fannie Hurst. "I hold no brief for her art," he told Conason; "in fact, I lean the other way. But, in studying, as I try to, the drivel in the *Post, Collier's, Liberty,* and that grade of widely-circulated magazines, I find that I prefer, after all, this abbreviated style of Fannie Hurst's to the long suffering, bloated, bilge water variety that the others rely upon." What she possessed, he argued, was "masterful technique—CRAFTSMANSHIP." Unfortunately, no editors responded this favorably to his writing. At the end of August, he received a succinct estimation of his work from Bye of the Putnam Syndicate; it "was appraised in this office as pointless."

Henry was sunk by his dream of popularity, June by her dream of New

York. In some deep essential way June had changed. When he first met her she had been enthusiastic about everything. But the nights at Wilson's and Raymo's and the Pepper Pot coarsened her, though she was only twenty-one. The continuous strife in their marriage had crushed her spirit. Her talk was artificial, practiced, like a sideshow pitchman's. The Village lured her. "We've got to get back, we've got to get back." For Henry everything went blank—the South seemed drained of its color: white houses, white trees, white roads, white skies, white dust, white buildings, white faces, white golf-balls hit into white sand traps in front of the verandah of the million-dollar Grove Park Inn, the "Finest Resort Hotel in the World." Only the blacks seemed alive. They moved with a gem-like brilliance, powerful and beautiful. Their rich, deep songs drifted from their cabins. But everything white, including himself and June, seemed dead. Henry lay inertly in bed, exhausted by heat and hunger, while June stalked around the room, naked, with a cigarette dangling from her lips, her hair wavy with the moist heat, the perspiration trickling down her belly.

Henry felt like a thoroughly beaten dog. By mid-September 1926, even he burned to get back to the city. But he was so thoroughly whipped that he could hardly get up the courage to stick out his thumb as a hitchhiker. Besides, he owed a month's rent and $80 in restaurant tabs; he couldn't afford to leave since he couldn't pay his debts and he was afraid of being clapped into jail if he skipped and got caught. "We've got to go, we've got to get back," June kept lamenting. And since they hadn't a cent, if they stayed they'd also end up in trouble. So they decided to run out. Early one morning, they packed up their belongings and made their way silently out to the highway. From Winston-Salem Henry wired his father for funds, as he had done from Florida. At Durham they awaited an answer. There a telegram from his father announced that he was sorry but, being dead broke himself, he had nothing to send. By the time they reached Richmond, Virginia, they were weak with hunger and desperate enough to try an old con that they had worked more than once. They picked out a good restaurant, one of the best places in town, and had a splendid meal. Afterwards they confessed to being broke. Almost always that would result in a tongue lashing but, with a woman involved, nothing more. In this case, however, the manager didn't hesitate for a moment to call the police. A local officer promptly arrived. Henry had to think fast. Of course, he explained, he had friends who would telegraph money to him. He begged to be allowed to send a wire to his friend, the eminent and wealthy artist Emil Schnellock, for money to pay the tab. With June making eyes at him, the policeman swallowed this story; he even paid for the telegram to Schnellock and lodged them in a hotel for the night. But in the middle of the night Henry and June skipped the hotel and set out on the road again. On the road—it seemed as if he had not stopped traveling since heading for Florida. Indeed, he had been on the move for nearly a decade, ever since he had started for California. And where had it gotten him? Only, finally, a return to the city, a dirty lodging for the night at Emil Conason's and the ugly, scabrous sights of lower New York, the soiled buildings and faces so worn and smudged they looked as if they had been wiped by a dirty eraser.

Thirteen

In the Catacomb

Obviously they were on a treadmill. They moved to Remsen Street again—to a different apartment, of course, but resumed their old routine. They even repeated their old arguments. June spruced herself up and got a hostess job at the Catacomb, a new arena for the old con games. Ashamed of their precarious existence, Henry started in on his same old search of a job and wound up as a salesman for a loose-leaf encyclopedia. Again, June ridiculed his efforts. "Stop this nonsense," she would say, "and get down to work"—by which she meant, quit selling and begin writing. Secretly, he was afraid he had completely dried up as a writer, and that was one reason he insisted upon "sacrificing" his career in order to work at a paying job. Her theme song was: "Don't be foolish, Val. You're not fit for business. If you'll just work seriously, I'll do anything for you." He was incapable, he must rely on her, he would regret it if he cut loose from her. She urged him to meet her at the Catacomb once or twice a day, to have lunch with her, to escort her home. Just like his mother, he felt, she wanted to squeeze him, make him smaller and smaller until she could put him in her suffocating womb—that was how he looked at it. It was damned insulting, he often told himself; but he never reflected very long on this subject before he admitted to himself that she was probably right: he was worthless, a worm.

The encyclopedia job, of course, came to nothing. The leads given him by the sales manager consisted of a little pile of grimy scraps of paper, coupons cut from a magazine by people who thought they were going to get free gifts. He'd arrange the leads into zones. Next, he'd try to figure out the character of each customer through his or her writing. He had memorized his sales pitch, of course—that was easy—but he found his mind making adjustments in it to suit the character he imagined. He might spend an hour or two going over his speech. Then, most likely, he'd start by traveling to the farthest address (incidentally, this gave him more time to read *The Magic Mountain* or one of the other books he carried with him to pass the hours on train or trolley). Thus, he might waste the day making his way to a house in Hoboken or Maspeth only to discover that the prospective customer had moved or died or been shipped to the looney bin. Then he would become discouraged and spend the rest of the day in his old haunts. Before the first month's end he barely glanced at the scraps before tossing them into the sewer, and he soon quit. He fell so low that he even tried to sell newspapers. But he didn't have the heart to be a paperboy at this age. A time came when he even tried to sell his own blood—but he proved to be anemic.

He closed his mind to his failures, but he could not prevent the revelations of his dreams. The fall of 1926 was like a dark night of the soul, a season in hell. More than once he dreamed that he was in the South again. He didn't know exactly where he was, but apparently he was trying to hitchhike somewhere at night. He saw the white sandy roads gleaming in the moonlight, the color of a skull. He was weak and hungry, and then terrified. Someone was pushing him into a dirty pen, backing him up against a broken fence. Then they reached inside his rectum with dirty paws and slashed his guts and privates into ribbons with a rusty jack-knife. Somehow, he found himself on a streetcar, which was like a hearse, and he was being dragged out of the old neighborhood and dumped on Decatur Street, the street of early sorrows. He felt a cruel joy in seeing the death of his hopes, even in dreams. By day he wandered desolately about New York, the port of misery, the enormous city with fire-and-mud-stained sky, where his loves had all crucified him and the torturers were awaiting him still. By night, in dreams, June, the "Queen of the Village" as some called her, the ghoul queen of a million dead souls, hovered over him. His heart was burning with cold fire: maggots were in his armpits and hair, and slugs feasted on his heart. He was by no means ready for the illuminations which might come out of such dark nights.

All June asked of him now was that he not interfere with her work—"the dirty work," as she called it. She imposed a number of unbreakable rules. First, it was not to be made clear to the Village that she was married. In consequence, he was never permitted to answer the bell, even if he was alone. Of course, it might be Joe or Emil Schnellock who was ringing, and so he was permitted to go to the window and push the curtains aside a fraction of an inch. A second corollary was: whenever he wished to leave the house, June must go out first to be sure the coast was clear. Third: when he came home after June was inside, he'd have to be cautious. At the door he'd whisper in a bitter, comic whorehouse routine: *"All right to come in now? All the customers gone?"* The fourth rule was: whenever June happened to bring one of her admirers home, Henry was to disappear in advance. June had worked out a set routine to play a John for a sucker. On her way home from the Catacomb with some fellow, she'd suddenly remember that there was not a thing to eat in the house, and she'd get the sucker to lay in a week's supplies from a nearby delicatessen. After the admirer had been feasted and treated to one of the cigars he had bought and had settled cosily into one of the chairs while he picked his teeth and eyed June as *chef-d'oeuvre,* she would complain of stuffiness, open the window and raise the shade. Henry, who would probably have become paralyzed by the cold while pacing the street waiting for this signal, would soon ring. "Well, Val Miller, the writer!— Isn't this a surprise!" "Just passing, by, thought I'd say hello." And so he'd be invited in to meet the other "old friend." The guy would eye the intruder with extreme annoyance and probably insult him grossly, but Henry would grit his teeth and hold on until the disappointed fellow left in the dawn. All these stratagems for a few day's supplies of Maxwell House coffee, paté, wurst, and pumpernickel.

June was changing. Asleep in the morning, her face still appeared fresh and virginal; her skin looked warm and creamy beside her blue-black hair. But as soon as she awoke, a mask of cunning cloaked and contorted her features. Each day she'd remake her face. She used makeup as a stageplayer does—to create a role. She would start with a good thick coat of grease, wiping it off with a turkish towel as an artist might begin by wiping his brushes. Then she would thinly coat her face with a liquid which hardened into a white, transparent death mask. Only one blue vein in her forehead showed through it. Beneath her eyes she rubbed circles of blue which seemed burned into her skin. Then she added a touch of rouge to her lips and finally a thorough dusting with a ghoulish green powder until her face had a fine cadaverous glow. She lingered a good long time over this *toilette* while Henry squirmed in agony and resentment. She wore no hat or stockings—only a coat of powder enveloped her legs—and no stays beneath her soft, sheer dresses. All her clothing was contrived to produce the illusion of veiled nudity. And finally, this created figure was baptised each day by a sprinkling of special perfume and wrapped (but only partly concealed) in a long, flowing black theatrical cape. "For Christ's sake, stop it," Henry would scream as she set about adding one more exotic touch. "Don't you see what you look like?" She would gaze into her mirror and snap back: "Like a whore, I suppose." Then she'd shrug her shoulders and repeat seductively: "I suppose you mean that I look like a whore?" Perhaps she'd shimmy her hips at him. And he'd fall for it and want her. Then he would have to apologize and declare that she looked truly dazzling, completely desirable. And more than likely she'd leave him abruptly when he finished praising her.

June always took center stage, allowing Henry only the role of a minor functionary or buffoon. What roles but these was he fit to play when he threw her into the arms of vultures? He acted like a stuffy uncomprehending German bourgeois who had stumbled into a cabaret and tried to make moral sense of it, and he resembled the professor in "The Blue Angel," Emmanuel Rath, in more ways than one. He kept strict account of the money June "borrowed" from her victims. If she had "borrowed" a hundred here or fifty there, then she "owed" these sums, he argued maniacally. And when she insisted that her company and conversation had amply compensated them, he would reply idiotically, that was hardly enough—what did she think she was, a goddess?

As soon as he gave up his job as encyclopedia salesman he began to drop in at the Catacomb, a dive where the "young and evil" congregated. But though June had earlier begged him never to leave her, she now made it clear that she would prefer him to make himself scarce. A fellow who mooned around like a sulky husband was unquestionably an inconvenience when every day brought new victims to the Catacomb. Where the famous had once come—O. Henry and Valentino, Frank Harris, Dreiser, and O'Neill—the tourists came now. She became angry when she caught Henry sneaking around the Catacomb after her, but he persisted, hovering outside where she couldn't see him. He soon discovered that whenever June encountered a new personality, she would lead him to a table by the basement window, and, putting her elbows squarely on the table, sit and talk and gaze admiringly into his eyes. At midnight, Henry would dare to stand in the dark just outside the window's railing and drink in June's rapt attention for another. He thrilled to know that if her attention wandered and she looked out the window, she would see nothing but a dark figure. Unknown to her she would after all be turning her sphinx-like smile to her husband.

If he begged her to reserve a night for him alone, if he implored her not to stay out all night again, she would hardly notice. Many nights, after hours of pacing about their room waiting for her, he would finally rush off to the el station and wait until several trains arrived without her, or go to the bridge plaza in the hope that he might catch a glimpse of her in one of the cabs that whizzed by. If he criticized her for indifference to him when she showed up at 4 a.m. or so, she'd fight back, blow for blow. It was fine for him to complain, she'd hiss, but what about all those times when she had begged for his company? Hadn't he previously lingered in the bathtub every morning so as to avoid walking her to the train and suffering through the stares that were always directed at her? Hadn't he once claimed as an excuse for not meeting her that the atmosphere of the Catacomb oppressed him? She'd go on and on until he recognized the truth in her accusations, and he would end up conscience-stricken and repentant.

Fourteen

The Fabulous Twins

June's lovers multiplied. But of all her betrayals, the worst came late in October 1926 when she arrived home without explanation after a three days' absence. Afraid to ask directly where she had been, he started his plaint about how she looked, when to his astonishment he saw a grotesque puppet dangling from the footboard of the bed. "That's Count Bruga," June exclaimed, clasping it to her breast, and explaining that the grotesque figure had been named after the hero of a recent Ben Hecht book. Hecht, in turn, had based his character upon the person of the poet Maxwell Bodenheim, whom Henry knew well. He had quite a literary reputation and June idolized him; but by 1927 he was ten years past his best days. Henry found him coarse, rotund, effeminate, and insipid and was driven wild to see Bodenheim paw June familiarly while she lapped up his line of sedulous flattery in a dark corner of the Catacomb.

The Count had violet hair of twisted silk, lavender eyelids, the mouth of a satyr, and pale cheeks. He wore a rich velvet jacket and a blouse of coffee-colored silk. On his head was set a huge black sombrero, *á la* Montparnasse. June set the figure on a dresser the better to admire it, murmuring rapturously about how it had more character than any human being. "There's genius in it, positive genius," she exlaimed.

Count Bruga—she might better have said Jean Kronski, who had made the cadaverous puppet. For it was Jean who had bewitched June, and Count

Bruga was her familiar. Jean soon became the very double of June, June's nightmare self. The decadent figure of Count Bruga opened another window into June's soul just at the moment when Henry had already glimpsed as much of her soul as he wished to perceive and far more than he understood. It was an abyss whose bottom Henry could never reach. All he knew at first was that a new phrase had entered June's speech: "My friend Jean." She said it unceasingly, lovingly, wonderingly; she could give dozens of tones to that phrase. And for the first time, he was jealous. Jealous of a female rival. Jean who had been orphaned and adopted, had only recently arrived in New York. She was about twenty-one. Her face was memorable, if not beautiful, and one acquaintance characterized it as "Lucrezia Borgia painted by Pinturicchio." One of those gifted and often doomed ciphers who instinctively catch on to the newest, most advanced modes of the day, she not only had made this grotesque puppet, she wrote expressionistic poems and painted surreal pictures. She had fallen right in with European *avant garde* doctrines in art and psychoanalytic studies. She was also devoted to Rimbaud, and seemed to be consumed at Rimbaud's rate without having much of his genius beyond the capacity for self-destruction.

Some of these details Henry gathered at once from June's disjointed rhapsodies about her friend Jean and some at a later time when the woman herself arrived on the scene. Jean moved to Pierrepont Street to be close to June; June was spending as much time in Jean's flat as at work. When June did come home, almost certainly Jean would be with her. Henry simply sat around the house numbed, hoping that they would appear. Yet he flew into an indignant frenzy or treated them with excessively ironical ceremony when they did. June and Jean, Jean and June—the twins became a fixation with him. He began to clutter the margins of *Psychopathia Sexualis* and Forel's *The Sexual Question* with the names *June* and *Jean*. Yet Jean humiliated him for this. One evening they walked in upon him while he was in his easy chair, reading. In her usual blunt way, June snatched Forel out of his hands and handed it over to Jean for inspection, as if to say, "Let's see what the boob is up to now." June read aloud some of the passages marked with Jean's name. But instead of being outraged, Jean found it amusing. He thought *that* described her or *that* or *that*? Ah, she assured him, she perhaps was far worse and certainly more complicated than a simpleton like Forel could imagine. Henry, she declared flatly, had old-fashioned ideas concerning the subject of sexuality: "Those books are out of date. I'll get you something more interesting." True to her word, the next time she showed up it was with books by Jung, Freud, and Stekel. She was a pathologic case, suffering from self-induced hyperesthesia, and whenever she encountered an analyst she was always ready to unburden herself to him. She totally bewitched Conason, who began by regarding her as an invert and ending by declaring her a genius. At first Conason tortured her with accusations, but at the end he fell for her so hard he almost tried to rape her. She was in love with the dazzling complexities of her neuroses, and Henry suspected that she had created some of them—stories of her love of trees and of her nude romps in a cemetery—out of books.

Before a month had passed, the two women and Henry decided to live together in a three-room basement apartment, formerly a laundry, on Henry Street. Even more than June, Jean was a creator of her own mythical life: gruesome fables of perversions, stories of her lesbian exhibitions for pay before a jaded millionaire, of her incarcerations in Bellevue, and of her marriage arranged as a newspaper stunt. The three of them were living in a fetid concoction of fears, suspicions, jealousies, lies. Each was the audience for the others' roles. Each was trying to deceive the others in long, carefully contrived inquisitions and in calculated confessions. Now and then a fragment of the truth might be revealed, but only for a tactical advantage, only as the opening move in the construction of a more monstrous lie. Every ounce of sincerity drained out of them; they lied out of habit and didn't bother to cover contradictions. In the morning June would tell Henry: "You're a god to me." In the evening, when she returned from the Catacomb, he would be a son-of-a-bitch. Jean would play up to him, praise him, decorate the wall with his portrait surrounded by skulls and serpents, and then mock him until he was buried beneath the sordid debris in the dream-dump of their tales.

He was shamed, too, by the fact that Jean pushed him into a subservient position. The least he could do for the benefit of living with such astonishing creatures, Jean intimated, was to pick up the tab. She urged him to get a job, condemning him for allowing June to gold-dig. To add to all his own failures, he was asked to go to work so that his wife could enjoy herself in bed with a psychotic woman.

Soon, to his astonishment and horror, Jean was sleeping in one of the twin beds with June. (Why had he insisted on twin beds?) One day, he found a letter from June to Jean which began; "Desperate, my lover." June treated Jean as she once treated Henry, that was obvious, always wanting Jean at her side, playing nurse-maid to her, even washing her feet, while Henry stood by neglected or was expected to worship Jean in order to keep

June's affections. He was not even allowed to tell Jean that he and June were married. "If I said we were married everybody in the Village would know about it," June said.

Before long the Henry Street flat was in terrible shape; everything was dirty, even the sheets. The windows were grimy, the floor littered, the air rank with fumes from the rusty oil stove. There was never any edible food in the cupboards; the shelves were stuffed with colored face powders, oils, shampoos, dyes, jumbled together with open paté tins and spoiled anchovies. What one took to be an open bottle of wine might turn out to be June's permanganate solution. Cigarette stubs were everywhere. When Henry prevented Jean from using his Funk and Wagnall's so that the pages would not be soiled and torn, or when he tried to sweep up the mess, they castigated his Germanic upbringing and told him that artists had always lived so, that he was bourgeois. No wonder he couldn't write and never would, they laughed. He felt as helpless as a puppet. He was becoming their depraved Count Bruga.

Only through some violent act, he believed, would he be able to claw up to the surface again. One night when June stayed away without word in an all-night debauch with Jean and one of her admirers, the wrestler Nat Pendleton, Henry dragged out his love letters, the photographs of himself and June, the manuscripts which he had written about her—"June the Peripatetic" and others—annotated them with desperate love messages and threw them about the room. He propped up Count Bruga and thrust his marriage certificate into the puppet's hand.

But at dawn, when the two friends flounced in, they looked at this stuff blandly, tittering: "another one of Val's gestures" . . . "his artistic temperament" . . . "a good joke." June didn't even bother to read the scribbled notes. Later on, he wrote fugitive notes to June and slipped them into her purse, but she went for days without bothering to read them and added them, unread or half-read, to the general litter, along with calling cards and empty matchbooks.

Finally he went to Conason and begged for some poison to end his misery. Conason solemnly and forcefully argued against suicide, but promised to help. Henry made him agree not to telegraph June until the next day when it would be all over. But Henry decided that he must see June once more and would wait until she came home, talk to her as of old, give her one more chance. Then, if she still showed her new disregard for him, he would kill himself while she slept. He waited until nightfall; still June did not come. He wrote a deposition willing his body to Conason. Then he wrote a fervent suicide letter and addressed it to June. Finally, he worked himself into such a frenzy that he took the pills, stripped, and opened all the windows to the cruel winter winds, indifferent whether he died from poison or from exposure. He liked the idea of June's coming in and finding his corpse. Just before he fell asleep he had an idea for a touching postscript and dragged his numb body out of bed to add a few words to his farewell letter. It wasn't death that he wanted, it was her, her love. Once June had claimed romantically that not even death could part them, but now since he could not have her, he preferred death, he wrote. He finished and waited in a fever of romantic anticipation to feel the first dank breath of the grave cross his brow, and then he dropped off.

Twelve hours later, feeling refreshed, he awoke from the opiate Conason had given him. June hadn't shown up all night. In the morning, however, Conason telegraphed June at the Catacomb. She rushed home, but Henry looked in the pink of health. He had managed to give only a bad imitation of Strindberg, who had jumped naked into the icy North Sea but had quickly run out. Strindberg too had remembered to telegraph his wife; but when she arrived he couldn't even manage a sneeze. To June's eyes, Henry was simply lolling about in bed after a good rest. She only half-read his suicide note. Yet it was like her, also, to want to comfort him in his misery, and she climbed into bed with him. Unfortunately, Jean showed up a few minutes later, and the fabulous twins went off together while Henry suffered the horrors of imagining their conversation about him: "another gesture" . . . "the poor boob" . . . "what did he say in the note?" . . . "how idiotic!" Later he found his theatrical suicide note crumpled up on the desk. Probably June never had finished reading it. He contented himself with another gesture, and in the bathroom he hung a sketch which Emil Schnellock had made of him, as if to say: *this is how you treat me.* But to his chagrin neither of the women noticed it there, so that finally he had to call their attention to it. On another occasion, in an exalted mood he wrote an assertive note to June, which concluded: "Don't worry kiddo, we're coming through." In fine fettle, he signed it "King Ludwig." Some days later, after a violent quarrel, he was rustling through her handbag for some evidence to confirm one of his suspicions, and there, unexpectedly, he found his note. On the back of it, like a grade, a black mark against his name, a dismissal of all his efforts, was scrawled: "FIVE YEARS". That said it all: it had been five years since he started *Clipped Wings,* five years of privation and yet no books, no fame, no money, no appreciation, hardly any finished pieces. Five years! *Mad* Ludwig!

Jean, he felt, had turned June against him. Henry fought against the Bruga woman. He schemed against her and attempted to discredit her by forcing her into examinations by Dr. Conason as well as inquisitions of his own. He attempted to embarrass June by walking into the Catacomb one day when the two women were sitting with a group of June's circle; he said to Jean straight out: "Tell us, are you a pervert or an invert?" June went white. Later she faced up to him: "Perhaps Jean is queer—invert, pervert, anything you like—but no matter what, I will never desert her. Is that enough?" He kept questioning her. She loved them both, she said, "though my love for you is not the same as my love for Jean." That was "platonic," she tried to explain. Though she admitted that they often did sequester themselves in Jean's room, that was merely to be able to kiss without embarrassing him. He wouldn't let it rest there, but kept saying, "That Bruga woman is a lesbian." "Well, then," June replied, "what do you suppose that makes me?" She said this in the same ironically sweet tone as she had learned to say, "You mean I look like a whore!" But then she launched her own attack. What about him? Wasn't there a queer tinge, perhaps even an outright streak of homosexuality, if it came to that, in his intimate relations to his chums, Stanley and Joe, Emil and Ned, and all the others? Why was he always calling Johnny Paul and Lester Reardon his idols, or talking about the long lost fellowship of the Xerxes Society? She went farther: the love of a woman for a woman was quite natural, fully in accord with her instincts, but that of a man for another man was perverted and depraved. He couldn't believe it and he reacted violently: "*My* friends? *My* behavior—made you suspicious of *me*?" he spluttered. "So you thought, did you, that I was falling in love with—who? Emil? God damn you. If I thought you meant that, I'd choke you, you bitch. But you're lying because you don't know how else to squirm out of the fact that Jean is a homo and so are you! You'd say anything. You're corrupt, poisoned, diseased. But if that's what you really think—all right then, tomorrow I get a red necktie . . . . Henry Miller, a homo to rent, weekly rates—moderate terms." She had hit a really dangerous spot and drove him to hysterics.

Then she was ready to turn around and take it all back: "You know how I love you. Don't twist this all around in your narrow, masculine way, don't probe and try to figure it out. Can't you see I'm growing?" He didn't know what he saw. He felt that June was playing one of her roles again—but instead of Stavrogin, now her favorite role was Gudrun to Jean's Ursula, in imitation of Lawrence's *Women in Love*. A shiver of disgust, of self-disgust, shot through him when he heard a poem by one of the Village esthetes which referred to "that magnificent half-woman, June." He cringed at the thought that June chose to sleep with Jean instead of him. Meanwhile, June's male lovers also lined up like empty milk bottles waiting to be collected. He winced when he spied June tiptoeing down the street with Nat Pendleton at 4 a.m. and heard her lie later about whom she had been with.

All these hatreds surfaced in an almost daily ritual when the three of them would sit down around a table in the middle room, the "gut table," and tear at each other with cross-examination and accusation and invective. They called this "modern frankness," it was fashionable, but it still hurt. June's voice stung like a silver whip. Jean's was harsh and heavy like a fist. They were clawing at each other's hearts with words, yet trying to smile. This couldn't keep up for long. When their analyses of their real situation became too cruel, to ease their suffering Henry invented the fiction of a play which he said he was trying to finish—would they help him? It concerned three characters—the husband, the wife, the other woman. How would they behave toward each other, those make-believe characters? How should their dilemmas be resolved? How would the play end? Each dramatized his own desires: Jean insisted upon the death of all three at the curtain's fall. The husband in such a case, Jean hinted, was likely to be at fault for not providing his wife with any romantic thrills; he would bring his tragedy upon himself. June supposed that the three would depart for Paris and live forever after in a contended haze of Pernod. Henry intervened: how could they be contented with that intolerable triangle?—if indeed, it was not a rectangle, or an octagon, since the wife in his play was also cheating on the husband with countless men? June became hysterical. The mask of the play dropped. "You want confession?" she cried. She confessed to horrors, she made herself a monster, and she heaped it all on his head like acid. Never did he expect to hear himself called a puritanical martinet, a teutonic pedant, bourgeois, and at last a foul fool. Jean chimed in, going so far as to imply that he, who was not yet forty, was already washed up, prematurely old, impotent as a writer and as a man.

And at the end of all this, Jean heartlessly told him: "It is good for you, this suffering. It will help you to write better." Some truth resided in her caustic remark, but since Henry never wrote except to gratify his ego he cursed Jean's cruelty. *Suffer in order to write?* Then he didn't want to write. To prove the truth of this he sacrificed a great pile of his manuscripts and wall charts in the open fireplace. It wasn't writing he wanted—he wanted June! Henceforth he vowed that he would write only letters. He took to signing these "The Failure."

Fifteen

Legendary Travails

"Legendary Travails"!—that was the title of a sketch he wrote describing the inferno at Henry Street. The travails were daily, if not yet legendary. Even June, who was the strongest of the three, finally broke down: "You people, who are so quick to accuse and torment me," she cried at the two of them, "let me see you do something for a change instead of tearing me to pieces." Later, when they were alone in their own room, she begged Henry: "O God, I feel so worn, so tired. Get me away from this. I don't want anyone in the world but you." But he was powerless to save himself, much less her. He still couldn't keep a job, even though he recently tried dishwashing, busing dishes, and running an elevator. He hitchhiked to Philadelphia to borrow a thousand dollars from his friend Blount. He asked for such an outrageous sum so that he wouldn't appear to be a lowdown panhandler. But he came back with a pittance, half of the rent they owed. June and Jean were so indifferent to him that no sooner had he returned than they left for a party without even asking whether he had had any success, assuming that he hadn't. June was weary of him. When he moved into Emil's, sleeping on the couch where he and June had once made love passionately, she didn't notice his absence. Another day he showed up at the Catacomb carrying his suitcase and he told June he was leaving to go West. He handed her a bunch of violets with a love note, clearly hoping to shock her into begging him to remain. *It won't be enough if she merely says, "You mustn't go"* —*no, she must beg me,* he told himself. But all she said was: "Perhaps it's better. Go for a little while, but let me know where you are." He hadn't actually planned to go anywhere and didn't know where to go. After a short trek, during which he got no further west than Philadelphia and Atlantic City, he turned around and hurried back. Certainly, he thought, June would miss him terribly by now—he had punished her enough. But instead of being thrilled at his return when he called from the ferry to announce his arrival, June told him it would be inconvenient to have him appear just then—she and Jean were having a party. And so for a quarter he flopped at the Mills Hotel among the other derelicts of the city.

Back at Henry Street his spirit died. He read the same four authors continuously—Spengler, Joyce, Proust, and Van Gogh. Each depressed him in a different way. He and June had once agreed to pack Jean off, but he was not surprised to see it was he who was being packed. June explained to him one day that she wanted to go away with Jean and during her absence to right her relations with Henry. She made him promise that he would not try to commit suicide while she was away.

He listened dully to their crazy conversation while he sat in Jean's room in the dark. Even when he heard them plotting out schemes to get enough money to go to Paris, he didn't believe they would leave. He watched them make puppets to sell in order to raise the passage money. All night long they sawed and hammered, driving the nails into the wood and into Henry's brain, until they had dozens of puppets on hand. But they could make no sales. Even Greenwich Village was not ready for the Count. New suckers arrived on the scene continuously, of course. June and Jean even picked up two sailors and tried to talk them into smuggling them aboard their Europe-bound ship. He still didn't believe they would leave even when June boasted to his face that she would have no difficulty getting along in Europe on her own. But by March 1927 the two friends had only one refrain on their lips: Paris, Montmartre, Tuileries, the Luxembourg Gardens, the Métro—the Paris of the American expatriate who has never been abroad. Henry was sick of Paris—he had large doses of it for *petit déjeuner, dejeuner* and *diner*.

He could not take the possibility of June's departure seriously; for at last he had gotten what promised to be a steady job—as a gravedigger, of all things, for the Queens County Park Commission. In April 1927 his boyhood friend Jimmy Pasta offered to make Henry his office assistant. First, in order to prevent any implication of political favoritism, Henry would serve a week's apprenticeship in the field, as a gravedigger, then be promoted into the office as a county park employee. In a pitiful way Henry felt quite excited about this job. He began to believe that he was rising out of his subterranean existence even if, he chuckled, he had to go down into the grave to do so.

On the Friday of his first week of work, he came home to witness the almost total disarray of the apartment. Half-packed trunks added to the general litter, everything was tossed this way or that; even Henry's portrait had been stuck in a drawer. (*So, someone had noticed at last!* He took it and put it back over the toilet.) The two friends tripped in at three o'clock, confused and elated. "Are you moving?" he queried. June came to sit on the bed and, holding his hand, spun the same old seamless filaments of silky talk into gauzy webs. "You won't mind if I go to Paris with Jean," she pleaded, putting her arms about him. "You'll follow when you can?" "Yes," he said, as he always did. Then he became angry. "What are you going to do in Paris with no money? How will I get there?—swim over? And what's going to happen to me without you here?" Though she begged for affection, he turned his back on her. Though he pushed her away he was horrified at the thought of losing her.

Saturday morning. When he awoke he found that June was already up, intending to spend some time with him before he left for work. She had even bought hothouse strawberries for his breakfast. She seemed chastened and ready to admit how unreasonable she had been. He in turn was ready to believe that she could soon be brought around to some plan for dumping Jean. When he was leaving the house she seemed reluctant to see him depart and walked outside with him. He beamed at the attention. "Today is payday. Tonight I'm going to bring you something special," he said. They were feeling a renewal of their old tenderness: his simple promise brought tears to her eyes. "I don't need a thing—really," she whispered. For the first time in years she stood outside and waved to him as he turned the corner. On the train, all the way to Queens, he assured himself that everything would be all right soon. And he worked his last day digging graves for others.

He brought presents of stockings and a brassiere when he descended, that evening, into the gloomy cellar. Even before he switched the light on, he knew that the room's aspect had altered. Then in a panic he saw that the trunks were gone. On an empty dresser lay a life-mask Jean had made of Henry. Fastened down by it was a note. He lay his package down gently and picked up the envelope addressed to him. June wrote that she had left a few minutes after saying goodbye. She and Jean were sailing on the *S.S. Suffren.*

She explained, as much as June ever explained, that she loved him too much to be able finally to say farewell to him—but it was not goodbye—they'd be together soon. . . . On a broken chair he sat down at the table where so many slashing verbal battles had occurred, and stared at the wreckage of the room.

The Danish landlady came in the unlatched door. At first she said nothing, she only put her arms around him. Then she began to give him June's other message: June had asked her to look after him, and in particular he was to promise that he would not attempt to do anything desperate to himself. For a long time he sobbed unrestrainedly in her arms. Later, when he was quiet, she left.

Then he sat facing the currents of his life which had led to this. Disconnected phrases and fragments stuck in his mind. *And now for the dirt. You're like a god to me. Desperate my lover. Nothing that concerns you, I love you both. Et forsan haec olim meminisse iuvabit* (Virgil's line, which he had inscribed above Jean's bed). *I can't, dear, Val is here. Suffering will help you to write better.* The phrases of Jean's poem "To H.V.M." were there, in the general litter of his mind:

> Let him live to prove
> dissection
> doesn't
> sleep
> with
> the
> sky.

He remembered mostly how Jean had castigated him as immature— calling him *baby* over and over—and how he had once overheard June defending her love for him by adopting the very terms of Jean's condemnation: "My love for Val is only like that of a mother for a child—that's all." Christ! it annoyed him when June harped on the mother business. She even complained, often, that he was inadequate as a lover—not in a physical but in an emotional way—because he was still tied to his mother's apron strings, he had never gotten to the point where he could accept his mother as a woman and so he couldn't accept any woman at all. Henry fumed when she spouted this drug-store psychology gotten from Jean.

He remembered their grotesque Christmas day of only a few months before. After a drunken Christmas eve, from which they emerged spent and exhausted, June had gotten into one of those sullen moods and stood pat on her insistence that she would not go with him to his parents' house without

Jean. They spent an hour or two trying to make Jean presentable. And then, despite all this, his worst fears were realized after dinner when the two women cuddled up together on the sofa and fell asleep.

He remembered all his humiliations, and he passed from grief to rage to despair to desperation, while he sat at the table. Pink bulbs gave the appearance of a deserted brothel. In the self-portrait which Henry had painted on the wall, his face had the appearance of a Chinese priest with a satyr's leer. It looked like his own face, only insane. He walked about the apartment, peering into every corner, feeling that he *was* becoming truly insane. Jean's room was even more bizarre; her paintings of skulls, serpents and mandalas were bitten into the plaster.

And then, at last, he started to break things. First he took down every picture on the wall and smashed them; even his own portrait he removed from the bathroom wall and tore into shreds. He pulled the curtains from the windows and spit and pissed on them. He ground his life-mask into powder under foot. He hurled the floor's litter, dirty glasses, sardine tins, soiled shirts, and torn magazines, at the frescoes on the wall—until from a corner he picked up a pair of silk stockings rolled in a ball.

They were June's. He put them to his nose and drew deep breaths. He kissed them. He used them to wipe the tears from his eyes. He caressed them. And finally he put them in his pocket where, in his secret grief, he could hold them. In the end he threw himself on the dirty sheets of his bed and cried and slept the night away.

Sixteen

The Spirit of St. Valentine

Hardly a week passed before Henry began to receive urgent cables from June; already broke, she begged for aid. Suddenly, when he saw that he was to be her victim in the telegram game, he realized that the job he thought would win her back had actually provided the peg on which she could hang her European trip. With a permanent job he would have the money to maintain her in Paris and, curiously, he was willing to do it. He had been dependent on June so long that now he rejoiced at the chance to help her. Even though it meant she would live away from him all the longer, he determined that he would send her almost every cent he made. He called his parents and arranged to move back with them. With hardly a glance at the debris of his sunken Henry Street life, he skipped out of the apartment one night, carrying only a few manuscripts and his Funk and Wagnall's dictionary.

As he sat in the taxi riding back to Decatur Street, he felt what he had felt so many times before—that the whole long circuit of his life was absolutely senseless and, what was more, doomed. He was being forced back to Decatur Street, back to taking the charity of his parents—though he was a grown man. A long time he had stayed away, managing to survive on his own. Then, when he returned from Florida in December of 1925, he had been obliged to come back briefly until he located June and got back on his feet. Now he was returning to the nest again, less than a year later, like a

135

whipped dog. A long time he had resisted the tailor shop, the firm of Henry Miller & Son; finally the business had fallen apart. Now he had the only job in the world he could get. This job that Jimmy Pasta had gotten him working for Queens County was an out-and-out charity. He seemed destined to become nothing in life—only a time-server, waiting with father and mother and their marginal hopes and vague desires, and with Lauretta and her silly jabber.

All along he had sensed how fictive June's life was, to what extent she had created herself out of books. But never until this taxi ride had he seen so clearly that he himself had been one of June's fictions: he was no more than a gusty emanation of her fantasy life, merely, like Jean, June's shameful double. It was June's fiction that he could be a writer—her idea, not his—her particular grotesque joke. Most of his pieces had been signed by June, and, in authoring him, she really had been their true author. Now that she was gone he lost all belief in himself.

He was, he told himself resignedly, not insane, not an artist—just an ordinary guy whose only talent was his personality. What he should do was find a woman who had never read a book after she finished school and never saw the inside of a dancehall, but had strong firm arms and rolled her sleeves up when she plunged her hands into a tub of dishes or clothes and whistled as she swept the house. Someone who would have a bundle of kids. Someone, in particular, who would discourage his illusions, keep his nose to the grindstone, and nod off with him after dinner, worn out with worry and work. In fact, why not go back to Beatrice and Barbara? This was not the first time the thought had come to him. Stanley kept him informed about their doings. Since ceasing to pay alimony he had given up the right to visit Barbara, but often he haunted the area around his old flat, hoping and fearing to see her.

Once, three children rushed by him as he stood before the big Catholic Church near where he and Bea had lived. He followed them, his eye on the little girl in the blue cape with the hood drawn up over her curly blonde head. For several blocks as they played he pursued them, thinking of buying some cakes for the children. All at once, something was wrong— the children ran into a store. He pushed into a doorway, almost out of sight. If they were in danger, he swore he'd protect them. Barbara's two companions poked their heads out of the doorway and seemed satisfied. Then Barbara scanned the street. When her eye fell on him, she jumped like a startled fawn. And at last he understood. They were afraid of him—he must have appeared to be the kidnapper about whom Brooklyn mothers warned their children. He walked ostentatiously out of the doorway as if to show that he wasn't lurking about ready to snatch them. A sidelong glance revealed they were edging out of the bakery door. He turned and started toward them but they scattered like little bunnies as he flew down the street after them. He wanted to stop, for he saw that in pursuing Barbara, he put her in danger of falling, but he couldn't stop—and he held his breath as she dashed blindly through the traffic across the street. Then he made no effort to catch her but stood on the corner accusing himself of being a bum. In a store window he caught a glimpse of his reflection. He even looked like a bum. He needed a shave; his khaki shirt was ragged. He saw the deeper ironies too: he had abandoned Barbara, he had neglected to pay his alimony, he had put her life in danger—yet he was indulging the idea of playing a bountiful prince by buying a few cakes for her and her friends.

That was a wretchedly low moment for him. No wonder that all during the four months he had lived at Henry Street he had been half-planning to return to Bea. One day he got Stanley Borowski to let him in the apartment when she was absent. Stanley showed him Barbara's few playthings: shamefully, he even pocketed one of them. As if he were home again, he sat at the kitchen table while Stanley robbed the icebox to make up a tasty snack. Not many days later, as he was waiting on the corner of Sixth Avenue for Stanley to come home, to his astonishment and chagrin Bea came hurrying down the street. What if she saw him? Maybe he'd have gone home with her, then and there, for good. But even though she almost brushed against him as he stood there in a wooden stupor, she didn't notice him. Was he so far gone that even a wife of four years could no longer recognize him? Could she forget him so fast? "No, Bea doesn't ask about you anymore," Stanley said. "But if you were to come back to her tomorrow, she'd throw her arms around you with joy."

Such was the progress of his thoughts as he rode down Evergreen Avenue. His parents were happy to see him. They were standing on the steps, awaiting his arrival, and smiled sadly at him as he walked up. Father stuck his hand out. Even mother did not make the comment which he had been dreading about his extravagance in taking a taxi. His family regarded food as a purgative for melancholy, and his mother had a rich spread prepared for him. Nothing was said about June. No reference was made to that unfortunate Christmas dinner or other events that had grieved his parents. Everything was as it had been, always: father sat at the head of the table, Henry assumed his familiar place opposite Mother. He had come home, where he was meant to be, where he had his very own napkin ring and fork and place at the table, where the furniture was old and worn and familiar, where the whole atmosphere assured him of the sanctity of simple life and warned him of the sins of presumption of which he had been only too guilty. If he needed any reminder of those sins all he had to do was reach in his coat pocket. He still carried June's silk stockings with him. When he went upstairs to his alcove room, he stuffed them into a drawer.

June meanwhile was sending a string of cables begging for money. He sent her most of his pay and occasionally borrowed fifty dollars for a treat—but this was never enough. June was always frantic and frenetic— she never seemed to have time to write letters. In three months' time he received only two letters from her and postcards of the Eiffel Tower, the Arch of Triumph, and Notre Dame, which he propped up on the mantlepiece. He, of course, wrote long letters to her; he never tired of putting the most trifling queries concerning Paris to her. What did she see when she walked out of her hotel on the Rue Princesse? Which streets were cobblestoned? Where did the workers live? What was the food like? Had she sampled any choice wines? Did she see any artists—was the Latin Quarter full of them? His imagination supplied the facts lacking in her telegraphic answers and he constructed a labyrinthine, magical Paris which became a significant part of his dream-life.

Never did he feel his own powerlessness more than the afternoon of May 21, 1927, when the news came over the wire that a young flier named Charles Lindbergh had made a heroic solo flight across the Atlantic, beginning not far distant from Miller's office and landing in Paris not far from June. While he sat in Brooklyn wondering where his wife was and whom her companions might be, this aviator had climbed into a single-engine plane and jumped the pond. Perhaps June was among the crowds that wildly received him at Le Bourget and threw him kisses that Henry wished to catch.

That same day, as this news flashed across the nation, Henry wrote a letter to June which was even more desperate than usual. He wailed about how much he missed her and announced his determination to commit suicide if she would not set a date for her return. He even fixed a limit during which she must reply by cable if she wished to head off his desperate act. Why should he not kill himself, he asked, since he was "the saddest fool of all?" To screw his fixation on death one dramatic turn higher, he composed a piece called "Cemetery Idyll" in the style of the old mezzotints. This he dispatched in the afternoon mail with his letter.

When work was over at five o'clock and all his co-workers had left the office Henry rolled a sheet into a typewriter, and following the dictations of his memory, began to set down notes for a book concerning his life with June, ending with her departure for Paris with Jean. The title in his mind was *Lovely Lesbians*. He began: "Chapter I. *Roses of Picardy*. Wilson's Dance Hall—first glimpse . . . discussing "Victoria" and June's likeness to her. Promise to send *Winesburg, Ohio,* Ben Hecht." This continued for hours. At one sitting he typed out twenty-six pages, a catalogue of events and crises, hieroglyphics by which memory might be revivified. He arranged the crucial four years of his life with June into eight chapters: "Roses of Picardy," "Alimony," "Cabaret," "The Failure," "Sidewalks of New York," "Speak Easy," "Double Hegira," and "The Captive." He might not be a writer, he admitted to himself, but every person had one book in him, the book of his own life, even though that might be called, like Sherwood Anderson's, *The Book of the Grotesque*. This one book of eight chapters was all he wished to write.

Immediately upon completing the outline for his planned book, he felt renewed and even before she received his suicidal letter, he cabled June to disregard it. For the first time, perhaps, a book seemed more important than his wife. He saw no way to begin the book. His strength had been consumed by the outline, the preparation. Instead, he went back over his outline and made corrections; in the weeks to come he added more than a dozen additional sheets of handwritten notes. He could not begin to write since he could not settle upon a view of reality. Certainly, he wanted to write about his life with June, and sometimes he could almost regard her as existing only in his book about her; but at other times what he still wanted most of all was June herself. She had not yet become a myth for him. He was worried about her safety. June, he learned, was not in Paris the day that Lindbergh landed there, she had gone to Munich. With whom? As usual, she was incommunicative. Yet a remark in a letter from her made clear— and he gave a jump at this—that June and Jean had finally quarrelled. The reasons were, as usual, clouded over; but the fact seemed to be that Jean had gone off to North Africa with two men, one of whom was a sophisticated Austrian writer with a Czech passport. June more than intimated that this fellow, Alfred Perlès, had first fallen for June herself and turned to Jean only when she would have nothing to do with him. Whether this rupture

between the extraordinary women meant that June's return would be
hastened Henry could not tell, though he concluded, happily, that this was
likely.

Yet a month passed, and it was the beginning of July before he got the
cable he had looked for so long: she would be arriving in a matter of days on
the *Berengaria*. Dutifully, he waited at the dock until the boat emptied. He
was hardly surprised that June was not aboard.

Seventeen

The Birth of Dion Moloch

A week later another telegram came, containing a similar message of
arrival. This time June did descend the gangplank. There she stood,
struggling with a black pasteboard trunk, an art album, books, canes from
the ivory coast, and a dilapidated Count Bruga, who was missing one leg.
Henry's heart sank—Bruga still!

But as he learned soon after she came sailing through customs, she
carried far more baggage with her—mental accumulations, new fictions.
More than ever, she longed for the exotic, the curious, the artistic, the
decadent. The album of George Grosz's *Ecce Homo,* her paperbacked copy of
the *Kama Sutra,* stubs from the Cirque d'Hiver, autographed manuscripts
of poems, a poster peeled from a pissoir on the Rue Blondel, handwritten
menus, a Zadkine sculpture—these were emblems of the materials with
which her mind was stuffed, new items with which her vision of the *outré,*
the bizarre, the exotic and erotic could play. He gathered from her talk that
she had sipped absinthe, that the music of the carousels and the street noises
of Montmartre were equally sweet, that a sight of Les Halles at dawn was
something not to be missed, that garlic and wine were spiritual restora-
tives. He pricked up his ears even more when she mentioned having seen
Hemingway at the Café Deux Magots, and having met Kokoschka, Paul
Rosenfeld, Augustus John, and Tihanyi at the Dôme. Not only did
Zadkine adore her, he took her one evening to the Bois de Boulogne. She

was also, to hear her tell it, chased by Cocteau and Picasso. She had to carry a revolver to protect herself from men. Her account of her Paris life was wrapped up and spiced with the most improbable adventures, including a cock-and-bull tale about swallowing a dose of poison, by which she accounted for her delay in arrival. But chiefly she came back singing the same song she had left with—Paris, Paris, Paris—only now Jean was out of the picture, and the refrain was: *"When WE go to Paris, Val...."*

Hardly had they moved into a nice furnished room at 180 Clinton Avenue when she began to hatch a plan which would get them to Europe together. Within a week Henry was plunged back into the same subterranean world that he had known in Henry Street. She hardly needed to argue him into quitting his job—this seemed so natural a part of his return to his former state of inertia and futility that it automatically followed her reappearance. Once again, money was coming in, chiefly from an admirer whom she called "Pop." Pop was old and ugly as a toad, according to June's account, but he was something of a connoisseur of literature; he relished Proust and Joyce. And what was more, he had detected, June reported to Henry, a genuine literary talent in "her" mezzotints. The fact that these and a few articles and stories had appeared under her name gave credence to her claim that she was an authoress; and her quick adaptation of "artistic" behavior from the books she read, as well as her recent immersion in Parisian art-life, combined to make Pop's belief in her talent plausible. She declared that he was prepared to support her while she tried her hand at a novel, and, if she could show enough discipline to complete the book, he promised to send her off to Europe for a year so she could perfect her writing talent in a congenial atmosphere. June brought Henry the news about this latest pigeon: she had done her job—all Henry had to do was write the novel.

Perhaps no one ever understood June. But Pop's analysis of June's lack of confidence as a writer certainly applied perfectly to Henry. Henry regarded Pop as his mortal enemy. Still, by asking June to write a novel, Pop had done Henry a favor. He forced him to write, to produce something every day. For more than ten years Henry had worked in water, producing only a few published pieces and a handful of manuscripts. Every time he had started to write he became convinced that he was inferior. He'd soon stop his typing in order to consult passages in Dostoievski, Arthur Machen, Edgar Saltus, Hamsun, Dreiser, Nietzsche, Pater, and his other favorite authors. He had tried to write "in the Hamsun style," "in the Rabelais style," and so on. He was hopelessly trying to write in the modes of others and thus preventing himself from finding what it might mean to write "in the Henry Miller style"—the one style whose existence he refused to acknowledge.

Pop's demand was just what Henry needed. But he was terrified at the prospect of having to put his literary ambitions to a test. "How can I write a novel, just like *that*!" he asked, snapping his fingers at June. "Just write a novel, any novel. You can, Val, I know you can!" she said casually, as if slinging words were as simple as pitching pennies.

He set the typewriter on the table. He changed the ribbon. He selected green and pink sheets for first and second carbons. He stacked his papers neatly. He read his favorite authors and reread his manuscripts and took walks, but there the blank pages sat for days. At last he wrote a title on the top of the first sheet: *This Gentile World*. (A little later he went back and crossed this out, writing *Moloch* over it, after the name of the hero.) Casting about in his files for a novel-length topic, Miller played it safe. He saw an opportunity to rescue the material in *Clipped Wings* by shifting the focus from the messengers to the adventures of the employment manager among his crew. The odd, the perverted and exotic characters formed the difficult world that this sensitive young man, Dion Moloch, has to face. The time of the novel roughly corresponds to the year 1923 in Miller's life. Beatrice, Conason, Muriel, Camilla, Sam Sattenstein, and others thicken the social density by appearing in the novel as representing ways of life which Moloch must avoid if he is not also to become a grotesque like the messengers whom he manages. Henry's personal experiences, thinly disguised as Dion's, provide the basic substance of the book. Of course, as he told Conason, "all the monstrosities [will be] sharpened and magnified."

He was not trying for much—only as much of a book as he could manage. He told Conason: "Oh, never fear! I'm not attempting another *Gulliver's Travels*. Wish I could. I'm not even thinking about *The Waste Land* or snotty evenings with Mr. Bloom on the banks of the Liffey. Lack erudition. No, just a plain tale about we—us and company. Sam? To be sure. None better. Will they wear disguises? Very thin, very thin, old man." At last it appeared that Miller had a clear sense of what he wanted to write. But as soon as he started the book he was in trouble. Even as he had begun to sense that he himself must be the central character of his own work he was constrained by the fact that the novel must be a made-to-order job: it was supposed to be June's work and therefore should have a female point of view. He tried to imagine how June would write about a character, Moloch. But after eighty pages hacked out on this pattern, when even June complained that the work was obviously masculine, he was lost and tossed the work away. Unfortunately, he made the mistake of trying to save portions of this draft, as one might hoard for re-use the scraps from a badly cut suit. Trying to make use of these, he couldn't get started again at all. June was becoming impatient: she had to show *something* to Pop, had to prove that she had made a start at least.

Henry couldn't tell his wife the truth, but he admitted to himself that he just couldn't figure out how to start a book about Henry Miller. Secretly he feared that his own story could have no interest for anyone else; when he came to look at it, his biography didn't hold much interest for himself. To him, all parts of his experience seemed about equal—he didn't seem to know how to arrange them—he couldn't see where his life began. If Pop hadn't been urgently requesting a look at June's work, he probably wouldn't have started at all. But under the pressure of these demands, he finally had to jump right in.

He made a false start. As soon as he wrote a first chapter he realized that there was a great deal of prior explanation necessary. The first chapter looked more and more like a middle chapter. So he began writing the book backwards and forwards from the center, like a tailor cutting at a bias. June brought the chapters to Pop one at a time. He didn't entirely see the logic of the book's progression, he admitted; but he was pleased by the evident speed with which she was piling up pages.

By the time Henry had written 200 pages he was in a panic again. That he had not yet been able to write the first chapter worried him. He had been told by the critics he admired that some inevitable form was required for a well-made book, a beginning and middle and end. True, form might be a complex matter, but even Joyce had found a definite form by borrowing Homer's, and Proust had found his in repetitions, counterpoints, and the regrouping of characters. But when Henry could not write the book's first chapter even when he was two-thirds of the way through it, he was convinced he could not satisfy even the most basic technical requirements of form. He decided that although he had been at work on the book for more than five months, it would be best to scrap it again: the book was inconsequential, unworthy of his talents, compromised, and incoherent. At this point June put her foot down. Pop, she said, liked the book; and though it was true he asked her questions about it which she could not answer, he had raised none of the objections about the book that the author himself was raising. Never once had Pop intimated that it could not have been written by a woman, never once that it was chaotic. Indeed, he liked the raw force of the book, its qualities of violence and abruptness as well as its scope. Henry didn't let June win this argument. "So," he said to her scornfully, "this is the opinion of a man who, you tell me, is supposed to enjoy Lawrence and Proust. He must be crazy." Then he went back to his typewriter and continued the book.

Toward the end of February 1928 Henry announced that he and June should take a holiday. After all, they had saved a little bundle from Pop's regular stipend and could afford a flyer, something to revive his faith in himself and to give him a new perspective so that he could finish *Moloch*. This was the kind of idea that appealed to June. Where should they go? Henry showed no indecision. "Montreal!" (He had been unconsciously smacking his lips over the prospect that Pop would come through and actually give June money to go to Paris.) French people—French food—French! As to details: Henry proposed that in order to save enough money for a swell hotel in Montreal, they should hitchhike up there. He was, of course, not surprised to learn from June that she couldn't leave New York on the date he set for his departure, and that she would set out by train a few days afterwards and meet him there. In the meantime, she had a certain plan to mature . . . a little swindle to bring off . . . an assignation to keep. . . . She didn't say any of these things exactly. She explained in her own fashion. Taken singly each one of her reasons was always fairly clear, like a thin veil; but she piled one veil upon another until Henry could see nothing.

He was surprised when June actually joined him in Montreal as planned, right on schedule. He took nearly three days hitchhiking, she went by train, and they arrived only a few hours apart. This beginning was perfect, and the rest of their little jaunt was caviar. They picked out a nice hotel. Their room looked foreign, quite unlike the shabby American flats they were used to. Henry felt exhilarated just to look out the window at the strange, un-American scene while June counterpointed everything he saw with a discourse on how this city was like Paris—this *lapin sauté* was nearly as good as one might feast on in Paris—this sight was just what one might observe everywhere in the French capital. Henry felt as if he were looking through Montreal's lenses and seeing Paris, as if Montreal were the eyepiece of a great telescope that pointed east. June preferred to sit about the hotel lobby, but Henry wanted to see everything and dragged her out into the streets and walked her into every quarter of Montreal until they were chilled and footsore. They had saved enough money to live well for a few days, and they had a marvellous time without a single thing to spoil it. He wrote post

cards and letters home to his friends about the superb food and the
wines—he never realized that there were so many kinds, and he wanted to
taste them all. All his senses vibrated with a single stupendous fact: he had
left America behind.

Maybe the joy of the trip gave him a beginning for his book. Anyway,
when they got back to New York and he sat at his typewriter, the first
chapter was there. He opened the novel in the only way it could begin—
with a satiric picture of himself, in a style concocted from H.L. Mencken,
James Branch Cabell, and the writers for the newly founded *New Yorker*.
Moloch begins:

> Dion Moloch walked with the dreamy stride of the noctambulo among
> the apparitions of the Bowery. I say "apparitions" because, as every sophis-
> ticated New Yorker knows, the Bowery is a thoroughfare where blasted
> souls are repaired for the price of a free lunch. . . .
>
> Though he was in the service of the Great American Telegraph Company
> he did not suffer from megalomania, dementia praecox, or any other of the
> fashionable nervous and mental disorders of the twentieth century.
>
> At any rate, he was not like a certain character out of Gogol who had to be
> informed when to blow his nose. He was in short, an American of three
> generations. He was definitely not Russian.

The body of the chapter is an exploration of Moloch's thoughts. Then Miller
looks at Moloch from on high again:

> What the rabble on the sidewalk observed . . . was a modest, sensitive
> individual of medium height, with the composite features of a scholar and
> faun. . . . A mortal with two legs to his trousers, like any other mortal in
> the Western hemisphere. Not a pedagogic sadist, like that trapeze artist
> from the Emerald Isle; not a great Socratic gad-fly stinging the thick hide of
> British philistinism; nor a Slav flirting with eternity in a bath of cock-
> roaches. No, just a man with suit and suspenders . . . and *B.V.D.'s for perfect
> crotch comfort.* A man whose name is un-Byzantine. An American of three
> generations, a husband and father, a modest, sensitive soul. . . . And yet,
> employment manager of the Great American Telegraph Company.

So the first chapter concluded. The next section of the book was drawn
from the chapter on Charles Candles in *Clipped Wings*: It was no longer a
study of the moron—it was beginning to be about Dion Moloch, if not yet
about Miller himself. Its directions shifted Miller away from the tone of
superciliousness and the attitude of determinism which had marred *Clipped
Wings* and almost all of his earlier work. Once, Miller had regarded most
people as types, museum exhibitions, laboratory subjects. In *Moloch* he

began to take a larger view of human multiplicity. "Nothing," he observes, "is further from the truth than that, given a certain impetus . . . the hero forthwith reacts in thus and such a manner. The grand metabolistic dynamics of the laboratory worker, which are so impressive in connection with rats and mental defectives, become inoperative when a truly human mind and organism is encountered. . . . Possibly twenty-five different courses of action presented themselves to our character." Henry, who had begun with determinism, had arrived at the threshold of romance. His novel was growing, and he was growing with it, in chunks.

Having written the first chapter of the book, his instincts, or rather his fantasies, told him what the novel's end must be. It must have surprised him to discover that though his book had fairly accurately portrayed his work at Western Union and the discontent in his marriage with Beatrice—called Paula in this book—yet, in the book Dion Moloch decides to go back to his wife. Identifying himself with Hamsun and his wife with Victoria, Dion resolves to renew his love for Paula. "If one could only get away," Dion muses. Miller, it appears would also have liked to solve his problems by getting away—even from June. Moloch imagines a revival of his love for his wife: "All the lies, the counterfeits, the baseness of his past was transmuted by her love into the gospel of devotion. The parched infidelities, like a barren soil in which they had struggled and starved together, promised to blossom and flower under the rivulets of this reawakened passion. Deep down in the rich subsoil of love hope took root." At June's behest Henry was writing his first novel; yet its story, ironically, dramatized his belief that if only he had gone home and thrown his arms around Beatrice on a particular night in 1923, he would not have suffered. He would have been happier had he never known June at all. His novel chose a course he could not choose. The end of his book proved to him that he was a mystery, even to himself.

But an even greater mystery was that he had, after all, actually completed the impossible novel. Perhaps the book *was* all he had damned it for being when he moaned his dissatisfactions to June: it was undoubtedly "wooden," "artificial," and "literary." His "inventions" may have been feeble and his account of his life distorted. But when he looked at the finished book, it mounted up into a gratifyingly monumental stack of 350 pages, and he glowed with pleasure. So, apparently, did Pop, since the money for June's *Wanderjahr* in Paris actually materialized. It all sounded so simple it seemed impossible: the novel was done; they had the money; he and June were to depart for Europe soon.

He was still possessed by a paranoic fear that Jean would suddenly arrive on the scene and snatch June away from him, that it would be June and Jean, who would set out on Pop's money, and he would be abandoned again. This fear was mixed up with his continuing guilt over his abandonment of Beatrice, which seemed to imply that it would be only just were he abandoned in turn. His anxieties came out in a recurring dream. In his dream the furnished room on Clinton Avenue became an open courtyard of an old castle in which he and June were sleeping. Accidentally, he looked through the window of the castle and discovered Jean inside a darkened room. He understood then that Jean had really secreted herself in this gloomy niche ever since her return from Europe. So it was true, as he had feared, that Jean had not remained in Europe when June left: the two women had returned together and June had been deceiving him with Jean all along. He made his way inside the labyrinthine castle to Jean's secret room where he found her kneeling in a nun's habit. Her body was crouched and twisted in such a grotesque fashion that on first look her whole pose, like a popular chromo of the day, resembled the shape of a human skull. She was groaning and crying and he was profoundly touched by her utter desolation. He simply watched her and observed her piteous condition. But when he emerged from the gloom of her cell into the courtyard again, the walls of the castle turned red and in the middle of this crimson room was a gorgeous panoplied bed on which Beatrice luxuriously reclined. He could not understand why, but this was a vision of horror which blotted out the rest of the dream.

Henry's personality was so fragile that he was likely to find terrible things if he examined himself. He knew that he must fix his eyes on some distant point called Paris and blot out all other sights. He resolved that it would not matter when June confessed: "Yes, Val, I slept with Pop—too many times to say." He told himself that he could never believe any of June's so-called confessions, since they were likely to be the opposite of the truth. He seemed to rely on her less than before. All through his life he had been sustained by others—a mother's love, friends' admiration, a June's adulation, a Challacombe's esteem. He had learned to value himself by others' regard for him. But in the spring of 1927, when June had deserted him, he had begun to learn that if he were to survive he must esteem himself. Slowly and haltingly and unacknowledged to himself, driven by his suffering, he was emerging from pain and coming to believe in his own identity. He was groping his way toward an axiom for his life: "Only get desperate enough, and everything will turn out well."

Eighteen

The Dream of Europe

Everything went smoothly. A slip in the cogs, however, could have wrecked everything: June might have blown the money on some further scheme; Pop might have changed his mind; Beatrice might have got wind that Henry had money and put the law on him; Henry himself might have lost heart. But between mid-March 1928, when they began their hurried arrangements, and mid-April, when they sailed, nothing interfered.

Henry drifted through this month like a somnambulist on a ledge, looking neither right nor left. His friends noticed that he seemed dazed, out of contact, as if he were really incapable of taking things in; he was leaving everything to June and trusting to fate. They sailed from New York as scheduled in April 1928 and came back nine months later, in 1929, when their money ran out. While he and June were in Europe his once-powerful ability to observe details and remember incidents disappeared almost completely. He often forgot where he had been, what he had done. Only what was happening to him—slowly being healed—mattered, not what he was doing.

Though it left only dapples, like sun spots, on his memory, Henry and June's actual route could be mapped. The crossing itself was a dream, slow and drifting and romantic in every sense. The French purser on the boat was a genuine *chauviniste* who sang the praises of his sweet country all the way over. Henry lapped them up while he floated luxuriously in an aura of sparkling conversation and sparkling wine, with ping-pong as an *hors d'oeuvre* and marvellous nights with June to end each day on the rolling ship. The *S.S. Paris* docked in Liverpool in late April 1928. They stayed in London for a short while before continuing to the Channel crossing. London was interesting but dreary. Henry didn't really like it, although he dutifully went around to all the sights that a few days and June's incurable habit of rising late could allow. London seemed dull since it was Paris toward which Henry's vision was leaping. Long before he arrived there, Paris had already become part of his imaginative experience.

It was the Paris he had dreamed into existence while June was there that he expected to see, and of course, he was bound to be disappointed. They landed at Le Havre, where his dream of Europe at once began to crumble. The first thing he saw was not some marvellous symbol of French grace or charm or artistic sensibility, but, in the background, coal-stained buildings and a scarred station; and, in the foreground, a grotesque figure whom, to his surprise, he recognized. It was the purser of the *S.S. Paris*. How many hours during their trans-Atlantic trip had he listened entranced to the purser's panegyrics about "la douce France" while they sat playing chess or drinking. Then this man had seemed the very incarnation of Europe. Now, he was already out of uniform and reduced to a clod, his trousers slumping over his shoetops, a shapeless cap plastered on his head, a satchel in one hand and a raincoat in the other, hopping awkwardly across the tracks, stripped of all glamour. He was probably heading for some hovel in the forlorn city. Henry saw a blighted townscape when he wanted to see only the glorious liberating Europe of his dreams; and he sat in the railroad car looking out of the window upon the grim, sooty city, refusing to believe that there could be any connection, except the iron bands of railroad tracks, between this city and Paris.

As the train rumbled southeast all he could see was the sameness. He knew theoretically that a French cow must resemble its American cousin, that a tree must be a tree and landscapes and even farm cottages much the same everywhere, but he wished it not to be so. If France could have been on the other side of the moon and peopled by strange creatures, he would have liked it more. But when the countryside seemed worn, and the towns they sped by were as shabby as the worst tenement sections of Brooklyn, he felt cheated.

At five o'clock, just as the sky turned lambent and all Paris began a frenzied rush, the boat train pulled into the Gare St. Lazare and he and June emerged from the station in search of a taxi. Then, when he was too occupied to expect it, Paris leaped up at him, and he forgot about the taxi and tried to take in everything at once, sunshine and shadow, buildings, clothes, faces, warm air, vehicles, posters—all—and all the while repeating to himself, *So this is Paris!* as if he could not believe he was really there and feared that the whole vision would turn at any moment into Flatbush, Brooklyn. June helped him. As they drove toward the St. Germain quarter, she was quickened by her own memories and gestured this way and that, almost shouting with glee *Ça y'est!*—there was the restaurant or café she had written about to him, the hotel she had mentioned, the park or the statue he had seen on postcards, or the buildings and streets he had read about.

Just as they wheeled down a boulevard toward their destination in the Rue Bonaparte, he caught a glimpse of a famous café, the Deux Magots, and felt somehow as if the literary history of the twentieth century could be as easily glimpsed. The hotel they pulled up to a moment later (without a reservation, of course) was the Hôtel de Paris, at 24 Rue Bonaparte: its very name seemed to guarantee that in it they would penetrate to the heart of the city. They leaped out of the cab. At times like this June often went into a frenzy of impulsive action. Henry hardly had time to breathe before June had served up her few words of French for the proprietor, had secured a room, and was dragging him and the garçon with his brightly colored vest and his rolled-up sleeves along behind her. Henry felt like a cubist creation ascending a staircase: everything came at him in pieces. The key was iron and enormous. The wallpaper was faded. The wardrobe was cracked and gouged and scarred. The mirror over the mantlepiece was stained. The carpet was threadbare and faded in spots.

He touched, as if tallying, the items of his new existence. So this was a French washstand, with its leaking faucets; this was a French window; this a *volet*; this a real *armoire*. And this—a *bidet*. Only after a while could he put the pieces together enough to realize the room was just as it had to be, centuries old, worn and faded and handled, caressed, and consecrated by the thousands of other bodies that had occupied it before they had. Drifting almost imperceptibly on the air of dust and stale urine and lysol and patchouli, the room's essential fragrance was the truly human sense of occupancy which the room conveyed. They threw open the windows and shutters and looked onto the courtyard where the garçon was already back at work repairing a bicycle. "Bon jour," he shouted merrily, "çą va?" And they, in their joy, beamed and like a couple of half-wits shouted back, "Ça va!" at him. They stood on the little balcony while the evening crept in with the tolling bells from St. Germain and watched the lights of Paris come on and yearned to be out on the streets, to see more, to experience more, to know more.

Henry was mad to see it all, and yet what he saw slipped through his mind without leaving a trace on his memory. They had plenty of money and were doing what tourists do, and, like tourists, forgetting what they did. What he experienced most deeply was the sense of being let loose again, like a child, to touch directly the sensuous delight of the open streets. Certain images, to be sure, hit him with great immediacy: the fleshy beauty, almost enough to produce an erection, of the statues in the Tuileries; the pornographic photos displayed in the window of a shop near the Folies Bergère; the Seine at night, the rush of its current scattering its reflections of lights and bridges and buildings; an old woman sleeping on a newspaper beside Notre-Dame; the beggars working the streets and cafés on Boulevard Sebastopol; strange streets, such as the Rue St. Martin, or the Rue Quincampeix. The area around the church of St. Sulpice, with the garish posters over the church door and the candles flickering inside behind the fat belfries, had a special fascination for him. Zola or Maupassant had gathered impressions while sitting on the benches of this square. Anatole France had particularly loved it. Henry recalled the praises which Stanley Borowski had sung of Anatole France's work. Now Henry was standing just where France had stood—France's spirit seemed almost palpably to be there still, as if he were preparing to turn the corner.

He was struck by how much Paris was the twin of his New York. Across the river from Place St. Sulpice, on the streets near Les Halles, the carts were stacked up, as around the Fulton Fish Market. The resemblances between the Dôme and Café Royale and between Montmartre (particularly in the Place du Tertre) and Greenwich Village were obvious. The junk piled up along the quais could be compared only to the push carts crowding the streets of New York's lower East Side. And traveling from the Champs Élysées to Clignancourt by métro was very much like going from Fifth Avenue to Corona on the subway. Paris still had, in most parts, the Brooklyn atmosphere of being a village, inhabited by earnest, hard-working folk who turned out their lights by 11 p.m. and rose early in the morning for work. Both had the same ramshackle look, worn by time and human usage. The Rue de Lapp vividly recalled the aura around the metal factory in the old neighborhood. Strangely, though it was Brooklyn he thought he wanted to escape, he was happily reminded of it. The old neighborhood was restored to him sensuously in Paris.

After a month, at the end of May 1928, he and June started on a journey which would bring them in an arc back to Paris around the beginning of August. Stopping here and there along the way, they took the train through northern France into Belgium, and then proceeded to Aachen, Bonn, Frankfurt, Heidelberg, Munich, Linz and Vienna. They stayed in Budapest for an extended time and then made the long rail journey through Roumania to Czernowitz, on the border of Russia, whence June's family came. Here they hoped to cross into the U.S.S.R. and to continue on to Kiev and Moscow. But at the border they were refused admission, and at Czernowitz went back, through Lemberg, into Cracow, then to Prague, Marienbad, back through southern Germany, into northern France, through Reims, and at last "home," to Paris.

These two and a half months passed in a whirl of sensation, leaving little impression on his memory. Henry's strongest sensation was of movement. Beside that, only broken images remained. He thought of Belgium as an extension of France. But just over the German border the spell of Paris was broken by the sudden hideous intrusion of European industrialism: at Aachen a mob of factory workers boarded the train. They seemed to regard the two American tourists with distaste, though they didn't hesitate to beg cigarettes; they threw ugly grimaces Henry's way, and showed no embarrassment in stripping off their shirts and washing each other with boorish gusto in June's presence. With their shaved heads they seemed to be machines themselves. That album of George Grosz's—Henry whispered to June—he had thought it was an exhibition of surrealism. But these Germans proved Grosz to be a painstaking photographic realist. Bonn seemed an improvement only because Henry's attitude toward it was more reverent: Beethoven had been born there. But Frankfurt helped to revive his first bad impressions; and though as they moved southward toward Munich he almost wept at the beauty of stretches of the scenery, he didn't like the signs of raw power, the industrialization, the evidences of hard work, the monarchical tendencies, or the high prices.

They escaped to Vienna with relief. And yet that too was disappointing. True, St. Stephen's was wonderful—far more splendid than Notre-Dame—but the rest of the city seemed to be dying, dreaming of a glorious past which had never really existed. Henry wrote to a friend: "the glorious old Vienna, city of romantic dreams, no longer exists. . . . Vienna is a morgue—and beyond that it stinks. Architecturally it could never have been very impressive. If you conjure up Broadway between Canal and Eighth Avenue you have the prevailing style of building existent in

Vienna." To make matters worse, in Vienna they had arranged to stay with a family to which June was distantly related. It was Cockroach Hall all over again: armies of bedbugs surged up and down the walls in open war—and the bedbugs were winning. June tactfully suggested to her relatives that surely the family was being inconvenienced, it would be better if the guests moved into a hotel. But they were hurt, they wouldn't hear of such a thing. Another night of torment. The next day Henry went out and purchased insecticide and a sprayer, smuggling it in and used it secretly. The best he could hope for was to slow the bugs down. Every morning the sheets were covered with blood.

Budapest was better and had an even better cathedral, with frescoes that Henry thought possessed the tones of the Incas and Mayas. The city seemed gay, immaculate, and colorful and the people cultivated and artistic, civilized to the fingertips. Henry liked it better than Paris. Once, he struck up a conversation with a Hungarian Jew who had emigrated to New York. His relatives remained, but he returned to Budapest because, he said, this city had a heart. Like good tourists Henry and June visited the medieval Matjes Kirche and the Roman cemetery and baths. The only complaint he had about Budapest was that here, of all places, he could find no gypsy orchestra as good as that in Papa Moscowitz's. But even this complaint was appealingly remedied one night. After sitting through a listless, spiritless performance of music in their hotel during dinner, he and June walked out disgusted and sauntered through the workingman's district on the Pest side. They decided to have a cup of coffee in a café before retiring. And while they were there a tough-looking peasant and his friend and a whore came in and, commandeering three musicians, sang one folk song after another.

In Roumania, too, it was the peasants who stuck in his mind—in native garb, barefooted, with big round eyes. And now that June was in her ancestral element, she too seemed to become more and more peasant-like. Everyone could see it. In Czernowitz, while they walked around town waiting for permission to cross into Russia, they were trailed by a string of peasants. If they stopped in a café, these devotees would drift in and seat themselves where they could silently watch June. Perhaps one or two of these love-struck souls, Henry speculated, might do away with themselves when June left.

They started back. Poland and Czechoslovakia (except for Prague) were horrors—worse than Germany, if that were possible. By the time the train arrived at Cracow, Henry had already observed several instances of belliger-

ence against the poor, timid Jews and decided that the Poles were the most
sullen and stupid people in Europe. But when a Polish tough came into
Henry's compartment with his girl and tried to give her Henry's seat, his
blood boiled and he refused point-blank. "He tried insisting so I sat down
and told him in feeble German to call a gendarme—I was not getting up.
Well, he goes out, by Jesus, and does bring a gendarme in. Then he picks on
a few inoffensive looking Jews in the compartment." Henry seldom hesitated to generalize from his experience, and he seldom took moderate views:
"The Poles," he wrote, "are the dirtiest, meanest brutes in Europe. I'd like
to disembowel the whole damned people."

What Henry hated most of all, what really brought the bile to the top of
his throat—were the toilets. His sense of sanitation absolutely rebelled at
the places that smelled like Sodom and Gomorrah and were lousy with all
manner of filth. "Christ, it would take a revolution to give Europe sanitary
toilets!" he complained. He wrote long accounts of the horrors of the
lavatory. Often, he said, the toilet was just a hole in the ground, "and when
you pull the chain the water comes up and swills around your ankles, giving
you a pleasant sensation of relaxation." Just to find a scrap-of paper was
heaven. "And when a toilet is clean one gets up and sings 'Onward,
Christian Soldiers!'" The result was that Henry memorized the locations of
the few toilets in Europe that were tolerable. His favorites were Parisian—
those in the American Express and the women's w.c. in the Dôme.

Finally, weary with traveling, they came back where they started. They
sank into Paris as into quicksand. June was interested in resuming her
acquaintance with the writers and artists she had met a year earlier. She
liked to sit all night in cafés with a chartreuse or a brandy—to sit and talk.
She hated the sunlight. Their Paris now came to be circumscribed by a few
favorite institutions: the Café Select, the American Express Office on the
Rue Scribe where they went almost every day to see if any remittances had
arrived, the Deux Magots, Zadkine's studio, the Dôme, the Gare de Lyon,
Montmartre, the Café Wepler, the Jardins du Luxembourg, the Rotonde,
the Café Zeyer, the Café des Mousquetaires. By the cafés Paris flowed, and
they took whatever the currents threw up—the artist Adolph Dehn and his
wife Mura; Alfred Perlès, the Austrian with whom Jean had gone to Africa;
the painter Hans Reichel, in his cups at the Dôme; the artist Kokoschka; a
German girl named Magda who fell in love with June; and Ossip
Zadkine—these (and the anonymous ones, the toothless hags and the
magnificent *poules,* the gendarmes and the waiters) were all food for the
hungry Americans and were washed down with talk, talk which began

nowhere and ended nowhere, but simply flowed in an endless gurgle. Sometimes, feeling empty and washed out, Henry would abandon the terrace and go back to the room. He was trying to re-read Spengler. But the cane chair in their room was uncomfortable and Spengler struck the wrong note in Paris. And so more often he'd lie back on the bed and feed on his thoughts while he listened to the Paris night, the music of horns and urinals.

He hardly would admit it to himself at first, but after two weeks of following June's artistic recipe for a perfect life in Paris he was unhappy. "This life of the boulevardier in the cafés and ateliers," he wrote to Emil Conason in New York, "is as stupid here as it might be anywhere else." He showed *Moloch* to a publisher, but it was soon returned to him, and this easily discouraged him from taking up any new literary endeavor. He didn't like the cafés, he found no romance in getting crocked on Pernod every night, he hated the toilets, he disapproved of Magda and Zadkine, and he liked June only when he had her alone. Everything was dismal.

Henry had never been good at solving dilemmas, but this time a golden idea occurred to him. Ever since he had arrived in Europe his heart had been jumping at the omnipresent sight of the bicycle riders. If only he had his Bohemian racing wheel still—he hadn't realized how much he had missed it. He talked to June about what a thrill flying along on a bike could be. An old, old dream of a bicycle tour was stirring in his mind. What the bike had meant in the old neighborhood, in his days of torment with Cora and Pauline, it could mean again: *away!*

And so he conceived the idea of a tour of France and Spain by bike. By this means, he told the dubious June, they would become immersed in the genuine peasant life of Europe, free to take the path they chose, or to take no path at all, and simply, if they wished, laze an afternoon away by the banks of the Yonne or Rhône. To be sure, June didn't precisely jump at the idea, but she had always been a good sport when it came to Henry's passions, and she did nothing to prevent him from dashing ahead. Soon he had purchased bicycles. On the Rue Visconti, where Balzac's publishing house had been, he taught June to ride. The only thing left was to plot out a sensible path for bicycle traffic. On one of the Dôme's marbletopped tables Zadkine drew out a rough sketch of the route they should follow to Marseilles, and he marked the towns to which particular attention was to be given *en route*. Henry committed the map to memory. June kept practicing riding her bike, weaving a wobbly line down the middle of the Rue Visconti. By the end of the first week of September 1928 she was still shaky and fearful of starting their trip in Paris traffic. So they put their bikes on a train for Fontainebleau where June practiced a little more before they set out.

The first part of the trip was a struggle, since June tired easily and they had to stop frequently. But they had memorable days. They stood on a romantic bridge at Auxerre and gazed at the trees waving in the glassy water below them. They found Vézélay especially fine.

Cycling became easier after Lyon, where the broad Rhône valley opened up. At Vienne they spent a romantic evening eating beside the roaring stream. The next day they gawked at the Annamite soldiers in the French army, who were quartered there. The countryside was astonishingly lovely. They visited most of the spots suggested by Zadkine; Henry was having the time of his life. But the trip soured. June turned weary and sick of it, wishing to be back in Paris. Besides, their money was running low. And so the last stretch of the trip, which was to be its highpoint, went flat. June insisted that they make no detours from the road but simply, doggedly, go on to Marseilles. She refused to look at another sight, no matter how lovely or historically important. She wouldn't pedal a foot farther than she had to. The beautiful dark green foliage of Avignon or the historic associations of that city with the Popes meant nothing to her. She could hardly be persuaded to stop at Nîmes to take in a bullfight.

She absolutely refused to linger in Tarascon, despite the fact that for days Henry had been singing of that city, which was so closely associated in his mind with Alphonse Daudet. At Stanley Borowski's recommendation Henry had read *Tartarin de Tarascon* when he and June had lived in Remsen Street. In his misery there he had dreamed of one day communing with Tartarin and Daudet's spirits in Tarascon. Now they rolled in at high noon. The heat was terrific and they sat desolately on a windswept, sunswept *terrasse* on the main street. The whole town seemed *ville morte,* locked behind iron shutters, exterminated by the hot blasts. As June had no interest in finding Daudet's house, they caught their breath and then spun down the white street, catching a glimpse of the towers of the Chateau de Beaucaire only from a distance. No, she would *not* turn aside. Exhausted, they finally arrived at Arles. Henry appreciated this city more for the memory of Van Gogh than for its fabulous history. But for June, Arles meant only a blessed rest, a bath, and a *fine* at the hotel.

At Marseilles they decided to travel east, to Italy, instead of to Spain. They bicycled to Ézes-Sur-Mer, where Nietzsche had written *Also Sprach Zarathustra.* Ézes was wonderful, but everything else was wrong. They were out of money. They got as far as Nice, where they sold the bicycles. After

that money was gone, they got a few handouts from a Georgia Negro who shined shoes on the Promenade des Anglais. The money they were expecting never reached them. It was like Asheville all over again: they were broke
- and desperate, and couldn't even raise money through sending desperate telegrams to friends.

Not knowing where to turn, they hitchhiked to Monte Carlo, secretly hoping that in this mecca of loose money something would turn up. Nothing did. In the little park in back of the gambling casino they sat clutching their stomachs with hunger. Everywhere they looked the scene was lush and luxuriant; even the foliage had all the delicate, deep rich green tones of American money. This was the world June desired, and in the midst of its luxury she was fighting off hunger pangs.

Suddenly, Henry saw a tear roll down her cheek and splash on the back of her hand. As in a trance, she raised her hand to brush away another tear, then gave up to her tears altogether. She sobbed and sobbed, as if every hope had been smashed, Henry felt guilty without knowing why, but could say nothing. He could not even raise his hand to touch her. He felt that walls had dropped between them, that something was at an end, but he didn't know what it was.

After they had been stuck in Nice for three weeks Henry talked the American Consul into disbursing money for June's fare to Paris. Once there, operating in the kind of haunts familiar to her, June managed to scrape up enough to telegraph Henry ticket-money for a train, with some left over to reclaim their promissory note from the consul.

Henry and June lingered on in Paris, as if unable to muster the strength to go home. Henry had written nothing, and when he tried to recall what he had seen, he realized he had learned nothing. Now, as he thought of his trip, it seemed always as it had been at Tarascon: the shutters were closed against him, he had never seen the Europe of his dreams. They drifted about Paris like a couple of ghosts, or sat in the cafés while the sun retreated and the weather turned cold. They were burned out and cold themselves.

They invited Zadkine to accompany them to the Ciquona dancehall for a *bon voyage* party on the night before sailing. They talked of prohibition in America while they quickly got tight. Everything started to go woozy for Henry. He began to act zany and to dance with a beautiful blonde with dark eyes. June looked annoyed, and Zadkine openly expressed his disgust with Henry for dancing with other girls. Henry didn't like the attentions that Zadkine paid to June. The more jealous he got the more he drank. The drunker he became, the more his jealousy flamed up. (*What had happened in the Bois de Boulogne when June and Zadkine had gone there late at night to stretch out on a blanket under the stars,* he'd like to know.) Henry began to feel reckless. He rubbed against the blonde on the floor, the way a smart aleck would try to do at a taxi-dancehall like Wilson's. Thinking of the place where he had first met June brought his mezzotint to mind. *Dime a dance. Can a girl keep her virtue?* He whispered to the blonde: "My last night in Paris." June looked disgusted. She was making faces at him. But the blonde was pressing back and whispering something in his ear. Then he had to go to the toilet ("Ou est le lavabo?" constituted a major portion of his French.) When he got there he found he had an erection and while he stood inside the *cabinet* holding it dumbly in his hand two American janes sailed in. When he got outside to the wash stand one of them gave him the eye. "Got to hurry," he mumbled to her. He had to hurry because June in her velvet suit or Zadkine with his goldknobbed cane, Zadkine with his beautiful neck ties, might come to fetch him. And then he had the woman in his arms. They were both pie-eyed. They tried to do it in the *cabinet* where no one could see them. But standing up or sitting down they couldn't seem to manage it, to get it in, until they stumbled together out of the latrine and heard the music coming from above. Suddenly he realized: *it's a waltz, my last waltz in Paris.* He tried to grab the woman and felt he was stumbling but he wanted to have a last dizzy waltz in Paris and they were dancing and he was so happy he came all over the front of her dress. She was angry that her beautiful dress was soiled. Her friend said something about the stink of the latrine and they unclasped enough to stumble upstairs and Henry remembered just in time to stuff it in and zip up his fly. Zadkine and June were waiting and giving him cold looks and Zadkine, waving his cane, said: "Let's all go to London tomorrow." And they all shouted "Yes!" And then they got back to the Hôtel de Paris and Henry stood in the midst of all the half-packed trunks and vomited on the beautiful gowns and the suits and the galoshes and the slippers and the briefcase and the unopened notebooks and Spengler and the cane chair and the bidet and the washstand—and all over the incredible French room. *So this is Paris!*

The next day they sailed. All the sick smells of Paris were in his nostrils, his eyes felt granulated and green bile rose around the bottom of his throat. That had been, he told himself, the best night he had experienced in Europe.

Nineteen

The Hand of the Dreamer

"Brother, can you spare a dime?" was the song that everyone would soon
be singing. Though the great Depression had not yet hit when Henry and
June returned to New York in January of 1929, Henry had been rehearsing
the tunes of depression and despair for a decade. He and June rented an
apartment near the corner of Fulton Street and Clinton Avenue. June began
to resume contacts with old friends, to attract new admirers, and to look for
a job, while he began to roam the streets aimlessly. He was learning to
become inert, as if he were burrowing in. If he found himself in a good
neighborhood, he'd try to make a touch: "Hey, mister, can you spare
enough for a cup of coffee?" But what he really wanted to say was, "I've been
to Europe and written a novel but I'm leading a dog's life, a life of pimp and
whore. Couldn't you help me out with a dollar or two dollars or a hundred
dollars?" He never said precisely that—but once, at least, he became so
depressed he trailed a fellow into a side street near Times Square, cornered
him, and threatened him with assault if he didn't come up with a good sum.

After a time the circles of his life started to contract around his own
apartment. Perhaps he'd only walk down Fulton Street to the Brooklyn
Bridge, or turn into Orange or Pineapple streets and make for a street called
Columbia Heights where a fine vista of the harbor awaited. By this process,
he eventually walked himself back to his apartment and to his desk where he
began the novel he had wanted to write when he had been sidetracked by
Moloch.

As he read and reread his notes concerning June, he felt as if his skin had burned away and his heart was transparently on display. He was writing the book of his life, and soon the writing became his life. His wife, his history, he himself, even his book, all became thoroughly fictive to him—only the writing was real.

Much of his past history, indeed, was actually broken away from his present, like smashed bridges in Salvator Rosa paintings. Not long after they returned from Europe June learned that in their absence Jean had made her way back to New York. There she had been committed again, and in the depressive cycle of her mania killed herself. Henry, for his part, learned from Stanley that Beatrice had married a man of some means, twenty-five years older than she. Ping! Ping!—it was as if the fates were knocking off his past with unerring accuracy. He sat at his desk, walled in by his notes, trying to write while feeling pinned at the dead center of a lifeless world.

Plan, his notes told him, was important. All his methodical habits urged him to plot out his work with care. He intended to write the book in four parts. The first would begin with his casual visit to Wilson's Dance hall and end with the surprise arrival of Beatrice at their apartment while he and June were in bed. The second part, portraying his own disintegration, would have its early climax in his loss of the Western Union job, then build up again with the arrival of Jean, and end with an account of his attempt at suicide. Part three, as he envisioned it, "should have tremendous wealth of incidents and characters, piled up crescendo, at lightning pace, allegro fortissimo, con furioso. No drawn out introspections—just facts, facts, facts." Here he would motivate his torment and jealousy of June through a thorough exposure of June's lies. He would portray himself as fighting against Jean for the love of his wife, but also fighting for truth against lies; for understanding against deception. The third section would bring him to the end of his original twenty-five pages of notes, with the departure of the "lovely lesbians" for Paris. But by the spring of 1929 he had extended his notes and was imagining a fourth section that would be "quiet, tranquil, breathing love, madness, suspense. Full of love letters, visions of Paris . . ." This section would tell the story of the hero's, Henry's, reconciliation with himself and the new understanding that resulted. The book would end with June's arrival at the dock, and with "the sight of her leaning over the rail, the very end being the attempt to express the sublime mystery of that face as it turned toward me, searching for me in the crowd."

For nearly two years he had told himself that this was the one book he wanted to write. But as he began to plan it, he began to depart from his

notes: the book was like quicksilver which wouldn't suffer even the most
delicate handling without wobbling.

And this was true not only of the plot. It was also true of his literary ideals
which were changing rapidly. As he began to write he told a friend that the
only good books were: *Ulysses, À la recherche du temps perdu, Hill of Dreams,
Wanderers, Against the Grain, Disenchanted, Closed All Night,* and *Decline of
the West.* But his notes had never been designed to produce that kind of
book; they forced him to write a book closer to the compendious super-
realism of Dreiser and Wasserman than to the works of his recent favorites.
He had overprepared: his imagination was stuffed with the paper wadding
of his notes, and when it fired it peppered his pages with a fusillade of spent
facts.

Worse still, June knew that the book was about her, and she took an
active interest in it. Almost literally, she stood at his side. Every time he
put his fingers to the machine he felt that she was beside him, waiting to be
titillated by his words about her. In fact, June spurred him on by swearing
she would clear up his confusions about all the lies she had told. Had he
really believed, that first night at Chin Lee's, that her father owned a string
of racing ponies? Well, she would reveal why she had said that, and, for the
sake of his book, expose the grand mysteries of her life. So, it was June who
insidiously began to make the book *her* book: he surrendered his imagination to her censure, giving her the right to say that he still did not
understand, that this or that account was still misleading, or unfair, or
badly proportioned. And this is precisely what she did say, over and over.
She didn't like his opening, the scene at Wilson's. And she didn't like the
next several tries he made any better, and she vetoed each in turn. By the
time he got to a version which she approved, Henry—the supposed hero of
the novel, whom June had named Tony Bring—had virtually dropped out
of the book except as a narrator. And, under June's directions, the story
rapidly threatened to become Jean's memorial. This first approved version
opened with a picture of Jean leaving her western home by train for New
York City, and reading a passage in a book in which she finds an emblem of
her own value: "Taken as I am and as I shall always be, I feel that I am a force
both of creation and of dissolution, that I am a real value, and have a right, a
place, a mission among men." With a grand thump Henry's book had
become a book about Henry's rival.

To accomplish her purpose, to keep control over the book, to make the
book hers, June began lying about her earlier deceptions, embroidering her
frauds, shattering even the smallest fragment of understanding once

achieved by Henry. She tried to persuade him to believe in even greater lies. He did, and he didn't, and in the abyss between these moods he wrote his novel. Whatever he wrote convinced him that what he had written was untrue, and so every new page completed entailed the destruction of two. To hasten on with the book, then, meant going backward all the more quickly with it, so that by the time he had written three or four hundred pages, he had a sheaf of manuscript sheets mounting only to the size of a slim novella. Should he compose any more, he would likely produce a short story, and possibly at last write his epic book altogether out of existence.

What he had at the end of ten months was only his notes, notes on notes, notes on how to rearrange his notes, notes made of passages saved from his manuscript, notes on how to reemploy these, and four hundred pages of typed manuscript which pretended to constitute a fictive narrative but really consisted of one long note on a novel he had not meant to write. One part of the book was a celebration of Jean; the other, an account of Henry's hatred for June and Jean ending in 1926 as Tony Bring murders his wife's lesbian lover. What Henry wanted in 1929, of course, was to wring June's neck by squeezing the truth out of her and getting it down on a page. But when he was not even prepared to curb his rhetoric or to minimize his own erudition, how could he ever get at the truth of his hatred for the woman he loved? He made a note of Velchaminor's remark in *The Eternal Husband*, the book which he regarded as Dostoievski's masterpiece: "Yes, it was from hatred that he loved me; that's the strongest of all loves." But he did not yet understand its application to himself. Thus, though the "Tony Bring manuscript" was completed, the book was far from finished. It didn't even have a title.

It was strange how the dead Jean continued to influence him. It was she, after all, who had given him his first real lessons in drawing and water-colors. Characteristically, it was a human skull and a bunch of flowers which she directed him to copy. And it was characteristic of Henry that just as he had the opportunity, even June's mandate, to work on the Great American Novel, he was seized by the mania to turn out watercolors.

Where had it all begun? Not with Jean of course. He had been interested in the magic of pictures as far back as he could remember. And his friend Emil Schnellock was a marvellous talker who spoke feelingly of the wonders of Italian art and prompted Henry to read Pater's *Renaissance,* which in turn led him to study Elie Faure's monumental history of art. He also remembered the exhibitions in the window of an art shop he passed each day as he walked to the tailor shop. One week it would be Hokusai, Utamaro, and

Hiroshige who allowed him a half-hour's respite preceding the humiliation of his apprenticeship; the next, Modigliani, Klee, and Kandinsky would save him; or Breughel, Van Eyck, and Van Gogh.

June had also hit just the right note in carrying the *Ecce Homo* album home. For some odd reason, Henry made a stab at copying the etching on the cover, taking it to be Grosz's self-caricature; and when he succeeded in achieving a resemblance he was so astonished and pleased he began to attempt to draw everything in sight.

In the summer of 1929, disgusted with his writing, the impulse to paint took powerful hold on him again. One evening as he was returning home along Livingston Street from an unsuccessful day of panhandling, he passed a department store window full of Turner prints. At home he got out a box of child's paints, a bad brush, and butcher's wrapping paper, added a newsprint pad and charcoal, pen and ink and pencils to this equipment, and proceeded to render battered felt hats, chairs with wrinkled coats draped over them, teapots, piles of shoes, the misshapen visages of Emil, Joe, and Conason, and at last father, mother, and Lauretta.

This mania only helped to convince his mother that he had become completely dippy. The reverse was probably true. Painting possibly preserved his sanity, and it certainly preserved his writing. None of the torments which were always working their way into his writing showed up when he dashed along *con furioso* with a brush, reckless of where he was going. When he wrote, he drove himself to tell the "truth" about his history; while painting he could be free from the words that gave him pain. He had no memory, only the present, as a painter. He wrote with his right hand or on the typewriter; but he painted—not actually but symbolically—with his left hand, the hand of the dreamer. Writing was serious, a test of self; but painting was the soul of play. Even when he was most abused, writing was somehow related to his impulse to dominate, to save his threatened maleness; while in painting he was blissfully docile and submissive. Somehow domination had come to be associated with suffering and regulation, whereas submission seemed to promise liberation and spontaneity. A city man and an American, he had had no opportunity to learn to meditate nor any likelihood of believing that sheer inertia could have any value. But in the midst of his despair over his book and his life, through his painting he groped his way toward an active contemplation and began to restore a semblance of reality to his harried existence.

There was no denying, however, that through painting he could never accomplish what he consciously desired—to prove to June that he had been worthy of her return. To please her was the motive which drove *Moloch,* and it lay behind his struggles in the coils of his new novel. He wanted to make everything right, to earn her respect, her admiration—yes, even her adulation, all over again. Failure as a writer, he came to believe, would be tantamount to admitting failure as a lover.

June, of course, was bent upon her private occupations. Under her name Henry was daily to turn out a 1500 word column, as if for the Hearst papers, in order to prove to an admirer that she might become a suitable reporter. For this she pulled in fifty to seventy-five dollars a week for nearly two months. As usual, other admirers were also following her around with their tongues out. One of them was named Oliver. Beginning in early January 1930 Henry had to compose affectionate and literary letters for June to copy in her feminine scrawl and send to Oliver. Whatever fate June had in store for Oliver, he was certainly destined to be the victim of another elaborate swindle. Another admirer's name slipped out, Stratford Corbett—"just an idealist who works for New York Life Insurance Company," June said. The same old webs.

Pop, naturally, was still basking in her affections. June believed that if she handled him right, he would cough up a lot of dough. It was on this note that she introduced the theme of Henry's return to Paris alone. She intimated that since Henry's temper was tender and undependable, it would be easier to conduct her negotiations with the old geezer if her husband were off stage. Pop was not as easy to dupe as her other admirers, but he had more dough, and June was busy weaving her most subtle spells about him. She argued persuasively and conclusively that Henry would be happier in Paris or Madrid. There he could finish his novel, the novel which sang her praises in curious ways, *her* novel. Left alone in New York, she would have a clear field to shuffle her cards and rearrange the pieces in a game whose rules only she knew. "Go. It would be good for you, good for your novel. Let me worry about the money. What more do you need to know? Trust me. I love you. God, Val, I love you, don't you know that?"

So he submerged his consciousness in watercolors and fiddled with his book while he waited for the working out of a destiny which he no longer understood, or cared to understand. He was tired of his old passions. He was tired of naming June's old lovers to himself but he couldn't stop dwelling on them: they were all in June's snares—Oliver and Pop and he, not to mention all the others who had loved her. Compulsively, torturing himself, he had counted them up—he even made lists of her lovers, a sort of masochistic catalog. As far as he could make out, forty-two men and sixteen women had loved her.

Now June and fate were arranging everything. When she was ready to spring the final swindle on Pop in February of 1930, the stars and planets swung into position. Mars and Venus were conjunct with Saturn on the degree of Henry Miller's natal sun. Saturn was in the Sixth House, Saturn was at Henry's zenith. But there was zero at the bone, zero weather, zero in his heart. These winter weeks added centuries to his age. Why *not* go to Europe?

June's talk was murky, impossible to penetrate. She rattled on and on. She had always managed to get him involved in her strategems. Usually it turned out that to mature her plans and to spring the snare his cooperation and even his active participation were required. Dimly he felt sometimes that he was really hoisting himself in the snares he helped her set. But he tried to learn not to ask questions. He already felt numb physically. Now he tried to numb his sensibilities. Whenever June started telling him about one of her schemes or began to make revelations he didn't care to hear, he tried to drag her into bed with him to restore his warmth and to return to his old securities. Much of the time he stayed in bed himself. Quite simply, he surrendered himself to her control and drifted in whatever direction her fancy or her strange designs pushed him.

So, driven by the stars, prodded by June, almost abandoned by his friends and operating under compulsions which he could not understand, he prepared to sail in late February to London on the steamship *American Banker*. He took the steamship tickets which she handed him. He swallowed whatever came his way, damnation or ordination.

One incident from his dead life stuck in his mind, the time, early in their relationship, when June had begged him to loan her fifty dollars—and when he assented immediately, she kneeled before him, clutching his legs like a lost child and crying, "You're my god!" If everything else died, this he could never expunge from his memory. Somewhere in that scene was the key to the past seven years, he felt. But though he pondered it often, he could never understand what it unlocked.

His sailing date came too quickly. He wanted to postpone his departure. June wouldn't hear of postponement. In fact, she informed him, he had to leave the house a day early—he couldn't even spend his last night in his own bed, with June is his arms. She couldn't go with him to the boat either. She had apparently arrived at a critical juncture in her schemes. Every now and then Pop's name came into her conversation, and obviously some connection existed between the necessity for his own speedy departure and her preoccupation with Pop. Finally, he followed all of her orders without understanding her motives for any of them. He simply took the tickets she handed him, rejoiced in a perfunctory goodbye kiss the way a Christian glories in a vision of his God, and stepped into the cold Brooklyn streets. A car followed him slowly as he shuffled down the avenue to the elevated line. He could not be sure who was driving, though he believed he recognized Pop. Did Pop arrive at the house just after he left it? Doubtless, that was part of the plot.

Henry boarded the train that he had ridden so often before, and got off near Delancey Street. All night he wandered aimlessly and alone around the East Side, penniless, unable to believe that he was actually leaving. Chilled and weary by the early morning, he stopped to rest and be warmed at the Jewish Chess Club on Fourteenth Street. Here he had his last vivid impressions of New York: the sight of dark faced men, wearied by their all-night matches, the stench of stale sweat and smoke mixed with the perfume of wet woollen overcoats steaming on coat racks and throwing off an odor of dirty rabbits crowded into a pen.

Finally, Henry made his way to the nearby studio of Emil Schnellock, his oldest and probably his best friend. With Emil, Emil of P.S. 85, he had had good times and many long talks. But now there seemed nothing much to say—only the same old question: "Do you have any loose dough about you?" June, characteristically, had forgotten all about this item. Emil produced a ten dollar bill. This was all the money Henry had to take on the ship with him.

And then he went aboard. Queer that he should have misgivings at being assigned to Cabin 13, for he had never been superstitious. But he was full of forebodings. A terrific impulse to give it all up and return ashore fought with a sullen sense that he was following an irrevocable destiny. He didn't want to go, but he couldn't stay.

Midwinter at the New York waterfront: the air was as cold as an iron rod and the snow stung the faces of the passengers at the rail. But Henry was so numb that to his surprise the air felt mild to him. The *American Banker* silently pulled out into the harbor but he could not feel it moving. He felt stunned, curiously surprised to see the New York harbor drifting by him. He almost forgot where he was going. He stared helplessly into the blankness of the snowstorm and could just barely make out the skyline. All about the boat the snow fell thickly in big flakes, which disappeared into the grey waters, disappeared utterly, without a trace. This gave him a strange feeling, as though the sky itself could drop and be silently swallowed by the waters.

And then skyline and harbor disappeared. Henry dove into the belly of the ship and threw himself on his bed, where he sobbed uncontrollably. It was as if he too had been swallowed by the sea.

He felt that now at last he had touched bottom, but he was wrong. He was like a swimmer who had just barely ducked his head beneath the surface. He had a long way to descend before he would sink into the bottom ooze, a long way before his bones would be picked clean by the sharp-toothed fishes so that his skeleton could at last be reassembled and his bones begin to dance again.

Henry, 3½ years old.

Henry, age 8 or 9, with his sister Loretta, his mother and father.

Pacific Palisades, ca. 1968.

The women from the film "Tropic of Cancer," 1969.

rue Princesse, Paris, 1969.

In his Grecian garb, Big Sur.

In Dutch doorway
of his Big Sur studio, 1951.

Two aspects of the Xerxes Society: sporting and serious.

Herman Bernhard   William Dewar   Alvak C. Burger
George A. Gifford   William H. Wilson, Jr.
Henry V. Miller, Sec.   George G. Wright, Pres.
Wm. F. Becker, Vice-Pres.

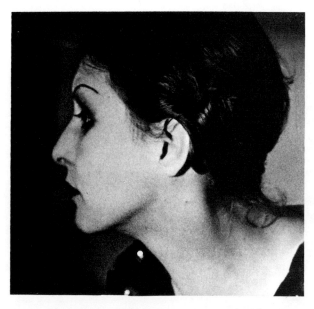

June ("Mona" of the *Tropics*), Henry's second wife.

With Lepska and their children, Valentine and Tony in 1950.

Val, Tony with clarinet, and Henry
in his unfinished studio, 1956.

Henry holding young Tony.

Henry and Eve
in Big Sur, 1953.

Henry and Eve beside the new tile mural by Ephraim Doner, 1958.

Valentine in 1978.

Tony in 1978.

Henry and Hoki, Pacific Palisades, 1968.

PARIS

One

Man of Letters

London matched his mood. It was dreary, unfriendly, impoverished. He felt joyless and lonely, and he had only a few dollars. June had promised she would have cabled a remittance to him through American Express, London. He had not been entirely convinced it would be there, and it wasn't.

So, it was back to the old game, on a international scale, of running up bills. His first problem was lodgings. He would have to take a room on a weekly basis to avoid paying in advance—preferably one including board. And if it could be cheap that would solve all his problems at once. At least he could stay alive until dough came from June. He soon discovered that London's cheaper hotels had no heating arrangements and no water in the rooms. They were simply "dinky, gloomy little rooms." Low as he was, the prospect of living in one of these made him feel even more desolate. Though it was the twenty-fifth of February 1930 when he arrived in London, the climate struck him at first as mild, like New York's in early fall. But he soon felt the difference in his bones. No sun pierced the fog and drizzle; and the damp, lonely rooms he looked at chilled him. It was damp and chill in his heart, and he was haunted by a vision of himself dying in one of these dismal rooms—"fine places to catch the 'con' in, to shrivel up and die in, without any of London's seven millions knowing it." He was afraid of dying alone; of being swallowed up by a pea-souper, as snow is swallowed up by the sea, lost without notice or recall. He finally chose the Melvin Private Hotel on

Gower Street, a pension where for three and a half guineas a week he could have room and board. He dumped his bags in the Melvin and burrowed in to await June's pleasure.

No depression of spirit ever prevented Henry from walking. He consoled himself by the feel of the ground moving under his bootsoles. Not a full day passed before he ventured out on investigative perambulations. His hotel was near the British Museum and the University of London. The exhibits in the Museum bowled him over, especially the magnificent displays of exotic and bizarre antiquities. An idea came to him for a sketch on the Japanese and Ceylonese Devil Dancer masks, in the manner of the mezzotints. Soon he began to stretch his American legs on the widening circles away from his hotel. He knocked about London's narrow streets, poked his nose between the little squat buildings of Whitechapel, and cocked his ear to the street cries, meandering where they beckoned. Like any tourist, he took in Dirty Dick's Pub, but he found it only "a filthy little wine cellar decorated with dead rats." He was a little shocked to discover that in the pubs the women came to drink right along with the men. He tried the underground trains, which he liked for their cleanliness and regularity and because— astonishingly—one could smoke in the cars while sitting in a plush seat with arms! The English, it seemed, had a civilized sense of comfort. But it was also on the tube that the division of classes in English society hit him hard. He could see the lower classes—a "vile, mean, servile lot, looking more like dwarfs and apes than human beings"—sitting side by side with the English gentleman, "often with his cutaway coat, spats, and silk top hat. He is quite a prince of a chap . . . . You can't beat him as a specimen of civilization and refinement." Between the classes there seemed to exist a gulf as wide as that between different species. It was no wonder, he felt, that there were agitators on many street corners airing their grievances. It was understandable that they had sizeable audiences. English workers had to exist on practically nothing. But Henry had nothing, nothing at all. And within a few days, London began to seem particularly expensive. What was the use of being able to smoke in the tube if a pack of cigarettes cost a whole shilling? What matter that fish and chips were a few pence, when Henry didn't have a single penny to lay out? Finally, after a week of tortuous waiting, Henry saw the clerk at American Express nod when he approached the desk. June sent enough to bail him out of the Melvin and get him just as far as Paris. No chance to get to Spain.

As the boat train pulled into Paris Henry sadly reflected that he had arrived in Paris twenty years too late. "Jesus," he wrote to Emil, "when I think of being thirty-eight, and poor, and unknown, I get furious." He had not kept pace with his own generation: he should have been publishing for two decades, yet he was still a raw recruit to the literary profession. Had he become an expatriate to Paris when he was twenty-one, instead of striking out for the Golden West, then he would have been the associate of Max Jacob, Cendrars, Apollinaire, Gauguin, Douanier Rousseau, Picabia, and all the others who had made such an artistic impact around the time of the First World War. Perhaps they would have welcomed him. But now he was thirty-eight years old. The careers of those his own age had in some cases already been completed, while for others, though the full blossoming was yet to come, the promise had already been partially fulfilled. He alone was still anonymous and was probably destined to remain so.

He admitted to himself that he had a few allies, a few advantages. June would probably support him—skimpily—with the franc at twenty-two to the dollar. Emil Schnellock, Joe O'Regan, a recent friend named Abe Elkus, who owned a Brooklyn dry-goods store, Emil Conason, and a few other pals wouldn't let him down. He had two valises and a trunk, containing well-tailored Fifth Avenue clothes made by Henry Miller, Gentleman's Tailor, in weights for all seasons. In the valise was a copy of Walt Whitman's *Leaves of Grass* and in a trunk the completed manuscript of *Moloch* and a draft of his novel about June. He had, finally, a will as yet unbroken, though terribly bent and battered, and best of all, a sense of fun. This showed in the inscription on the back of more than one envelop mailed from Paris:

> Return to: Henry V. Miller
> Man of Letters
> % American Express
> 11 Rue Scribe
> Vive la France! Liberté, Egalité, Fraternité
> Pax Vobiscum

He hated the fact that his potential had gone so long unrealized, but he was not content to let it die.

Each day removed a century from his past. He was terribly lonely and heartsick for June, and had not a friend in Paris (except Zadkine, whom he wished to avoid) to give him solace. Yet he needed to get away from others, to learn to move with the flow of life, to follow the rhythm of his own body, to run with the arterial rush of the streets. By being alone he could, possibly, discover a self that his parents, his friends, his jobs, his loves, his life in America had long suppressed. It was really the first time in his thirty-eight years that he could not assume someone else would take care of him, as his parents, Pauline, Beatrice, and June had. He never handled solitude well. By lavishing so much attention on him from the time of his earliest youth, his parents had taught him to believe that he would always be cherished and nurtured. Though he had differed with them over almost every possible issue by 1930, he was still very much tied to them. By loving him so much, they, unfortunately, made him dependent on their aid.

But now he *was* alone. No sooner had he arrived in Paris than he realized he did not have the passage money to return, even if he wished to do so. He had no Emil nearby, good for a touch, no mother and father to move in with. Accustomed to indulging himself, watching his pennies was repugnant to him. His natural instinct was to treat himself to Paris. But he had to foresee a time when he might have no resources at all, when he would have no room, no daily glass of Anjou, no shaving soap, and perhaps not even a precious scrap of paper to wipe himself; when he would try to work but, lacking a work permit, would be refused.

Henry had hung on the edge of disaster often, but he could always, when he began to sink, count on a helping hand. Now he was merged into the life of the nameless crowd, moving as others did, gawking at the sights that stirred the crowd, swept down the streets the crowd moved along. It was a kind of uterine life, a swimming without consciousness or speech in an indiscriminate sea, a reduction to the most basic impulses—warmth, hunger, sensation. He was wholly ruled by two simple mottos which Paris gave him: *Fay ce que vouldras!*—Rabelais's invitation—and *Defendez-vous contre la syphilis!*—the warning written beneath a leering skull which he found inscribed in every pissoir of the city. When he had so little to live by these two axioms served as well as any.

His life began to settle into a certain unity, like splinters drifting together on a flood. Every movement that he made was new, but each one set a pattern for his future behavior. At first he tried to stay in familiar paths, of course. Upon arriving in Paris, for instance, he went directly to the Hôtel de Paris, where he had stayed with June. In a sidewalk restaurant on the Boulevard St. Germain he ate his first meal in Paris. He was excited and scared. Even his speech broke down—because though he wanted to order *légumes,* he simply couldn't remember *"haricots verts."* He rolled something-or-other off his tongue, but by the blank look on the waiter's face he knew he had made a mistake; and having misplaced this word, he lost confidence in the French he possessed. All he could do was jabber in

English and make signs—but how could sign-language convey "beans"? In America, Henry's feelings of superiority derived from his facility with words: deciding to be a writer was capitalizing on this talent, stressing his superiority. But at this instant he realized that in France he was as helpless and talent-less as a baby who had to grunt and wave his arms in order to make his wishes known. He was reduced to a strange, stupid object by his American desire for beans. Well, let them give him what they wished, then. *Fay ce que vouldras!*

The next day he left the hotel with its reminders of June for a somewhat less grand room on Rue Bonaparte: The Hôtel St. Germain des Prés, at number 36. The name sounded distinguished and looked well in letters or on post cards to friends, and Auguste Comte had lived here for four years. (That was more than a century earlier, however, and hinted at the antiquity more than the distinction of the hotel: the paper still on some of the walls probably started to peel during Comte's time.) The important thing was that it was cheap. For 500 francs a month—twenty American dollars—he secured a room five stories up, just below the mansard roof. There was a bath right outside his room which he could use for five francs the visit. The dormers let in little light, the ceiling sloped precipitously, the yellowish paper was stained and peeling, there was no carpet on the floor, the ventilation was inadequate, the radiators tepid, the rooms musty and draughty—but Henry rejoiced that this Paris room was his alone.

Better still, a number of painters lived on the opposite side of the street; they hung their canvases out on the balconies to dry, face front, dotting the gray buildings with color. Every time Henry passed into his hotel, he went by an art shop whose prices seemed so ridiculously low that it occurred to him he might just as well do a little painting on the side. Then he too could hang his own productions out, like posters proclaiming to the odd-numbered Rue Bonaparte side: here, too, lives an artist, Henry Miller.

In his quarter around Rue Bonaparte, many art galleries clustered. Turning a corner to come upon a gouache by Max Jacob, a Kandinsky woodcut, a Miró oil, a Laurencin watercolor, a Lurçat, or a Cocteau displayed in a window, was like coming upon Europe itself, its sophistication, its earnestness raised to the last notch of perfection. One could walk into these shops and turn over the works stacked in the bins, pulling out works of genius like fish out of a tank. Yet, Henry felt that most contemporary European art smelled of geometry and betrayed minds as arid as stale encyclopedias. Far superior to the intellectualism of cubism, he felt, was the Oceanic and African Exposition held at the Théatre Pigalle. In this exhibit, he wrote to Emil Schnellock, was the direct, the autochthonous, "the expression of peoples in various strata of civilization who have not been touched yet by the white heart rot of a bogus white culture." Perhaps he himself had really been meant to be a denizen of Easter Island or one of the lost Grimaldi men. Perhaps he should even chuck the difficult job of the writer and give himself to the brush. Or, better still, like D.H. Lawrence and Max Jacob, he might be writer, wit, saint, and painter rolled in one.

A mere glance at the map of Paris showed what he dimly knew, that the city was laced with streets consecrated to the memory of writers—Balzac, Eugène Sue, Rousseau, Baudelaire, Cervantes, Villon, Victor Hugo. But more than this, it was a city whose very history was bonded together with the history of literature. He marked his map of Paris and set out to find these historic streets and to see the houses of Rousseau and other immortals. He was still a tourist in the world of art. Twenty years had passed since he asked Boardman Robinson how to go about writing: yet Henry had still not learned that Robinson told him the truth when he said you just write. Henry still believed that there was a mystic passageway into the art world, a password, a button, or a special handshake such as the Xerxes Society had. And so he wanted to see the Paris of the artists, and to try to see what they saw. At the American Library on the Boulevard Raspail he found two books that became his chief guides: Arthur B. Maurice's *The Paris of the Novelists* and Francis Carco's *Bohemia*. Sitting at the big redwood table brought to the American Library all the way from California, he went through these books, making copious notes and circling spots on his map, and planning ways to swipe these books. Maurice's book gave him just what he wanted, the locations in Paris which had provided the inspiration for various scenes in fiction; but its prose was rather flat. Carco's was the opposite, full of color and life, and much better than Mürger's more famous book on bohemia—but a little hazy as to geography. Not long after reading *Bohemia,* to his astonishment he happened upon the announcement of a reading of poems by Carco. In the lobby outside the Théatre de Noctambules, piles of Carco's books, fifty or more different titles, were for sale. Carco was bohemia incarnate. After reading Carco and Maurice, whenever Henry looked from his own humble window in the Hôtel St. Germain des Prés he imagined himself out in the streets, which now seemed drenched with an artistic presence.

Often lost on the Paris streets, he was self-conscious about asking directions of strangers. "Où est le Boulevard Victor Hugo?" He asked this question of a dozen passersby, only to be met with bewilderment or a shrug.

Henry began shaking his own head. What was the matter with these Frenchmen? Not only didn't any of them know the city streets, no one ever seemed to have so much as heard the name of the great French novelist, otherwise how could they all be so mystified over what should be a familiar name? At last he button-holed an intelligent looking guy and pointed to the map. "Ah, *Veector Oogo!*" Henry swore that thereafter he would wander aimlessly rather than be thus humiliated. He felt that he was humiliated all along the line. He hadn't passed a week in Paris before his resolve not to contact Zadkine broke down in the face of his absolute loneliness. But when he did visit the painter's studio he sat on his hands for a whole Saturday afternoon listening to the painter and his friends jabber in French, German, Russian, and Hungarian, now and then throwing a condescending bit of English in for his benefit. Implicitly, he felt they were showing him up as helpless just where he was strongest, in language, and he burned with resentment.

Everyday, as he started out from his hotel, he paused before the entrance to Elie Faure's lodgings on the Boulevard St. Germain, always too shy to call upon the great man, since all he had to tell him was that he, a nobody, revered him with all his heart. And he couldn't tell him even that, fluently. And so he passed on. After all, he was on his way to the American Express. Every day he took the same route and every day heard the same answer from the clerk. "Nothing for Henry Miller." Once he had performed this obligatory ritual, for the rest of the day he was free to do as he wished— providing it didn't cost too much. June had never wanted to look at the museums, and so they were still new to him. On one visit to the Bib-liothéque Nationale he asked in lame French to be directed to the famous chess collection with pieces dating from the time of Charlemagne. Fortu-nately he accosted one of the directors, who spoke a little English, and they had a pleasant five-minute conversation. "Have you ever been to Provence?" the director asked, quickly adding: "Go as soon as you can. You will never regret it." Such things stuck in Henry's mind.

In many ways he was ready to go to the French countryside, for the metropolitan life of Paris struck him as false and artificial, just like New York. He was annoyed, for instance, by the homosexuals who paraded about the Jardins du Luxembourg, "where even the gendarmes had to be careful lest they lose their pants." "If I were prefect of the Police," he announced to Emil, "I'd have them all rounded up and make paté de foie gras of them." Montparnasse, where numerous fake artists congregated, he found a "very, very sad place"; and his compatriots at the Dôme and Coupole were dubbed "insufferable idiots." He disliked the ostentation and the superficial elegance of American women in Paris. They were all dressed beautifully but used foul language; they looked like angels but acted like whores. The French common man, he felt, was not much better; coarse and brutal, he treated women "like dogs," Miller complained; he had "no chivalry, not even the slightest respect." French vulgarity was shown, too, in the stupid French love of pictures in which women were presented, skirts up, wearing only fancy drawers or stockings. Still, the longer he stayed in Paris the more he learned to feel its romance—in the Passage Jouffroy and the Rue de Vanves, streets which always held a sense of mystery for him; in the Place d'Italie, which appeared sinister and menacing at night; in the area around the Closerie des Lilas, where one-man orchestras, tumblers and weightlifters put on their acts; in the district near the École Militaire and the Champ de Mars, where *chaumières* and factories were intermingled very much as in Williamsburg; in the Rue Pasteur Wagener, where the whores sailed out of their tenements "like birds of prey and ran, like a river of semen," down to the Boulevard Beaumarchais. He didn't come to see the charm of these places all at once; every day he had to learn Paris.

Miller's first Sunday in Paris, as much as any day, set the tone for his Paris life. Though he still suffered a little from a cold caught in London, a few days in Paris had washed the fog out of his nostrils and he decided that he would rise early (June had never allowed him to do so), observe the early morning life of Paris, and make a holiday of this never-to-be-repeated first Sunday.

He was awakened early by the cries of the street vendors, each singing his own tune. He leaped out of bed, determined to see St. Severin before breakfast. Paris awoke early and the housewives were already hurrying about the winding streets, ducking into stores or rushing home with armfuls of provisions. The streetcleaners were still at their tasks: with long brooms made of bunches of thin hemp they swept the debris of the street into the streams of water that flowed swiftly along the curbs into the mysterious sewers. The air was cool but the sun was strong and imparted a delicate glow to the air, like light diffused and reflected from gray walls.

He walked along the Seine, repeating to himself the name of each bridge as he passed it, yet taking in the whole often-spanned river as he had seen it rendered on many canvases, on many postcards, in many dreams. On both sides of the river men with long poles dropped lines into the slightly ruffled water; their shadows wavered and trembled insubstantially on the surface. In the distance, as the river meandered and turned, the houses above its banks seemed to dip affectionately toward the water until they embraced. That morning a direct engagement with an authentic, immemorial Paris seemed possible. Those who strolled the banks of the Seine, crossed its bridges, or stood on them taking in the whole aspect—as he himself did—were indistinguishable, he felt, from others who on earlier days had done the same. He was hardly more than a particle in a moving stream, anonymous but alive and glowing, like a warm drop of a wonderful French liqueur.

Toward eleven a.m. he retraced his steps to his hotel and climbed the five flights to his room. Until one, he worked on his novel about June and Jean, adding a page or two. But he was unable to stay off the streets for long. He went in the direction of the Gare Montparnasse, keeping his eyes open for the famous literary cafés. On many of the main streets he passed open air exhibitions where artists mingled with the bourgeoisie who were out *en masse* to survey the week's artistic productions. Most of the painting was abominable, but, clothed picturesquely in corduroys and black berets, with huge pipes stuck into big beards, the artists fulfilled every expectation. Henry made his way to the Deux Magots and found a quiet table. He had his first Pernod alone. He opened the manuscript of his novel and read over what he had added to it a short while ago, making corrections here and there, and, on the whole, feeling quite smugly satisfied that he was doing just what a literary artist might be expected to do at midday—sipping a Pernod and dabbling with the punctuation of his book-in-progress. Perhaps, unseen by him, tourists were nudging each other and pointing him out. He preened a little, he yearned to be a local sight.

Promenading over to the ancient Église St. Germain he took a turn around its garden, where the gargoyles, long ago fallen or removed from the church, lay propped on pedestals, like sacrificial heads of pre-Christian monsters. Then he made for the section beyond the Gare Montparnasse, on the other side of the Avenue du Maine, where the railroad yards spread out. The sky, turned leaden with the afternoon, blended right into the gray stone walls, the gray buildings, the gray paved streets and dusty windows. A marvelous circus-like scene opened before him, all his senses were jumping, as if he were in a surrealist painting. The tattered idiots of Chagall, the grotesques of Goya, the one-eyed monsters of Picasso, all passed in review, brushing against him, crying out, mumbling and stumbling. The horse butchers were doing a tremendous business at the center of the activity. The dripping carcasses, split open and hung on pegs, looked monstrous, antediluvian. Two or three dwarfs, grunting, trying to hoist one up on a hook, looked imbecilic, like the midgets of Velásquez; or deformed, like Fantin-Latour's gnomes. Here, only a few blocks from the anemic Dôme with its phony bohemian frou-frou, was an utterly different world, brutal but powerful, its only meaning the meaningless procession of life.

Back in his room, Miller felt a little uncertain about how to proceed with his novel. Though he had utterly scrapped the conclusion of his first version in which the husband melodramatically murders his wife's lesbian lover, he was still trying to use many of the book's earlier episodes and couldn't see what possible end they could come to. Once the real Jean was dead, he didn't need to kill her in fantasy. The meaning of the book was clouded. The book seemed lifeless; it paled beside the life of muscle and sinew. He started to think of doing an account of Paris—not a guide book exactly, but of his impressions, and—naturally—he thought of calling it "Paris and Me."

Full of ideas, he walked to the Boulevard St. Germain for Sunday dinner and he started a letter to Emil on the back of the handwritten menu. The pages mounted up, the letter flowed so easily, that he understood he must have been writing it unconsciously all day. So long had he been used to composing books in his mind that to walk the streets was tantamount to creation. So he wrote on, between the courses of a glorious twenty-two franc à la carte dinner, topped off by a café crème at fr. 2.50. What if he had busted 100 franc notes with astonishing rapidity during his first few days in Paris? Soon enough, he felt, he would really know the city and find the dives where he could get a dinner for twelve francs or breakfast for fifty centimes. "So, all in all, men, I am content," he wrote to Schnellock (instructing him to circulate his letters to Ned, Conason, Joe, and Elkus). "I will write here. I will live quietly and quite alone. And each day I will see a little more of Paris, study it, learn it as I would a book. It is worth the effort. To know Paris is to know a great deal. How vastly different from New York. What eloquent surprises at every turn of the street. To get lost here is an adventure extraordinary. The streets sing, the stones talk. The houses drip history, glory, romance."

That was a big mouthful to swallow with dinner, but Henry resolved that he would not be one of the imbeciles who lives in the cafés, merely posing as an artist. He would really examine Paris life. Already, in order to learn the language, he was using a French dictionary to translate Paul Morand's book on New York. In doing so, he was, of course, also learning from Morand the art of gathering and recording impressions—with an eye toward doing for Morand's Paris what Morand had done for Henry's New York.

In the evening of that first Sunday, back at the hotel, Henry translated Morand for a while, often turning to the dictionary. As his first Sunday in Paris drew to a close he dreamed that he would write such a book. After a time, dizzy with syntax, he closed Morand's work and wrote a long letter to June. It was still not bedtime when he finished, and because he had no friends and nothing else to do, he turned back to work on his novel just as he had done for the last few nights. Worn and excited, he finally went to bed alone, yearning for June, at the end of his first Sunday in Paris.

Two

Paris and Me!

The idea of the Paris book took hold: it made him feel that he had a purpose for being in Paris; merely circulating, surrendering to chance encounters, was his job. Anything he did, any way the streets took him, might turn up an interesting sight. Besides, Henry Miller was sick of being Dion Moloch or Tony Bring—what a relief it was to write in the first person, to think his own thoughts. Why pretend that he was interested in "characters"—he was really engaged only with himself. Everyone of his friends knew that in whatever he wrote he was his own hero and that the incidents were drawn from his life. So he resolved that whatever he thought he would say (if only he could tell what he *really* thought); he would report his true experiences (if only he could be sure what his experiences were). In his former misery he had felt that life was unreal, entirely fictional, that he could make no sense out of existence. Now he stumbled toward the idea, born from happy optimism, that what was real was anything that happened to *him*: reality was simply *his* fiction of it. Accordingly, he resolved to make his letters as full and truthful a report on his experiences as possible, and to use these as the basis of a book about Paris. To be sure, Henry knew that earlier writers, from Horace to Oliver Goldsmith, had written travel letters, and he saw that his own reports resembled the skeptical but naïve, humorous style of the letters in Mark Twain's *Innocents Abroad*. Many of his epistles were twenty or more pages long and arrived in Emil's mailbox

190

complete with literary titles like "Spring on the Trottoirs," "The Lion of the Louvre," and "Six Day Bike Race." They were Paris updates of his New York mezzotints, but more flowing and more rhapsodic: he dreamed that his book would someday stand on the shelves of the American Club besides *Bohemia* and *The Paris of the Novelists*.

Maybe others had disarranged Henry's life, but he himself was as much as ever addicted to regularity and order in personal behavior. He wasn't in Paris more than a week when he drew up a formal work schedule and started a program to knock out one long letter each week for later use in a connected narrative. In his exalted desire to see all, to see it rapidly, and to be sure he gathered enough material to fill his quota of pages, he raced around Paris as if he were practicing for the Tour de France. Naturally, his travels soon ran far ahead of his ability to record them. He was forced into taking copious notes of ten to fifteen pages a day, until his notebooks bulged with unused material. By the end of his first month he lost account of what he had gotten into the letters and what remained condensed in his notes, and he pleaded with Emil to tell him what he had covered. "Here are a few of the things I am in doubt about: have I touched upon them yet?"

The Legend of the Pissoirs
Ham and Iron Fair, Boulevard Richard Lenoir
Flea Market, Clignancourt—veritable objects of art for a song, including
    Oceanic, African, Melanesian, Siamese, etc.
Kandinsky, Lurçat, Miró, Czobel, Dufresne
Surrealism—2nd Manifesto (Aragon, Breton, Soupault et alia)
Abattoir Hippophagique, Ville Malakoff, Place Violet
Place Vauban—Last Man of Europe sleeping under the Capitol
Willy—"Le Troisième Sexe"
Charlemagne's Chess Pieces—the macaroni guy at Bibliothèque
Rue Blomet and other rues
Grand Guignol—Cent Lignes Émues and "Le Griffe"—Stupendous!
The Mummies at the Trocadero—where Zadkine, Maillol, all of them, big
    and little, got their first inspiration—and their last . . .
The Mussulman's Cemetery at Père Lachaise
Toilets on the right bank and toilets on the left
The Lesbians at the Jockey Club and the fairies at Rue de Lapp
The Idiot in French—with a French Madame for Nastasya Fillipovna
The Madonna des Sandwichs—Rue Mademoiselle
The Cosmos on the flat at Galerie Zac—Mexican show
Dufresne's marvellous pink-meat nudes—bit canvas, déjeuner.

By the time that Schnellock's answer arrived Henry was swamped with additional notes. He started a whole series of sketches on the impressions evoked by the streets named after writers and artists. He met a man of about his age, Guy Hickok of the Brooklyn *Eagle,* who had also been making investigations of Paris, and he picked Hickok's brains for exotic spots. One evening toward the end of March, Hickok treated Henry to a fine meal in a café opposite the Madeleine. During dinner Henry told him about the strangest place he had discovered—Cité Nortier, with its Ufa setting— and in exchange Hickok took him to his favorite spot, a small winding street below Buttes-Chaumont called Rue Asselin, a sinister alley where the whores who catered to the Arabs and Algerians hopped about like vultures sharpening their claws. Henry added this to the list of places about which he wished to write fully. By the end of March, when he had been in Paris less than a month, he already had made enough observations to last him for years. But there was no damming the creative flow once it was released. It was only a question of finding enough time and adequate outlets for it. His loneliness kept him working, and the joy of working kept new ideas coming. Henry even wrote a letter to Morand effusively praising his analysis of New York. Then he continued right on and penned a similar letter to Maurice Dekobra, whose *Sèche L'Amerique* he was also studying as a model for a book on France. The former answered him politely, which led Henry to begin thinking of making Morand's acquaintance and offering his services as an expert on American civilization. The enthusiasm flowed back into his novel; he did extensive revisions, added a hundred pages to it, and gave it a French title: *Trés lesbienne.*

Meanwhile, Henry was being exposed to other influences. At the Club de L'Ecran, Salle Adyar, Place Rapp, was a Theosophical Center with a little auditorium and a screen where intellectuals met to see and discuss the latest productions of experimental filmmakers. During the post-screening discussions he was reserved (he could barely follow the rapidly spoken comments, and he was certainly wary of exposing the poverty of his own spoken French), but internally he was exploding. After a showing of Buñuel's surrealist *Un Chien andalou,* Miller could no longer keep quiet. He went home and in English composed a long letter, "as crazy as his film, and crazier," to the director. Unfortunately, Miller's surrealism did not provoke Buñel to respond.

Not many weeks later, however, Henry was equally excited by another film, Germaine Dulac's *La Souriante Madame Beudet.* He wrote a long missive to this director and got a quick response; he received an invitation to Madame Dulac's residence. Henry gloated that though he couldn't participate in the foolish chatter of the French film buffs at the Club de

L'Ecran, it was he whom the director herself wished to interview. He showed up at her door in a fever of high expectancy. A maid ushered him in and a butler brought him to Madame Dulac's study. Inside, the spacious room was softly, theatrically lighted so that it appeared almost like a grotto. The high ceiling was darkened and seemed to reach upward into space like the inaccessible ceiling of a cathedral. But the walls, covered with bookcases, were glowing with the rich deep tones of polished wood and fine leather-bound books. Between the bookcases the walls were dotted with antique maps, old sea charts. And all about the room stood large, luminous tanks in which exotic fish swam.

He looked about this marvelous room until Madame Dulac—looking like an exotic fish herself—came swimming toward him from its recesses. He was a little surprised to see that she had dressed in male rig and to feel the firm handshake she gave him, but he was flattered by the pleasure she showed in welcoming him. She motioned him to a chair, a fine antique, and she sat herself regally behind a massive desk placed on top of a dais. He sat there realizing the room was everything he wanted, a dream room, just what a writer would need. Someday, he vowed, he would have a room like this himself. But he also paid close attention to what she was saying in her low murmurous voice: his letter had interested her not only because he had obviously seen many films and had such an appreciation of her own efforts, but especially because he was an American. "And why do I place emphasis on this fact?" Madame Dulac asked. "Because the Americans have broken new ground in making films with sound." Planning to make a sound picture, she wanted to hear Henry's account of the sound films he had seen in America and get his ideas about how to use sound experimentally. As they talked, Henry kept trying to think of bright observations about the film of the future as well as praise for her work, and especially he tried to bring the conversation around to a discussion of new American actresses— particularly one player who was destined to make a stunning success. Had Madame Dulac ever heard about June Mansfield, the writer and actress? She hadn't, of course; but Henry was always able to talk splendidly about June, and he painted her mythically, as a fabulous creature, topping the portrait off with just a hint of June as *très lesbienne*. The director walked to his side, stood over him, and put her hand heavily on his shoulder while he talked of June. "Yes," she breathed, June seemed just the person for Mme. Dulac's first sound film. Even while Henry continued to talk with Dulac, he was mentally writing to June about the prospects of her stardom, and he was imagining a letter to Emil containing some of his choice observations about the cinema, with his missive to Buñuel thrown in.

Henry was so obsessed in his writing that he failed to notice how much the experiences which filled the books cost. His funds dwindled at an alarming rate. Entrances to films, purchases of books and newspapers, the cost of the métro, the sampling of new wines, the substantial meals which he liked to consume, his afternoon glass of Anjou, his evening Pernod, all added up. It seemed foolish to him only in retrospect that he might walk out of his quarter to a less expensive district in order to save three francs in a cheap restaurant, only, upon his arrival, to be suddenly struck with a new literary idea, then dive into a taxi at five francs and hurry back to Rue Bonaparte before the idea faded away. By the beginning of April Henry was down to fifty francs and had only a day or two remaining on his paid-up rent at the Hôtel St. Germain.

That he had to be troubled by finances just as he was getting into the rhythm of his literary work irritated Henry. In his view, his troubles were all traceable to June's irresponsibility. Though she had not written a line to him in the six weeks since he had left New York, she had cabled several times, but the cables contained only gossamer rainbows, puffed-up hopes; through them all sang the maddening refrain: *Money on its way. Am writing.* . . . But no letters and no money ever came. He wrote to her constantly, in rambling monologues, of his dazzling adventures *à la vie Parisienne;* he wrote fervently, in romantic rhapsodies, of his love for her. But by the time six weeks had passed, Henry's letters withered like his spirit and turned into telegraphic, crabbed calls for help in which such words as "desperate," "despair," "prisoner," and "hungry" figured prominently. At last, certain he would never get a written response from June, he had to beg his friends for money. "Don't let me get lost 'in a bohemian world'," he wrote to his New York chums. No answer: he *had* called into a void. He couldn't work with such worries on his mind. April in Paris found Henry desperate.

Aid finally came from a totally unforseeable direction. One sunny day after a fruitless visit to the American Express he walked up to the Folies-Bergère, where he liked to hang about in the alley by the back door, dreaming that one of the chorus-girls would pick him up. An open truck clattered up beside him. In heavy, guttural French the driver called out to Henry to give a hand with the load of iron barrels of insecticide he had to roll inside. Henry's answer was couched in French almost as bad as the other fellow's. But, he made clear, he'd be glad to help (thinking that once inside he might be able to peek at some of the luscious beauties backstage). Soon he and the truck driver, who was Russian, got into a conversation. With some difficulty, Henry made him understand that he was poverty-stricken—would not the driver at least offer him the price of a little meal and a package of cigarettes in return for his assistance? That an American should be out of funds perplexed the Russian. "But, ah," he beamed, "a sizeable money transfer would soon be at the American Express." Henry nodded slightly at this; he had not yet lost hope. Suddenly the Russian expressed himself as elated at Henry's temporary distress. Since he hoped to go to America he must take English lessons. In exchange for instruction he offered Henry lodging at his apartment in Suresnes, a big Russian meal *tout compris* every day, and even a few francs extra should Henry accompany him on the truck and help roll the big barrels into the roach-and-lice-infested glamour spots of Paris.

Though this would indeed solve his urgent problem of food and lodging, Henry didn't want to become a vagabond or fall into an anonymous working class, and he shook his head, No. But perhaps, the driver urged, he would change his mind; he pressed a little sum for carfare upon Henry, and gave him directions.

This day was an anniversary. He had been in Paris for exactly a month, his paid-up days at the hotel were just about exhausted. He had only a few coins in his pocket. He simply had no choice but to accept the providential offer. Accordingly, he made his decision in a kind of carefree, desperate manner, as if he were mentally hitching up his pants, like Charlie Chaplin. Under the stern eye of the concierge he removed his bags from the hotel and toted them over to the American Club, where he stored almost everything he had. In the afternoon (after one more fruitless visit to Rue Scribe) he descended into the métro, emerged at the end of the line, mounted an autobus for the trip around the Bois de Boulogne, and finally arrived in Suresnes, where a sizeable colony of Russian emigrés had settled.

Still clutching the illusion that he led an independent, self-reliant existence, he did not go directly to the address he had been given. In the restaurant Louis Varnier he lingered over a café and wrote a letter to Emil lamenting that in a month he had made no friends in Paris to whom he could turn for aid. Finally, he stumbled to the address he had been given and got a royal warm-hearted greeting to which, in his melancholy, he couldn't respond.

One night was enough to show him that he had made a mistake. Certainly, his host had kind intentions, put a big meal before him, and told intriguing tales about his father, who had been the commander of the famous battleship *Potemkin* when the rebellion occurred. Nevertheless,

Henry couldn't get over the disorder and filth of the rooms or tolerate the way the family indolently threw scraps from the table to the dogs. Worst of all was the pallet which Henry was given to sleep on. Several gallons of insecticide must have been poured on the pad. It had been thoroughly pickled and had a rancid smell.

The next morning, when he got out of the truck at the Place Perreire he accepted a few francs for that evening's carfare, but was too embarrassed to tell his new friend he would not be back. Henry stood outside the American Express office for an hour, hoping to see a familiar American face. But he had no patience and left for Montparnasse on the chance that he might spot someone he knew, like Guy Hickok, sitting in one of the cafés. Hickok had convinced Henry not to go on to Spain, pointing out that in Madrid living *en marge* would be much more difficult. But now Henry couldn't even see how to survive in Paris. After all the discouragements, especially of the previous two days, Henry was thoroughly depressed. He couldn't go on begging and pleading for handouts, chasing about Paris after a familiar face. Even though there were no familiar faces in view, Henry sat down in the Dôme and ordered a drink. A reckoning had to come, but he ordered more drinks and let the saucers pile up. He had to keep drinking; for once he stopped the check would arrive. The only plan he had was to offer the waiter a cheap gold watch in settlement. Beyond that he vaguely hoped that Providence, in the form of a well-heeled American, would soon come to his deliverance.

Alfred Perlès, the Austrian who had had an affair with Jean Kronski, saved him by stopping by the Dôme on his way home from work on the Port Edition of the *Chicago Tribune*. Recognizing Henry, whom he had met in 1928, Perlès joined him. Their talk started out on the note of remembrance: "Remember that rainy evening when we first met on the Rue Delambre?" Of course! And what had the other been doing since—the food? the girls? the writing? Was there enough of each? There was, of course, never enough money, and so there was no point in discussing that. And the saucers mounted still higher. A very friendly conversationalist, Perlès wanted to know what had happened to Jean (one of what he called his "distinguished cunts") and June (whom he disliked). Henry found him an attentive listener for his sad story. Perlès explained in turn that he had been scraping along in Paris as a writer of feature stories for the newspapers. His specialties were curiosities, sketches of Paris, and previews of artistic events. "Anna Pavlova Dances," "Poisonous Potions Brewed from Fly Paper," "A Talk with Scapini, Blind Veteran," "Who's Who Abroad," and

"Literary Cafés of Paris" were some of the many articles whose regular production kept him sheltered and fed while he ground out a few sentences each day on a novel he was writing in French. He got along, he survived—sometimes he flourished. He knew how to find a cheap meal, how to sneak a friend into a hotel, how to cadge a little money, how to get a drink on the cuff, and how to get girls into his bed. He existed on the margin—but he existed, he was an old hand at living by his wits in Paris—just the kind of teacher Henry needed.

More important for the present, on this particular April evening, Perlès also had his pay from the *Tribune* in his pocket. Finally the truth that Henry was flat came out. Perlès examined the gold watch dubiously. It didn't look like much to him; even coming from an American it wasn't likely to impress the proprietor. Why not let him pay? And for that matter, why not stay in his room since Henry had no other place to go? Late that night the two conspirators tip-toed up the stairs of the Hôtel Central on the Rue du Maine. The next day Perlès paid a week's rent for him, loaned him a shirt, and bought him a tooth brush. A little over a month in Paris: Henry was already in his third home and had reduced his possessions to the barest minimum, as if stripping for a race.

The American Express was Henry's haunt now. Every morning at nine o'clock he could be found outside the door waiting for it to open. At one o'clock he reappeared. At five he made a last desperate sortie. On Saturday he loitered until the last moment, when the company closed at six o'clock. Finally, a cablegram arrived from June marked: "Tuesday. Money being telegraphed today." But Wednesday, Thursday, Friday, and Saturday passed and nothing came. The same webs of illusion. Henry fidgeted with anxiety, unable to think of anything but money, uninterested in his notebooks, his novel, or even Paris itself. He simply lay in bed, inert. He stared at the ceiling, worried about June, wished himself back in New York, and tried to calculate how much his winter clothes, his heavy Montagnac, his leather bags, and his trunk would bring on the used goods market. Saturday night and Sunday he wrote a barrage of letters to his New York friends and June complaining bitterly about "callous treatment." It was fortunate, he said sardonically, that he contracted a case of dysentery which allowed him to eat only oranges and bananas. What might his fate have been, he grimly joked, if he had contracted some malefic germ which made him unquenchably desire *cervelles* or *entrecôtes grillés*?

When the American Express office opened on Monday morning, however, the long awaited cable with the needed funds, more than he expected, had arrived. This little money worked amazing magic: Henry's intestinal disorders cleared up, he wrote a long letter to Emil discussing his literary plans, optimistically predicting that his notes would yield at least two hundred pages in addition to the fifty he had already written on his Paris book. He slipped a long essay called "With the Wine Merchants" into his letter. He was so full of ideas, he told Emil, that if he could only employ a stenographer to accompany him to bed, he could write twenty-four hours a day and turn out at least one book a month.

Fred Perlès even persuaded him to offer *Moloch* to Henri Müller, an intelligent critic who knew English and worked at Grasset's where he was Blaise Cendrars's editor. (With Fred's aid, Henry was translating Cendrars's *Moravagine* and being influenced by this sprawling, tumultuous book.) Though Müller declared *Moloch* unpublishable in France, he recommended a suitable Berlin firm, to which Henry sent it. Müller also urged Miller to write less realistically and recommended two surrealist books to him, Breton's *Manifesto du Surréalisme* and Philippe Soupault's *Un homme coupé en tranches*. "I believe in it with all my heart," Henry wrote to Schnellock concerning the second book. "It is an emancipation from classicism, realism, naturalism, and all the other outmoded isms of the past and present." He decided, he added, to revise his work-in-progress in order to see the story of his life with June through a surrealistic lens like Soupault's, and "describe incomprehensibly the drama going on in a soul standing at Forty-Second Street and Broadway." This book would definitely be "firmer knit, racier," and "more integrated" than *Moloch.*

His encounter with surrealism gave him several new ideas. It wasn't long before he tossed off a sketch describing an interview with a female artist named Madame Zanzerhof who paints only portraits of General Grant. Real alarm clocks, which keep only sidereal time, adorn her canvases. Her house is strange: "the bed looked like the kitchen and the kitchen was an alkali sink dotted with *mesas* and sagebrush. The curtains were nailed to the windows and perforated with bullet holes. There were no shadows in her pictures, but there were bread knives and roller skates and lawnmowers." This was a little lame, closer perhaps to vaudeville than surrealism, but it got Henry away from his realistic penchant. Soon, his surrealist pages mounted up in stacks beside those of the Paris notebooks and the novels.

Three

Life is a Sandwich

June began to establish a pattern in her communications. About once a month a cable would arrive stating that money was about to be cabled. A week or so later—a week during which Miller went into a fit of depression and did nothing—about twenty-five dollars would arrive. Occasionally he received a donation from Schnellock. Somehow, though, however he tried, he never seemed to be able to make his money stretch until funds arrived: the last five days of each thirty were devoted to hanging about the cafés, moving out of hotels, looking up friends, or squeezing his stomach on a bench in the Luxembourg Gardens to keep down the pangs of hunger. He was in love with Paris most of the month and wanted to stay there, but at the end of every month he was engulfed by a black despair. "I get no mail at all," he wrote, "—except morbid letters from the folks, explaining the terrible conditions there." June only cabled, never wrote. Apparently she moved around a lot. Henry had to write her in care of the Pepper Pot, though he suspected that the joint had been closed and none of his news was reaching her. Every letter seemed a gamble, like a bet on a race whose outcome he couldn't discover. Given the uncertainty of his existence, Henry couldn't be blamed much for handling his money imprudently. He hated to feel pinched and cornered by anything, and so he usually ended up pissing his money away on temporary pleasures.

Henry had been in Paris for two months, yet remained celibate. In the beginning of his stay he followed the prostitutes around, eyeing them from a distance but acting skittish whenever one approached him. Later, he found a certain pleasure in exchanging a few words with these women, knowing that by saying the right word he could have his choice of them. But he was still cautious, aware of the warnings in the *pissoirs,* afraid of the filthy rooms they might lead him to, and wary of the *apaches* who might lie in wait for him in a dark hallway. When June sent him the usual sum in May it bucked Henry up, and he decided to give himself a treat. With his pockets jingling, he put away a good meal with a bottle of wine, then, feeling especially affluent, sauntered down the Champs-Élyseés, rhapsodizing to himself dizzily. He couldn't help noticing that on this elegant boulevard the girls had a class and beauty lacking in the denizens of most other rues. Several of them gave him a wink or made a little kissing sound. He tried to keep his mind on the literary letter he was planning to write about the Champs-Élyseés and remember details that should be entered in his notebooks. But he found himself fingering the bills in his pocket. And at every encounter he weakened a little more. He dodged six girls. Then a lulu walked right up to him and took him by the arm. He just gave up and let her lead him to the slaughter.

The price, so far as he could make it out, sounded fine. She chattered away and never gave up her hold on him until she got him inside the room. By this time he was beginning to feel a little nervous, but he was resolved to go through with it—for fear of hurting the girl's feelings. Bit by bit the cost increased. Besides herself, the girl explained, *monsieur l'Americaine* would please pay for the room—nice but expensive—and a few francs for the *preservatif,* and of course something for the maid, and even perhaps, for the special pleasures she offered, an extra *soupçon* for herself. Feeling like an idiot Henry peeled off bill by bill as she smiled at him sensually.

Then it was all business. Monsieur would please undress. She got him down on his back and started to work with her mouth. As he watched her she looked like a machine; the slurping noises she made sounded ridiculous. He lay back, feeling cold as a mackerel, and stared at the ceiling. It looked like a movie screen on which he could almost see projected a skull and cross bones above the legend: *défendez-vous contre le syphilis!* The skull looked like his own bald head. He could almost feel his skin falling off. Christ! His only thought was: *one hundred and seventy-seven francs, enough to last me ten days, thrown away, and I'm probably contracting syphilis in the bargain.* He remembered his visit to the American hospital, when the doctor had shown him some ghastly fellows far gone with the clap, and he groaned and writhed in agony. The girl looked up at him in astonishment. "Don't I please you?" He didn't know what to say, but he made a weary, Byronic gesture and waved her away. "No, I'm just sad," he said. He dressed quickly, and as soon as he got outside he made a bee-line for a taxi. He wanted to get back to his room as fast as he could and give himself a good scrubbing. Another five francs for the cab! *Défendez-vous!*

With Germaine Daugeard everything was different. One Sunday in June he took an excursion to Clignancourt. On his way back he spotted Germaine parading the Boulevard Beaumarchais and he stopped and waited for her to pick him up. He was a little more on his guard now (and had quite a bit less money) and so when they repaired to a café, he told her frankly that he couldn't afford her, even though it was clear that she was a cheap factory girl type. If she liked, they might take in a film, though, or have a lunch on the Rue de Lapp. Germaine was easy to get along with, and once she understood the situation, she came to terms with little haggling. After all, she hinted, since he was a writer and she a painter's model, they were fellow artists of a sort. A little courtesy to the trade. Twenty francs would suffice, and he could come to her hotel on the Rue Amelot for a mere five francs extra. It was flattering to him to be treated so well, and this time he enjoyed himself royally. Afterwards, he took her to dinner and spoke a lot of French and sign language—and promised to meet her again. Obviously she liked him. He was her *"grand ami,"* as she put it in the quaint blue pneumatiques she sent to his hotel. Certainly she had her *maquereau,* but she favored Henry. He couldn't quite get out of her why she liked him. But one day he put two and two together as the result of a casual remark she let drop about his clothes. She enjoyed sitting with him in the café when he wore his itchy typically American upper-class outfit of knickerbockers and loud golf socks. No Frenchman would wear such an outfit; it definitely identified her companion as an American. And it made her, Germaine Daugeard, feel distinguished, someone special, when she sat with him at the Café l'Éléphant. Once or twice, when he was out of funds altogether, she took him to her hotel room, "for love." She whispered frankly: "When you have money we will go to another hotel, stay all night, lie in each other's arms."

There seemed, however, little prospect of enacting this vision. Where was the money to come from? *Moloch* was all too evidently a flop, while the second novel was bogged down. No one had yet heard of any American magazine that had paid for a surrealist story or sketch; he hadn't even the slightest idea where he could send his "Portrait of General Grant." His only remaining hope lay in his book about Paris. He wanted to write it in such a way as to make a popular sale possible, to make it, as he told Emil, "a rollicking book . . . popular, saleable, palatable." He wanted it to have the gusto of personal observation as well as a wide appeal.

This was a bad sign. Miller, who had given up business for writing, always secretly wanted to justify his break with commerce through having a popular literary success, and yet he always became fearful and anxious whenever he saw himself begin to turn writing into a business. By the early summer of 1930, however, after nearly four months in Paris, his funds were so predictably marginal and he was so afraid of starving that on Perlès's advice he had adopted the expedient of eating oatmeal, the cheapest nutritious food, three times a day. He had to have money to survive, but if he made a mere business out of his writing, then all his sufferings would have gone for nothing. The conditions of his existence obliged him to make choices while he wished only to drift back into childhood, when he didn't have to make choices. The most insoluble of his conflicts was over his separation from June. Though he wanted to have her with him, he could not be sure she would come if he asked her. And if she did come he would be lost, since he needed her to remain in New York where she could work her old magic on the customers at the Pepper Pot and send him money. Without her he hadn't the inspiration for his art, he told himself; but had she been with him he would have had to chuck art and work his heart out even to earn their daily oatmeal. He could barely acknowledge to himself that the "clients" and "victims" into whose clutches he was fearful June might fall were those whose donations were keeping him in Paris. He was caught in a labyrinth of needs and necessities, rebelling against fate and accusing himself of his many blunders. With so many contradictions to solve, he didn't solve any. Nothing went right. He couldn't even retrieve from June the letters he had written to her about Paris. Though he begged her to return these documents so that he could plunder them for use in his travel book, June never answered.

Henry was so depressed that he began to dwell upon suicide again, and to reread Strindberg's pitiful account of his own attempt at putting an end to his life. Within walking distance of Henry's lodgings was the Pension Orfila, where Strindberg had resided during his lowest period. Driven by a self-tormenting longing for June, one day at the beginning of July Henry walked into the Pension Orfila and demanded to see the room once occupied by Strindberg. As luck would have it, the dark, cramped room was vacant and it was offered to Henry. Somehow this coincidence brought him to his senses. He saw, past his own self-pity, that compared to Strindberg he had suffered little. Descending the stairs, he hurried to the clean, well-lighted

U.S. Club library, where he sat at the redwood table weeping for all his losses, yet saying ironically to himself, over and over: "Not yet the Pension Orfila!"

He hadn't totally despaired, but he was out of money again. One night he was obliged to sleep under a bridge along the Seine. He thought of all the living bodies that had dropped into it, as if it were a flowing cemetery, but a dogged hope kept him company. The next day he took up his old station outside the American Express. Nothing came from June, but just before closing time, a taxi sped up to the door and a fellow whom Henry recognized dashed into the office. Henry caught up with him at the information desk and stuck out his hand with a "Hello," before he realized who it was—one of his messengers at Western Union, Jacobus H. Dun. Seven years earlier, the Salvation Army director had sent Dun, down on his luck, to Henry, the telegraph company's personnel manager. With an obvious air of style and full of stories of Europe, Dun had appealed to Henry instantly. He moved in with Henry and Beatrice until payday. Then, a mere ten days after being hired, he met an old acquaintance, the head of an engineering firm, at the door of the Flatiron Building, who employed him on the spot for a job in Europe. The very idea of this astonishing development excited Henry so greatly that he had tried to incorporate it into *Clipped Wings*.

Now here was Dun standing before Henry in the offices of the American Express. "Henry Miller. I knew I would find you in Europe some day," he exclaimed. Dun wanted to know if Henry was still writing. Yes, he said, he was gathering material for a book "that would make the bourgeoisie fall on their buttocks." And Madame Miller—Beatrice? Henry explained. Ah yes, Dun said, nodding his head in sad wisdom. He admitted that he remembered hearing the silky voice of the new wife, June, on the phone once when she called Henry at the office. Henry wanted to know all about Dun's adventures. Had he ever sold those paintings? What was he doing now? Dun revealed that he was leading a tour party for American Express—London, Rome, Budapest, Munich, Berlin—the route that Henry had taken with June. In winter, he managed a travel office in Tunis. He had arrived in Paris only an hour before, had money, and declared himself anxious to give his old boss a treat. Henry led him to the Alba. Dun paid Henry's room rent, then took him for a splendid dinner, followed by a serious bout of drinking, which started with Vichy ("to cleanse the stomach" Dun said) and continued through vintage wines, beer, Pernod, vodka, and kirsch.

In the process of climbing up from Western Union messenger to his present position Dun had turned into a thorough bore, egotistical, opinionated, and bombastic; his only redeeming quality was his ability to drink himself senseless. More than anything else, when he was far in his cups, Dun liked to talk about what he called the "European attitude toward love." He got started on this topic in relation to Henry's divorce. Americans, he kept obnoxiously saying, were Puritans who did not understand sexuality. Henry, Dun said, needed to free himself of this one-woman devotion, to take sex more casually and with greater sophistication. Henry, who was in a state of terrible anguish over not having heard from June, was tormented by visions of her unfaithfulness. But Dun kept singing the praises of promiscuous sex and kept saying that what he himself liked best was to "sandwich" a girl with another fellow, or another woman. Everybody of sophistication in Europe, he suggested, was "sandwiching it." Indeed, wouldn't Henry like to tackle some young wench with him at a whore house? At the Bar Dominique, Dun became a little more reckless after his sixth vodka. What did Henry suppose the new Madame Miller was doing? Doubtless, Dun hinted, they were sandwiching it in America too. That made Henry furious and provoked Dun into a vituperative personal attack on Henry; he hit home just where Henry was most vulnerable, calling him a narrow-minded American Puritan.

Henry felt an almost irresistible impulse to punch Dun in the nose, but he kept his eye upon the main chance of borrowing money from him. He felt cold, like a Raskolnikov, and was determined to get what he could even if he had to murder the bugger. Finally, Dun reeled outside, blind drunk, and collapsed. Henry settled him on a bench, lifted his money, and left. An hour later, he strolled back. Dun was snoring peacefully. Henry spit on him and walked on. The next morning, at the Alba, after unsuccessfully begging Dun for a 500 franc loan, Henry hissed coldly to him: "Remember this, if you ever again ask me about my wife, or mention the sound of her voice, I'll let go at you . . . I'll chew you alive."

He did squeeze a loan of a few hundred francs out of Dun finally, but he could not get over the agitation concerning June's activities which Dun had triggered. On the Fourth of July all his thoughts turned toward America. He had left his country and lost his wife—and for what? He sat alone in his room at the Alba and got quietly and quickly drunk. It was the second Fourth of July that he and June had been separated. Only three years earlier, on Independence Day, June had been in Europe with Jean. At least then he had had a few letters from her. Now he had not even a picture, nothing but cablegrams telling of letters which never came. Her last cable announced: "sending letter on *S.S. Europa.*" The heat in Paris was terrific on the Fourth. Even when he stripped down to his drawers, the perspiration poured from him. For the last two weeks he had been so bothered by a feverish feeling and hives he had even gone to a druggist to get some relief. That his blood was overheated, the druggist said, made him break out in *les boutons rouge*. Perhaps, Henry felt, his blood was being thickened and overenriched by spermatozoa too long stored up. Perhaps, as the pharmacist recommended, he should give up wine and eggs, visit a wench now and then, and forget his wife. He didn't want anyone else, only June. But suppose June was really lost to him?

He sat drearily in his room dreaming of June and drinking and wishing for anything but independence. Sometime in the later stages of the melancholy which increased with the wine Henry started to type a letter to June. "If that note which is coming on the *Europa* is only a feeble message then I am indeed done for," he wailed. "And if there is none at all . . .? If I am to go to the American Express, like I once went to the dock, Jesus, June, all my guts will spill out." He figured it up. The *Europa* would not dock at Cherbourg until the tenth—that meant the eleventh or twelfth before he would have her letter; over a week to wait. He had become so over-excited by Dun's comments about what June was doing that he felt he "couldn't stand it a moment longer, that I must get right up and start to walk home. If it weren't for that ocean between us surely I would start out and walk to you, crawl to you." He kept tormenting himself with recollections of June's passionate nature and images of the eruption of her sexuality: like hot wires, scenes of their love-making whipped around in his mind. How would June be able to stand living as a celibate? He recalled a time when, lacking money, they had been living apart for a mere week or two, when June developed a tic as the result of sexual frustration. She threatened to throw herself in the river if Henry didn't sleep with her. How could she do without sex for months, then?

As Henry continued to drink and write, he began to think of her with other men. He pictured her walking around her room, nude in the New York heat, her blue-black hair curling, and the beads of perspiration standing out on her neck and upper lip. He thought of her silky, squirming crotch with its reddish brown lips and the little fluttering ridges in its upper channel and he remembered everything they did, how salty she tasted, and how she would moan: "Fuck me, Val, put it in up to the hilt!" And then the visions came of June in someone else's arms. "Yes, I will put it down in cold type," he wrote to her. "I am foolish enough to believe that you would not want to kiss anyone but me." But he didn't believe his own foolishness and he pictured himself "sandwiched" in among all of June's lovers. At last he fell into a drunken sleep.

In the light of day he realized that June could join him if she could find work in Paris, and he set out to convince Germaine Dulac that June should star in her first talkie. Miss Mansfield's voice, he insisted in several notes, was like the sweep of silk. Another of his schemes was inspired by the abhorred Jac Dun. Henry consulted a travel bureau agent and had some hopes of getting a job as a guide (at five bucks a day and expenses) for European tour parties. By July, he believed he was on to an even better job. He went to see the American Consul in Paris and came away feeling that with his business and writing experience he might land a vice-consul's job, most likely in Bucharest or Copenhagen, at about $2,000 per year. This seemed more than a pipe dream, and he wrote to Emil Conason, whom he gave as a reference, urging him to prepare a recommendation containing "the usual crap" of general praise.

None of these jobs ever materialized, of course. Once Henry believed he had been born under a lucky star, but now he was haunted by fear of starvation and destitution. He was mindful of the terrible prospect offered by the line from Rimbaud quoted in Carco's *Bohemia*: "Always, when one roams the streets at night, hungry and thirsty, there is some one who chases you, pursues you, some one who waits at the turn of the street in order to unmask himself!" That line kept running through his head as he walked out each day from the Alba onto the Rue de Vanves, a street that was like the gate to purgatory, with its musty odors and stale exhalations. It was mostly his own face he met in the visages of the weary, tenacious souls drifting there—himself that he unmasked on this street.

Four

Cinema Days: June to the Rescue
and Other Catastrophes

And yet even here, on the Rue de Vanves, angels resided. One day, hungry for companionship, Henry struck up a conversation with a big bear of a fellow who was tottering on a ladder, posting the week's feature on the marquee outside the Cinéma Vanves, a movie theater only a few doors from Henry's hotel. The man was another emigré from Russia and, like Henry's earlier Russian benefactor, he, Eugene Pachoutinsky, was thrilled to have a chat with an American. He was a man of all work around the theater; after posting the features on the marquee, he would repair to the inside of the house and bang out a rousing, rattling piano accompaniment to the silent films. This time he invited Henry to accompany him to the corner café. After they had conversed awhile and played a game of chess Henry overcame his embarrassment and explained that since he had no money for food, perhaps Eugene would buy him a bite to eat rather than another drink. Obviously, it was astonishing to one and all that an American (who must be rich according to Parisian dogma) should seek the aid of a Russian exile, but Eugene responded grandly and began to teach Henry what he had learned about how to survive *en marge*. Henry, he suggested, should build up a steady clientele of French bourgeois who wished to learn English. As if he were Henry's business agent he wrote out a sign and posted it in the café window:

Leçons d'Anglais
Adresse à M. Miller, 60 Rue de Vanves
Prix modeste

But Henry's days at the Alba were already numbered. By early July he owed a week's rent and the proprietress regarded him closely with her piercing, glittering eyes. Early each morning he left his room and not until nightfall did he return, afraid to face her needling questions: "When do you expect to get your money?" "Any day now, any day," he'd mumble until he wearied of his own evasions. Finally the proprietress at the Alba named a date when he would have to pay up or vacate. But where else could he go? Eugene suggested the Salvation Army on the Rue de Rome. He gave that a try, but his inquiry at the Salvation Army produced the same result as it had done in Jacksonville. Instead of a bed and a meal, he was handed a list of hotels by the clerk.

Things looked bad when it came time to leave the Alba. But as soon as he actually cleared out and strolled down to the corner café for a drink with Eugene and his boss, Robert Girardot, he felt free again. His friends took the measure of his plight in one gulp: he was a writer; he had nearly finished the novel he had started in America; and he had had enough energy left over to write a substantial part of a book on Paris which was composed on new principles . . . yet at the moment—he was broke. *Alors!* The solution was evident: at night he could flop in Monsieur Robert's office in the Cinéma Vanves itself. As for a supply of ready cash, beyond language lessons, a practical solution for that also existed. Eugene directed Henry to a second-hand clothing dealer on the Rue Sts.-Perès, where Henry disposed of four worn suits—suits made by Heinrich Miller—at a price so low that the shame-faced dealer also treated him to a big feed at an excellent restaurant. After all these years he was temporarily in the clothing business again—in the used clothing trade, like June's father. He sold other clothing to friends of Eugene, Russian seamen and workers. Like a fighter stripping for a match, he cast off unnecessary weight until at last he reached his single, essential outfit: a slouch hat with ventilators all around the sweat band, flannel pants, a worn sweater, an ancient tweed jacket, and sneakers. (As a reserve—and for Germaine's delectation—he also kept the scratchy knick-erbocker suit he had borrowed from Joe O'Regan). Dressed in this odd, informal assortment of rags and tatters, he looked like a city Whitman. So he resolved his fundamental problems of lodging and food money. If the free shower at the U.S. Club happened to be in order, which was seldom, so much the better. For entertainment, he could take in the cinema and for society it cost nothing to croon "Ochi Chornia" with the Pachoutinsky boys just as if he were back in the Little Hungary on Second Avenue.

But staying at the Cinéma Vanves turned out to be hell. Every night

Monsieur Robert turned the key on the office door. Then the trouble started. Henry tossed all night, feeling imprisoned and suffocated, endangered by fire and tormented by vague fears. The one window in the office was boarded up; the oxygen seemed to have been sucked out of the air, leaving only the odor of disinfectants, varnish, and celluloid to breathe; the dank air seeped through his body like embalming fluid. Henry's temples throbbed and his heart labored and leaped erratically. When he did sleep, he dreamed that he was in Madame Dulac's subterranean studio, with pop-eyed fish blowing bubbles at him. When these bubbles burst strange images leaped from them, scenes from the films he saw during the day, fragments of his Paris rambles, memories of June. His fear of starvation sometimes reached an almost hysterical pitch in his dreams. An obscene sight he had seen through a restaurant window, of a man feeding paté to a dog, reappeared in many dreams, until he saw himself as a mutt and dreamed that he would be locked in the Cinéma Vanves and made to starve while just outside his window food was lavished and wasted.

Finally, Girardot removed the boards from the window—but it was still covered by heavy iron bars. Even when Henry stood on a table beneath the window he could not see the street. But he lay on his overcoat and listened and slept a little. Every morning before dawn a little cart rumbled by with a tinkling of tiny bells, followed by the sound of a weird, unearthly song. Henry never saw the cart or the singer, but in his dreams he saw a demented North African chanting a litany for a son he had lost in the war. Thereafter, until nine o'clock when Eugene—like a zoo keeper—came to unlock his cage, Henry sat at the desk suffering from hunger pains, dreaming of juicy breakfasts such as he once had at home, of eggs, ham, sausage, hot cakes, waffles, pfannkuchen, strudel, and muffins piled high, washed down with steaming mugs of hot chocolate.

Influenced to some extent by Gide's sketch of Dostoievski, which he read in French at this time, Henry began to feel that his little cell in the Cinéma Vanves was an apt symbol of what he must accept: that he was locked in Paris with no hope of release; and—worst of all—he must live without June or anyone else to aid him. This time there was to be no flight, no easy avoidance. If he couldn't accept Paris, he would be destroyed by it. Thus, he learned to concentrate his energies and follow a routine, to work at about the same hours every day, to eat in the same few places, to take the same seat at the Dôme every night after eight. In doing so, he brought a semblance of order into his existence, even though it was threatened on every side by disorder and dissolution. Equally important, the regularity of his routine began to provide him naturally with a circle of friends and acquaintances. By the end of July, after five months, he began to live in Paris.

Through Alfred Perlès he acquired one new friend and guide to Paris, the Hungarian photographer Brassai, from whom Henry learned the sordid side of Pigalle, the naughty brothels on the Rue Blondel, and Chez Jean on the Rue Victor Masse, where exhibitions of sodomy were staged. He even posed for a few of the pornographic photos which Brassai distributed for the insatiable tourist trade. Brassai was a marvellous companion, a person with gusto, one who laughed easily, postured theatrically, and often winked gleefully; but since Henry didn't understand Hungarian and Brassai knew only a few words of English, little conversation between them was possible. Most of Henry's friends were Americans. Tex Carnahan, a painter and part-time secretary of the U.S. Club, was always good for a handout. Frank Mechau, from Colorado, was another painter who was willing to treat Henry and whose wife Paula struck him as a second edition of June. Another painter, Fred Kann, talked interestingly of Tibet, Theosophy, the occult, and the Orient, and treated Henry to fine wines and swell food at the Restaurant des Gourmets. Wambly Bald wrote a column for the *Tribune* on the bohemian life of Paris and made it a point to know everyone. Sensing that Henry would be a rich source for gossip, he cultivated him. "Give me something for my column. Who's in Paris now? Who's coming to Paris? Who's left? What's been happening?"—he'd always ask. Henry fed him gossip, went with him to interview arriving celebrities (such as Djuna Barnes and Countee Cullen), and occasionally wrote part of the column himself, for ten francs.

In early September 1930, Henry was sitting at the Dôme looking for one of these friends when he spotted an old acquaintance, Nanavati the pearl merchant, whom he had met about ten years before through some of the Hindu messengers he had employed at Western Union. At that time Henry's imagination had built up Nanavati's Paris apartment, at 54 Rue Lafayette, into something oriental and rajah-like in its splendor; and now, in as subtle a way as possible he let the pearl merchant know that at present he was without a fixed domicile, and he would consider becoming his guest for an indefinite period. "Come join me, Endee," Nanavati urged. Endee would be welcome, and perhaps he in turn would consent to perform a few simple chores around the apartment. When Henry actually stood before the building, his heart sank, it looked so run-down. Once he entered the flat, fourth-floor rear, his dreams deflated. Nanavati could offer him only a few rough wool blankets, a dusty pallet in a roach and bed-bug infested corner, and musty vegetables or bread without butter. Another Cockroach Hall! And for this, every day Henry swept the carpets, washed the breakfast dishes, prepared the vegetables for lunch, and scoured the toilets.

At Nanavati's, miserable and humiliated, Henry reached a level of blank despair different from his earlier times of disappointment. He had accepted his poverty and separation from June without giving up faith in a better future, but now he believed that he had fallen so low he had lost any reason for hope. He felt utterly lost, his work suspended, and his future closed. He went to Joinvu and tried to get a job as an extra at Paramount Studios, but he was never even called. He was, clearly, superfluous. In his worst moment, he sat disconsolately in Nanavati's rooms and Lucienne Boyer's "Dans la Fuinic" came on the radio. He felt then that his whole life, nearly forty years of it, was written in smoke. All up the flue! Two years before, he had heard that very song for the first time in the Hôtel Princesse, where it drifted into their window from an upstairs room. Now June was smoke too. He was so poor he had to pawn his wedding ring. *Soit!*

He seemed to be drifting into nothingness. Lacking a work permit on his *carte d'identit*é he had no way of earning money, and thus no prospect of escaping Nanavati's. Every morning, Nanavati pursued him with directions. "Endee, why don't you show a little more energy in sweeping the carpets?" "Endee, the onions were cut in the wrong direction." "Endee, please to polish the bidet." At night he was obliged to take the Hindus, businessmen or missionary followers of Gandhi who showed up at Nanavati's on tours of the risqué sights of Paris, Chez Jean, the brothels along the Boulevard de la Chapelle, or the house of mystery on the Rue du Faubourg St. Martin. The time spent at Nanavati's was the nadir of his worst period—life looked so dark he hadn't the tiniest particle of hope left. But eventually this hopelessness was transformed into a subject for fiction and turned him into a novelist.

For seven months there had been no letter from June. Now, suddenly, in late September, she sent a money-transfer and announced in a cable that she would arrive on the *Majestic* before the end of the month!

This was astonishing, unbelievable. The thrill of it overwhelmed him. What could he do for her when she arrived? What little treats could he prepare for her? What if she did not come? For days he hopped around like a frantic bird. Work of any sort was out of the question, he was so preoccupied with thoughts of June. "But Endee," Nanavati would intone, "the carpets are not clean, the toilet goes boomboom all night. You must do something about this, Endee." Henry did just enough to cajole a few sous out of his Hindu host. He borrowed 50 francs from Eugene. He drifted about impatiently. By the time the day of June's arrival came he was beside himself. No letter of explanation or other communication had followed the telegram. Was she drunk or hysterical or jesting cruelly when she sent it? Was this one more torture? On the day the *S.S. Majestic* was due Henry yearned to go to the Gare St. Lazare and just sit there all day, even though the boat train was not scheduled to arrive from Cherbourg until evening. He knocked about Paris so long in an attempt to hold back this desire that when he started for the station he was flustered and frantic because he got going later than he should have. To his horror, when he ascended from the métro and ran into the station, he was quite late. The empty boat train was already steaming contentedly in the station.

June was nowhere in sight. Henry searched the station. Nowhere. *So she has not come after all,* he thought with bitterness. He trembled, like a beaker of nitroglycerine about to explode. He didn't give way to any emotion for fear he couldn't stop it once it started. He took the métro back to Montparnasse and went to look for a friend, any friend. Suddenly, as the customers sitting in the Dôme came into sight, he saw her, a pale, heavy-faced woman with burning eyes dreamily lifting a milkish yellow Pernod to the evening. She was wearing the little velvet suit which he adored—it always gave him a knifelike thrill to imagine her cool, ripely firm muscular body under the creamy, soft velvet. He went toward her as if carried by a conveyor belt, unable to speak or cry out, his eyes wet. She seemed to be rising out of a sea of starry glasses, eyes, saucers, noses, bottles, fingers, and window-panes. "Never again will I let you suffer this way—never again!" she cried to him, like a lost soul herself.

Her talk started to unwind as if from an endless bobbin. She never stopped, she only paused for his questions. Why hadn't she waited for him at the station? Stepping off the train without a penny in her purse and not seeing Henry around she had naturally jumped into a cab, directed the driver to the Hôtel de Paris, asked the patrone to pay her cab fare, dropped her black pasteboard trunk in her room and then casually sauntered downstairs—the imperious Madame Miller gracing the hotel—and borrowed a hundred francs from the landlord—nothing easier. And then, naturally, she plumped herself down in a chair in the Dôme where she could wait in comfort for Henry. Her conversation assumed the improbable and proceeded to the impossible. As she talked, her eyes darted about, she was watchful and alert as if fearing attack; her hands and shoulders continuously moved in jerky fashion; she sat poised for flight. And all the while a river of perversion streamed out of her, about Bodenheim and Romany Marie and Pop, and the dirty atmosphere of New York and swell apartments. "Do you remember when Romany Marie promised to go down on the sailor? No? That was after you left? I thought you were still there." He was hurt and troubled that she hadn't seemed to notice his absence with the same sharpness that it contained for him.

June was always a mystery, but for once, when she started to talk about how anxious she was to make movies for Gaumont or Paramount, how she was *dying* to meet Germaine Dulac, Henry seized the key to her sudden transatlantic voyage. In his mind he went back over the effusive letters that he had sent urging her to join him. Had he really told her that the big studios needed an actress of just her type and her voice? Had he really urged her to throw up whatever she was working at in New York? Had he overdone the account of his session with Germaine Dulac—or made her seem too attractive by calling her one of the "celebrated *lesbiennes* of Paris?" Yes! . . . But he had simply been spinning romantic fantasies. How *could* she have believed him? *Why didn't she know better?* She never heeded his pleas, but she had been taken in by his fantasies. *Dans la Fuinic!* She was so much a fantasist herself that once he gave her a seed of dreams she built monstrous schemes from it. She was already dreaming of being a big star and having a fine apartment, perhaps a stone house in the country, champagne, fine liqueurs, tickets for the theater, friends, parties in cafés—everything they always wanted. And this was why she had brought nothing but flimsy evening dresses with slits and peek-a-boos in them *à la* Olga Tchekhova. He was a Hindu's houseboy while June was planning an existence based on an income of a few hundred thousand!

In the Hôtel de Paris time had been frozen. They mounted the steps in a dizzy, honeymoon mood—it was 1928 there still. He touched the walls and the old things as if he could draw June's aroma out of the upholstery and halls that had once felt her touch and still gloriously and painfully retained a sense of her presence. He opened the window and looked on the courtyard where they had repaired their bicycles and once listened to Lucienne Boyer's voice drifting out of an upstairs room. They sat in bed and smoked and talked and made love, and finally slept. At five o'clock in the morning they were awakened by bed-bugs swarming all over them—June's hair was alive with the insects. There was nothing to do but to get up, dress, and walk the streets until morning, when they moved into the Hôtel des États-Unis on the Boulevard du Montparnasse, where they could get a room with a much-needed bath. That night found them at the Coupole where they

drank and talked and played chess until three a.m. In the early hours of the
morning, Henry pushed his drink and the ashtrays aside, beamed at June
and wrote a letter to a friend in New York which concluded: "Seems now
that I'm beginning a new life again."

But during their seven months of separation they had taken separate
paths. Before long they were bickering steadily. June had already had as
large a dose of misery and poverty as she could stand in New York; she
simply couldn't start over again in Paris. Henry was soon miserable because
June destroyed his whole routine of organized poverty. The quarrels started
every morning when June leaped out of bed to close the window before she
lit a cigarette and began to fill the room with smoke. They continued with
her slurs on France, her complaints about the room, the noise of the toilets,
the meager breakfasts, and the cold. Henry hated the smell of smoke before
breakfast, he defended France and condemned the automats, the doll-faced
women, and the vicious dollar-sign atmosphere of New York. As for her
complaints about the cold, why hadn't she brought her heavy cape, short
woolen skirts, and her heavy bathrobe instead of flimsy rags? The disputes
increased as June applied her cadaverous green make-up. They continued
through lunch, when June insisted that they drink Pernods (to help produce a nice yellow-green complexion?), and increased as they sat in the cafés
while June made him help her write letters asking Oliver and other friends
at home for money. Late at night, their bitter words fizzled with Chartreuse
and Benedictine, and the day ended dismally, like a burnt-out cigar. They
fought like two ravaged skeletons rattling bare bones at each other. He
wrote in his notebook: "When I listen to her wild chatter, that optimistic
birdseed about the future, which she brought duty-free from America, I feel
that I am back in the Ice-Age."

Whenever their money equalled their hotel bill, they paid up and moved
so as not to lose their remaining luggage. On this plan they were out of the
États-Unis by the eighth of October. They transferred into the Hôtel des
Écoles, a building on the Rue Delambre decorated with limestone satyrs,
because two Hindu girls from Kashmir guaranteed their rent there. After a
few weeks, they skipped back to the Hôtel Princesse. Henry tried to earn
some money—he gave English lessons to a businessman in Neuilly—but
four dollars a week made no real difference. Finally, in early November
1930, a little over a month after her arrival, June left France, as broke as
when she arrived.

The money for her return fare had to be raised from telegrams sent to her
new friends in New York. She had come with high hopes, but they were all

illusions. Most heartbreaking of all was her suspicion that Henry may have deceived her—at the least he deceived himself—concerning the intensity of Germaine Dulac's interest in her. She never had so much as an interview with the famous film director, though as soon as she had been safely shipped away Henry was up to his old tricks and was writing home to urge June to make a determined effort to get into the theater in New York. Then, he told her, with recent acting experience she should present herself back in Paris in the winter. He wrote that he had "succeeded in getting a promise . . . of a job [for June] in the first English talkie to be directed by Mme. Germaine Dulac." He said this confidently—but his confidence broke down, and he added: "that won't be until January at least." It would have been clear to anyone that he just wanted to attract June back to Paris with a ruse that had "worked" once.

She halfheartedly encouraged him to come home. She urged Henry to follow her back to New York, repeating to him the words of Stavrogin, "An individual out of touch with his country has lost God." But though Henry yearned to pursue her, he was beginning to feel that his own case demonstrated the opposite—he had always been lost in New York. June's departure was a relief. He began to write airy letters to Joe O'Regan and Schnellock and Conason, inviting them to join him in his "happy life of shame." His books looked good to him again.

Slowly he began to realize that Paris was good for him because it was a slaughterhouse of dreams, a perfect zero. The only law in Paris was—reality. He believed that he had learned a little from Paris how to look skeptically upon fantasies, while June was still living at the rancid heart of the fat American dream. June's visit rid him of one more of his false gods—June herself.

Five

Ballade d'Hiver

Henry struggled just to survive. Trying to live on ten francs a day, he moved from one cheap hotel to another, traveling light and flopping in rooms that had no heat or water or electricity. By late November, when the Paris drizzle started, he was prepared to give up. Shaking with hunger and cold, he sat down to appeal to his friends for aid in a chain-letter which he started with Abe Elkus. His life, he wrote, was more miserable than a dog's. He had made plans, checked schedules and so on, and fixed upon the cheap boat of the America-French Line which sailed every Saturday from Le Havre to New York at a fare of about $90 including the boat train. He counted on raising the fare between his friends and his parents. He moaned with guilt and humiliation that he was sick from the daily struggle.

His friends couldn't aid him; his parents had no money. He had no way to get home, to be saved from his misery. He thought that this was a disaster, but it really saved him. For though he could not know it at the time, by late November 1930, he had already begun the process of recovery, the climb upward from his low point. The previous six months had crushed the weak, dependent Henry and had given him the ability to survive without aid. At the very time that he had been trying desperately to raise money to return home, his victory in Paris was already assured.

Fred Kann put him up in his studio on the Rue Froidevaux near the Montparnasse Cemetery. He introduced Henry to two of his acquaintances. One was the painter John Nichols, an exuberant young artist with considerable talent but little discipline. The other was Richard Galen Osborn, a graduate of Yale College and Yale Law School, a sensitive and slightly unstable would-be writer who was working in the legal department of the Paris branch of the National City Bank. Osborn was from an old Connecticut family; he was unmarried and he had a respectable, well-paying position. He wasn't wealthy, but he had more free cash than anyone else Henry knew. He had taken this Paris position in order to enjoy himself for a few years before settling down to a Wall Street office, and he was not stinting on any of his pleasures—lodging or food or romance.

Osborn's apartment was well situated at 2 Rue Auguste-Bartholdi. Soon, Henry was skipping up the 129 steps to the seventh-floor atelier several times a day. Osborn urged that the place was too large for him to occupy alone, with its sitting room and coal stove, large bedroom and separate kitchen, and he invited Henry to move in. It was not long before Henry realized that Dick must have seldom been alone, for a succession of *filles de joie* presented themselves at his door like succulent dishes waiting to be tasted. Osborn had carried a little sign from Bridgeport which he hung on the bedroom wall and which never ceased to provide him with merriment. "No tickee, no shirtee," it said. Dicko liked to point that out, with a sly giggle, to the girls he brought to the room. But of Henry he asked nothing.

Now that Henry was securely installed in a flat, with nothing to do but keep the fire going, he could take a casual view of the world. He let his beard grow. To his astonishment, it came in with a slightly reddish tint. It gave him the appearance, according to one of his friends, of "something between a *clochard* and a Tyrolean Christ." When he looked out of Osborn's window he could watch the students of the École Militarie drill with sword and bayonet, playing at the glory of battle while they sank ankle-deep into the mud of the field. It was a grand and comic sight. If he raised his eyes and looked beyond the soaked field, there was the Place Dupleix, its colored awnings rolled down to shield a few patrons from the rain; and beyond that, the Champ de Mars and the Eiffel Tower were in view against the slate-gray sky.

When Henry turned from the window, he had two choices. Every day, before leaving for work, Osborn silently put ten francs on the table. He hoped, he often said, that Henry would get himself a good meal with it. But Henry was on his own diet, and when he pocketed the bill and went out, it was two paquets of Gauloises Bleu, *café nature, croissants,* postage, and métro fare that consumed his daily dole. Osborn always placed the money beside the typewriter; for he could also count on Henry's working. At 2 Auguste-Bartholdi, Henry felt a lift in his spirits and he resumed work on his novel about June and Jean, now definitively entitled *Crazy Cock*. He wrote three entirely new concluding chapters and gave the whole a thorough rewriting, reading his revisions to Osborn in the evenings. Osborn's hearty applause gave Henry confidence. (He blithely ignored the fact that Osborn also declared its style "old-fashioned.") "It is just likely," he wrote to Schnellock, "it will create a sensation. It is just possible I will be made." If ever he got a chance to relate in *Vanity Fair* or another magazine the picturesque story of his tribulations during the composition of the novel he expected to become "the romantic guy of America—*sans doute.*"

After finishing *Crazy Cock* Henry went right on to a series of sketches about his down-and-out-life-in-Paris and to a novella about his nights in the "Cinéma Vanves." The literary influences upon him were obvious. Yet, from the artist-type of *la vie bohème,* Cocteau's clowns, Dostoievski's mad saints, Dreiser's dreary city men, Grosz's grotesques, Strindberg's poor sex-driven devils, Cendrars's men of gusto, Duhamel's skeptical observers, and a multitude of hints in the works of other writers, Henry began to create a character whom he dubbed himself. Squarely in the center of his new literary work was this figure of a vagabond artist, reckless and irresponsible, childish and thoroughly unscrupulous; pulsating with sensuous vigor, but also zany, always on the edge of insanity; saintly, but ready to become a criminal at the slightest provocation. The kernel of this character's philosophy resided in his insistence that his own survival was the most important thing in the universe—at least to him. His views on the relations of the sexes rapidly closed on the conviction that prostitutes were the only women who were pure and honest.

This new character and the themes associated with him adorned two stories. The first was titled "Mademoiselle Claude." This was actually a story about Germaine Daugeard of the Boulevard Beaumarchais, who demanded nothing of Henry but kindness and a little cash. He even had daydreams of removing her from her profession and making her his mistress, supporting her and even pampering her with lavish gifts. Obviously, that was a kind of obliquely Puritan fantasy, a desire to do something for her in return for having made her prostitute herself for him; it resembled his attachment to Pauline. Besides, like Pauline, how *grateful* Germaine would be! And she would be faithful to him. A faithful whore—he reveled in that fantasy. He poured out his affection for her in his story "Mademoiselle Claude," the first really effective piece of writing he had ever done. For the title he used the name of a far more selective and stylish whore named Claude, whose uppish airs and fussy manner in bed actually gave Henry a swift pain in the ass. "Previously, when I began to write this tale," the story began,

I set out by saying that Mlle. Claude was a whore. She is a whore, of course, and I'm not trying to deny it, but what I say now is—if Mlle. Claude is a whore then what name shall I find for the other women I know? Somehow the word whore isn't big enough. Mlle. Claude is more than a whore. I don't know what to call her. Maybe just Mlle. Claude. *Soit.*

Around this same time Miller wrote another story about a prostitute, a surrealist sketch which he called "Bezeque." This told of an encounter with a prostitute who feeds him a yarn about her dying mother—a genteel whore with a firstclass diploma on her bedroom wall, whose money he snatches before he tiptoes from her apartment.

Taken together, these two stories constituted a real breakthrough in Miller's literary career. He had hit upon a theme which mirrored his newly formed convictions and a voice and tone which made his convictions persuasive. He believed that both stories were publishable. Along with an article on Buñuel's *"L'Age d'Or"* he sent "Mademoiselle Claude" to Samuel Putnam's *avant-garde* journal *The New Review,* while he decided to ship "Bezeque" to a New York agent named Madeleine Boyd for possible publication in America.

Certainly Miller's sketches were indebted to many literary influences, but the way he brought these influences together was directly traceable to the influence of his friend Alfred Perlès. Perlès survived on his wits, he knew the marginal life in Vienna and Paris well, and the morals of life *en marge* suited him perfectly. An emigré, he instinctively understood the appropriateness of the maxim: "It is wise to be shifty in a strange country." A second maxim naturally followed, which applied especially to wine, laughter, and women: "Get as much as possible and don't be too choosy." Perlès's epicurean sense of life balanced Miller's romanticism, it helped Henry crystallize his literary invention of a character who had Henry's experiences but the attitudes of Perlès toward life.

By the winter of 1930-31 Henry's considerable capacity for friendship finally began to bear fruit on foreign soil. Perlès, Eugene, Anatole and Leon Pachoutinsky, Fred Kann, Wambly Bald, John Nichols, Frank and Paula Mechau, Dick Osborn, Walter Freeman (at Dick's bank), and Tex Carnahan made a round dozen allies and gave Henry the warm fraternal feeling of a bohemian Xerxes Society. People helped him because they liked him. If, for instance, Perlès got Henry his first commission for a feature article in the Paris edition of the Chicago *Tribune,* Dick Osborn led Henry to the material for his article. Osborn liked to have good times, he was friendly and sociable, and only too glad to have Henry come along, gratis, on his excursions. Every night when he came home from the bank, he'd shout gleefully in his bad French: "Ce soir, Henri, nous vouldras fait un rigolo!"—a perfectly untranslatable suggestion which, like "No tickee, no shirtee," nonetheless conveyed to a fellow American a perfectly clear meaning: *Let's have a fucking bash for ourselves!* One night Dick treated Henry to a show at the Cirque Medrano, with its glorious bareback riders, clowns, trained seals, jugglers and acrobats, often portrayed by Seurat. The show hit Henry just right, making him recall that he had once aspired to be a clown. At least he could write about clowns. Perhaps he could clown as a writer. He advised himself in his notebook: "Go again! Write it up!" Perlès carried the article to Elliot Paul, formerly an editor of *transition* and now managing the feature section of the Paris Edition of the Sunday *Tribune.* When the article (the first piece of Miller's printed abroad) came out in early 1931 it was splendidly illustrated by a reproduction of a Seurat painting. A few weeks later, he placed another article, "Six Day Bike Race," in the *Tribune.* Though this had the title of one of his earlier mezzotints, both of his *Tribune* articles were flowing and exuberant unlike the crabbed and artificially elegant mezzotints. And these were *not* signed "June E. Mansfield."

The sheets began to roll rapidly in and out of the typewriter, with its violet ribbon favored by Henry. In early 1931 the stars were all propitious: not only was he pounding away at the machine, he began to make huge wall-charts, the first clear indication that he was overflowing with ideas, that his imagination was gushing with such force that he could only get it down on the run, in notes and diagrams. In earlier years, when he had exercised restraint and control, it had been clear that he was fearful of exposing his inadequacies; he had been afraid that if once he let himself go, someone would say, "Is that all? Is that really all?" But now that he began to produce charts, diagrams, schemes, schedules, journals and notebooks, these were signs that he felt confident, ready to expose himself completely. On the wall beside the typewriter he tacked two sheets of brown wrapping paper, one by two feet each. He divided these into six columns and headed them "Words." On them he wrote, Osborn remembered, "scientific words, descriptive words, mythological terms, archaic and obsolete expressions, crapulous words, insulting words, explosive words, garnered from the weirdest sources." He also considerably expanded his "Paris Notebook" by copying out extracts from the books he liked, pasting in newspaper clippings or menus and copies of his letters to Emil, and composing long disquisitions on art. So, he spent his days writing and making purposeful plans to write; yet, by the evening when Osborn came home, Miller was still fresh as a daisy and ready to argue with his host's literary values and literary idols, Anatole France and Joseph Conrad. Miller extolled the virtues of Proust, Gide, Valéry, Duhamel, Cocteau, Spengler, and Faure. As Henry talked and gestured, John Nichols, who often visited, occupied himself by painting Miller's portrait, bearded, looking like a cunning old satyr. (On the chance that someone would fail to perceive the sensual qualities of Miller which Nichols wanted to stress, he painted a window next to Henry and through it offered a highly phallic glimpse of the Eiffel Tower.) After all the talk was over, too tired to write, Henry often began to paint. Under Nichols's influence, he wielded the brush and sponge with reckless abandon—but *abandon* was now his byword in everything, and he felt that by increasing his speed and destroying premeditation he made a leap forward in painterly technique. Osborn remarked that around this time Henry's enthusiasms made him appear to be in a continuous state of intoxication; but Dick understood that *au fond* he was clear-seeing and level-headed: he had been so restricted by life that to regain balance he had to be excessive.

The year started out with a lucky sign. On New Year's Eve, the last night of 1930, Henry stepped into a taxi after a pary at the Coupole; the taxi driver had been partying, too, and as soon as he got his vehicle to its highest speed, the cab went out of control and hurtled head-on into another car. The force of the collision was so terrific that Henry's taxi flipped right over, the glass side window smashed to bits right beside Henry and slivers flew all about inside. Yet he wasn't even scratched. He celebrated this New Year's nursing a case of the piles and resolving to walk a few miles every day. Somehow, his stars seemed to be right, everything appeared to be falling into place. The new year promised to be merry and bright. Miller placed a few articles in the *Tribune* under the names of regular staff writers and got a kickback from them. He wrote up a couple of items for Bald and built up credit with the columnist. He even managed to get several paying jobs of ghost writing. When a new brothel on the Boulevard Edgar-Quinet advertised for the American trade, Henry wrote up a promotional handbill. Then, he met a retired New York fur merchant named Louis Atlas who hired him to write a series on prominent Jews in Paris. Henry squeezed out four or five columns—one on Fred Kann, for instance—at twenty-five francs a throw. These were dispatched to a syndicate of Jewish newspapers in New York and appeared, translated into Yiddish, under Atlas's signature.

One thing followed another. In March of 1931, a young man named Millard Fillmore Osman showed up, on June's recommendation, to solicit Henry's aid in writing his thesis for an advanced degree in psychology at the Sorbonne. Osman's topic concerned the situation of crippled and mentally retarded children in New York, Paris, and other large cities. Henry moved into Osman's apartment on Rue Denfert-Rochereau, began to read through the psychology texts stacked on the mantlepiece, and spent hours discussing them with Osman in order to write intelligently about the plight of the crippled. Osman treated Henry to big American-style breakfasts and dinners, handed him packs of cigarettes, got his wedding ring out of pawn, gave him valuable presents (such as rolls of toilet paper marked "Extra Fine," old ties, and darned socks) and a few francs a week. But Henry remained with Osman for six weeks and ground out his thesis for only one reason: to eke out every possible crumb of information about June. Osman was full of gossip and liked to chatter. To hear him tell it, he had lived with June—in a purely Platonic way—along with a third person. Man or woman, Henry could never worm out of Osman who that third person was, though Osman certainly delighted in gossiping about the doings of the Village denizens. Henry bristled when Osman said, "Yes, of course I know Pop—he's not bad looking at all, certainly not a monster." Annoying as he found Osman, Henry still suffered from the impulse, where June was concerned, to follow up every clue, sort out every bit of evidence, and compile an iron-clad case against her. Even though he loved her and wanted her to be innocent, he was always trying to prove her guilty of infidelity. He kept on pumping Osman until he was convinced that he had sucked him dry.

Despite intensive cross-examination Henry got very little from Osman beside food and lodging. Yet, if he had not gone to live with Osman he would probably not have met Walter Lowenfels, who lived at 16 Rue Denfert-Rochereau, close to Osman's apartment. Living in the south of Paris with his wife and child, Lowenfels didn't hang around the Montparnasse cafés. Lowenfels was a serious writer, the first published author of the experimental tradition Henry had met. Since arriving in Paris five years earlier, Lowenfels had published two slender volumes of poetry. The first of these books, *USA With Music,* was a bitter attack upon the superficial values of American life and paralleled Henry's own views. The other, *Apollinaire: An Elegy,* was the first of a projected series of elegiac volumes which Lowenfels intended to assemble under the general title *Some Deaths.* Lowenfels' thesis was that the modern world had "died" by stressing dead functional values. *Apollinaire* struck the note of the series: "the world is mourning the world's own death/dying in its own creation in Apollinaire." When Miller met Lowenfels in April, 1931, he was working on an elegy for D.H. Lawrence and contemplating another one, for Hart Crane. These were Lowenfels' contribution to the "death school" of writing on which he and his philosopher friend, Michael Fraenkel, were collaborating.

Henry's mind had always been elastic, quick to see connections, and though he didn't at first make much sense out of this elegaic mumbo-jumbo of the death-speakers he saw some of its connections with what he had read in Spengler, Lawrence, and Nietzsche; under Lowenfels' influence he soon began to assemble his own version of the death-gospel. He asked for Lowenfels's opinion on his article "Buñuel, or Thus Cometh to an End Everywhere the Golden Age," which Samuel Putnam had accepted for *The New Review.* In this essay Miller argued that Buñel's surrealism proved that civilized man worships decay and putrefaction. Only by wiping out all of society could the diseased organism be disinfected. These views were tinder for Lowenfels. They started to swap articles. Lowenfels showed Miller an essay he was preparing for *This Quarter.* "We go dead inside, therefore our words go dead. If one goes dead inside there is no background for emotions. . . . Everything and everyone dries up in a world of talk," he wrote. Soon, Henry was stopping by the Lowenfels apartment daily, sometimes he took their little girl for a walk in the Luxembourg gardens, often he stayed for one of Lillian's splendid dinners. And unrelentingly, in the liveliest possible way, he and Walter would hammer at the death-theme.

One day Lowenfels gave Miller a tip about a person who would make a fine subject for one of the articles he was doing for Louis Atlas. A prominent American Jew in Paris, he said, was Michael Fraenkel, whose Carrefour Editions had published Lowenfels' *USA.* A naturalized American of Russian extraction, as an immigrant lad Fraenkel had peddled papers in New York. Later he became a professor of English, made a modest fortune in the book trade, and increased it on the Stock Exchange before moving to Paris in 1926 to devote himself to philosophy and literature. Fraenkel had already published *Werther's Younger Brother* and several delicate poems in *transition.* He was Walter's acknowledged master in the death-school of literature. At the same time, Lowenfels was telling Fraenkel about Henry. Here was a guy he said, who was full of life, strange quirks, unrealized talents, and an inexhaustible power of disputation. Lowenfels whetted Fraenkel's appetite by mentioning that Miller had read most of the same philosophers that Michael had studied. But he had a somewhat different slant on them. Certainly, these two should meet. "Take him on," Walter winked, "he's just your meat."

Six

The Villa Seurat:
An Instinctivist Portrait

The interview was arranged. Henry emerged from Métro Alesia, walked a few blocks down the Boulevard Alesia until he came to a corner café, turned right for a few short blocks, then left into the Rue Villa Seurat. He halted before number 18 at the bottom of the *impasse*. The houses in this neighborhood, at the south central outskirts of Paris, had all been built after World War I. It was far from being a bohemian neighborhood; yet a number of artists and writers who were intending to settle fairly permanently in Paris and wanted apartments with cooking facilities of their own had migrated here from Montparnasse. Dali lived nearby. Artaud and Foujita lived on Villa Seurat itself; Derain had moved from the street not long before Henry arrived. Number 18 was a three-storied affair, with a studio apartment set back on top. Henry walked up one step, opened the double doors and just inside them turned to the left where, at the base of the winding stairs, he knocked on Fraenkel's door.

The man who opened the door was a Trotsky in miniature. Shorter and thinner than Henry with dark bushy hair and a dark goatee made to seem even darker than they were by his pallor, Fraenkel concentrated most of his life in his bright, piercing eyes, and in his talk, which revealed a mind that darted about, like his eyes, with a fierce fire. He seemed to be buried alive in the tomb of his flesh. All his vigor, all his ruthless intellect, went into one theme—death. Beckoning Henry to enter, the quick little man threw himself on his couch in the shuttered room and began to talk decisively, as if

225

each sentence were a pin pushed into a map. Before long it was clear that this map was of a cemetery. Every sentence knocked off another illusion, another public hero, another hope. Ping! Ping! Ping!—just like a shooting gallery, with Michael Fraenkel, master marksman, pulling the trigger. He seemed able to speak only in one tense: "You have died" was the refrain of his talk.

He took Henry under his wing and began to teach him his catechism. The only way to overcome death, Fraenkel began, was by living it out, not attempting to engage in the sham of life, since that would be impossibly self-deceptive. Only by living out his disease could a man liquidate it. Perhaps this idea had been borrowed at a distance from *The Birth of Tragedy* or Nietzsche's correspondence with Brandes, but Fraenkel gave it a special twist and made it a world-view encompassing all experience. Always interested in the personal detail and trying to imagine how to write up a newspaper article out of this interview, Henry wanted to know something about Fraenkel's career. How had he arrived at these ideas? Michael started in by talking about the frenzied, masturbative existence of the American businessman who compensated for the unreality of his life with an hysterical and self-defeating desire to live, to enjoy, to possess. He had been such a man, he confessed. Then he screwed the pitch of the talk up a degree to speak of D.H. Lawrence's perception of this condition; and, still higher, to speak of his own "Weather Paper," an essay which had occupied him for the last two years. All action, he proved, was futile. The weather was blowing from the north, from the Ice Age, and the weather would not change. Fraenkel fascinated Henry and almost everyone else who came into contact with him with his brilliant fanaticism; he put all his ideas in their extreme forms, where they burned brightest. He had placed his own book, *Werther's Younger Brother,* on his shelf between the Bible and Nietzsche.

Though all of this conversation promised to produce little that would satisfy Louis Atlas, it put Henry's head in a whirl. That night Henry remained as a guest and the next day he moved into Michael's flat, sleeping in the living room. For the next two months, in the Villa Seurat or at Lowenfels's apartment, the two spokesmen for the death cult stacked up the corpses of western civilization. These were genuine intellectuals such as Henry had never had much chance to know, and he wanted to learn from them and felt a keen sense of competition with them. Occasionally, they made their way to a café where they resumed their conversational *danse macabre* over a nice stewed *lapin,* a fluffy omelette, or a tasty *tripes à la mode de*

Caen. Henry was nourished by the meals and dazzled by the talks. In his mind the death theme marinated with Kann's occultism, Perlès' bohemianism, Dostoievski's spiritualism, Hamsun's sexism, and with his own experience in America and Paris. He felt unhinged from his axis, and he believed that if he were to find a center in all this he might, like Van Gogh, have to put his hand in the flame.

Lowenfels and Fraenkel believed that men who understood the disintegration of the modern world to be a stubborn fact should be anonymous as writers, undifferentiated from an audience whose death they shared. The days of personal authorship were over. The best the writer could hope for was creative suicide: anonymity. They had collaborated on a twenty-nine page pamphlet arguing this point, titled *Anonymous: The Need for Anonymity* (1930): "The Anonymous struggle to project the completed novel, or poem, becomes the struggle for a world ideal, creation; not the advancement of any one poet's 'standing, or recognition.' . . . If he is an artist, that is enough." While Henry agreed with the logic of this, he couldn't help feeling it a little hypocritical since, after all, Fraenkel had enough money to publish his own works (including *Anonymous*), while Henry had to take whatever kind of publication he could and was publishing articles anonymously, quite against his will. His essays on Jews in Paris were signed by Atlas; those in the Sunday *Tribune* appeared under Perlès's name. As a staff writer, Fred had had an easy access to the Sunday feature pages, while these would have been generally closed to Henry, and Miller sorely needed the fifty francs a column paid for features. "Gobelins Tapestries," "Prismatoidal Scenery," "Paris in Ut-Mineur," "Promenade Without Spats" "Mummies and Other Things," and "Rue Lourmel in Fog"—essays which earned him 350 francs ($16) in all—appeared in this manner during the winter and spring of 1931. These, of course, were assembled from drafts of his Paris book and from the copies he had kept of letters written to Schnellock. He revised these with an eye toward a loosely impressionistic, sometimes amusingly surrealist style. "The hour to visit the Gobelins district," he wrote, for example, ". . . is toward *le crépuscule*. It would be better still to go when you have a nightmare, but then you might forget your *carte d'identité* and your revolver. And you might walk into a hospital by mistake and have your insides removed before you woke up."

Miller, as the ease of this style suggests, had acquired enough stability and confidence to roll with blows that would once have thrown him into a melancholic sweat. In July 1931, when Fraenkel sublet his apartment and moved out of 18 Villa Seurat, the dislocation meant nothing to Henry.

Now he had plenty of mental and physical resources to ease him along. Henry merely moved his few things, consisting mostly of manuscripts, into Perlès's room at the Hôtel Central. As for food, his solution to this problem was devised with Fred Kann one day as they sat together on a bench just below the Coupole. Hungry, Henry was speculating about how much he might get by rehocking his wedding ring. (A plaint about the wedding ring was almost infallibly good for a touch.) "I've doped it out," he told Kann. "Now I could live on just about six dollars a week. But what does it matter? Even if I said three dollars a week, I wouldn't be any nearer to a solution." It wasn't that he never had money, he said. Until recently, he'd been able to pick up the loose change lying about the Villa Seurat and occasionally relieve the pockets of Michael's coats of the weight of a few coins or bills. June and some of his friends still sent him money now and then, and he earned a few dollars by writing. And when worse came to worst he could beg Wambly Bald for money: Bald sometimes tossed a handful of centimes in the gutter for Henry to pursue like a pointer; occasionally, he'd give Henry a few sous for shining his shoes and he'd let him flop in his flat. But, as Henry told Kann, he just couldn't get enough money regularly for food. Kann assured Henry he would help him and went on to mention all the others who would be glad to come to his aid. Suddenly, the idea of a "schedule" of meals divided among his numerous friends occurred to them almost simultaneously.

With Teutonic thoroughness, on the following day Henry proceeded to carry out this plan. First, he listed each of his friends on a separate three by five inch card. He selected the most promising fourteen and arranged them by day and hour according to their capabilities to entertain him. Osborn, who worked at the bank, for instance, had to be reserved for the weekend. Then, with his card file, Henry sauntered over to the Dôme, sat down confidently there, called for stationery, pen and ink, and wrote letters to a dozen or so friends. "I have just hit upon a practical solution to my difficulties," he began. "I have lined up the best friends I have here for a meal once a week regularly . . . . I feel sure you won't mind if I include you in my list?" This arrangement, he said, would not only distribute the burden equally and be a tremendous relief to him, but, "it will permit me to work with a free heart and mind." Above his signature he concluded the letters with: "Yours for 'happier days'." The plan worked to perfection, as the answers which he got from Frank and Paula Mechau, Michael, Walter, Zadkine, Kann, and Ned Calmer soon showed. Each one of his friends had some special preference. Bald, for instance, agreed to give Henry lunch on

Tuesdays, since it was on that evening that his column was due and Henry's gossip helped to stuff his space. Then, schedule in hand, on the very next Sunday evening, Henry appeared at Osborn's door and started to eat his way happily through the week, until he reappeared at Dick's once again. This plan worked so well, indeed, that after some time Henry became discriminating. He revised his list, dropping off the bores and confining his visits to the select group of friends who combined wit with rare wines and tender cuts of beef.

Not all the dinners went smoothly. During his Monday night handout from Joseph and Bertha Schrank at number 7 Rue Huysmans he walked on difficult ground. Though Henry didn't find much to interest him in the successful plays that Joe had written for the Broadway stage, he was swept off his feet by the lovely face, milk-white skin, and full breasts of Bertha, and he was soon writing long surrealist love letters to her. Every Monday night he dined with the Schranks and listened to Joe's self-centered remarks on the drama he was planning for the new season, while Henry and Bertha groped for each other under the table. After dinner, Bertha would play the piano, her husband sitting back coolly and smoking a fine cigar. Whatever piece she tried, he always remarked: "Play that other one that you were practicing." Henry was not clear himself just why he was so taken with Bertha, but to any person acquainted with Henry since 1917 the reasons would have been obvious. She reminded him strongly of his affection for Beatrice and June. Like his first wife, she played the piano—the first time he met her she said she would play "just for him." To see a beautiful woman sitting in her own home at the piano affected him strongly. She couldn't help but bring Beatrice to mind; even their names were similar. Her skill was certainly not on a par with Beatrice's. But with the first chord he was lost, his heart was singing. He leaped with excitement to the piano, gave an exhibition of his crosshand technique and came up with a brilliant idea. It would be no trouble at all for him to drop around to the house to coach Bertha on the proper execution of the andante and legato and so aid her in keeping the "Moonlight Sonata" from sounding as if it had been written by Richard Rodgers.

What really made him mad about Bertha he concealed even from himself: physically she reminded him of June. Actually, Bertha saw this before he did. They saw each other a lot during the summer of 1931, while Joe was in New York readying a play for fall production. Once when she was in his room, Chambre 29 at the Hôtel Central, she looked hard at the photograph of June on the wall. "She's a very beautiful woman," she said.

"There's something strange about her, something elusive. . . ." He tried to change the conversation while he edged her toward the bed. "When are we going to Russia?" he asked. "Do you think I can get a job as a proofreader there?" (More than once they had spoken of running away to the Soviet Union: Bertha was interested in the social experiments there.) "Wait," she said, pushing him away, "look at me closely. Don't you find a resemblance . . ." Her eyes swung over to the photograph. "I've forgotten all about her," Henry hastened to say, "and she's forgotten about me too." But Bertha was right. She might have been June's sister. He tried to kiss her. "Don't do that. It's no use," she said. "All right, " he said. "It's true that there's a resemblance, a great resemblance, I saw that right from the start. But it doesn't mean anything—it's just a coincidence—you're different, thoroughly different." But she would not be convinced. "Sometimes when you embrace me," she remarked, "you're not thinking of me at all—it's her you're thinking of." "That's ridiculous," he replied, and he pretended to be hurt at her implication, but he protested no more, for what she had said was true. He tried to get things going once more. "No, I don't expect ever to see June again." (That was a lie and he knew it: he wanted nothing more than to have June in his arms again.) Then he said lamely: "Marry, me, leave Joe and marry me." She looked ruefully at him. "I can't be sure of anything until June is here again. Only then can you choose between us. You don't know your own mind now, and I—I feel like someone who's playing an understudy." Yes, he thought, as he pictured a chorus line of all the women he had ever loved, she *was* an understudy to many others and all were interchangeable links in a chain that stretched from the time he could first remember seeing a feminine shape bending over his bed.

In September 1931 when Joe returned, Bertha simply said: "Henry, no more words of love. Joe has come back with a heart full of love." So their affair was over, and Henry realized that he was completely indifferent about losing Bertha. Now that the romance was over all he regretted was: that her thumbs had been too large, that she would not give him back his love letters even though he needed them for use in his book, and that like a dim-witted ass he had fucked himself out of a fine Monday night dinner—just for romance!

By this time, however, he had gotten a $12 a week job on the *Tribune* as a proofreader of stock exchange quotations. That was about double what he needed to live on in Paris. Never expert in economizing, however, he found no difficulty in spending his salary. As if getting ready for a new leap, he mopped up his earlier literary projects and shipped off all his completed stories and sketches to the literary agent Madeleine Boyd, who exhibited bracing confidence in him. Under the guidance of Michael Fraenkel who declared that *Crazy Cock* was "inexorably flat, sterile, insipid," and "smelled of the nineteenth century," Henry reduced the novel by half, down to 300 pages: this was like editing Dostoievski with a guillotine. He submitted the book to Edward Titus, who operated a little press—and Titus promptly lost the manuscript. (A pity. But Henry had plenty of earlier versions.) The important thing was that Henry underwent a fundamental intellectual reorientation, a profound change which was completed during the summer of 1931. Michael might say that he had recognized at last that he was dead. Kann might have seen his change as a visionary experience. But it was simpler, really. It was the—thoroughly groundless—hope that comes from the feeling that one has experienced the worst misery possible. Some years later Miller expressed the lesson he learned during this time when he advised Walker Winslow: "It's very good to get down to desperation—always works." Henry himself felt—and it was really a feeling, a subtle alteration in his relation to the world that he experienced, not an "idea"—that he no longer had any claims upon the world or the world upon him. He seemed to see the whole pattern of his life clearly laid out. Now he no longer bemoaned his bad fate. He was going toward his destiny—that was all. Had he been accused of the greatest crimes, he felt, he could have gladly answered: "Guilty! Guilty on all counts. Guilty in every possible way." Suddenly it seemed that his guilt and shame had fallen from him. He had believed that when June left him in 1927 or when he was forced to depart for Paris in 1930, he had hit bottom. Again, at Nanavati's he had felt the same. That really had been his nadir in misery. But his fall had been noisy, full of complaint—too full of an ego that had not yet been extinguished by despair. By late summer, 1931, he achieved the gift of numbness and indifference which made both hope and despair seem irrelevant. Now, very simply and very quietly he knew that he had reached zero as a value. The past and the future seemed alike: he had achieved nothing in the past, he hoped for nothing in the future. He had only wanted to write, he felt now, in order to avoid life. Now his delusions fell away, even his last delusion—that he was destined for acclaim as an author. Now that he had somehow discovered that he did live, the need to write no longer seemed so all-engrossing, and he realized that if he wished to do so he *could* write. But he was no longer *compelled* to write, he no longer needed to become the "romantic idol of America," to become famous, to make a commercial success. To write was—just to write—if it pleased him.

It was as simple as that. And out of that simple vision he began to think of a new book, not a novel like *Crazy Cock,* but as truthful an account as he could make it of his first year—a happy, irresponsible year—in Paris.

His life became simpler while he lived at the Hôtel Central and frequently saw Alfred Perlès, who lived in the same hotel. At eight o'clock every morning, he'd open the door of the next room, Fred's room, for a morning chat. Later he'd work steadily, but without the frenzy which had driven him at Osborn's, reading, taking notes, making out enormous charts, painting, and writing. He started what he called "an album of my Paris life," *la vie quotidienne,* with observations on Salavin, snatches of French songs, pen pictures of Les Halles, and imaginary interviews with "distinguished cunts." The paper he chose for the journal was stout enough to take a wash, and he mixed watercolors with literary improvisations. On off days he helped Fred to write features for the Port Edition of the *Herald Tribune.* Mostly they rewrote old articles from back numbers of the supplement; by imaginative rephrasing Henry and Fred turned out tourist articles on resorts that they had never seen, such as Split, Hvar, and Majorca.

But Henry didn't really feel much compulsion to work. Why labor when he could enjoy the view from his window overlooking the little park of the Place du Maine? French mammas came in the morning to sit on the wooden benches and watch their toddlers. Around noon the vagabonds and sandwichmen of the quarter took their places, eating a simple meal of bread and cheese and drinking their *vin ordinaire* from green bottles. Later, the whores patrolled the area from the park to the Boulevard Edgar-Quinet. He liked these girls, they were simple and business-like, and at five francs (the price of two packs of Gauloises Bleu), they had the distinction of being the cheapest prostitutes in Paris.

In the early afternoon, Henry usually went out scouting for someone to buy him a meal. Lots of people around Montparnasse recognized him: he had even been written up in Bald's "La Vie de Bohème" column. Bald wrote: "Henry Miller's study of a maquereau in 'Mademoiselle Claude' is unique." Americans who visited Paris and left came back to find Miller in the same haunts. "Still hanging on, old fellow?" they'd say and invite him to join their table. "What's been happening in Paris?" they all wanted to know, and he could easily keep up an entertaining patter through a late lunch, café crème, and a few drinks.

He might go back to the hotel and continue work afterwards, or meet a friend or two and sit about talking until evening and he had to go to work at the *Tribune.* Sometimes, on his way to work he'd cut through the Luxembourg Gardens, walk down the Rue de Seine, and cross the river to the Avenue de l'Opéra, passing the American Express, a route that he took from long familiarity—even though he had lost hope of hearing from June. Just as often he avoided the American Express office and winding his way across the river and through a tangle of streets, he'd emerge from the Rue Notre-Dame des Victoires into Rue Montmartre, with the big electric arrow pointing to the Folies Bergère, and make his way through the congestion of the Rue Lafayette to the offices of *Le Petit Journal* where the *Tribune* was produced. Before work he'd take his evening meal, often with Fred Perlès at Giolotte's, a lazy jovial place. Life seemed swift and easy and delightful, he shed his cares, and he felt like a boy again.

He and Fred perpetrated a wonderful hoax on Samuel Putnam in mid summer 1931. Putnam had accepted "'Mademoiselle Claude'," he said, "because I felt that it was a good expression of Montparnasse life in that era and of a prevalent type of expatriate—the Henry Miller type." But when Putnam decided to return to New York for July and August and to entrust the contents of the fall number of the *New Review* to Henry to see through the press, he didn't count on his running true to type and *actually* behaving like a mad artist. The material for that issue, Putnam reasoned, had already been collected, selected, and arranged. All that remained to be done was to keep the printer at his work, read proof, and make corrections in galleys. It was to be an especially good issue, with a contribution by Robert McAlmon which Putnam particularly valued. But just as soon as the editor was safely packed away on the boat train, the new assistant editor, Miller, and *his* assistant, Fred Perlès, went into action. No journal edited by them, they vowed, would have a story by McAlmon in it. McAlmon was chucked out. They tossed a few poems out and slashed some lines here and there from the ones that remained. Having made a start, they set out to revamp the remaining contents according to their own tastes. Henry's story, of course, remained. An article on Rilke by Fred went in. Henry added a few rhapsodic passages to it. *"I never read Rilke,"* he wrote to Schnellock. "But I think, after what I wrote, that he must be wonderful!"

They were just getting started. Everything seemed to be going along in such fine fashion it occurred to them to give the subscribers to the *New Review* a bonus by printing up a literary manifesto as a special free supplement to the regular number. When they got down to it, this statement parodied the kind of manifestoes that Parisian journals had announced in support of a score of *isms* over the last two decades. Henry and Fred announced "The New Instinctivism": "a proclamation of rebellion against the puerilities in art and and literature, a manifesto of disgust, a gob of spit in the cuspidor of postwar conceits, a healthy crap in the cradle of still-born deities." The essence of the New Instinctivism, they explained, was "nothing more *and nothing less* than being *for* or *against*—instinctively." There was to be nothing in between. In consequence, the mock-manifesto came out squarely against almost everything and for little else than the liberation of the "element of violence in man without which he ceases to be creative"; it supported the destruction of every civilizing influence strangling creativity. "The only thing that is important now is to rebel, to fight, to destroy. Anarchy? Yes, but not Anarchism . . . Are you tired of your wife? Fuck her! Are you weary of politics? Don't vote! Are you disgusted with your job? Throw it up! Whatever you want to do, do . . . and don't tip your hat first."

Twenty typed pages of "The New Instinctivism" went off to the printer with the new selections they had made for the magazine. Perhaps all this might have been printed without objection had they written their dogmatic proclamation in English, but about a third of the instinctivist bombast was in French, and some of it was libelous. A little concerned, especially since he was liable under French law, the printer sent the galleys to Putnam to check. It wasn't long before the inevitable cables flew from New York to Paris. Putnam had every right to be angry—instinctively and otherwise. But in fact, he took a rather conciliatory tone, speaking of "misunderstanding" and "regret." Doubtless the two instinctivist authors were *against* Putnam, for he killed their manifesto in galleys. This was not unfitting, however, since, after all, they had also expressly announced their thorough-going opposition to the movement called "The New Instinctivism."

Seven

Happier Days—And Newer Disasters

Henry continued to help Bald with his column. In early September 1931 after receiving a long awaited telegram from June, Henry gave Wambly a paragraph of considerably more interest to himself than to Bald's readers: "June Mansfield will be back in a couple of weeks . . . When she left she said she wanted to start her novel, *Happier Days.* In New York, June ran a Bohemian hell-hole called the Fire Bird. It had a Stravinsky setting. The decor was executed by Jean Kronski, one of her friends . . . ."

The undertone of satiric bitterness in these observations marked the distance Henry had come during the year. To his surprise, he found that he was not, after all, so terribly happy about the prospect of June's return. Even before June's arrival he began building up his defenses against her, reminding himself of her disturbing behavior, particularly of the pain she had given him in her association with Jean. He wanted her but he was rejecting her in advance. And so he was at loose ends, not even sure when she would arrive, knowing only that in her usual peremptory way she had cabled out of the blue that she was taking the first available boat to join him. Though he could never get used to them he knew June's habits. Very likely, he realized, he would not hear from her again until she showed up on his doorstep or tapped him on the shoulder as he sipped a Pernod in the Coupole.

He didn't work much, only paraded about like a cadet waiting for the battle to begin. On a Saturday night in late September he went to Princess

Lieven's studio to watch Helba Huara perform Incan dances. These excited him so much he decided to write about them before retiring. But first he drifted over to the Dôme to wait for Bald to come along and buy him a drink. Wambly didn't show up at once, but it wasn't long before a group of youngsters invited him to their table. He was disgusted with their unfavorable remarks about France and the *New Review,* and he had left them when he spotted two prostitutes hanging about the corner; one of them he particularly liked. It was easy to strike up a conversation, they were sociable and not pushing him, and eventually he made a date with the nicer one for later in the evening. He proceeded back to the tables and had hardly gotten seated when a stranger came up in back of him and tapped him on the shoulder. "June's sitting over there," he said.

For a moment he was confused. Why had she sent an emissary to him instead of rushing over to him herself? Why, when he was preparing an offensive against her, did she immediately put him on the defensive, as if he had to pay her court? How long had she been watching him? Why hadn't she come, thrown her arms around him, and kissed him simply and affectionately?

When he turned to her he shuddered. She looked like a corpse. She had lost weight and all the lush roundness of her figure had turned sharp and angular. Her eyes burned. She looked perverse, strange, unworldly. Her face was whitened like a clown's. She seemed to be unable to move, except dreamily, zombie-like, feverishly. Had she been reading Fraenkel's *Werther's Younger Brother?* Should he walk up to her and say, as Michael would have done, "You have died?"

Before he knew it, however, he was beside her. He took her in his arms, feeling her thin body beneath her coat and listening to her speaking hectically, uncontrollably—he couldn't understand what she was saying, hearing only words like "privation" and "suffering." As he drew her close to him, he looked over her shoulder and saw the effeminate stranger standing behind her, leering demoniacally. He looked like a painted puppet—a living Bruga. Henry felt tenderly protective. He felt that now she had been restored to him by a miracle and that he should rescue her from her perversions and delusions. He felt that he wanted to smash her false gods. He wanted to be her God again. He rejoiced that she sank into his arms, babbling about how much she had missed him.

These feelings dissipated bit by bit. As they were about to leave the Dôme, Bald came up. He said he had been looking everywhere to inform Henry that his wife had been in Paris for some time. Yes, June admitted,

she had arrived more than thirty-six hours before. So, she had been in the
city all the previous day: while he had been eating dinner at the Closerie des
Lilas with Fraenkel, while he had gone over to visit the Schranks, engaging
in a meaningless conversation about poisons. It burned him up that she
hadn't found him. He was annoyed, besides, that she sent a messenger to
him instead of rushing to him herself. And he felt deceived in his urge to
protect her.

He accompanied June to her room in the Hôtel Princesse with its garish
red wallpaper, and there, amid the disorder of her wardrobe, on the bed lay
Count Bruga. Bruga!—hadn't he put that monster to its final rest in *Crazy
Cock,* recently finished? Hadn't June gotten over Jean Kronski yet? Bruga,
the ghoulish symbol of Jean, still haunted him, recalling his defeats in the
Henry Street hell. "Until Bruga is destroyed," he now said to June, "there
will never be peace between us." But he felt that the fact that she had
brought this puppet with her had spoiled and soiled everything about their
reunion.

This time the harrowing battles started almost at once. Everything she
did and said annoyed him, most of all her inability to enjoy anything
simple. "She spoke cryptically even about the simplest things," Lillian
Lowenfels thought. The truth was plain enough. A part of June's spirit had
died: she had lost heart in Clinton or Remsen or Henry Street, or in the
miserable furnished room on Hancock Street when he was writing for
Snappy Stories; her hopes had been blasted in Asheville; her fantasies had
been wasted in a beautiful garden in Monte Carlo. And in place of her heart
a hard shell had grown which gave the appearance of life. Perhaps it had
been all his fault. He had asked her to bear too much. His greatest crime
was in resting all his faith and trust on her; for no one could bear such a
burden. He turned his wife to stone by making a goddess out of her. The
hero of *Crazy Cock,* Tony Bring, had called his wife "his vulture." Yes, June
wanted to eat the marrow out of his new life because he had turned her into
one of the living dead. She had returned to Paris to accuse him of crimes
against her. She intimated that she knew he was mixed up with another
woman: she was in possession of "certain facts" about a "particular person."
(June always spoke as if she were in a Russian novel.) He thought at first
that she had read "Mademoiselle Claude" and was annoyed at his confession
that he liked whores. She denied this. (Actually, it turned out that she
wanted to meet Germaine and Claude, get to know them.) Had she guessed
at his affair with Bertha? Had Osman told her anything? Or, more likely,
had a female friend of the Schranks who had returned to New York a few

days before June's departure for Paris given the game away? (June volunteered that she had in fact talked to Cherie over the phone.) He stood half undressed in her room while June berated him and Count Bruga seemed to leer in triumph. Previously, he would have pushed everything else aside to occupy himself exclusively with June, even if only to quarrel. But the distance which his own transformation put between them kept him from becoming wholly a slave to sullen debate. The real June seemed like an anachronism. He had "fixed" her, like a specimen, in *Crazy Cock*.

And besides, he had started to write another book about himself and June, an autobiographical account of his first year in Paris ending with June's first visit. The idea had come to him during the month while he was living with Fraenkel in the Villa Seurat. This was the book that would eventually be called *Tropic of Cancer*, of course. By the fall of 1931 he had just gotten started and only a few pages had actually been written. Yet the book seemed to know where it was going. It was a book of vision beginning exactly where his visionary experiences had begun: "I am living in the Villa Seurat, the guest of Michael Fraenkel. There is not a crumb of dirt anywhere, nor a chair misplaced. We are all alone here and we are dead." He was writing of his vision, not composing a novel—that was clear to him—and that was why the real names were called for. He did not know what the title would be, but he believed that he would sign the book "Anonymous": he was the anonymous observer of the truth of other people's deaths. Such a book, he knew, must be "a libel, slander, defamation of character," and he intended to go the whole way. To prevent any falsification he made a silent compact with himself not to change a single line or to attempt to polish or perfect his style or thoughts. For he was not writing literature, and any attempt to embellish his vision through form could only weaken it. Very early, then, he was intent upon using the method of automatic writing and such forms as the letter, the journal, the diary, and the doodle, which did not allow for the accustomed kinds of literary perfection. He was bound to run into trouble. After completing the first half dozen pages, Henry showed the manuscript to Fraenkel. His objection was immediate and straightforward: he did not want Henry to use his real name. All right, he told Michael, that could certainly be altered. But he had no intention of making any such alteration. He swore in his journal that if necessary, he would delude even his teacher, Fraenkel.

June was annoyed by the same few pages and by what he told her of his plans for the rest, especially about her part in the book, like the scene with the bugs in her hair. She didn't at all favor his idea of telling the truth about his bohemian experiences during his first year in Paris: that would let everyone know she was married to a bum. Henry counterattacked, saying that he found the humble girls of the Paris streets more appealing, more womanly, than any American female. Did June suppose that because women in New York worked for a living and had learned to swear like men and fuck whomever they pleased, they should be worshipped? Was she herself feminine because she employed feminine wiles cunningly to get whatever she wanted, bamboozling this sucker and flimflamming that one? "I want you to know," he told her, "what it is to live, to be just man and woman, without any address if needs be, without rouge or lipstick, without a mink coat."

After such unfavorable reactions to his new book by Michael and June he was somewhat hesitant about sending the early pages to a young married woman writer whom he had met through Osborn. This was Anaïs Guiler, whose husband, Hugo, was an official in Dick's bank—he was Osborn's boss, in fact. Dick had been telling Henry marvellous tales about the young woman. He first engaged Henry's interest by showing him an article she had written on D.H. Lawrence, under her maiden name, Anaïs Nin. The article, Henry thought, was fine except for its idealization of Lawrence. Lawrence—Lowenfels and Fraenkel were full of him and that had made Henry rebel against him. Still, it excited Henry to think of a young woman writing in praise of *Lady Chatterley's Lover,* a book still banned for sale outside France. She herself, to hear Osborn tell it, was beautiful—and a figure of mystery. Her father was the Spanish pianist and composer Joacquin Nin; he and the Danish singer Rosa Culmell met in Cuba and married. Born in France in Neuilly, in February 1903, their daughter had a proper Spanish Catholic name, Juana Edelmira Antolina Rosa Nin Y Castellano; but from the first her parents called her by the Greek name Anaïs. As a child she had been taken all about Europe. Her parents separated when the girl was eleven and she was taken by her mother to New York City. Extremely bright and with a highly developed verbal capacity, she learned English and soon started a hopeless plan to read her way alphabetically through the books in one of the local branches of the New York Public Library.

At about the same time, this precocious girl began to keep a diary which she addressed to the father whom she felt had abandoned her. At first she wrote this work in French, but later she shifted to English. Though subsequently she moved back to France with her family, the American experience had struck deep, linguistically at least, and she continued to write and to do most of her reading in English. Indeed, she had completed a

book of literary criticism and appreciation, *D.H. Lawrence: An Unprofes-
sional Study,* soon to be published by Edward Titus' Black Manikin Press,
the very same publisher who Henry was hoping would bring out *Crazy
Cock.*

Her sympathy for Lawrence gave Henry some hope that she would not be
offended by his freedom of expression when he nervously accepted an
invitation to dine at the Guiler's house at Louveciennes, a town lying to the
west of Paris. The forty-five minute train ride set him up. It was not unlike
an elevated excursion to an outlying district of New York—like a ride to
Bergen Beach. Everything seemed slightly touched by the extraordinary
and mythical. The station, where a chauffeur was awaiting his arrival, was
hidden by big fine spruce trees. The railroad bistro and café looked like
subjects from Vlaminck or Utrillo oils. Louveciennes had been built by the
Romans in the fourth century, and though few evidences of their presence
remained, the spell of the antique was certainly prevalent in the high,
crumbling, ivy-cascaded limestone walls beside which the road to the house
at 2 bis, Rue de Monbuisson went. The house which the Guilers occupied
was a subsidiary building on the estate of the legendary Madame DuBarry.

The villa had a romantic setting. The garden had been allowed to grow a
little wild as if the life there was too primitive to be entirely civilized. This
effect, like all the others connected with Anaïs, was carefully calculated: the
filigreed bronze Arabian lamp which hung above the entrance was designed
to give a romantically Moorish effect to the threshold and to confer a soft
pink glow to the faces of those who passed under it. The interior was
Moorish, its disorder took form as the release of the imagination upon stone
and wood. On the apricot and peach-blossom walls astrologic charts, exotic
pictures, and beaten copper ornaments hung in the shadows of violet-blue
lamps. On tables stood bowls filled with curious stones. The carved wood
bookcases were painted black, and the merest glance at them showed that
they were filled with volumes in German, French, Spanish, and English—
everything written on William Blake, anything that touched upon
psychoanalysis, sumptuous albums of the great painters. The effect of the
whole was of a jewel box.

But the woman herself, Anaïs, was obviously its chief treasure. Henry
compared her beauty to two movie stars—Marcelle Chantal in *L'Ordonnance*
or Miriam Hopkins in *Haute Pègre*: all three women had the same sort of
lustrous hair; the same kind of burning eyes; the same fine network of facial
bones, delicate yet strong as steel wires; the same oval shaped face. Even an
Osborn could see that. But she also had, Henry felt, many qualities which

Dick missed: the beauty of the European woman, depths that lay just below the surface, a tragic tone, an energy playing against her exquisite costume, an elegantly tranquil sway, as if her fully composed poise were finally a mask for full-blooded vulnerability. Her depths were evident in her conversation: how different from June's cheap remarks on *Lady Chatterley's Lover* was her appreciation of Lawrence.

Though inwardly Henry and Anaïs were really more alike than anyone could guess, at the time that they met they were like an actor and actress assigned the task of creating totally different characters. By the inclination of her exquisite personality as well as by her position as the young wife of a bank vice-President, Anaïs was assigned the role of the refined woman. Henry was playing the part of the Great American Hobo Artist, which Edmund Wilson would later call "the Henry Miller type." A portrait of Miller as a happy, slightly mad vagabond of the Paris streets had recently appeared in Wambly Bald's column. " 'Montparnasse is a great place [says Miller]. Everyone likes to help a fellow who is broke. A couple of days ago, a girl I hardly knew stopped me on the street. I told her about my status, so she took me home with her and sewed a couple of buttons on my coat and trousers. People are swell, do you see what I mean? They worry about you.' " Henry was, the portrait concluded, "a legitimate child of Montparnasse, the salt of the Quarter. He represents the classic color that has not faded since Mürger and other optimists." Accompanying the column was a caricature of "Henry Val Miller" done by Brassai, showing him looking unshaven and a little seedy, but wearing his slouch hat at a rakish angle as he sits at a café table clutching a glass while an opened bottle of wine chills. A pen is stuck in his coat pocket and a copy of the *New Review* lies unopened beside the wine. Henry wrote the column himself and it reflected the view which he wished others to have of him. But he was bigger than the role he was playing. And Anaïs Nin Guiler was deeper than the role she had been assigned. Anaïs's husband was quiet, even a little boyish, but to Henry's eyes he seemed to lack any inner passion for life. Henry could find no common ground with her cousin, Eduardo, whose passions were astrologic, medieval, and monkish. Nor was there any point of reference in his own experience by which he could come to grips with the exotic setting which Anaïs had so conspicuously made for herself. Nevertheless, by the time the evening drew to a close she had mentioned her diary, as if that might be a bond between them, and he had responded by promising to send her the opening pages of his autobiographical novel. That night, as he waited at the station to return to Paris, he looked out at the surrounding country and saw the Seine moving silently below him and beyond that the wonderful twinkling lights of Paris. And whether he knew it consciously or not his life had been altered.

June, with her incredible instincts, was angry when he arrived at the Select where she and Osborn sat out the evening waiting for him. Dick had undoubtedly been regaling her with stories of Anaïs and when Henry was uncharacteristically quiet about his dinner she was immediately suspicious. June frankly cast all relations in sexual terms, and she had urged Henry to go alone to Louveciennes so that he would not be hampered by the competition of two women. But she had by no means expected him to be as affected as he obviously was, and right there in the café she let him know that he had better not be thinking of two-timing her with this married woman. When a second invitation to dinner at the Guilers arrived at Henry's door, June did not refuse to go. If a sexual contest was to be waged with Henry as the prize, June would be prepared. Anticipating Anaïs's polished elegance, she dressed in her most outrageously bohemian finery; a red velvet dress, her heavy cape, and a dirty fedora. Henry could see what was likely to follow, and as they left their hotel he warned her to watch her language, a remark not calculated to allay June's suspicions.

He was, however, watching his own language. He had delayed showing Anaïs his autobiographical writing, fearing that his new book might be a little strong and reveal him to be a crude barbarian with a dirty mind. But he had underestimated the flexibility and versatility of the young woman's mind. She was as fascinated by the crudities of life as by life's perfume, and certainly she was interested in strangeness, whatever forms it took. Even June, who must have surprised her, was swallowed whole. Indeed, to her own astonishment, June soon found Anaïs courting *her*. This perplexed her and made her suspicious at the same time that she found herself liking her rival very much indeed. Eventually, June dropped most of her reservations and began to return the compliment by wooing Anaïs as she had Jean, giving her little gifts and even telling her secrets about Henry—exposing her husband to ridicule in order to win the affections of her rival. In a sense June became part of the silent compact which had been made between Anaïs and Henry; Anaïs used June, a woman who held Henry in an invisible vise, in order to understand Henry's deepest secrets.

At the same time, Henry was pulling out of June's hold. He was no longer June's puppet, Tony Bring. That broken, miserable hero of *Crazy Cock* and the Henry of 1931 exhibited the same scars, but Henry's no longer bled. All fall Henry waged a battle for supremacy over June, with Osborn and Perlès aiding him against her. He used *Crazy Cock*—a book which June disliked intensely—to show up her weaknesses, she complained. By late November he was convinced that June had probably come to Paris so suddenly because she had some intimations of unfaithfulness on his part, was sick of her life with him, regarded him as a poor sap, and wanted to get rid of him. She came to castigate him for his sins, to crush him like a poor worm, and then leave him for good. But when she found him healthy, she wavered: she desired to bend him once again to slavish adoration before abandoning him; and this, which had once been so easy, was precisely what she now found difficult to accomplish. Even her most telling tactic— accusing him of being so tied to his mother that he couldn't understand a real woman—didn't work. The climax to their skirmishes occurred on Christmas Eve 1931 in the Hôtel Princesse when she made him confess his infidelities. She informed him that in a matter of days she would return to New York and probably divorce him there. She simply couldn't forgive him for his adoration of Bertha, in whom she saw too much of herself. "I'll never marry any one again," she screamed. "No one is good enough for me, no one appreciates all the sacrifices I'm willing to make. No, I won't go near a man even—except when I get so hot I can't hold back. And then I'll fuck anyone and everyone. I'll do the choosing. I'll just tell them I want a good fuck." She said this ferociously with a cold glint in her eyes, like a bayonet flashing out of the dark— straight for the heart.

Eight

Walled In

June's capacity for argument was inexhaustible. She could have criticized Henry all winter long—if he had been ready to take his punishment in Paris. However, he had managed to land a job in Dijon, a place that in June's view was uninhabitable, and so in early January 1932 she debarked for New York as he prepared to go to the mustard capital of the world. Beginning with the new term, he would assume the position of *répétiteur d'anglais,* assistant in English, at the Lycée Carnot, a French preparatory school. When all of his other efforts to get a job of some sort had failed, Hugh Guiler had recommended him to Dr. Krans of the American University Union, who in turn arranged for him to assume this exchange position usually reserved for younger Americans engaged in advanced university studies of French. Both Krans and Monsieur Declos of the Office Nationale des Universités Françaises, warned Henry that the lycée had a "Spartan regime" which defeated the expectations of the previous two English instructors. Both were unclear about the rate of compensation, but by the time June left his nerves were terribly frayed and he was looking forward to Dijon as a consumptive looks to Switzerland, as a restorative. Besides, in a longer view he dreamed of a permanent place where he could work quietly. He assumed that at the Lycée Carnot he would earn a salary of about 500 francs a month in addition to bed and board. This meant (he figured to himself, ignoring all obstacles) that soon he could save enough to pay off his debts, to continue on to Spain, and perhaps even make a place in Spain for himself and June. Only a few days before he left for Dijon he wrote to Joe O'Regan: "The world is cracking. We're going to fall back into the Dark Ages." He was looking for a haven from catastrophe.

But his first view of Dijon made him wish to fly back to Paris: better the Dark Ages than the Ice Age. Blanketed by a thick fog, its streets crusted with frozen snow and its elms roped with frost, Dijon was not the glamorous old summer city through which he had bicycled in the summer of 1928 with June. The school had a mean "barrack-room" atmosphere. His introduction to the school gave him intimations about the petty, miserable life to which the position condemned him. Leaving his luggage at the station, he located the lycée buildings and applied at the gate for admission. He was met by a half-wit and led to the office of Monsieur le Censeur. With his whining tone of high authority, his icy confinement to the business at hand, his shiny frock coat, and his wig, this personage seemed a caricature of a French schoolmaster. After a formal discourse on Henry's responsibilities, he passed him on to Monsieur l'Économe. This dreary looking person had another bourgeois sermon all prepared, and he delivered this nonsense as if reading from tablets of gold. The Chef des Garçons, looking like the dwarf in Hamsun's *Mysteries,* fetched him and delivered a panegyric on the school's regulations. Then he turned Henry over to a servant with a wooden leg who accompanied Henry to the station to pick up his luggage. After a good deal of huffing and puffing this fellow ushered Henry into his room, gave him a quick lesson (in obscure French) on how to light his stove and how to conserve wood; told him where to wash, where to eat, when to appear for work. Everything seemed as regulated as a clock and everything was doled out to the last pinch.

That first night Henry managed to get his stove going, but it went out before morning and he awoke to a frigid dawn in a morgue-like cell. This was worse than Monsieur Robert's office in the Rue de Vanves. He pulled the thin covers over his head. A bell struck six sharply like ice ringing on ice, sending shivers through Henry: it had exactly the same dismal tone as the cemetery bell which sounded everytime a hearse passed through the gates at the Cemetery Montparnasse. How often had he heard that when he had lived with Kann on the Rue Froideveaux, right next to the graveyard. To arise from bed in such a deadly atmosphere prepared him to feel that the people, the houses, the quality of mind, the dining hall, manners— everything was frozen, congealed into misery and stupidity. In his classes he railed against the school and tried to infect the students and surveillants with the spirit of rebellion. Downfall and disaster were his themes; Spengler provided him with examples. Besides, evidences of decline were obvious in Dijon, a once noble city.

However, the work wasn't arduous, involving only nine hours of tutorials each week. On his first day, as he lounged beside the stove smoking, he turned the lesson in English conversation into a discussion (adapted from Gourmont) of the physiology of the elephant's sex life. The boys perked up—this certainly was an improvement over "John Gilpin's Ride," the bumpty-bump ballad which the English professor had been trying to get them to memorize. With none of the insistence upon social difference which a Frenchman in his place would have relished, Henry soon made friends with the assistants and the students. It astonished them when he revealed that he, an American, loved France, old France in particular, better than his own country, and that he preferred wines to gin, Rabelais to Sinclair Lewis, Proust to Jack London. They were surprised to see that he knew Paris more intimately than any Frenchman at the school; was eager to make a first-hand inspection of Dijon's bordellos on the Rue Philibert Papillon; and could sing dirty songs in tune and dance in step at the Brasserie Miroir, where the tunes of Massenet and Rudolph were sentimentally rendered by a French cabaret orchestra.

The biggest drawback was that the job carried no stipend beyond bed and board. "The difference between that little pittance and no pittance is that difference between life and death," he wrote to Osborn. Naturally, he appealed to Declos and Krans. Once, Henry had begged his friends not to abandon him to a bohemian world. Later, under Fraenkel's influence, he had vowed to be an Anonymous Artist. Now, however, he was sunk into the fat of French bourgeois school life and threatened with the anonymity of a schoolmaster marooned in the provinces. This terrified him and he sent out appeals to all and sundry. By the time that the answers to his initial squawks for aid arrived from his friends in Paris, some of his terror had abated and he was prepared to stick things out until March when the sun and his Easter vacation were both supposed to arrive. The Guilers were particularly helpful. First a letter arrived from Hugo giving instructions on channels through which to appeal for a stipend. The next day both a telegram and a letter containing money came from Anaïs. The first assured him of their willingness to aid and the second invited him to take up residence in their villa should he be obliged to leave the lycée. He said in reply that he believed their very interest itself would sustain him. Besides, he went on rather ebulliently, his French was improving in leaps: he had gobbled up *Vol de Nuit* as well as the most recent issue of *La Nouvelle Revue*

Francaise and was taking Proust in large doses. Albertine, he told Anaïs, fascinated him, reminding him as she did of June. By now "June" had almost become a secret code, a password, a bond, between them; he traded his notes on "The Mansfield Woman" for Anaïs's diary observations on June. Each confessed an intention to write a novel involving June.

At Dijon Henry wrote little besides letters, but he had a superabundance of time to reflect upon Albertine, June, Proust, Dostoievski, and a thousand other themes.

His mind seemed to be so bursting with ideas, he told Anaïs, even five isolated minutes of his thoughts would be worth a book. Though she failed to sell any of the pieces he submitted, his agent in New York urged him to attempt a "modern Trilby." Stupid as Henry thought this idea, he reread Du Maurier's novel with a good deal of pleasure. Perhaps he thought, an oblique satire on *Trilby* could fit into his autobiographical book. Most of his thinking, however, was going into other projects. Anaïs pronounced *Moloch* publishable if he could cut the 300 page manuscript in half, and he agreed to follow her suggestions for deletions. Even if only a hundred good pages remained after her surgery, the result would be, he said, "French proportions"—in the tradition of Flaubert instead of Dreiser. "I think that I would agree with you on whatever you wanted to cut," he wrote from Dijon. "And after you get through with it I believe I would have sufficient enthusiasm to make further revisions myself." He objected only to her complaints about the effect of hypersexuality in his presentation of all his unsatisfying love affairs. Henry responded vigorously. He contended that he had no more than a normal interest in love, pointing out that when many years of romance were concentrated in one book the effect was bound to be exaggerated. Most of his love affairs, he implied, were not as important in actuality as they were in their effects upon his own sensibility. Cora, for instance, had turned out to be "a wet rag. . . . But when I dream of her, as I sometimes do, she is magnificent." However, as he said to Anaïs, Cora could go if it saved the novel. Secretly, however, both of them knew that the book was not worth all this labor, and *Moloch* peacefully expired.

He took up *Crazy Cock* next, and suddenly he understood what it was all of his friends had criticized in the novel. Even Perlès, usually so mild and kind, had disliked the book so much that one day in the summer of 1931 he had quite literally taken sheafs of it and torn them apart. More gently than Fred, Anaïs pointed to its major literary defect—that the husband in the book, though *said* to be an interesting character, an impulsive lover, a writer, an adventurer, was palely rendered. Jean Kronski and June were done with bold, emphatic strokes, but Tony Bring was a bloodless abstraction, a mere observer who speaks of his suffering but never makes the reader feel it. "I couldn't find you," she told Henry. "I would only see a man who was telling a story." Henry was attached to the book through its deep personal meanings, but even he was at last obliged to agree that it was hardly more than an exhibition of "le spleen anglais." He had plotted and planned the novel down to its last comma, but his elaborate preparations had suffocated his imagination. At last he himself wrote off *Crazy Cock* in a notebook entry which condemned it as an expression of "the vilest crap that ever was." He turned to a list of twenty-six articles—mostly in letters to Emil or as remnants of the old Paris book—which he might be able to sell, including "The Last Man of Europe," "Toilets on the Left Bank and Elsewhere," and "From My Paris Window." "The New Instinctivism" was posted to Emil in the hopes that he or George Buzby, editor of *USA,* might be able to sell it for its "smut value." "It's meant to be humorous, you know," he remarked somewhat dubiously.

So at Dijon he marked time and prepared for a big push. The stipend never came through, the cold never abated, and his loneliness increased. When Perlès telegraphed in late February that he had been authorized by the editor to offer Henry a permanent job on the *Tribune* as assistant finance editor at the salary of 1200 francs a month for working 8:30 p.m. to 1:00 a.m. everyday—with the likelihood of an increase—the Dijon winter and his isolation had become thoroughly intolerable, and he leaped at the chance. His students gave him a sendoff. He rejected their first plan—to carry him to the station in an open barouche—but as he was leaving they gathered around him in the hall, raised their voices in the chorus of an obscene French song, and gave him three cheers. "See you in Paris at Easter!" they shouted. He felt strange and elated to realize that if these French boys did show up in Paris, he, an American, would have to show them around.

Immediately upon arriving in the capital he went straight to the Hôtel Central to join Perlès. It was as if everything had been planned for his homecoming. Fred opened the door, stark naked. Out of the room drifted an odor of life, concocted of wine, ink, semen, cheese, women, and bread. There was little Alf beaming in the midst of all this abundance, with a joyous welcome on his lips and a "distinguished cunt" in his bed.

Having made his leap over the walls at Dijon, Henry was ready to break out of the strait jacket of literary self-deception as exemplified in his first two novels. He was no longer willing to write "mere literature" in the conventional sense. He came slowly to his new book with the wise instinct that it was too important to hurry.

Nine

The Last Book

The new book. The first book. In dismissing *Crazy Cock*, Fraenkel had urged him: "Write as you talk. Write as you live. Write as you feel and think. Just sit down before the machine and let go . . . Evacuate the trenches!" That was good advice and Henry followed it. He decided to find out how he did live and think and feel. Inspired now by the mere existence of Anaïs's *Journal intime* (which he had not yet read in its entirety), and accepting the logic of the confessional impulse from which her book had sprung, he decided to compose his own autobiography as a diary. He called it "The Last Book." Later he called it "The Tropic of Capricorn" and finally *The Tropic of Cancer*.

Probably to conserve paper, but with a nice gesture of dismissal for his previous work, he turned over the sheets of his original Tony Bring manuscript and rolled the clean side upward into the typewriter. Osborn was on his mind, and he began the logbook of his desperate life with the story of Osborn, himself, and Irene, the Russian princess. This was an account of a woman who lived with them and preyed on the two of them, especially upon Dick, while assuring them of the truth of the most outlandish tales of her past and keeping them away from her by claiming that she had a dose.

At once the line between fiction and reportage broke down. Whatever Henry said was true *was* true, at least for that moment. The only rule that remained was the drive to digress. Soon, everything was going into the diary, all the stories of his Paris years. "It's like a big, public garbage can," he wrote to Ned Schnellock. "Only the mangy cats are missing. But I'll get them in yet." In they went. He pillaged his notebooks for additional material, observations, quotations, questions. Some he even pasted in, along with newspaper clippings and menus. A description of Wambly Bald's room went in along with a catalogue of the labels and brand names of the liquors from which Bald distilled his column. One day while he was writing, the voice of a woman singing "Never wanted to . . . What am I to do?" drifted into his room. The song and her rich, dark voice went into the book. He wrote to Bertha, hoping to put some of his love letters in the book. They didn't go in: she replied that on the day that his actions had ceased to correspond with his words she had destroyed his letters. *The bitch,* he growled as he castigated her in his diary. From "Bezeque" he extracted the story of the prostitute with the dying mother. The Cirque Medrano was revisited. That went in. George Grosz's paintings, as well as Grosz's and Spengler's ideas about "the late-city man," were inserted. Herbert Wilkie of Valier, Montana, and Marseilles appeared, a "confessed pederast." Nanavati, Eugene, Fred, Germaine, Putnam, Zadkine, Claude, Fraenkel, and Lowenfels appeared, each pursuing his own identity, illumined by his own mania. The higher mathematics of the gospel of death were formularized. The whole Dijon episode was spun out with high humor. For good seasoning, Papini, Duhamel's *Salavin,* Rabelais, Proust, Whitman, Annie Besant's *The Ancient Wisdom,* and Keyserling's *Creative Understanding* were stirred in. Henry had given up any desire to defend himself. Defenseless, his single motto now was *fais ce que voudras:* do anything—so long as it yields ecstasy.

Certainly, there were many presences here, but Miller was finding his own voice among theirs as he pounded his typewriter in the Hôtel Central in a room next to Fred's. He radiated the excitement of his self-discovery. In those days, as Perlès has beautifully said, his friends walked in his shadow, "and even his shadow was warm." He expanded in every direction: everything he did took on a new dimension. He was up every morning at six. With mountains of books piled high on his worktable, enormous charts tacked to he walls, Beethoven or jazz or an African laughing record blaring at full volume from the victrola (a present from Anaïs), his typewriter racing over the speed limit, the gargantuan became commonplace and it almost seemed as if the tiny hotel room could not contain him.

As a matter of practical fact, it was obvious to Henry and Fred that they would save money and live more pleasantly by renting an apartment together; not only would they be able to divide the rent, they would be able to prepare their own meals, as they could not do in the hotel. Fred's affections settled upon a flat in a recently built row of apartment buildings at 4 Avenue Anatole France in Clichy, just on the outskirts of Paris. It did not particularly appeal to Henry for it was like being transported back 3,000 miles and twenty years to the apartment rows put up above Central Park. Henry would have preferred a studio or grand, old-fashioned Parisian hotel apartment. At the Clichy place the look was functional modern, the architecture was undistinguished; the interiors were plain and angular, unmarked by time or human use. Much as in some tough areas of New York, there was a spot on the way to the apartment that was dangerous to cross at night, along the junkyards between the Porte Clichy, with its trolley terminals and garages, and the beginning of Clichy itself. But the kitchen and bathroom decided the issue: to Fred's eyes these were glorious. The fixtures were new, the faucets didn't drip, the toilet seat was intact, and the bowl didn't run all night. In addition, there were two bedrooms separated by a hallway, which made it possible for Henry and Fred to come and go quite separately or entertain friends privately. (Fred had a young woman named Paulette living with him.)

The French would have said that Henry had at last established a *domicile fixe*. But after years of transience Henry could not dare to call the Clichy flat more than "pseudo-permanent." For Fred, so long relegated to the shabby and second hand, the bourgeois modernity of the place was marvellous. For Henry it was a simple financial arrangement, based on the fact that the rent was far below ordinary hotel rates. At 5,100 francs plus the tax at the end of the year, they could afford to agree that if either one lost his job the other would support him.

Before the middle of March 1932 they moved their few belongings into Avenue Anatole France. Henry, of course, promptly lost his job—though not directly as the result of any calculation of his own. As early as the second of March, the accounting office at the *Tribune* had asked him to put his Work Permit on file. Since arriving in Paris he had never registered for employment. Now, when he did so, he was refused a permit. For this reason, before the middle of March he received a notice of termination from the *Tribune* and two weeks later, on the twenty-fifth, his dismissal came in a letter from Jules Frantz, the managing editor. When Henry accused Jules of injustice—for there were a number of Americans who were working at the *Tribune* without permits—Frantz hung his head and muttered some excuses about "economy" and promised to allow Henry to go downstairs as a proofreader again for the vacation period. But though he excoriated Frantz, in truth Henry was secretly gratified. Again, he told himself, he owed his salvation to the French. Nothing, he felt, could be lower than the depths to which he had fallen at Nanavati's or the Cinéma Vanves so how could he concern himself over the mere loss of a newspaper job? Everything that happened was exactly what was meant to happen. To convert defeats into triumphs—that was as much as he could ask. For the first time, Henry was thoroughly convinced that he had lived out his fate and had a destiny to fulfill.

Besides, he was working at such a pace now that the extra four and a half hours that he had gained by his dismissal from the paper were put to immediate and good use. He was so full of energy that he hardly seemed to need sleep—no more than five hours. He slept, he claimed, only for the pleasure of dreaming. He dreamed constantly: of the books he would read (loaned by Anaïs or filched from the American library), of the watercolors he would make (influenced by Klee, Chagall, and Picasso), and, above all, of the books he would write. There was a depression all over the world; literary men, like the economy, had diminished expectations. Miller was one of the few American writers who by 1932 still preserved the grandiloquent hope of the twenties: to compose works as great as any that had ever been written. Many others wanted only to compose something "proletarian," something superior to Gorki. Henry was ready to take on the *Iliad,* Rabelais, Joyce, Proust—and the Holy Ghost, if need be. At this moment he was sure about his destiny. He *had* to write a certain number of pages each day, he told Alf, "for the sake of posterity."

Now he arranged his life like pieces on a chess board—in little ordered graduated rows, so much space for everything and everything having a place. He lived as he had wished to live in Remsen Street (without the disorder introduced by June), a simple, bare, Japanese life. Each morning he arose, washed thoroughly and straightened up after himself, raised the curtains, and, though naked, inspected the doings in the courtyard, then dressed and made his bed. His Teutonic habits of orderliness prevailed until the matter of work came up—then he'd explode. Sometimes as he began to prepare his morning meal he'd notice a book he had left unfinished the night before. Then he'd forget breakfast altogether. Instead of clearing a place for his plate, he'd pick up an enormous tome by Rank, Jung, or Keyserling and start in reading. This was a promising sign. Soon there'd be a pencil in his hand and he'd be annotating the margins, at first sparsely, then copiously. From that stage to the next required only a jump to the typewriter, usually to copy out a particularly meaty passage. Then he'd toss the book aside in order to start right into squeezing the juices out of it, possibly in a letter to Emil or Anaïs. By now his fingers would be flying over the keys, as if he had leaped with hardly a transition from the "Moonlight Sonata" to the "Minute Waltz." He went like lightning once he turned to work on his novel. The associations that had begun in his reading would accumulate and bubble into new blendings which went far beyond their origin. Those were the days when writing was as easy as singing—no wonder that even as he was typing he'd occasionally burst into song. Ten or more sheets might easily roll in and out of his typewriter before he was ready, having missed breakfast, to stop for lunch. He didn't worry any more about losing an idea. For the first time in his life, to begin writing seemed no harder than turning on a tap. Like running water, the stream of recollections, words, and ideas was always there—he had only to turn on the faucet to have the flow begin or snap it off to give the illusion that it had ceased.

After lunch, which would sometimes be washed down with a fresh Vouvray or a Muscadet, he'd arrange everything neatly and go through his daily ceremony: he'd undress completely, put on his pajamas, and tuck himself into bed for a nice nap. This seemed to his friends to be an incredibly self-indulgent luxury—but it was a necessity of his routine: his sleep not only, as he claimed, put "velvet in his vertebrae," it was a deliberate damming of the stream until, on its own, it overflowed its banks. His dreams, which he cultivated, were also part of his work, imparting new angles and different directions to the thoughts of the morning. The nap was also, clearly, a beautiful return to his childhood, whose bourgeois tranquility the Clichy flat recalled. He was like a child tucked into his bed for his afternoon nap, a good boy. So much of his adult life had destroyed his dreams, he was committed now to dreaming his way backward to childhood, and forward to art, again.

Upon awakening, he might even hold back the headwaters a little longer while he took an excursion on his bicycle or by foot. By the time he sat down at the typewriter again his fingers were itching to slaughter the machine, like a drummer. The flood would rumble along for several hours of the late afternoon. On this work schedule, twenty, thirty, forty, and—on one day—forty-five pages (with two carbons) would be stacked up beside the laboring typewriter before dinner. He would have been playing music all day, keeping time to the music, and by the end, a triumphal column of records would be piled next to the victrola. All the ashtrays would be filled with Gauloises Bleues. A visitor could count the stubs and figure that there would be one burnt-out Bleu for each page he had produced. And, far from being tired, Henry would be full of vinegar, ready to reach for a bottle—of a velvety Nuits St. Georges, say—when Fred sat down at the kitchen table for a chat.

Fred was working on a novel of his own in just the opposite way from Henry's volcanic outpourings. As Paulette put it: "Monseiur Henri can type much faster than you, and when he sits at his typewriter he goes on for hours without a stop." Henry was unconcerned about his productivity because he produced so much, while Fred avoided that concern by deliberately limiting his writing to no more than two pages a day. If he reached the bottom of that second page (and most often he didn't reach it) he'd stop abruptly, even in the middle of a sentence. To Fred this procedure was eminently clear and perfectly rational. As he often explained it: "Two pages a day, 365 days in the year, that makes 730 pages. If I can do 250 in a year I'll be satisfied. I'm not writing a *roman fleuve.*" He was in fact writing a book in French called *Sentiments limitrophes*—a book of "peripheral feelings," a work about the fragments of his memory and the streams of association flowing between memories. Although these memories went back to his childhood, they also included recent ones and involved portraits of Henry, June, and Anaïs Nin. Henry was certain that he himself could not match the delicate power and transparency, like that of a perfect watercolor, of Alf's book. Fred's writing he thought of as a "subtle distillation" and declared that he liked it better than anything he could do himself. But though their methods of composition were different, the books shared a similar view of the flexibility and rapidity of the faculty of memory, were influenced by Proust's treatment of recollection, and had some of the same materials—their mutual acquaintances. And finally, they were, as Henry wrote to Alf after both volumes were published, "companion books in misery and loneliness."

In the evening, then, Henry and Fred were likely to loaf over a bottle of wine and talk about their work of the day, add up their funds, and discuss the women upon the horizon. If they lingered long enough to open a second bottle of wine and both started to feel euphoric, Fred might suddenly stop the conversation and seize Henry by the arm, begging him to take him along to America should he ever return. Then he'd urge Henry to give him an account of his travels in that fabulous place, America. Once Henry got started on the subject of places in the United States, no natural end to his monologue was foreseeable: it was like mentioning the decline of the

western world, painting, sex, or the role of the artist to him. Just ask him
for a good description of Miami or mention Santa Fe and he'd be on the
wing. He had his own especially favorite places, such as Mobile Bay and Big
Sur, and concerning these places he had never seen he could spin dazzling
improvisations. But no matter how long he rambled on, at the end Alf
would always pipe up with the demand: *"Now* tell me about Arizona." It
was not one of Henry's specialties, and he'd sometimes growl: "The hell
with Arizona. I'm going to bed. I've told you all I know." "Then tell me
again," Fred would ask in a tone of blissful expectation. They'd both have
had a skinful of wine and Fred's eyes would be shining with tears of joy.
Almost invariably, Henry would start in again, inventing freely. Very
likely, he'd become newly interested in the subject and begin to talk about
the places he wanted to visit before he died—Mexico, India, Greece, the
land of Saladin, Tibet. From the last he expected to go to Devechan; but
before that time came, Henry would ruminate, there'd be time to see
Fillmore Place once again as well as the bayous at the mouth of the
Mississippi. When he finished, perhaps an hour later, Fred would grate-
fully raise a ruby glass of Porto *sec* to him and say: "Now tell me about
Arizona!"

Such epic expressions of their *sentiments limitrophes* were reserved for
special occasions and demanded Fred's night off from work for proper
elaboration. Occasionally, one of Miller's friends would arrive. Fraenkel,
still deep in the writing of his gospels of anonymity and death, often came
to mull over his ideas. Start him anywhere and soon Fraenkel would be in
the cemetery and battlefield, tallying up the corpses. At this point, Fred
was likely to take himself off to the Restaurant de l'Escargot if he had any
cash, or, if he didn't, to Giolotte's on the Rue Lamartine, where the staff of
the *Tribune*—housed just across the street—could run up tabs. Henry and
Michael would monumentally occupy the apartment, jabbering about
"creative suicide" to their heart's content. But if he had ever been, Henry
was no longer on Fraenkel's side. Fraenkel was right in every particular but
one: everyone was dead—everyone but Henry himself. For him, the gospel
of death became a measure of his own triumph. As Michael became more
and more convincing, Henry became more and more justified. All the
people he wrote about—Bertha, Bald, Fred, and even Fraenkel—were like
so many cold corpses in transparent caskets. He, Henry, danced alone in the
graveyard, picking flowers.

For Michael, that was a definite and unwelcome compromise. But it was
just as he had feared. Even before Henry left for Dijon, Fraenkel had

cautioned him: "The reason I wanted you to commit suicide that evening at the Lowenfels' . . . I was afraid, terribly afraid, that some day you'd go back on me; die on my hands. And I would be left high and dry with my idea of you simply, and nothing to sustain it. I should never forgive you for that." He meant that he wanted Henry to commit creative suicide by admitting that his life was a death. By the spring of 1932, however, Henry came alive for himself. Now, Michael's once-respected letter was inserted into "The Last Book" as an instance of the gospel of mumbo-jumbo.

Richard Osborn actually did threaten to die on their hands. During the winter while Henry was in Dijon, Dick experienced a complete mental breakdown with paranoic delusions. The hospital on the outskirts of Paris in which he was incarcerated was literally nightmarish and at least part of Osborn's fears had real basis. He had been living with a younger French girl named Jeanne who had become pregnant—or at least he *thought* she was pregnant and he believed he was the father. He'd knocked her up—he kept mumbling to himself as if even biology was persecuting him. None of his Paris friends would have predicted the next development. His Bridgeport morals reasserted themselves: he *wanted* to marry her, the woman he had ruined. He was preparing to die, hoping to die—and his mind was dying—but he was determined to "do the right thing" first.

In the asylum Osborn was raving: his mind was shooting fragments in every direction. He suspected that while he was out during the day Jeanne had had men up to the apartment. He had gotten the clap and given it to her, he said with tears streaming down his face. But the next moment he'd claim that it was Jeanne, the little slut, who'd given him the dose and pretended to have gotten it from him. He couldn't bear to leave her, he wailed. But then, he'd say, he was desperate to escape from her but had no chance, she'd track him down and claw his eyes out if he tried to defect. He wanted to marry the poor girl. But as soon as he said that he'd turn around and curse his fate: now he'd be stuck in a provincial town forever. Christ!—all he had wanted was a fling in Paris before settling down to a practice in corporation law, with a nice house in Bridgeport and an office in Wall Street. His mind had collapsed: he was paralyzed by fears of others and accusations of himself.

Henry vowed to save the poor devil, no matter how desperate the required measures might be. He tried to penetrate the fogs of Osborn's paranoia to discover what had actually happened. Henry talked to some of Jeanne's friends and neighbors and concluded that she was not pregnant, only growing fat from indolence. After a while he simply gave up and decided that the truth was irrelevant. The main thing was to save Dick. Some time later, when Osborn was released from the hospital and allowed to return to Paris, Henry determined that he should light out, abandon Jeanne, and return to America. There was nowhere in France that he could hide from Jeanne if in fact she decided to track him down. Certainly, as soon as Dick got back to Paris, she seized him like a spider; she didn't quite devour him, but she wouldn't let him out of her sight. One day in late July, Henry ran into him on the Right Bank. "I'm just on my way to the bank to draw out some money," he said uneasily, "I've got to be back in a half-hour. I don't know what to do." It was a sunny, breezy Paris day. Outwardly Osborn looked like a healthy American—well-dressed, bareheaded, with a little paunch. But there was a dizziness in his eyes. "You've got to help me out of this," he suddenly urged Henry with desperation in his voice. "I don't belong here. I wish I were home." He started to blubber and go to pieces. He groaned about his disgust with the cruelty and sterility of the French, a people he once adored. It even drove him crazy, he said, to have to speak incessantly in French.

Henry's thoughts were going fast and he took Dick's arm. He formed a crazy scheme—crazy enough to work. Henry decided to break his plan easily to Osborn—otherwise sheer panic might follow. "I'm going to help you," he said. "Let's have a drink." Dick looked at him with horror. Hysteria danced behind his eyes. To have a drink, to invite Jeanne's displeasure, to be late returning from his errand, to put his trust in this irresponsible Henry Miller—sounded crazy to Osborn. "Relax, sit down. Let's have a whiskey, an American whiskey," Henry said. The whiskey did it. As the American liquor arrived, looking velvety and golden brown, his eyes brimmed with tears. He seized Henry as if he were his last friend and sang the praises of their native land, which he said he dared not hope to see again. The garçon arrived with a second drink. "Bottoms up!" Henry commanded. Dick downed it at once. "Listen," Henry said, "if I were in your boots, I'd go—I'd go to America, without hesitation, today." Osborn glanced about, as if the mere whispering of such an idea would be enough to bring Jeanne down on his head. "How much do you have in the bank? Is it yours or Jeanne's father's?" Henry asked. Getting satisfactory answers to both questions, he outlined his plan. He gave his voice the air of command and authority. The plan was insanely simple. At once—hatless—lacking a cane—abandoning his mackintosh, his manuscripts, and even his Yale diploma—without returning to his apartment to pick up a toothbrush—Osborn was to board a boat to his native land. In hardly more than a week,

Henry reminded him, he'd be back in Bridgeport. The slapstick plan was so preposterous that Osborn went right along with it. Henry had never acted decisively in any of his own crises, but he had become desperate enough to learn to be resourceful. "Jesus, Osborn," Henry said to buck him up, "why by tonight you'll be in London up to your ears in English."

Henry shepherded him through the ordeals of the bank, the British consulate, and American Express, with a pause at a fine restaurant and a farewell bottle of wine, the finest on the menu. With Dick's money stuffed into his pockets he was pretty exhilarated by the events himself. By the time they were on their way to the Gare du Nord in a cab, he had changed all but about 2,500 francs of Dick's money into traveler's checks and pounds. In great confusion Osborn tried to explain how to break the news to Jeanne and was getting muddled and feeling responsible and preparing to collapse on Henry's hands. But now Henry was determined to see it through. "Never mind that," he told Dick. "How much dough do you want to give her?—that's all!" Osborn looked ready to faint: "How much do you have?" "About 2,000 francs, more than she deserves," Henry replied. "I don't know . . ." Osborn said weakly, wanting to go and wanting to stay. "All right, I'll give her all this French money," Henry said, holding up the two-thousand.

So it was settled. Henry pocketed the dough and promised to see Jeanne the very next day, and he pushed the tottering wreck onto the boat train, and Dick was off toward America.

America!—how much Henry himself had wanted to return to his country. Once, he had begged his friends and his wife to send him the funds to come home, fearful that he would starve to death in France. He had been as desperate to get out as Osborn was. So, as he sat in a café on the Place Lafayette, he counted Osborn's money up to a total of 2,800 francs—$125. That was enough for a ticket to America. Who would ever know if Jeanne never got the money at all? Even if Osborn did write to her, who would believe him, a crazy fellow who had performed the kind of act unthinkable to the French—boarding a boat for London without picking up his reversible or planting his hat firmly on his head! If Henry wanted to follow Dick to America, then, he had but to take a train to Le Havre or Cherbourg and wait for a departure. It was the first time since he had been in Paris that he had any choice about his own fate. He sat in the Place Lafayette and let his thoughts drift. All the defects that Osborn found in French life were there all right—the selfishness and indifference, the insistence on the reasonable and restrained, the petty severity and mean puritanism—there for Frenchmen at least. But for an American, like himself, who had not caved in, an American who knew where his next meal was coming from, France was just fine, he could ask no more. The way the colored awnings were gently flapping in the breeze, the chestnut trees spilling gold sequins in blond beer, the clock ringing in a church tower—these all seemed to be a part of the flow of the seasons, the sweep of time, and yet for the very same reason to be unchanging. It was not the whiskey or the wine or the last Pernod he shared with Dick that flowed through him—it was the golden stream of the life about him gliding by and then through him and becoming his life. Now that it came to a choice about returning to America, he discovered that the Paris which he had never chosen had chosen him. It was like his first Sunday in Paris: he would stay and live and write—he felt that same conviction again, only now it was born from experience and not innocence and was likely to last. He and Dick, that day, both made their way home.

This did not imply that Henry wasn't pleased with the escape plan which he had led Osborn to execute. He decided at once to vote himself a sizeable commission of eight hundred francs. He sent an even 2,000 francs to Jeanne by postal check that very afternoon. He enclosed a note written with his left hand, shakily, like Osborn's writing, saying: *"Chère Jeanne. Je suis parti pour l'Amerique. O."* His haste could have been an error of a major sort, since Jeanne rapidly checked the schedules of French departures and was on a train that very evening to Le Havre where she kept her eye upon the departing steamship *Rochambeau* until it sailed. Fortunately Dick was departing that same day from Cherbourg for London on the *Olympic.*

Henry put his story into "The Last Book" even before Osborn landed in America. By this time the book was far enough advanced for him to take the chance of showing it to Lowenfels. Walter sensed its importance after reading the first fifty pages and wrote out eight pages of commentary on them. "He is careful to surround himself with dead people," Lowenfels remarked. "Naturally he adores Fraenkel. . . . Miller recognizes Fraenkel's death as the real thing, and so idolizes it. The others, the living dead, he had only to annihilate by—what? It's not contempt. It's that he is so alive nothing else can exist. It's like being close to the sun." "This book should be called," Lowenfels announced, "I am the only man in the world that's alive." For a while Henry actually thought of calling the novel "Cockeyed in Paris." At the end of the month he proposed two more titles to Anaïs: "I Sing the Equator" and "Tropic of Cancer." The first was an apt allusion to Whitman, but Anaïs' interests in astrology predisposed her to prefer the second. The title had several associations for Henry. Into his notebook he had copied an excerpt from the *Satyricon*: "I was born myself under Cancer, and therefore stand on my feet, as having large possessions both by Sea and Land!" Cancer is the crab, a creature who can move in many directions, the fabulous beast of the Chinese sagas. Cancer is the sign of the poet who observes and exposes the disease of a civilization which is proceeding in the wrong direction. Cancer is also the sign of death in life, with affinities to Nietzsche's doctrine of eternal recurrence as well as to Buddhist Doctrine.

Tropic of Cancer is about the critical early period of Miller's poverty and personal despair in Paris. He uses his encounters with Bertha, Eugene Pachoutinsky, Fraenkel, Nanavati, Perlès, Osborn, and others as symbols of the fragments into which his life had fallen. Death and nausea hover about him. He begins as he had begun the book in his earliest draft (though the real names were finally eliminated):

I am living in the Villa Borghese. There is not a crumb of dirt anywhere, nor a chair misplaced. We are all alone here and we are dead.

But though death is the prison house about which he writes, it is the living artist who is writing the book. Surely he was right: in his worst days in Paris Henry Val Miller had really died from failure of the heart. But a new desperado had been reborn:

I have no money, no resources, no hopes. I am the happiest man alive . . .
To sing you must first open your mouth. You must have a pair of lungs, and a little knowledge of music. It is not necessary to have an accordion, or a guitar. The essential thing is to *want* to sing. This then is a song. I am singing.

Song, food, words, physical sensations of sex and many other kinds, the lunacy of acceptance, these bubble to the surface of the narrative even as Miller recounts his dark days—of hunger, decay, pain, cold, and the sense of personal extinction. The story he is telling, of course, is fundamentally an explanation of the book in which the story is told. How did such a book come to be written?—a book that is "a gob of spit in the face of Art, a kick in the pants to God, Man, Destiny, Time, Love, Beauty"? Such a book, he implies, could have been accomplished only through the death of the conventional artist and his resurrection into a new man who sees with new eyes and tells his tale in accordance with a new compact with the world. At the time of his writing the main character of the book and Miller were not at all identical. He had come out of his desperation in order to write—but he wrote from the point of view gained through his harrowing experiences.

This, then, is not an autobiography in the usual sense, though filled with chunks of the actual. It is an autobiography of Miller's present perspective on his past experience, which he changes freely to suit his present mood. The most brilliantly achieved instance of this kind of autobiographic transmutation occurs in the closing scene. Here, Henry Miller tells of how Val Miller saved Osborn (Fillmore) from the clutches of his French fiancée. In fact, Henry had delivered most of the francs left by Osborn to the girl. But in the autobiographic romance of *Tropic of Cancer* he pockets all the dough, since that is what such an artist as he now sees himself to be would do. And in the book the money turns into a radiant symbol, a warm comforting bulge in his pocket. Under the spell of his money, he understands for the first time how joyous Paris is. He sits by the Seine and feels the river swelling and flowing through him with its burst of new freedom: "In the wonderful peace that fell over me it seemed as if I had climbed to the top of a high mountain; for a little while I would be able to look around me, to take in the meaning of the landscape." His first look, of course, will be at the spiritual geography of his life in Paris. At the end of the book the man who can write the book is born.

Although he had not quite completed *Tropic of Cancer,* Miller was already trying to find a publisher for it. Michael Fraenkel had openly asserted his belief that Henry was "doing something greater than *Ulysses,*" and he proposed to have the type set in Bruges and issue the book under his own Carrefour imprint. But Michael was in a bad state emotionally. Arguments with Lowenfels and domestic problems had rendered him almost as ineffectual as Osborn; all day long he sat in a cold room too broken and helpless to be able even to make up his mind to go out. Henry hesitated to entrust the book to him; he made up a list of other "little presses." First, however, Anaïs encouraged him to try for commercial publication. She asked her friend Dr. Krans (through whom Henry had been placed at the Lycée Carnot) to recommend Miller to a Paris literary agent named William Aspenwall Bradley. Wambly Bald had mentioned Bradley in the same column in which he reviewed "Mademoiselle Claude," asserting that Bradley "has encouraged and assisted more buds than any other angel we know." Soon, Henry received a cordial letter in which the agent requested that he bring his books around to his office on the Rue Saint-Louis in the Île de la Cité.

Henry left the manuscripts of *Crazy Cock* and *Tropic of Cancer* and waited—not too patiently. Bradley answered within a week: "I have been through both the books now, and should like very much to talk them over with you—especially the *Tropic of Cancer,* which is magnificent." Could Henry come to see him by the end of the week? he inquired. In their first talk, Bradley was discouraging about *Crazy Cock,* but he softened his criticism by persuading Henry that the novel suffered terribly through comparison with the later, richer book: he dismissed *Crazy Cock* in about two minutes. But what would Henry think of seeing *Tropic of Cancer* published in a limited edition of 500 copies at 500 francs apiece by the Obelisk Press? Miller's first reaction was revealing. Though Anaïs was with him, he cried out: "If only June could have been here to enjoy this with me. To think that all we dreamed of is happening and she doesn't even know about it." His second reaction was curious—a kind of backpedalling loss of confidence exactly at the moment of his triumph. Out of some deep-seated need for self-justification, Henry wanted to force *Crazy Cock* down their throats. *Tropic of Cancer* was not the book he wanted to write, he crazily asserted, not the story he really wanted to tell. He had promised himself in 1927 that he would dedicate himself to writing the story of his life with June. And like a pilgrim of little faith who settles for the first shrine he sees, he had merely written a book recounting his own miserable history. *Crazy Cock* was the story he wanted to tell. If they wanted *Tropic of Cancer* they must take *Crazy Cock* too!

Just when this defiant mood was fully upon him, Henry received a letter from Samuel Putnam, who was in New York. On behalf of Covici-Friede, Publishers he inquired if Henry had any work to submit; Covici had read and liked "Mademoiselle Claude." Now, stubbornly, Henry was enraged that interest should be taken in such a "weak" story, a *jeu d'esprit* done with his left hand. It was humiliating, he decided, to be admired by such buggers. In letters to Lowenfels, Anaïs, Putnam, and Emil he ranted and raved. If Americans wanted a book by him now, they would have to take *Crazy Cock*. He wanted it to be a big success in the United States, he said, so that he could take down his pants and show his ass to his countrymen and say: "I'm crapping on it, disowning it. So much for you, America, of thee I sing! That's just the kind of shit you've been eating for the last fifteen years!" Having said all of this, he went on outrageously to propose that either Lowenfels or Putnam should undertake the publication of *Crazy Cock*. Wouldn't it be an apt gesture of the New Instinctivism for him to bring out a book which its author would publically castigate just as the public began to praise it? To Henry's surprise Putnam actually read the manuscript and said he believed it to be "a Covici-Friede book." ("I think he's crazy," Miller told Schnellock—but he did send the book to the

Covici-Friede editors.) Typed on the title page was a one-sentence foreword ("Apologies to Michael Fraenkel") and a Preface only slightly longer ("Good-bye to the novel, sanity, and good health. Hello angels!"). It was another man, he told Emil, who had written *Crazy Cock,* a man whom Henry now saw as an imposter; and he was defecating on that man too, the hollow American puppet he had left behind.

His fury over American interest in his writing also worked its way into *Tropic of Cancer,* which he expanded now that its publication by Obelisk Press seemed guaranteed. At around the same time *Crazy Cock* was being considered by Covici-Friede, Henry was excising everything but the "fire and dynamite" from *Tropic of Cancer.* Determined to affront readers and to make his book completely unacceptable to the public taste, he added several new sections whose frankness would be almost certain to offend. He also added a contentious preface in which he connected his own world-view of contemporary disease with the surrealist savagery of Luis Buñuel and with Duhamel's violent attack upon American values in *Salavin.* Such a prefatory critical *tour de force,* he felt, would throw the critics overboard or sink their ship. He ruthlessly followed Fraenkel's logic, signed his book "Henry Miller, Pseudonym," and then went one step further and typed a new title page: "'Tropic of Cancer' by Anonymous." Last, he vowed that the fact of publication being merely an incidental occasion in his expression of himself, he would not revise in order to please the public, mollify the censors, or perfect his art. Only his own integrity, he decided, mattered to him. He was even willing, if need be, to accept expulsion from France as a consequence of the publication of *Cancer* and to wander the earth like an untouchable.

Jack Kahane might have been dismayed had he known of these resolutions; for as editor and owner of the Obelisk Press, he was drawing up a contract for the publication of *Tropic of Cancer.* By the terms of this document, Miller agreed to give Obelisk Press world rights to publish his book in English in return for a 10% royalty and an option on his succeeding two books. That last provision of the contract was far from being an empty gesture. From Kahane's side it indicated faith in this new writer. From Miller's it promised at least a reading for future books. Indeed, as he signed the contract he had already written sixty pages of his next production, a book which he was inevitably calling *Tropic of Capricorn.*

Ten

She-Who-Must-Be-Obeyed

Miller's personality was immeasureably stronger in 1932 than it had ever been before. Certainly the satisfaction which he felt over the composition of the *Tropic of Cancer* helped give him confidence. Certainly, his ability to pull himself out of hell without aid taught him calmness. But what really confirmed his new belief in himself was what he was always looking for—the belief of another person in him. In 1932 this person was Anaïs Nin. She made him feel as if his stars had all been rearranged by her appearance on the horizon, as if a new fate were in store for him. The astrological metaphor is apt. In her house at Louveciennes, the stars ruled. Her cousin, Eduardo Sanchez, was an adept in the science. Also one of Anaïs's analysts, René Allendy (author of *Paracelse, le Medecin Maudit*), used astrology as one of his interpretive instruments. In the spring of 1932 Hugo Guiler, assisted by Allendy, did Henry's "interesting but unfortunate" chart. Hugo remarked that Henry's ruling planet, Mars, was "out of harmony" with the rest of existence, but to everyone's surprise Anaïs broke out: "Mars is the planet that has only one friend—Venus. My ruling planet is Venus."

Venus was involved, but also more than Venus. Though outwardly Anaïs conferred the impression of ethereality, there was nothing bloodless about her belief in Henry. By the summer of 1932, when Fred Perlès's earnings, divided among himself, Paulette, and Henry, were all too obviously insufficient to sustain them all, Anaïs began to make regular contributions to the household so that Henry would not be obliged to waste his time

265

looking for a job or begin his transient existence anew. The United States was ready to come off the gold standard, but she moved him onto it. For the first time since he had lost his job at Western Union he was secure financially. Anaïs Nin was a giver by nature, she was gentle and not given to the kind of domination that June exercised when she sacrificed for him. She supported him unconditionally, without demanding that she be glorified or even that he be grateful. The money she gave him was important, for Henry was still neurotically afraid of starving to death. But equally important was the aura of personal, psychic security which her complete acceptance of him conveyed when she gave him money for the rent or food or bought or borrowed books for him, when she surprised him with a victrola and Bach records, when she chose and purchased new curtains for Clichy, or came there to prepare a lunch for two. Once she showed him an entry in her *Journal intime*: "I will always stand by him, with him, against the world. I will laugh *with him* even if it is against me." That was her precise attitude and her behavior conveyed it without deviation.

The house at Louveciennes, which he visited often these days, contributed to the sense of security which he felt. The Watteau-like Louveciennes scene, the green pastures dotted with cows, the trees moving in the clear breezes, the whole quiet pastoral atmosphere came to have a healing effect upon him, as the country had never done earlier in his life. The interior of Anaïs' house was calculated to produce a similar effect of calm. Everything seemed to be formulated, polished, categorized, filed away, and unchangeably labelled. Coming from Paris to Louveciennes was like entering another civilization, China or Egypt or Araby, where everything had long ago arrived at its final determinations, and against the background of which the individual could confidently stand. Even the room that was now set aside exclusively for Henry's use gave the feeling of stability. Once the billiard room of the 200-year old DuBarry estate, it now had a huge handmade desk with compartments on either side to hold files, whiskey bottles, paints, carbons, supplies—everything he needed to settle in. The room was richly furnished not just with utilitarian items, but with objects of art, such as an Alexandrian hand mirror with a turquoise and onyx handle. Henry's room was a reminder of the beauty of art above man's struggles and mischances.

Anaïs helped him to believe again in an ideal conception of woman; and since for him the idea of woman was very intimately related to his notion of himself, this renewal really helped to restore his self-confidence. As Henry adopted Anaïs's person as the feminine ideal, he accepted her conception of him as the correct one. Inwardly he had not yet freed himself from the ghosts of his anxieties over his previous disappointments, but all the fears which still haunted him Anaïs took on herself. She encouraged him to stress the affirmatory attitudes that remained at the bottom of his personality. She led him, in short, around the recent agonies of his rosy crucifixion at June's hands to the Rosicrucian idealism of his youth. Once, at a moment of great exaltation which occurred while he was in the midst of writing a fourteen-page letter to Anaïs concerning Rank's ideas, he brought himself up short, going in back of his analysis to the heart of his reeducation: "*You* have been the teacher—not Rank, nor even Nietzsche, nor Spengler. All these, unfortunately, receive the acknowledgment, but in them lies the dead skeleton of the idea. In you was the vivification, the living example, the guide who conducted me through the labyrinth of self to unravel the riddle of myself, to come to the mysteries . . . . If one goes the whole way with you, if one *can* go the whole way, indeed, one is rewarded by a different product entirely, something quite unpragmatic, something, and I am glad to say it, *unreal*. One is privileged in the end to drink of wisdom. I say this very, very romantically! It is sheer romanticism in this day and age to speak of the value of wisdom, for it is a value that is no longer wanted. It has no efficacy in this world of reality which had been created, because this world of reality is a world of death. It is the bitter unreality, the world that lies outside of the psychologist's ken, the world to which we *should* never become wholly adapted, that you have led me."

Such wisdom—and Henry very much needed her wisdom—was the Neptunian side of Anaïs's character, but Venus never dipped far below the horizon. "Come and be my husband for a few days," she would write from Louveciennes whenever Hugo remained away on business. Alone together, they were often quiet, eating in the garden under the ancient trees, washing the dishes or mending the furnace, savoring the best wines that the Louveciennes merchant could provide, walking the dogs across the gravel paths at night, dancing to the music of the victrola, reading and talking. They left little notes around the house for each other to find, even love notes on the pillow of the sleeping one. Henry was soaring. The more he knew her, the more mythical, ever-changing, did Anaïs seem. He called her *Schneewittchen,* Snow-white, but he also detected Moorish, Jewish, and African forebears in her. Like Ayesha, she had to be obeyed—but she demanded nothing but his good. Henry was soon writing to friends that Anaïs was the first woman whom he had truly loved, the first to make him happy and to give him the conviction that the feelings of a man and woman for each other could be inexhaustible. That Fraenkel and Osborn had been gripped with a kind of paralysis in France while Henry had flourished was due to her, he confessed openly. Not surprisingly, he began to quietly predict to his friends that there would soon be another marriage. Henry assured Michael Fraenkel and other friends that in his opinion Anaïs could not remain married to Hugo, "a man without ecstasy." In October 1932 he wrote decisively to Emil Schnellock: "My next wife is Anaïs."

The same old story. He wanted to marry—but where was the money? Hugo held the purse strings.

Henry conceived a number of money-making schemes. He started to calculate royalties he could earn from *Tropic of Cancer.* He made contact with Paul Morand to discuss the possibility of translating his French lectures into English for an American tour. He thought this might publicize his book-in-progress on Paris and sell it to Knopf or a similar publisher. He believed that the sole impediment to a life with Anaïs was economic. In his euphoria, Henry had almost forgotten that he was still married himself. Of course he didn't look to June for support anymore—as Anaïs looked to Hugo—but he certainly was still emotionally tied to her, more than he supposed. If any confirmation of this were needed, one had merely to read the manuscript of *Tropic of Capricorn,* which he started in the summer of 1932. Quite simply, he was beginning to tell the story of *Crazy Cock* all over again, compulsively; once again he was trying to make something out of the notes he had compiled in 1927. Once these looked as though they might save him, but now they might sink him; they had become a fixation, as if he could not be rid of June until he broke her spell by writing this book. Without question, work on *Tropic of Capricorn* always produced anxiety. He worked easily, impulsively, on his other projects, but when he was hammering at *Tropic of Capricorn* everyone knew it, for then he would lock himself in his room for hours on end until he finally emerged looking worn and harried.

If any further proof of the power which June still wielded were needed, she proved it once and for all by reappearing in Paris in late October of 1932 and immediately putting him under her spell. Having written but four letters to him during his two and a half years in Paris, in mid October she followed her usual habits of telegraphic mystery and cabled him in care of Bald at the *Tribune:* "Returning to Paris the end of October. Letter following. Please write me care Elkus. Forgive, love you June New York." He wrote back at once, calmly asking her to bring all his old manuscripts, but it didn't take long for his fears to float to the surface. A week after receiving her cable he panicked while sitting in a little park some distance from Clichy.

Perhaps—he suddenly thought—June was already in the Clichy apartment reading his manuscripts of the *Tropics* and tearing them to bits in anger. He rushed back, but of course June hadn't arrived, nor did she write or cable for the next two weeks, as if her original message had been produced by the scratching of sparrows on the telegraph wire.

But toward the end of the month word reached him that June's appearance was imminent. For safekeeping he returned Anaïs's letters to her and asked her to keep his manuscript copies of *Tropic of Cancer, Tropic of Capricorn,* and his Paris notebook. Soon he began to breathe easier and even, astonishingly, he began anticipating June's arrival with glee. He laid in a small supply of Pernod and whiskey and some other little surprises for his wife. As if they were precious holy documents he pocketed the four letters June had mailed to Paris and carried them around so that he could read them while sitting in cafés. He imagined himself in love with her again and he decided (as he wrote in a notebook) that to have her with him he would be willing to destroy his own book, accuse himself of criminal acts, and retract every accusation he had ever made against her. On a late October afternoon he sat in the Café Wepler and not only justified June, he castigated himself for having ever complained in letters to her. Certainly, she had suffered— her loneliness may have been more terrible than his. Now, from her letters he could see that this was true. "As for my good spirits," she had written to him in 1930, in her first letter, "how could you believe that?" She was willing, she insisted, to "commit robbery, murder, anything to make you happy and to be with you soon, not as the woman everyone knows, but as an insignificant little housewife, lover, friend . . . ." He sat in the dingy café reading these words and yearned to have her with him, sure that nothing and no one else mattered.

Near the end of the month June arrived. Evasive as ever, she went directly to the Hôtel Princesse and announced her arrival to Henry by *pneu.* Although Henry and Fred did not arrive home until late that evening, Henry insisted on going immediately to Montparnasse. He and Fred bicycled into Paris to the Rue Princesse only to find June already asleep. She was astonished that they would bother her so late at night and declared that not only didn't she intend to accompany them to Clichy that very evening, but that she had taken her room for ten days. (Enough time for Henry to hustle up money for the rent.)

The days to come unlocked their separate griefs. As always, June seemed bent on rearranging his life and his mind. Her indiscriminate chatter tumbled out like a bubbling stream of lava that hardens even as it sears the countryside. Her interest in the hard-surface life of America annoyed him; she demanded that Fred and Henry accompany her to a screening of *Scarface* and afterwards insisted that it was a "marvellous picture, better than any phony surrealism done by Buñuel and *that* crowd." (June never hesitated to mock Henry's idols.) "Yes, there is vitality there," Henry agreed, "but it's the decaying luminosity of a corpse, sterile and dead." He began to think of June like this—her hectic energy was the seething of putrefaction.

Henry had never ceased to injure himself or his wife with his desire to pluck the truth out of mystery. Now that he was surrounded again by June's enigmas, he reached out for intelligible guides. Two of these were closely connected: the work of Marcel Proust and the insights of Anaïs. June had first called his attention to Proust in 1926, making him a present of a translation. For the last six months, however, Henry had been struggling with the French of Proust's massive *À la recherche du temps perdu;* he was intensely involved because he had to pick out the meaning word by word. By November, June herself was saying, *"I am* Albertine" in the same way she used to announce "I am Stavrogin" or "Now I am Henriette." If this were so, then he *could* penetrate June's thoughts, her attitudes, her real longings and desires, her true being, by understanding the truths about Albertine whom Proust lay bare in the course of his novel. June, he told Anaïs, was certainly similar to Albertine—though obviously more complicated, more fully orchestrated in her human dimensions. After reading about Proust's woman he was "on fire"; Proust seemed "to take the words out of my mouth, to rob me of my very own experiences, sensations, reflections, introspections, suspicions, sadness, torture." If June could be understood through Proust, excellent; if for such understanding Henry might be required to make a thorough investigation of Jung's theory of introversion, he would not shrink from the study. For every word June babbled, Henry recorded an observation about her in his notebook. For every mysterious clue she dropped, he copied out long passages from the works of Proust, Jung, or Lawrence. He also pressed Anaïs into his investigations. He was disturbed when Anaïs revealed to him that Albertine was really Albert, and that Proust's real model for the situation being described had been a homosexual one. For a moment he paused: was he creating his own betrayal? When June was so attractive, how could Anaïs not fall in love with her and at last line up with June against him? Was Anaïs fascinated by June because she desired to discover what it was in her that so attracted Henry or because June was truly fascinating? (He showed Anaïs copies of his love letters to June.) Did June go around saying that

Anaïs was wonderful because that was so patently true or because she sensed that Anaïs was her competitor for Henry and wanted to test her rival? Even privately, none of them could have responded adequately to such questions: almost by magnetic attraction they had become so close to each other, separate identities were hard to distinguish. At the deepest core of these attractions was a truth which each of the three concealed—each loved himself or herself more than he could ever love anyone else. What were the two women for Henry except the image of *his* capacity to love and his need to be loved? What were the two others for June but an audience for whom she could play her parts, an arena for her continuous transformation— hermaphrodite and homunculus? What was deeper in the attraction of Henry and June for Anaïs than her desire to be perfect for both of them, as she was—secretly—perfect for herself? In the others each saw the androgynous shapes of his own desires; in order to strengthen himself, each invented the others' qualities as imitations of his own.

If Henry had become thoroughly muddled by June, the potentials for ambiguity were multiplied by the addition of Anaïs to the circle. An invisible, emotional ballet was in progress in which each of them was engaged in a shifting dance of attraction and repulsion. Anaïs now saw June very frequently, more than she was seeing Henry. To be sure, at least one of the reasons for this was that she was thereby unselfishly trying to give Henry free time for his work, and also to wean him from his all-too obvious need for June's company. Yet it was also true that she and June exchanged pieces of jewelry as a token of intimate affection. Henry thanked Anaïs for saving him from being crushed by June; yet he made as little effort to see Anaïs as to see June and appeared quite content to work in peace and solitude, with neither woman nearby. If anything, he seemed to prefer June's company. On her side, June began to treat Anaïs as she had Jean and to spread her veils of mystery over their relationship. Extravagantly she'd "defend" her relationship with Anaïs while never exactly saying just what their relationship really was. And she'd warn Henry that he would never be able to understand the nature or depth of either Anaïs or herself.

Henry tried to convince Anaïs that it was her faith alone that preserved him although at this very time he could think of no subject for conversation except June, June, June. Anaïs was sharing with Henry her intimate relations with June in the same manner that June had shared with Jean the secrets of her life with Henry. She was betraying June in order to bind Henry to her. But in addition, she was responding with her own special attractions by letting Henry read her diary notes on June and, later, the short manuscript called "Alraune" (June), a novella that she wrote about the triangular relation. If Henry could not find the explanation for June in Proust, perhaps he would be obliged to take the interpretation of Anaïs or of the psychoanalyst, Otto Rank, whose theory of the multiple personality Anaïs borrowed to interpret June. According to Rank's explanation, June's escapades, her rapid transformations, her roles, must be understood as the absolute fragmentation of her self: what she did in one case bore no relation to any other. June could hold herself sacred and yet give herself to temptations of any sort of corruption without noticing the contradiction. Or perhaps her multiplicity was meant to satisfy Henry's multiple needs. In Nin's book, Alraune tells the character called Mandra (Anaïs) that Rab (Henry) didn't want simplicity and so she had learned to reinvent herself continuously and exotically for him; she could preserve his love only by telling him lies! Miller spent days poring over Anaïs's "Alraune" manuscript, interlining her typing with handwritten corrections and silently arguing with Anaïs in the margin about her views of June, herself, and him. But none of this brought him the conviction that he had himself reached a true understanding of the subjects which most preoccupied him. Even though June was on the spot, to scrutinize to his heart's desire, he never saw her clearly. By the time that June had been in Paris for two months, she was a greater mystery than ever.

For a time Fred almost threatened to turn the Henry-June-Anaïs triangle into a quadrangle. He treated June as a natural enemy, a moral moron, a pathologic liar, and a bore. June disliked Fred intensely in return. Fred began to fall in love with Anaïs, who loved Henry, who loved June, and this made a deep tangle of affections and hatreds. Perlès was not entirely joking when, in badinage, he proposed that Anaïs revenge herself on Henry for his inattention by falling in love with himself. He was ready, he wittily declared, to volunteer his person for a campaign to make Henry jealous. Much of this talk was dropped in Henry's presence and was an affectionate kind of sexual joking, letting Henry and Anaïs know that he liked them both, approving their choice of each other. But beneath his irony Fred was at least a little serious. The strained situation came to a head one day when Fred took Henry to task for his continuing devotion to June and his neglect of Anaïs. Perlès was not entirely surprised to see that Henry was inclined to defend his wife, but he was astonished to see Anaïs taking June's side against him, with Henry. Was it true, then, that Anaïs was also in June's spell? The truth, as Anaïs explained when she met Fred privately, was that she was afraid that criticizing June would lose Henry to her. She tried to make June love her so that Henry would do so as well.

June had them all in her web, but she herself tore it asunder. She and Henry and Fred had argued so violently at Clichy that one day June moved out to live with friends in Montparnasse. Until then, Henry had virtually given up writing for fear that June would use whatever he wrote as evidence against him. When she moved out, however, he took his copies of the *Tropics* back from Anaïs and resumed work. By early October 1932 Henry had completed 146 pages of *Tropic of Capricorn*. But since June's arrival he had been able to write only thirteen new pages. Once June was out of the way he realized that he was steaming with ideas for both *Tropics*, new sections concerning June's mysteries. Then, one evening in late November Henry's worst fears were realized. He walked into his room at 4 Avenue Anatole France and found June reading *Cancer* and waiting to pounce. She screamed the cruelest accusations he had ever heard: he had utterly distorted her, he had revealed his lack of understanding or talent of any sort by magnifying and vulgarizing insignificant details, and he had made his meanness evident to everyone. Everything she had done for him, the innumerable sacrifices she had made—all were wasted. "You are the greatest enemy I have in the world," she cried at him. "I'm going to kill you. I read your letters as if God had written them, and all the while you were defaming me with your low filthy mind, your disgusting words." Raging, slashing out at him, she handed him one of Anaïs' letters to her. "Read this. You think you love her, but she's just a little lesbian. She'd be dead without you. And you—you only love her because you're a homo yourself." She cruelly called him "empty as Santa Claus is the day after Christmas." The revilement poured out like filth from a sewer. She even accused him and Fred and Anaïs of trying to poison her—that was why she had been ill with nausea and diarrhoea all the while she stayed at Clichy. She warned him that if ever he published a book mentioning her she'd have him in the courts. Then she changed her mind. "No, I want it published just as it is so the whole world can see what sort of person you are. When I read *Crazy Cock* it nearly killed me, but this is too funny, it's so distorted. You think you know all about me but there are a dozen other men who know me better than you do. All you prove is that your own mind is petty and small. Now you'll expose yourself to everyone." He was reeling under her attacks by the time she got up, trembling, to go. "You can find our marriage license and my wedding ring at the bottom of the Seine if you care to look. From now on I'm going to be an Alice in Wonderland," she howled as she pushed her way out of the room.

He stood there unable to move, wanting to run after her and make her
stop and say: "Yes, I've called you whore and cheat, and defamed you. It is
my task now to crucify you. Nothing can interfere with that. But if this is
my hate, my love will come later. Even when you shout that you would like
to cut my heart out, even were you doing so, still I would cry, 'I love you,
June.' I am making you immortal, don't you see? Never has a man been
willing to say these things about the woman he loves." But he did not chase
her. Instead, he collapsed on the bed, in dumb grief. Thrown on the floor he
found a ball of toilet paper wrapped around the earrings and bracelet given
to June by Anaïs. And in June's loose, childish scrawl was written: "Will
you get a divorce as soon as possible?" *The bitch,* he thought. *Now I'll never
get my manuscripts back.*

But she was not finished with him. The ties between them were too
strong to be severed even by the scalpels of such hate. Afraid that Henry
would fall into June's clutches and be destroyed by her, Fred and Anaïs
decided to pack Henry off to London for a vacation until the holidays were
over. The idea of spending a Christmas in Dickens's London held a childlike
attraction that persuaded Henry to accept the passage money. Besides, a
jaunt over to London also offered him the chance to meet Rebecca West and
other literary luminaries who might help him to get his works published in
England. He go a visa and a round trip ticket. Fred helped him to pack his
manuscripts, his notebooks, and his personal papers. Never one to travel
light, he stuffed two valises. He changed about forty dollars of the money
Anaïs had given him into pounds.

The English bank notes were in his wallet and his other effects were piled
up in the hall the night before his scheduled departure when June unexpectedly arrived. She was starving in the flat of the fairy with whom she was
staying, June complained, and accused Henry of not caring what happened
to her. After a terrific scene Henry forked over the entire contents of his
wallet to her—and she marched out triumphant. By the time Fred returned
from the paper at 2 a.m. Henry had reached a state of intellectual paralysis
and drunken self-pity nearly as total as Osborn's had been. His whole
attitude could have been summed up in Osborn's very plea, "What are you
going to do to save me?" And in fact, Perlès rose to the occasion and acted
with the same dispatch as Henry had in Osborn's case. He emptied his own
wallet—containing a little less than 200 francs—and in the morning he
shipped Henry's valises, a carton of manuscripts, and even his typewriter
directly to London. Once his manuscripts were on their way Henry had no
choice but to go. Through the same gates at the Gare du Nord that Osborn

had walked a few months before, Henry went toward the train with something of the same feeling of dislocation and dread that Dick must have had. He sat on the train as the December night fell and made the crossing in a bitter dark. The further he got from Paris the better he felt.

The trouble began when he arrived on the English side of the channel, in Newhaven, and had to answer the questions of the British Customs inspector. How much money was he bringing into the country? The official said courteously—but outrightly—that his suspicions were aroused. To him, Miller looked like a man who had come to England carrying every one of his earthly possessions—even his typewriter—as if intending to stay a good long time. Yet he had but a mere 178 francs—the equivalent of one English pound. As soon as he started to grill him, Henry realized that the inspector believed that Miller intended to be admitted into England and then become a public charge. Perhaps Mr. Miller had already paid for a hotel room in advance? the inspector was saying. No? Did he have any friends in England who would accept financial responsibility for him? No? Henry felt like a displaced person, an immigrant on Ellis Island, and he became flustered and tried to put on a big front. Their questions were misplaced, he implied, for he was an author and should be respected. This didn't help matters. By this time the other passengers had been cleared through and several officials joined in the cross-examination. "But would you tell us the titles of some of the books you have written?" they requested. He mentioned *Tropic of Cancer,* which was to appear in February. They clucked their tongues at that. "You don't mean to say, Mr. Miller, that you are writing about diseases?" "No," he said and, though he began to feel that anything he said now would be wrong, he attempted an explanation: "No, it's about geography." Geography didn't seem any more feasible than diseases did. They came back to the subject of money. Didn't he know that on this very day England had met her war debt to America? From this he understood exactly what the problem was. These petty officials were resentful of the fact that England, poor England, had been forced to pay debts to the affluent United States, and they were taking their resentment out on Henry with his American passport. They implied that America was probably also sending its derelicts over to fair Albion's Isle through the port of Newhaven. In some subtle way they seemed to hold Henry responsible for America's bloody crimes.

At the conclusion of the examination a big black X was drawn through Henry's visa and he was given over to a constable until he could be returned to Dieppe in the morning. Suddenly, in a panic, he remembered that his bags had been passed through customs and were rattling toward London. Wouldn't the constable do something about getting them back? he pleaded. Yes—for a little tip for the constable. The telegrapher was instructed to wire ahead of the train. (A few shillings for the telegrapher.) Then he was locked in a large room, bare but for the benches, just as if he had tried to smuggle American cancer germs into Britain. In the morning he was given breakfast. (A tip left for the waiter.) Well, he thought, England may have paid its war debt, but these limeys had fucked him good and proper. They sent him back to France on the first boat, practically penniless. But somehow his spirits revived. Though it was late December he stood out on the prow and looked toward France. The wind from the Channel seemed to blow the odors of musty rooms out of his mind. As they came in sight of Land's End, the water glittered, the seabirds dived and whirled in great arcs, and the houses and hills gleamed in the distance. Inwardly he rejoiced and his pulses sang; but consciously he was worried, since his French visa had expired and if he was unable to convince the French authorities that he had a means of support, he might indeed face deportation back to America. Perhaps, he speculated, he'd be cuffed and chained and sent back on the very same boat that June was taking.

But everything was reversed on the French side of the Channel. When the clerk who was inspecting his passport noticed that he was a writer, an *écrivain,* he immediately assumed a deferential tone of respect. Did Monsieur Millair know where he was stopping in France? *Bon.* Would he, good sir, take a moment to put his visa in order? *Très bon!* Could the official, perhaps, be of any service? Henry shook hands warmly with the clerk, who escorted him to the train platform. "Bonne chance, Monsieur Millair," he called. Henry knew that the attention accorded him was not personal, but it was just because of this that he rejoiced. His acceptance by this official was born of respect for his profession and therefore no matter what he did, whether his books were good or bad, he would still be accepted. That made his return to Dieppe seem like a homecoming. Soon he was laughing with his friends, glad to be back, delighted at having a good story to tell. Eventually he would write out the account; but immediately on his return he told it in his own special blend of conversational wit. He related his tale as if he expected to get a pie in the face at any moment.

Fred and Anaïs were not quite so joyful about this turn of events until he agreed to allow June to believe that he would be in England until after the time set for her departure. Sequestered at Louveciennes, he waited out the days until her sailing. As usual, June showed no inclination to aid herself.

She made no move to get the steamship tickets. She simply announced to everyone that she was sailing at such-and-such a date and then smiled innocently, folded her hands, and sat back for the fates to take care of her. Doubtless, she reasoned, there were enough people who wanted to be rid of her that she was bound to be shipped off. A few days before the departure, Fred delivered a ticket to her door. She supposed that it was he who had raised the dough for her passage, but of course it was Anaïs who did so. Fred took on the job of seeing June to the train. She departed the day after Christmas, on Henry's birthday, still unaware that he was hiding out nearby. She had probably spent a miserable Christmas, as Henry had, and she was feeling very blue the morning of departure. The world looked strange to her. She repeated to Fred what she had said to Henry the last time she had seen him: "I feel like Alice in Wonderland." But she managed to brighten up. Those were the days when young men and women were supposed to be "game" and smile at disappointments. As though she were placing a grocery order with Fred she said: "Tell Henry to send me a divorce as quick as possible." Then she skipped onto the train.

Eleven

Clichy Days and Nightmare Nights

Clichy was quiet now that June was gone. 1933 promised to be a dream of a year. Henry worked steadily and the work was fine. Anaïs visited him regularly, at least twice a week, during the day. Occasionally they went out for lunch; more often she'd prepare *dejeuner à deux*. She was a marvellous cook; her Spanish ancestry was in evidence when she produced a paëlla or a juicy fowl. Henry himself was rapidly becoming an adequate cook: he especially liked to choose fine cheeses and to prepare beefsteaks—choice cuts only—with *salade de mâche* and *betteraves,* Vouvray for an *aperitif* and St. Emilion for the meal. After lunch with Anaïs he'd push the dishes to one side and read from his manuscript, show her his watercolors, or explain a wall chart that might interpret world history through a color wheel.

Yet for all its peaceful appearance, 1933 was a year of dreams—murderous dreams. The days were quiet in Clichy, but the nights were full of the horrors that, somehow, he had strength enough to recognize in himself. Anaïs's interest in psychoanalysis affected Henry very deeply even though he thought of himself as an opponent of psychoanalysis. "When Germaine lifted her dress and showed me her little pussy," he was fond of saying to Anaïs, "she cured me more effectively than the whole crew of Freud, Jung, Adler, and Stekel could have done." Obviously, this was a pose by a sophisticated, complex man trying to persuade himself that the world was simple. But he never persuaded anyone else that he believed his simple spoutings. Whenever he got going in that vein in Fraenkel's presence, Michael would slaughter him grimly; Anaïs gently talked him around to her way of thinking, and Fred just laughed at him. Henry really had no defense: after all, it was clear that he greatly admired the work of Otto Rank, psychoanalyst and author of *Art and Artist* and *The Trauma of Birth*. Rank had already undertaken an extended analysis of Anaïs, who introduced Henry to him. In November of 1933, when Henry felt he had lost perspective on his revisions of *Tropic of Cancer*, Rank agreed to offer him an opinion on the manuscript. Henry was nervous about this but Rank inspired trust, and eventually he read the novel and praised it for its vivid presentation of a personality. Henry found him not only penetrating but also sane and kind, very human, and these personal qualities drew him to Rank's ideas. So Rank became such a frequent subject for discussion that Henry almost felt he was getting a course of Rankian analysis through Anaïs. Far more than Freud, Rank was willing to understand human life in terms of its poetic configurations, as if the psychologist was a critic. He was less interested in patients needing to be cured (Freud's subject) than in the artist figure, who needs to be understood. For him, a work of art constituted a kind of apocalypse of the mind in which society and the neuroses it produced were symbolically killed, while the artistic work lived on, the healthy child of neurosis. After much discussion with Anaïs, Henry concluded that if a work of art was made from neurosis, then the artist had to become as conscious as possible of his own sicknesses in order to make the best use of them in his work.

Everyone after Freud knew, of course, that the best place to catch one's neuroses was in dreams. With the encouragement of Anaïs and Rank, and possessed by a spirit of adventure as if he were setting out on a dangerous voyage, Henry decided to plunge into the deep waters of his mind, to face his ills and to try to turn them into art. He believed that in *Tropic of Capricorn*, which was coming along slowly, he had closely approached the core of his psychic terrors. If he could go all the way, he told himself, right through his hunger to his neurotic fear of starvation, through his failure with June to the causes for that failure—if, as Michael put it, he could die all the way—*then* what a book he could write. So Henry set out on a program of remembering, recording, and analyzing his dreams. He found that he could fish the most minute details out of the well of memory, and he realized that precisely because he could remember so much, his task was to remember everything—to remember so much that he would be able to transcend his old life and create a new one. He never believed that he could cure his neuroses simply by recognizing them in dreams: he didn't want a cure, he wanted a new life. "Dream true!" he used to admonish Joe O'Regan. That was what he was trying to do.

As early as September of 1932 he had started to keep a dreambook; but his conflicts with June had made the days so nightmarish that he had no time for dreams. Every night he sank into bed as into a bog, thankful if he could obliterate his consciousness. After he made it through Christmas of 1932 and June sailed and his birthday passed in the fumes of miserable memory, his dreams resumed. He attempted to stimulate them by a simple device of the surrealists. Every night before retiring he recorded whatever came into his mind in his notebook. This "automatic writing" was like dreaming with his eyes open: surprising names and places and events began to pop up telegraphically on the page. Before long, his mind would be dancing a jig. While the tap was still turned on, he'd throw himself into bed and try to sleep. Hardly would he have cautioned himself, *Don't forget your dreams,* when he would fall off and the images started flowing. He was so intent on possessing his dreams in their entirety that he often found himself retracing old dreams in the midst of a dream and saying to himself: *There, this is the very thing you were trying to remember!*

Henry's dream devices worked almost too well. Healed by Anaïs and cheered by Fred he had gotten fabulously healthy—strong enough to endure the phantasms of his worst fears. The dreams came, after a while, with hardly the need for a stimulus of any sort. Once he was in a dream, preposterous as it might have been, everything in it seemed perfectly logical, part of a pattern whose purposefulness was undeniable even if inexplicable. The atmosphere of his dream world seemed to be constructed along the lines of a Wagnerian opera or a German expressionist movie. Some stage technician seemed to be trying out his background effects: snow-capped mountains, tropical suns, colored lights, clouds of blue fog, and painted, artificial stage sets, all appeared in his dreams and gave them a Coney Island atmosphere. One after another his deepest fantasies came tumbling out like a loop-the-loop as he plunged through the laughing face of reality. He dreamed his way back to young manhood, adolescence and infantile fears.

Beatrice came down a Flatbush street wheeling a baby carriage, but Barbara was not in it, she was fully matured. Naturally Henry wanted to know what street they were on and so he pulled his notebook out of his pocket to look up the address of their home, when Bea seized him and said, "Yes, this is the street. Don't you remember? 244 Sixth Avenue." Then they go to a restaurant, but his wife begins to behave like a trollop, causing a stranger to insult her. "You can see what she is," he says apologetically to Henry. And so Henry takes her home to look her over carefully. As he inspects her vagina it suddenly assumes the shape of a billiard ball with little teeth in it which lock and unlock like gears. "A remarkable instrument," he sighs. "You ought to put radium hands on it!"

From his bed he hears his mother groaning and cursing father for his drunkenness and he realizes he is back in Decatur Street. Osman is next to him saying, "Isn't this fine, Henry?" and trying to bugger him. The sheets are so twisted around him that he is beginning to strangle, but he manages to free himself and mount a woman with big breasts who is lying next to him. She resembles Bertha and he is ready to screw her when suddenly he sees a shadow—June's shadow—fall against mother's bedroom door. Her finger points ominously and her whole figure seems poised to witness the scene.

The shadow of a cross falls over the foot of the bed onto which he is chained—the chains clank loudly while an anchor is lowered. Mother is at his side, saying to him: "You better call the police. Father isn't home yet." She goes to Henry's bureau and removes his revolver. If father doesn't commit suicide, Henry wonders, how are they going to collect the insurance? In the middle room of their railroad flat mother stands in her chemise crying like a madwoman while making her toilette, powdering her arm pits, bosom, and crotch with a big puff, then using an atomizer to spray the same areas with vile perfume. Disgusted at this behavior and blaming father for it, Henry thinks: "It certainly would be better if the old buzzard killed himself!"

Though they are sitting in a semi-circle in the middle room, he no longer recognizes any of his relatives. He does not even recognize the old, familiar Decatur Street rooms, since everything in them is rearranged. Nevertheless, he leaps out of bed in his nightshirt and clowns around, pulling the beards of his uncles, twitting his aunts, teasing his cousins. No one shows either approval or disapproval. Even so, he starts to show them his notebook, which will expose him in the most damaging light, for in his notebooks are recorded thoughts and acts that he doesn't wish his staid relatives to know about. Besides, in showing his notebooks, the colored envelopes containing letters which Anaïs sent him from the Tyrol fall out. At once, he becomes conscience-stricken and fearful that these will be seen—even more so when Hugo shows up. His fears do not diminish even though Hugo urges him: "That's fine, Henry. Go ahead and show them."

He walks off in disgust, but just as he is climbing into a ditch, he hears his name mentioned on the other side of the embankment. "He's just a nobody," Uncle Gustave is telling a stranger, who replies: "But everyone is talking about him—surely he must be of some account." "No, I tell you, he's completely worthless."

On lower Broadway one moment and at the Bedford Avenue Fountain the next, he is trying to shove his way through a great crowd to catch a glimpse of the parade. The troops, it turns out, are a disorderly group of French toughs. Having just returned to America, Henry feels a kinship with these fellows and is soon swinging along at the head of the column. He leads them into a building and up an ancient spiral stair, like that leading to an old fortress dungeon. Just as he is about to go through a doorway, one of the Frenchmen shouts that he is trying to trap them and pulls him back.

He has escorted Gertrude Imhof home and before he has a chance to bid her goodbye she asks him casually if he'd like to have a fuck. At once he is squeezing her enormous buttocks and trying to screw her standing up. He manages to go off all right, but just as he does so she takes a huge pair of old blunt scissors from the table and begins to cut away at a string attached to a condom he had inserted inside her. He's paralyzed with fear that she will snip his penis off—indeed, as she cuts away it seems that the string is a living fibre attached to his own body, it *is* his penis, and though the pain is quite bearable, he is very nervous.

He is in the midst of an elaborate lie concerning how much he enjoys swimming in rough seas when he becomes so aware of the terrible truth of an incident during a thunderstorm at Coney Island when he was caught beyond the lifelines and almost drowned, that he breaks off his story, sinks into his luxurious leather seat, and resumes his reading. Over his shoulder a girl he loves and her lover are also reading the work. It is his own book, he realizes, in which they are all so engrossed. One of its passages is particularly fascinating and though it is unintelligible they repeat it over and over intently. This connects to another dream, he realizes, in which he is seeking the dream book which will provide the key to all his books. How obvious it should have been all along, he thinks that the dream book should be the book he wrote himself, the book which opened his heart. The ultra-modern suburban train pauses at Darmstadt to have its engines changed. The station is glass, rising to a steeple as in a church. Somehow the steel shed looks like the open book on his lap: the opened volume also seems to be crystal with its ribs showing through. "In my heart," he whispers to himself," there is a little glass bell and under the bell there is an edelweiss." Though all the earth is covered with a diamond-like frost, at his words it blooms magnificently and all his cares fall from him.

On his way home in the dark he is obliged to go through a forest, a patch of woods which he can almost remember from his childhood. Standing on a bridge he sees that all the roads run through the woods in parallel lines—all lead home—and yet they are all covered with snow and absolutely impassable. Bald is with him and as they stand there, suddenly a couple in evening dress begin to walk across the ice-cold stream. The man, Billy Ayres, leads the woman right into the stream despite the fact that she is clad only in a light evening dress with a bare back. The water rises right up to the crack in her rear, but she is unperturbed. At first this seems astonishing, but it conveys the impression of something beautiful, delicate, like a flower made of ice.

In a train station of a foreign country, while Henry is changing in a deserted salon with peeling red wallpaper, his mother enters and informs him that she is also departing on the ten o'clock train. It is already ten minutes before the hour and she has not even begun to dress. He informs her firmly he will wait ten minutes—no more! She promises to be on time and goes out; but no sooner does she do so than he leaves. "Let her take care of herself," he mumbles. But he has trouble getting tickets himself, the procedure is too complicated for him to remember. When he finally does make his way to the gangplank, his parents are already there waiting for him, looking very worn and old-fashioned. To make matters worse, as he tries to go up the gangplank pretending that he is not with them, whom does he meet but a boyhood friend who is pretentiously overdresed in a frockcoat. Henry was always sure that this fellow would come to nothing, and so he inquires how it is he is now so well off. He has married a dowager for her money, he explains: "It's very simple. I sit and do her telephoning— that's all!"

Such was the dream-cinema which unreeled in Henry's mind all through 1933, particularly from January to September. His dreams cast a strange, super-real shadow upon his everyday occupations. Finally he began to see that day or night he always pursued the same goals: to recapture his past, to deepen his imagination, to realize his own identity, to pass into a state of cosmic consciousness—to dream true! He was transfixed by the realization that every event in his past had not only connections with other events but a meaning and purpose in the development of his psyche. This implied that, though unnoticed, the present was having the same significant effects upon him and that he must consciously attempt to become as aware of the present as his dreams had obliged him to be of the past. To see clearly was really, then, to see prophetically; for to understand his present was to know the future and fate of his ego. His dreams gave him the assurance that he had a full, rich inner life.

Perhaps most important, he came to grips with the psychological chain binding all his loves together. In 1935, he wrote in the third volume of his dream book:

And thinking of . . . the questions A[naïs] and others put to me about my mother, my possible worship of her (unconsciously) and of how this affected my whole love life, I must confess there is an enigma here worth penetrating. Because I see that in the women I loved there was always a dual nature—I prostrated myself before them, worshipped them, trusted them blindly, *and* I regarded them as *cruel*. And perhaps the root of it lies in my attitude towards my mother, when a child: first, a very trusting, dependent nature, early disillusioned by her stupidities and brutalities; secondly, coming to hate her, and taking my father's part, because I could understand his weaknesses, his greater human qualities. And I transferred this dual nature of love (the worship and hatred) to all the women I encountered, and created each time anew the same conflicts, even when there may have been no reason, no necessity for them—that is, as regards the essential nature of these women, of their relation with me.

Such understanding marked an almost immeasurable advance in psychic health over just a short period. And Anaïs and his dreams were his instruments.

Miller never published his "Dream Book," though in October, 1933, he did type up his dream transcriptions and analyses, devise an analytical table of contents for them, and design a typed and painted title page: "To Anaïs Nin/ Original M.S. of Dream Book/ from Henry Miller." This dream book, nonetheless, stood behind the work of that year and was to cast its glow over his writing until the end of the thirties.

Twelve

The Lost Book

The keys tapped across the pages as if the sentences he typed out already stood in little rows in his head, merely waiting to be transcribed. Nothing could stifle the flow. Rejections which would have paralysed him a year or two before rolled off his back; elaborate projects now were outlined in notebooks and on gigantic wall charts; hopes he would never have entertained, even privately, he now openly acknowledged.

By the time that he received word that Covici-Friede had "so kindly rejected" *Crazy Cock* in the beginning of January 1933, he was rather glad and prepared to pillage the book for the sake of *Tropic of Capricorn* since both books had the same subject. Part of the reason he had moved so slowly on *Tropic of Capricorn* was that his earlier book had robbed the later, richer one of material. Now, however, the rejection of *Crazy Cock,* he wrote to Pascal Covici, gave him "a moment of exuberance."

Miller needed exuberance, for he was working on three major projects simultaneously: revisions of *Tropic of Cancer;* composition of *Tropic of Capricorn*; and the outline for a critical work on D.H. Lawrence which he had started early in November 1932. In accepting *Tropic of Cancer* for Obelisk Press, Jack Kahane had remarked that the influence of Lawrence was evident. To Henry's annoyance he kept speaking of Lawrence as "your great favorite" and finally proposed that Miller write a *plaquette* on Lawrence of a hundred pages or so which the Obelisk press would issue in advance of

Tropic of Cancer in order to give Henry the sort of prestige as a thinker which would disarm the critics in advance and force them to take the novel seriously. Well aware of the financial success in a limited edition of *Lady Chatterley's Lover,* Kahane was also very wary of the censors and possible criminal consequences. Kahane intended to guard against these by publishing the book only in a private limited English language edition (Fachette would not even consider publishing a French edition). A critical work on Lawrence, he reasoned, would give Miller something of the status which had protected Lawrence and his publishers from prosecution. So Kahane said: "Write this pamphlet on your favorite, Lawrence. You haven't very much else to do now." Though he was busier than ever, Henry took this task—proving to the world that he was a thinker—as a challenge. He started almost immediately and soon wrote to Osborn that he was "knocking the shit" out of Joyce in a new book he had undertaken. In contrast to Lawrence, he considered Joyce "dead as a doornail," and Proust as well, and was planning to call this essay, *Brochure,* or "The Universe of Death," a title borrowed from Lawrence's *Fantasia of the Unconscious.*

Miller began writing without the slightest idea of what he wished to say. It didn't occur to him that what drove him along might have been a sense of competition with Lawrence: he didn't want anyone to suppose he was Lawrence's disciple—he wanted to prove himself Lawrence's superior and he wanted to dispatch him along with Joyce and Proust. After writing well over a hundred pages based on this motive, however, he began to suspect he had made a mistake. He wasn't sure that Lawrence really deserved such harsh treatment. Was it possible, he had to ask himself, that he condemned Lawrence willfully just because Anaïs and Michael and Walter (and even more distantly, Emil Schnellock) all supported him so completely? Not only did he have doubts about his treatment of Lawrence, more fundamentally, Henry's imagination in 1933 inclined him toward positive thinking.

As the original conception of *Brochure* shifted, another book began to grow up inside it, a treatise on the "Thinkers" or "Life-givers" (Spengler, Nietzsche, Faure, Maurice Bucke, Whitman, Fraenkel, Rank, and Jung) who counterbalanced the modern "death-eaters" (Lawrence, Joyce, Proust). In *Brochure,* as in the "Dream Book," he was trying to see what made him tick by writing about the powerful intelligences that had influenced him. If they had some unity, so did he. All of his favorites were systematizers, thinkers who offered comprehensive explanations of the universe, and that, of course, was exactly what he wished to do. But he believed that these apparently different thinkers really shared some basic understanding of reality. He designed intricate charts to demonstrate elaborate underground systems of relationships among them. By January of 1933, this effort had broken down completely and Henry's good spirits with it. Lost, he aimlessly copied several hundred pages of extracts from the works of his favorites, but when he was finished he hadn't the slightest idea how they fit together.

Next, influenced by Anaïs and a reading of "The Crown" and *Apocalypse* he began to reverse himself on Lawrence. From having thought Lawrence weak as an artist, he began to find him dominated by ideas and a supreme thinker. Finally, he began to fall in love with the man. Thus, the short critical book which Henry undertook at Kahane's behest went through a series of transformations. In April of 1933, he started his third version. By this time his notes had assumed tremendous proportions: the extracts alone constituted more than 200 pages. He had no idea how he would reduce them to any sort of order in a consecutive argument. At the urging of an inner spirit which "dictated" to him, he wrote a hundred new pages. He argued that although Lawrence had failed as a writer, his works represented the drama of his attempt to experience his death creatively. But the similarity of this idea to Fraenkel's troubled him: Michael, who was nothing if not sensitive, might well consider Henry to have plagiarized from his "Weather" paper. Besides, Henry himself had mocked the death dogma in *Tropic of Cancer*—and if it were now to provide an illuminating interpretation of Lawrence, what did this mean for his views there? One of his books was ready to negate his other book.

Miller started again. He arranged a list of forty-five topics drawn from his notes under four topical headings: "The Malady: Disintegration of Ego," "Man as Universe," "Function of Art," and "Man as History." But broad as these headings were, many of his topics floated about rather uneasily. Where should "Magic of Sex," "Hamlet-Faust Cycle," "Keyserling's Spiral Evolution of Man" or "Obscenity" be placed? And where would Lawrence, Joyce, or Proust fit? He started again by devising a thematic index to suit these writers, and he managed to reduce his scheme to twelve items, such as "Individual Soul," "Woman vs. Man," and "Homosexuality." He realized that something was amiss with a conception that could be divided indifferently into one scheme or another. He suspected that he was imposing gratuitous ideas upon his material. Aware that Emil Schnellock (to whom he had been sending his manuscripts) must be utterly confused, Henry tried to explain his intentions, and then he realized that he himself was as confused as anyone and he admitted to Emil "that God only knows when I shall come to the end." The basic problem was that he was trying to join several books together—a *plaquette* on Lawrence, a cultural psychology for his age, a history of his own intellectual gestation, and an attack upon modernity. He admitted to himself that his plans contained the seeds of several books. But instead of discarding most of his material, he astonishingly inferred that he must write *four* separate books: slender brochures on Joyce and Proust, a good-sized tome on Lawrence, and a book of cultural-philosophic theory, "a book divorced from names," in which all his themes were orchestrated.

Eight months on the Lawrence book—yet everyday it grew larger and more ungovernable. By June 1933, the best he hoped for was to finish the book by the end of the year. Kahane had delayed the publication of *Tropic of Cancer* in anticipation of the swift completion of this critical work, which he intended to publish in advance of the novel. Though Miller endorsed this plan and did indeed wish to make absolutely clear what he stood for and against, he floundered, toiling on the project all summer. A year after the *plaquette* on Lawrence had been suggested to him, then, he returned to his starting point. Surely, he felt, out of the hundreds of pages of notes and writing he could quarry a little pamphlet on Lawrence, only Lawrence. Resolutely he wrote out the title: "The World of Lawrence." From his various drafts—which often conflicted with each other due to his frequent changes of mind—he pulled out 225 manuscript pages and tried to stick them together. Instead of going back over these pages to smooth out their differences, Miller decided to let the contradictions stand. The truth was that he was helpless to do otherwise, yet he attempted to justify this curious critical procedure in a "preface" which he placed in the middle of the book. He let contradictions stand, he explained, because they showed his previous ignorance. The important thing—he told himself as much as his reader—was that he now "get into action" in setting forth a final, lucid view of Lawrence.

It was a bad sign, then, that he started to draw up more plans instead of writing. Another wall chart was tacked up, called the "Tree of Life," in which he attempted to interpret Lawrence as an apostle for a new way of life and to explain the symbolic system whence his ideas flowed. At last the fundamental source of Henry's difficulty in completing the book was obvious: he had thoroughly blurred the line between Lawrence and himself. Sometimes he almost felt that the spirit of Lawrence had "composed" the chart and was "dictating" the book to him, sometimes that he was "possessed" by Lawrence. "Lawrence," he wrote, "has meant so much to me . . .

because I saw in his struggle my own struggle with the world. When he denounces the world I feel that I am denouncing the world too—in the very same words." He simply could not write the book in Henry Miller's words.

Finally, by October of 1933, he had lost all understanding of his own work. He went to Lowenfels for aid. Walter read his manuscript and came back shaking his head. He could make absolutely nothing of it. Henry turned to Anaïs. More gently she remarked that whatever it was he had tried to say he had not succeeded in saying anything coherent.

A year of work had ended in a complete disaster. He declared himself a fool to have put several other books he had planned aside for the work on Lawrence. He had elaborately planned a work called "Palace of Entrails," an unfilmable scenario, a kind of anthology of film ideas, and a burlesque of Anaïs's "Alraune." He had also outlined a critical book on the cinema and another, longer book—titled "Self-Portrait"—displaying himself through his dreams in a kind of diary of his nightlife. He hadn't gotten anywhere with these works. Most important of all, his elaborate chart for *Tropic of Capricorn* began to fade on his wall, although he said it was the one book he wanted to write. He had to ask himself whether it wasn't true that he had taken on other projects in order to avoid telling the truth about his life with June. "The World of Lawrence" had stalled everything. Henry was frustrated because with all these works bulging in his head, he was squeezing out so little, and his head was aching from all it still held.

Thirteen

"All the Loose Ends That Were Flapping About Inside Me"

June remained a spike in his brain. No one, least of all Henry himself, could have said whether or not he was still in love with her, but again and again it was proved that he was very much tied to her. He had done nothing about getting the divorce that June had demanded. The tie that still bound him hand and foot came close to strangling him in May 1933. Osborn posted a forty-two page letter to Henry, but Henry didn't get beyond the first page before he was fuming over the news of June. Osborn had bumped into her at a restaurant in Patchin Place, in Greenwich Village. "She seemed very bitter at the mention of your name and said she wanted to know nothing or hear nothing concerning you but was curious enough to ask if I knew whether your book had been published over there." She was escorted, Osborn wrote, by "a rather nice looking young fellow considerably your junior in years."

The phrasing was vintage Osborn—stilted and ludicrous—but it pierced Henry's heart. He saw her looking scornfully at Dick, speaking insolently, hanging on a man considerably Henry's "junior in years"— what a phrase! (That could only be Stratford Corbett, a healthy piece of meat who lived on Patchin Place.) So that was why on her last visit June had said to Henry more then once, as they were climbing into bed: "God, Val, how thin you look"—doubtless, she had Corbett's athletic figure in mind.

For several hours he brooded over Osborn's letter. Late in the evening he poured out his despair in a twelve-page suicidal letter to Emil Schnellock. He could not continue life, he explained, with June hating him. But why should she hate him?—she had committed crimes against him, not the reverse. But whatever she did, he said, he could never get over his love, never escape her. So, though he had no hope of regaining her love, he pleaded with Emil to beg her to stop hating him.

But as he rambled on loosely, emptying a bottle of wine beside him, his tone changed to a defense of himself. He admitted that he would not be content to have June stop hating him, he wanted her to love him slavishly. He wrote: "I want her to get down on her knees and *beg me to forgive her.* I want her to weep until her heart breaks, her dirty little mean petty Jewish heart that failed to recognize a great soul when it had one. Who is June, *in reality?* Don't you think I know? Don't you think all your little sarcasms and ironies, your petty innuendoes lodged in my brain? . . . Sure I know who June Smith-Smerth-Mansfield-Miller-Cunt-Balls-whore was. I know her down to the roots of her insatiable cunt. I know her soul inside out, because it was so thin that you could turn it inside out like a sleeve. I knew June, better than any of you did. But I loved her . . . I could love her and at the same time I could ridicule her." It angered him to think that she could believe she had the right to hate him. He wanted to perform one grand gesture that would show her how wrong she was, some act that would put him in the proper light. And so there was one thing he wanted Emil to tell her: if his suicide would soothe her conscience, he would gladly do away with himself.

Perhaps, he said as he continued, it was all his fault—he was a dreamer who wanted to be somebody and he believed in others so much that he pushed them about for his own sake. He had pushed June—into selling candy, being a hostess, pushed her toward other men, and into whatever sacrifices were necessary to keep him going. Now she wanted only to hate him and to have a little love from a young man "considerably his junior in years," et cetera. He confessed that he wished, wished desperately now, that he had never written a word, that he worked for New York Life and was an idealist, that he could be that naïve, stupid young fellow, believing in June and hanging on her every word in a Greenwich Village restaurant. But he couldn't be; she regarded him as her enemy. And so, all she had to do was say the word and he would commit suicide, and nothing he had ever written, neither the *Tropic of Cancer* nor the *Tropic of Capricorn,* would ever be issued. "I would have liked to think," he wanted Emil to tell her for him, "that it was eternal, this love of ours. But since it isn't or wasn't what can I do? I can blow my brains out or jump in the Seine." Perhaps the thought of that would make her twitter, and as she lay in the arms of a young man, considerably his junior in years, she would tell him of the wormy, flyblown writer who had committed suicide for her titillation. Then as June went from one man to another in the future, she could give herself an air of glamor by speaking of the guy who wrote books about her and killed himself for her love. He was roaring drunk by the time he came to the twelfth page of his letter, and he knew then what it all came down to: Emil was to inform her "Hurt, Hurt, I loved her. Tell her." Then Henry dropped off to sleep. But the drunken composition of this long letter released his conflicts over June. When he awoke he felt quite refreshed. Laughing, he read his letter over, then added a postscript: "If I say my heart is breaking never believe me. It is just literature. Should you ever see the said Mansfield-Smith-Smerth-Miller woman tell her to go fuck herself—tell her I said so." This abrupt turn-about was pure Henry Miller. He was certainly more intact emotionally than his original letter indicated, but far more obsessed with June than his flippant postscript suggested.

He brooded for two weeks after this episode and wrote nothing, even though he still faced the problem of a conclusion for *Tropic of Cancer.* Finally, in early June of 1933 he attempted to resolve his personal problems and complete his book in one stroke, by ending with a literary letter to June marked: *"Dernières pages."* This ending for the book, he explains, was made possible by Anaïs, who taught him what real sacrifice was. Until he met Anaïs he had believed that June's sacrifices were selfless. To do June justice he must express his contempt for her: that is the meaning of *Tropic of Cancer.*

Such a conclusion should have impelled him to resume *Tropic of Capricorn,* but his novel was giving him as much trouble as the Lawrence brochure and for much the same reason: he had overprepared his lines, he was like an actor still thumbing through a greasy worn script for a play which should have opened years before. He had scanned his forty pages of notes enough times to have memorized them, he never gave them a chance to seep from the memory into his imagination. Now he revised them once again and then wrote an elaborate outline. In June of 1933 he could not see that the novel and the brochure on Lawrence both became unmanageable because he refused to select from his experience or to depart from his minutely particularized plans. When he tried the opposite method— simply to write automatically and let the sweep of his style and the leap of his intuitions carry him to the insights, he was equally unsuccessful. He tried an unpremeditated opening and it was a disaster. "The most difficult thing for me is to write this first line," he started, "—a piece of sincere insincerity, a clue to my character, to everything that follows. The hardest thing for me is to begin, because I have never known a beginning nor an end." The book, he said, was merely a book—not a novel, a story, a slice of life, a fantasy, a biography or even an autobiography—just a book: if it were anything other than itself, it could only be called a funeral. He wrote in order to give a decent burial to the deeds recorded in his book: "it is *my* book, *my* life, *my* creation": it was anything he, the author, wished it to be.

So much for his aesthetics. They made an opening—but where would he go from there without falling into the trap of constructing a novel, when what he really wished to do was rinse his pages with his red blood? He had announced an aesthetic that put him in a corner. He liked his principles but now that he was faced with *doing,* how could he write a book that was *nothing* but a book?

Since he had no answer he laid *Tropic of Capricorn* aside and picked up "Self-Portrait." Though he originally regarded "Self-Portrait" as a note to "The Universe of Death" or the coda to "The World of Lawrence," he always planned it as a personal statement and instead of following a grand plan, he let this book take shape easily, naturally, by looking at himself, or portraying his experience, in a variety of ways. "There are huge blocks of my life which are gone forever," he wrote. "Huge blocks gone, scattered, wasted in talk, action, reminiscence, dream. There was never any time when I was living *one* life. . . . Wherever I was, whatever I was engaged in, I was leading multiple lives." By resisting the temptation to present the essence of his personality he kept his novel fluid enough for him to improvise on his various selves, as husband, friend, son, writer, painter, exile, and dreamer. The essence of the book was its insistence on rambles, excursions, walks. Miller pictured himself strolling through Paris, through his past, through continents, through his dreams, his roving mind, the seasons—toward the possession of a new territory and a renewed consciousness. Unconsciously, he had adapted the form of *A Man Cut in Slices* which had been steeping in his mind for many years and had influenced *Tropic of Cancer.* He was bent not on giving his readers slices of life but his own self sliced into transparent cubist pieces—a self seen now this way, now that, a self existing only in its multiplicity.

Finally he had rediscovered the method that suited his talent and he breathed a sigh of relief at his progress. First came a sketch about his childhood, a rhapsody about the origin of his mind, called "The Fourteenth Ward." This evoked his sensuous delights as a small boy on the streets in the old neighborhood as if it were his first day of spring. In the next section, "The Third or Fourth Day of Spring," he remembers the house on Driggs Avenue, and he associates the sense of wonder it conveyed, with Paris. In "A Saturday Afternoon" he continues his ramble about Paris and writes comically about French urinals. Miller followed these with a series of sketches on the development of his artistic sensibility. In "The Angel is my Watermark," a piece destined to be among the best known of his writings, he outlined the genesis of one of his own watercolors. "The Tailor Shop" gave an account of his frustration when he dreamed of being a writer but worked in his father's tailor-shop. A burlesque, "Jabberwhorl Cronstadt,"on the conversation of Walter Lowenfels an artist who put most of his art into speech, followed. Then came an account of Henry's own dreams, based on the records of his dream book, which exhibited the sources of art in images rather than words, in interior creations rather than social palaver. In this section, called "Into the Night Life", Miller was trying to write in the style of what Stuart Gilbert had called the "Language of Night." As if using an *impasto* technique, he wanted to lay down on his pages large smears of the irrational along with his more detailed etchings. This put the section called "Into the Night Life" at the affective and aesthetic center of the book. The title came from a line of Freud's which Gottfried Benn said contained the whole of modern psychology: "Into the night life seems to be exiled what once ruled during the day." Following were three sections, "Walking Up and Down in China," "Burlesk," and "Megalopolitan Maniac," which were designed to exhibit Miller's present point of view. Anarchic, improvisational, and rhapsodic, the book was an urban *Walden* exhibiting a number of elemental contrasts—between civilization and the self, death and life, society and the womb, past and present, bondage and liberation. His plan for the book not only allowed him but obliged him to weld the most contradictory impulses into one ramble. Very wisely he told Walter: "Don't look for realism, verisimilitude, simulacrum, honesty, justice. Look for the passion that animates me. . . ."

In "Self-Portrait" Miller neither felt that he had to prove himself a thinker, as he had in his work on Lawrence, nor did he have a story to tell which continually triggered his neuroses, as was the case in *Tropic of Capricorn*. For once he kept his work purely exuberant. He wrote as if he were dreaming. His only elaborately developed scheme for "Self-Portrait" was inaccessible to rationality: it consisted of a color chart and it helped to give this book a great resemblance to the work of the action painters in the nineteen forties and fifties. Convinced that "life writes itself in terms of color," in the fall of 1933 he took painting lessons from Hilaire Hiler—one of the modern masters of color—with the hope that he would learn how to visualize the vast material of his present and future books in graphic and symbolic form. Experience was represented by red, idea by blue, and the unconscious by yellow. These primary colors symbolized the primary states of being. Violet, the strong mingling of thought and experience, symbolizes the dream state; orange is the product of the combination of experience with the unconscious and symbolizes the life of the streets. White is no color at all and suggests the pre-natal, while black is the absence of color, death. When the inability to live or the yearning for extinction invades the primary impulses of man, a pale life, a gray or brown life, results. Only in that perfect time when the strong impulses of the unconscious mix vitally with idea does spring (green) appear. At present, Henry believed, green was drenched with black: it was a "Black Spring." He had arrived at a concept and a title! Since contemporary life is so infused with death, Henry argues, new forms of literature should smell of the tomb; literature should become a funerary art. He had been unmistakably influenced by Lawrence's *Apocalypse*. (In *Brochure* he wrote: "No. We want no rebirth. We want death—death of everything. We want only enough language, enough intelligibility, to deliver our own funeral oration.") He aligned his imagination with the apocalyptic tradition. His own book, as he saw it in the epilogue, was a painting of the end of the world: "This is one of the strange black springs which visits man at periodic intervals. A spring without hope. A spring without buds or fragrance. A cast-iron, intellectual spring that leaves a stain of rust and melancholy. . . . The women move forward grotesquely as if they knew that inside the shell of the womb there reclined on his elbow an idiot with a buttercup in his mouth and his lips rotting." Miller intended *Black Spring* to deliver the world's funeral oration. But it would also be a rearticulation of the new ideology of the artist bent on restoring creativity to man by balancing the three primary colors and states of being in his work. It was an articulation of himself. Even as everything tumbled around him he proclaimed that he himself was the man of the future. The world was black but it was a green springtime for him. The grand insanity of his book, as Anaïs told him, "was inspired by life and not by life's absence." With Rimbaud he could shout exultantly: *"Moi, je suis intact!"*

Black Spring, as he had definitely named the book by September 1933, constituted a rupture with accepted mores just as much as *Tropic of Cancer* did, though on the surface it was far less offensive. Both books stressed the necessity for movement, receptivity, self-expansion, and circulation of many kinds—on the streets, in the blood, of ideas. Miller liked *Black Spring* better than his first novel, particularly for its stress on the artist and the metamorphic imagination. Henry meant *Black Spring* as an assertion of the artist's future. Michael Fraenkel had attempted to persuade him that all the artist could do was commit "creative suicide"; Lowenfels had shouted at him, "No more poems!" They talked and talked about death, until they were blue as corpses and hoarse as old crones, and yet Henry was unconvinced. He seemed to be agreeing that the black death was everywhere. But he made the weather change. He slipped out from under the shroud the death-eaters had sewn for him and went right on, into a green horizon.

Fourteen

Anaïs, Anaïs, Anaïs

Excursions—real ones, on rail or road—were in the air all through 1933, and not just as a metaphor for *Black Spring*. Anaïs was full of plans for trips, and Henry was in the mood for a little vacation. As early as March she was planning to accompany Hugo to the New York office and to remain for at least a month there. But she didn't want to leave Henry behind, abandoned, and she contrived to find funds so that Henry could also make the crossing. Many and many a time previously he had stated conclusively that he wanted to remain just where he was in Paris, and never see his native land again. But just as soon as Anaïs began talking of visiting New York, he admitted that he did long to see the city once more to observe "American cunts in their native habitat." By May Anaïs decided not to accompany Hugo to New York; she and Henry planned a trip through the Chateau country, Andorra, the Pyrenees, and Spain. But this didn't come off because Anaïs's horoscope declared a European trip unwise, so they spoke of going to Constantinople, Athens, Bagdad, Smyrna, and Fez, perhaps India, in the late fall. "I don't believe in the fucking stuff," Henry wrote Emil, "but if the horoscope says we are going . . . then well and good, I'm going and no kick about it. A man must take what comes his way, whether it be hail or snow or hot ginger and fried mullets." Eventually, Guiler returned, the plans for the vacation were dropped, and Henry found he had to make himself scarce at Louveciennes. Finally, he settled for a cycling vacation with Fred through France to Luxembourg. The bicycle jaunt was a short one, and he was soon back in Clichy listening to the angels that drove him on.

He was most free, he felt, when tied to his typewriter. Ever since he had met Anaïs Nin he had been persuaded that he had a destiny to work out, not a fate to suffer. He felt that somehow every one of his actions was part of a life-work, that there was a "great plan" which was directing his existence, giving it order and imbuing it with significance. To put this another way—a way in which Henry increasingly put it to himself—he had an inkling that he was more than a writer: writing was merely the instrument through which he was practising sainthood. "Above all," he confided to Emil, to whom he entrusted his manuscripts to be preserved for posterity, "I have made some sort of synthesis, which is fine for my soul. All the loose ends that were flapping about inside me are being gathered and knit together. I am seeing things whole, living whole, fucking whole. A holy man, Emil. A just man, a hero—to myself anyway."

He had always been driven by an obsession for order, but now he attempted to organize his life for the sake of his destiny. This desire was expressed most vividly in the "Work Schedule" which he tacked on his wall to remind himself constantly of his responsibility to realize his future. In the prudent and aphoristic manner of a Benjamin Franklin he divided his Work Schedule into several sections and counselled himself, under the heading of "Commandments": "Work on one thing at a time until finished. . . . Don't be nervous, work calmly . . . work according to Program and not according to Mood. Stop at appointed time! When you can't create you can work. Cement a little every day, rather than add new fertilizers. Keep human! See people, go places, drink if you feel like it. . . . Discard the Program *if* you feel like it—but go back to it next day. . . . Write first and always. Painting, music, friends, cinema, all these come afterwards." He divided his days into sections; so much work, so much typing, so much converse with friends, so many minutes for walking, reading, painting, revising—but absolutely "no intrusions" on his plan and "no diversions" from it. He divided his literary work into a "Major" and a "Minor" program, the first consisting of twelve and the second of ten projects. He laid down rules for a "Painting Program" which could occupy him when he was too tired or too empty to write: "Do Self-Portraits—as many as possible," as an aid to writing, but "Do nothing except to be connected with books, ideas—always personal and practical. Paintings should supplement and reinforce my literature."

This surge of confidence in himself and his future was certainly fostered by Anaïs' belief in him. No matter where he looked in his room in Clichy was a token from her—his desk, books, lamp, suits, valise, ashtrays, victrola, couch covers, curtains; when he wrote in his notebook, fountain-pen and paper were both from her. He went to Louveciennes as often as possible and drank up the fine wines in the cellar. She was aware that he had not gotten over his neurotic fear of starvation. The meals she prepared for him were always huge. When Anaïs saw the pit of confusion into which he had fallen in his work on Lawrence, she took up his notes and tried to help him make sense of them, even though the spirit of the book was inimical to her own much more personal work on Lawrence. She counselled him on other work, she always stood ready to talk his artistic problems over with him, she gave him an audience—the first one that he had ever really had. She let him know that she wanted him near her. In the winter of 1934, when she moved out of the draughty house in the country and into the Passy section of Paris, near the Trocadéro and Tour Eiffel districts, Henry left Fred in Clichy and moved to an apartment on the Rue des Marronniers, to be near her. He was the first person whom she allowed to read her complete "Diary"; he spoke of this work with reverence and always insisted that she had exposed herself more completely and with greater artistry than he could ever hope to do. Henry vigorously opposed Anaïs's analyst, Otto Rank, who insisted that she abandon her diary. He supported her in her belief that the diary was a healthy act of creativity. In the book that he often called her "unfinished symphony" of the struggles in her very soul, he perceived a realization of the form which he felt contemporary art must have. Since he believed that her journal would be immortal, he begged her permission to be allowed to contribute to it. (He wrote six pages in it.)

Thus, they joined together to aid each other. She helped him with *Tropic of Cancer* and his work on Lawrence. He, in turn, once rose to a splendid defense of her work when he learned that, at the suggestion of the agent William A. Bradley, the journal might be published in a drastically condensed form. "Since you are the one who has inspired the premeditated abortion of Anaïs Nin's Journal," he wrote at once, ". . . I am addressing myself to you directly in order to warn you that I shall use all my influence, and it is not inconsiderable, to belittle and ridicule your suggestions. Consider this an insolence, if you like. I have only one concern, and that is the preservation of what I consider a valuable document—more than that, a work of art."

By the end of 1933 Henry had forgotten all about the torments of his two

marriages and wanted nothing more than to marry Anaïs. Though he
wanted to demonstrate in his writing that "the great artist is he who
conquers the romantic in himself," he thought very romantically. Henry
felt that if only he could solve the money problem everything else would fall
into line. Anaïs dreaded the impoverished existence he had led with June.
One reason that Henry was writing so feverishly, on a merciless schedule,
was that only through writing, so far as he could see, did he have any chance
of earning a living.

Very probably Anaïs had reservations about these matrimonial plans that
she never revealed to Henry. And Miller, even though he wouldn't admit it
to himself, also had very considerable feelings of guilt; for he was placing
Hugo in the same triangular situation which had so often and so deeply
pained Henry himself when his own wife June had given her attention or
affection to others. Miller should have listened to his dreams. In one dream
he was sitting in a large studio room similar to that at Louveciennes. From
across the table, Anaïs's mother castigated him for destroying her daughter's life—he was a tramp, she said, who would bring Anaïs only unhappiness. Anaïs's brother, who resembled Hugo in the dream, sat in an easy
chair listening. Henry became so enraged that at every remark he shouted
back: "What do you mean by that?" At last he leaped over the table and
attempted to strangle the mother—who at once changed into the mother of
his old friend Karl Karsten, a woman who had always been his model for the
ideal mother. If this dream did not reveal enough, another was even more
explicit. In it he discovered that one of Fred's sisters had fallen in love with
him from reading his work. "That's a man I could be happy with," she cried
in the very language that Anaïs had once used about him. But the sister had
a husband, a clean-cut, official banker-type dressed in a blue suit. When
Henry realized that she was married, he drew the man aside for a chat,
confessed his love for his wife, and advised the banker to drag her away. In
yet a third dream, Henry is with Joe O'Regan in his dreary Decatur Street
parlor watching over his and Anaïs's child. He removes the baby from its
warm crib and, after fondling it, places it in a bed that is as cold as ice. At
this moment he hears a car pull up and Joe, who is at the window, tells him
to go downstairs to open the door for Anaïs. He opens the door steathily and
Anaïs slips in (just as June used to do when escorted home by a stranger)
while Hugo, thinly clad, stands out on the icy steps looking wan and
mystified.

When Henry had had to face June's many liaisons, he had always held on
to the belief that they were practical necessities, not romances. Now that he

placed Hugo in the terrible position he once occupied himself, unconsciously he treated love in the same unsentimental way that he believed Pop and Oliver and Marder and Strat had done. So Henry pulled back from Anaïs even as he was saying he wanted to marry her. He had a secret urge to debase their relationship. This was dramatically manifested in Henry's frank and detailed descriptions to Anaïs of the prostitutes he went with or the numerous women he and Fred brought up to their apartment in Clichy. By a curious inversion, he used a whore named Nys whom he met in the Café Wepler to lavish his romantic inclinations upon, and he freely whispered to her the words of love and treated her with the self-effacing chivalry which he wanted to give to Anaïs. By his own admission in letters home, the girl was a duplicate of June, and he described his relations with Nys in detail to Anaïs. He let Anaïs know, for instance, that after a time of wonderful intimacy with her at Louveciennes, pocketing a few hundred francs which she had given him to buy a suit, he stopped off in the Wepler, ran into Nys and ended up paying her 200 francs to allow him to kneel before her and "suck her off." Anaïs was bewildered though she said nothing; but this whole episode angered Perlès (who was infatuated with Anaïs) and it temporarily soured him on Henry. "And you try to tell me you're in love with Anaïs?" he shot out. Of course he was, Henry insisted. Perhaps, he further suggested, Anaïs might have gotten a perverse pleasure from watching him grovelling at the whore's feet. He demeaned the romantic illusions in his relation to Anaïs because he felt guilty toward Hugo and—even more seriously—he was unconsciously afraid that Anaïs would refuse him, if he ever were in a position to propose marriage. Thus, though he yearned to hold her to him, he acted to destroy their relationship. If he could not have her romantically—which to him meant marriage—he could not act romantically toward her. Not while she remained married to Hugo.

On the surface the wedge that this matter of marriage was driving between them was imperceptible. They supported each other in every other possible way. Anaïs went to London in the spring of 1934 to renew her acquaintance with Rebecca West and the other English writers whom she had met following the publication of her first book, and she took *Tropic of Cancer, Black Spring,* and fragments of "The World of Lawrence" with her. Having been completely rewritten for the third time, *Tropic of Cancer* was going through the press, though with the current fluctuations in the value of the pound, franc, and dollar, just when it would appear was still uncertain. Even this late Henry still hoped to arrange a more favorable contract. If Miller could assume the costs of production, Kahane agreed, the Obelisk Press would distribute the book and take merely an outlet's percentage of Henry's profits. On this basis Anaïs persuaded Hugo to pay the printing costs.

Having failed to complete the "brochure" on Lawrence that was intended to prepare the way of the book with the critics (and the censors), Henry next bent his mind to come up with alternate solutions. He may have lost interest in *Tropic of Cancer* (finding it difficult himself to believe that it was all true and not just an exercise in surrealism), but he was still interested in its fate with the critics and he certainly didn't want to see it suppressed. Kahane suggested that Miller get someone to write a preface for it. He approached Walter Lowenfels first, recalling the notes he had written on the first fifty pages. Walter agreed and did write a special kind of preface, somewhat derived from the dogmas of *Anonymous*. His avant-garde idea was to write a preface under Henry's name, as if Miller were introducing his novel by quoting random notes written by a friend. "My publisher," he has Miller say, "thinks this book needs an introduction, a sort of prophylactic jacket, I guess he had in mind, through which the contents can be touched by any reader without danger of infection. A few professional sentences, strictly antiseptic, to show what a serious chap I am, and that, no matter how diseased or horrible this book, the author's dignity (and thus his publisher's) is not to be questioned. In brief, something to stamp the book as literature, not smut."

This too obviously gave the game away. Besides, Henry wasn't comfortable signing a preface written by Lowenfels. Next he turned to Anaïs. She moved in influential circles with friends like Rank and Antonin Artaud, and she had attracted serious attention with her Lawrence book. Henry reversed Lowenfels's procedure by proposing to Anaïs that they collaborate on a preface which she alone would sign. She had already made an appraisal of the book in her journal, and they lifted sentences from this, doing the short appreciation with verve and a good deal of secret merriment. When they claimed that the aim of the book was to present a "resurrection of the emotions," that sounded serious enough—but what they meant by "resurrection," Henry confessed to his friends, was "erection," and so on. In the end they worked out a preface with a reputable tone, barely concealing the tongue-in-cheek, and the book was complete.

Then, at the last moment Hugo blew up and refused to pay the printing costs, saying he wouldn't give a cent to aid his "greatest enemy." Well, Henry concluded, there was no point in losing sleep over this. But Anaïs was adamant. She herself raised the money for the cost of production, about $600, and inserted into the contract an agreement by which the net receipts of the sales would be divided equally between the author and publisher after the deduction of royalties.

Meanwhile, Henry had to find a permanent abode—with Anaïs' help, of course. For a while, he planned to rent Peter Neagoe's fancy studio on the Rue Dounier (the street on which Braque and Derain lived) just off the Parc Montsouris. However, Walter Lowenfels, who had been working a little as a rental agent, let Henry know that in Fraenkel's old house, 18 Rue Villa Seurat, a vacancy existed on the upper right (Michael had occupied the ground floor left), an empty studio, with a sun parlor, bath and stream heat, a luxurious apartment, at $40.00 a month. (Artaud had vacated it only a month earlier.) Walter, who had recently been converted to social concerns, was about to return to America. He supplied the apartment with some household necessities and his record collection, ranging from "Body and Soul" to "Variations on a Theme by Haydn." On September 1, 1934, the very day that *Tropic of Cancer* was published, Henry moved into the Villa Seurat. Kahane appeared at the door, carrying the first copy. To Henry the cover looked horrible: it showed a crab crushing a nude female in its claws; Jack Kahane's 16-year-old son Maurice had executed it to save his father the cost of a cover designer. But in Henry's joy, that was easily put aside. As gestures of gratitude, he mailed the first copy to Fraenkel, sent another to Osborn, and gave copies to Anaïs and Walter. He considered sending a copy to Bruce Barton inscribed: "To the biggest shit on this earth, with my sincere compliments!" He screwed the loud needle into the arm of the victrola which Anaïs had given him and put Walter's records on the machine—good, sentimental American songs of Stephen Foster, like "Old Black Joe," "My Old Kentucky Home," and "Swanee River." The music flowed through his body as the Seine is said to do in the last passage of the novel—a river of music—as Mobile Bay and his dream places flowed through him. America, the past, his visions, the spirits of his friends, his old lost, longed-for selves drifted in the studio with the sun and the birds and the wild flowers. He felt that he had never been so happy.

The day had a tranquil, joyous character that set it apart from the days of excitement which followed as the responses to *Tropic of Cancer* began to reach him. Lots of people were excited about the book, feeling a new literary spirit in it. Osborn wrote that Henry had gotten Irene, the Russian princess, "down pat." Marcel Duchamp praised the book to everyone he met; Duchamp's wife, Mary Reynolds, designed a presentation illustration

for Henry (which he gave to Anaïs) of a body crab climbing out of the pubic
delta under a magnifying glass. One day the great Swiss-French writer, one
of Henry's heroes, Blaise Cendrars, pulled his hulk up the stairs to extend
the hand of friendship, one artist to another. Henry, he said, was in the
great moral tradition of French writing, a noteworthy successor to the
innumerable foreigners (like Cendrars himself) who had come to Paris to
find their talents and had learned to love and celebrate France above their
own country. (He also said these things in a review in *Orbes* which appeared
in the summer of 1935.) A letter arrived from Ezra Pound, who declared
that in *Tropic of Cancer* Miller had out-Ulyssesed Joyce and made a contribution to literature infinitely more valuable than that of "the weak minded
Woolf female" and her kind. Havelock Ellis wrote to praise its psychological truth. When a letter arrived from T.S. Eliot asserting that *Tropic of
Cancer* was unquestionably superior to *Lady Chatterley's Lover,* even Henry
began to wonder if they weren't all crazy—or kidding him. But he decided
to believe in himself. His first book was published and he was singing for
joy.

Fifteen

Wonders and Portents

Up near the ceiling Henry wrote on the Villa Seurat wall: "Jetzt musste ein Wunder gescheh'n." 1934 had been a wonder year for him, he had never really had one like it. At the very end of the year he completed *Black Spring.* Death was its ostensible subject, as it had been in *Tropic of Cancer;* but again the real inner subject is the life of the narrator who can tell stories of disaster and yet remain full of joy, laughing in the face of apocalypse. The first book gave the history of his survival, the second an account of his artistic life. In *Tropic of Cancer* he showed how much endurance the artist needed; in *Black Spring,* the art that came after the rigors of existence had been experienced and transcended. This meant that he should be able to go on and finish his various works-in-progress.

Writing obsessed him between early 1935 and the end of 1938. He bore in like a creature hibernating in the cave of his imagination. For the most part his outward life was uneventful, but now and again a few events drew him into a social context. On December 20, 1934, Henry was divorced from June by proxy in Mexico City. His old pal, William Dewar, had handled the whole divorce for him, and no complications developed at all. Now possibly, he might find a way to marry Anaïs. She, indeed seemed to have discovered a way to earn money—maybe lots of it. After assisting Rank in his analyses for some time, she decided to set up as an analyst. Rank and Allendy promised to refer patients to her. Anaïs had been analyzed down to the last atom by eminent practitioners and knew every technique. She could ask sharp, insightful questions, was by nature a good listener, and had a natural grace which would set her patients at ease. Her idea appealed to Henry for himself. Since his days at Western Union he had had a lot of pride in his ability to analyze the neuroses of others. He had never undergone analysis, only a quick interview with Rank, but he had no doubt that Anaïs could easily teach him the techniques of psychoanalytic counselling. Then he could be worked into her practice, and pretty soon the two of them would be interviewing like crazy and the dough would be rolling in. At 100 francs an hour, he calculated, he and Anaïs would need only a few patients a day to establish a regular source of income.

But Henry's calculations didn't take Otto Rank into account. Though world-famous, the psychotherapist could command only small sums in Paris. He decided to move his practice to New York where psychoanalysis was definitely in fashion. To Henry's complete surprise and dismay, Rank urged Anaïs to come and help him during his early days. Feeling that she owed a great deal to Rank, she could hardly refuse. Before Henry could blink, Rank was steaming toward America with Anaïs at his side. A few days before the end of 1934, unable to stand separation from Anaïs for more than a month, Henry was impulsively bobbing along in her wake toward the wintry land and the dismal shores he had left behind nearly five years before. He had no illusions that he was returning to his homeland crowned by success. Anaïs had to cable money to him for the passage. Though he carried with him a list of publishers and other writers he hoped to meet, what did he have to show for five years abroad but the publication of one book which had sold a hundred copies and could not legally be imported into the United States? He expected to be scorned; but he was lonely for Anaïs, and he felt that if they did not bind their lives together and discover a means of livelihood now, they never would do so.

For months he hadn't so much as glanced at his manuscript of the *Tropic of Capricorn*. Now, as he prepared to take it with him, he read it over and was completely disgusted. He discarded everything he had written except the title. Despite this radical act he looked forward to taking up the book afresh. Perhaps, he thought, it was fitting that the book should be written in New York City, the very place where the history of his misfortunes had unfolded. This sunny spirit didn't last long. As soon as he boarded the *S.S. Champlain* a feeling of malaise settled upon him like the fog on the sea. He felt that he might not be allowed into New York. He was not a criminal or an alien, yet he felt like an outlaw and couldn't help remembering the refusal of the English authorities to admit him. In bleak letters to friends he predicted that he might be jailed as a peddler of smut on arrival at Ellis Island; he actually made serious plans for getting released on bail if necessary. Consciously convinced that he hated the very idea of returning to America, he promised himself that he wouldn't even go on deck to get a glimpse of the skyline as the ship sailed into New York Harbor; but at the last moment, he dashed onto the deck and leaned on the rail with the rest of the third-class passengers to watch the buildings rise out of the sea. This imparted no thrill, only the recollection of all his old failures, but it hinted that he still secretly hoped for personal and literary success on native grounds.

Henry found a room in the Barbizon-Plaza hotel, where Anaïs and Rank were staying; but after a short stay, he moved into the less expensive Roger Williams apartments at 28 East Thirty-first Street. Before he had been in New York a week it was clear that he wasn't going to make any friends among New York writers. Walter Lowenfels patiently explained that Henry's bohemianism was decadent and decidedly unwelcome among the New York literati whose politics had shifted visibly to the left during his absence. The only question they found worth asking of an artist was which he supported—fascism or communism? This talk sounded like gibberish to Miller, whose fundamental anarchism held that all political systems were unnecessary; he had no illusions that he, personally, had any other interests but his own to protect, and he attacked Walter's support of the United Front and his sympathy for the "masses." Whether under fascism or communism, "when the mob rules that means I'll have my throat cut," he told Walter. When civilization itself was the source of corruption, who could choose between the Soviet, democratic, or Nazi varieties? Certainly, he admitted, anyone who saw the world for what it was would wish to alter it. Obviously, the whole of civilization was in a terrible mess—in Russia as well as in Germany. But could one correct the evident ills by getting rid of Hitler and Mussolini? By ousting Stalin? They were just expressions of what most people wanted, and there were hundreds of gangsters waiting to take over should these fall. Society could be improved only when enlightened individuals behaved differently from the masses, not by replacing one ideology or system with another. Never consciously worked out, Henry's political position was a mélange of pre-World War One native anarchism. He abhorred civilization and therefore couldn't believe in reform or political change: when all civilization was defective, one simply chose the system that "suited" him with no utopian illusions. His rebelliousness worried the conservatives, while his detachment disturbed his radical acquaintances.

He couldn't discover a common ground with many writers. Through Hilaire Hiler, now living in New York, he met a few—William Carlos Williams, Nathanael West, James T. Farrell, and William Saroyan (he became friendly only with the last). Predictably, he had no better luck with publishers, who were uniformly agreed that he could not be printed in the United States. Only Alfred and Blanche Knopf encouraged him to write something that could be slipped by the American censors. With so little response from fellow artists and intellectuals Henry felt isolated and alone in New York. Indeed, he couldn't even revive a vital connection with the city of his birth. Nothing in Manhattan seemed familiar.

The old neighborhood in Brooklyn had decayed so completely he felt as if he must have lived there in ancient times. One snowy night he took Anaïs on a tour—but what was there to see? His grammar school was levelled; the tin factory had burned down. The Presbyterian Church, which often appeared in his dreams, had been strangely used; it had been converted into a Synagogue. The Novelty had been turned into a movie palace. The saloons were gone, gone long ago, and the ferry boats no longer bumped out of the slips at the end of Grand Street. Where were his dream streets?   The geography seemed to twist in new ways and streets that he played on as a child he could no longer find. He also took Anaïs to inspect those fabulous places about which he had written in *Crazy Cock*. But these too looked cracked and worn to him, as if their magic had disappeared with June. The apartment on Henry Street which he had shared with June and Jean had become a Chop Suey joint. Henry's fresco of himself as a Mandarin was still on the wall, but it looked quite horrible above the booths.

One bit of good fortune counterbalanced these disappointments. Rank performed the miracle that Henry had hoped for in Paris. His practice was an immediate success, and he soon referred the overflow of patients to Anaïs. She in turn referred some to Henry. By the end of February 1935 Miller was seeing four patients a day. Psychoanalysis was all a tautological game of clichés, he believed, in which most of the patients' illnesses and fears were manufactured from the psychoanalytic jargon of newspapers and magazines. All the analyst had to do was answer in the same clichés in order to "heal" these commonplaces. He became a serious man of affairs, Henry V. Miller, again. By mid-March he was feeling successful and convinced that by putting on the professional gown for a few months each year he could live nicely. From a little measure of St. Augustine, an ounce of Emerson, a pinch of the Old Testament, a tincture of Forel and Freud, and a sprinkling of Lao-Tse, he compounded a general prescription for ills. Most of his patients congratulated him for bringing them "relief"—at least enough to tide them over to the next session. By the end of April, however, he was disgusted with the job because he hadn't cured anyone; he had merely taught the patients forms of adjustment to their maladies. Henry wanted to perform more radical surgery.

He felt that he was temporizing, evading his important work. Even worse, his relation with Anaïs was still unsettled; she was busy and so was he. Their intimacy didn't grow. No decisions were made; they hesitated even to discuss their future. Their love was withering mysteriously. With Rank settled in New York, Anaïs said she had to get back to Hugo and she returned to Paris in May 1935. Henry hung around until the end of the summer, but he deserted his patients. At the last, he had no more money than in the beginning, just enough to put aside to buy his return ticket. On his final night in New York he wandered around, broke, and finally went to visit a female friend at midnight. She bought him a sandwich—it was almost as if his return to his native land came down to this: a ham and cheese on rye, the American dream.

Sixteen

"Alone in My Private Glory"

Paris was home. There, he was not willing to be defeated. Almost as soon as he got back, in October 1935, he started a tremendous campaign of letter writing to everyone who might help him, not so much to succeed—this much he did not quite hope for—but at least to be recognized for what he had already accomplished. In one sense at least New York had given him courage and presumption. He had inspected modern American letters and came to the conclusion that he was superior to all his contemporaries. After finishing *Black Spring* in April 1935, he had written triumphantly to Fred Perlès:

When I read my own pages (weeping and cheering) I look out over other men's work here in America—and there are only two or three I need consider at all as rivals—they are nothing. I am alone, the field to myself, but alas, unrecognized and unchampioned. Alone in my private glory. But good. I swear it. The only book that gave me qualms, which I hesitated to open for fear it would depress me by its brilliance and certitude, was "Of Time and the River" and I opened it last night and this morning I have no qualms, no fears, no hesitations. I am beyond that and beyond all Americans writing here in my native tongue. I have moved out of the realm of fine upholstery, of life garni, of charlotte russes and chocolate éclairs, of corn rippers and whataboys. I am Huey the Kingfish allotting to each his private parts and to myself my own kingdom which is the earth.

His assertion that he was the champion of the world had a hollow sound, even to him, since few of his countrymen had so much as heard his name. Without a "reputation," he saw, his books, with their limited circulation, might easily drop into oblivion. This realization prompted him to begin a grand self-publicizing campaign immediately upon arrival in the Villa Seurat. His correspondence mounted to such proportions that to the young French writer Raymond Queneau it seemed as if the Villa Seurat flat was a *maison d'une commerce*. Often Queneau would meet Henry at a café for an aperitif in the early evening; Henry's arms would always be filled with thick envelopes addressed to individuals in all parts of the globe. Obviously, Queneau thought, Henry was ruining himself with the cost of stamps. But from Henry's point of view, he was writing letters to the world, whether the world wrote back to him or not.

Two of his letters, however, brought surprising results immediately: they became his second and third published works, appearing in October 1935. No form, clearly, was closer to Miller's imagination than the letter. The best of his writing always resembled the casual flow of an epistle to a familiar old friend interested in all his secrets. *What Are You Going To Do About Alf?* is written in the epistle style as an appeal for funds to help support Alfred Perlès so that he could work full time on his own literary projects. Here was a writer, Henry explained, who had to waste his time working on minor journalism when he had already proved himself capable of high literary achievement. With only a small income Fred could go to Ibiza, live cheaply, and finish his current work. As exemplars Fraenkel and Eduardo Sanchez donated the cost of printing, and Henry offered to be Fred's collection agent: "Send your checks, by the week or by the month, to me, Henry Miller, 18 Villa Seurat (14e). Keep firing until we stay Stop!" Certainly, the few contributions that trickled into the Villa Seurat never left Henry's pockets and Fred remained just where he was, in the Rue des Artistes. But Miller did not really expect to collect money with his letter: its importance, rather, was its expression of an artist's attitude. The second work, *Aller Retour New York,* was an attempt to write the longest letter ever published. Addressed to Perlès, it mounted to 147 printed pages. In describing to his friend how an artist would respond to returning to his native land, Miller argued that the writer was necessary to his culture, since most of society had reached such an advanced state of decay it could be redeemed only by the artist's understanding, sensibility, and ecstacy. *What Are You Going to Do About Alf?* and *Aller Retour New York* share the same concern for the preservation of the artist and a sense of artistic community in the modern world.

Less than a month after returning to Paris Henry was drawn into what was possibly the most elaborate scheme of artistic collaboration in the twentieth century. It started in the most casual fashion. Michael Fraenkel was also back in Paris and he had been cajoled into treating Henry and Perlès to drinks at the Café Zeyer; the day was November 1, All Saints' Day. In repayment for the *fines à l'eau,* they rather merrily discussed the death theme for Michael's benefit. But for Henry there were personal overtones to the discussion. Something had happened to him in New York: he hadn't written much, his relation with Anaïs had deteriorated, he began to believe that at the age of forty-four he was imaginatively dying and sexually washed up. Suddenly, while Michael was making a point about a poem by Wallace Stevens, Henry interrupted: "We might as well kill thirteen blackbirds with one stone. Instead of just talking about death, why not write on it? We could knock out a thousand pages in no time!" Fraenkel chimed in: "A thousand pages—no less!" "And no more, either!" Perlès echoed. "No more and no less even if we have to stop in the middle of a sentence," Henry said, "a thousand pages on all the varieties of death!"

But how should such an improvisational book be written? Fraenkel came up with the solution first: he'd start the discussion off through a letter to Henry, with a carbon to Fred; then each would reply separately with carbons to the other. After that it was every man's death for itself. Eventually, their agreement would emerge: sooner or later all three would figuratively arrive at the graveside. In the meantime, at the least, they'd be actively living out their deaths. But, Fred insisted, they'd also be talking in a higher mumbo-jumbo if they couldn't come up with a more concrete subject—any subject. Michael and Henry agreed—but what should it be? Fred suggested *The Merry Widow*—with the Hungarian operetta in mind. That was excellent, brilliant, so far as Fraenkel was concerned: the deadly spider, the female who stings her mate: the connections between sex, procreation, and death leaped to mind. Alternately, Henry suggested that *Hamlet* was a richer theme and this was adopted. (Michael had written on the play in *Werther's Younger Brother.* They decided to pick up where he had left off.) Immediately, *Hamlet* letters were added to Henry's already mountainous correspondence. And to his other friends he wrote letters about the letters he addressed to Michael and Fred, explaining to Count Keyserling, for instance, that their real subject was reality—super-reality, surreality, dream reality—and the art based on the multiple conception of reality. The *Hamlet* letters would be a kind of artists' cathedral, a vast outline of the themes, plots, myths, fables, fictions, and characters which future artists would employ. This notion was, as Henry confided to Huntington Cairns, "colossal in its pretentiousness," but he quite seriously believed in the destructive and regenerative role of the artist. The opening letters set the pace for the rest: Michael was dogged, systematic, and disciplined, while Henry danced or skipped about, ran in circles or did intellectual somersaults. Fred wrote his first letter in elegant French, posing metaphysical and editorial problems with nice discrimination. Michael was bent on defending *Bastard Death* while Henry was anxious to quote a few meaty passages on "The Sacred Body" from *The World of Lawrence.* Fred refused to be "Hamletized" in this fashion and pointed out that they were both talking through their hats. "I am only concerned with my own body. Sacred or not," he declared, "it's my body and, for the time being, at least, I am satisfied with it." This was too mundane a view for Fraenkel or Miller to tolerate and they ignored Fred, who soon stopped writing.

In Paris, in the fall of 1935 Miller not only wrote voluminous and numerous *"Hamlet* letters," he also proposed to edit a pamphlet called "Three Essays in Weather Counterpoint: Homage to Walter Lowenfels," which would feature Walter's "Mental Climate," Michael's "The Weather," and Henry's "The Universe of Death." He sold the five-year-old surrealist sketch, "Portrait of General Grant," to *Night and Day* (London), and almost had a section of the Lawrence book accepted by T.S. Eliot for *The Criterion.* What is more, he had plans for two collections of short pieces. Still fascinated by the idea of the long-defunct *Clipped Wings,* he intended to tell the stories of lost souls such as Gladys Miller, Camilla Fedrant, and Max Bickel of the Rue Jean Jacques Rousseau. Perhaps he would include fantasies on Michael Fraenkel in Hong Kong or on Jean Kronski in the asylum. His other project was a collection of a dozen essays—mostly already written—including "The Universe of Death," "The Cosmological Eye" (on Hans Reichel), and comments on films by Buñuel and Machaty. He wrote up an amusing burlesque on Ezra Pound's economic theories of Social Credit. Mocking a phrase of Pound's for his title—"Money and How It Gets That Way"—Henry wrote a double-talk treatise purporting to solve the problems of economic depression. He begins in Periclean Greece with a history of money, goes through Minoan culture, and soon arrives at the present to announce his basic economic principle: *"Money has no life of its own except as money.* To the man in the street, unaccustomed to thinking of money in abstract terms, this obvious truism may smack of casuistry. Yet nothing could be more simple and consistent than this reduction to tautology, since money in any period whatever of man's history has, like life itself, never been found to represent the absence of money. *Money is,* and

whatever form or shape it may assume it is never more nor less than money."
(In due course, one or two economic theorists took Miller's burlesque
seriously and referred to it with approval.) With such a spate of work in
progress it was little wonder that Henry retreated more and more into his
flat. Not only did the Villa Seurat resemble a business office in the volume of
mail that poured from it, Henry himself was like a busy American executive. There was little time for fun. Outside his door he frequently pinned
notes: "Am out for the day, possibly for a fortnight" or *"La maison ne fait pas
de crédit."*

Miller's basic problem was that he had no genuine publishing outlet, yet
he was rapidly producing publishable work, and so he had to solve not only
artistic, but also production and distribution problems. Obelisk Press dealt
mostly in smutty books for the English-speaking tourist trade; Kahane
would be interested only occasionally in a book like *The World of Lawrence* as
a front to establish an author's respectability. Therefore Henry virtually had
to guarantee Kahane's printing costs in order to interest him in any of his
literary projects. Miller needed to bring in money by writing, but he found
himself shelling out money.

Despite these economic difficulties, 1935 and 1936 showed that his
work was making its way, becoming known. Twice a day, when the mail
arrived, Miller dashed downstairs to find letters of praise from critics such as
Cyril Connolly; and still better, from young admirers. One such letter came
from a Harvard undergraduate named James Laughlin IV, who wrote to ask
permission to reprint the first ten pages of *Aller Retour New York* in the
Harvard Advocate. (Laughlin subsequently reported that the Boston police
had fallen upon the *Advocate* offices, destroyed the issue and jailed the
editors. So, Miller told himself, *the germ has been planted despite official
precautions, even in the United States!*) From the other end of the world, Corfu,
Greece, a twenty-year-old named Lawrence Durrell wrote a letter containing an appreciation of *Tropic of Cancer* which made Henry jump. "I have just
read *Tropic of Cancer* again," Durrell began, ". . . It strikes me as the only
really man-sized piece of work which this century can boast of. . . . I did not
imagine anything like it could be written: and yet, curiously, reading it, I
seemed to recognize it as something which I knew we were all ready for."

Like a magnet Henry drew others to the Villa Seurat. Perlès moved into
the nearby Impasse Rouet. Hans Reichel, the German painter, lived in the
same street; he gave Henry lessons in watercolor, but even more usefully he
was a model of artistic dedication. David Edgar, a young American painter
who never painted, provided the opposite example. Neurotic, lovable, and

without financial worries, Edgar (like the young Henry Miller) had assorted interests in Zen, Rudolf Steiner, Madame Blavatsky, anthroposophy, E. Graham Howe and young, blonde female American art students. Abraham Rattner, another American painter, resided in Paris only briefly, but his intricate, brilliantly colored paintings made a great impression on Miller. Like the others he was often at Henry's house. Anaïs Nin continued to support Miller—and at least two afternoons a week, while Hugo took lessons from Reichel, she visited Henry. She also introduced him to a Swiss-French astrologer named Conrad Moricand, who had been an intimate friend of Max Jacob. Before introducing the two men Anaïs brought Moricand the date, place, and time of Henry's birth and asked him to cast his horoscope. Moricand was a true sensitive, and Henry thought the work he produced had "astonishing" accuracies, especially in its emphasis upon the "death instincts." When they met, Moricand's comments on Henry's chart gave Miller reason to believe that his private sense of destiny had a cosmological *raison d'etre,* and this cemented his relation with the astrologer. Other Europeans were pulled onto the periphery of Henry's cosmopolitan circle: Raymond Queneau; Roger and Jacques Klein, French artists living in the Rue des Artistes; the shy and unsuccessful painter Gregorie Michonze; and the photographer Brassai. Finally, below Henry's apartment, on the ground floor right, lived a young American abstract painter named Betty Ryan, the granddaughter of Thomas Fortune Ryan, who left an estate of 160 million dollars. She had, as one of her acquaintances said, "a flower-like grace," a soft voice, a "Rolls Royce manner," and sparkling eyes. Perlès, Reichel, and Miller all acknowledged themselves half-ready to fall in love with her.

The members of the group aided each other. Queneau reviewed *Tropic of Cancer* and *Black Spring* in the *N.R.F.* Miller became the editor of the "Siana Series," books to be distributed through Obelisk Press. ("Siana"—Anaïs spelled backward—was invented by Perlès.) Anaïs Nin supported the series financially and Miller intended to publish a book by each member of his inner circle. *Aller Retour New York,* the first volume published, was followed by Richard Thoma's *Tragedy in Blue* and Anaïs's *House of Incest* (the extension of *Alraune).* Henry did write a preface for Fraenkel's *Bastard Death,* wrote about Nin's diary in *The Criterion,* and printed the essay—Un Être Étoilique—in a separate pamphlet in 1937. With Nin's encouragement he planned to edit a series of "Booster Broadsides," including *The New Instinctivism, En marge des sentiments limotrophes* by Perlès, *Incognit in America* (poems) by Osborn, and *The Neurotic at Home and Abroad* by David Edgar.

Miller also wrote a book, published in 1937, which he said in a prefatory note, was "directly inspired by a phantasy called *The House of Incest* written by Anaïs Nin." This was *Scenario (A Film With Sound)*, an extraordinary piece of literary surrealism which was just as extraordinarily illustrated by a frontispiece drawn by Abe Rattner. Finally, in printer's dummies which Durrell got from Faber & Faber, Miller wrote a number of personal books for his friends. Perlès celebrated the group in his book *Le Quatour en Ré-Majeur*. Betty Ryan's friend Radmilla Djoukic of Belgrade sculpted Henry's bust. Reichel gave them painting lessons, Moricand did their horoscopes, Edgar loaned them esoteric books, and Betty Ryan gave them dinners.

These writers and painters who congregated around Henry at the Villa Seurat made everything from nothing—even as the powers of Europe seemed bent on making nothing of everything. Spain was the scene of a bloody modern war in which Hitler and Mussolini tested their weaponry. When Spain fell, France seemed likely to follow, though whether it would fall to the fascists or let the communists take over wasn't yet clear. England seemed doomed. And the United States?—its citizens were absorbed in the Townsend Plan, Technocracy, the Chapel of the Little Flower, baseball, and brain-breathing. To Henry and his friends no sane spot seemed left in the world, except for the little corner of it called the Villa Seurat. Everyone in the group felt this, and it drew the artists and writers closer together, into one cozy circle of light, before that glow too should be extinguished by the more violent blazes of war. Many artists all over the world were giving up the struggle: some were shouldering guns; others were devoting themselves to the Revolution, while others had been numbed and dazed into inaction. But the Villa Seurat was a kind of warm, sustaining place of mutual encouragement. In 1936 and 1937 its members felt like survivors and looked around strangely at the conflagration which had overtaken their fellows. They were dancing in the glow of the coming war, dancing like ghosts in the Villa Seurat.

The Villa Seurat was becoming as legendary as Camelot in medieval Europe; at least those who lived or congregated there thought so. From the perspective of Corfu, too, the Villa Seurat, Lawrence Durrell told Henry, seemed like "an immense factory, rather like the Walt Disney Studio, with you in the centre, surrounded by a few hundred active typewriters. . . ." Even at his distance, Durrell sensed the collaborative spirit of the Villa Seurat and proposed to aid in getting recognition for Miller. A sheaf of adulatory letters and a few reviews of *Tropic of Cancer* had resulted from

Miller's enormous correspondence. Miller told Durrell he had conceived the scheme of printing a brochure containing the most interesting comments. In addition he intended to write himself letters he would have *liked* to receive. He hoped to illustrate this collection with a photograph of himself astride a bicycle, add his horoscope to it, have it translated into a dozen languages, and then distribute it *gratis* to the world's leading newspapers and magazines. Durrell attempted to supplement the letters by writing to various well-known authors for statements about *Tropic of Cancer*. The answers which he received were not so adulatory as those that had been volunteered. George Bernard Shaw, for instance, observed: "This fellow can write: but he has totally failed to give any artistic value to his verbatim reports of bad language." Then, some of Henry's correspondents demurred at the publication of their original comments. In mid-1935, after reading a copy of the book mailed to him by Miller, T.S. Eliot had written: *"Tropic of Cancer* seems to me a very remarkable book . . . a rather magnificent piece of work. There is writing in it as good as any I have seen for a long time. Several friends to whom I have shown it, including Mr. Herbert Read, share my admiration. . . . Without drawing any general comparisons, your own book is a great deal better both in depth of insight and of course in the actual writing than *Lady Chatterley's Lover."* Naturally, Miller asked Eliot's permission to put his comment into print. In two letters Eliot carefully modified his observations: the comparison to Lawrence, he said, was irrelevant. It would, furthermore, be improper in a published letter for him to mention opinions other than his own. Thus, qualified, Eliot's comment was reduced to one sentence—"a very remarkable book . . . a rather magnificent piece of work." Nonetheless, Henry gave that to Kahane and it appeared on the paper cover of the second printing of *Cancer*. Finally, only a fragment of Henry's plan for the brochure was realized when he issued a selection of "Opinions of This Writer's Work" printed on four sides of a folded sheet and distributed by Obelisk Press in 1938.

Though the project of self-advertisement into which Henry drew Durrell eventually fizzled, in 1937 Durrell was drawn in person to Paris and to number 18 Villa Seurat. Fresh from Greece, a natural story teller with a touch of the exotic and a flash of the Celtic about him, Durrell was soon leading them all in hearty laughter. He was a man of contrasts: of Irish descent, he had been born in India in sight of Tibet. Educated conventionally, he had a most unconventional turn of mind. Idolizing Henry and his success in conveying the truth of his personality in bold experimental prose, under a pseudonym (Charles Norden) Durrell was already on his way to becoming a commercially successful, slick novelist. Short and stocky, he was big-hearted and had an imagination that danced from the social to the cosmological. Henry was overwhelmed by him.

Durrell and his lovely wife Nancy were installed in the flat of Betty Ryan who was traveling. Anaïs came over from the Quai de Passy, where she was living, to meet them. Talking bound them all together: conversation in the Villa Seurat was made of subtle distillations which would have been mysterious and incomprehensible anywhere else. Durrell became part of the conversation as soon as he arrived.

In many ways that first day of Durrell's visit was the high point of Henry's literary life. Taken as a whole, late 1936 to early 1938 were his best years, and Durrell, Miller's first real disciple, showed up right in the middle of these.

Conrad Moricand was not nearly as personally attractive as Durrell, but his influence upon Henry's imagination was greater than Durrell's—far greater than most of Miller's friends recognized. A man who seemed to have concentrated all his will and energy and even his physical powers on one object, Moricand lived astrology, he consulted his horoscope daily, and he saw astrological effigies everywhere—in religion, in art, in psychology, in literature. Moricand's method was poetic, intuitive, mystical, and elliptical. An afternoon with him was like a leap into myth itself, in which everything in the world took on new and strange significance, and history had new heroes, such as Hermes Trismegistus, Akhenaton, and Paracelsus; while other figures of historic importance, like Plotinus, Heraclitus, Jacob Boehme, and Meister Eckhardt seemed more meaningful than ever before. So Henry thought, and in 1938 he spent at least one afternoon a week at Moricand's Montmartre apartment. Moricand was constantly opening Henry's eyes with his magical reinterpretations. Did Henry suppose from reading *Contes Drôlatiques,* for instance, that Balzac was a pedestrian realist? Moricand urged him to read *Seraphita* and *Louis Lambert.* He handed Henry the ten-page manuscript of his own essay, "L'Oeuvre et le génie de Balzac devant l'Astrologie" which was about to appear in the *Revue de Paris.* Quickly Henry read the two books and concluded that Moricand was absolutely right. Balzac was swimming in a Neptunian world.

At one time Miller had scorned astrology. When Hugo cast his horoscope at Louveciennes he wrote privately to Emil Schnellock: "I am full of Mars and Venus—you didn't need to know that . . . I am the crab (cancre), which moves sideways, flops over on its side and can't get up again. I move through strange tropics and deal in high explosives, embalming fluid, . . .

fluted snot, peccadilloes and porcupines' toes. Because of Uranus, which crosses my longitudinal, I am inordinately fond of cunt, not chitterlings, and water bottles." But Moricand's appearance coincided exactly with Miller's rejection of mechanical rationalism, and as a substitute Moricand offered Henry a comprehensively symbolic interpretation of the universe. Henry commissioned Moricand to do horoscopes for all his friends, for correspondents like Count Keyserling, and even for imaginary personages. He wholly accepted Moricand's contention that a horoscope was at least a "portrait matricule," an outline of the potential self which the individual could achieve if he understood his destiny.

Henry's sense of destiny was confirmed not only by the horoscope Moricand made but also by other clairvoyants. Bijoux, an ex-whore, read his hand and gave an account of his past life that was accurate to the smallest detail. Then she went on to make numerous strange predictions: he would live beyond the age of eighty, take many voyages, realize enormous financial success, achieve artistic recognition, and marry at least one beautiful young girl. An American exile named Jessica Hensley who examined his chart on the very day that *Black Spring* was published, predicted fame and success abroad through the amazingly wide circulation of his books. But everyone predicted fame; he had given the stars a good deal of cooperation through his vast correspondence and his various subsidiary efforts at publicizing himself, and fame was coming. By early 1938, four years after its publication, *Tropic of Cancer* still sold steadily, having gone into its third printing. The book was translated into Czechoslovakian under the title *Obratnik Raka* and had on its cover a drawing by Matisse! The limits which censorship had placed upon its circulation had not killed the book; instead, it gained a legendary reputation. An American expatriate in Paris, Eve Adams, sold copies to American tourists at the Dôme. Miller was by now so prominent a "figure" that Eve Adams found that she could even sell his watercolors for fifty francs each. Infrequently, too, a *pneu* or a letter from Kahane would be delivered, inviting Henry to lunch with Baroness So-and-So who had read his books and wanted to see him in the flesh.

Much more surprisingly, American and even English publishers seemed quite anxious to consider his work. In 1936, T.S. Eliot wrote that Faber & Faber would like to see a copy of *Black Spring,* and Simon and Schuster informed him they were interested in seeing any novel he had written which could be published in the United States. Bennett Cerf of Random House stopped by the offices of Obelisk Press to pick up copies of *Tropic of Cancer* and *Black Spring* in order to study the possibility of somehow bringing out editions in America. In 1937, Alfred Knopf made Henry an outright gift of $100 and asked, in return, only that Henry show him the next three books he wrote, whatever these might be. Blanche Knopf was particularly interested in publishing the letters he had written to Emil Schnellock if ever he could get them assembled and properly edited. The Knopf lawyers had counselled against the publication of *Black Spring,* but Henry considered authorizing an expurgated version for American sales. Both Faber & Faber and Knopf asked to consider a collection of pieces which Henry assembled under the title of *Max and the White Phagocytes.* This book, which eventually appeared in September 1938, combined stories and essays which he had once thought to publish in separate volumes. "Max," the tale which gave the collection part of its title, may well be the best short story which Miller was ever to write. Its subject is the encounter between Max Bickel, an aging American Jewish tailor living in great poverty in Paris, and Henry Miller, the narrator, who is himself living on the margin of things economically but is nowise in such desperate straits as Max. Like the hero of *Tropic of Cancer,* Max wants human contact even more than a handout. Miller meets him during his wanderings about Paris in search of literary material. In contrast to Fraenkel, who heartlessly brushes Max aside, the narrator will be measured as an artist by his ability to meet this old man on human grounds. In doing so, Miller finely blended sentimentality and cynicism, sympathy and scorn.

However, Faber & Faber and Knopf rejected *Max and the White Phagocytes* in October 1937. Unable to issue his banned books, they were lukewarm about his comic, critical, and philosophical work. (Even so, Miller planned to publish a second collection, *Plasma and Magma,* in 1939.) Certainly, critical interest in his work continued. H.L. Mencken told him that it would be some time before he received acclaim, but when it came it would be like a landslide; and Mencken capped his prediction with an inscribed copy of *The American Language.* In January 1937, the first critical review appearing in the United States of Miller's work declared him an "extraordinary writer"; this was written by Herbert Faulkner West, a Professor of English at Dartmouth. Before 1937 was over Henry had begun a correspondence with a much more influential critic than Herbert West— V.F.Calverton. Refusing to accept the radical party line that Miller was "decadent" artistically and "unreliable" politically, Calverton informed Miller that he planned a book-length study of his works and their social significance. To interest Calverton was a triumph for Miller, since Calverton was the leading radicial critic in America, and all other radicals ignored

Miller completely or else condemned him on political principles. Calverton's interest was a sign that Miller's literary power was great enough to transcend mere political judgments.

But this was not the last or the greatest surprise in the war between art and politics. One of the early Miller fans was Huntington Cairns, a young Washington attorney with literary interests. In fact, Cairns was the person who had first interested Calverton in Miller. What was most amusing— and, Miller thought, significant—was that Cairns was the attorney that the U.S. Customs Office consulted about the books that could be legally imported into America. In essence, Cairns was the unofficial censor of the United States! Though obliged by the laws to recommend that *Tropic of Cancer* be banned, he freely told Henry his high opinion of its literary merit. When he could win even the censor to his side, Miller thought, the rest would be easy.

Seventeen

Historia Calamitatum

Henry was convinced that with such support rumbling below the ground, his next book would blow the top off. He had tried to tell the story of *Tropic of Capricorn* so often and in so many ways that he at last began to see that its meaning resided not in the straightforward account of his suffering at the hands of June and Jean, but precisely in the confused criss-cross of tracks and cross-purposes, the contradictions, ambiguities, and mysteries to which his personality had been subjected. It was not, then, the "truthful" story of his life with June, but of his own confusions and sufferings, that he had to tell. He had his notes, now more than ten years old, and his lists of events, ideas, styles to employ, characters, wall charts, and graphs. But these did not contain the real story he had to tell; it was not in his anecdotal life that he could find a pattern. He had to make a hopeless leap into the blue. He took the leap and found that instead of falling flat on his face like a burlesque comedian, he was flying high. He simply gave up his notes, his impulse to justify his own conduct, and his search for truth, and opened himself to his story. Magically, a new self—a Henry Miller that didn't exist when the notes were planned or *Crazy Cock* was written—took over the story and began to shape it.

As soon as he was cut loose from his notes, better perspectives on his life and outside affinities offered themselves for guidance: Jung's "On the Psychology of the Unconscious," Breton's *Nadja,* Dante's *Comedy,* Una in

Spencer's *Faerie Queen,* Eduardo Sanchez's theories of apocotastasis, Keyserling's *From Suffering to Fulfillment,* Proust, Fenollosa's concept of the ideo-
gram, and the Book of Revelations. In *Tropic of Cancer* Miller had managed
to see himself from several disjunct perspectives. His great advantage in
telling that story was that the experiences which formed his subject were
recent and had therefore not yet fused with his more permanent compulsions and fixations. In some sections of *Black Spring,* especially "The
Fourteenth Ward" and "The Tailor Shop," Miller had managed to treat
materials deeply intertwined with long past defeats. Yet he had managed to
write about them in a lively fashion. These instances were especially potent
in showing him the paths along which he should proceed in *Tropic of
Capricorn.* Two remarks by Ralph Waldo Emerson which Miller happened
upon in a history of American literature startled him. The first stated that
"novels will give way, by and by, to diaries or autobiographies—
captivating books, if only a man knew how to choose among his experiences
that which is really his experience, and how to record truth truly." "Life,"
Emerson wrote in the other, "consists in what a man is thinking all day."
These gave Miller a point of view and a psychological method. But a book
which Fraenkel loaned him, Peter Abelard's *Historia Calamitatum,* really
gave him the thematic key which unlocked the others. Miller had so far
been unable to write his story because at every point it always quickly came
down to a record of his outer tortures, a complaint against the world.
Abelard, however, disposed of his own castration in a paragraph, while
insisting that he suffered real pains from his moral conflicts; so Henry gave
up his grievances and concentrated on his anguishes—these existed beyond
suffering. He felt like the character in *A Man Without A Name,* a film by
Werner Kraus which he had seen with Fred Perlès and Walter Freeman in
1932 at the Studio L'Étoile. The hero, who suffers from amnesia, is at last
asked to choose a name. "Gottlieb Leberecht Müller" is the identity he
chooses, and his friends come to him with gifts and say: "We are going to
celebrate your birthday—you have just been born—you have a new name
and you are going to lead a new life."

Casting aside all the pages he had written three years earlier, in mid 1936
Miller started *Tropic of Capricorn* afresh. "It is only recently that I came upon
Abelard's celebrated autobiography: it has given me the courage to begin
my own story, the story of *my* misfortunes, which until now seemed
impossible to relate . . . . Even to unfold this story will be of no avail: at the
best I shall earn the right to enter that Purgatory which we have made of life
because we have ceased to love or even to understand the meaning of love."

These lines were also eventually cut, being a prelude to an attitude rather than a part of the story; but they started the dictation going again. This time he didn't put his energy into notes; instead he cried: *Je t'écoute! Vas-y!* and prepared to transcribe whenever his angels sang. By mid 1937 he had finished the interlude called "The Land of Fuck," which he considered the best writing he had ever done. In conversations with friends he characterized it as a piece of symbolic prose (despite its surface obscenity) in the metaphysical tradition of Plotinus. There were, he told Calverton, "at least two hundred pages in it the like of which hasn't been seen yet in English literature." By the end of August 1938 a near final draft of the book was completed. Miller declared his own novel "a thousand times better than Joyce or St. Augustine."

Three parts were discernible in it. In the first, Miller portrays himself as an ordinary, unillumined citizen of a world that is dead, even though the corpse is still twitching furiously. Due to his position as the personnel manager of the Cosmodemonic Telegraph Company, he has a ringside seat at the madness and chaos of modern civilization. Henry Miller, Ph.D., the hero-narrator, a man with a wife and a child, is in danger of accepting the madness of civilization as a norm and living by the regulations of the insane. What saves him from complete acceptance of this artificial society is the obvious plight of his messengers and co-workers and, more positively, his explorations in the "Land of Fuck." "Fucking" is Miller's metaphor for the awakening of the Uranian power of the senses. His hero is kept from dying in the civilized world by the sensuous powers called into being by lovemaking—not romantic love, which is tainted by civilization, but physical ecstasy. He maintains contact with the primitive, pre-civilized men, and loses his societal identity, becoming an anonymous man, a man of joy. But the novel itself is not written from the point of view of a merely sensual man. Saved from destruction in civilization by sex and the release it stands for, the hero's self is really given new birth by his discovery of the powers of imagination which rest upon natural sensuality. The hero takes a new name, Gottlieb Leberecht Müller, the god-loving, right-living man, since he is utterly freed from bitterness, suffering, and fruitless opposition to society. Far from being a primitive, he is an artist in whom, as he presents himself, the currents of modern experimental writing, dadaism and surrealism, have culminated. At the same time, he is a kind of Christ, who, like the savior in *The Brothers Karamazov,* will speak words issuing in a new gospel, a new phase of history. His new bible proclaims: save yourself by embracing ecstasy.

The book was dedicated to Her—his wife June—the magical Ayesha-anima of his psyche who, like Dante's Beatrice, draws the Henry-hero through the Inferno of civilization and the Purgatorio of sensuality into the Paradiso of the liberated imagination. Smashed as a woman but refined and reassembled as a myth, June is seen in *Tropic of Capricorn* as an instrument for the hero's confusion and, finally, his salvation. She represents an imaginative mystery which, at the end of the book, he pledges to follow.

That conclusion was splendid for the book, but ominous for Henry's career. Just when he had managed triumphantly to free himself in *Tropic of Capricorn* from the impulse to adhere slavishly to his notes and the desire to tell the whole truth about his life with June, he ended the book by implying that he was only just beginning to tell the story! Anyone who knew him well might have suspected that he was about to slide back to a repetition of the same old compulsions. That was precisely what happened. He had created a work of art; but this was not what he really wanted: more than anything else he desired self-justification against June. Therefore, no sooner had he made his revisions and regarded *Tropic of Capricorn* as complete than he began to tell his friends that *Tropic of Capricorn* was merely a portal to a great epic romance which he planned to write, a colossal series of books—at least seven or eight volumes long—which would give the full history of his life with June. *Tropic of Capricorn,* the astonishing book which he had started to write more than a decade before, had now metamorphosed like a character in Ovid. Even as it was completed it became introductory to the work of a lifetime.

He was in no hurry to follow up *Capricorn,* so—as it were, with his left hand—he took up some minor projects. The newspapers of 1938 and the "News of the Day" documentaries at the theaters were filled with scenes of war, including the ghastly indiscriminate bombings of populations in Madrid and Shanghai. Miller turned his sense of comic irony upon this stupidity and the cruelty of man in a sketch which he titled "The All-Intelligent Explosive Rocket." Here he announced the invention of a "cerebrated explosive" which would seek out only that which it was commanded to destory. For instance, "used by Communists and Anarchists it would destroy nothing but Fascist men and materials, women and children included, if necessary." "The All-Intelligent Explosive Rocket" was an effective though a minor piece of satire, but no one else seemed to be able to take the war as offering any possibilities for comedy, and none of Henry's friends gave him much encouragement. A second project was called "The Sleeping Sleeper Asleep." Miller thought of it as a long scenario, a surreal dream piece revolving around the general idea of a sleeper who dreams she is awake or vice-versa. Henry was ready to pull some material out of his own dream book for use here, but he never could get a firm hold on a mode for presenting it. Worked on throughout 1938, "The Sleeping Sleeper Asleep" remained a series of drafts which started in confusion and ended in silence. A third project was far more grandiose in its presumption; but it was, like the others, an assertion of Miller's belief in his creative energy. He extended his plan to write short sketches about each of his friends by proposing to write a series of ten or twelve connected novelettes on the members of the Villa Seurat circle—his initial idea was to write the book in French. Its title would be "Some Pleasant Monsters" (later, "Astrological Effigies"). Naturally, he continued the correspondence concerning *Hamlet;* by November of 1938, he had only 150 more pages of his share of 500 pages to finish.

For Henry, who had once sweated over every sentence and destroyed as much as he wrote, writing was now as easy as thinking. The words oozed out like oil, and though he blotted many, he saved more. This was his great period, when his dreams seemed to be marching in a straight line to realization. He was the center of a circle of enlightened artists, good friends, angelic creatures. In Anaïs Nin he had found a perfect woman, and he was troubled only by the fact that he had not really been able to get any closer to her after the New York trip. His books were coming out and he was receiving praise from all quarters. He believed that Mencken was right— that recognition would come like a landslide, but he felt that it would come sooner than Mencken thought. He sat in the Villa Seurat like the ruler of a magical kingdom. He was the man he had once dreamed of being, and every day was his birthday.

Eighteen

The Last of the Best Days

Since Henry was doing so much, obviously he could do more. But he hardly supposed that soon he would also be working on two magazines. His involvement with *The Booster* was the more important and came about through a comic chain of accidents. In the spring of 1937, the *Chicago Tribune* closed its Paris office and Alfred Perlès was out of a job. Very shortly thereafter Fred was summoned to the village of Ozoir-la-Ferriére, about twenty miles east of Paris, to discuss a position with the president of the American Country Club of France. For a few years, the businessman explained, he had sponsored a club magazine, *The Boosters,* in order to print club notes and, not incidentally, to lend class to the club. The magazine paid its way since those sporting goods manufacturers and food and beverage purveyors who supplied the club took ads in it. But he found the editorial side of the venture a little uncongenial and recognized his own deficiencies as a journalist. Fred was hired to run the sheet and instructed to do his best to bring in further advertisers. Eventually, the president himself tired of the journal altogether, and one day he startled Fred by making him a proposition: in exchange for his promise to retain the name, to indicate that *The Booster* (now singular) had been founded by The American Country Club of France, and to continue to run two pages of club notes in every issue, Fred could have the magazine, *gratis,* to edit just as he pleased.

It looked like a typical American businessman's gift: the Club would continue to gain prestige from its association with the journal, while running its items free and saving the editor's salary, while *The Booster* remained the same white elephant it had always been. But after brief consultation with the desperadoes in the Villa Seurat, Fred decided to take it and to turn it into a literary magazine devoted to the gang's special interests: in a spirit of fun they would represent craziness, irresponsibility, and indecency. Just for the hell of it, they decided, they would boost everything—almost everything. It was as if "The New Instinctivism" had been revived and turned inside out to serve as the basis for an editorial position. Advertising support was guaranteed, at least for the first few issues, until the advertising offices of Johnnie Walker Scotch, Hanan shoes, and Spalding golf equipment noticed the curious copy surrounding their ads. Before the advertisers pulled out, the editors might have a chance to get the magazine established and attract support of their own. Perhaps by the time the capitalists had departed, the artists would have arrived. In the interim Henry, who ran the new *Booster* and appointed himself Associate Editor, made a concerted effort to drum up subscriptions.

Henry's correspondence factory went into action again. By early August 1937 he sent out a "special begging letter to celebrities" which announced that *The Booster* had passed into the hands of Perlès and a capable "staff of untrained editors." "We are modest, diffident, rather negative on the whole, except that we intend to boost, baste, and lambast when and wherever possible. Mostly we shall boost. We like to boost, and of course to begin with we are going to boost ourselves. . . . We do not intend to make a 'success' of the Booster," he concluded this appeal. "On the contrary, our aim is to run it into the ground as quickly as possible." After such a beginning and with five hundred subscribers, they could only go full steam ahead, and by September 1937 the first issue was ready. Henry boosted it in advance with a placard handout describing the magazine as a "non-successful, non-political, non-cultural review," whose editors supported Food, Plagues, and Epilepsy, and opposed Peace, Moderation, Rheumatism and all other isms. The cover of the first issue was done by Nancy Durrell, Anaïs was listed as Society Editor, Henry as Fashion Editor, and Fraenkel as heading the Department of Metaphysics and Metempsychosis. William Saroyan also joined the staff.

The second number contained a story by Saroyan, as well as a column "For Men Only" by Henry Miller, Earl of Selvege. Henry's column was wacky but not offensive. However, Durrell was responsible for the first trouble the magazine got into. The president of the American Club had been puzzled by the contents of the first issue, but it did seem lively, and he frankly regarded the contents as subsidiary to the publicity purpose of the magazine. But he was obviously aghast to see that in the second issue Durrell had introduced an Eskimo story concerning a bachelor who is swallowed by the vagina of a beautiful young girl. This particular story led to a telegram from the American Country Club firmly condemning the journal as pornographic. The editors consulted. If vaginas were so eminently capable of getting the bourgeois upset, then they should have vaginas in abundance. They decided to make their Christmas issue an "Air-Conditioned Womb Number," even if this spelled the magazine's demise. Miller's article "The Enormous Womb" led off the fracas. "As far as I can make out," Henry began, "there is never anything but womb. First and last there is the womb of Nature; then there is the Mother's Womb; and finally there is the womb in which we have our life and being and which we call the world." Beneath the surface *jeu d'esprit* of this essay and the other pieces in it, the "Air-Conditioned Womb Number" was very seriously concerned, as Miller wrote to Fraenkel, with death, bastard death and the possibilities of rebirth in the modern world. So far as Miller and Perlès were concerned, however, the magazine was a dead duck. For a while they thought of raising the price of the womb number from 5 to 100 francs and selling it privately to porno-collectors and lascivious shut-ins. But eventually this issue was distributed to the regular subscribers and the magazine was dismembered. Its title was changed to *Delta* and its contents were thenceforth selected largely by Durrell, who assumed financial responsibility.

In the meantime, at the suggestion of Raymond Queneau, Henry became one of the nine editors of a serious French revue, *Volontés*. Though he made only a small editorial contribution, a number of his shorter works or extracts from works in progress appeared in it translated into French by Georges Pelorson, its editor-in-chief. Acceptance by French writers was meaningful to Miller, since, with his books banned in English-speaking countries, he received very little public notice from his countrymen and had to look for his main support to the literati of his adopted nation.

The censors constituted a primary problem in the sociology of distribution and the dynamics of reputation; but the economics of authorship still offered his most pressing personal dilemma. Money was the problem— how, in any circumstances or by any contrivance, to get it. Not since he had talked his way into Western Union had Henry exhibited any capacity for making money: the only talent he had shown was for survival. Nothing associated with commerce ever seemed to work for him. For instance, in December of 1937 he founded the "Villa Seurat Series" in what seemed to be a thoroughly business-like way. Nancy Durrell guaranteed the money for the printing costs of three books—one each by Miller *(Max and the White Phagocytes)*, Durrell *(The Black Book)* and Nin *(Winter of Artifice)*. Kahane agreed to distribute these books through the facilities of Obelisk Press at a commission of 20% of sales. But the brochure that Miller wrote for advertising purposes showed that he knew the series was designed, like *The Booster*, to self-destruct commercially. This Villa Seurat Series, he explained, was founded in response to the demand of writers, not readers: its goal was the publication of books for which no commercial audience existed. The unprintable, unwritable book, "the demonological forecast of the century's trends," was the kind of book he intended to make available to the thinking public. When Nancy's money supporting three publications ran out, the series folded. All that remained were the business-like contracts neatly filed in Henry's papers. He was also attempting to place his work in American magazines that paid, such as *Esquire,* and he wrote circulars to numerous American booksellers asking them to place orders for broadsides which had not yet been published. (If he got enough orders he'd publish the *plaquette.*)

Henry struck a less common—but a little more certain—way of making money when he attempted to have his banned books smuggled into the United States to be sold at a profit. He worked out a scheme by which he mailed books, one at a time, to his new agent Marion Saunders; then by letter he informed Joe O'Regan to pick the copies up from her. Henry paid a little less than a dollar for author's copies, and Joe peddled them to the Gotham Book Mart for $3.00 each or turned them over to individual buyers at $5.00. Henry would thus get back a dollar or even more on every copy handled in this manner. It was difficult to get several copies past customs at one time; but when friends left Paris for the States he usually loaded them down with copies to dispose of in the same manner. Anaïs held the unofficial book-smuggling record by managing to bring in fifty copies on one trip. These profits were tiny, but Henry was living on an economic margin where every dollar counted. He saw that there was a market for his books in America and he followed up the smuggling racket by trying to arrange for the "pirating" of his own books. After the publication of *Tropic of Cancer* he had gotten in touch with Stanley Rose, a well-known Hollywood bookseller who had already served a jail term for printing and distributing pornography. Henry suggested that Rose pirate the novel and pay him royalties under the counter. During his 1936 visit to New York he actively looked for a subterranean outlet for his banned books. Anaïs aided him by consulting a judge about the legal aspects of book piracy. The essential question was: could Henry make a contract with a pirate, receive royalties and yet avoid prosecution? This was an amazing question, but in fact the answer seemed to be, *possibly yes*—even though he would be duping the censors and screwing his publisher Kahane. He also followed up a lead that Simon & Schuster sometimes issued private *de luxe* editions of forbidden works. He made some contacts, also without results, with a New York printer named Guy Dilsere, alias Gaborse, who often pirated banned works. All this was like working in the dark, and before he left New York in 1936 Henry turned to Joe O'Regan with the suggestion that he arrange for the printing of an American edition himself.

Finally, when none of the piracy schemes seemed possible, he took another tack altogether. In circular letters of 1937 and 1938 which began "I NEED DOUGH," he approached a few dozen known collectors. To those interested in literary rarities, he proposed to sell books which he had critically annotated in his own hand; he had ready "for prompt delivery," at ten guineas a book, Emerson's *Essays, Ulysses,* Keyserling's *America Set Free,* Dostoievski's *The Eternal Husband,* two books by Rank, Spengler's *The Decline of the West,* Nietzsche's *The Birth of Tragedy,* and St. Augustine's *The City of God.* He was also ready to sell watercolors and even an old pair of his moccasins (should the latter be desired by a museum) as well as his notebooks, unpublished material, and the drafts and revised copies of all his published work, at prices ranging from $120.00 to $1000.00. For 1500 francs he would compose a little book in a printer's dummy written in pen and ink especially for the buyer. (Apparently, however, not a single collector expressed the slightest interest in any of these items.)

As if matters were not bad enough, the urgency of his scrambles for money was certainly increased by a letter he received from his father in December of 1937, telling a simple tale of woe. Some months before, the elder Miller explained, he had given up his independent tailor shop and joined a Fifty-third Street firm in Manhattan. By the previous year his total earnings had fallen to less than $2,000, nearly every penny of which was consumed in business overhead, and so he was now reduced to working on a 10% commission basis. The rent which he collected from a tenant at 1063 Decatur Street paid the taxes on the house, but this still left no money for food. His savings were gone. Commissions were few and far between. Henry's mother kept up a good face and often regaled her neighbors with stories of her son's success as a writer in Europe, where he was being royally entertained by his admirers. Heinrich knew that he was probably as impoverished as they were, but they couldn't really accept that. Privately he poured out his troubles to Henry and begged him to send a pittance for himself: he never had a cent of his own in his pocket anymore, he wailed.

Deeply touched, even if as short of cash as usual, Henry sent a little enclosure and promised to do whatever he could. Next, he saw that he might turn a profit with the letter. He typed out his father's letter and a phony answer intended to elicit pity, and he sent these to Rebecca West, Somerset Maugham, T.S. Eliot, and others, asking implicitly for a mite to pass on to his dad. "I certainly do feel bad reading your letter," he began. "I hardly know what to say to you. In a few years I shall probably be in the same position that you are now in. I don't want to make you feel bad either, but I must confess that when that day comes I shall probably commit suicide." He spoke about the small returns his work brought despite its critical success. He confessed that he had been obliged to dismiss all his scruples and to beg, borrow, or steal, if necessary. "To be a writer is almost worse than being a tailor, I can assure you," he concluded. "I am sorry now that I did not learn a trade when I was young. . . ." Henry's inner circle of friends took the letter as a good dadaist joke, worthy of printing in *The Booster*. Those who knew him only by reputation or from having read *Tropic of Cancer* were probably already convinced of his unscrupulousness and took him at his word. No one, in any event, sent him any money.

In the last years of the 1930s Henry certainly experienced many dismal days, but somehow they became secondary to his central joy. All in all, these were good years, lucky years, for Miller. He had no money, it is true, but who else did? Compared to his early years in Paris he was certainly well off: he had begun to go onto the gold standard at about the same time that the rest of the world was slipping into an age of silver—and much tarnished silver at that. By the late '30s he often thanked his lucky stars. But he also had Jupiter there to save him whenever he needed saving and he had survived pretty much unscathed.

These days Henry liked to climb up to the roof of his studio late at night and take a look at Jupiter, his lucky planet. One night in August 1938, though Jupiter was sailing across the heavens, Henry had bad luck as he climbed back down the iron ladder. He lost his footing and crashed through a plate glass door on the studio terrace, falling into his bedroom. For the moment he lay still, wondering where Jupiter had been and pondering whether he was about to be lifted up above the planets. The moistness he felt under him was unmistakably his own blood. But he shook himself. Nothing was broken, only his back was full of glass. He hopped around, his feet picking up splinters. He had to be taken to the hospital for stitches but was returned that night to his house. Conrad Moricand was the first visitor to arrive. The astrologer held in his hand a detailed astrological description of an accident threatening Henry. Moricand's intelligence was a little late. Henry wanted to know why Jupiter had let him down. Well, Moricand hypothesized, Jupiter had kept him alive at least. Besides, this accident allowed him a little vacation from all his labors, with the best of care and the pleasure of visits from all his friends.

Nineteen

Salut au Monde

For a long time the change in Henry occurred almost imperceptibly and by slow degrees, but it seemed to be complete by early 1939. All his friends perceived this alteration, though few could describe it: it was easier to name some crucial instances of change. The most revelatory involved his plans for a novel whose 1942 publication Henry began to announce in 1939. Tentatively titled *Draco and the Ecliptic,* this book was to be the seal and capstone of his autobiographical works by giving occult, symbolic significance to the sequence. The title derived from Frederick Carter's *The Dragon of the Apocalypse,* and the substance of the book, which always remained fuzzy, was compounded from Lawrence's *Apocalypse,* James Hilton's *Lost Horizon,* the writings of Lao-tse, and the fact that Henry's own horoscope showed him crossing his ecliptic in 1942. Properly speaking, he wrote to Keyserling, the book, a "joyous book of the mystic," would not be written by Henry Val Miller of Brooklyn and Paris, but by the author who had been awakened from that corpse: Gottleib Leberecht Müller. He told Schnellock that the book would describe "the heaven beyond heaven," and be the prelude for his next stage of life, in Tibet or Shangri-La. After that book he would write no more. At other times, however, he gave different slants on it: it would be, he predicted, a book of beginnings and endings, an alchemical work, an exploration of the mystery of literary creation, a book including all the elements of experience which he had otherwise left out of his work, an analysis of the pattern of his life. These explanations were not so much contradictory as revelatory of the fact that *Draco and the Ecliptic* was a title in search of a vision. It was the first vivid signal that he wanted to be a spiritual writer. More, his plans for *Draco and the Ecliptic* indicated that he was turning out of the current of experimental modernist writing in which the *Tropics* and *Black Spring* had been composed, and was thinking of his future work in terms of the visionary traditions of Blake and Lawrence. Miller, at least, saw himself as unifying the impulses which these two writers had separately represented. One English critic had already dubbed Henry the "Sage of Villa Seurat," and more and more he was playing the role of the wisdom-giver. Once he had simply wanted to tell his story, now he wished to convince people of the benefits of knowledge acquired through suffering. Nin, Moricand, and David Edgar had urged Henry to study various versions of the occult and mystical traditions, and Keyserling had set him on a particular road by praising him not as a novelist so much as a philosophical visionary. He had always yearned to synthesize even the irreconcilable, for his temperament yearned for unity and order. Now a jigsaw lay before him and he started to put it together. If the pieces didn't fit, if it was necessary to trim the edges, he did so gladly. But he never threw a piece away. New influences had adhered to his earliest ones. Nijinsky, American apocalyptic utopianism, Brunhubner's "Le Message de Pluto," Hebrew mysticism, Jungian analysis, Faure's conception of China, Berdyaev's theology, Zen, the Egyptian *Book of the Dead, The World's Desire,* the *I'Ching,* Christian Science, Theosophy, Romain Rolland's book on Ramakrishna, Krishnamurti; Dane Rudhyar's "The Artist as Avatar," John Cowper Powys, Maeterlinck's *Wisdom and Destiny,* the life of Milarepa, Paul Claudel's *Connaissance de l'Est*—these were all part of what Henry himself called the "divine jumble" to which he opened his sensibility and his reconciling intelligence. Nothing, he became convinced, would be gained by straightening out the disarray; when the pieces didn't fit at all, he threw them in a box, his own mind, and called their proximity their order. For him, the quickening of the spiritual pulse was sufficient.

Inevitably, this meant that not only was he losing interest in the narrative of his life, the full exploration of his personal perplexities, he was even losing his enthusiasm for any literature except this special sort. When the purpose of composition became the statement of vision, then the discussion of literary merit, with its emphasis on drama and tension and confusion, seemed superfluous. If he were to write at all, Henry began to say, it would be for the men of 2500 A.D. Still better, he would give up literature for the perfection of silence, and become, as he once told Durrell, "more and more ignorant, more quiet, more vegetative, more ruminative, more omnivorous, carnivorous, herbivorous. I want to stand still and dance inside. . . ." The very reasons which had impelled him to write had disappeared, at least on the surface. He felt he had achieved wisdom. What, then, did he need with books?

He began to paint much more than he wrote. Earlier in the decade he had continually warned himself not to let the watercolor bug distract him from his literary work. But after 1935 most of his new friends and acquaintances were painters—in addition to Hiler, Reichel, and Betty Ryan, there were Picasso, Man Ray, Jean Helion, Max Ernst, and Joan Miró. Writing seemed like a lonely occupation now. Painting was sociable: he could lean over Picasso's shoulder to watch him do an ink portrait of Man Ray and chat with both while the work went on. Besides, now that he was at last earning a little money from writing, it was tainted for him, unconsciously, by the stain of commerce from which he had fled in order to write. But his painting was thoroughly non-commercial. He never knew what was going to emerge at the other end of the brush—or whether he should sign the finished product Henry Miller, Crazy George Insel, or Jesus H. Christ. He liked that feeling; writing he identified with consciousness, and he was tired of his own ego. Painting, on the contrary, gave him a feeling of anonymity and unpremeditated wisdom.

The same feelings were behind the brief revival of his enthusiasm for musical performance. He was much more interested in his collection of records than in his library, he told Joe O'Regan in 1937, for music was "the ultimate. I wish I could compose. I am definitely becoming a musician," he said. "Music," he wrote to Osborn, "blots literature out completely." And to Durrell he confided: "That's what I want to do eventually—write music. . . . That's *the* art."

Perhaps the planet Jupiter had protected Henry from personal disaster; but it was not inclined to save Europe. The cuts on the soles of Henry's feet and on his back were scarcely healed when the patches and plasters which the Allies had pasted on Europe after World War I were tearing loose. Henry could announce in a *Booster* blurb that he was against peace, and that he believed with his whole heart in the obliteration of modern civilization for the sake of a new order. But he was also, for himself, against war and disinclined to believe that the *Neue Ordnung* of *Das Dritte Reich* was what he had been plumping for. It seemed most unlikely that human transcendence would emerge from the rattle of machine guns, poison gas, aerial bombardment, splintered bones and broken towers. No one as yet had invented an "All Intelligent Explosive Rocket" and, anyway, the best men were not those in possession of the weapons. Suddenly, in the summer of 1938 Henry was struck with great force by the possibility that after all his struggles his head might be blown off. A descendant of two grandfathers who had fled their native land to evade military service, he had left his own country only to find that he had been fleeing toward a new conflagration. In August 1938 everyone expected the war to begin. Europe seemed like a bullring in which the toreros had gone mad and were crying for blood, waving their black and brown and red capes wildly. And France looked like a lazy, contented cow mincing around somewhat uneasily while it waited for a sharp blow behind its head.

Henry was in no mood to write, but he was in no mood to be splattered with France's blood either, and he began to make plans to slip out of the arena. Everybody was leaving. Fred decided to go to England and Henry gave him a sendoff. Then Fraenkel departed for Puerto Rico. Miller wrote to Larry Durrell that he might soon debark for Greece (then Istanbul, Dalmatia, Mobile, Santa Fe, Timbuctoo, Easter Island, Indo-China, India, and Tibet). The main idea, in any event, was: *Escape!*

In September 1938 with the Munich crisis looming, Henry stored some of his manuscripts with Kahane. He kept only a single, slender, bound volume imprinted "June" which contained all his notes for the remaining volumes of *Capri.orn*. Thinking Bordeaux the safest and best port for departure, he lit out for the west coast of France, prepared to take the first sailing for either Greece or America. Carrying only two valises, a cane given him by Moricand, and his typewriter, he declared himself almost ready to swim. And swimming, indeed, did seem like his only option for a time, since he had neglected to bring enough money for a transatlantic fare. Trusting to the gods and with a residual faith in June's old telegraphic dodge, he sat in his room at the Hotel Majestic on the Rue de Condé and wrote out cables. The period of silence and expectation which always followed this maneuver was intolerable. In several letters he lashed out against the Germans, whose barbarism had destroyed his tranquil life in Paris. He even vowed to abandon all his earlier literary plans and to devote the rest of his career to defamations of Germany.

But suddenly the money started to pour in. Huntington Cairns cabled $50; Laughlin, the editor of New Directions, sent $200 as an advance against royalties for the American rights to all of Henry's books, past and future; Kahane, for all his fabled miserliness, wired 3,000 francs as an advance on Obelisk Press books. Relieved though he was to have the price of a first-class ticket to America, Henry was now informed that no boats were leaving Bordeaux for America in the immediate future. To get home he would be obliged to make a break for Le Havre or Cherbourg. But to do so seemed insane since the trains all went through Paris, and that city, from all reports, was congested to immobility by frightened people in flight. And suppose he arrived in Paris, only to be caught there just as the war broke out? He was in a remote box in Bordeaux, but somehow that seemed better than placing himself in a crowded box. As always when he was perplexed, he stopped his thrashings and simply did nothing. This time his instincts were right.

On the day that Hitler's forces were announced to strike against France the sky was clear (one would be able to see the flights of bombers approaching from some distance), the sun was glistening on the waters (which would make the port a perfect target), and the breeze blew lightly from the sea (no need for the bombardiers to make wind adjustments). It was a perfect day for a catastrophe. People and motor cars and horse carts dashed about without any direction beyond the urge to move. The war was supposed to begin at 2:00 p.m. Henry strolled out of his hotel to a restaurant where he ordered a fine lunch with wine. Toward the end of his meal he began to wonder vaguely how to estimate the time at which the first dark wave of bombs would fall from the fleecy clouds. But he was sure of neither the air-speed nor the distance involved, and since time itself would produce the answer, he gave up worrying. It was, in any event, an excellent day, he had had a splendid lunch, and so he wandered over to the park, the Allées de Tourny, to loaf on a bench. What better place to watch the show?

But the crisis had been averted through secret meetings in Munich. Though deprived of a spectacle, Henry didn't complain. His hysteria passed, and the western world seemed to settle into sullen anticipation. After a time he returned to Paris and resumed work. But Paris was irredeemably altered for him. There was no doubt in his mind that he was destined to bolt sooner or later. He made his plans against that time and, as it were, lived in the Villa Seurat with his valises packed and his hat and coat on.

The Henry Miller of 1939 was a very different creature from Val Miller, alias June Mansfield, of March 1930. But the world he lived in hadn't changed its ways at all. Power and possessions were still its preoccupations. The Munich Crisis of 1938, anyone could see, was not a false alarm, it was the warning gong for the first round of the battle-royal. Henry had his own weapons prepared. Now that Obelisk Press had published several of his books, he worked out a new arrangement with Kahane by which he received 500 francs a month against royalties. Forty copies of the first editions of *Cancer* and *Black Spring* which he shipped off to the Gotham Book Mart passed through customs and brought him a return of $200.

With enough money to travel, he spent the month of May 1939 preparing to leave the Villa Seurat forever, after four years and nine months in residence. He sold or gave away all of his possessions. He left his notebooks and manuscripts with a storage company in Louveciennes for safekeeping. At the American Embassy he left his permanent address: 1063 Decatur Street, Brooklyn.

He was ready to go. He planned to spend a few weeks in the south of France, then sail for the States where he would travel through the South and Southwest and then around the world as conditions permitted. He even contacted a friend who was editor of a Chicago daily to try to arrange a commission for travel articles. However, encouraged by Durrell, he decided to head for Greece instead. As much as he dreaded the war, he also feared the prospect of being locked in his own country. In Corfu, he hoped, he might be able to weather the war.

Now that his plans were made, he was feeling easy and peaceful, ready for new adventures. Just before the end of May he ran into Queneau, and they had a drink for old times' sake. Everywhere in Paris old friends were making farewell toasts. He had been worried earlier, he told his friend, but now he was above the war. "Even if I were put in a concentration camp," he said, "it wouldn't matter."

On the last day of May he picked up his valise and typewriter and went to the Port d'Orléans to take the night train for Rocamadour. He was sitting on the terrace of a nearby hotel having a last drink when a one-armed figure with a familiar face rumbled into sight: Blaise Cendrars—the very first man to review *Tropic of Cancer*. Only a few minutes remained before Henry had to board the train, and they talked briefly about the war. Then Henry dashed for the train, away from Cendrars, away from Paris, into the night.

He spent a quiet month of June in Rocamadour and on Bastille Day in Marseilles, Miller boarded an antiquated boat which looked as big as a troop ship, the *Théophile Gautier*. He had a second-class ticket and found the accommodations poor: he was assigned a cabin with three others, a Turk, a Syrian, and a Greek. The boat proceeded south very slowly.

Quietly, easily, it moved toward the Tyrrhenian Sea until suddenly the coast of France sank into the calm, sun-lit waters like an old Atlantis abandoned by its citizens, who without sorrow, cried *Salut au monde* as they steered their course towards other capes and ancient shores.

Emil Schnellock,
watercolor mentor, 1943.

Henry and Alfred Perlès in 1955.

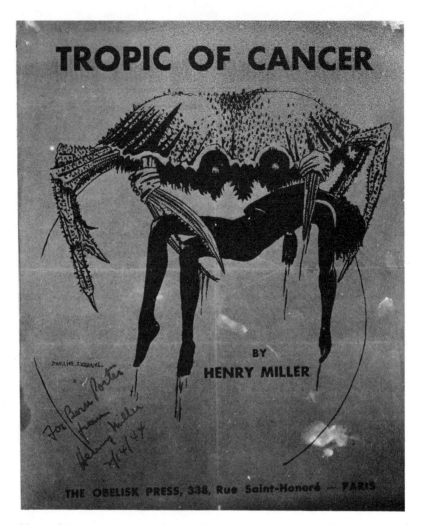

Tropic of Cancer was first published in 1934.

Miller and "the Colossus" setting out.

Durrell and Katsimbalis
in Athens.

Katsimbalis and F.J. Temple, 1966.

Joseph Delteil, 1970.

Anaïs, Henry, and Jean Varda.

Anaïs at Louveciennes

Lawrence Durrell, Lawrence Clark Powell and Henry
at UCLA during Henry's 80th Birthday celebration, 1971.

Henry and Ephraim Doner,
Big Sur, 1969.

Abraham Rattner's map for Henry, commemorating their journey across
America.

Rattner, ca. 1938.

Henry and Rattner in Paris, 1969.

Henry and Joe Gray, Pacific Palisades.

Henry and Emil White
earst's Castle, San Simeon.

Emil White, 1977.

Henry and Benny Bufano.

Harrydick Ross in Big Sur.

Caryl Hill, 1962

Henry's shack at Anderson Creek, Big Sur,
where he wrote *Into the Night Life*.

Henry and Lawrence Clark Powell, Big Sur, ca. 1951.

PASSAGE TO AMERICA

One

Journey to an Antique Land

La morte et resurrection d'amour—that title kept running through Henry's head as the boat sailed east. If America had nearly killed him, body and soul, the decade he spent in Europe had nourished his capacity to love. Anaïs, Fred, Michael, Germaine, Nys, Reichel, Betty Ryan, and all the others had raised him from the pit. Paris had breathed a warm new life into him.

His friends were scattered now. True, Anaïs had been with him in Aix-en-Provence just before he left Marseilles for Athens. Years before, Henry had told all his friends that she would be his next wife. That hope had never quite died, even though it was disappointed again and again. *When everything else in the world is falling apart, then perhaps Anaïs and I will join together at last,* he tought when she met him in Marseilles. *What would be easier than for Anaïs to step abard the Théophile Gautier?* He never pushed this proposal, for Anaïs made it perfectly clear that she had come to say goodbye. They talked over old times and they were happy together. She planned to return to Paris and simply sit in her apartment at 12 Rue Cassini in the Fourteenth Arrondisement, she wrote to Fred. Thence she would be able to continue to send money to Henry, until some miracle picked her up and put her down in America. She flatly refused to break with her husband. On July 14—Bastille Day—1939, Anaïs and Henry went in separate directions, one by train and the other by ship. Without realizing it, they gave up their last real possibility of a life together.

So, Henry was alone on a boat to Piraeus, alone again on the open seas. He was not so much liberated as cut loose, set adrift again, for he had had to give up almost everything he had achieved. All he had left was the revival of love, the renewal of his sense of joy. But that, of course, was the best thing he had found. He was alone at forty-seven—but intact.

Conrad Moricand had stressed the theme of a sea voyage in the horoscope he made for Miller: "The image which this chart evokes is that of some great sea monster which plunges tirelessly, and with the suppleness of a shark, to the nethermost depths of the sea in order to continually bring back to the surface the trophies of an unknown world." Miller did have the strength that Moricand saw. Properly understood, the "unknown world" which he seized was his own being. Now he was journeying toward an antique world, and he hoped to find something other than ego there.

Before long Henry had made the acquaintances of some of the Italians, Turks, Syrians, and Greeks aboard the boat. Ever since his first day in Paris, when he forgot the word for "beans," Henry had not been shy about jabbering away in his own special language consisting of Brooklyn idiom, slangy French, sign language, pantomime, grimaces, grunts, and groans. He certainly had to make use of this language now in order to be understood among the general babel. And if he didn't always make himself perfectly understood, that didn't matter, since the exuberance which he obviously put into the attempt to communicate invariably succeeded in establishing the human contact—a smile, an embrace, a hand placed on the shoulder.

When the *Théophile Gautier* laid over at Naples for eight hours, Miller, still the tourist that he had been in 1928, rushed ashore to take a friendly look at the crowded, tenement life of the city, which reminded Henry of New York. Then he dashed down to inspect Pompeii even though he knew such frenzied tourism was absurd. He was fleeing France to escape the Axis onslaught; yet here he was inspecting antique ruins in the heart of one of the two great Fascist powers. Even as he inspected the crushed Pompeii, he envisioned the buildings of modern Naples smashed by the coming holocaust. Past and future, Pompeii and Naples were sister cities in disaster—but basically irrelevant to him, merely a pause in his flight from counterfeit Montparnasse toward the real Mount Parnassus. He and civilization were traveling different historic arcs.

Miller knew what he was leaving and he idealized what he was going toward. In a special sense the war had come at exactly the right time for him. He really had tired of Paris—he called it "a city of sewers." In a sense, he had also tired of literature. Once, when his life was in shambles, he had believed that art was superior to life and had desired nothing more than to be a writer, to use literature to understand a life—his own—which had become foreign and completely mysterious to him. Then he had managed to achieve his dream and live his life through art. And as soon as he did so, he began to mourn the loss of the wild, unpredictable, adventurous life he had led. *Black Spring* and the "Dream Book" set him on a new path by reminding him of the importance of his childhood. He yearned to get out of the city atmosphere and draw in gulps of fresh air.

In Greece he expected to breathe free. He knew little about the actual conditions of the country, but he knew exactly what his ideal of Greece was like and whence it came. From his youthful reading of Bulfinch, only a delicious, sweet aroma of pleasure remained. But more recently Betty Ryan, who had lived in Greece, had spoken about it often. In love with her during 1938, Henry had naturally absorbed her love for the country. And Durrell had been bombarding Miller with letters concerning the glories of Greece and inviting him to share them. From all these sources Miller had constructed a vision of an ancient, primitive land whose main character he associated with simple human fellowship, personal directness, and the basic elements, water especially. Greece would be like a womb—a pastoral, Cyclopean world, truly what Larry called a "heraldic" world, able to satisfy Henry's yearning for both deep human contact on an emotional plane and for the visionary experience of wonder on an imaginative level. Every mile he traveled seemed to confirm this vision. Even on the big slow old tub of a boat that was lumbering down the southern Italian coast, Miller had intimations of the new world he felt destined to experience. Standing at the prow and making toward unfamiliar shores with a fresh wind in his face, Henry was stirred by the old, old memories of his first ambition, to be a pilot. He could almost imagine that at last he had become one.

On July 19, five days after leaving Marseilles, his boat bobbed into the port of Piraeus. Raymond Queneau's translation of "Via Dieppe-Newhaven" had just appeared in *Volontés*. What a contrast! The Greek officials were human: the formalities were minimal and he soon passed through the gates to the docks where tour guides waited to greet him with impersonal friendliness. They swarmed about him, they showed their teeth in fine grins, they treated him aimiably, and they put themselves at his disposal. Although the sun was blazing and he was wearing his woolen knickers and cap, Miller couldn't resist taking a peek at the Acropolis, and he let himself and a shipmate be led away by one of the guides. By the time the frenzied taxi had spun through the narrow streets and over the hills, he was wringing wet. He decided to sit at the base of the Acropolis under a tree and dream about the ancient life of Athens, rather than make the climb in the hot sun.

Later, with the sure instincts of a city dweller, Henry found his way to a café where Athens literary society often met, the Old Brazil Coffee House on Stadium Street. He wasn't able to make clear to the waiter what it was he wanted to order until a couple of Greek students who spoke English came to his aid. After some literary talk he asked one of them, Nikos Gatsos, if they ever read American writers. Nikos said "Yes" but explained that Greek students did not care for American literature particularly—it was too flat, too prosaic. Didn't they admire any American writers, then? Henry asked. "Well, one anyway—someone you have never heard of—" Gatsos said tentatively. And that was? "Henry Miller, an American writer living in Paris!" "But *I* am Henry Miller," he said flabbergasted. Gatsos was polite. "No, pardon me. The Henry Miller I speak of is a writer, the author of the *Tropic of Cancer,* who resides in Paris." It was a slapstick scene. Miller took out identification, passport, photos, and so on, trying to prove that he was *the* Henry Miller. The student tried patiently to explain that in America "Henry Miller" was a common name, while Miller spun out stories about his life in Paris and New York, trying simply to prove that he was himself. These Greeks were too logical to accept such a coincidence. But at last Henry wore them down, and they talked on for several hours. When they were parting, Miller stopped them: "Say, where can you get laid around here?" They were embarrassed and pretended not to understand. It was not a question one should ask a young, very proper Greek student. They were sorry, they couldn't help him. But it proved he was the real Henry Miller!

Henry went to a hotel in Athens. The heat was still terrific, like one of those unforgettably sweltering nights in New York City when people slept on fire escapes or even climbed into bathtubs seeking relief. In the hotel dining room he ate ice cream and drank water and then ate ice cream again. When this failed he ordered hot tea (" something hot will cool you off," his mother used to insist). But nothing worked and the heat lay like a slab of marble on his chest.

The next morning Miller made his way back to the dock where the *Théophile Gautier* was stoking up for the trip to Corfu. Unable to get through the Corinth Canal, which had been blocked by a landslide, the boat chugged around the Peloponnesus, taking over a day longer than usual. But it gave Henry a chance to feel and understand the keys to Greece: *land* and *water*. The land was never out of sight from the water, and some arm of the sea was visible from almost anywhere on land. As the port of Corfu came into view, Henry looked for Durrell's familiar figure. No one. Then, as the boat chugged to the dock a car pulled up and a short chunky man and a slender woman stepped out in the dust. Convinced that boats and trains never arrived or departed on time in Greece, Durrell had arrived on time simply by being a day late. They were joking and laughing as of old before they even got started toward Durrell's house at Kalami.

Miller was ready to be affected by Greece from the moment he decided to go there. Until his arrival at Corfu, however, he had been preoccupied with time, fearful that the war would start—worried that, having abandoned France, he would never reach Corfu. Once settled at Kalami he simply forgot about time, history, the bloody strife of humankind, and the daily news of Hitler's threats; and he felt a sense of liberation and release.

Many months before, the Villa Seurat had resembled a factory, with its flood of correspondence pouring from the second floor, the people coming and going without cessation. Henry had been the flywheel of activity. But in Corfu, everything stopped. Like the boats tied up off Kalami, Henry simply floated, and it was delicious to drift. He promised himself that for a year he would write nothing but letters. He avoided the radio and refused to read newspapers. His only books were those about the soul's growth, like Madam Blavatsky's *The Secret Doctrine* and Nijinsky's *Diary*. He let his beard grow, sat in the sun on the rocks facing Albania, and swam in the nude. He wished he could regress through all the stages of civilization and become an animal by simplifying his needs; then a vegetable by empyting his mind; and finally, like a character in a Greek tale, turn into a rock, land, sun, or water. He absolutely believed that the Greek experience, the sunlit Mediterranean vision, would give him guidance.

But soon he was forced to abandon his dreaming. When the King returned to Athens in the late summer of 1939 everyone took this as a sign that war for Greece was imminent, and Miller and the Durrells left Corfu for the capital. Larry was in a sweat to go off to fight against Italy in the Albanian campaign. Miller didn't feel the slightest twinge of desire to be blown to smithereens on Kalami's rocky coast and had no intention of fighting for anyone, anywhere. Kalami or Athens were one to him. The only advantage to Athens was the chance for new acquaintances. Durrell generally avoided Englishmen abroad, but he had a number of friends among Greek writers and artists who spoke English. They were, indeed, leading figures in the modern renascence of Greek literature. Many were translators, since the group aimed at absorbing modern European literature into Greek and also making Greek literature known in Europe. Two members of the group, Dr. Theodore Stephanides and George C. Katsimbalis, had translated Palamas' *Poems* and produced an anthology of *Modern Greek Poets* in English. George Seferiades, who wrote under the name of Seferis, was translating Eliot and other modern writers and writing imagistic verse about the Greek landscape and character. Through Seferis, Miller met several other writers who congregated around Katsimbalis's journal *Ta Nea Grammata (New Letters)*, where work by Lawrence, Breton, Rimbaud, Lorca, and Giraudoux appeared. The painter Ghikas also joined this group. Internationalist in style, they were all cosmopolitan and very serious about their art, but they also felt close to their country—particularly now that the war was edging so close to its border. Katsimbalis, a teller of colossal tales and a man of enormous gusto, immediately reminded Miller of Blaise Cendrars: he seemed able to fill a room all by himself. Keenly interested in American literature, well acquainted with Paris and London, a tireless monologuist, he swept Henry along in endless strophes and antistrophes of talk, like a drama in which he spoke all the parts. Katsimbalis urged Miller to make a contribution to his magazine. As a result, Miller was in Greece for less than two months when he broke his vow and wrote "Reflections on Writing" which was inspired by a talk with Katsimbalis. (It would appear in *Ta Nea Grammata* in Katsimbalis's translation in 1940.) "Even now," Miller says in this essay, "I do not consider myself a writer, in the ordinary sense of the word. I am a man telling the story of his life, a process which appears more and more inexhaustible as I go on." He finished the essay in Corfu, when he returned there alone. But when Nancy Durrell drove to Corfu to pick up some supplies, he returned with her to Athens for a dose of artistic, urban, intellectual life. The sun and the water in Corfu were as dazzling as ever, but he was itching for the play of minds again.

One day as Miller sat with Katsimbalis, Seferis, and Ghikas in the Lumides Cafe the conversation touched on the possibility that much that was venerable in Greece would soon be destroyed. Before this happened, someone suggested, they should take one more trip, like bachelors on a final fling. They used Miller as an excuse to indulge in a sentimental journey: this American, this man of letters who was so obviously in accord with Greek life, should be shown their country. So, with little prior preparation, they visited the ancient Greek scenes that might soon be blown off the map. Ghikas and Seferis went as far as Ghikas's ancestral home in Hydra. The painter guided Henry around the island. Then Miller and Katsimbalis continued on alone for a journey of two months. Henry simply put himself in Katsimbalis's hands like a baby. It was as if he were being picked up by this colossus and put down in Poros, then again in Nauplia, Epidaurus, and Mycenae. To be taken care of so completely made everything seem easy. Somehow Henry began to feel that he was not *on* a way to a changed life, a revivified consciousness—in a mystical sense he *was* the route he must take. Behind every rock in Greece seemed to hover a broken column, a fragment of a frieze, some ancient secret. Everything seemed to have two sides, two natures, a spiritual significance behind the human fact. On his tour with Katsimbalis, though he was covered with dust and sweat, Henry felt like a holy man. He tried to describe this: "Each station . . . marked a progression into a new spiritual latitude and longitude. There is only one analogy I can make to explain the nature of this illuminating voyage which began at Poros and ended at Tripolis . . . I must refer the reader to the accension of Seraphita . . . It was a voyage into the light."

In Hydra, Seferis had started a poem about Miller, *"Les Anges Sont Blancs."* Its details were drawn from the *Tropics* and Miller's constant references to Louis Lambert. This *was* an angelic time for Henry—everyone noticed it. Back in Athens, where he lived at the Grande Bretagne Hotel on Constitution Square, Miller went around to Seferis's house one night to hear the finished poem about himself. With him he carried a little mystical book on the Immaculate Heart he had written for Seferis. It was late and Seferiades was already in bed when Henry arrived. But he got up and the two writers talked. Stirred by the poem, Henry started thinking of the "angel" in man, which inevitably led to that angelic personage Nijinsky. The theme of the angelic preoccupied Miller.

The spiritual wisdom of the ages, in any of its forms, now held enormous fascination for him. Whenever he met Ghikas the painter (chiefly in the Apotzos, an old fashioned café whose walls were covered with hundreds of old posters), they talked about Indian philosophy, yoga, magic, and Zen—all interests of Ghikas' which Henry shared. They traded books with each other, Henry giving the painter an edition of Lao-Tse. Ghikas was privately convinced that Miller was experiencing a period of unconscious purification. One day, Henry mentioned that he was thinking of writing a very short book about his stay in Greece, an episode in his series of autobiographical romances. Ghikas laughed and said: "That will be a book without sex, then." Henry didn't understand. But Ghikas said: "If you came to Greece as a Parisian bohemian, you have become a pilgrim. The places you have seen and the people you have met; the rich history in every object in Greece; the mountains and sea and rocks and marbles; and above all, the simplicity of life and the absolute purity of line and light here—these have altered your point of view. Henceforth your writing must be different." Henry was on the defensive at once—*he* wanted to change, but he hadn't counted on having his writing changed. He insisted to Ghikas that he could write a book about Athens just like *Tropic of Cancer*—but, when he was alone, he wondered.

Ghikas had, in fact, quite accurately understood Henry's renewal of vision, the restoration of his sense of wonder. "In Crete," Miller wrote to Huntington Cairns, "I expect to see something phenomenal. I am sure of it. I don't want beauty and harmony. I want to see the origins of things—the autochthonous . . . ." Crete was everything he expected: the land itself was dark and bloody, pre-Christian, an apt setting for the ancient ruins at Knossos and Phaestos. It made him think of the primitive, long unsettled American land. He experienced the same feeling everywhere in Greece. From the heights of Phaestos (and later on the plains of Thebes and at Delphi) he had a weird awareness of the ghostly presence of the autochthonous man, the redskin with his wigwams and signal fires. He knew that he would soon be going back to America, and he was already creating the American scene in Grecian terms. Greece, he told himself, was what America needed, and Greece was what the American dream aimed at. He believed that he now understood the possibilities of his own country and he even began to look forward to a return to America, the still primitive land. Moreover, everywhere he went in Greece he ran into Greek men who had spent a few years in Chicago, Detroit, or New York and now wished to be back in the States. Certainly, that gave him a certain amount of hope for his native land.

Many things were driving Henry back to the country of his early sorrows. First of all, his finances were now in a state of confusion. His economic lifeline came from the Obelisk Press. Kahane had continued to send Henry a monthly stipend against royalties. These had been adequate to support him in Greece, but in September 1939 Kahane died. Though his young son Maurice promised to keep paying royalties, France was in turmoil. Maurice was about to join the army and it seemed highly unlikely that Henry's regular monthly payment could be long maintained. Already, war restrictions prevented money from being sent out of the combating countries. On the other hand, for the first time American publication seemed possible. James Laughlin, who had once printed "Glittering Pie" in the *Harvard Advocate,* had started a press called New Directions. He wanted to publish a collection of Miller's short pieces drawn from *Max and the White Phagocytes,* titled *The Cosmological Eye.* G. Legman was planning to issue a pirated letter-press edition of *Tropic of Cancer* and offered to pay royalties. Henry encouraged him to pirate the book, whether he himself got paid or not. Furthermore, some of Henry's friends (Frances Steloff of the Gotham Book Mart, William Saroyan, Ben Abramson of the Argus Book Shop, and Laughlin) wrote to him saying that they had pooled enough money to buy him a homeward bound ticket. They preferred to send him a ticket, Laughlin wryly said, because, "Too many times have there been sad experiences with people sending you money to come home." And finally, Anaïs had made her way to New York and he yearned to see her.

The fates conspired to advance his desire. On December 5, 1939 the American Minister to Greece, Lincoln MacVeagh, ordered all American civilians out of the country. Henry had a horror of being torpedoed. "The Germans are sinking everything in sight, the bloody idiots," he wrote to Cairns. But practically speaking, as he wrote Emil Schnellock, his choice was only between the chance of being torpedoed from below and the certainty, if he stayed, of being bombed from above. He refused, at last, to consider the possibility of either; he leaped like a Cretan off the horns of his dilemma. Not long before his boat was supposed to leave he started to travel again—to Eleusis with Ghikas; and to Sparta and the Peloponnesus with the Durrells. Christmas in Sparta was dull and damp with steady rain. The chill penetrated even into the cavernous café where Henry, Nancy and Larry Durrell ate their holiday dinners. The table top was as cold as a tombstone; the plates on the table were so dank that the grease congealed on the lamb even as it was being set down before them. The food looked like lead and the Spartan wine tasted poisonous. In short, in Henry's experience it was a typical Christmas, consisting of sour smells, upset stomachs, and misery—just what St. Nicholas ordered. It would not have been much different had the sun been shining gloriously, of course. Nor was his forty-eighth birthday any better: December 26, 1939 was spent on the drafty, rattling train from Tripolis to Athens. Only the mail waiting for him at the Grande Bretagne Hotel cheered him up a little, especially the money postals and cables. He had his birthday dinner with Katsimbalis and Seferis, but no one had much to say.

He had one foot in America already. Accompanied by Ghikas, on the twenty-seventh of December 1939 he went to the boat at around 11 a.m., while it was still being loaded. Henry carried a small suitcase. He wore a battered gray hat and his old gray overcoat and looked a little gray himself—sad and apprehensive.

He was certainly not overjoyed at being forced back to America. The vessel was an American cargo boat with a crew of tough American merchant sailors. When Henry stepped on board the *Exochorda,* he felt he was back in the States. Ghikas came aboard with him, but it did no good. From this gray boat, even the Greek light on the horizon seemed gray. There was no *ouzo,* no *retzina* aboard. He and Ghikas downed a raw whiskey and the painter left with few words. Miller wandered about nervously until the ship finally sailed into the gray fogs lying off the harbor. Resolutely, he faced backward, gazing, gazing, gazing at the light over the hills until the hills disappeared into the sea and only the light, the light of Attica, was left. When that too was consumed by the gray waters it was as if a flame had suddenly been snuffed out, leaving ashes behind.

The question was: *What does the future hold?* Not many weeks before Miller was to leave Athens, Katsimbalis took him to an Armenian sooth-sayer named Aram Hourabedian in whom Katsimbalis had great faith. The man had studied the Kabbalah, astrology, occult lore, and the mystical sciences of Arabia. Like many others, he read Miller's fortune. Miller had made many enemies, the soothsayer remarked, and had led a schizophrenic life, but he was soon to achieve a unity of vision and person and win the greatest kinds of honors. He would go on many journeys. Finally, on his third visit to the Orient, he would vanish into the light. In the meantime, Henry had a marvellous career before him, with triumphs on all fronts and the certainty of a charmed life. "I want you to remember my words," he intoned, "when danger confronts you again—that however perilous the situation you must never give up, you will be saved. You are like a ship with two rudders: when one gives out the other will function."

Rudders, indeed! Henry thought as he sailed out across the lonely seas on the *Exochorda.* If a German U-boat were patrolling the Mediterranean he might do better with a pair of wings. Yet that visit to the soothsayer provided him materials for days of reflection during the voyage. There were many alarms, and as each one proved false, he began to feel that he was genuinely protected. Most of the passengers sat sullenly eating their way through enormous meals and listening to the war news on the radio. (Miller was dying to talk to one of them, the philosopher Jacques Maritain, who sat at the next table, but his shyness prevented him from breathing a single word.) The further he steamed from Greece the more he also believed that Ghikas had been right. He *had* reached another level of vision there. Perhaps like one of the sages mentioned in Jewish tradition, he held the universe together—perhaps it was his sidereal rudder that steered the boat through its perilous course, perhaps the soothsayer too was right. And if so, the return to America, half compelled and half wished, was merely another pilgrimage, like Whitman's passage to India—or more than India. Wasn't it clear now that he was moving upward and that his return to the United States was simply a stop on the Great Circle route he was traveling, and that it provided the opportunity for one more purification? Even Greece, as he now saw it, had been such a stage—it was, as he had written to V.F. Calverton, "the world of nature, par excellence. One just breathes here, and it is enough." Had he arrived in Greece at the age of twenty-five he would have been content to become merely a natural man. But his humiliations and sufferings in New York and the decade of growth toward artistic consciousness in Paris had blocked him from so simple a resolution. He didn't understand what his American stage would be, for he didn't entirely understand his destiny. But he felt thoroughly convinced that America would be an interlude—this land of fuck, where one *is* fucked—on his way to something older than Greece, something with even more ancient form. America, he thought, would give him the opportunity to exhaust his ego once and for all in the final orgy of completing the story of his life in a sequel to *Tropic of Capricorn,* "The Rosy Crucifixion," which would be his final work. "And then," he told Osborn, "silence. After I complete my program I shall probably go to Tibet and become a sage and a seer." Like Rimbaud, and even more than Rimbaud, he was preparing to quit literature "in full plenitude."

Although the boat was crowded and dreary and tossed through gray wintry seas, the colors of Miller's imagination lit up the whole homeward voyage. Previously in America he had felt that he was running away from something—himself mainly. Now that the boat went relentlessly west, he believed that he was going toward something, his next level of awareness, whatever that might be.

Two

A Man with No Fortune and a Name To Come

It was a new decade. He left Greece in 1939 and docked in America in 1940. The ship stopped in Boston before proceeding to New York. Henry wandered through a Boston railway station and was amazed to see the piles of books and magazines for sale. Had Americans suddenly become a nation of readers? Perhaps a revolution had occurred in America? Was the persistent European belief that a new man and a new order would arise on the American continent really to be fulfilled? But when he arrived in New York his hopes came down. Yes, he decided, Americans were creating a new order, but it was of a machine world in which there was no place for man, much less the gods.

Miller waited alone at the dock for Anaïs Nin to meet his boat as promised. He carried a present for her: a sixty-eight page essay which he had written by hand in a blank notebook and embellished with two pencil sketches and two watercolors. He had titled it *The Heaven Beyond Heaven* and inscribed it to Anaïs "aboard the 'Exochorda' 1/12/40." Greece, he explained, was his "heaven beyond heaven," his Thirteenth House, as far as he could get in his ecliptic. In his mind the Greek world and Anaïs (with her Greek name) were connected: both were perfectly human, both had saved him. But Anaïs did not meet the boat. She was home nursing the flu. Just as penniless as ever, carrying $10, the same amount he had left with in 1930, Henry didn't even have enough money to pay the duty on the other gifts he had brought home. He made his way by cab over to the Royalton Hotel, near Times Square, and settled down, alone, in a little, worn room in the heart of the cruelest city in the world. A typical homecoming. He was still exultant about his spiritual growth in Greece, but he knew he was back in the rat trap again.

If anyone was a man with no fortune and a name to come, he was. Though he had published several books, in America only one collection of his essays, *The Cosmological Eye* (1939), had appeared. He was known to few readers or critics or even fellow writers. He didn't intend to remain unknown for long. Henry always had a sure instinct for nosing out fellow artists and he had gone to the Royalton because writers often stayed there. At this very time, he learned from the desk clerk, Sherwood Anderson was in the hotel. He sent Anderson a shy note and subsequently arranged to meet him in a nearby bar. John Dos Passos was sitting with Anderson when Henry came up and both greeted him warmly. Suddenly he was sitting side by side with two of the writers whom he had admired for almost twenty years. Henry felt awkward, bothered by a sense that he was still a novice to them. But they edged into talk about America, Anderson speaking wonderfully about American small towns and the still-evident continuity of American life; and both struck him as deeply American. Again Henry's American dreams revived: if the country could produce such men as these, who kept their American faith even on close contact with native conditions, then there must be something vital in the country. He felt the same over again when he met other American artists: Kenneth Patchen, Carl Van Vechten, Alfred Stieglitz, and John Marin. In the face of such evidence, who could deny that it was possible to be an artist in America?

New York City, to be sure, held many ghosts. He was unhappy with Anaïs, unable to get as close to her as he wanted. June he might meet coming around any corner. He thought often, with a revival of the same old painful frustration, of his daughter, Barbara. He looked curiously into the faces of the young girls he passed. Would he even recognize Barbara? More than anything, his parents haunted him. He wrote them of his expected return, and he was aware that they expected him to join them at Decatur Street—to visit them at least. But he kept making excuses to himself—he had to run down to Washington with his Paris friend, Caresse Crosby, he was busy writing, and so on—until January and February had passed without his making the trek across the river.

Like a recuperating patient, he made his way home to Brooklyn in stages, visiting the old neighborhood several times with Anaïs and other friends.

Finally, he arranged to visit his parents. After such a long absence he
wanted to return bearing presents, to do something grand, to show that all
these years had not been wasted, that he had not betrayed his parents' hopes
after all. But he was flat broke and he came close to sending a message that
he was unable to come. At the last moment, however, he had sold a
manuscript to a collector for $50 and spent it all on gifts. Once home he
itched with uneasiness all evening, as if he were mentally rocking from one
foot to another. The house breathed an even more abject air of poverty than
he had remembered. This was what he feared—but he realized that now he
was stronger than his guilt: he could face his humiliations down and face his
parents—sick and poor and helpless, yet pathetically anxious to keep up
the old air of respectability and to welcome him back. "Do you remember
this?—and this?—and this?"—they kept asking—"the day you planted
these lilacs, the nights we sat on these steps, this day—that day?" What
most tore him apart was his realization that they didn't expect anything at
all of him. Although his father was dying from cancer and they were living
in poverty, they could now accept him for himself. They expected
nothing—that he was with them was enough. To him this turnabout was
abrupt. But he could not easily forgive his mother the demands she had
once made to earn her love; he did not forget her cold, critical eye. As he was
taking leave, she cried out. "Oh, Henry, there's a thread on your coat!" and
hurried to pick it off. It still bothered him that her affection could be stirred
only by his deficiencies, but he embraced each of them rapidly and then
rushed off toward the elevated railways, weeping, weeping for the little
Henry who had never gotten the bronco from Texas, for the young man who
had to hide in the closet when mother's friends called during the day so that
they wouldn't know that he wasn't working, and for himself, unable on his
own to attract a direct expression of love. He hated his mother for not being
able to give him the affection he craved, and he burned to perform some
great act of love himself in order to give a demonstration of what love was.

So, he suggested that he drop in every morning and clean out the bag into
which his father's excretions drained, but they wouldn't hear of it. Instead,
he came over in the afternoons to sit with his father in the sun, jawing about
the old days of the tailor shop and the Wolcott Bar and telling him all about
Europe. He began to recognize himself in his father and his father in himself
and to admit his love for the old man. He brought whatever little treats he
could. But he wanted to do more. He wrote to Cairns and others that he was
desperate for money and was willing to "take anything from anybody, like a
dog takes a bone." He circulated his manuscripts to New York dealers and

collectors, hoping to make a sale. He did get a meager $200 advance from Laughlin for the collection initially called "The Enormous Womb" and later published as *The Wisdom of the Heart.* An Oklahoma pornography collector's agent offered Miller one dollar a page to compose private works of pornography, but his imagination rebelled at being expected to pour out such garbage.

After making a valiant try (which the patron thought "too poetic") in two tales of about seventy pages each—"Mara-Marignan Marinated" and "Quiet Days in Clichy," written in May and June 1940, Miller simply found that he couldn't write acceptable pornography. Still, Henry's name, as the author of *Tropic of Cancer,* was worth money, and he farmed out the job to an acquaintance with the suggestion that she simply take the cast of *Cancer* and the Paris scene and run amok with it. Seven sketches, qualifying as sheer pornography, resulted. The titles had weakly humorous twists, such as "France in My Pants," "Sous les Toits de Paris" (crudely punning on "Under the Twats of Paris"), and "Le Rue de Screw;" and though they were as far as possible from Miller's style and subject, the oil millionaire lapped them up. *Tropic of Cancer* would have bored the shit out of him. So Miller had returned to the United States, where his books couldn't be sold, to become a fumbling pornographer and even to have his pornography ghost-written. That was the way, in America, to earn enough money to visit his parents with arms full of gifts.

Yet his Greek experience, followed by the reunion with his parents, gave him a new slant on himself and his future. Anaïs was right in saying that his reconciliation with his family humanized him by turning his pity outward. His pity and his confrontation of guilt touched off emotional springs which stirred his imagination. As early as the second week of March 1940 he wrote to Cairns, for instance: "I was cracked wide open here by the parental tragedy. Has done me good—I will write some heart-breaking stuff . . . ." He felt like writing again and so, in his old methodical way, he got his life properly arranged to make writing possible. He moved into spacious bachelor quarters in Caresse Crosby's apartment house at 137 East Fifty-fourth Street, set up his pens, ink, block of paper, and typewriter on a table at a window overlooking a courtyard, and sat down, as if he were back in Clichy or the Villa Seurat. His favorite, most natural subject was Henry Miller and how he got that way: he enjoyed nothing more than writing about how he had written one of his books. In mid-March 1940 he continued the themes of his Greek essay, "Reflections on Writing," in a long essay attempting to explain the heavy emphasis he had placed upon sex in his previous books. Titled "The World of Sex," this essay was completed in a few weeks and is Miller's best statement on his own work. Obviously, "The World of Sex" was closely connected in an emotional way to his attempt to write sheer pornography: his inability to do so forced him to explain what he did hope to achieve in treating sexuality frankly. From another point of view the essay was a companion to the witty, lively treatment of sex in the two connected tales, "Quiet Days in Clichy" and "Mara-Marignan Marinated." With vibrant good humor Miller played with the comedy and the mythology of sex in these tales.

But his most serious work during this period was of quite a different sort. These essays and tales were done with his left hand while he concentrated on his Greek experience in a book that began with a five-page sketch of Katsimbalis. Miller didn't want to see his account of Greece buried in a mere collection with pieces of less consequence, and he quite deliberately expanded his portrait of Katsimbalis. By May of 1940 he had finished eighty pages and vowed to go on to make a full-length book. Ready to lengthen his text with the observations of other travel writers, he studied Pierre Roussel's *Delos* and Fernand Robert's *Epidaure;* but once he got into the work his imagination required no prodding: it flowed unprompted from the deep engagement of the two contrary but primary sources of his sensibility—the child-like sense of wonder and the yearning for wisdom and antiquity—*sagesse.* Greece provided a perfect subject for the fusion of these impulses, and Miller naturally adopted the lyrical style of the oracular sage. *The Colossus of Maroussi* was primarily a confession of what had happened to Henry Miller between July and December 1939, for his return to his native land, the uncertainty of his future, and his surprising reunion with his parents all tended to hold his focus inward during mid 1940. Where had he come from? Where was he going? Who was he, and who might he *become?* Such questions were natural under the circumstances and they kept his Greek book very personal, nowise resembling a travelogue. *The Colossus of Maroussi,* then, was not finally a recognizable portrait of Katsimbalis, the "Colossus." Rather it embodied the gusto, the rhapsodic strain which had been quickened in his sensibility by Greece and Katsimbalis. He confessed in the book itself that anyone who had read *Death in Venice* would understand the emotions which he, a northerner and Teuton, had felt for the warm south and the generous Mediterranean people. Above all, it was an earnest of his spiritual renewal. What Gauguin had found in Tahiti and D.H. Lawrence in Mexico, Miller had experienced in Greece.

But because his own fundamental impulses were so deeply satisfied,

Miller also caught something of the essence of Greece. Almost certainly, he did not know that Winckelmann had characterized Greek art as possessing "Edele Einfalt und stille Grosse"—noble simplicity and tranquil sublimity—but he had discerned the same character, the "naked strength of the people, their purity, their nobility, their resignation"; and he wished to absorb these traits into himself and his work. What did he need, then, with the devices that he had used in his earlier works—particularly in *Black Spring* and *Capricorn*—of the fantastic, the surreal, and the absurd, when the liberation of the imagination could be achieved merely by a steadfast inspection of the real? Why plunge into the life of the night when the blazing sun of Greece gave back to the viewer the colors of his humanity? Why retreat into dreams to recapture the child when the child-man of the race still resided in Attica? He never took a high tone with his book; he steadfastly held to the personal, as if to say: I don't know what Greece would be like for you, but I can tell you how it was *for me*.

In July Miller went to Bowling Green, Virginia, to visit Caresse Crosby. The painter John Dudley, his wife Flo, and Salvador Dali and his wife were already guests at her house. It wasn't long before Henry rather freely expressed his view that the Dalis spoiled the place by always acting "like a couple of shrewd bedbugs," attempting to manage everyone else's lives. The air became increasingly electric and Henry would have returned to New York except that he continued to be short of money. The last he had heard of possible Obelisk Press royalties was in March 1940, when Maurice Kahane wrote to promise continuance of Miller's monthly 500 francs payments. Then Paris fell and the young editor fell silent—either in a prison camp or dead. Hopelessly, Miller wrote to the old Obelisk Press address in the Place Vendôme: "Does the Obelisk Press still exist?" He expected no answer and he got none. Instead, he imagined sausage-faced German officers opening his letter and burning his manuscripts. *The Cosmological Eye* took years to earn the small advance. Victor Weybright of the American branch of Penguin Books offered Miller a $1,000 advance for his authorization to publish a rewritten, expurgated version of the *Tropic of Cancer*, solely with the intention of capitalizing on the *sub rosa* notoriety of the novel. Henry couldn't agree to do that any more than he could write pornography. To John Slocum of Russell & Volkening, who had replaced Marion Saunders as his literary agent, he turned over five book-length manuscripts and twenty-two articles or sketches, all unpublished or published obscurely. And Slocum couldn't place a single one! The *Nation* refused a sketch, *The New Yorker* turned down three, Malcolm Cowley vetoed a piece for the *New Republic*. Miller's work was refused by *Twelve Arts Monthly, Esquire,* and *The Kenyon Review*. To top all this, even a magazine emanating from Madison, Wisconsin, called *Diogenes*—a magazine that had requested a piece from Miller—turned down the contribution he sent, "Creative Death." And he had offered it *gratis!* So he sat in Virginia, hands in his empty pockets, cursing the Dalis and smouldering like a doused fire.

   The Colossus of Maroussi, he felt, would change his luck. At Miller's request, Slocum sent part one, about a hundred pages, to Blanche Knopf. Early in August she sent him a copy of a report by Harold Strauss, one of the Knopf editors. The book, Strauss advised, was "very difficult to classify. It appears to be a travel book and yet actually it is no more than Mr. Miller's private animadversions on life, art, and philosophy." He recommended rejection. The book was rejected without further discussion. A week later Frank V. Morley refused the book for Harcourt, Brace. Ten consecutive commercial publishers in New York rejected *The Colossus;* their consensus was that no readers would be interested in Greece (notwithstanding, Will Durant's huge book on ancient Greek philosophy and civilization was selling unexpectedly well). What *did* the publishers want then? Henry asked John Slocum. Though vague and heavily qualified, the answer was: with their country in a critical period, hovering at the edge of war, Americans had turned inward and were interested in their own nation. "Why not give us a book on America?" the editors echoed each other.

   Miraculously, this fell right into Henry's plans. Long before leaving Paris he had been telling friends that some day he would return to take a close look at the United States. He had told Count Keyserling in 1936 that he was "an American myself, not just a hundred percent, but a hundred *and one.*" Yet he felt he had "lived through, *lived out* . . . my American life" and could be objective about it. In July 1938 he had described a book to Kahane which he called *America, the Air-Conditioned Nightmare.* His outline proposed such chapters as: "Mississippi Mud," "The Grand Canyon and the Culebra Cut," "Celluloid City (Hollywood)," and so on—fifty chapters in all. "To write the American nightmare thing," he said, "I must revisit America for the last time soon. I want desperately to get to Arizona, and travel up and down the Mississippi . . . . A travel book of impressions— nothing preconceived. If I get a break now I will hop a boat and go. Because after that voyage I expect to go far away from Europe—maybe to Tibet, or at least to the frontier." Now, in 1940, editors demanded books about America, and he wanted to write one: these coincidences were golden.

   Everything fell into place with a final accident. The illustrator of

Scenario, his friend Abraham Rattner, mentioned that he dreamed of taking a trip across the United States. They planned to travel together and eventually to produce a deluxe book recounting their impressions, the text by Miller and the sketches by Rattner. The publishers whom Slocum approached unanimously looked unfavorably upon Rattner's part in the project: with the increase in printing costs due to the war, elaborate illustrations would make the book too expensive. But editors were definitely interested in a former expatriate's fresh observations on his native land. Doubleday, Doran & Co. proposed a contract which specified that the book must be free of pornography and offered Miller an advance of $500—only about a quarter of the sum he needed for the tour he planned. He got the advance increased to $750, signed the contract and collected his money in late August 1940. He also applied (rather diffidently) to the John Simon Guggenheim Foundation for a grant. The anticipation of rejection hovered about his application:

I plan to make a journey by automobile through these United States beginning some time in October, 1940 . . . The significance of the book would be for posterity to decide. For me it represents the fulfillment of a vow.
I have no plan . . . . I simply wish to see with my own eyes what America is now like . . . .
My ultimate purpose as a writer, since it is requested that I state it, is that of every sincere artist—to fulfill myself and thus, inadvertently, enrich the lives of men and women everywhere now and forever after.
. . . Your aid would be welcome but not indispensable. It would perhaps enable me to do the task with less worry. The venture is primarily a joyous one. To have money in my pocket, for a change, might increase the joy of labor.

Instead of solving his problems, signing a contract for *The Air-Conditioned Nightmare* simply presented him with new ones. With such limited funds he could make his tour only with difficulty. The miserly economics he would confront—in transportation, food, and living accommodations—would very likely color his whole outlook on the trip and sour his mind and his book. How would Mobile look after a greasy breakfast? How splendid would even the pueblos be after a sleepless night in a seedy motor-court? How vigorous would Chicago seem with the smells of the slaughter houses in his nostrils? What would California look like when he recalled his earlier failures there? Wouldn't most of the fun be drained from the journey if Abe Rattner didn't go along? Moreover, now that he had contracted to do the book, he had to decide what kind of book he meant to write. Whenever he thought of his long-anticipated "American Nightmare" book, his mind was filled with contradictory or at least conflicting impulses, all laid one over the other like geological strata. Its condemnatory approach to America was allied with books like Duhamel's *Scènes de la vie future* and Celine's *Death on the Installment Plan*. But due to the influence of Henry's Greek experience and his awareness of D.H. Lawrence's appreciation of the American Southwest, Henry also began with a strongly positive view. He hoped to experience the American dream of Edenic renewal. "I want to fall in love with the country if possible," he wrote to Herbert West. "If it's not too 'air-conditioned'." His forebodings and his hopes were equally evident. Now it remained to journey about America. And so he began.

Three

The Air-Conditioned Nightmare

Much later Henry Miller would regret that he had started at all and would decide that he had wasted a year in traveling around America. He should never have taken the trip. He was as ambivalent about America as about his own identity. Certainly, after nearly a decade of living abroad he was homesick for the sights and sounds of his native land. But what he really missed was the ideal America of his dreams. The real America was the arena in which he had failed ten years earlier. The real sights and sounds seemed ugly, tasteless, bourgeois to him—the real America threatened the stability that he had managed to achieve in France.

Simply to travel around America would have put difficult, almost impossible, pressures on Miller's psyche. But the basic personal problems he would have faced in any event were compounded and multiplied by the penurious circumstances under which he'd have to travel. He simply didn't have enough money to travel across the nation, much less to have any of the comforts and little pleasures that might relieve and cheer a bored, exhausted traveler. His plan was doomed to end badly, and it did.

He tried to plan so as to provide for companionship and interesting visits, and free bed and board, as frequently as possible. With his usual efficiency he charted out his itinerary and he studied the map and racked his brains to think of people he knew along the way. In his notebook he made lists of people whose hospitality he could count upon. With some friends,

375

such as Huntington Cairns, he made an honest confession of his poverty and asked for help in a manly way. He wrote to Sherwood Anderson, among other acquaintances, that he hoped to be able to stop and visit. He had never before lectured at a college, and though he was persuaded that he was incapable of speaking before a college audience, he was willing to give it a try. Following the advice of Henry Volkening, who became Miller's agent when John Slocum left the firm, Miller wrote to Allen Tate at Princeton and to Herbert West at Dartmouth, saying that for a small fee he could give a little discussion-talk to students interested in writing. "As a can opener," he planned some reflections on how to write, then he would talk about the processes of creativity, and then get the kids to talk, too. He told Tate and West that he was certain the students would relish this far more than the kind of "sticky aesthetico-critical dope" that other lecturers usually "dished out." (Unfortunately, he didn't give his talk at either university.)

Despite his financial difficulties and the predictable problems of the trip Miller put a lot of thought into his journey and had considerable hopes for success. The largest part of the letters he wrote had nothing at all to do with bed and board. He asked questions about the most interesting places to visit. He was curious about his country and he dreamed of seeing its best face.

The great poet of America, Walt Whitman, was on his mind these days. Whitman had also been a failure in the early part of his life, then he had found himself and had become a powerful writer through his positive vision of America and of the new American man. Miller hoped for the same thing; he would have liked to be a second Whitman. With all the symbolic identification implied in the act, Miller kept the log of his tour in a printer's dummy for a large-format edition of *Leaves of Grass* which he picked up in the storehouse at Doubleday, Doran & Co., the publisher of this Whitman volume and the prospective publisher of Miller's book of American travels.

Just before he began the journey Miller was introduced to the burlesque queen, Gypsy Rose Lee, at the World's Fair in Flushing Meadows. When he told her of his plans she said seductively, "Well *I* could think of a lot of better things to do than to tour America!" But Henry wanted to believe that she was wrong. He had become obsessed with the idea of seeing his country. In the back of his mind, of course, was the realization that the War had made him come back to the United States and would prevent him from going abroad—who knew for how long? And therefore, as he secretly knew, he had to find a home in America, some part of it that could nourish him, some American place that could be a France or Greece to him.

Henry made his final plans in the late summer and early autumn of 1940. First he purchased a 1932 Buick sedan for $100. Then he received a hurried driver's training course from Kenneth Patchen. By the time he was ready to begin his journey the best that could be said for his driving was that he would have a chance to learn as he went along.

On October 24 he started the trip. With Abe Rattner beside him, Miller steered the car through the traffic of lower New York, pulled onto Canal Street and followed the stream of traffic into the Holland Tunnel. He was nervous anyway, but he was unnerved by the descent into the humming tunnel which went under the Hudson River and came out in New Jersey. By the time he got onto the gigantic skyway that led from the tunnel he felt that he was nearing a state of nervous collapse and he had to pull to the side of the road to compose himself.

Henry's travels lasted for more than a year. Rattner accompanied him part of the way, but during the majority of the time he was alone. Eventually, he made the trip in several great arcs slicing across the country, since he wanted to visit every part of it. In the first swing he went from New York south through Asheville, North Carolina (where he reexperienced his tragic days there with June), then Charleston, South Carolina, through Georgia into Florida, then west to Louisiana and ended in Natchez, Mississippi.

Receiving the news that his father was seriously ill, Henry cut the first wing of his trip short in Natchez. He wanted to hurry back to New York. As usual, he only had a few dollars in his pocket. To drive was completely out of the question when time was so important, but he didn't have the money for the plane tickets. He was stuck in Natchez, feeling terribly frustrated, until at last Anaïs telegraphed thirty dollars to him. Henry dashed home to be with his father in his last sickness. But he didn't arrive in time. Two hours before he got to New York his father died.

This was a shock. For the next few weeks Henry was miserable. The funeral seemed cold and the arrangements brutal. He and his mother had a wake in the Decatur Street house. Then the burial took place in Evergreen Cemetery, a place in which his father had liked to take walks on sunny days. Henry visited his father's grave several times. The days were bitterly cold that winter. The cemetery looked desolate at first, but after a while Henry began to enjoy sitting beside his father's grave. He spent hours meditating about his father and soon found that he really missed him. Now that it was too late to tell him so, he realized that he loved the tailor. He began to feel something restored in himself. But his emotional reconciliation to his father also had its frustrating sides. Not only did he wish he had been a better son, Henry was reminded of how poor a father he himself had been: he accused himself of losing both his father and his daughter through his own selfishness. He found, too, that his acceptance of a part of his family made him yearn all the more for a home of his own.

On March 2, 1941 Henry resumed his travels. He took the train to Ohio and Michigan and Wisconsin, stayed in Chicago for a while, then returned to Natchez to pick up the car. The fellowship awards of the John Simon Guggenheim Foundation were announced around this time, and Henry was not one of the successful candidates. He vowed that if he ever did write a book based on this trip, at its end he would print a list of the nonentities who won Guggenheims, along with their ridiculous projects. (When *The Air-Conditioned Nightmare* was published the list was in it.)

From Natchez he drove up to Arkansas, where he picked up Route 66 going west. This led him to the California coast and Hollywood, where he settled down to begin writing *The Air-Conditioned Nightmare*. Finally, he made the trip back to New York by the northern route, doubling back through Wyoming and Iowa, and finally coming into upper New York State. He had driven "25,000 miles," he wrote in his notebook wearily, and concluded it was "a year wasted."

Miller was not a good traveler, but under the circumstances few people could have found much pleasure in the trip. Driving exhausted him, he was forced to put up in poor motels and tourist cabins, he hated the food that he could get in cheap restaurants along the road or in the heart of cities. Worse, still, he couldn't really settle down to write, he didn't have time to think. He filled his dummy of *Leaves of Grass* with notes, itineraries, watercolors and doodles. He tried to write up his account haphazardly, during times when the trip was stalled due to heavy rains, or while he got the car overhauled, or when he waited for needed money to arrive.

All the damp, rain-drenched motor courts, the alkali food, the artificiality of many of the sights, the lack of money, his fatigue and eyestrain—all these worked their way into the fabric of the book he was trying to write. Not since *Tropic of Cancer* had he been so bitter. He felt like a failure all over again in that he had frittered away the joyous attitude toward life he had expressed in *Black Spring*, *Tropic of Capricorn* and *The Colossus of Maroussi*. This reappearance of a sour attitude discouraged Henry—he wondered if his powers were fading with age; he felt again that he had started out as a writer too late in life. He was especially disheartened over the fact that the book was going badly. He confessed to himself that in his pride and arrogance he had believed he had attained mastery as a writer, but now he had to admit that he was a failure in this area too.

By mid-September 1941 Miller felt unhappy in California, as well as discouraged with his own accomplishment. Besides, he missed Anaïs, he was lonely. He wired her and told her this, and she sent him a moneygram which enabled him to make the return across the continent. His work on the book began in earnest once he returned to New York in October of 1941. He surveyed the whole journey to see what it meant. Certainly, he had experienced some good times. He had had some good visits with friends such as Jasper Deeter, director of the Hedgerow Theatre in Pennsylvania, and an eighty-year-old Louisiana doctor-painter named Marion Souchon. He had found a few people in California that he liked, such as John Steinbeck and his friend Ed Ricketts, and also the poet William Everson (later Brother Antonius), and the novelists Aben Kandel and Aldous Huxley. His old friend Hilaire Hiler, from whom he had taken painting lessons in Paris, had been working on the sensational murals at the San Francisco aquarium and he liked seeing Hiler again. Perhaps his most enjoyable days had been in California.

Meeting two young artists, Gilbert Neiman and his wife Margaret, "both poor, both enthusiastic and divinely out of this world" (as Henry told Eva Sikelianou), had given him other human contacts which sustained him, though even this friendship would impart little warmth to his book. Many a day he had taken the trolley downtown from Hollywood to South Bunker Hill Avenue, where the Neimans lived. This district was seedy and run down, filled with slatternly buildings surrounded by empty lots and rubbish piles, but it had made Henry feel at home—it was a comfortable, shabby feeling, reminding him sometimes of the "old neighborhood" and sometimes of the thirteenth arrondissement. Often he and the Neimans had eaten on the wooden terrace which overlooked the ravine. They would drink a Beaulieu Cabernet and Margaret would relate her dreams or talk about the pixies and fairies of Eldorado, Arkansas. Both Neimans would speak of Mexico. Gilbert would talk wonderfully of writers, particularly of D.H. Lawrence, Cendrars, Waldo Frank, and Rilke. If Man Ray and his wife Julie dropped in, the talk would inevitably come around to the Marquis de Sade, one of Ray's specialities. Toward night Bunker Hill took on a special, crepuscular aspect, it seemed very French to Henry's eyes. Looking from the Neiman's terrace Henry saw Paris; Bunker Hill seemed to have the same cream-colored, red-tinted hue that Montmartre had when seen from Fred Kann's balcony above the Montparnasse Cemetery. The Eiffel Tower had

been placed on the left instead of the far right and read "Richfield" instead
of "Citröen"—but the tangle of streets beneath it looked like an assemblage
of the Rue St. Maur, the Avenue Wagram where it approaches the Place des
Ternes, the Rue de Sevres, and the Rue des Irlandais. The Neimans were
good, enthusiastic talkers, too, and enthusiasts for art. This had almost
made him feel as if he were back among his friends in the Villa Seurat.

In his final notes for the journey Miller listed more than fifty memorable
sights or events experienced during his trip. He had seen the moonflower
opening at Bunker Hill; been shown a film of the original scenes of
Shangri-la in Tibet; interviewed John Barrymore in bed ("the most real and
natural person I ever met"); discovered Krishnamurti; and traveled the
spectacularly wild, primitive country between Hearst Castle and
Carmel—"Jeffers' country." In San Francisco, too, he had finally arranged
for the publication of *The Colossus of Maroussi* for a one hundred dollar
advance.

But in the final casting-up, he had to consider the trip a colossal
disappointment. Toward the beginning of his travels, Henry had stopped to
see Anaïs Nin's cousin Eduardo Sanchez in Biltmore Forest, North
Carolina. Eduardo made an histrological chart for Miller titled "The Way of
the World," which showed Henry's sun under the equatorial line. According to this graph the way of the world was downward, and the astrological
weather would not change. "The Way of the World" turned out to be
accurate: Miller's sun never really did get over the horizon during this year.
The good times were few and far between—the bad predominated. An-
napolis had seemed "sterile, puerile and vapid—a polished shit hole of
buttons and discipline." Portsmouth, New Hampshire had looked as bad as
a Hieronymous Bosch scene; Detroit like a mechanical monster. He
thought that the people in Milwaukee looked like giant sloths marinated in
the suds of Pabst Blue Ribbon beer. "I'd rather eat horse shit in Mallorca
than Charlotte Russe in Cleveland!" he scratched into his notebook. Main
Street in Los Angeles, he recorded, was a sewer, full of mechanical and
human junk; at twilight it looked like the Yangtze River filled with floating
corpses. The whole downtown was like a public toilet, with no Emil
Jannings to mop it up. At the Hollywood parties he had gone to, affecta-
tion, artificiality, and stupidity were abundantly present. He had listened
to the silly talk, the false intellectualism, the phony mysticism, and he
understood that these were the masks of hard, driving materialism. After
touring R.K.O. he had concluded that the movie studios were dreary:
movie making was a "terrible grind" in which technical exactitude, cer-

tainly not human emotions, was central. He had promptly rejected a feeler about his interest in script writing. "It would drive me mad in a week," he remarked.

Naturally, he had been lonely; Rattner had gone only as far as New Orleans before returning to New York to arrange an exhibition of his paintings. Alone, Henry had talked to himself and made up imaginary companions to tell his tales of woe. He had been especially lonely for a woman. In Asheville, he wrote in his notebook: "Jesus, June, if you were only with me now! . . . Death comes to the Archbishop and to love and to Valentine too!" In Hollywood he had been reduced to asking the script-writer Gordon Kahn to provide him with a list of whores—"reasonable ones and free of disease, if possible."

Anytime he thought of love, he thought of June. From his hotel in Hollywood, the Gilbert, he had walked to a nearby park, in which a statue of Valentino had been placed by the "Women of America." It was located at the corner of June and Selma streets, not far from Mansfield Street. He couldn't resist associating all these, and he wrote in his notebook; "Fresh wounds for sale. Take a telegram:—to June—I am sitting in the park corner of June and Selma. Where are you sitting now? . . . I love you. Valentine, Valentine." The park, he said grimly, would be "a nice quiet place to commit suicide." During the time he spent in California, particularly, both June and Anaïs had been very much on his mind, so much that he saw them, or people who looked like them, everywhere. When he had met the actress Luise Rainer, whose birthday was on he same day as June's, he identified her with both June and Anaïs: she resembled June in this way, Anaïs in that. He had tried to flirt with her, but nothing came of it.

Long before he was finished Miller hated the book he was writing. He felt that if it was not unpublishable—and he suspected it was—Doubleday would be sure to reject it anyway. He would have rejected it himself, since he felt it was his worst writing since *Moloch*.

He really didn't want to see the book published—he just planned to send a carbon of the final version to the Library of Congress, sell the original manuscript to a private collector, and pay his advance back to Doubleday. He was even a little afraid that the book might get him into trouble. After all, 1941 was no year to publish an unmitigated attack on American achievement, American values, and the American future; during wartime especially, anyone who sniped at Americanism from within seemed like a spy or a shirker. Miller had written over 400 manuscript pages by December 7, 1941 when the news of the Japanese attack on Pearl Harbor was announced. It was obvious then that *The Air-Conditioned Nightmare,* as conceived and written from its title to its conclusion, would be unpalatable to the American public, with or without obscenity. The Government was rounding up Japanese-Americans to impound them. Miller worried that his book might bring such a storm of criticism down upon him that he also might be clapped in a cell for the duration. What was he—a pornographer, a man without a job, a faithless husband who had deserted his wife and child, a man with detectives on his trail trying to get him for back alimony owed to Beatrice to the tune of $20,000, a vagabond, drifter and outlaw? Would anyone object if he were locked up to assist the war effort?

Nevertheless, he plugged on with *The Air-Conditioned Nightmare.* On Christmas Day, 1941, he approached the conclusion of his book. Over 500 pages were completed. Christmas always dampened his spirit, but he worked doggedly all the day, with nothing to eat. In a delirium of hunger and melancholy he finally wrote "Finis" at the bottom of his manuscript late on Christmas Day. Then he went out on the prowl and ended up about midnight in a drug store. He felt no joy, no hope in the future or sense of accomplishment in the past. The place was ghastly. He confessed to the lowly workers that he had no money and was looking for a handout. The two clerks who were left to run the place while all the other employees celebrated, staked him to a meal of the leftover Christmas special in return for his offer to help them clean up. Having eaten, Henry began to feel set up by the warm food and the fact that he had completed a book. When their chores were over, he was moved to deliver a euphoric speech to the clerks, a Christmas speech. "The Gods are coming back to earth," he began. He spoke about the new age, the age of Aquarius, that was ready to dawn, when all that they had known of civilization—war and famine and books— would be wiped out for good, and a new, more human, age would begin. It took audacity to say this, he admitted, just as the war was beginning in earnest, but he concluded: "This is no horse shit. I'm telling you the truth!" They took it wonderfully and gave him a cheer.

The next day was his fiftieth birthday. He looked at his "completed book" through bloodshot eyes and saw nothing but its incompleteness. He started an epilogue, a "cadenza à la Webber and Fields," telegraphically shoving into the book all that he had not otherwise included. But still he was not satisfied. Later, he wrote an imaginary conversation between himself and Rattner for the conclusion. But his first instinct on Christmas night had been sound; the book really had been finished then. His additions only threatened to produce other additions. On January 12, 1942 he wrote to his agent Henry Volkening that he had decided not to offer the book for publication, since it was "a fiasco." He proposed to use his royalty earnings from other books to make reparation for the advances he had received on *The Air-Conditioned Nightmare*.

Failure or not, *The Air-Conditioned Nightmare* was a fresh installment in the story of his life. In no sense had he ever intended to give an exact guide to America. Rather, he was improvising on the theme of America and of his relation to it, and thus was writing a purely subjective book, an account of his debate with himself about his native land. He wrote it in the way that he used to improvise in Clichy for Alfred Perlès's sake. Now he saw that the book would have been better if he hadn't traveled at all, but just transcribed one of the rhapsodies he always started when Perlès would plead with him: *Tell me about Arizona, Joey!*

Four

Ventilating the Soul

The transcontinental trip had not only proved superfluous, it washed most of the joy out of the book he had dreamed of writing. Even worse, during the eighteen months that it took him to tour the country and then write *The Air-Conditioned Nightmare,* he did no work at all on the history of his calamities with June, with the result that even as he was planning and writing one book he regretted postponing the other, much more important, book. All he had, more than four years after deciding to write this book, was a title—*The Rosy Crucifixion*—a sheaf of notes, and a hundred pages written during the summer of 1940. Finally, in January 1942 he resumed work on *The Rosy Crucifixion* and by June finished a draft. But he was not satisfied: it seemed incomplete, partial, unresolved. Far from getting closer to it, the "truth" seemed to elude him more completely as he went on. Miller's work had not gone at all well since his return to the United States. Perhaps he hurried too much, had too little time for reflection. Perhaps without a romance he felt lonely and unsure. He sorely missed a constant literary or artistic companion—some Osborn or Perlès or Nin or Rattner. Whatever the combination of reasons, he floundered in his writing, uncertain of his direction, unsure whether he should even *be* writing. Briefly he picked up old, tired projects, like "The Sleeping Sleeper Asleep." But in the end his enthusiasm for everything fizzled out.

He was floundering emotionally too. He wanted to believe that he had "turned a spiritual corner," as he told Huntington Cairns, but he wondered if he wasn't simply declining in energy. He was, Anaïs Nin noted, "resigned, mystical, quiet." The death of his father had affected him profoundly. Once he had thought the old man a blight on existence, now he missed him. During the bleak, frigid winter of 1942 he often went to visit his father's grave in Evergreen Cemetery. As he sat on an iron bench gazing at the strangely carved angels and reading the queer French and Alsatian family names and looking beyond the cemetery at the ragged New York skyline, he felt strangely at ease with death. If it were permitted, he felt, he could even take out his father's bones and play happily with them, like an idiot, so simple had death become for him and so close did he feel to his father. He wrote in his notebook: "The old man's death left something beautiful in its wake. Have lost all terror of being near the dead. Could sit up now with a corpse and enjoy a few meditative moments. Soon I'll be there myself. Pleasant anticipation. No fear of worms. The worms are here—in life."

Romance always stirred his mind and body and rescued him from inertia; and, early in 1942, Henry's unconscious instincts for preservation impelled him to seek a woman to adore. Like all of his loves she would need to combine sensual with Neptunian qualities and look like one of the figures in a Puvis de Chavannes fresco. During the spring of 1942, he attached himself passionately to a young woman who possessed that combination of the impulsive Slavic and the soft Mediterranean character which had so obsessed him in June. He immediately declared her "divine." The divine Laure had a marvellous bearing and an almost classically sculptured head; in her veins ran Polish, Basque, and Peruvian blood. She *was* June all over again. She had the same condescending attitude in accepting adoration, the same inclination to tyrannize, the same monstrous willfulness. Henry encouraged all these qualities in a woman, of course, by his own complete self-effacement. When he was in love Henry abused himself in every possible way, he surrendered everything—except the relentless will to possess the loved one completely. He would sacrifice everything in order to triumph. Love for him always involved great romantic moments of revelation and outbursts of emotion.

Like June, Laure astonished him with a monumental eruption of passion; her will broke down in one rush of surrender, as if the winter snows all melted simultaneously and came roaring, full of debris, into a channel which could barely contain the boiling flow. These were the kinds of moments that Henry lived for—times when he felt he was adored for himself alone and could worship a woman without reserve. He never could keep a love affair at this pitch of madness. Any woman must eventually appear to draw back from absolute self-abasement or weary of her lover's humiliation. Few people could accept being made into a god and a slave at one and the same time. Henry, of course, also hedged his declarations with private doubts and public hesitations. He felt that Laure was resisting him willfully and he was right. In May 1942, Laure decided to break away and left New York for Hollywood.

Now there was nothing to keep Henry in New York. He hated the city, he did not feel his mother needed him or his company (nor did he want hers). Most of his old New York friends had been dispersed by the war or economic opportunity (Emil Schnellock had gone to teach in a Virginia college). Worst of all, Anaïs had told him that she must reject the emotionalism which had given her pain so often. She couldn't do what he begged her to do—give up her husband. And so she attacked him for asking too much of her. They never really made a conclusive break or had a devastating argument, but he heard from friends that she regarded him as a traitor. They had lost their "accord," and she felt reproachful. Once, they had been deeply in love and that had bridged their enormous differences, but when the love frittered away, a gulf was left between them. With no woman to love in New York—and he desperately needed one after the rupture with Anaïs—New York City meant nothing to him. Laure's departure led him to California. If he had lost June and Anaïs, he'd have both back—in this new woman. By a happy coincidence his young friends Margaret and Gilbert Neiman had just moved into a cottage in Beverly Glen, an area in west Los Angeles just north of Sunset Boulevard, and they offered him a room of his own with them. By the second week of June 1942 Henry was on the train in pursuit of Laure.

There were other reasons for going to California. He had concluded from his tour of America that if any promise remained in the United States, it was in California. "This is the vital spot (for people like us) in America. It is quite unexhaustible," he had written to Anaïs Nin. Of California cities, Los Angeles had the most European air for him—the aroma of colonial Spain still lingered and so many emigrés had come from Europe due to the war that a congress of all nations seemed to have gathered in Los Angeles. "Am going to ventilate my soul," Henry wrote to Herbert West as he started toward Los Angeles. He wanted to leave the past behind and open himself to a new mental climate. The old weather forecasts, such as Michael Fraenkel's prediction of the spirit's coming ice-age, no longer held. Miller went to California for its warmth, its liveliness, its promise. He almost forgot that his ostensible reason for traveling west was to chase the divine Laure. Indeed, though he saw her again, their brief love affair expired as quietly as a Hollywood option. But Henry found himself surprisingly happy. He settled in at the Neimans, started to write, and began to sign his letters "Henry Valentine of the Glen."

The Beverly Glen cabin was really just a three-room shack situated in the still wild hills north of Sunset Boulevard. The area in back of the house was covered with trees and flowers, and wild animals and birds scuttled through the underbrush. He slept on a cot in a room that was too tiny to serve as anything other than a sleeping room. During the day he worked on a table in the garage. After a few weeks he became friends with the Jordans, who lived in a substantial house next to the Neimans. He accepted a larger bedroom in their house, returning to Gilbert and Margaret's for meals and companionship. Near Beverly Glen was Bel Air Estates, a luxurious new development. And just south of Bel Air, about a mile from Henry's room, was the UCLA campus, where he could use the library; and beyond that was Westwood Village where he could ramble about.

Past fifty, he knew that he should be able to take care of himself; but he was still an object of charity. Rather reluctantly, he began to think of accepting a job as a scriptwriter in the movie mills. That the studios *were* mills for "the lowest and craziest work a man could do," he had seen when he visited Hollywood in the summer of 1941 and talked with Waldo Salt and other young screen writers. They confessed their shame and admitted that the fabulous sums they earned did them no good. In 1941 he had casually ignored hints that he would find a place waiting for him in the studios. For more than a month after settling in Beverly Glen, though he dreamed of having money, he couldn't bring himself to approach those people who earlier had wanted him, and offer his services. Instead he fantasized that some adventurous producer might put *Scenario* on the screen. This was obviously impossible and it made him speculate about what films he would make if anything were possible. This idea so completely absorbed him that he wrote out a story idea which he headed "Notes for Imaginary Exotic Film":

Starring Merle Oberon, Ingrid Bergman, Irene Dunne, Miriam Hopkins, Barbara Stanwyck, Judy Canova, Michele Morgan, Simone Simon, among others. Full length plot—serious drama of love. Love scenes to be carried out in full. When a Gabin, for example, kisses a girl passionately, he should run hand up her dress, strip her, lay her. Then proceed as normally—with

plot. Little interludes—surrealistic—using stars of pornographic
world—the anonymous monsters, such as French telegraph boy, Negress
who blinks eye before camera, etc. Scenes in hotels, peep shows, subway
crushes, exhibitionists. George Grosz treatment, via Dali-Būnuel—with a
dash of de Sade. Sessions with psychoanalyst. Dreams in toto—enacted
with Disney technique. Technicolor fucks. Hollywood dramas—fucking
machines. Rape with broken bottles. Caligari nightmares. Jealousy as in
"Eternal Husband." Banquets à la Giono. In short a prolonged & endless
fiesta of eating, drinking, fucking, loving, murdering. Directed by Marcel
Duchamp & John Ford. Throw in a little Boogie Woogie too—and the
Mona Lisa.

This, of course, was his way of defending himself against Hollywood,
mocking it even as he prepared to court it. Then, to his surprise, he was
actually offered screen work.

Marcel Friedman, a Viennese emigré whom Henry had met in New York
the previous year, purchased the exclusive rights to sell Jacob Wasserman's
The Maurizius Case to the movies, and he solicited Henry's aid in adapting it
to the screen. *The Maurizius Case* was just the kind of metaphysical novel,
concerning guilt and redemption, that never failed to seize Henry's attention. Friedman had no difficulty in convincing him that it would make a
wonderful film, and he went busily to work writing up a synopsis and a
rough adaptation of the novel. Until the book was purchased by a studio,
Friedman explained, he himself would have no money to pay Henry. So, he
wrote "on speculation" for fifteen percent of the eventual profits, profits
which seemed pretty certain. Henry was in the Hollywood business to the
extent that he was writing a screen treatment which might possibly be
made into a film. He had told himself that he would work in Hollywood
only for money, yet he found himself laboring without a penny. He had
achieved the worst of both worlds of movie-making. In any event, he wrote
up an adaptation of the novel with a good deal of enthusiasm, handed it over
to Friedman, and sat back to count his chickens.

Then the Hollywood merry-go-round started. He had been told that
during the last few years, while Wasserman's estate had been confused,
Hollywood producers clamored to buy rights to his books. But now no one
seemed keenly interested, Wasserman had to be "sold." Meanwhile, Miller
had caught a slight case of Hollywood fever. He was hoping that he would
get assigned to do the script, even though he had no screen credits. But the
advice he gave in the addenda to his synopsis killed any chance that he
would be trusted with the film. He wrote: "To do it properly would require
miles and miles of film. More film than even an Eisenstein demands. . . . In

short, I would gamble my entire fortune and the fortunes of my colleagues on the success of this one picture." Anyway, *The Maurizius Case* never sold. Finally, Friedman paid Henry a mere $100 as an outright purchase price for his synopsis.

Miller didn't give up. He was tenacious once an idea lodged in his head. For a time he believed that he might get film work through Marlene Dietrich's secretary. Later, he hoped that Erich Maria Remarque, who was rumored to admire his work, would help him. Through a girl he met in an agency he believed that he might be hired and earn a "substantial sum" for doing an adaptation of Graham Greene's *Brighton Rock*. The director Josef von Sternberg was rumored to have read all of Miller's books and Miller was said to be the "one man in the world that he wanted most to meet." He had first editions of the *Tropics* in his legendary $100,000 erotica collection. Henry fantasized that after he met Sternberg and won his friendship, the director would beg him to accept a sumptuous salary, and finally they would make films together (perhaps one or two erotic ones on the side—for private circulation.) But though he let the director know of his interest in meeting, Von Sternberg never evinced the slightest interest in a professional association. Next, Miller contacted Budd Schulberg, whom he believed could help him get work in Mexican movies. He also briefly speculated on an adaptation of a Stefan Zweig novel. "A couple of French Jewish refugees from the cinema are after me to collaborate," he reported. He was approached about ghost-writing books for a superannuated actor. He played with the notion of writing a book or film about John Barrymore—once a drinking friend of Henry's father—whom he visited more than once and thought one of the most alive men in Hollywood, despite his age. He contacted Donald Friede, who had temporarily given up book publishing to work for the Myron Selznick agency. But the publisher-turned-agent was a flat disappointment. Friede told Henry in unambiguous terms that only experienced screen writers were wanted. As for *The Maurizius Case,* he added, that novel had gone begging around Hollywood for years.

In addition to everything elese, he wrote to Nin, "There's another thing works against me, the fact that everybody regards me as 'pure'. Everybody expresses terrific disappointment that I should compromise. Nobody seems really convinced that I am willing to do as the others. This is also my fault. Bad acting, no doubt. But you know, when I see the fawning, lying, cheating, conniving, etc. I get absolutely disgusted. I can't switch over into that role very easily." Possibly he was rationalizing. He did devote nearly four months of effort to the movie business. But he continued to be ambiguously blessed with an inability to secure any position at all. In early December 1942 he made one last try for a Hollywood job. At the Myron Selznick agency he met with an agent named Donohue and described his qualifications in full. After their meeting Henry went home and penned a note to him. "I thought, when I came to Hollywood, that I would eventually meet a man to whom the story of my life and tribulations would have meaning. A man who would have faith in me, not just because of my ability to write, but because of what I am, what I represent. I believe that there ought to be a place for me in Hollywood. There ought to be a job somewhere for an American writer who has tried to tell the truth about his experiences, who has resisted all temptation to prostitute his work, and who believes that he has something of value to give to the world." In reply, a telegram came from the agency urgently summoning Miller to a meeting. Yes, after beating around the bush Donohue said he was ready to get Miller work—if he was really serious. According to the account given by Miller, Donohue simply asked him: "What we wish to know, Mr. Miller," he said, "is: couldn't you just write plain shit, wrapped in cellophane, with a little touch of sacrifice in it? Sacrifice is very important these days." *Shit wrapped in cellophane—a nice glossy, sanitary package!*—that was all Donohue wanted, after Henry had poured out his heart to him.

As his fifty-first birthday rolled around, Henry Miller, the author of eleven books, had been in Hollywood, the city of gold, for six months and he had earned exactly $100. He thought of returning to New York to hunt up a job, but he couldn't even raise the fare. He applied for a Los Angeles library job, but the pay was thirty-five cents an hour for thirty hours per week. He looked into a job doing translations from French at a better budgeted library in Pasadena, but that didn't pan out. Next, he made a try for a position interviewing ex-convicts at the Bureau of Probation. But, he was informed, his lack of a college degree barred him from personnel work. He was advised to try the Juvenile branch, which he did—unsuccessfully. He got introductions to the personnel directors of two big aircraft factories and offered to fill any job from riveter to personnel manager. Gilbert Neiman, who had gone to Sacramento to organize the Mexican immigrant laboring force on which maintenance of agricultural production depended, wrote Henry that if he could pretend to speak a little Spanish he might get a job as a field director. Next, he tried the Office of War Information which was taking on writers who could grind out cheery propaganda. The California office had no place for him. (Not long afterwards, however, the New

York Office of War Information asked him—as a distinguished writer on Greece—to provide, *gratis,* a message to be broadcast to the Greeks: "Please . . . interpret for them the American scene, American ideals, and aims in regard to Greece and Europe at large," he was requested.) "Between you and me, Huntington old man," he wrote to Cairns, "I am most serious when I say that if in the next two to three weeks I don't land some sort of job which will keep me afloat, I intend to go back to the Western Union, preferably in Beverly Hills, and work as a foot messenger. That I know I can do!" Finally, in the spring of 1943, Henry was reduced to a level he had sworn never to reach: he was so low he wrote to editors of journals for books to review. Word came back from *Tomorrow,* the *Nation,* the *New Republic,* and the New York *Tribune* that he would be sent some volumes, at about $10 a review. He began by reviewing a short life of Kierkegaard and followed this with several others during 1943.

Meanwhile, Scorpio was rising and dragging Mars, the Moon, and Uranus after it, the warm Santa Ana winds were blowing, and the "fragrance of cunt was in the air." Most of the available women were what his friend Savington Crampton labelled "neurotic cunt." One of the girls who had volunteered to do some typing for him—as it happened the work was on *The Rosy Crucifixion*—broke down and offered herself to him while sitting before the machine. To be seduced by typing—that rather shocked Miller. Another liked to crawl in bed with him and get psychoanalyzed for a warmup—she required a good long foreplay on her oedipal complexes, oral fixations, and neurotic hysterias, with a twist of Freud and a twitch of Adler. While the Neimans were away in Sacramento, Henry was invited to dine at a neighbor's house. The wife kept hinting that she didn't get enough sex. "Why couldn't there be ten or fifteen men around, all waiting for it, holding it in their hands like broom sticks? I could just go from one to the other," she'd say right out, with her husband in the next room. Occasionally her friends arrived to take nude sunbaths and they usually called Henry over to brush the lizards away while they rolled around, browning themselves all over. "I don't bother you, do I?" one sunbather asked occasionally, carefully exhibiting those parts that did bother him. Another of the same neurotic crew, a woman named Jean, had been brought around by his *Hamlet*—of all books!—to the point of trying to seduce him. She even tried to persuade him to climb into bed with her and her husband. "My husband knows I'm schizophrenic," she whispered. Another husband offered his wife to Henry—"You might like her, she's a mental whore," he explained. That was what he *didn't* want, mental whores and neurotic cunts—

cold-hearting fucking. He wanted a Pauline, a June, an Anaïs—a woman who would love him passionately yet ask nothing of him. But after all, he had deserted Pauline and betrayed June into all her betrayals. And he had finally asked too much of Anaïs. He dreamed of winning her back—as he had wanted Beatrice and June after losing them. But he had to admit that their love affair was over.

Now what Henry wanted was what he always wanted: "a woman to worship"—which is to say a woman to worship him. He was looking for romance, not just a lay with some neurotic dame. "I need a mate now," he wrote to Savington Crampton. "Now more than ever I can make a woman happy, and enrich her. But I refuse to make an alliance just for the sake of sex. I want to be used up thoroughly. I want to give her everything I've got."

Five

Sevasty-Sevasty

"Revered one!"—that was the English meaning of Sevasty. Sevasty Koutsaftis was the name of a lovely young Greek girl with whom Henry fell in love. The name itself infatuated him. He was still in love with Greece—more than ever. ("Anaïs" was also Greek.) Ever since he sailed from Piraeus three years before, life for him had declined. Only *The Colossus of Maroussi* had been a real joy—during the writing he felt sun-flooded, like the land. Anything Greek enchanted him and thus the effect of a lively young Greek woman was monumental. Besides, from the beginning Sevasty was associated with *The Colossus of Maroussi,* for Henry had met her as a possible translator of that book. Always keenly interested in foreign translations of his work, Henry was particularly anxious to have this book translated into Greek. With the Axis forces occupying or attacking every part of the country, it was out of the question to negotiate with anyone in Greece concerning a translation. Henry turned for advice to Lawrence Clark Powell, the librarian at UCLA whom he had met in Dijon a decade before. Powell said he knew a young, very intelligent Greek girl named Sevasty, formerly a cataloger at UCLA, who spoke Greek and French and Italian as well as English. She was good to look at and very eager to do translating work. With Henry's permission a copy of the *Colossus* was given to her. She soon wrote to Henry with praise for it.

And so a meeting was arranged. She was certainly everything that Powell said, Greek through and through. She reminded Miller of certain statues he had seen in Greece. And this Aphrodite was now working as a secretary in a Lockheed defense plant! With hardly a second look, Henry fell hard for her, the only way he ever fell in love. "Am head over heels," he wrote to Emil Schnellock, "—about like I was when I met June. Anything may happen." Sevasty was not experienced enough to undertake such an extensive translation as *The Colossus of Maroussi* required, but discussion of the book gave her and Henry an excuse for numerous meetings. She was an interesting, lively, contradictory young woman. Henry saw—or believed he saw—the solidity and strength and wholeness of the Greek earth . But she was also extremely sensitive and high strung. She wrote imagistic poetry and though Henry professed not to understand them, he sent a sheaf of her verses to his friend Tambimuttu, editor of *Poetry-London*.

It was a clear sign that conversation had developed into romance when Henry also wrote a poem (his second: the only other had been inspired by Camilla Fedrant.) The poem was an overflow of his dreams and desires. Recently he had done his best watercolor, which he named "Sevasty-Sevasty"; and, like all his watercolors, this poem came without premeditation. He needed only to take pencil in hand and record the images. It rolled out like a chinese scroll. One evening, after a long conversation with Sevasty, Miller walked restlessly all the way from Beverly Glen to Hollywood and Vine, then took the trolley back as far as Doheny Drive and walked home from there. Beverly Canyon was lighted from Sunset Boulevard by a wondrous moon, a rich ripe moon in Aries. He thought about Sevasty's poems. Sometimes, when he slept at her house—her mother and sister keeping hawklike eyes on them—she'd write a poem and tip toe into his room and slip it under his pillow. Well, he thought as he got home, alone, there would be no poem for him tonight. Exhausted, he fell into bed.

The next morning he was awakened by a female friend who brought the makings for a marvellous lunch. While eating she talked mysteriously about "the dark empire of the mothers." After she left, Henry took his regular afternoon nap and slept soundly again. When he awoke, there was a poem sitting on the edge of his mind, waiting to be written, a dream poem, made of Sevasty, the moon and the night and the rich repast and talk about the dark myths of the soul.

It started with a line that ran insistently through his head: "The one I love is with flower." It was promise he was speaking of, the moon in Aries:

The one I love grown big with flower
Wheels within the lunar hour
Birds of Jade in milky fire
Mitigate the heart's desire.

Fragments of French danced in his head as if he were writing the poem in two languages at once—in sidereal language! *Au dessus deux oiseaux—un qui parle, un qui écoute,* birds on the wing, like two lovers, merged in space, *sans corps, sans nom:*

The heart is like a lake of light
Flower, moon, milk of fire . . .

The one I love, revered one, Sevasty.

This dream-poem was the climax of his romance with Sevasty, however. Well before Henry's poem was published in *Harper's Bazaar,* he and Sevasty had parted for good. Sevasty, in her curious combination of the Mediterranean and the harsh, almost Icelandic mind, was like June resurrected: she resisted him even as she enticed him, and in June 1943 she told him she could go no farther—she wanted to break off entirely. He resisted this. It was a harsh blow coming in the midst of a generally low period for Miller. He was over fifty, an accomplished writer, but he seemed stalled. Now he was threatened with another personal failure: he still felt he had the heart of a young man, ready for love—but who would accept his offering?

Sevasty began to write him long cruel letters about her resemblance to Rimbaud. (Shades of Jean Kronski!—this was a bad sign.) For a while Henry held out hope. In August 1943 a Hollywood medium named Rose Feine told him that he and Sevasty were meant for each other and would soon travel together—perhaps to Greece—and would be married suddenly. She advised Henry: "You've been alone too much. Sevasty gave and was rejected. She is ready now for real love—because of suffering." No oracle was ever more wrong. Hardly a week passed before Henry received a definitive letter from Sevasty, a "cold, cruel" logical letter which rejected him with absolute finality. "I know now what the wall is, and I know it's insurmountable," he wrote to her. "But Sevasty, no matter how hopeless the situation, I can't stop loving you . . . . It's for you to make what you will of such a love. . . . For myself I have no hopes of any kind. I stand before the wall and cry to you on the other side to accept what you can and will." To many of his friends he wrote of his suffering. He confided to Eva Sikelianou, the wife of the great Greek writer: "But real anguish is frightful. I only *thought* before that I knew what it was. Now I *know.*"

Henry associated the figure of Rimbaud with personal defeat. The appearance of Rimbaud in Sevasty's letter was a curse. Jean Kronski had adored the French poet; and in 1943 there was not only Sevasty but a strange young man named Pierce Harwell, whom Anaïs had sent to Henry and who almost seemed to be a Rimbaud himself. Something told Henry that he better protect himself by taking a close look at Rimbaud.

In the summer of 1943, Henry began reading the *Saison en Enfer* in a combatative spirit. But despite his bad associations, strangely enough Rimbaud conquered him. He had thought the Frenchman his foe—but now in the poems and also in biographies by Jean-Marie Carre and Enid Starkie, Miller discovered amazing parallels to his own thoughts and experiences. Soon he was rejoicing in his anguish over Sevasty's cruelty. He rather blithely told Herbert West that suffering "never hurts the writing" and he began to plan a little autobiographical book about his pain. Toward the end of September he had a final meeting with Sevasty at his place. "I love you . . . I always will," were his last words. But even while he was saying his romantic goodbyes and pledging his troth, he was thinking about how to write up this encounter effectively. A few minutes after Sevasty closed the door he sat down at the table he used for a desk and typed on a sheet, "My Life with Sevasty." For a moment he reflected that he had already ceased to love Sevasty (he wasn't really sure that he knew what she looked like any more. His mind drifted and he began to wonder whether it wasn't even true that Sevasty's mother was better looking than the daughter . . . . Perhaps he should look her up on the sly and give her a tumble?) Sevasty herself was already becoming mythical, one more of all the Maras and Monas he had known, interchangeable with all the other women he had loved. He planned to present his life with Sevasty in a book resembling Gerard de Nerval's *Dreams and Life*. He told Herbert West: "I can breathe freely again. What a relief!" By the time he received an affectionate letter from Sevasty a few months later, hinting at the possibility of a renewal of relations, he could toss it aside casually—it "now means nothing," he remarked to a friend.

Six

The Green House Thatched with Women's Hair

By the fall of 1943, painting meant almost everything to Henry. He was living further up the Glen, occupying three rooms over the garage of a house rented by his old Paris friend Richard Thoma. No longer cramped—with only a bed, a backless chair and a table in the three rooms—he had room to paint and plenty of wall space to hang up his productions. If only he had money for art materials! This problem was solved in a quite unexpected and unpremeditated way. One day he went into the Westwood Village art shop run by Attilio Bowinkel and asked for a box of the cheapest water paints he sold. The owner politely inquired whether he could use any other supplies, but Henry admitted that he could afford nothing else. "Choose what you like, then," Bowinkel grandly said, "—paper, paints, brushes, whatever you need. It's a gift!" A few days later, the dealer stopped by in the Glen and left with a few of Henry's watercolors, promising to display them in the shop. Bright and early the next day, Henry was down in Westwood, hopping around with excitement, to see how his works appeared—all matted and framed, *and* for sale. Wonderful! And even more wonderful, later that very day an M.G.M. producer named Arthur Freed who owned paintings by several modern European masters, strolled by the shop and noticed the paintings. Satisfied that these were by the same Henry Miller who had written *Tropic of Cancer* Freed bought the whole lot at a good price. This gave Henry such a tremendous lift that in the next six months he completed 128 paintings.

Then, when the Neimans decided to move to Colorado, Henry wrote to
his old artist friend John Dudley, recently separated from his wife, and
proposed that they take over the Neimans' cottage, turn it into a studio,
and paint together. Dudley soon arrived. Though Dudley's melancholia
and alcoholism kept him from doing much painting, he proved to be a
splendid companion and an excellent critic. They soon established a pattern
of life much like that shared by Miller with Fred Perlès. The cottage offered
few comforts, only a few remnants of furniture in the three small rooms, and
a tiny heater which struggled in vain to mitigate the damp chill that rolled
down from the hills. But it was a home, like Clichy. Henry brightened
things by tacking up his watercolors and chalking or painting various
mottoes on the wall: "Dreadful are the mornings of a drunkard" (an
admonition for Dudley), "If suicide is on your mind give me a ring" (satire
on Henry himself), "When I hear the word culture I reach for my revolver"
(inscribed at the entrance to the kitchen), and above the door of Henry's
room "S'Agapo" (Greek for "I love you"—a reminder of Sevasty). During
the day, Henry usually went to Thoma's garage to write. But toward
evening, he'd appear at 1212 Beverly Glen, now known as the "House of
Analysis" or the "Green House Thatched with Women's Hair." Then the
fun would begin. Dudley often stood at Henry's side criticizing as the first
washes were laid down. Attentive to Dudley's technical advice, Henry
always started cautiously. But after a few bright splashes blossomed against
the wash, Henry no longer listened as he danced his brush over the paper
until unforeseen shapes began to appear. When Henry paused, Dudley
often tried to show him how to proceed on the basis of an analysis of color
value or structure. But as Dudley was weighing this or that approach,
Henry would lunge at the painting, sponging out a section, maybe leaving
just the ghost of the former image, or even blotting out everything by
massive applications of Chinese white. Sometimes he'd take a tree branch or
a handful of pine needles and paint with them. Sometimes things got so
heated that even Dudley would grab a brush and start from the other end of
the paper. All the while the victrola would be playing anything from
"These Foolish Things" to a Varèse composition—full blast. These, as
Miller remarked in a letter to Alfred Stieglitz, were "Holy Nights."

The cabin became a gallery to display Henry's work, and he wrote up a
little invitational leaflet for advertisement: "At 1212 N. Beverly Glen
Blvd., West Los Angeles, the blissful abode of John Dudley (ambulatory
paranoic) and his pupil Henry Miller . . . there will be henceforth a
permanent exhibition of aquarelles and allied media, both inside and out,

weather permitting, including kitchen and lavatory wings. Due to per-
petual impoverishment no refreshments will be available but the Master
and his pupil will always welcome the advent of an occasional bottle—for
the Master Bourbon, for his pupil *French wines and liqueurs* . . . . It goes
without saying that the masterpieces on exhibition are for sale." The
advertisement ended with the strict promise: "Ladies will be treated with
respect." And the visitors did come, fellow artists and sometimes customers. Knud Merrild, the Danish painter, was often there and frequently told
of his days in New Mexico with D.H. Lawrence. Man and Julie Ray would
drive up from Hollywood in their white Mercedes, sometimes bringing a
camera to catch on film some of the strange doings in The Green House,
sometimes to propose a chess problem, and always with some fresh
thoughts on the divine Marquis. Once, the Los Angeles Chief of Police
escorted the director of an art museum there in a limousine. Occasionally,
the guests would stay on, all day and all night. Perhaps in the morning the
rains would prevent Henry's departure to Thoma's and he'd have to sit in a
room full of people, alcoholic fragrances, smoke, the din of talk, the clatter
of dishes, and do what writing he could. Anyway, there was a certain
splendid hallucinatory quality in all of this, and sometimes the guests
would depart with watercolors at prices ranging from five to twenty-five
dollars. (At Bowinkel's, the prices ran from $25 to $75.)

To Henry's complete surprise painting seemed to have solved his financial problems. In October 1943 Clara Grossman of the American Contemporary Gallery in Hollywood offered to give him a show. Always wise in
self-promotion, Henry wrote to *Time* magazine: "If you would come to draw
attention to the show . . . it would be of great help to me and I would deeply
appreciate it." From his friends he borrowed about twenty of his best
paintings (most of them given away) so that the exhibition list would show
the owner's name next to the title. This, Henry wrote to a friend, would
give his exhibition "the stereotyped air of authenticity." He raised his
prices to from $25 to $100 and even before the show opened sold a half
dozen at fifty dollars. *Town and Country* gave him and the show a write-up in
the December number, printed some black and white reproductions, and
generally pronounced his paintings original and worthy of attention. Soon,
Henry was devoting seven hours a day to painting and entertaining potential buyers. All his writing languished, but he was not dismayed. "Well,
Emil, ol' top," he wrote to Schnellock, "it sure will be strange and ironical
if I make my living as a water colorist, won't it?"

Nor was he content to rely upon painting for his sole income. In the early

fall of 1943 he mailed an "Open Letter to All and Sundry" to a sizeable list
of people prominent in the arts and media. In this little plea Henry
described his impoverishment; but declaring himself unwilling to sacrifice
his art to commercial concerns, he announced that he was ready to mail
watercolors to patrons who sent him money or articles of clothing. This
letter should have been titled "What Are You Going to Do About Henry?"
But now the appeal worked: by October 1, he had received $400: $300
more came in during October and November. (This $700 was nearly two
times the amount he had earned during the whole of the previous year.)
This personal but limited solicitation worked so well that Henry began to
build grandiose schemes upon it. He placed his letter in *Circle* magazine
and then in the *New Republic,* where it caused a lot of comment. "I think,"
James T. Farrell wrote to Miller, "that I can well understand your feelings of
indignation, independence, and rebellion . . . . A serious American writer
has no alternatives other than those of continuing as a rebel, or else of
becoming a hack, prostituting himself and his talents." Farrell also enclosed a check, and a good bit of money trickled in from others. Not all the
responses were sympathetic. One novelist mocked Henry's plea and mailed
him a pair of socks with the message that these "formerly adorned the feet of
the great American writer, Henry Morton Robinson (me)." Miller never
sent Robinson a watercolor—but he did wear the socks and he went right
on to hatch other begging schemes. One was designed on the model of his
round-robin dinners in Paris. Miller compiled a list of acquaintances who
could be hit up regularly for small sums, "Dollar a Week Patrons," such as
Arthur Freed, Dudley Nichols, and James Agee. It didn't prove to be a
lucrative list, but he got some aid from Melpo Niarchos and, more
important, the assurance that if he were ever in desperate straits he could
count on her for aid. (He never took any help from her, but characteristically he paid her the compliment of dedicating one of his books, *Sunday
After the War,* to her.) He felt confident enough in November 1943 to turn
down an offer from Freed of a screenwriting contract at M.G.M. "The door
is always open for you," Freed said. That was all Henry wanted, really.

As 1943 approached its end Miller tried in vain to make sense out of the
year. The first half seemed to consist of nothing but disaster and the second
half almost unmodified good fortune. First he had been rejected by
everyone, on every occasion, then he was an instant success wherever he
turned. Moreover, 1943 had speeded the dynamics of his literary reputation. Numerous new friends and admirers appeared. Paul Weiss, of the
Bryn Mawr philosophy department, praised Henry's original mind and

genuine power and characterized himself as an "ardent Millerite." Ben Abramson was planning to publish *Tropic of Capricorn*. A young scientist named Bern Porter evidenced a great interest in Henry's work and promised to set up a press to publish any new Miller material, at his own cost. A young dock worker and aspiring writer named Harry Herschkowitz sent him three dollars a week and sometimes took up a collection from his fellow workers. "As long as I am unfortunate enough to work for a living," Harry wrote, "I shall send you three dollars a week." George Leite, editor of *Circle*, was also bent on seeing everything Miller wrote in print. He worked as a taxi driver during the day, and out of the small sums he made, even though he had a wife and child, he sent Henry gifts "every now and then, always at a crucial moment, for he had a nose for my needs." Frieda Lawrence and Henry began to conduct a lively correspondence; Lawrence's widow often remarked on the striking spiritual and artistic resemblances between Miller and her husband. 1943, then, ended as a good year, a rich year.

The only lack Miller felt was in not having a woman close to him. Rejections by Laure and Sevasty had stung him. But he had not entirely lost hope. Toward the end of the year he wrote touchingly to Abe Rattner: "I've almost gotten to believe that I'm no good for a woman . . . . Sometimes I feel like advertising for a sick whore, some one who is dejected and despairing, offering to share my life with her. A simple peasant woman, or a Negress or an Indian would do."

Seven

A Paradise for the Artist

Of course, a woman was not all that Miller lacked. Problems with his writing irritated his sensibility. To write effectively he had to have a home, but as 1943 ended he had not yet resolved the question of where he would settle permanently. Some times he thought of joining Fraenkel in Mexico; at others he considered meeting Perlès in England as soon as the war ended—both men were associated with the happy days in Paris. But he had no funds for either venture. After the first burst of response to his "Open Letter" and the initial interest in his painting, his income dried up: he had paid off his debts but nothing was left for himself. He was alone and poverty ridden and rootless. Christmas Day presented the same tidings of bad cheer as it had on previous years: he had to borrow a dollar from a friend in order to get himself a Christmas dinner.

However, in January 1944 he developed other schemes to solve the money problem. After his luck turned bad and several plans fizzled, he made up a form letter urging some patron of literature to send him $50 for fifty weeks. He drew up a list of friends and sent off scores of mimeographed pleas based on this $50-50 plan. He explained in his letter that since he returned to America, he had been able to make only four or five hundred dollars per annum, except for the previous year when he had earned $1400 from the sale of watercolors. But even then, after using this windfall to pay off all his small debts, according to his calculations he still owed $24,000. Thus, when all was said and done he had really gained only three pairs of woolen socks, a plaid woolen shirt, a pair of corduroy pants, and some good watercolor paper. He just couldn't go on in this fashion, he complained, dribbling away his time and talents. He needed a regular stipend so that he could go to Mexico and concentrate on finishing the major works, especially *The Air-Conditioned Nightmare* and *The Rosy Crucifixion*. Were he relieved of all other cares and concerns he would be able to finish up his fictions and simply live by living simply. "All I want is fifty dollars per week for fifty weeks. In that time I shall have accomplished what I set out to do." He stipulated that he would be willing to have the loan repaid through Russell & Volkening from future royalties, indeed that he would repay $5,000 for the $2,500 borrowed, because "once I have finished the books in question I do not care whether I write another book or not. I can get along quite well if I have nothing on my mind but the business of getting along."

He explained that since he expected seventeen of his books or pamphlets to be issued in 1944, he was a good risk. "Will some one take a chance on me?" he plaintively concluded.

At first there was little response. Fifty dollars came from Abramson of the Argus Bookstore (but then Ben never sent royalties on the Miller books he had pirated.) Another fifty arrived from the actress Geraldine Fitzgerald. While not sending anything himself this time, Huntington Cairns wrote that he believed he had lined up a patron. Finally, at the end of April 1944, a letter arrived from Henry Volkening: "A strange and perhaps miraculous thing has happened. A gentleman was in here yesterday who insists upon being completely anonymous. He wants, he says, to set up a $2,500 trust account in a bank, with you as the beneficiary, and with the bank being instructed to send you from this sum for as long as it lasts, either $50 a week or $200 a month." Volkening was fearful that the guy "might be a screwball," but it appeared that he was actually on the level, since he deposited $300 in the bank at once and thereafter began to make payments of $200 a month. Miller had written in *The World of Sex* that anyone who helped an artist should donate anonymously, and apparently this mysterious benefactor had read that book carefully, for he followed Henry's advice to the letter. His nearest revelation to Miller was to write anonymously: "Tchelitchew is my painter/Miller is my author/Robicsek is my psychologist." He expected no interest, would not tie up Henry's royalties, and only asked for repayment when (if ever) Henry could afford to make it.

He himself was by no means rich, he said; indeed, he was borrowing the money he sent.

The first remittance of $200 arrived on the third of May 1944. That same day, with no hesitation, Henry sent $100 to Anaïs Nin, and promised to split the rest of his windfall with her in order to pay for the printing of the first twenty volumes of her diary. On his own he promised to mail out advertisements, postcards, and circular letters urging readers to subscribe. With little delay, Anaïs accepted his offer but announced that she planned to condense the first twenty volumes into one. Henry then mailed $50 a month (half of his remaining hundred) to Harry Herschkowitz as a gesture of artistic fellowship with a young writer who had exhibited faith in him. This left Miller himself fifty dollars per month. Naturally, he dashed off a letter to Cairns explaining how he had disposed of three-quarters of his funds and urging him to continue to seek another patron. And he also tried to explain his vision of a vital community of artists. In aiding Anaïs and Harry with the little he had, he wrote to Cairns, he had begun to give that vision embodiment: "I think you know that I shall never appropriate for myself more than I need. It happens that I have become a vital center of some sort: a transformer, as it were. Especially where artists are concerned. Indeed, in making public my plight, as I have done now on a few occasions, I have thought much more about the condition of American artists as a whole than I have of myself. . . . Artists will always spring up, and a few will survive, no matter how bad the conditions. But it is the public which suffers, and until the body of the American public realizes the nature and extent of its deprivation no amelioration can be hoped for."

The idea of a paradise for artists was in the forefront of his thoughts because several months earlier he thought that he had found the perfect place for himself. In February 1944 he visited with the painter, Jean Varda, and his wife, Virginia, in Monterey, California. Like Abe Rattner, Varda was a master colorist, a bright vibrant painter and a marvellous conversationalist, "a 3-ring circus, a sage, a saint, a tightrope-walker all in one," as Miller told Knud Merrild. Although Miller had left Los Angeles with only seven dollars in his pocket and bitterness in his heart, his spirit of fun revived soon after he arrived at Varda's red barn, and his thoughts turned to the area around Monterey as a possible home. Ever since he had driven along this rugged coast in 1941 he thought it "superb country," fascinating for its primitivity. Varda drove him around, bringing him as far as Big Sur to meet his friend Lynda Sargent, a distant relative of the great portrait painter. They arrived during a violent downpour but when the skies cleared he was invited to take a hot sulphur bath at Slade's Springs. Nature at Big Sur obviously had both a savage and a smiling face. Friendly, artistic folks lived there too. Furthermore the spirit of Robinson Jeffers and the ghosts of Jack London and George Sterling hung in the misty atmosphere. Had Henry wanted to go to Tibet?—Big Sur seemed, he wrote to a friend, "the nearest to Tibet one can find in this country of bustle and hustle."

Big Sur felt like home and he made it his home. Lynda Sargent let him share her Log House (later the site of the Nepenthe Restaurant) while she helped him find lodgings of his own. ("No monkey business between us either," Miller told Herbert West). He stayed at Lynda's during March and April. In May 1944, the ex-mayor of Carmel, Keith Evans, who was then in the service, offered his cabin on Partington Ridge for the duration of the war, and Henry had a home. (He could have had it free, but when he had money he paid ten dollars a month for it.) Settling in Big Sur was a sudden but not a quixotic decision. Because the rent was nil, his chief need would be firewood since the sea often threw a beautifully iridescent but icy cold cloak of fog over the whole region. He even got a good stock of supplies— wood, blankets, linens, a hogshead of kerosene, food, and even an axe— from Lynda, who was moving away. (The owner had sold her cabin to Orson Welles for Rita Hayworth.)

Henry had practical justification for choosing to settle in Big Sur; but his reasons were not entirely practical. The yearning for a paradise for artists was much in his mind, and he clearly felt an aura of freedom in the wild area. The change from France to Partington Ridge seemed almost tantamount to saying: from art to life, civilization to primitivity, self to selflessness. "I am doing my utmost," he wrote to Knud Merrild just before moving up on the ridge, "to make a sort of paradise now, not only for myself but for all those I believe in. I do not want to get to the top alone, like those vultures and hyenas of Lawrence's. There are already fifteen or twenty people in the world like ourselves. We should aid one another to the limit, I believe. Make a world of poetic, viable reality in the midst of negation and a world of corruption. We could do it." Especially now that he was rewriting *The Air-Conditioned Nightmare* he felt more and more convinced that America was fundamentally (as he wrote to Osbert Sitwell) "a desert in which the sensitive man or woman spills his unwanted seed—like camels pissing in the dark somewhere in Arabia." Yet, in America—especially in Big Sur—he believed, as the earliest settlers had believed, that man could make a new start.

Partington Ridge had no: telegraph, telephone, sewage system, waste disposal, electricity, butane tanks, or refrigeration. Alternatively it did have: miles of scrubby bush, skunks, snakes, a few buzzards, and almost impenetrable jungles of poison oak. It also had: an astonishing forty mile view of the ragged, majestic coast, a steep mile and a half climb up from the road until one stood a thousand feet above the sea, infrequent mail deliveries, violent winter rains, flies, sulphur baths six miles south, blazing sun and dense fogs, and, despite the general air of solitude, neighbors hidden in every nook and cranny, neighbors who gathered to chat and wait for the mail, or appeared out of nowhere bringing gifts and sage advice for the newcomer. In this early period at Big Sur Henry often dressed in a long robe, cinched at the waist, with a Mandarin collar, wore a coolie hat, and carried a gnarled walking stick. He said his morning prayers—usually he prayed for money—to a small carved Chinese God and an assortment of other objects decorating his mantelpiece. He liked to affect the role of a Tibetan monk.

But he certainly didn't have an easy life. A city dweller, Miller hadn't quite realized what physical labors would be required to maintain existence. The mail and the groceries and supplies were delivered three times a week at the base of the ridge, a mile and a half below his house. On Henry's way down, the hill offered a pleasant stroll. The breeze felt cool on his neck. The little wooden cart which he made to haul supplies up the hill was empty on the way down and rolled easily. He felt like an ancient oriental sage who had become a hermit on this isolated ridge. On his way down this ridge Henry was elated, saying to himself: *This is the California that men dreamed of years ago, this is the Pacific that Balboa looked out on, this is the face of the earth as the Creator intended it to look.* But all this changed after he picked up his supplies and started up the hill. The path seemed to have increased about five times its previous distance. Curses were substituted for prayers. Dragging his load up the hill in a wooden wagon, sweating like a spavined ox and muttering under his breath, he began to feel like a coolie laborer, not a monk. He felt he was being fried in the blistering sun before he was halfway up. Then he'd start cursing Lynda for not leaving him her car. By the time he got to the turn of the road at Nicholas Roosevelt's driveway, he'd have divested himself of every article of clothing except his jock-strap. And when he finally succeeded in dragging his supplies up to his own place, his work for the day was only starting. He'd have to hike off to the forest and scrounge for dead limbs for fuel, fill his cart again and haul the timber back to the house, then saw and chop it. If he wanted a hot lunch or coffee (as he usually did) he'd have to make a fire. Then he'd have to store all the supplies and clean up the dishes. The labor seemed endless. He took a nap every afternoon—he really needed it. Afterwards, he often hiked into the woods with his sadfaced, thoughtful dog, Pascal, following a narrow path which led to a stream where the water was blocked with fallen tree trunks and boulders, making a little pool amid the great redwoods. A little further, the river bed became deeper, hemming the stream in, like oriental meditation walls. Tired and meditative, Henry would often sit down at this stop for a long while, contemplating the curious tree stumps that were shaped like a Japanese idol, a giraffe, a falling cow, two mummers . . . . By the time he got back to the cabin, the day would be shot.

Unabating labor and fatigue gave Miller every excuse not to resume his long delayed literary work—but in fact he finally continued work on *The Rosy Crucifixion* and started several other pieces in these early days at Big Sur. "I get an idea a day up here," he told Bern Porter. "The air is bracing, invigorating, worth a hundred Beverly Glens." His first original work on Partington Ridge was a short essay on Knud Merrild, called "A Holiday in Paint," stressing that "the effort of the few creative artists in our time is . . . one of liberation." He revised "Of Art and the Future," an essay drafted at Lynda's, and wrote "Varda, the Master Builder" for publication in *Circle*. He wrote a preface for an edition of Haniel Long's Cabeza de Vaca book, retitled *The Power Within Us,* and also "discovered" the fiction writer Albert Cossery and George Dibben, a self-styled citizen of the world and author of *Quest*. He came back to Rimbaud with even more fascination than before and attempted a translation of *A Season in Hell.* His correspondence also mounted. "I get so many letters from young people," he told a friend, "all striving and searching and struggling—full of despair," and he simply had to answer them.

Yet he had a superabundance of energy. The more he wrote the more able he seemed. This would have been the time to put aside all his minor projects and concentrate once and for all on *The Rosy Crucifixion.* But he did not see then that this was the moment, in the early fall of 1944, when for a few glowing months he had the chance of his life. If only he had said, *Now I am settled into an abode which, though it may be utterly different from the Villa Seurat, offers the same possibility for work. It is time to clear the decks, drop the scattered writing of essays, forget about supporting* Circle *or getting* Porter *to print the pamphlets, sever correspondence with all and sundry, and above all keep my mind fastened on those great moments when* Tropic of Cancer *came to an end, when* Black Spring *flowed out of the* "Dream Book," *when* Tropic of Capricorn *blossomed into life. Give up the painting too. And deepest of all, feel again, each day, the emptiness and abandonment of those days at Nanavati's. Then, washed clean of desire and hope and any delusion, anonymously write the book I wish to write as if it were the first and last book to be written. Now, all that I've learned and every particle of concentration I possess I will focus on the one book worthy of this moment:* The Rosy Crucifixion.

But he said nothing of the kind and the moment passed.

He let his mind flow in many directions. Maybe he was too happy in his new home to work on the story of his misery with June. Maybe he was revelling in a new-found self-sufficiency. Maybe the hard work required by existence on the ridge left him too tired to focus his energies on this difficult story. In any event, he kept interrupting work on *The Rosy Crucifixion* with new ideas, and he revived the idea he once had of making the still-undefined *Draco and the Ecliptic* the capstone of his "Rosy Crucifixion" story. But the days when he could force himself into a rigid writing schedule, as he had done at Clichy, were over. He wanted to do everything and give up nothing: he had lost his discipline. He wanted so much that he would never again have anything fully. It was a bad sign that he began to replan his long novel instead of finishing it; he decided that he would do it in three volumes, and the enormity of this new plan helped to put off completion of the book. It was a bad sign too, that he painted so often—enough to have three shows during the year—at Santa Barbara, Washington, D.C., and London. Once he had been forced to relinquish everything—even his self-esteem. Life had demanded of him: relinquish, relinquish—but now he would relinquish nothing.

Yet he felt happy. He was, as he liked to say, pissing warm and drinking cold. After so many years, he was merry and bright again. Despite the long hours he had to devote merely to the necessities of life, the next three years at Big Sur were the happiest of his life. Ever since he had met June he had been a wanderer but Henry had never wanted to be dispossessed. A deep instinct for friendship made him always search for some vital human contact, for a community, and not just an imaginary one of artists. He had been naturally drawn to communities, but most had held together only briefly—the Xerxes Society, his circle at Western Union, his emigré friends in Paris.

Now at Big Sur he created another community of friends. He remembered a young man he had met in Chicago two years before, named Emil White. (Years earlier White had worked at Western Union while Miller was personnel manager, but they had scarcely met then.) White was just the kind of person Henry liked, an Austrian socialist with a European appreciation for fine food, books, and women. Now, in 1944, Henry promptly wrote to White in the Yukon, where he had gone to evade the draft, and invited him to Big Sur.

White became his constant companion. Like Fred Perlès he was a helper, an admirer, and a devoted friend. He became the central friend that Henry was always seeking. There never was any tension between them. Under Miller's influence White began to paint well—but only, as he jovially said, as a bait for women. Eventually he would write the *Big Sur Guide* in which Henry had a prominent place. He read a lot, and his tastes were similar to Henry's; even before they had met he had been a fan of Miller's writing. He relieved Henry of some of the chores which had kept him from writing. Emil often lugged supplies up the hill and brought news of the outside world. Occasionally he'd find a bottle of wine or some other delicacy, and often he'd put together a feast for the two of them. He even began to help Henry out with his correspondence and packaged and mailed out Miller's books and pamphlets that people all over the country were ordering directly from the author. He also got in touch with Anaïs Nin and went a long way in beginning to settle the differences between Anaïs and Henry, which continued to grieve Miller. Above all, he was a good man, a kind, soft-spoken person who put himself at Henry's disposal without in any way suggesting either that he did not have a life of his own, or that he expected a reward in return. "There are some men," Henry would write many years later, "whose devotion goes beyond the bounds of friendship. Such a man is Emil White. For twenty-five years I've known that I could depend upon Emil for anything—and I mean anything."

White was the central figure in the shifting group of friends that came to surround Miller. These included writers like Maud Oakes, Walker Winslow (Harold Maine), Lillian Bos Ross, and George Leite; the sculptor Benny Bufano; a few Hollywood admirers, like Leon Shamroy, who bought paintings and often provided supplies; the Israeli artist Bezalel Schatz; the German pianist Gerhardt Muench; and a host of Big Sur neighbors and residents—Norman Mini; Harrydick Ross; Jean Wharton; and numerous others, including Noel Young, an aspiring young novelist who took refuge with Miller and became a life-long friend and finally Miller's publisher.

If Emil White in some measure took the place of Perlès, Ephraim Doner, a painter who lived in Carmel Highlands, became another Schnellock. A vigorous artist and an even a more vigorous man, Doner could converse on all manner of topics, from the works of Dostoievski to the Russian Revolution, from Zionism to French wines. And, of course, he knew an enormous amount about art and was acquainted with many of the artists Miller had known in Paris. In fact, they had once met at a party in Paris. Now they resumed their talk, for talk, after all, was what Henry liked most to do. And he and White and Doner and many other visitors often sat up late in a little kerosene-lit cabin and roamed all around the world in conversation. To Henry the circles of light which fell upon them from the lamps seemed halos—jolly, clownish halos, for these were happy and holy times, these first years at Big Sur.

Eight

Other Bright Messengers

"All I need is a cunt. And I think I'll have that soon too," Henry wrote to Bern Porter in April 1944. At this time he was conducting, of all things, a long distance mail-order romance with another June—June Lancaster, a woman he had never seen. *Another June!* —indeed, it was through Janice Pelham, a close friend of the first June, that Henry heard about this June Lancaster. Many strange parallels existed between the two Junes. June Lancaster was an artists' model, having posed in Columbia University art classes for Henry's old friends Frank Mechau and Tex Carnahan, as well as in George Grosz's class at the Art Students League. One of the photographs she sent him was a nude—it excited him because it revealed a kind of heaviness, an evidence of sensuality, like the other June's body. She was a dancer, too, and had worked in nightclubs as a taxi-dancer, as June Mansfield had. There was undoubtedly a connection here too. Like the earlier June she appeared to be a creature of moods, with many per-sonalities. "Keep on being metamorphic," Henry urged her. She needed no encouraging along those lines; for she saw herself as a person of many personalities. She wrote to him: "I'm a composite—or 'collage' . . . of the following: a female Thoreau—Manhattan Troglodyte—Lady Flying-Dutchman &, last & perhaps most painfully, something of a 'Eurydice with tears on her lips.' . . . Like Saint Joan I hear angelic voices!" June all over again! "I knew immediately," June Lancaster said at the outset of their correspondence, "that the similarity of my name was the reason prompting this." Very soon he was suggesting that she call him Val, the name he liked best, the name by which the first June had always addressed him. To Knud Merrild he wrote: "Did I tell you that I found another *June!* . . . I wonder what it will be like this time." Weeks before meeting June Lancaster, he wrote to Larry Durrell: "She is almost a copy of the first June. I am crazy about her." Finally, he urged the second June to join him in Big Sur, to be June transfigured and renewed and in her own person create an image worthy of completing *The Rosy Crucifixion.* Henry could admit the resemblance to June, but it took him a long time to acknowledge that in June Lancaster—as also with Laure and Sevasty—he was attempting to regain his daughter Barbara's love. "I guess my malady now," he said offhandedly to Harry Herschkowitz, "is that I'm continuously falling in love with my daughter."

At this point Harry Herschkowitz arrived in New York, threatening to write the Great American Novel and putting himself at Henry's service. Henry's faith in Herschkowitz's literary talents was unfounded—he had little talent and less self-discipline. On his own hook he began to plead Miller's case with June Lancaster and he screwed things up royally. He couldn't make up his mind about June. In one letter he would describe her as "really alive, enthusiastic," with "an attractive warm face," while in the next Harry was likely to call her "narcissistic," selfish, and too absorbed in the "Art-freedom idea" of independence and the fulfillment of her career as a dancer. If Harry could have put into words what he thought he was doing on Miller's behalf in New York, he would have flatly explained that he was thinking entirely with his prick and trying to lay every girl in sight so that he could select just the right one for Henry. Eventually, indeed, he convinced himself that if he didn't do something drastic to tie her to his cause, June would give up Henry. And so he came up with the ridiculous idea that he could save June for Henry by screwing her too.

That actually worked: through Harry, June surrendered to Henry. By the end of April 1944, she telegrammed that she would be in Big Sur before the month was out. Signing herself "June Bliss" she added: "I hope I will fulfill all your expectations."

But she didn't. As soon as she arrived Miller saw that she wasn't June, she wasn't Barbara. She hung around the house, like a rag doll, waiting for someone to take her up. She cooked a little—badly. She hummed and danced in the woods—a neighbor thought he caught a glimpse of her dancing nude one afternoon in the forest. She watched Henry. He hardly noticed her. He found her ordinary, hardly a continuation of the fabulous June Smith-Smerth-Mansfield-Miller woman. And after a brief stay, June Lancaster went back to New York, alone.

Hardly more than three months had passed when Henry was called back to Brooklyn himself. His mother was gravely ill with cancer. This time he made haste; he claimed that he could never be reconciled to his mother, but just the same he didn't want to fail his duty to be with her at the end as he had failed his father. But his mother triumphed over his best intentions again. She made a fine recovery after her operation. She didn't need her son by her side, and Henry was certainly not inclined to hang around. Two young critics of French literaure, Henri Peyre and Wallace Fowlie, heard that Miller was in the east and arranged a watercolor show at Yale University in New Haven, Connecticut.

Henry still didn't have a woman to love and he craved affection. Perhaps especially since his mother had seemed close to death his thoughts were often on some romantic, ideal, possible woman to give him the womanly affection he craved. Harry Herschkowitz had been mistaken in sending June Lancaster to Big Sur to join Henry. But he had not given up the idea of finding the right girl for Henry. When Miller arrived in New York to be with his mother, he met two sisters who had emigrated from Poland. They spoke English with an accent—which Henry, still in love with his ideal of the "European Woman," found attractive—and were both pretty and serious. One was a twenty year old named Janina Martha Lepska, and he found himself very attracted to her, though it hardly seemed as if a serious affair could possibly develop with her. Not only was he more than twice her age, she had serious, intellectual plans. In the Spring she had graduated from Bryn Mawr, and come Fall she planned to do graduate work at Yale in the philosophy of history.

Henry restlessly marked time in New York until his mother was strong enough to be out of danger. Then, in early October 1944 he made a leap up to Yale to see his admirers, to be present at his show of watercolors, and to see Lepska once again. He enjoyed this visit—it was a break and it gave him the chance to talk to young admirers about literature. He spent hours talking to Yale students in little groups of four or five. Finally, the president of Yale invited Henry to give a public lecture and offered him a thousand dollar honorarium—a year's wages by Miller's standard! His public shyness emerged. "If anyone needs that dough, I do," he told Fowlie, "but I've never given a lecture and I never will."

Of course, he saw Lepska several times, and he convinced himself that she somehow resembled his June. She had the same firm but fine slavic features as June, and a similar quickness, a kind of agitation of manner which excited Henry, making him feel the presence of a quick beat of impulsive life in her. She was slavic like June, but blond, Nordic like his high school flame Cora Seward; Henry saw in her the combination of the Latin and Teutonic traits that Anaïs Nin had exhibited to perfection. Like Anaïs, too, she was strong but elegant and delicate (Walker Winslow spoke of her "Dresden figurine" beauty). What was more, Lepska was interested in his ideas and interested—if he read the signs right—in *him*. Of course, he was lost. He would do anything to win this woman—even if nothing came of it but a long-distance heartache. The most obvious way to keep himself before her was through his works; and in early November he dashed off a quick message to Bern Porter asking him to send *The Plight of the Creative Artist in the United States of America* to the girl, while he went off to Dartmouth to visit Professor Herbert West.

Despite his vow at Yale not to lecture, at Dartmouth Miller gave his first and last college address. On this occasion it was evident for the first time that in a subterranean way Miller was acquiring a special reputation. He had become an aesthetic celebrity, attracting fervent devotees and furious detractors. On the surface his lecture seemed simple enough: its subject was the creative spirit in art and civilization. To his surprise, however, he was heckled by one member of the audience. And not long after, an article on Miller's visit to Dartmouth, written by this same heckler, appeared in *New Currents*. Titled "Odyssey of a Stool-Pigeon," it classed Henry unfavorably with Gide, Pound, and Hamsun as a particularly evil example of those artists who were anti-patriotic, anti-social, and anti-American. The author hinted broadly that Miller was a subversive and a traitor. This was dangerous talk during wartime and, as a result, Miller and West were both visited by the FBI. Miller was a little worried: if agents were looking for "combustible material" they could certainly find plenty of tinder in his books. (In particular, he had recently finished an anti-war piece, *Murder the Murderer*, which he was afraid to publish—it didn't appear until after the War.) Nothing came of this episode at Dartmouth, but it was the first sign that conservatives saw Miller's work and person as subversive to established social values; and it was the first of scores of newspaper and magazine articles branding him a moral moron and a menace to society.

Nonetheless, Henry continued to circulate in the east among friends and admirers. He and Lepska went to Bryn Mawr to see Paul Weiss who, like Keyserling, saw a philosophical position in Miller's work. He went to Bridgeport where he stayed *chez* Richard Osborn. Something had happened to Osborn long ago in Paris: he had never snapped back after his breakdown over Jeanne. He no longer suggested that they *fait un rigolo.* Paris had sent him off his track and Bridgeport had locked him in a mood of melancholy hopelessness. Martha Lepska went to nearby New Haven while Henry paused at Osborn's only briefly. He saw that in his absence Lepska had taken the message of *Plight of the Creative Artist* to heart. Though she had a rational, mathematical mind, she was seriously involved in the arts. He invited her to come to California with him and she accepted. It was clear that some deep familial, conventional impulse impelled Henry to present Lepska to his friends for approval. Then they went to Washington, D.C. to stay with Caresse Crosby. (During this visit for posterity and the Library of Congress archives, Miller recorded selections from books banned in America, *Black Spring* and *Tropic of Capricorn.*) After a short while they proceeded south to Fredericksburg, Virginia, where Emil Schnellock was teaching—at Mary Washington College for women. Early in December they started west. In Boulder, Colorado, they stayed with Margaret and Gilbert Neiman, and here on December 18, 1944, Henry and Lepska were married during a near conjunction of the moon and Venus. They then spent a week in San Francisco with the Rexroths before visiting Varda in Monterey who drove them to Big Sur.

He hadn't planned to marry Lepska, he told a friend years later—it just happened that he rescued her from Yale, and the rest followed. Behind the sudden impulse was the shadow of his mother; his mother's illness had brought him east and contact with his mother always made him reach out— blindly almost—for what he felt she had never given him: unearned affection. He had always fought against his mother because he wanted her to accept him purely on his own account, not for what he would "do" for her. If a woman believed in him he would do anything for her, but if she had to test him he would do nothing. Whenever a woman looked his way he was ready to melt, because with each new woman he experienced anew the possibility that he would receive the acceptance he felt his mother had not given him since the cradle. "Perhaps I took revenge upon my mother by my incestuous alliance with Pauline," he meditated once. Pauline loved him even when he betrayed her; and he came back to her in order to betray her all over again and thus to prove that she would forgive him anything. Henry came to understand his attachment to his mother by confronting it in his work on D.H. Lawrence, and Lawrence's emphasis on the "incest-motive" was one of the things that made this study such a struggle for Henry. Lawrence insisted that "incest-craving" was as normal as sexual marriage and should not be repressed. Miller's own mother-fixation wouldn't allow him to go this far, but the problem had been opened for him and he turned to Jung for aid in seeing the mythological dimensions of the mother figure. Into his notebook he had copied all of Jung's references to the mother in the *Psychology of the Unconscious*. Now, ten years later, in his work on Rimbaud he was tracing out the same story, of the violent effort to separate the budding personality from the mother. "I feel," he wrote in his Rimbaud study, "that it was the same with Lawrence and with Rimbaud. All the rebelliousness which I share with them derives from this problem." When his mother's illness had forced him back to her, he rebounded by becoming attached to Lepska. "I am very happy," Miller wrote to Knud Merrild two days after his third marriage.

But amazingly soon after Henry was removed from the pressures which proximity to his mother put on him, he wondered why he had married Lepska. For her part, she had not really anticipated how rigorous life in Big Sur would be. She accepted Big Sur life with few grumbles, but her passion for order tore the heart out of the place for Henry. Clearly Lepska was not to blame for the tension that soon began to develop between them. True, she was a disciplinarian by temperament—but this would not have depressed some other person as it did Henry, for it was clear that she was trying to be his protector. But in protecting him from interruptions she didn't realize that he loved intrusions—he preferred seeing his friends to writing his books—and through her good intentions she alienated his friends and turned them, and eventually Henry, against her. Henry had thought that this Polish girl was Slavic, like June; but she turned out to be Germanic—like his mother. His own training, to be sure, had addicted him to order; but his spirit was also soothed by chaos. Henry soon felt Lepska was tyrannizing him, and he rebelled against being subjected to someone else's schedule. Lepska not only put order into his life, she taught him how to live in Big Sur, for she had been raised in a rural area in Poland and far better than he she knew how to get along under fairly primitive conditions. To make things worse, all the Big Sur wives were on her side: they marvelled at the way Lepska had "taken hold" of her new husband and her new life, making the most of both and never complaining. The neighbors regarded Lepska as a model wife—and later as a model mother. Look at what she had to put up with. First of all, Evans soon returned to claim his house, and Henry and Lepska had to move into a former convict's cabin on Anderson Creek, so ramshackled that it rented for $7.50 a month. Lepska had to cook on an ancient wood-burning stove and tolerate a cantankerous, odd, old writer for a husband. Yet she remained undepressed and, to all appearances, cheery. She must have been a saint—the neighbors agreed. But Henry wasn't pleased by the neighbors' views or Lepska's grim cheeriness. The more spry she became, the more he was driven into moroseness. Wasn't it wonderful, they said to Henry, the way she managed to keep everything neat as a pin, the way she slaved so he could concentrate on his work? Why was he so grumpy most of the time, then? And why, with such a helpmate, did he manage to get far less work done than when he had to care entirely for himself?

And then in March, Lepska became pregnant and Henry's heart leaped into life again. All his terrible suffering over his abandonment of his daughter, Barbara, suffering that he still experienced, began to diminish. He lived the last month of Lepska's term in a fever of anxiety and impatience. And then, finally, in November of 1945, she gave birh to a daughter. "It's a girl, Valentine—dark eyes—Slavic—perfect form & features. Born superconscious," he wrote to Huntington Cairns the day after she was born in a hospital in Berkeley. She was named Valentine— Henry's middle name, Lepska's father's name and Henry's maternal grandfather's name. He lavished upon her all the love he had pent up for his lost daughter. Before Valentine was a month old he told Durrell: "She's a little beauty, an angel, and I'm madly in love with her. Gives no trouble at all. Sleeps perpetually and hardly ever cries. A real back-to-the-womber." Unfortunately, Valentine's birth increased the differences between Henry and Lepska. Henry gave all his attention to the child. For Lepska, the arrival of a child meant that she had to hold all the more tightly to the reins of order. When she began to tell him how to regulate his work schedule, open, sullen war broke out. The more he was aware that she was guarding him so he could work, the more he felt like a prisoner, paralyzed in his writing, and impelled to flee his studio. The education and general rearing of Valentine also became a bone of contention over which they snarled and snapped. Certainly, Lepska felt that Henry was putting Val first—what was more, that he was spoiling her absurdly. The child, she said over and over, in many different ways, had to be disciplined, controlled; she ridiculed Henry's ideas concerning the child's need for freedom. She derided all of his romantic notions about the life of the child, the needs of children—it was as if she jeered at his dreams. But Henry was determined to create the natural life he felt his parents had prevented him from having. He took Valentine for long walks in the woods, along the deer trails, until she was exhausted. He called her a "little Mongolian" or a "wild Indian," he argued that there was absolutely no reason in the world to consider sending her to school. This remained a sore point between Henry and Lepska from that time on.

Nine

Money and How It Came His Way

Troubled by a general, grudging tone of bitterness, generally impoverished and tied down to a routine of hard physical labor, Miller went for long stretches during the years 1945 to 1949 when he did not write at all. During this period, too, he experienced a number of personal and psychological tensions. His relations with Lepska deteriorated completely. Again, as in the period of his worst years with June, he began to lose confidence in himself, to proclaim himself a has-been, irresponsible, selfish, ineffectual. The necessities of the arduous life at Big Sur, a mountainous correspondence, and a continuous scramble for money, all distracted him from serious writing.

He wrote in flashes of confidence, periodic occasions when he managed to regain or invent a reconciliation with himself and believe in the capacity of literature to make a difference in the world. He no longer felt the joy that had once given his writing vividness and verve. Now he grimly cranked out a steady succession of works; but something in his imagination had relaxed, consolidated, ceased to go forward. Most of his work in the mid-to-late forties emphasized the same ideas, had the same tone. He wrote more quickly than ever before and usually contented himself with one quick polish of a typescript. His style became smoother—and more predictable.

Bern Porter stood by ready to print whatever was unsuitable for New Directions. A number of magazines, some of which paid, were prepared to accept whatever Henry offered, and he produced dozens of articles. Printers of fine books, fans of Miller, encouraged him to give them a try, and he did offer short works to several. Many of these works were reprints, or had been written earlier. *The Angel Is My Watermark* was reprinted from *Black Spring* by Holve-Barrows of Fullerton in 1944. A selection of his letters to Emil Schnellock, written from Paris, was issued by Porter in 1944. *The Air-Conditioned Nightmare* was finally published, by New Directions, in 1945. Porter reissued *Money and How It Gets That Way* in 1945. In the following year he assembled the Henry Miller *Miscellanea*, made of work written as early as 1924. Separately the Colt Press and the Motive Book Shop of Waco, Texas, published editions of the essay on Wasserman's *Maurizius* trilogy. *Murder the Murderer*, completed in 1944, appeared in 1946. In several critiques or prefaces—a review of Haniel Long and an introduction to Thoreau's essays, for instance—he rehashed earlier favorites. *Remember to Remember, Sunday After the War,* and *The Wisdom of the Heart,* all were collections of previously published work. *The Waters Reglitterized,* an essay on "water color in some of its more liquid phases," begun in February 1939, was published by John Kidis in 1950. Miller's most original work during this period was the study of Rimbaud which was issued in two parts as "When Do Angels Cease to Resemble Themselves?" in the New Directions anthologies of 1946 and 1949. Even this work had originated in 1941 as an attempt to translate *A Season in Hell.*

So, his work in the late forties was that of consolidation and engaged the imagination of revision rather than vision. This was most true of all with regard to his work on *The Rosy Crucifixion*; by 1946 the manuscript mounted to over a thousand pages and had an epigraph from the Tibetan sage Milerepa on its title page: "It was written; and it had to be. Behold to where it has led." By the end of 1948 he had finished more than 1500 pages, too long to be the single-volume sequel to *Tropic of Capricorn* that he had planned in 1939. By 1948 he had divided his completed material into two volumes, retitled *Sexus* and *Plexus.* The rest of the story he intended to complete under the title of *Nexus.*

From a physical point of view the most striking work he produced during this time was *Into the Night Life*—the dream chapter from *Black Spring*—beautifully printed and illustrated in collaboration with the Palestinian artist Bezalel Schatz. It was Schatz's idea to execute an entire book by the serigraph process; he would do the design and art work, and Henry would

inscribe a text which would be serigraphed exactly as written, with varia-
tions in style and writing instrument to suit the flow of the narrative and the
mood of the moment. "The sentence from Freud, from which the title
derives," Henry gleefully noted, "as well as his signature, are also in Henry
Miller's handwriting, it being impossible to resurrect Freud to do the job
himself." The work started in February of 1946. They believed the job
would take a few months to execute, but a year of labor passed before 800
copies went to the binder, and even this was accomplished only by collaborative work by both authors from 8 a.m. to 2 p.m. daily. Each color
they wished to employ had to be put individually on silk fabric fastened in a
wooden frame. Then the fabric was inked with a roller and the paper, one
sheet at a time, pressed against it. Each sheet was hung on Henry's
clothesline to dry. To achieve the final state required 220 stencils to make an
eighty-page book. The materials alone cost $73.00 a copy and they planned
to sell this fabulous book for a mere $100. It was the most sumptuous
expression of Miller's vision of artistic collaboration. Schatz gave the key to
the work: "The Chinese, the Hindus, the Persians, as well as the medieval
monks, created works like these instinctively. In our day this sort of
collaboration is conspicuously absent." And Miller added: "We hope and
believe that it will inspire other artists." Henry took out a "Permit to
Engage in Business as a Seller" in July 1947 and with the aid of friends
started to peddle the volume, insisting that Schatz take the first $2,000
they collected: "I can bide my time," Henry said. The first $2,000 came
quickly: Henry and Schatz and Benny Bufano, the sculptor, made a swing
through Hollywood and sold eighteen copies in five days. But the sales
languished, and it was a long time before Henry collected his share.
However, people seemed to be willing to give him much of what he needed
or desired in order to keep him alive. In Big Sur he never was in danger of
starving or desperately lacking the necessities of life. It was only the
problem of actual money which he seemed unable to solve. True, some
money trickled in from the sales of watercolors. But his royalties from the
four books published by New Directions before 1945 (*The Cosmological Eye,
The Colossus of Maroussi, The Wisdom of the Heart,* and *Sunday after the War*)
earned him hardly more than a thousand dollars a year. Even *The Air-
Conditioned Nightmare,* finally published by New Directions in 1945, sold
poorly.

Henry knew well how to bide his time. In 1944, with the liberation of
France, his financial picture had begun to change. He received a message
from an officer in the Merchant Marine, a reader of Miller's, that he was

prepared to deliver two trunks consigned to Miller by the moving-van man at Louveciennes—trunks stored when Miller departed for Greece—which contained his most precious manuscripts, the original *Tropic of Cancer* and *The World of Lawrence*. Then, in mid October 1944, Miller received a letter from Jack Kahane's son, now renamed Maurice Girodias ("Practically everybody had a new name in France," he explained) announcing that he was resuming publication with the firm of Editions du Chêne. "Your books have not been seized by the Germans," he said in a postscript; "all the stuff you left with me is all right." Then less than three months after this news, Girodias sent him a detailed report. Henry's books continued to sell unexpectedly well, the publisher explained off-handedly. With a sublime capacity for evasion about money which seemed calculated to drive Henry mad, he wrote on and on, going through innumerable petty details concerning the press, his operations, and so on. Then he finally got to the point. One detail leaped out from the page. Miller's accumulated royalty amounted to 410,000 francs. Forty thousand dollars! *410,000 francs. Yes, forty thousand dollars.* Henry sat down and smoked a cigarette. Here, in his $7.50-a-month shack, owing the mailman-grocer $200, without a car, without a bank account, he suddenly found himself in possession of more money than had passed through his hands during his whole lifetime.

Or, almost in possession. For when Girodias's letter was read closely, it became clear that French postwar regulations in the *Office des Changes* prohibited the exportation of such a sum. Perhaps the French economy would crumble if one impoverished American author were paid his royalties. So, Henry was in America and his money was in Paris. How *did* money get that way? The only feasible suggestion that Girodias could make was for Henry to come to France, buy an estate, and live like a king.

It was a happy thought, a dazzling thought, and Lepska joined Girodias in urging it. He could buy antiques for a song, sweep up pictures by Miró, Picasso, Braque, and Soutine, invest in a nice steady French business. Who else in France had 410,000 francs? But for Henry this plan was absolutely out of the question. He refused point blank even to consider going abroad. For one thing, his mother was still in dangerous health and he had vowed that he would stand ready, in case of her death, to take complete care of his sister Lauretta, who was helpless and had no one else. For another, he was worried about Val. She was still a baby, after all, and he felt that it would be unmerciful to subject her to the hazards of travel, the changes in diet and water, the difficulties of getting proper food for her in postwar France, the uncertainties of medical care. He doted on her, he would not take her, and he refused to go without her. The best he could do was to buy an "estate" from his Big Sur friend Jean Wharton—a house high up on Partington Ridge that certainly was a big improvement over his shack on Anderson Creek. (This, however, is the house that became permanently identified with Miller's life in Big Sur.) Still, he didn't have the few thousand dollars—in the United States, at least—to pay for the house he had "bought." On paper he was wealthy, but he had to live in a borrowed house.

And so he began, in his old resourceful way, to think up strategems to get some of those funds out of France. Delay was the first of his disasters: time began to take his money away from him even before he got his hands on it. Two months after his first good news, bad news arrived: the franc was devalued in January of 1946, its dollar value decreased by a third: forty thousand dollars suddenly became about twenty-five. However, the sales kept booming, and additional royalties accumulated; Miller's books were reprinted in batches of 10,000 copies each and sold out quickly. Fees for translation and reprint rights swelled the royalties even more rapidly than devaluation diminished them. He decided that he wished to turn half of the royalties over to Anaïs Nin, and he beseeched Hugo Guiler to help collect the funds through the Paris branch of the National City Bank, of which he was an officer. But even with Guiler's aid, only a mite got deposited in Anaïs's Paris account, and Henry got nothing at all.

By June of 1947, after several devaluations, the sum owing to Henry was 4,470,000 francs. But he still couldn't get it out of France. As fast as the money accumulated in the bank, it fell on the exchange. The most obvious and simple solution would have been to instruct a factor to purchase easily transportable goods, such as jewels, against his Editions du Chêne account. But Henry always devised strategems too elaborate to work. He had an idea, which he regarded as absolutely brilliant, to exchange royalties with French authors owed money in the United States. (Of all French authors only Albert Cossery agreed to this exchange and Miller collected only a few hundred dollars.) In an even more cumbersome scheme Henry urged friends or acquaintances who were going to France—Caresse Crosby, for instance—to pay him dollars before departure and collect francs from Girodias upon arrival in France. He did work such a swap several times, but it was so piecemeal and undependable that it was almost as unsatisfactory as having no money at all. With royalties again flowing from France, Miller terminated his relationships with his New York agent, Henry Volkening, and his English agent, Patience Ross of Heath and Company; and he contracted with a Paris firm, Agence Hoffman, on the Rue Caumartin.

Hoffman began to break some of the funds loose, little chunks at a time, Early in 1946, he collected a token payment of $2500, then $2000, and later $3038 more. By May 1947, Henry's account showed a credit of 3,714,000 francs or $37,250.00. "Little hope is offered me as to when I will receive the money. This is quite a blow to me, as you can imagine," he wrote Huntington Cairns. Despite the enormous sum owed him, he never had a cent to spare, he was still continually in debt and now he was continually harassed by creditors and would-be borrowers who had heard about his "good fortune."

He even received a begging letter from June, stating that she was ill and poor, and had been deserted by her present husband. She pleaded in the most simple, pitiable way for any little amount he could spare. This letter hit him hard. June begging him for money—on her knees! His image of a hard, self-sufficient June shattered like glass against the reality of this letter. Henry was really upset. He was humiliated and angry, too, to realize that though June assumed he was wealthy, he couldn't shower her with aid as he would have liked to do. Immediately, he sent June the small sum he could scrape up, then kept sending ten or twenty dollars at a time. How could he make June believe that he was not deceiving her and that the reports of his vast earnings were true in theory but far from true in fact?

Even the federal government made its appearance, and Henry found that he owed United States taxes on his earnings—$800 worth by August of 1947. Since he owed taxes on profits whether he could collect them or not, the more he made, the deeper he would fall into debt. He was in serious trouble with the government. Agence Hoffman saved him from disaster in the fall of 1947 by managing to get out a hundred dollars every few days during a period of relaxation in the *Office des Changes*. Then by mid 1948, Girodias was officially authorized to pay Miller $500 per month. Even so, Henry still had a million and a half francs in Paris which he had not been able to get into America. At one point in the late forties he was so desperate for money that he conceived a plan that for sheer impracticality rivalled his previous junkets to Florida and North Carolina. He explained it to Girodias: "Come the worst, I have made up my mind to ship my wife and child home to her parents in the East, and then go on the road, from town to town, hitch-hiking my way, with one copy of the hundred-dollar book [*Into the Night Life*] under my arm. I would travel without a bag, buying change of linen as I go along. Just a tooth brush, that's all I need. And I would let the book carry me along, make friends for me—as it has already—and trust to Providence to get somewhere eventually."

He never executed this plan, but he never accumulated any funds. By the end of 1949, he had just managed to pay off his debts and to keep up with his taxes—and he had scraped through only by his sales of watercolors. Once, when he found that he gave concern to a French friend by a description of his poor economic circumstance, he had to explain his position:

I am sorry if I gave you uneasiness about my own precarious situation. When I think of the conditions under which the great majority are living I know I am well off. Besides, I refuse to be defeated. Lacking hard cash I have become a barterer. I needed certain essentials desperately—food-stuffs, clothing, tires, postage stamps, et cetera. I sat down and, with the few post cards I had on hand, I wrote a few people to make me a gift of post cards. Then I wrote to my friends, my admirers, any one I thought a good prospect, that if they would furnish me the items I listed I would in return (and in good measure) send what I have to dispose of, viz. books, records, mss., paintings, prints. I had to do this when I first came to California and I have to do it now once again, despite my increased output and my growing fame. If you are at the bottom you have to start from the bottom. The results have been encouraging. If you can go direct to your man you are not apt to be deserted or betrayed. Publishers may be undependable, the public may be fickle, but the human being, if you can reach him, is always 'there', and he is ready to manifest it by showing his good heart. Under the present order of things one can wait until Doomsday to receive his just reward.

His woes were not only financial. His success in France made him famous. This was not all to the good by any means. For instance, a *Harper's Magazine* (April 1947) article on "Sex and Anarchy in Big Sur" inspired the *San Francisco Examiner* to villify the Henry Miller "cults" of hate and violence and anti-Americanism at Big Sur. The American public was assured that his behavior was dirty, scandalous, and immoral. The result was obvious: several printed references to the "Henry Miller colony" appeared in newspapers and journals. And many readers journeyed to Big Sur. Some articles attracted the dissatisfied, others the "debauched," others the bohemian and the early experimenters with drugs. Mail poured in from correspondents who demanded an answer or required Miller to admit them to his colony. Visitors began to arrive at his door at dawn and continued all day. Some were psychotic and demanded that Henry live up to his reputation—expose himself, say, or deliver a tirade against America. Others blamed Miller for the defection of a wife or daughter and threatened to strangle him.

Miller was certainly not responsible for the reputation which journalists fashioned and sensation seekers accepted. For most Big Sur residents, including Henry and his friends, there was no "hate" in Big Sur, and there was more love and certainly more companionship and mutual collaboration, than sex. Sex was not by any means out of Henry's mind, but he was bent on fashioning a new public image, as a happy clown and a man of wisdom. He corresponded with Krishnamurti (on stationery emblazoned with his own photo), he wore a Yemen amulet which Schatz had given him, he practiced sainthood in public. He rid himself of all desire for success. He rejected offers that he had once solicited—to collaborate on a variety of film and television projects—to review books, to travel to the Orient or Tibet and to write up his experience. He was content to settle into the life of Big Sur.

He was also attracting renewed artistic attention. The *Nation* reported in 1949 that Americans returning from France were bringing back copies of *Tropic of Cancer* and *Tropic of Capricorn* bound into one volume and wrapped in a dust jacket on which the title *Jane Eyre* was printed. Exhibitions of his paintings were held in a San Francisco museum, at Harvard, and at Dartmouth. A thesis on his work was written at Columbia University. He was the subject of two books, one of them written by Nicholas Moore and published in England, and the other a collection of essays edited by Bern Porter. Titled *The Happy Rock: A Book About Henry Miller,* this collection had contributions by Durrell, Fraenkel, Perlès, Paul Rosenfeld, William Carlos Williams, Philip Lamantia, Wallace Fowlie, Osbert Sitwell, Kenneth Patchen, and Paul Weiss. Young writers like Robert Creeley wrote to him for advice. In the next few years, he was the subject of rather favorable critical essays by Edmund Wilson, Frederick Hoffman, Philip Wylie, Philip Rahv, and Herbert Read. John Cowper Powys, whose lectures Miller had attended as a young man, began to champion him around 1950. Powys declared enthusiastically: "Where Henry Miller is specially great . . . is in *two things. . . . .* 1st in his descriptions of odd fantastic grotesque quaint queer eccentric pathetic & big tragically endearing human figures that he has met and made friends with all over Europe & America. In his descriptions of these odd fish he reaches at times a point of humorous perception and of imaginative pity almost Shakespearean, and 2nd in his profoundly mystical—there's no other word for it—interpretation of certain landscapes and certain towns and coasts and cities and provinces into whose very souls . . . he lives or burrows." Lawrence Durrell announced plans to edit a *Henry Miller Reader* and to write a book about Miller. So, with his major books still banned in America, Miller suffered all of the penalties of fame but enjoyed few of its profits.

Ten

Devils in Paradise

Nothing could have been more foolhardy than to bring an outsider into his domestic wrangles, but this is precisely what Henry did. In mid-1946 Henry had received a plea from Conrad Moricand who had heard reports of Miller's fabulous book sales. He was in Vevey, poverty-stricken, and he asked Henry to take him in. Miller's first response was practical—that it would be impossible to offer him a haven at Big Sur; not only was he short of funds himself, the shack at Anderson Creek was totally inadequate to house Moricand. And besides, Henry explained, he and Lepska were nearing a possible separation. The best he could do was to send Moricand food, cigarettes, and money. But his refusal gnawed at him and in a fine exhibition of his own plenitude of spirit in March of 1947 he cabled: "Do not despair. Our home is yours."

Moricand accepted at once, but the arrangements were difficult to make. Apparently destitute, he would be allowed in the country on alien status only if a citizen of the United States would guarantee that he would not become a public charge once he had gained entry. Accordingly, Henry signed an affidavit making himself financially responsible for Moricand. He purchased tickets for the journey from Vevey (at a price equal to the sum of his American royalties for the previous six months) and paid Moricand's

427

$165 hotel bill. When all this was done, Moricand was so neurotic and inert, he couldn't face the journey. Miller refused to be defeated and asked Caresse Crosby, who was in Europe, to aid in packing Moricand off. Caresse, he remarked, "could extricate the devil himself if she wanted to." The phrase was ominously prescient. For hardly had Moricand arrived, in February of 1948, than he proved almost to *be* the devil himself, and it was Henry who was soon in need of extrication. If Henry and Lepska had been leading a purgatorial existence, Moricand plunged them into hell.

Quite possibly, the astrologer had not consulted the stars before he departed for America; he certainly had not formed a very accurate picture of Henry's life and must have imagined it to be far more grand than it was. When he arrived, he declared himself totally discontented with the arrangements made for him. He was a city man, a cosmopolitan, accustomed to cultural surroundings, and he found it difficult and mentally confining to live in the unrefined country. He thought the climate harsh and extreme, unhealthily damp and uncomfortably cold. Soon he developed several illnesses. It was absolutely necessary, he complained to Henry, for him to have the use of a bathtub—otherwise there was no relief for his skin disease—but even in his new house on Partington Ridge Henry had only a shower. Moricand didn't like his room either. Miller offered to give him the very room which he himself used for a study, a room which he cherished for its bright, cheery atmosphere. But though Moricand took the room, he declared it barely habitable. He shut the windows, tacked curtains over them to keep the sunlight out and refused to open his door, and then wailed that the room was humid and full of noxious fumes from his oil stove.

Pregnant again, Lepska was not exactly happy waiting on Moricand, but he attached himself like a leech to Lepska and all day long he poured out a sulphurous stream of woes and miseries. He castigated the little "spoiled brat" of a girl, Valentine, and her "silly chatter", her "lack of manners," Henry's "foolish indulgence." He made it clear that he was terribly disappointed in his hosts too—and after all their promises. Surely Lepska could do a little more for him, surely Henry could show more concern. By being so miserable and so full of complaints and accusations, Moricand pushed Henry deeper into depression. In Paris, Moricand had made a fuss in praise of Henry's mystical intuitions and his depth of knowledge; but now he told Henry that he regarded him as a solid dolt. By the end of March 1948 he announced that he simply could not tolerate life at Big Sur. Henry would have to extricate him from it in some noble aristocratic way. Moricand made it clear that this was definitely Henry's responsibility. He himself was content with suggesting that the best plan of all would be for Henry to find him some suitable position and location in Europe and establish him luxuriously in it.

Henry was nearly at his wits' end. He wrote to Girodias to recommend Moricand for a reader's position, but for weeks no answer came. In the meantime Moricand developed a terrible itch. This, he implied, was the result of a nervous condition caused by his ill treatment. It was Henry's duty to see that he was cured. Moricand moved to Monterey for regular medical treatment and Henry had to rent a hotel room with private bath in Monterey so that Moricand could stroll over to the hospital at his leisure. Moricand's demands ate up the little money that Henry could scrape together.

Next, Moricand moved to a good hotel in San Francisco. Between the end of March and the end of May, Henry's expenses for him amounted to over $275. To rub salt into the wounds he gave an interview to the San Francisco *Chronicle* vilifying Miller for having deserted him.

Finally Henry resolved to be rid of this incubus. He arranged transatlantic passage for Moricand and sent him a $150 moneygram for his cross-country fare. Moricand spent the $150 but did not debark, flatly asserting that he could not rely on Henry's promises and categorically stating that he would not budge until Henry guaranteed him one thousand dollars upon his arrival in Paris. Otherwise, he would simply remain in the United States where Miller was obligated to support him. Did Miller suppose that he was ready to return to poverty?

At this Henry broke off all communications with him. Then Moricand turned his appeals to Werner Jost, the Swiss Vice-Consul in San Francisco, and filed a complaint against his mentor, despite the fact that by this time Henry had spent about $3,000 for Moricand's support, some of which he had to borrow. Moricand explained to Jost that he was utterly helpless and forlorn, a man without resources, cursed by fate and friendless, a man who had been betrayed by Miller, that hypocrite who had induced him to emigrate to America with promises of security. He told the same story to a San Francisco lawyer who threatened Henry that he would "bring the matter to the proper authorities." And finally, he started to write an autobiographical account, titled "Bel Abbes à Big Sur" in which he proposed to expose Henry's cruelty toward him. Miller found that he had to defend himself from every side against this devil who had crept into his paradise, and after dispatching defensive letters to all the accusers whom Moricand had set upon him, he took the offensive and wrote an account of Moricand's fiendish ways, called "Paradise Lost" (later called "A Devil in

Paradise" and incorporated into *Big Sur and the Oranges of Hieronymous Bosch*).

This long essay concerning his tribulations in *l'affaire* Moricand came easily. Miller had a fast grip upon his conception right from the beginning. True, he had had many troubles in Big Sur—with everything ranging from money to his wife to rattlesnakes—but never had his life been so soured as it had been by Moricand. Big Sur *before* Moricand's arrival did seem, by comparison, a real paradise. Written easily and with a wit born as a protection against exasperation, "A Devil in Paradise" was one of the best works composed during this period. The encounter with Moricand generated the kind of misery in Henry that he had experienced in 1930 and 1931 in Paris. And hopeless misery was, for him, the first spark of the creative fire.

Miller's troubles came even from France, where he was most successful. In March of 1946, the *President du Cartel d'Action sociale et morale,* Daniel Parker, had registered complaints against Les Editions du Chêne (for *Tropic of Capricorn*) and Editions Denöel (for *Tropic of Cancer*) under the provisions of an anti-pornography law of 1939. An official committee was formed to decide the case. To everyone's astonishment, it found against Miller, determined that he *was* a pornographer, and proposed to bring sanctions against the distribution of his work. At this point, however, Claude-Edmonde Magny and Maurice Nadeau, then literary editor of *Combat,* appealed to the writers of France to protest this restriction of freedom of expression and to defend Henry Miller. Thus, a *Comité de défense d'Henri Miller* was created, which included André Breton, Albert Camus, Paul Eluard, and Jean-Paul Sartre. Even André Gide, who read Miller's *Black Spring* for the first time, joined.

Parker counter-attacked by issuing a pamphlet titled: *Que faut-il penser de l'Affaire Miller?* in which he argued that Miller's publishers should be prosecuted and Miller himself given medical treatment as a psychopath. The battle began. Any time one opened a French paper, some reference to Miller might be found. Articles ranged all the way from serious defenses of Miller's work to spurious reports that Miller had been seen in the nude atop a New York skyscraper, painting a watercolor of a luscious blonde. Over 200 articles about him were published within four months. Girodias gleefully reported: "You are more praised, argued about, hated and admired than any French writer has been since Baudelaire, Rimbaud or Verlaine. People mention your name continually: critics write about 'Ford, Capra, ces Henry Millers du cinèma,' etc." People spoke of *"Le Cas Miller"* as they had once discussed the Dreyfus affair. The only thing that worried Girodias was that the furor over the books would reveal the fact that the demand had been so great for Miller's books he had had to resort to using blackmarket paper. Finally, the *Société des gens de lettres* and Girodias brought suit against Daniel Parker, charging him with libel and slander in attacking the books and asking that the case against Miller be dismissed.

This settled matters in France in Miller's favor. But of course it had no effect upon the views of authorities or writers in the United States. When a bookseller was sentenced to three years in prison for selling *Tropic of Cancer* and *Tropic of Capricorn* not a single American writer came to Miller's defense. No committees were established to defend his work or to urge its free circulation.

Strictly on his own terms Miller was counterattacking by agreeing to release *Sexus* for publication, a book which deliberately revived "the mantic and the obscene." "As you know," Miller wrote to Girodias, "I did wish to see all three books come out at once, primarily because I didn't want false conclusions drawn from a reading of Book One which is so heavily loaded with sexual experiences—saturated, is probably the word." But since Girodias' firm was on shaky ground and needed a good seller to buoy it up, Miller agreed to the separate publication of *Sexus* in 1949, shortly after his victory over the vice crusader. This was a miscalculation. *Sexus* raised a new furor even in France. Before a thousand copies had been sold, the book was supressed for offending the morals of the French public and in December 1950 the Minister of Interior decreed that *Sexus* could not be published in France in any language. The French writers who had earlier defended Henry were now strangely silent, and the reason for their silence emerged very soon. They were unsure about how to defend the book; they themselves felt that the sex in it was "excessive." Maurice Nadeau, who had led in the formation of the previous defense committee for Miller, wrote to inquire if the author himself regarded the book as "frankly obscene." What was Henry's purpose? Miller was no help. "In the autobiographical narratives," he replied, "I have no purpose! I am simply relating my life story . . . ." Pierre Lesdain, an influential editor and translator, wrote to ask if *Sexus* was better or worse than Miller's other books, in the author's opinion. Henry responded that he could not tell.

Miller soon found that many of his friends deplored the book. With Pierre Lesdain, he would shrug off criticism with a remark like, "Perhaps I *have* deteriorated. If so, *tant pis pour moi!*" But a full scale attack from Durrell could hardly be brushed aside so lightly. "You may not like R.C. at

all," he warned Durrell several months before publication. "In some ways it
is a reversion to pre-Tropic writing." Still, he could hardly have been
prepared for Larry's response. "Received Sexus from Paris and am mid-way
through Volume II. I must confess I'm bitterly disappointed in it, despite
the fact that it contains some of your very best writing to date. But my dear
Henry, the moral vulgarity of so much of it is artistically painful. These
silly, meaningless scenes which have no raison d'être, no humour, just
childish explosions of obscenity—what a pity, what a terrible pity for a
major artist not to have critical sense enough to husband his forces, to keep
his talent aimed at the target. What on earth possessed you to leave so much
twaddle in?" Miller was unaffected by the attack because he knew precisely
what effects he had wanted to achieve in this book. Though he listened to
Durrell's criticism he never allowed him to instruct him. "This time the
Englishman in him got the upper hand, I fear," he wrote to Lesdain. Then
he set about to instruct Durrell:

What I want to tell you is this—(I said it before and I repeat it solemnly: I
am writing exactly what I want to write and the way I want to do it.)
Perhaps it's twaddle, perhaps not. The fact that I put in everything under
the sun may be, as you think, because I have lost all sense of values. Again,
it may not. I am trying to reproduce in words a book of my life which to me
has the utmost significance—every bit of it. Not because I am infatuated
with my own ego. You should be able to perceive that only a man without
ego could write thus about himself. (Or else I am really crazy. In which
case, pray for me.) Since 1927 I have carried inside me the material of this
book. Do you suppose it's possible that I could have a miscarriage after such
a period of gestation? Perhaps it's a monster I'm giving birth to. But really,
I don't care. The paramount thing is for me to get it out of my system—and
in doing so to reveal what I was and am. I made a herculean effort to
represent myself for what I then was. The only artistry I endeavored to
employ was the capturing of that other self, those other days. I've been as
sincere as I possibly could, maybe too sincere, because it certainly is not a
lovely picture I made of myself. In justice, however, I think you, you
particularly, should be able to read between the lines, to reconcile truth
seeker with artist, liar, playboy and what not.
                                    * * *
Larry, I can never go back on what I've written. If it was not good, it was
true; if it was not artistic, it was sincere; if it was in bad taste, it was on the
side of life. If I were a braggart and an egotist I might have written more
gloriously. There is a poverty and sterility I tried to capture which few men
have known. Far better to have been a gallows-bird! But I have only this one
life to record. That passion you sense to be lacking has been put into the
minus side. That life of "senseless activity," which the sages have ever

condemned as death—that was what I set out to record. But as I say towards the end of Book 2, I suffered out of ignorance, and thus was highly instructed. Perhaps in the summing up, my life will be seen to be a huge pyramid erected over a minus sign. Still, nevertheless, a pyramid. Perhaps better understood when placed upside down.

Two weeks later, he returned to this subject: "More and more, as I think of your words, Larry, I smile to myself, especially when you refer to the inane or inept or trifling conversational passages, some of them quite long too. I was rather proud of myself for having caught these so well. It is as if I took a few steps backward—towards an outmoded realism—but not really. I don't know how to explain what it is which, to my mind, saves this work from being 'realistic' in the crude, vulgar sense. But I am sure of it. Perhaps you have to examine more closely the work of certain painters who, though masters, were able to deal with 'trifles.' I think that the 'trifle' was very important in my life—if you get what I mean." It was the truth of life that he was trying to get into his art—even if it became necessary to seem to sacrifice art in order to do so—even if he were to be castigated—or imprisoned—by his enemies and abandoned by his friends.

Entirely undeterred, in late 1949, he completed *Plexus*, making wall charts and doing a lot of rewriting of his earlier draft. In his notebook he advised himself: "Quicken pace of narrative, pile incidents pell-mell, faster, faster—till by time of quitting Remsen Street it goes like lightning." He was writing steadily as he had not done for ten years. The book burst out like a symphony that drowned out all the minor distractions of Big Sur. Not since *Tropic of Capricorn* had his inspiration tank been so quickly filled up and his inner dictation so active. He could hardly turn it off. As soon as he arrived in his little studio each morning, his inner voice took entire possession of his will and made him write. For hours at a time, words, sentences, paragraphs, and whole sections tumbled out like pieces of coal from a sack. He no longer knew why he wrote—he simply wrote.

Eleven

Life's Traces

Instead of continuing on to *Nexus* and the completion of *The Rosy Crucifixion* Miller turned to another kind of autobiography, a history of reading. *Books in My Life* had its genesis in 1950 in a suggestion by Lawrence Clark Powell, librarian at UCLA who periodically drove to Big Sur to loan Miller books and also to collect his manuscripts and correspondence for the "Henry Miller Archives" in the UCLA Special Collections library. One evening after dinner, Miller happened to mention that Raymond Queneau, now the chief reader for Gallimard, was making a collection from various authors of lists of the hundred books which had most influenced each, and Miller had been asked for his list. (John Cowper Powys had had the original idea in *One Hundred Best Books*.) To Powell, Miller spoke feelingly, as he often did, of the books he had read as a child, the magic of books, the splendor of the stacks in public libraries. Finally Powell interrupted: "Why don't you say something like that in a little script that I can have printed up for the friends of the library?" Miller jumped at the idea, since (as he told a bibliographer friend) such an account "should complement my life story"; it would "supplement the autobiographical 'novels' I have written—round out the picture of my life, so to speak." He plunged right in and on index cards drew up a list of 5,000 books that he could recall reading. (D.H.

434

Lawrence and Maurice Maeterlinck represented the largest number of titles.) Soon, as if he were filling a shopping list, Powell began to truck boxes of books from UCLA to Big Sur, and Henry's friends supplied volumes that Powell could not. Once, in his notebook for *Tropic of Capricorn*, he had observed concerning his tendency to digress: "It is impossible for me to write even the most fantastic tale without mention of books and authors . . . books and authors are a vital part of me, they too are in my blood, carried along with my living, part of my hate and love." Books *were* his life: as a man of imagination he certainly should be able to write an autobiography of his reading.

Like most of Miller's works, this excursus on his reading was a cautionary tale—an attempt to discourage reading by showing how much time he had wasted in reading worthless books. But it also soon became exhuberant as did most of his other works. It was an account of the way he had come through a vast amount of dross and *dreck* and yet at last did discover in some books that vital material of imagination which everyone sought in literature. It is, like much of his other work, a moralizing book, with an aroma of Lord Chesterfield and an eighteenth-century spirit of instruction hovering about it. First he titled it "The World of Books," then "The Quick and the Dead" (the two kinds of books), and finally—alluding to Nerval's *Dreams in Life*—*Books in My Life*. That was really the best title, since he wished to emphasize the intimate connections between life and literature. Though burdened with correspondence and plagued by visitors he wrote *Books in My Life* quickly, turning out as many as 100 pages in one month. By January 1951, almost exactly a year from the day he had begun the script, he finished a revised, third, final draft.

A genuine calmness came over Henry during this period. Whatever he did, he would stand still, he felt, as if in the storm's eye. By 1950 he began to feel that he had lived through his suffering. His desires quieted. "What I fail to accomplish in this life," he wrote, "I may do in the next . . . I make little or no plans for the future. I do what I can each day and let the future take care of itself." He believed that he had lived his desires through and achieved liberation. This had been his whole story, he began to see. Whether he wrote about friends, critically interpreted the work of others, analyzed the defects of his native land, revealed his happy life of shame in Paris, or narrated his adventures on the streets or in the study, his was a simple tale—of liberation.

But his own life was imprisoning him in the consequences of personal failure. Even the birth of a son on August 28, 1948 had not been able to restore peace with Lepska. Indeed the baby had intensified disputes about child-rearing. (Henry named his son Henry Tony—the name June had once said she would name their son, the name of Henry's first alter ego, Tony Bring, of *Crazy Cock.*)

Lepska had increasingly felt that she was unappreciated and that she was wasting her life in bitter quarrels. She fell in love with a biophysicist and in July 1951 she left Henry and took the children to stay with her parents in New York. In October she returned to Big Sur to work out arrangements with Henry for the children and a divorce. Miller begged to be allowed to care for them first. Had he wanted full custody of the children, he feared that if he had to fight Lepska for them in a court a judge would probably be unsympathetic towards the author of *Sexus,* a book suppressed even in France, and would refuse to allow him to keep an angelic daughter who was just starting school and a boy three years her junior. "If I didn't have my two kids my life would be miserable," he told Durrell. They agreed that the children would spend six months with Henry and alternate six months with Lepska. With the help of his friend Walker Winslow Henry tried to be mother and father to his young children. Soon, however, Henry began to wonder whether Lepska's kindness was one more of the tortures she was determined to inflict upon him. He had never realized how difficult the children were—how impossible it was to take care of them alone. Nonetheless, he vowed he would raise them—he could count on neighbors like Dorothy Herbert and Winslow for aid. Then, finally, he began to scrutinize his willfullness with his intelligence. He wrote to Lepska to come up and take Tony away until the time when he would be able to care properly for the boy. Almost at once he regretted this compromise and, having secured the services of a young woman, brought Tony back with him. But his helper soon decamped, and Henry was simply not able to prepare meals, entertain Tony, wash clothes, mend toys, pack Val off to school, keep the linen fresh, do the shopping, answer his correspondence, paint, travel to San Francisco, take long walks with the kids, play games with them, and, in general, give them an ideal life with father. He could hardly keep up with what the children required, much less what they demanded.

At this point Walker Winslow interceded. One morning he knocked on Henry's studio door. "There's only one thing I can do for you, Henry," he began, "even if it makes you my enemy, and that is to tell you that you've reached the limit of your endurance. You can't manage the kids all alone, much as you love them. And to insist that you can is merely an obsession, a continuation of your argument with Lepska. Are you insisting on keeping the children out of love for them and concern for their welfare or a secret desire to punish your wife? It won't work. It won't bring you happiness. If you do have any peace now and then, it's only a makeshift one, ready to fly apart at any moment. You're not getting anywhere this way. I came here to help you. If you insist on going through with it, I won't desert you, but how long can you hold out? You're a bundle of nerves now. Frankly, Henry, you're licked—but you won't admit it to yourself."

Miller stood at the studio door and listened quietly as Winslow uttered Henry's worst fears, yet he felt relieved that the decision might be lifted from his hands. He promised Winslow to think about his words overnight; and the next day he sent Lepska a telegram asking her to take the children. "Walker," he wailed, "I'm throwing in the sponge." But a few lonely days later, he moaned in self-accusation that had he only been able to hold out a little longer, tried harder, and had more courage, he would still have the children with him. He was sore at Winslow for catching him in a moment of weakness and exhaustion. And he wept over the things that the children had left behind . . . the toys and tops and pieces of outgrown clothing, the fingerprints on the wall, the drinking tumblers and spoons . . . as if tears could bring them back. He blamed himself for being a failure as a father.

Now he was alone with plenty of time for writing, but he found that he had lost almost all desire and certainly all spontaneity. He wanted to write *Nexus* and finish his trilogy, but there was a wall between himself and his experience. He summoned the dictation, but no voice so much as whispered. Was he too old? Had his recent sufferings at last killed his capacity to be stirred by his ancient griefs? He had become a writer just to tell this one story. To have suffered, to have been castigated as an offender of public morals, to have been subjected to a million annoyances—and *not* to finish his story—wouldn't that mean that he had become a writer for nothing? Self-doubts and unanswerable questions preyed on him. He had to ask himself: Was he washed up as a writer?—finally failing, where he had always failed, in trying to tell this one story?

He had no long period in which to give these questions a thorough test. Just when Henry felt he was finished as a lover and probably as a writer, he suddenly found that a very pretty, intelligent young woman was in love with him! In late November 1951, Eve McClure began to write to him from her home in Beverly Hills. In her first letter she mentioned that she was Bezalel Schatz's sister-in-law and, being often in Big Sur, they had stopped at his house several times only to find it closed. But recently she had read *Tropic of Capricorn* and she wanted "to see the reality of the genius that produced such a work of art." Her letters were genuine and vivacious and soon Henry was writing back and sending her books. He heard from Schatz that she gave "glowing accounts" of him to her family.

In March of 1952, during a visit to the children at Long Beach, Miller used the excuse of Val's measles and his own cold to stay in southern California and meet Eve. He found her absolutely beautiful. Of course she was young—still in her twenties—but she seemed quite entranced with him and they got along wonderfully. If the gods took his talent with one hand, perhaps they would give him a wife with the other. Henry had a twinkle in his eye again, but this sixty year old man and this twenty-eight year old woman were both shy about declaring to each other or anyone else that it was virtually love at first sight. They acted as if they were con-spirators and left little love notes for each other at the Special Collections desk at UCLA library. When he drove back to Big Sur, Eve went with him. Miller was simply ecstatic. To describe Eve to his friends he had to compare her to his great love. She "reminds me in many ways of Anaïs," he wrote Durrell, "like Anaïs again, she brings with her the feeling of ease and abundance." "She's all I hoped for and more. A pure gift from the gods," he told an acquaintance. She gave him exactly what he desired: a free, unconditional offer of her love. Eve was a tender, all-giving, understand-ing, and gracious woman, an especially fine cook, a great reader, and a sensitive artist. She smiled a lot and she looked good smiling. "I tell you," Miller wrote to Durrell, "I feel like a new man—and about fifty years younger! . . . It's like living on velour, to be with her."

With Eve to help him Henry realized that he could have the children in Big Sur for the summers and for alternate years, and this gave him great joy. Eve and Emil White built a swimming pool for the kids and in its sides embedded sea shells, coins, and tiles—"so beautiful," Henry said, "you can bury me in this." He hurried through a property settlement, involving joint ownership of the house, with Lepska. Through a revival of his "Dollar a Week Campaign" ("Keep up till I say stop"), he collected some money from his old friends. He also mailed out a printed advertisement offering his books and paintings "at prices no higher . . . than ordinary ground burial rates." He advised his customers to order "in carload lots," making it clear that "due to the ever-increasing cost of living plus exorbitant taxation," he needed all the dough he could lay his hands on.

Again, in 1952 life seemed wonderful to him. He had everything he wanted—a woman who was young and vibrant, and a real home, a place to bring the children. Val and Tony gave him enormous pleasure. By loving them and doing little things for them, he made peace with his own childhood, and he felt sunny and contented. He still had a wonderful sense of play, and the children gave him plenty of chance to play. Eve loved the children in a splendid, natural way. She was tender and good with them, truly concerned about them, and they responded well to her. Henry glowed as he watched her care for them. She was the kind of miracle he had always dreamed of in a woman. So with her and the kids, the house in Big Sur came alive for him again. Eight years after he first arrived, he regained his original vision of the paradise he had discovered there. Between 1944 and 1947 he had been supremely happy in Big Sur, until troubles with Lepska and the appearance of several devils had sent him out of paradise, sore and restless. Now, in 1952, the gates opened and for the next three years life was merry again.

Like tumblers in a lock everything seemed to fall into place. He suddenly found that for the first time since 1940 he wanted to return to Europe; this was part of his sense of renewal and triumph, this revival of his spirit of adventure. He felt like a child and wanted to indulge himself and Eve.

On New Year's Eve 1952, they set down at Le Bourget airfield in a fog and snowstorm and started a seven-month visit which was mostly a disappointment to him. Europe seemed to be in rapid decline. (How could it live up to his dreams?) Europe was destined, he believed, to be caught in a cross-fire between Russia and the United States. He found dry-rot wherever he looked in Europe. "We are in the Apocalyptic Era" was the constant refrain of his letters home. Even in his first few days in Paris he was unexpectedly morose: every corner he turned faced him with a recollection of defeat. True, he was praised on every hand, he heard a continuous roar of adulation. But he was bothered by the questions of reporters and he couldn't help noticing that the cheers were mostly for books he had written nearly twenty years before. What had he done in the last ten years that his admirers considered worthy of praise? What writing, indeed, had he done at all in the last two years? He was in the middle of the longest dry period he had ever experienced and the praise that resounded about him sounded hollow. Strange to say, he actually did feel an itch to write—maybe Paris gave him that, too—but he had no typewriter and anyway he never wrote well on the wing. The frustration of this literary impulse irritated him.

Besides, he found the weather unexpectedly cold, he caught the flu, he longed for Big Sur with its restorative sulphur baths, and he missed the children very much.

For a while his spirits revived. Enthusiastic about everything, Eve fell in love with France: she declared herself ready to become a citizen. Besides, they were soon cozily installed in the Latin Quarter *chez* Maurice Nadeau and visited by old friends like Georges Belmont, Hans Reichel, Brassai, and even the long lost Eugene Pachoutinsky of the Cinéma Vanves. Correa & Cie, his principal French-language publishers, gave Henry a wonderful reception at which hundreds of the most distinguished men of the city appeared. In France his face was as famous as a movie star's and people just wanted to see him. Some attempted to embrace him in gratitude for his writing.

A little worn out by all of this, he accompanied his publisher, Edmond Buchet, to his little house outside Paris at Le Vésinet, for a rest. The cold fog congealed his good humor again. Once each day Henry walked past the house of Utrillo, hoping to see him, but the artist never showed his face: *he would have to be truly mad to come out in this cold,* Henry thought, wondering what he himself was doing in this cold. All day he dreamed of Big Sur and all night of the sunny south of France and all the good friends in Provence who had urged him to visit them. At the end of January he and Eve left for Monte Carlo. Bad memories of his early days in Monte Carlo made the place seem like a morgue, and they hurriedly departed for Le Ciotat, near Marseilles, where the French actor Michel Simon opened his house to Miller. The town was a little wild, a little like Big Sur, but the Mistral was blowing, blowing, blowing and the only way Miller could get warm was to huddle in the kitchen before an open fire.

Eve and Henry drifted around a bit until the Schatzes came from Jerusalem to join them and all together they met the Delteils at Montpellier for a holiday jaunt to Spain. Miller had always wanted to go to that country and it seemed that even as they crossed the border, below Peripignan, the sun came out. Perlès met them in Barcelona and for two solid days it was like old times—anything might set them roaring. They sat at sidewalk cafés laughing unrestrainedly and reminiscing grandly, playing as they had always done.

For the next month they toured Spain. With its incredible ranges of color in sky and earth and its immense vistas and rugged features (reminding him often of Big Sur), the Spanish landscape seemed wonderful to Miller. He enjoyed everything. When they at last left Spain by way of Andorra, he decided that he was glad not to have made it there in 1930. Had he done so, he would have written nothing. He might have become a humble fisherman, or a smuggler. He would have had friends and a sturdy wife and doubtless been surrounded by children. Or perhaps he would have been slaughtered in the bloody revolution.

If a paradise existed anywhere, it was in Big Sur, whither they returned at the end of August 1953. Eve agreed that Big Sur was the real paradise. "What is 'paradise' to Henry," Eve wrote to Emil White, "—*is* a paradise for me, too, Emil . . . I am *happy* there—as I have never been before." For the first time in his life Henry experienced a love that continued to grow. "We love—increasingly," Eve wrote to Emil. "All is and will be better and better—with the rich years ahead." No longer harassed, no longer feeling driven, Henry could settle down happily in Big Sur. By no means did he vow never to leave Big Sur again—he was in fact thinking of at last going to Japan since his books and even his paintings were selling well there—but he was delighted to be home. And it was time for him to receive visitors himself. Four important guests came in rapid succession to Big Sur.

First of all, in the fall of 1953, the Greek colossus, George Katsimbalis, came to the United States on a mission of cultural exchange and made straight for Big Sur. No sooner had Katsimbalis left than the critic Van Wyck Brooks and his wife Gladys arrived. Brooks had become a Miller devotee, and was to propose Henry for election to the National Institute of Arts and Letters.

Wonderful though they were, these visits were overshadowed when Henry's daughter Barbara suddenly appeared. He had believed her to be lost to him. More than twenty years earlier he had told Osborn he would never give up the hope that someday he'd be able to "reach the girl and be able to tell her things in a straightforward way." He sent her a lot of postcards from Europe, but never got an answer. Around 1940 he had enlisted the aid of his then agent John Slocum, Joe O'Regan, and numerous other friends, in vain attempts to communicate with her. He lost sight of her around 1944—though ironically at the time that Henry had settled down in Big Sur, Beatrice and Barbara had moved to Pasadena, California, not more than twenty miles from his former Beverly Glen lodgings. Then in February 1954, out of the blue, the postman delivered a letter from her, marked: "Henry Miller, Big Sur, California." She explained that she had only recently happened upon an article about his life in Big Sur which appeared in the December 1951 issue of *Family Circle*. Until she saw that, she had not known where he lived or how to get in touch with him. But she had been thinking of him for the last few years and no longer had any reservations about meeting him: in fact, she was hoping to do so. This was the fulfillment of his oldest dream. He replied the same day, inviting her to pay him a visit, and she came in June. Barbara and he got along immediately, just as he had dreamed. Naturally, he saw himself in her. She was built like him, slender and wiry, and was about his height. When she grinned, her cheek bones stood out, just as his did. She played the piano—that reminded him, not altogether unpleasantly, of Beatrice and his own piano-playing days. Best of all, she had turned out well: she was obviously a hard-working, spirited girl, and held no grudges against him. He reveled in seeing Barbara and Val together; they all got along, and he felt tremendous joy.

Finally, in November, another visitor arrived. Alfred Perlès came to stay with Henry in order to write the last section of his biography, *My Friend, Henry Miller*. It was more the story of a friendly relationship than a narrative of Henry's life. It was written from the "soul's memory" and was decidedly casual about dates; but it sparkled with laughter of those old times. The two friends walked the hills, painted together, took trips to Los Angeles and San Francisco, read and wrote, and above all made merry.

On his way home to England Fred Perlès stopped in at 1063 Decatur Street, Brooklyn, for a few moments, and reported: "Lauretta tried to explain the television set to me but I told her I wasn't mechanically minded. She may be a simpleton but she's very warm and friendly, and resembles you a little, Joey. I liked her very much. Both seem to be quite happy, I asked if there was anything I or you could do for them, but they're apparently O.K. and in need of nothing. Then I told them, before leaving, what a big and important guy you are, Joey, that I was sent all the way from England to write a book about you, and your mother said 'Henry was always a good boy.' But there was a tear in her eye. Lauretta kept explaining the television set to me. I embraced them both tenderly and left after about half an hour."

Twelve

A Womb in Which the Sun is Bursting

In 1956 Miller planned to resume work on *Nexus*. But as soon as he started to write the conclusion of *The Rosy Crucifixion*, an inner voice kept urging: "Now is the time to tell the world about your quiet life in remote Big Sur." He headed his first page "Peace and Solitude: A Free Fantasia" and started right in. "It flows out like water," he observed, "I'm at it all day long like a madness." This book was a potpourri in which Miller assembled a variety of elements and forced them together. One of the leading themes was contained in the earlier piece on Moricand called "A Devil in Paradise." Moricand, however, is not the only devil in the book. Lepska is his female counterpart. Henry doesn't even attempt to treat Lepska or Moricand realistically or to account for his third wife's good qualities; rather he uses devices of distortion and surrealism, as Bosch did in his paintings, to portray his fellow humans as devils; his special targets are those whose approach to life is rigid. Miller's main point was that any person who is tied to any system is bound to become selfish; in contrast, the man who has left system behind and takes experience as it comes will take a generous, wholesome, flexible view of existence.

The Moricand section, Miller told his agent Hoffman, was "a most important part of the book, since it features the rejection of Paradise," and it pleased him most. "I nailed him to the cross and then incinerated him—with love and tenderness plus a few flame-throwers," he chortled to Schatz. Other sections of the book took up the theme of a Paradise Lost from other angles. Like the hero of *Lost Horizon*, Henry portrayed himself seeking a paradise he had lost—through Moricand or through other friends who failed him. In a very striking way the book is also a confession that he was attracted to Moricand, for instance, because, in fact, he himself resembled Moricand in so many ways. But if Miller saw himself in the monster, then, could he worm his way back into paradise again? He had to rid himself of the Moricand in him. So he continued the story of his life through an account of the Big Sur environment in which he had lived for a decade. It had the pastoral character of *Walden;* Miller's depiction of his friends resembles Thoreau's chapter, "Brute Neighbors." Also influenced by a book by William Franger, Miller fused a stream of fantasy with his autobiographical potpourri by embroidering freely on the themes of Hieronymus Bosch's apocalyptic triptych *The Millennium,* and to point up this association, he gave the book its final title: *Big Sur and the Oranges of Hieronymous Bosch.*

In January 1956, when he was working on a section called "In the Beginning," he received word that his mother was dying of cancer of the liver. His mother was very low when he arrived at her bedside in the first week of February. But three tedious, terrible months passed in New York before she died, while he longed to be back in Big Sur, to complete his book or to build it up further, and to see his children. The only work he did was a set of records titled *Henry Miller Recalls and Reflects,* arranged by Ben Grauer of NBC. So much preoccupation with his mother ate at him since he had never really come to terms with his relationship to her. He slept poorly. An old dream, a suppressed memory of being taken to a park by his mother, haunted him. They were going to hear Adelina Patti sing. Somehow he knew this was the first day of creation. Suddenly, everything turned green, a beautiful, rich sap green, as thick and liquid as if it had been squeezed out of a gigantic tube. The words of the twenty-third Psalm seemed to be colors, which flashed and danced like golden notes. He ran toward his mother, through green hills and golden sun, past black shadows deep as wells and dark as an eclipse. There was his mother, Patti herself, singing and twirling her luxurious green parasol. She, his mother, called to him to run to her. She was waiting for him. Neither a woman nor a mother, she was but a great parasol of a womb in which the sun was bursting in seeds of flame. In guilty dignity, he walked up to her and said: "I am here . . . I have come."

Yet, in his waking hours he insisted that his mother had always been an obstacle to him. Eve argued against him, "When she dies, you will miss her." That made him angry: "Never!" he said. "I was through with her long ago, her death will mean nothing to me. There was never anything between us!" But they struggled with each other right to the end. Even when she was dying she never lost her strength of will. But he was stronger now. "Christ!" Eve wrote to Emil White, "—I saw a demonstration of her 'strength' day before yesterday that scared me . . . . You should have seen Henry handle her! I'm certain he actually enjoyed it—the first time in his life he ever had the power-over-the-throne, I'll bet." Louise never ceased to reproach him for being a failure or to order him about as though she were an empress. Often, he refused to visit her, sending his young friend Vincent Birge in his place. When Henry came himself she'd torment him by saying that Vincent was a nice boy, the kind of young man she had wished Henry to be. On her very deathbed she was still berating him. Once, toward the end, she even pushed herself up in bed to do so. At this he became angry. "You're ill now," he cried. "No more such talk!"—and he pushed her back. A few days later she died. "A new life begins," he wrote to a friend. "Day by day—that's the motto now."

Once home he polished off *Big Sur and the Oranges of Hieronymous Bosch* quickly, for he was preoccupied with a variety of petty annoyances: getting Lauretta settled in a nearby rest home, learning from Lepska that Tony had broken his collarbone and needed money for medical expenses, and fearing that Beatrice was preparing to sue him for all the alimony owed her since 1924! But once it was published, *Big Sur and the Oranges of Hieronymous Bosch* became the greatest annoyance of all; for now that it was even more widely known that he lived on Partington Ridge in Big Sur, a steady procession of pilgrims made their way up the hill. He had so many visitors and so much mail, he complained in despair, that even by using form letters he couldn't find time to answer all the extra correspondence—requiring two or three hours a day—that the book had inspired. What was it the visitors wanted? Most simply desired to tell their friends they had seen Henry Miller. Some stood silently waiting for him to drop some pearls of wisdom: they saw him as their guru. Many wished him to hear their life story in minute detail. Most demanded his time as if it were of no value. Some made it quite clear that they considered themselves his guests: When would lunch be ready? How about a little drink before lunch just to wet the whistle while they read a new story to him? Some saw no impropriety in arriving at night, rousing him out of bed: he and Eve were once awakened at 2 a.m. by a couple opening the door to their room with a flashlight in hand. Several young men and women, who had read of the way Henry had sponged off a variety of people, proposed that he should take them in for a year or two. Some hinted that a stipend of a hundred or so a month would suit them fine. About five book manuscripts arrived in the mail every week. Two enterprising fellows arrived to request that he will his cock to them. A few women showed up who proposed that he make more immediate use of it.

In inducting him into the National Institute of Arts and Letters in 1957 Louise Bogan cited Miller's "originality and richness of technique," his "boldness of approach and intense curiosity." He was honored in 1959, as few authors are, by the founding of an organization devoted to his work, "The Henry Miller Literary Society," founded by Eddie Schwartz in Minneapolis; its newsletter achieved international circulation. No living American writer had a greater international reputation. Rumors began to circulate that he was a strong candidate for the Nobel Prize. Yet in Big Sur he was harrassed by admirers, pursued by creditors, and worried by debts. He found time only to rework old materials. He took two tales written in 1940—"Quiet Days in Clichy" and "Mara-Marignan Marinated"—and fused them, under the first title, into a short novel that was perhaps his best work of fiction since *Tropic of Capricorn* and certainly suggests the enormous talent for literary legerdemain which Henry could still summon. He made a superbly charming and breezy book out of two ordinary tales. Next he took up *The World of Sex* and extensively rewrote it for publication by Girodias' new Olympia Press. The result was again a brilliant success.

Miller's tendency was always to look backward whenever he had lost the way forward and to lose himself in writing whenever he lost his path in life. He definitely lost himself in his writing following his mother's death. He wrote a great deal, of a rather unpredictable and uneven sort, skipping without direction from sexual rhapsodies to metaphysical clichés, from amusing literary fantasies to work-a-day introductions requested by publishers (Gallimard gave him $150 for a few pages on *The Odyssey* and he got the same amount for introducing Jack Kerouac's *The Subterraneans.*) Though some of this work in the late fifties had marvellous flashes, even the best pieces also showed evidence of old habits, old attitudes, old perceptions, and old catchwords. Durrell and other friends were worried that America had softened his critical faculties. "Give up the self-indulgent," they urged, "and sharpen up the Bowie-Miller blades again!"

In the fall of 1958 Miller was reminded in the most vivid manner possible that time was passing, though his "real" work lay unfinished. Hans Reichel and Emil Schnellock both died rather suddenly. On Thanksgiving Day, within a week after hearing the news of these deaths, Henry had a vision. At sundown he walked into the hills with his dogs. Everything was aglow. Clearly silhouetted against the transparent sky were horses and riders moving across the spine of the mountain's crest. He tried to draw the attention of the dogs to them and even bent over the big one to point his head in the right direction. Then, as he straightened up, he felt he saw a huge, pale blue bird, a condor it might have been judging by its enormous wingspan, come hurtling towards him, through the liquid air. He ducked to avoid being struck. But just before the thing reached him it turned into a glittering, spinning propeller blade for a moment, and then vanished abruptly. Not long after, Michael Fraenkel also died. The signs looked ominous, as if his old friends were clay pigeons set up for picking off by ghostly propellers. A little uneasily, Henry began to write in his letters: "Reichel . . . Schnellock . . . Fraenkel . . . who's next?"

A sense of fatality pulled him up short. Immediately, he went through the files and papers accumulated in his studio, threw away everything inessential and put the rest in order. He turned his entire correspondence over to Eve. He retired by 9 p.m. and arose at 5 a.m. This, he felt, was his last push, his last chance to finish his life story. Working for a few months at a pitch that was near madness, he finished *Nexus* by the end of January 1959, with a marvellous litany of farewell to America. By early April the book was thoroughly revised. Some of his friends were sure that he expected to die when he put an end to *Nexus*. Instead, he vowed to continue his tale in still another book. He wasn't finished with the story of his life after all. There was always one more episode in it to write. But he delayed starting the second, "concluding" volume of *Nexus*. And he lived on.

Thirteen

We Who Make Life Unliveable

Though he was the most famous living author of banned books, Miller had devoted comparatively little attention to questions of a theoretical sort concerning the nature of pornography and obscenity, before May of 1957, when the Attorney General of Norway ordered *Sexus* seized on the grounds that it was "obscene writing" and instituted proceedings against two booksellers. In June 1958 these defendants were found guilty and appealed to the Norwegian Supreme Court. For the benefit of the defense in the case brought against *Sexus* in Oslo, Henry wrote a resounding apologia in the form of a long letter to the defense attorney, Trygive Hirsch. A fervent plea for the freedom to read, this essay stands with D.H. Lawrence's "Pornography and Obscenity" and "À Propos of *Lady Chatterley's Lover.*" Miller came to the heart of the legal question through discussing the aesthetics of his "auto-romances":

To be precise, the question is—are the author of these questionable works and the man who goes by the name of Henry Miller one and the same person? My answer is yes. And I am also one with the protagonist of these 'autobiographical romances.' That is perhaps harder to swallow. But why? Because I have been 'utterly shameless' in revealing every aspect of my life. I am not the first author to have adopted the confessional approach, to have revealed life nakedly, or to have used language supposedly unfit for the ears of school girls. Were I a saint recounting his life of sin, perhaps these bald statements relating to my sex habits would be found enlightening, particularly by priests and medicos. They might even be found instructive.

But I am not a saint . . . . No, I am not a saint, thank heaven! nor even a propagandist of a new order. I am simply a man; a man born to write, who has taken as his theme the story of his life, a rich life, a merry life, despite the ups and downs, despite the barriers and obstacles (many of his own making), despite the handicaps imposed by stupid codes and conventions. Indeed, I hope that I have made more than that clear, because whatever I may say about my own life which is only *a* life, is merely a means of talking about life itself, and what I have tried, desperately sometimes, to make clear is this, that I look upon life itself as good, good no matter on what terms, that I believe it is *we* who make it unliveable, *we,* not the gods, not fate, not circumstance.

"This trial," he said—the trial of life itself, really—"has been going on since the days of Prometheus."

His letter was published under the title of "Defense of the Freedom to Read" in the summer of 1959 issue of *The Evergreen Review,* a publication of the Grove Press. The owner of the press, Barney Rosset, saw of course that given American laws against obscenity such a statement could be used to supreme advantage in an attack upon censorship in the United States. Thus, when Miller and Eve took the children to Europe in the summer of 1959 Rosset asked Girodias to bring him and Miller together informally at a lunch. Clearly, Miller saw, the two publishers had something on their minds. Rosset mentioned that Vladimir Nabokov's *Lolita,* originally published by Girodias' Olympia Press, had been originally banned in the United States but recently its free circulation in a Putnam edition had been protected by court decisions. At this very time, Rosset said, he was getting ready to publish *Lady Chatterley's Lover* and to fight through the courts for freedom to sell it. He expected to win—but this would not satisfy him. Nothing would do but victory against censorship on all fronts. And that would only come when the right of anyone to buy *Tropic of Cancer* and *Tropic of Capricorn* was established! He wanted this, he added, not for its commercial success, for he was willing to exhaust his resources in court, but as his contribution to the growth of freedom in the United States. He put his proposition on practical and moral grounds. Henry, who had done so much to free American writing, might do as much for Ameican reading by allowing Grove Press to present his case as an offensive against American censorship. He and Girodias joined together to urge Henry to give Grove the American rights to publish *Tropic of Cancer* and *Tropic of Capricorn* in this country. Certainly, Rosset said, Miller didn't have to make a decision at once but why not think about it, consider the prospect? Miller explained that as long ago as 1939, K.S. Giniger, the owner of Signet Press, had consulted an attorney about setting up a test case on the admissibility of the books into the United States. In 1944, Miller and James Laughlin had discussed a possible New Directions edition with blanks for the offensive words and instructions on how to contact Miller for printed up lists of words which could be pasted in. In 1948 Penguin books had made Miller an "unacceptable offer" to print *Cancer* in an expurgated edition. One of the distributors of the so-called Mexican edition (Medusa-Impenta de Mexico) had been sent to jail for ten years. As recently as 1953 George Oldhausen of the ACLU in San Francisco had lost a case concerning the banning of *Tropic of Cancer*. When two film makers—James B. Harris and Stanley Kubrick—approached him in 1958 about adapting the *Tropics* to the screen, he was cold. "No," he said, "I am going to hold out to the day when we really have freedom of expression." Such a time, he believed, would "probably not [come] in my time, if ever."

So, Miller shrugged Rosset's idea off as a pipe dream, but he continued to lend an ear to Rosset's campaign of gentle persuasion, and he couldn't help but speculate from time to time whether he would live to see his books sold openly in America. He always concluded that the answer was obvious— NO! He was certainly not writing objectionable books anymore, only minor essays or literary commentaries like those which he contributed to the discussion of his work in Perlès and Durrell's *Art and Outrage* or pleasant texts for illustrated books, like *To Paint is to Love Again*, (Henry's only commissioned piece, suggested by his friend Bill Webb).

He had, he felt, enough troubles without raising the hackles of the authorities. His problems could be divided into two categories. The first was sheer physical decline—he had recurrent trouble with his ear drum and his hip, resulting in a series of operations beginning in 1960. The second involved problems with wives. Beatrice was apparently simmering over the way she had been represented in *My Friend, Henry Miller* and *Sexus* and she might boil over and sue him at any time. Lepska was divorced again in 1958 and wrote to him that she had money problems, that her life was sterile.

And trouble in his once velvety marriage with Eve came after seven years. (This seven-year cycle in Henry's affections remained remarkably constant from Pauline onward.) In 1960 it was time for another woman to arrive on Henry's amorous horizon.

Actually, Henry was by no means entirely to blame for the breakup of his marriage. At the least Eve shared the blame. Eve really loved Henry, and she yearned to be good to him. But she was pulled in many directions—by her strong sexual drives; by her feeling that she was approaching middle age without having accomplished anything on her own (she wanted to be an artist and she had lots of talent); by alcohol; and by simply being married to a famous man and having to be both an intellectual companion to him and a mother to his children. Finding these more than she could reconsile, she began to drift away from Henry.

For his part, he responded to this by drifting towards a new, positive relationship. One night in the fall of 1959 Henry walked alone into the Nepenthe bar in Big Sur and noticed a lovely young woman, a waitress there, dancing with a man he knew. "How can you find any pleasure in dancing with homosexuals?" he asked her. Perhaps his spirit of competition was aroused. The woman answered pleasantly and they talked on at length. Her name was Caryl Hill. She had grown up in the area, been married and divorced and had a child. For a time she had attended the University of California at Berkeley. She was eager and enthusiastic and liberated; serious about things she smiled and laughed easily—and she certainly smiled a lot at Henry. Within a few days he was back at Nepenthe looking for her.

The third time he saw her he and Eve came together to the bar, and Eve started drinking and refused to leave. When Henry walked outside to sit and wait in the car, Caryl followed him out and slid into the seat next to him. Henry was delighted—romance was in the air again.

Later that same fall, while Eve stayed for extended periods in Berkeley to be near her ill mother, Henry began to have a serious affair with Caryl. Caryl sometimes posed nude for the drawing class Eve attended and Eve found it strangely awkward to be intensely inspecting the body of a woman with whom her husband was sleeping. One afternoon when Caryl was at the house she spoke out directly: "I know you and Henry are very fond of each other," she said to them, "and of course love is a great thing and no one should stand in its way, and even a temporary flirtation can be very exciting, so why don't you two just go right upstairs to bed, I really mean it." It was an act of dissimulation, of course, a desperate one: she thought that if she could treat the matter contemptuously she could rob it of all its romance. But the result wasn't entirely what Eve expected. Henry actually found the prospect exciting—sleeping with a young woman right in the same house with his wife! But Caryl saw that Eve was suffering, even though Eve tried to give her some of her sexiest nightgowns to wear. Caryl went up and tucked Henry into bed, and then found Eve and comforted her, assuring her that Henry really did love her. Eve sobbed about her supposed failures, and Caryl stayed with her until she became quiet and fell asleep.

Eve was driven on all sides by problems—not only her own, but Henry's, and in general by her share in the complexity of his life. In addition to all the other sources of tension in her life, Eve had taken over part of Henry's correspondence and sometimes had to respond to demanding or pleading letters from Henry's former loves, June, Lepska, and Anaïs. Eve was a good, loving person who wanted to keep a home together for Henry and the children and herself, but now she felt continually awkward and embarrassed, unsure of herself and of Henry. She couldn't deal with him, his wives, and all the visitors he attracted, and now a new girl friend. Besides, she was hurt by what she interpreted as Henry's indifference to her emotions; his hints that he might take a trip in the spring to Japan, Siam, and Burma sounded as though he wanted to toss her aside. When he actually went ahead and accepted an invitation to be a judge at the 1960 International Film Festival in Cannes and said he would go over by himself, she despaired. What was worse, she became aware that he intended to have Caryl join him in Europe. Then, shamed, Eve started to drink very heavily and she never really stopped. She gave up on their marriage, and because she felt guilty, she gave up on herself.

Henry definitely decided to go to Europe, spend some time alone on business and pleasure, then have Caryl meet him in Cannes just at the conclusion of the Festival. From his point of view, too, his marriage to Eve was coming to an end.

Before the International Film Festival started Miller journeyed to Hamburg to visit his German publisher, Ledig Rowohlt, whom he had met on his previous trip to Europe. Henry was glad to leave his problems behind him in Big Sur, and now he was ready to play. In many ways he was returning to his childhood. When his plane touched down in Hanover, for instance, he cajoled a stewardess off the plane for a cozy drink. The result? They both missed the plane as it continued on into Hamburg. Five or six journalists and photographers who awaited his arrival in Hamburg had to cool their heels for another hour until the next flight came in. So did Rowohlt's assistant, who was waiting in the terminal to greet him with a big bouquet of roses. Once he saw her, he forgot all about the stewardess. Frau Renate Gerhardt was a young, very attractive, dark, German woman who spoke English beautifully and handled the English-language books at Rowohlt Verlag. With her short dark hair and big eyes she reminded him instantly of one of his old idols, the Italian actress Falconetti, who had made a lasting impression on him as Joan of Arc in the Delteil-Dreyer silent film. He had been loquacious and bouncy everywhere he had gone: but beyond explaining about the stewardess episode in guarded terms he didn't seem to have anything to say to Renate. He was morose and shy, signs that a person he could love was at hand. Renate chattily explained that following World War II she and her husband had been the first translators into German of Eliot and Pound and they had also translated the first chapter of *Tropic of Cancer* in their magazine, *Fragmenten*. Talk of translation led her to observe that the Rowohlt translation of *Tropic of Cancer* was not especially good: with shocking insensitivity the translator invariably chose the pornographic rather than the obscene word. She began to give him examples of what she meant, and he found himself blushing and excited to hear a beautiful girl talk in four-letter words. His ears perked up when she said her husband had been dead for seven years. Within a few days he was telling her flirtatiously how much he "looked up" to her, how wonderful she was. He was ready to fall in love all over again.

The International Film Festival itself interrupted this new romance. He had to leave Germany for Cannes. But he enjoyed himself at the Festival. As a judge Henry had the chance to be a gadfly and to make some outrageous suggestions for the prize. Then, near the conclusion of the judging Caryl joined him in Cannes, and he enjoyed having her there, taking her around with him, helping her to enjoy herself, and showing her off. He liked Caryl. But he was thinking seriously about Renate, and he pushed Caryl toward other men. For the rest, he enjoyed being with Durrell again, in Cannes and at Durrell's home in Nîmes. That was a highpoint. Durrell always put Henry in fine spirits. After the judging was over, Miller took Caryl to visit his friends in southern France and Italy.

Meanwhile, Eve had been examining their marriage. In mid-May she decided to act. First she wrote to Lepska, with whom she had become good friends. For years, she said, there hadn't "been any sort of marriage, union" between herself and Henry. Now with Henry floating around Europe with "a foolish choice for a companion"—looking, to Eve's eyes, ridiculous and making her look ridiculous—she felt she had at last to admit failure. She wanted Lepska to know that so far as she was concerned the children could always have a place with her. She hoped to remain in Big Sur—perhaps she could simply stay on there as Henry's secretary and business manager, a job she was filling anyway. Then she took a deep breath and wrote to Henry that it was time to get a divorce, not because of Caryl but because she honestly believed that there was no longer any reason for them to remain together, living a lie. "I've no rancour or hurt or anything," she concluded, "but a desire to do what I know is right, and become more and more myself."

Eve's was a good letter, written in the true Henry Miller vein, and Henry took it in good fashion. Her letter caught up with Henry while he and Caryl were at the house of Feltrinelli, his Italian publisher. He was saddened at first—then elated. "I think all you say is quite right," he responded. He begged her not to feel guilty about anything, not to accuse herself: "We're still friends." More than anything else he was relieved, though every time he added up his alimony payments and the support for Lauretta that he had to shell out every month, he felt a little sore. He talked about remarriage with Caryl, but neither of them took that seriously. Caryl, he remarked to a friend, was "not his type." They returned to the United States separately.

Miller told everyone that things were merry and bright for him again. But secretly, inwardly, he was miserable. He didn't want to be out of love—he wanted Renate Gerhardt. She *was* his type. He found that he missed her terribly, especially after returning to the United States. He wrote to her that though his marriage was over he didn't despair of the future. (He was hinting he would consider marrying again.) He felt he could go "on—like some wandering ghost—on to some new phase of existence—who knows what, who cares? But life!" In August 1960 he said: "Deep down all's well. It's simply like shifting gears on your car. One day a new pattern—and the old falls away like a dead snake's skin." He realized that nothing serious had passed between him and Renate—they had merely spent a few days of fun together. Consciously he was convinced that a man approaching seventy could hardly expect to keep attracting young women, but secretly he believed that he might yet win Renate's love. And so, unexpectedly soon he returned to Europe and parked himself and his used Fiat in front of the offices of Rowohlt Verlag, or at Renate's apartment at Schaumannskamp 29.

When he was with Renate they stayed up every night sipping gin and tonic and getting drunk on conversation. Whenever he took short trips, he wrote her letters signed "St. Valentine," as he had done with June. One note he even signed "Gottlieb Leberecht Muller." "It's such a wonderful thing," he told Renate, "to be able to worship someone—in a healthy, natural earthy way." "Love me, as I love you," he urged her. "You are everything." He informed Ben Grauer and other friends that he had found "a new life and love." To his amusement he learned from Eve that news of his divorce had brought two marriage proposals from young women. "Amazing!" he commented, but he begged Eve to "let them down easy": "Tell them I am already taken." He *was*, he felt, "already taken." Within a month he and Renate were talking about getting married, planning a life together.

But, as always, everyday problems began to wear the romance away. Where would they live? Although Henry was sure that America was his real home, Renate insisted that for her children's sakes it must be Europe. She was afraid of the drug scene in America. Henry thought about his own children. Would Val, now fifteen, be ready to leave her friends? Would thirteen-year-old Tony, who had developed a passion for surfing, find any satisfactory European equivalent? This wavering, this indecision, set a bad tone. Both were worried that any compromise would be the end of romance. "More and more I ask myself—can I possibly give you all that you deserve? Be very frank—cruel, if you like—with me," Henry wrote her. If she did have any doubts, he wanted to avoid the "years of misery" that his fears were forecasting.

Settled in his hotel on Rosenplatz Strasse in Reinbeck, he played: Rowohlt set up a ping pong table in his office and Henry spent hours demolishing the employees with his mean cut and snap roll. The company Mercedes and a driver awaited his command. He tossed off a preface to a Gallimard edition to Elie Faure's *History of Art* and wrote a crazy mock-German burlesque called "Ein Üngebumbette Fuchselbiss." He checked the galleys of the Rowohlt translation of *Nexus*. He dashed off several fine, vibrantly colored watercolors. He was happy, life's sap was flowing through his veins.

But the holidays brought their melancholy reminders. He was alone. Renate had to attend her ill father and on Christmas day 1960 Henry made up a big pot of spaghetti for dinner so that he would have enough leftovers for his 69th birthday. He felt like a leftover himself. This kind of misery and self-pity always turned him, for comfort, back to writing. Just recently, Traugott Krieschke in the theatre division of Rowohlt's had insisted that Henry was a "natural dramatist." Now Miller sat down and found himself writing a play. Saroyan's *The Time of Your Life,* Beckett's *Waiting for Godot,* and Ionesco's *The Bald Soprano* were on Miller's mind. Less consciously but certainly in the background was such a Broadway comedy as George Kelly's *The Show Off* (1924). After three days, he finished *Just Wild About Harry,* a "melomelo in three acts," an absurd work, very much in the vein of vaudeville. The play concerns a young man named Harry, various ludicrous characters, and improbable actions. All this was made to seem even more absurd by being mixed with popular songs from Henry's youth. Henry had cured his blues by writing the zany play.

In March 1961, full of hope, he began a six-month quest to find *the* place, some perfect house in Europe where he and Renate and their children could settle down and be happy. It looked simple—but it proved to be a trip as frustrating and harrowing as his trip around America two decades before: Europe was a nightmare—and not even air-conditioned. He told everyone that he could settle almost anywhere, but unconsciously he kept one reservation: the place had to be perfect. Germany was depressing, the Ticino was *too* perfect, Sete was mosquito-ridden in the summer, Ischia was infested with phony artists, Portugal was hot as a furnace, Spain was impoverished-looking. His battered Fiat well symbolized his trip: it broke down in rush-hour traffic in Milan, it was dented in a collision in Padua and damaged in Lisbon, it broke down in Garda and outside Strasbourg. The car also symbolized Miller's state of mind by the end of the quest: if anything he was the more broken and bent. He was very restless, possessed by a sense that his life, though unfulfilled, was coming to a close. Though it made him feel utterly lost and helpless and confused, and even guilty, he couldn't find any place that suited him. Continuously he wrote back to Renate for reassurance: he needed to hear from her constantly; when he did not, he fell into a state of remorsefulness and self-accusation. To make matters worse, he had promised Val and Tony that by the time school let out for summer vacation, he'd have found a place for them. Finally, on the first of June 1961, thoroughly licked, he had to wire Lepska not to plan on his taking the children. He told Eve: "I seem to have gone to pieces completely. I almost thought I would have to go to a sanitarium. Every setback, every failure to find the place, made me more nervous, more anguished, more helpless. Finally, I realized I would have to give up—and that almost knocked me out. I not only feel terribly guilty but a complete failure— helpless." He abhorred the idea of any further travels but he hated to admit defeat. He sensed Renate's disappointment and her unspoken accusations irritated him.

They didn't quarrel. What was worse, Renate insisted on a serious, realistic assessment of their chances together, and that, obviously, turned up uncountable problems. During the day he meditated sourly over the difficulties of life and joked about committing suicide, and at night he often was awakened with a start by the sound of his teeth grinding. What was his destiny? he kept wondering. One astrologer told him that Renate was just right for him, another that she was all wrong. When the stars were uncertain, how could *he* expect to be positive? He simply threw up his hands, left his destiny to the future, and did what every impulse of his being urged him to do: get out of his insoluble predicament and return to America. On the other hand he wasn't anxious to face his woes at home. He was broke, he still owed a sizeable tax bill, he felt empty and harassed, and he believed his life had been smashed to smithereens.

Fourteen

Over the Equator

He was in no state, certainly, to face his second wife, June, and she was
waiting for his arrival in New York. This came as no surprise—Henry
expected her. He had made plans a long time in advance to stop over in New
York City on his way back from Europe and he proposed that June meet
him. Without her knowing it, of course, he had kept informed about her
ever since their divorce. She had married Stratford Corbett, but something
had happened to her, something had snapped in the late thirties: Emil
Schnellock reported that she was dressing severely, like a nun, and looked
cadaverous and ill. "I have not the courage to see her, and yet I must see her
one day—there must be a reckoning," Miller wrote to Claude Houghton.
But the war came, Corbett became an Air Force captain, June followed him
to Texas and Florida, and then he abandoned her at the end of 1942, and she
dropped out of sight. When she had written to Henry begging for aid at the
end of the war, she was living miserably in a dump on Clinton Avenue, near
many of their old haunts. She weighed only sixty-seven pounds. All
through the late forties and early fifties June cried for help constantly,
begging Henry piteously for money, food, his books, snapshots of himself
and his family, his watercolors—anything. She moaned that she was broke
and starving, never had any meat to eat, needed penicillin, that her teeth

458

were gone and her eyes were bad, that she needed money for medical treatments. She lived in a single room in a bad area, on Ninety-fifth near Riverside Drive. Henry enlisted the aid of Annette Kar Baxter, a professor at Barnard who had written a book about him, to help June out by regular visits and little attentions.

Finally, in September of 1961, they met. It was like living out the coda to *The Rosy Crucifixion,* the book that after so many years he had still failed to complete. June gazed at him with admiration. She told him that he looked "wonderfully well, rakish, handsome, dapper, full of energy and exhilaration." But he was stunned. She had become old! Though she was only fifty-eight she was reduced in every way, not only physically but in spirit. All of her old mystery was gone, blown away by the winds of time. He found the whole meeting terribly heart-wrenching and blighting. And yet he felt, he confessed to himself, a spark of pleasure and triumph at this horrible finale to his grand passion. Could he write an account of this meeting, he told himself, it would a make a marvellous pendant to his autobiographical romances. Its theme would be: June was stronger—but *he* had won. But he knew he could not write it.

This "reckoning" with June was the first of two meetings with old and still powerful loves. He had hardly recovered from seeing June when he began preparing to receive Anaïs Nin in California. She herself was the one who proposed they settle their differences. Hearing from Anaïs was quite a surprise—he had really despaired of a reconciliation. As recently as 1955 she had become furious when she learned from the galleys that Alfred Perlès had written about her in *My Friend, Henry Miller.* Insisting that no one must ever know she had any relation to Henry, she finally threatened to sue Perlès if he did not expunge her name from the book. Eventually Perlès was forced to give in to this threat and invent a name for the inventress. On this occasion Miller pointed out to her that, after all, their association had been public and could scarcely be entirely hidden. He was right, of course. An occasional gossip column even linked them together, adding heat periodically to her simmering displeasure. Walter Winchell, for instance, wrote in July 1955: "Miller . . . had a romance with French novelist Anaïs Nin, whose works were also naughty-biographical . . . A friend once cracked: 'It was very romantic, they had the only boudoir in Paris with twin typewriters.'"

But Miller's increasing fame due to the publication of *Tropic of Cancer*—with Nin's preface—gave her an idea. In the spring of 1962, just sixteen years after their last meeting, Anaïs came to tell him of it. The

reunion went off beautifully. To Henry she was "still the same"—a fabulous, mythical creature. Just to be in her presence made life seem radiant
again. She had the same bright angelic smile in her eyes, the same flashing
perceptions. She was still veiled in mystery, as Neptunian as ever.

Her idea was simple. Some time earlier she had learned that Henry had
placed the letters she had written to him in the Special Collections Division
at UCLA, along with his own papers. Partly with an eye toward self-
protection, she had proposed to Powell to "trade" the letters Miller had sent
her for those of hers in UCLA. The trade was made. Now she had the idea of
making a publishable collection of those letters of Miller's—a collection
which would show his own early development and hint at her importance in
furthering it. Would he allow her—or her agent—to edit and select from
his letters to put together a volume called *Letters to Anaïs Nin?* Perhaps a
successful volume would prepare the way for the first volume of the
abridgement of her diary which at last she wanted to issue. Henry was
dazzled at the very idea that after all these years he could do something to
please Anaïs, and he leaped at the idea. He went further, in his old generous
way, and insisted that since his letters really belonged to her, she must take
the royalties from the publication.

First he was reconciled with June—then with Anaïs! These were great
victories for him.

He had been winning on all fronts. When he returned to the United
States in 1961 *Tropic of Cancer* was in every bookstore in New York! It was
the best-selling book in America, and he had found himself the most
famous and widely-discussed author in the country.

Behind the publication of the book lay a series of negotiations. For a long
time Henry Miller was steadfastly opposed to the publication of his own
book in America. Asserting his belief that he would be able to defend *Tropic
of Cancer* in the courts, in April 1959 Barney Rosset of Grove Press proposed
a contract to Michael Hoffman to pay Miller a $10,000 advance and to
assume the costs of all litigation involving the books, even up to the
Supreme Court, and at his own expense. But this offer only opened the
negotiations. From here on, it was a matter of offer, refusal, and counter-
offer. Rosset next offered $2,500 for an option binding Miller within the
next four years to allow no other publisher than Grove Press to issue the
Tropics. Miller also waved that proposition aside, but this time he tried to
explain his position. Partly, he was concerned about personal attacks and
retribution, including arrest, against him: he would not be altogether
surprised to see American Legionnaires show up at his door with buckets of

tar and bags of feathers—such things did happen in the land of the free! However, he was much more afraid of the favorable publicity that publication would generate: photographers, reporters, newshounds, radio and television men, and thousands of autograph seekers would show up, and the mail would pour in, he would be deluged by his so-called "success." To become more famous than he was already would be still more difficult. And what would he get in return? Certainly not money—Hachette would take 40% of the royalties, Agence Hoffman 10% and the tax collector would take half of the rest. If he were lucky he'd have enough left to hire a secretary to answer his mail and an accountant to calculate his liabilities.

Early in 1960, Rosset and Girodias took a new tack. They reminded Miller that the *Tropics* were not protected by U.S. copyright and could be pirated on a large scale—perhaps in bowdlerized editions. Rosset, offering a carrot, also proposed to increase the advance. Again, Miller responded negatively in a letter to Girodias: "We all need money to live. The question is—how much? At what point does it cease to nourish one? With all my ups and downs I have managed to live. What I need will come to me, when I need it, that I am certain of. [But] . . . the more I earn the more problems I have and the less I enjoy what I do earn. I must take care of my children until they are of age; after that, it is their own look out. I see no way to protect anyone through money, through security of any kind. On the contrary, I regard all forms of security as a menace to the progress or development of character." He was not at all opposed to the present circumstance, when people who wanted to read his books had to smuggle them into the country or pay exorbitantly for them. Fine—he thought— the higher prices gave the books added prestige; the difficulty of obtaining them gave them a special status. They made their way, they *were* read, despite every measure the authorities could take. Yet the question of the copyright did bother Miller. After he had held out all these years, a sleazy publisher might arrive on the scene, expurgate the books enough to protect himself legally, and then issue them as if they were the long-awaited *Tropics*.

Events started to move more quickly. Karl Shapiro, the well-known critic and poet, published a very favorable article on Miller in the magazine *Two Cities*. Miller felt that Shapiro's appreciation would "hit like a bomb" and prepare the way for appreciation of his books. He started to take a new view of the usefulness of money as Rosset repeatedly upped the ante. The "drastic changes in my life which I'd like to make right now," he explained to the publisher, would "demand a whacking sum." Meanwhile, Hoffman had been working to hammer out a practical contract. James Laughlin, who believed that years would pass before the *Tropics* could be sold openly, agreed to release Miller from any claims New Directions had. Rosset agreed to separate *Tropic of Cancer* and *Tropic of Capricorn* and to deal with each in a separate contract, as publications to appear one at a time. The new proposal for *Cancer* involved $10,000 as an outright option payment and $40,000 guaranteed against royalties payable immediately upon the execution of a contract for publication on a definite date. Still, Henry balked. It took him until midsummer, 1960, to form his position. He devised a kind of scenario of the future. Suppose Rosset succeeded in having the book published in America? His admirers would hound Miller into seclusion. Suppose Rosset was wrong? For Rosset the whole episode would be high adventure, no matter what the result; but for Miller, the anguish of sensational trials would be torture.

Miller was content with things as they stood:

I have been waging guerilla warfare with my compatriots. To my own way of thinking, I have already won out over them. What I have written cannot be nullified; my works will continue to be circulated in one way or another until they have reached their natural end. The very fact that my books are obtained only with difficulty enhances the prospect of their furtherance. Why go through the torture and mockery of a sensational trial to make them available to any and every one? Of what value, to me, these additional readers? All that I could hope to acquire thus would be more fame and more money. By now I know that one's true fame is kept alive by the good opinion of a thinking few. As for a sudden increase in fortune, it would undoubtedly cause me more harm than good.

Part of my reluctance to wage open combat with our American authorities arises from the fact that I see no evidence of genuine revolt in the people themselves. We have no real radicals, no body of men and women who have the desire, the courage, or the power to initiate a fundamental change in our outlook or in our way of life. We are moving steadily in the opposite direction of Whitman's democratic vision. Every decade we surrender more and more of our privileges and rights because we are determined to live in comfort and security at any price. The nascent, intermittent liberalism which arises from a senseless ease and prosperity strikes me as a tainted and decadent sort. Whatever concessions are made to the mob are made with an eye to lull and stifle any real revolt. We grow more and more Roman every day.

It is not enough, under such an illusory form of freedom and democracy, to win the privilege of reading anything one pleases—usually more trash—but to obtain the right to read books which are distasteful, obnoxious, insidious and dangerous not only to public taste but to those in power.

How can the people wrest such rights and privileges from their appointed representatives when they do not even suspect that they are living in a state of subjugation? When they imagine themselves to be "a free people"? To win a legal battle here or there, even if sensationally, means nothing. One does not acquire real liberty through these operatic victories. There has to be an understanding of what freedom means, and of what it entails. Freedom from what or for what, in other words. From boyhood times I have heard and read much of these sporadic victories both in the courts of the land and on the battlefield, yet all I see is a mob which continues to accept the illusion created by its masters that we are living in a state of freedom.

What I mean to say is that to be hailed and accepted by an unthinking public as the Petronius of our time would afford me no satisfaction. And that is how, if by some freak of fortune *Tropic of Cancer* won out over the courts, I would be regarded. I would triumph as the King of Smut. I would be given the liberty to thrill, to amuse, to shock, but not to edify or instruct, not to inspire revolt. Certainly you must be aware that throughout my autobiographical works, including *The Colossus of Maroussi, The Books in My Life, Hamlet, Big Sur* and the *Oranges,* the overlying thought is to inspire and to awaken, not merely to titillate and amuse the reader. In the process of delivering myself, of submitting to the discipline of writing, I have come to realize that it is I myself who was awakened, that my hidden purpose in writing the story of my life was to free myself of the devils that possessed me. In short, I have no desire to alter or instruct any one now. Naturally, there are still lapses and contradictions both in my utterance and in my behavior, but the primary thing to know—at least *I* know it:—is that I have come to regard the ills and misfortunes which dogged my steps as resulting largely from my own ignorance and inadequacy and not as the random blows of fate. I also know that anything I may accomplish for the benefit of others can only be done indirectly or obliquely. The game—of writing, living, being—has come to be for me the end in itself.

Does all this make any sense to you? It is difficult, after spreading one's thoughts through so many books, to recapitulate or give the essence in a mere letter. You may possibly conclude that I am a fool or an idiot, that I am throwing away my chances, or that my vision is temporarily beclouded. All I can say now, in justification of my stand, is that in pursuing my own way, even blindly, no evil befalls me. My strength and security come from within. I must trust my own intuitions.

Pushed to the wall over whether to have the *Tropics* appear in America, Miller uttered his most noble expression of his convictions as a writer. But even as Miller pondered this problem, Rosset received news that another firm was definitely planning to pirate *Tropic of Cancer* and sell it, possibly in expurgated form, in the United States. As it happened, when Rosset urgently cabled this news, asking permission to go ahead, Miller was in Europe, in the midst of his romance with Renate; these were the best days of his life, he felt, and his spirits were exceptionally high and he took up the challenge and gave the green light. Hurriedly, Rosset flew from New York and Hoffman from Paris to meet Henry in Hamburg. Rosset put down $10,000 and guaranteed to bear all legal expenses and damages and to protect Miller from court appearances. And Miller took up his pen and signed. This was historic news! Within a week Leonard Lyons reported in his New York *Post* column that "Grove Press, which published 'Lady Chatterley's Lover' here, will fight the censors again with Henry Miller's 'Tropic of Cancer.'"

On June 24, 1961, *Tropic of Cancer* was published in the United States. The reviews of *Tropic of Cancer* were terrific; the commentary in the news was almost completely positive. 68,000 copies sold in a week. By the end of the first year the sales totalled about 100,000 copies in hardbound and over a million in paperback. This twenty-seven-year-old book was the "blockbuster" of the year.

But Miller's predictions were right. He was lucky to be in Europe, for the troubles started immediately: several booksellers were arrested and parallel suits were brought against Grove Press. One of the first cases occurred in Los Angeles where Bradley Smith was arrested for selling the book. This trial set the precedent for the ridiculous way the courts were likely to treat his book. Henry's old friend Lawrence Clark Powell defended the book as a "social document"—but when the prosecutor requested him to read a particular passage, he refused to misrepresent the book by reading sections out of context. A UCLA professor of American literature argued that there was nothing "shameful or morbid" in the book, but also refused to read any parts of it aloud. Robert Kirsch of the Los Angeles *Times* and Jack Hirschman the poet defended the novel by placing it in the tradition of Pepys, Casanova, and St. Augustine; Hirschman surprised the court by calling *Cancer* a "deeply religious book." On the other hand, the well-known Shakesperian scholar at USC, Frank Baxter, declared the book obscene; and the novelist Leon Uris spoke of it as the "perverted, irrational bubbling from an unhealthy mind." Dr. Howard McDonald, the President of Los Angeles State College, also testified for the prosecution that the book was obscene, but under cross examination he admitted that he had never heard of *The Sun Also Rises, Butterfield 8, Lolita,* or Matisse. On such testimony Smith was convicted. In Illinois, on the contrary, only a few days before Smith's conviction, Judge Samuel B. Epstein of the Superior Court declared that *Tropic of Cancer* was "lewd, vile, vulgar, and [contained] revolting language," but was not obscene under the law. He forbade the city of

Chicago and six suburbs from interfering with its sale. This important decision was widely cited in subsequent litigations. Around the same time 198 American writers, including Saul Bellow, John Dos Passos, Lillian Hellman, Alfred Kazin, Norman Mailer, Bernard Malamud, William Styron, Robert Penn Warren, and Edmund Wilson, signed a statement supporting Miller and condemning censorship.

These early decisions seemed to represent the division which existed in cases occurring all over the country. Before the trials were completed, Miller would become the most litigated author in history: the various cases would provide enough material to fill several dozen volumes and would require an entire book to analyze them. During the first year after publication, Grove Press itself had had to fight sixty cases and spend over $100,000 in legal fees. Even the Epstein decision was immediately appealed by the Counsel of the City of Chicago; and the famous lawyer Elmer Gertz had to fight the case all over again in the Court of Appeals. By March of 1963, the various trials came to a head: a reviewing court in New York, the highest Court in California, the Illinois Supreme Court, and the United States Supreme Court, were all considering whether Miller's work was protected under the law. That month, at Gertz's request, Miller produced a noble defense of his book in an open letter addressed to the United States Supreme Court, which was reprinted in the Chicago *Sun Times.* He and Gertz anticipated victory and they were victorious, but this is what Miller's victory meant: he lost his anonymity, he could not return to Big Sur, he owed a staggering tax, his time was consumed by consultations with lawyers, and certain pages of his books were read in back rooms, under cover. He was indeed the King of Smut.

Fifteen

A New Life Revisited, and Other Burlesques

When Miller returned to California in the fall 1961, his chief desire was to be near his children. It was impossible to live in Big Sur, what with Eve still there—and she was now living next door with Harrydick Ross. Henry took a furnished room in Pacific Palisades, near the children, who were living on Las Lomas with their mother. So terrified was he of a steady stream of intrusions, he only let a few people know of his whereabouts. To be famous was tantamount to being a criminal. The room cost him $65.00 a month. Like the old Henry Street flat it seemed to be buried underground. Crowded with a refrigerator, a heater, two big armchairs, two dinette chairs, two tables, two dressers, a cot, and a screen, it allowed him just enough space to turn around. He was back to the uterine life again.

But he strolled over to see the kids as often as possible, hiked around the Palisades, and sometimes even hitchhiked along Sunset to get to Hollywood, as he had done in those Beverly Glen days when he was broke. Indeed, he was poorer than he had been since that time; for now he had no house and no patrons. He had already spent his Grove Press advance and still owed taxes on it, he wanted to pay child support, and an additional $250 a month to Eve, fees for Lauretta's care, taxes, and maintenance on the Big Sur property; he wanted to send small sums to June, Barbara, and others,

466

buy presents for the kids, and help out old friends like Walker Winslow who were "cornered and helpless." One day, with no money in his own pocket at all, he stopped at a bank in Pacific Palisades to cash a check and was refused. He was not known to the manager and didn't have an account there. Outside, in front of the bookstore next to the bank, was a display rack filled with dark blue paperback copies of *Tropic of Cancer.* He gazed at them blankly. He walked away feeling as if he had not written the book, as if he had been accused of passing bad checks by signing the name "Henry Miller" to them, as if he were a counterfeit of himself. He tried to work on the second volume of *Nexus,* but after completing 110 pages he lost interest in the tale and could no longer remember the details of his European journey with June. What a simple-minded, pleasant dolt he had been then. And how wretched he felt now. No wonder his Christmas card for 1961 had such a dismal message (quoted from Whitman): "Go on, my dear Americans, whip your horses to the utmost—excitement! money! politics! . . . You are in a fair way to create a whole nation of lunatics."

But poor or not, Henry had an output like a factory, Henry Miller, Inc. George Wickes began to edit the correspondence between Miller and Durrell. Grove Press sent *Tropic of Capricorn* and *Black Spring* to the printer. The Miller stock was booming, but the chief shareholder had a cash-flow problem. That the money disappeared so rapidly was partly his own fault. During the final negotiations, his agent, Dr. Hoffman, had suggested an arrangement which would have put Miller's European royalties in a Swiss bank instead of sending them to America and subjecting them to enormous taxes. Hoffman and others went further and tentatively proposed other means of avoiding substantial payments. They argued that having suffered years of povery, Miller might in justice claim a large profit. But he stood firm against all such schemes and insisted on taking no measures to prevent large deductions from his income. The result was that the United States Treasury collected about 75% of his royalties and he kept falling behind in payments. By 1962 he was nearly $15,000 in arrears for 1961 and had to use his royalties from *Tropic of Capricorn* to pay the tax on *Tropic of Cancer.* What would he use to pay taxes on earnings from *Tropic of Capricorn?* This situation resembled the crazy conditions in France in the mid-forties—and with the same books. *Tropic of Cancer* and *Tropic of Capricorn* were earning plenty of money, but it was like quicksilver.

These years he moved around a lot because he really had no place to go. In 1962 he was in Mallorca to serve on the jury for the Formentor prize in literature, in Minnesota to meet the members of the Henry Miller Literary

Society, in Edinburgh for a Writer's Conference, in Berlin to see Renate . . . By now he and Renate had drifted apart. Neither spoke any longer of his living in Europe or her going to America. They were fixed on separate paths. If there were any doubt, it was dispelled in late October 1962, when young Tony wrote plaintively to him: "It's been a long time since you've been home. Maybe when you come home it will be for good." That appeal decided Henry. He loved his children and preferred to deny himself rather than them. Henry told Renate that life looked "terribly bleak" to him and it was "queer and unnatural" for him to leave her: "I had such dreams, such hopes—and now all seems gray, dreary, monstrous, futile." Then characteristically, he rebounded. *Well, fuck a duck,* he said to himself and hurried home.

Actually, Lepska had in mind buying a new, larger house, and she was counting on Henry's assistance. The children were growing up, she convincingly argued to the indulgent father, and they needed a place where their friends could come. Besides, she continued, if she could find a large enough house, with a little wing, and if (with his help) she could afford to buy it, then he could come to live with them; he could live separately and quite cosily but be right at hand for the children's sakes. Henry liked the idea. Since his divorce from Eve in April of 1961 he had been alone, and he hated it. Besides, he believed he would be a good influence on the children, a salutary counteragent to Lepska's rigid discipline, a spirit of freedom that would bring their growing rebelliousness to a halt. From a tax standpoint, too, the purchase of a good, expensive house with deductible high interest payments, seemed sound. He dreamed of having a separate wing for his exclusive use and even a swimming pool for exercise now that his hip socket was giving him such pain that he could no longer take long walks or ride his bicycle as often as he would have liked.

In February of 1963, the whole family moved into a nice two-story house on Ocampo Drive with a swimming pool and a study for Henry. He paid for the house, but Lepska paid for its remodelling. During the time that Henry had been at loose ends, Lepska had raised the children on her own, but now they would all live together again—this looked like a happy solution, and it was. He remained in his own part of the house during the day but took his evening meal with Lepska and the children. George Wickes, who visited him there, described the domestic scene warmly: "As I arrived, Henry was helping Val with her French lesson—translating Rimbaud, whom she pronounced crazy, off beat. She didn't seem to think that 'Henry knew anything about Rimbaud either. Then, during dinner, Tony (who is almost a caricature of a teenager, with his exaggerated poses and a mop of platinum blonde hair) was explaining sexual reproduction—of amoebas, to be sure, but some of his remarks were memorable, dismissing the old man as one who wouldn't know anything about such matters . . . . All tease him in a rather heartwarming way, even Lepska, and he obviously loves it."

Sixteen

Cancer, Schmanser, What's the Difference so Long as You're Healthy?

A rumor circulated that a warrant for Miller's arrest had been issued in Brooklyn. It spread even as far as England and reached Alfred Perlès. Fred naturally took it as a joke and offered to dispatch the British Navy on a rescue mission if Henry were clapped in jail. But it could not be true, Fred said, since by 1963 *Tropic of Cancer* had been published even in England— selling 40,000 copies the first day of publication—and after all, England was the stodgiest place on earth.

He was quite mistaken in this assumption. The most puritanical spot in the world was Henry's hometown, Brooklyn, New York, and its authorities were highly insulted that a native of the Fourteenth Ward, Brooklyn, should have been the perpetrator of a book so full of "filth." In early 1964 the District Attorney of the Borough of Brooklyn issued an order for Miller's arrest and extradition from California to Brooklyn to answer charges in the Criminal Court of New York, Kings County, in a case brought against him and Grove Press. It was alleged that, as the District Attorney's brief put it, "on or about and between January 1, 1961, and June 30, 1962, in the County of Kings [Henry Miller] prepared and authored said [obscene] book"—as if he had written it while the printer stood at his side setting type. For several months it actually appeared that the Brooklyn authorities might clap Henry into jail "as a common criminal." His lawyers filed an application to show cause and also filed a motion of interlocutory injunction against Nelson A. Rockefeller, Governor of the State of New York, and Edward S. Silver, District Attorney of Kings County, in which Miller pointed out that at the time he actually wrote *Tropic of Cancer*, Grove Press did not exist and Barney Rosset was twelve years old. He agreed to remain in the United States while the temporary restraining order was in effect. This concession was a mistake of great magnitude: it meant that Miller was locked in the United States until the time that the case was completely settled and the extradition order abrogated. Even in mid-1964, when the Supreme Court declared the sale of *Cancer* constitutionally protected, the Brooklyn case went forward against Grove Press, and the charges against him were not dismissed until October 1964. The case went into history—into Elmer Gertz's *A Handful of Clients* (1965) and even university text books like Milton R. Konvitz's *First Amendment Freedoms: Selected Cases*. Last, the whole legal process was summarized by E.R. Hutchison in Tropic of Cancer *on Trial: A Case History of Censorship*.

Finally all this litigation prodded Miller's imagination and he began a one-act burlesque in the manner of *Just Wild About Harry* on censorship: judges, lawyers, and government officials talked in the idiotic idioms of their professions about a writer accused of obscenity.

Tropic of Cancer, this novel that he hadn't intended to write, was nothing but trouble now, and when film makers became interested in it, anything could happen. In 1962, Joseph E. Levine purchased the film rights to *Tropic of Cancer* and announced that he planned to make a two million dollar film from the book and that Henry Miller himself would be a consultant on the production. For the first few months the production went along smoothly; then one disaster after another, quite apart from any question of censorship, started to haunt the film. Bernard Wolfe produced a weak script, which was rejected. Next, Levine became involved in legal suits over the film—first with his partners, and subsequently with the actress Carroll Baker, who was fired from the film even before shooting started. As part owner of the film rights Miller himself was entangled in these litigations for four years. In the meantime, Shirley Mac Laine wanted to play June, but the production was stalled by litigation. Then Perlès complicated the whole picture by proposing to design a "Henry Miller" film for Hildegard Knef—in which she would play all the female roles—and he actually wrote a scenario called "Beyond the Tropics" which unfortunately invaded material sold to Levine.

Not for several years did *Tropic of Cancer* actually reach the screen and then it was, as Pauline Kael remarked, "so much less than the book that it almost seems deliberately intended to reduce Miller . . . to pipsqueak size."

Meanwhile Miller was busy being famous. He was in demand at Hollywood parties. Ava Gardner, Kim Novak, and Yvette Mimieux corresponded with him. Miss Novak sent him samples of her poetry. He had a "light romance" with Ziva Rodam, a young Israeli actress. She inspired Jewish themes in several of his watercolors. His advice on love and sex was widely solicited: his romantic essay on love was published in *Elle,* the French journal edited by Blaise Cendrars's daughter Miriam. In English the same essay was bought by *Mademoiselle* at its "top price" of $750 and printed as "Love and How It Gets That Way." In March 1963 he studied silkscreening with nuns of Immaculate Heart College in Hollywood. There, surrounded by bevies of approving Sisters, he turned out nearly a hundred paintings in less than three months. His painting improved considerably; he made watercolors, he told Nicolas Nabokov, "as easily and as frequently as I make water and, you know, by dint of turning them out so regularly I almost feel that I have become a painter." He appeared on several segments of the Steve Allen Show; he was a character in a Shelley Berman recording. He showed up on several talk shows and seemed to enjoy himself. He saw no reason to take things seriously. Maybe his mind, like his hip socket, had worn smooth.

Fame nailed him on its cross and wouldn't let him down. Someone was always hounding him into one project or another. Would he authorize a new edition, another translation, a film adaptation, a staged reading, an opera libretto, a radio production? Would he give an interview, appear on television, write a preface, donate money, bail a friend out, blurb a book, or autograph a dozen or so copies of those once-banned books—beginning his inscription: "To my dear friend" even though he had never heard of the person before? Worse, his life was filled by visits to businessmen, producers, technicians, financiers, lawyers, accountants, and tax advisors. He had leaped out of Big Sur and landed plump on Wilshire Boulevard, gone from a shanty-like writer's studio to corporate offices, from writing books to signing checks. He even resorted to forming a corporation for tax purposes: Rellim Productions, it was called—spelling his name backwards—and he did feel turned inside out. A mere ten years before he had made do on $1000 a year; now he spent more each month. After earning over $200,000 in three years from the sales of various books, chiefly the *Tropics,* and donating manuscripts, other documents, and watercolors worth $30,000 to universities, museums, libraries, and other non-profit institutions, he had a measly $1500 in the savings bank not earmarked for tax payments.

No one would believe that he was just short of bankruptcy and no one would loan him money. Even Larry Durrell, whose "Alexandria Quartet" was making such a splash, declared he couldn't loan Henry anything, when he was approached during a financial emergency in 1963. In 1964 Miller could get an advance of only $2500 from Rosset: he had already taken $5000 from unearned royalties. And he had already borrowed $3500 out of Lauretta's account. By the end of 1964, Miller had given away about $100,000 to friends in need, leaving himself with only a pittance against the bills and taxes he had accumulated. To Renate Gerhardt alone he had sent sixty thousand dollars between 1962 and 1964 as investments in her publishing house.

The price that Miller had paid for "success" was worry, sleepless nights, and notoriety. He had no time whatsoever for writing, except for articles which might sell immediately, and he soon found that though the big-paying magazines like *Playboy* liked to have his *name* in them, they found his writing quite unsuitable. Sometimes, like Midas, he wished he were a poor man again. And since his thoughts were likely to be painful, he emptied his mind and tried not to think of anything at all. He was seventy-three in 1964, but there was no trace of senility in this blankness of mind, only a kind of blind yearning for rest from care, the care that thinking brought. He had headaches and his eyes hurt him; his arteries seemed to be growing rigid, and he lived in constant pain. Sometimes as he lay awake at night, his mind throwing gigantic panoramas of his life on the dark walls, he felt five hundred years old, but no wiser than he had ever been.

Seventeen

Another Goethe

And he was lonely. Tony had been seized with the desire to enroll in a Military Academy in Carlsbad, California, and so he began to board away from home during 1964. Then Valentine married a young man named Ralph Day. Everyone thought her new name was "cunning," especially since she was married on Valentine's Day, 1964. The name was fine, but the man was wrong and the marriage was soon in trouble. In April 1964 Lepska, who had remarried, also moved out of the house—presenting Henry with a "whacking" bill for all the furniture in it. Now that he suddenly had the whole house to himself, Miller felt like a ghost drifting about in vast spaces. He quipped to friends that there was so much room he intended to get himself a pair of roller skates in order to make his way around. But he bided his time, amusing himself with a string of young women who came around to keep him company, until early September when Tony decided to quit the Academy and Val and her husband moved in with him. This began one of the most contented periods of Miller's life.

The only thing worrying him was the possible American publication of *Sexus*. Miller himself had come to regard *Sexus* as pornographic, not just obscene. When Girodias was assembling material in his own defense and appealed to Miller for a statement, Henry admitted in a letter to the French

Minister of the Interior that his book possessed "scabrous, obscene, [and] immoral" incidents. Finally, in March 1964 Girodias was convicted of having "outraged public morality in France," sentenced to a year in prison, fined 7000 francs, and deprived of his right to publish in France for twenty years. If France took such extreme measures, Miller reasonably asked, what charges might the Government of the United States bring against *Sexus*?

To Miller's horror, one day a man appeared at his door to inform him that he was about to issue *Sexus, Plexus,* and *Nexus* (Volume I) as "Greenleaf Classics." He explained that although the books were not copyrighted in the United States, he was willing to offer Miller the usual author's contract. Miller refused. The man shrugged: his edition would be out in a week's time, he casually announced. Rapidly, Grove Press produced a photo offset edition at a low price within ten days and mounted an effective publicity campaign designed to persuade booksellers into refusing to stock the pirated edition. Then, to head off a similar emergency, Grove issued *The Rosy Crucifixion,* as well as *The World of Sex* and *Quiet Days in Clichy.* Miller waited for the governmental axe to fall, but nothing happened. Not a single one was vigorously prosecuted. Once these books might have created a storm of controversy, but now there was no great opposition. Americans seemed to feel that "the Miller case," the fight against censorship, had been settled over *Tropic of Cancer.* Very few persons live to see the triumph of a great cultural revolution for which they are mainly responsible. But Miller did live to see a total reversal in American laws and social mores concerning the circulation of explicitly sexual writing, largely as a result of his own books. As H.L. Mencken had predicted thirty years earlier, his triumph came quickly, like a landslide, when at last it came.

After mid-1964 he began to say that it was unlikely that he would ever finish the second volume of *Nexus,* despite the fact that he had so often termed this the only story he ever wanted to complete. Publicly, he told Bernard Wolfe in an interview for *Playboy* in 1964 that the entire trilogy was "a record I want to make of my life, no matter how long it takes or how many volumes." But privately he was explaining or justifying in many different ways his inability to complete the book. He told Maxwell Geismar that artistically it would be better to have the series end with the first volume of *Nexus* instead of with the actual final dissolving. That which is so well hinted at "does not have to be literally completed . . .," he argued.

From this time onward his letters and his public statements show a perceptible relaxation. He read very little—mostly he went back to old favorites. In years past he had uncovered a dozen new literary devotions every year. The only new writer who really sparked his enthusiam during these years was I.B. Singer. He became devoted to television. He was fully prepared to be sublimely foolish, the biggest fool on earth, and he liked to tell his friends that to be childish in one's old age was the greatest of treats. He was simply unable to do concentrated work. Even the composition of a short preface he found a task of large proportions. In the case of one photograph album for which he had promised a foreword, he ended up returning the photos and explaining: "I am finding it more and more difficult to write about anything." Pained by his osteo-arthritis and finding no relief in drugs, he fell into a lethargy from which he could not revive himself. When his energy went, his talent went with it. What did it matter, he often asked, if he finished his work or not? This was a sensible question. He had written millions of words; and if he had not yet penetrated to the heart of the mystery of life, another few thousand words were not likely to uncover it. Who had ever done so? —not Dostoievski, not Strindberg, not Hamsun. Had Hesse done so? Or Balzac? Rider Haggard? or Richard Jeffries? Shakespeare? No, none of them. He told his friends (and himself) that he refused to be a drudge, a victim of his own art. Instead, he let himself float in a tide of impulse, following the promptings of his heart. Wasn't such serenity what he had been seeking all along?

Trouble with the children distracted him. Val was divorced in 1966. At loose ends, she borrowed money from him to purchase a ski shop in Aspen, Colorado. He had always hoped that Val would write, but now she showed no inclination to do so. He had certainly steadfastly preached to both children against formal codes and intellectualism; except for brief enrollments at Santa Monica Junior College, neither went to college for long. Rather than be drafted and have no choice of assignment, Tony enlisted in the Army and was then shipped to Fort Ord. There was a war in Viet Nam and Henry was worried that Tony might be sent there. Henry had secretly hoped that both children would become interested in some kind of service, like the Peace Corps or Vista, but neither seemed destined for that. Yet, how could he complain that they were drifting when he was drifting himself?

He no longer worried about death. But Eve's death in August 1965 at Big Sur shocked him. By nature, Eve had a lot of courage and energy and optimism. She still possessed pluck, but her drive had worn out. She no longer had confidence in herself. She wrote to Henry in 1962 that she couldn't rid herself of pangs of guilt and failure, she was continually looking backwards to her mistakes with him. She was afraid of alcoholism, but she kept on drinking and her depression increased. At last she gave up entirely and drank herself to death.

After experiencing a brief period of intense sadness, Henry rebounded with a strong instinct not to fall into Eve's melancholy. By an effort of great will he picked up his spirits, he put an end to his drift, he tried to get his sap flowing again. He fell in love in every direction. About two weeks after Eve's death, he told a friend that he was in love with four women simultaneously—a Jewish woman from New York, a beauty in Leipzig (an actress, painter, and pianist), a Chinese movie actress named Lisa Lu, and a Japanese jazz singer—the last he called his "anata bakari," his one and only love.

He was approaching seventy-three. This, he recalled, was just a year short of the age at which Goethe had fallen in love with a nineteen-year-old girl. Henry was obsessed with this whole episode and Goethe's poem about it. He read the story often and thought about its application to himself. He wanted to be in love. One of Miller's visitors had written on his wall: "Though lovers may be lost, love shall not." He believed that—he felt that he still had the heart of a lover, and he was fully prepared to fall in love again.

His old friend Emil White hit exactly the chord that had reverberated in the back of Henry's mind for some years when he wrote from Japan that Miller should go to that country to find "one last wife." He had always been fascinated by the whole notion of the Geisha and dreamed of having a perfect Geisha for a wife—being loved without discrimination and, if need be, without desert. Certainly he was still yearning for the mother he had been deprived of, as he showed when he read Prevalakis' novel *The Sun of Death* in 1965 and told the author that he had fallen in love with Aunt Roussaki—the kind of ideal mother he would have chosen, "all love and understanding, plus the wisdom of the earth." Along with his continuing attachment to an image of the ideal Greek woman, the ideal image of the devoted Oriental woman shimmered in his mind.

It was the Japanese jazz singer, Hiroko Tokuda, who fascinated him most. In the summer of 1966, Henry met her at a party in the house of one of his doctors, an internist named Lee Siegel. It was apparent on first glance that Hoki was a very modern young Japanese woman, far more accustomed to mini-skirts than to brocaded kimonos. Before coming to southern California in 1965 she had acted and sung in Japanese films. She had also studied music, piano, and fine arts at Alma College in Ontario and had developed into an accomplished jazz singer and pianist. Miller didn't pay much attention to her at the party. However, she telephoned him the very next day. "Hello, this is your little friend from Tokyo speaking," she began. He didn't recognize her voice at first, but he soon got to know it well. Hiroko deeply attracted Henry for many reasons, and soon he began unconsciously to think of her as his "one last wife." Though Miller accepted her modern appearance, he professed to see a traditional woman beneath her surface sparkle. She was young—twenty-seven years old—and vivacious; she perked up his spirits by her brightness and quickness. And so they dated occasionally, and Henry often dropped in on her show at the Grand Star Restaurant in Chinatown. Certainly, he saw that she smiled equally on him and all the others who sat along her piano bar, yet he hung around in an agitated state of exquisite torture, as if all her smiles were really for him. Ever a romantic, he even came early in the evening to sit by her before the other customers arrived in order to create the illusion that she sang for him only.

All night, until the lanterns were darkened, she sang of love—she knew songs with "Love" in the title in English, French, Spanish, Italian, and Japanese. And he was St. Valentine once again. Hoki, Henry felt, designed her whole life around the assumption that if she smiled and sang sentimental songs in an appealing sexy way she could make men fall in love with her. She gave her smile to one and all, as any entertainer must, to anyone who sat at the piano bar and particularly to anyone who stuffed a bill into her glass. She sang to the customers as easily as June had once danced with them at Wilson's. "They don't mean a thing, they're meaningless"—that's what she and June both said. As before, Henry believed and didn't believe. Still, it was a sure sign that something amorous was at hand when Henry wrote lyrics for a song for Hoki. It was the third poem of his life. Though he claimed that he was trying with all his might not to lose his heart (after all, Goethe's young sweetheart had rejected him), he fell in love as easily as ever. He began to call Saturday night "Japanese night" at his house and he persuaded Hoki to teach him Japanese, to appear regularly at Japanese night, and to become his chief partner at ping pong.

After several months, thousands of smiles, and hundreds of love songs, late night phone calls, unsent and unanswered letters, Mah-jongg games, and competition with rival sugar-daddies, Henry found himself in love. He awakened in the middle of the night thinking about her, he scribbled notes to her at 3 a.m., and, in the early hours of the morning he painted pictures of her on the walls of his living room and study. He wanted to know all about her, all her past loves, to pin her down like a specimen he could observe. And, like June, she told him whatever he wanted to know—she tried to convince him that she was a devil. Above all, she was a mystery, and Henry loved that.

Meanwhile, during 1967 more than one story had appeared in newspaper and magazine gossips columns, even in Tokyo itself, concerning this love affair between a young Japanese girl and the famous author, whose books were very popular in Japan. Henry took the opportunity to write to her father and express his regret for these gossipy accounts, then to confess his love for Hoki. "To me," he wrote, "though she is a 'modern' young Japanese, she symbolizes much that is authentically Japanese, qualities, I mean, which your countrymen have tried to preserve in their womanhood. What more can I say?" Before he closed, Miller asked if by any chance Rokuro Tokuda recalled the hour of Hoki's birth. He was, of course, turning to his astrologers to see if she might be "right" for him. The answers were favorable, and he was elated.

These days he ceased talking about Goethe's disappointment, but he often spoke of how Pablo Casals had married a twenty-year old when he was eighty. Hoki resisted his advances, frequently declaring her admiration for him and deprecating her own worthiness by stressing her faults and shortcomings. "And so," as Miller wrote, "we have this reportedly famous old man (75, no less!) pursuing a young will-o'-the-wisp. The old man very romantic, the young songstress quite down to earth. She has to be down to earth because it's her business to make men fall in love, do foolish things, buy expensive gowns and ·jewels." At each of his advances she retreated and so, though they swung like a pendulum, they got nowhere.

Things might have continued this way forever except for the unwitting but timely intervention of the United States Immigration Office, which informed Hoki that, her visa having expired, she must leave the country. Henry proposed that she marry him instead. And suddenly she accepted. Their romance was made even more exciting by this conspiracy to triumph over the authorities. They quickly took out a license to marry, and on September 10, 1967 the ceremony was performed. Hiroko wore a white mini-dress with a scoop neck and Henry an Ivy League-cut gray plaid suit with a turquoise-studded silver Navajo belt buckle. The tiny emeralds in the ring which Henry slipped on her finger he declared to have come from "King Solomon's Mines." She told the newsmen: "I'm nervous but very happy." Miller clowned about like a boy and continued to do so when he and Hoki appeared on "The Today Show" the next day.

A week later, still beaming, they left for Paris for a honeymoon trip planned around a *vernissage* of a show of new gouaches and water-colors by Miller. As usual, the journalists were waiting for his arrival at Orly. Miller was asked by a reporter for *Le Figaro* if he considered himself primarily a writer or painter. In his French, still good and still pronounced with a Brooklyn accent, he answered without hesitation: *"Pour moi, c'est l'ange qui peint et le diable qui écrit."* Whatever he said, however bad his accent, he was a hero in France. The opening of his show at the Daniel Gevis Gallery in the Rue de Bac was so mobbed that he had literally to be rescued from the crowds by police.

In a very striking way, his life with Hoki recapitulated his days with June. Hoki was mysterious to him not simply because she was Japanese, or over forty years younger than he, but because, like June, when she told him of her life, even the truth sounded made up. She seemed to be yielding, worshipful, ready to throw herself at his feet, but she could also act distant, indifferent, and imperious. Her male acquaintances often showed up, and Henry was jealous of them. She brought her female friends home and two of them moved in. Before long, Henry was depressed and angry and frustrated again. In fact he again began to feel the same helpless *Weltschmerz* that had gnawed at him in his adolescence. And so he returned, as he had always done for comfort, to his typewriter and began to compose a melancholy account of his love life, called *Insomnia—or, The Devil at Large.* This book contained his best writing in a decade.

"First it was a broken toe, then a broken brow, and finally a broken heart," he began. During the year he had courted Hoki he had often awakened in the middle of the night with a pain in the toe and a pain in the heart. Now he had the same pains again, though the toe was healed. He had begun to make paintings, made of "sayings," a writer's dream-painting in which words *were* pictures. These paintings and inscriptions were still on the wall as he wrote *Insomnia.* He stared at the maze of female faces and copied off the lines: "The icy white maiden-head of love's logic!" "The gorilla who feels his wings growing!," "A splinter buried in the quick of the soul," "Hoki Doki," "My Japanese Sand Man." Many others were there in the shadows, green and red and brown words staring back at him like eyes.

Hoki was a creature of the night, and she was often out late at night— still playing Mah-jongg, perhaps? It was a game she said she was passionate about, and she stayed out late playing it. He was as much a detective as ever—like an unhappy scorpion he stung himself in his investigations, even though he knew he was acting foolishly, a famous stupid romantic old man wailing in the palace of the heart's entrails. He reread Hamsun's

Mysteries, as if Herr Nagel's plight would explain his own. All those tunes she sang ran around his head. What did they all say?—just love, love, love, the greatest the world has known, love at instant request, love for the one and only one, love, many-splendored love, love as a cure for loneliness, love as a cure for all ills—for broken toes and broken hearts and broken bodies, bodies running down with arthritic pains and incurable aches, love strong enough to fly the lover to the moon—"I wish you health and, more than wealth, I wish you love!" But after the piano bar had closed and the Chop Suey was all cleared away, and the Mah-jongg boards were stowed in the closets, then where was love—*aishite 'ru*—and at 3 a.m., where was Hoki? Miller never saw the bottom of any mystery, the end of any myth. At last he ended up believing her, even when he believed she was lying, and believing her to be lying when he knew she was telling the truth. Shades of June!—she turned everything around.

So, as he had often done before, Miller turned his anguish into clowning and his clowning into literature. And he wrote himself not into happiness but into indifference about the cause of his suffering. When he wrote, he always won in the icy Mah-jongg of his own agony. *Insomnia* was like slipping a stiletto from the folds of his kimono. Another dame knocked off, another love enshrined in prose. Perhaps, he despaired, he would never learn, old man as he was, to live love the way the flower lives beauty. But he could live literature so, and that allowed him to survive his seasons of anguish.

Hoki moved out of the Pacific Palisades house after two years of marriage. By 1970 she rented her own apartment in Santa Monica and opened a boutique on Sunset Strip. Though she returned periodically and left again—to Henry it was obvious that the grand love, a love worthy of romantic insomnia, had duped him once more. There he was, nearly eighty, still seeking someone to worship—and someone who would unreservedly worship him—and finally seeking rejection by ferreting out the faults of the beloved. All he wanted was an angel ("to worship and adore") and all he did diabolically was to find the flaw in anyone he chose. He always sought the absolute, the perfect, he always pursued a fugitive, impossible something.

So Miller drifted into the decade of the 1970s, feeling more and more like a creature of some antique age. He felt left behind by civilization, when once he had believed himself to be its advance guard. As early as 1942 he had expressed confidence that his work would some day have its proper influence. Though he then told Theodore Schroeder that he knew "no man can hope, in his lifetime, to radically alter the existent mores," he had also asserted: "I know my voice is felt, and that my influence will increase with time." Perhaps it seemed to some that the changes in censorship laws brought about largely by the litigation over the *Tropics* fully justified Miller's confidence. To many he even seemed, by his work, to have indeed altered the "existent mores" during his own lifetime.

Yet now he had his doubts. To an interviewer who was praising him in 1976 for his influence, he retorted: "Sexual revolution? Linda Lovelace? Oh I consider it a misfortune for us that we have created these things. . . . Really, I am . . . amazed and disgusted." He went on to say that his ideas had changed. "More and more I don't think the way I did when I wrote those books [the *Tropics*] . . . I don't give much of a damn for sex and all that business." It was not a sexual revolution he had intended to further, he felt, but a revolution in sensibility, an upheaval in consciousness. He had had his influence, his works had made their way, but he was apprehensive. "Young people nowadays," he said, "don't seem to have that special something which *we* had when we were young . . . . There's such a gap between me and the younger generation. Maybe I'm just an old man, too old to appreciate and understand them, but I don't see any *reverence* in the young."

His illnesses increased. He lost his chief amusements: painting became difficult, ping-pong nearly impossible. He could only read large-print books—but, anyway, he was content with his old favorites, Dostoievski and Hamsun and Marie Corelli, and generally uninterested in discovering new writers on his own. By the end of his eighty-fifth year he was bedridden or moved about in a wheelchair. On the rare occasions that he ventured out of his house, say to visit Jacob Gimpel's master class in piano, he was carried up and down stairs. Mostly, though, he was content to remain in his house, avoiding the pain that movement produced, and evading a world which was too often surprising. "I have everything I want in this house," he said, ". . . If I go outside, I'm nobody again."

Sometimes he dreamed his old dream of finding "the spot," the perfect European abode; or of returning to Big Sur. But then he'd have to find new doctors. He no longer talked of disappearing into the mists of the Tibetan mountains. He stayed in Pacific Palisades and distributed his books and paintings in preparation for his demise. "I'd hate to see the revenue people take anything," he grumbled.

He continued to write, however, even though physical infirmities obliged him to compose—not without pain—in longhand. For his old friend Noel Young, the owner of the Capra Press in Santa Barbara, he produced a series of chapbooks in the early 1970s. The most interesting of these was projected in 1972, and written during the next two years; called *Book of Friends,* this volume gave some new information and a new slant on Miller's friends during his youth in Brooklyn. After the publication of this work in 1975, Miller announced that it was but the first in a series of books in which he would write of later friends in Greece and California. What was more, he wrote letters to newspapers, gave interviews, and produced blurbs. As early as 1963 he had remarked: "I never know what I will do from day to day. Most likely I will die at the typewriter." He wrote something almost every day—that habit remained, and daily he summoned strength for it. Nonetheless, he ceased altogether to talk of finishing the book of his life by completing the second volume of *Nexus.*

Hiroko left for good in 1974. Through the 1970s Miller fell in love continuously: his major literary efforts went into love letters. By 1976 he was in love with a young Chinese actress. But he declared he had no plans to marry for a sixth time. "Marriage," he said wryly, "kills love."

Val established residence in the old house at Big Sur and eventually began work on a diary. Tony also showed some inclinations to write; he turned out a screen treatment which pleased his father. But, Miller felt, both children were "timid about writing because of me—I'm their handicap, I'm not good for them. I ought to die . . . and then they can get on with their work." Tony moved into the house to take care of his father, and together they lived "a sweet, peaceful, contented life."

He made reconciliations with his life—but they were not those of a man surrendering. He showed the same old strength of will that had always saved him, carried him through his miseries. Perhaps, after all, that was what he had gotten from his mother: he had inherited her strength. After all these years of struggle perhaps he finally also made peace with his mother. In 1977 he wrote a chapbook, *Mother, China, and the World Beyond,* in which he imagined his own death. It begins: "I didn't quite realize I had died . . . until I saw my mother approaching." She greets him warmly, and suddenly for the first time, his love for her flows out: " 'Mother, dear Mother,' " he says in a rush of emotion. Then they talk about their past lives, and Henry asks the crucial questions of his life; for ultimately his loves, his writing, his life all revolved around the real Her—his mother:

After hearing so much from her lips that made sense to me I decided to ask her outright why she had always been so cold to me. I particularly wanted to know why she never had a word of comfort for me when she knew my heart was breaking. Couldn't she help me locate Cora now, I wondered.

No, the only way to find someone here was to think hard, wish for them and they would appear. She thought it quite possible that Cora had already returned to earth.

"She was a good girl," she said, "only I didn't see very much in her. I knew you were suffering but I felt that you had to work it out yourself. I always believed in letting people do as they wish, even if they wanted to kill themselves."

I decided to say no more about Cora but to try to find her on my own. My mother, however, ventured to add a few more words. "The real place to look for her," she said, "is on earth. That's the whole purpose of love—to find your other half. Sometimes the search goes on for a thousand years."

These observations bowled me over. "Why Mother," I exclaimed, "you sound as if you had read Marie Corelli."

* * *

But I was not through questioning my mother about the things which had estranged us in life. I realized, of course, from the moment I encountered her that she was an entirely different person here. How good it was to exchange thoughts with her. Below we hardly spoke to one another.

"Mother," I began, "do you remember a woman I wanted to marry who was considerably older than myself? Do you recall the day I told you about her—we were sitting in the kitchen—and you took a big carving knife and threatened to plunge it into me if I said another word about marriage? If, as you said a moment ago, you believed in letting people do as they wish, why did you become so furious, so violent?"

"Because," she replied, "you were out of your mind. It was only an infatuation, not true love.

"However," she added, "you did go and live with her a few years, even if you didn't marry her. And they were years of torment and distress, weren't they?"

I shook my head affirmatively. "But mother, no matter if it were an infatuation, she was a good woman. You should have felt a little compassion for her."

For answer she replied, "Sometimes one runs out of compassion. The world below was so full of misery that if one felt sorry for everyone who was in distress one could shed rivers of tears. When I return to earth this time I am sure I shall have more courage and strength than before."

Having endured much suffering, misery, humiliation, I could appreciate her words. I had one more vital question to put to her.

"Mother," I began, "I have never been able to believe that you preferred to see me become a tailor rather than a writer. Was that true or did you have some other reason?"

"I'm only too glad you asked me that question. Of course I never meant to imply a tailor was more important than a writer. (Though I must confess that since being here I have arrived at the conclusion that one thing is no better than another. I have met some very wonderful souls here, and they were people of no account on earth.) But I am wandering afield. I wanted you to be with your father, to guide him and protect him. I couldn't bear to see him go to the dogs. That's the real reason I wanted you to be a tailor."

Finally, they prepare to part, and, his fears and doubts all purged after eighty-six years, Miller says farewell to his mother in just the way he had always dreamed of doing—

When I looked up I perceived my mother some distance away. She appeared to be on her way out. Looking more carefully, I observed that she was waving to me, waving goodbye.

With that I stood up, my eyes wet with tears, and giving a mighty shout, I cried: "Mother, I love you. I love you! Do you hear me?"

At the end, then, he had his triumph—and his reconciliation.

He was very ill. His circulatory problems increased and he had a series of operations to open up the flow of blood to his heart, including the implant of a plastic vein which his body rejected. The third of his operations brought on shock which caused a stroke that left him blind in one eye and deaf in one ear and partly paralyzed on his right side. He was sick—but never weak. He continued to write and in the fall of 1977 miraculously finished *My Bike and Other Friends,* chiefly concerning his acquaintances in Big Sur. He was dying, yet still insisting on his life of joy.

On his front door he posted a sign: *"When a man has reached old age and has fulfilled his mission, he has a right to confront the idea of death in peace. He has no need of other men, he knows them already and has seen enough of them. What he needs is peace. It is not seemly to seek out such a man, plague him with chatter, and make him suffer banalities. One should pass by the door of his house as if no one lived there."* He never gave up his hold on life even when he was convinced that death was imminent. He had lived his live on his own terms and he wanted to die in the same way. His will was never paralyzed. He was not giving in to death—*he* was *preparing* to die.

In 1953 he had written to an acquaintance about his despair: "If I could go backwards like a taperecorder, I'd erase every word." But he never really despaired. He kept writing, he made warmly received appearances at the Actors Studio, he found his close relationship to his son a source of continuous pleasure, he continued to correspond with his friends.

Was he willing to erase his contribution to the book of life? That was out of his hands; he lived in his books and in innumerable hearts. Besides, he was always marked out, he felt, for a special destiny. In 1976, Uranus had traveled all around the zodiac. "It's right where it started when I was born," he mused. "Most people don't live to see it—and when it happens, great things take place."

Preparing to die? Rather say, preparing to live, preparing always, for some new, unimaginable ecstasy.

Epilogue

The Final Dissolving

Miller always complained that the books about him misrepresented his intentions, his ideas, his work. Critics, he thought, made distinctions he resisted and failed to see the fine discriminations that he did make. Nicholas Moore's chapbook of 1943 was followed by the essays in the *Happy Rock*, Perlès' book, Durrell's and Perlès' *Art and Outrage*, Sidney Omarr's astrological portrait, Annette Kar Baxter's intellectual study of Miller as expatriate, Walter Schmiele's brief biographical sketch published in German by Rowohlt, and F.J. Temple's pamphlet in French, and several scholarly bibliographies. In the late sixties several books on his work appeared and he despaired over every one. Now that he was famous, critics could take a free and easy ride on Miller's reputation while debunking him or exposing him to gossip—as Kingsley Widmer and Kenneth Dick did. In *Sexual Politics*, Kate Millet took the worst of Widmer's cynicism and of Dick's sensationalism and with little interest in discrimination of any sort classed Miller with Lawrence and Mailer as foes to women's liberation. Miller tossed off most attacks, but he was stung by this one. As he saw it, both men and women were falsely enslaved. "Neither man nor woman," he wrote in 1961, "has yet found the way to freedom. Freedom can be found only together, not separately, just as 'poetry must be made by all'." He knew that he himself could never be content until the unity in the universe was restored. He shook his head over Kate Millet's misrepresentations. Hadn't he again and again stressed the importance of the truths of the female sensibility, especially in praising Anaïs Nin? Hadn't his own theme always been liberation? Hadn't he even written a blurb for a feminist collection titled *The Bold New Woman* (and later, for Erica Jong's *Fear of Flying*)?

However, he wasn't any more satisfied by his supporters. He made an attempt to follow the arguments by which Norman Mailer defended Miller (and himself) in *The Prisoner of Sex,* but Mailer seemed to make everything too complicated. "I never read a thing Norman Mailer ever wrote," he told an interviewer for the Los Angeles *Free Press* in 1976. "Not even the thing he wrote defending me against the feminists. I started to read it but I couldn't stand it. . . . you see, I hate the New York type—the ultra-sophisticated, analytical, critical of everything." He was no more favorably disposed toward Mailer's extravagant praise of him in an essay published first in *The New American Review* and later used as an introduction to Mailer's selection *Genius and Lust.* "When I see the shits who are writing today . . . I'm sick and angry," Miller said before seeing Mailer's collection. "Even Norman Mailer. He's doing me a great favor, he's compiling a book about me, and according to my agent, Mailer's book is going to make me . . . I've started to read his stuff, but it's too much, I can't stand it, I don't like that kind of writing." (Yet he was tickled when Mailer visited him and Tony came in to ask for Mailer's autograph. Mailer wrote: "From Norman Mailer, at the foot of the Master." That pleased Henry. "The man has charm," he said.)

Academic criticism on Miller began in the sixties. Miller wasn't much happier with those supposedly responsible, serious university critics who sought to put him in what they regarded as his proper place—as if he needed to fill a pigeon hole in literary history. William Gordon, for one, saw him as a writer influenced by Rank, while Jane Nelson thought that the writings of Carl Gustav Jung provided the most useful critical methodology for understanding his work. A brief pamphlet by George Wickes hit the most balanced view of Miller.

Miller soon began to deplore the kind of "acceptance" that this stream of books suggested and to regard these critics much as he had once regarded the intruders at Big Sur. He wanted to shut the door in their faces, to pretend that he was not at home. Even more, he found that critics now possessed an annoying tendency to think their own thoughts and an unwillingness to take the same view of him that he had spent so much energy in projecting for himself. The problem was that he had created a Henry Miller, the hero of his autobiographical romances, which, for him, was the true Miller, while the critics seemed intent upon going in back of it, to the "real" Henry Miller which each one saw quite differently. As far back as the publication of Perlès's book, he had shown a tendency to censor his critics. At first this took form in his desire to "help"—in Perlès' case, Henry extensively revised the book about himself. He wished to supervise works by scholars or critics about him: William Gordon's published collection of the letters which Miller wrote to him concerning his work-in-progress shows this desire, and so does his correspondence with Wickes and Schmiele and Temple. He wished his critics to see him as he saw himself. He resisted interpretations differing from his own.

He did everything he could to leave a certain kind of Henry Miller to posterity. He repeated the same stories in interview after interview. In the case of the preparation of his letters to both Durrell and Nin he supervised the script very carefully and insisted on many deletions of personal material. He argued with George Wickes about the edition which Wickes prepared of Miller's correspondence with Emil Schnellock, the long awaited *Letters to Emil*. Wickes finally threw up his hands and abandoned the project. For Miller the difference between truth and fiction was no longer significant: in any event, he preferred the fictions. So Henry Miller began to suppress the truth about himself! —the very idea seemed improbable, impossible, and absurd. No one, he began insisting, could ever write his biography adequately. There was talk in the late sixties that Richard Elman of Columbia College would like to write Miller's life. "Who does he think he is—a wizard?" Miller asked sharply. Anyone could write about his life, he said, but he would give neither aid nor comfort to such a foolhardy endeavor.

It was around this time, in the summer of 1970, that Lawrence Clark Powell, drove down to the University of California, Irvine to visit me. As he left he said: "You're the very one to write Henry's biography. I'll call him up and say I think so." And, to my surprise, later than evening Henry's friend Robert Snyder got on the phone and said: "Come up Saturday. Talk to Henry. Play some ping pong!"

Miller himself opened the door, looking smaller than I had expected, and led me into the family room, where some chairs were arranged around a low table.

In the center of the room was a ping pong table. At the far end was a piano, with some large blown-up photographs of Henry Miller tacked to the wall behind it. Scriabin's Fifth Piano Sonata was playing on the phonograph.

"Well, Mr. Martin," he started, "I don't like American biographies. They're too full of details. They tell the reader everything he doesn't want to know." But after a few minutes he mentioned some biographies he liked. "If you wanted to do a biography like Chesterton's on Dickens, or Gide's on Dostoievski—a marvellous portrait even though Gide was all wrong—or Delteil's work on St. Francis—those are the sort of books I would like to have done about me, purely poetical evocations, in which the facts don't matter in the slightest. Why, you could even invent the facts. I'd prefer that. So long as you were interesting, I wouldn't care."

I tried to suggest that the actual facts themselves might be fascinating, and not unpoetical. But Miller was already shifting his ground. I saw the Miller magic. He had started out in measured tones to disparage biography. But slowly, as a wave builds, he began to rhapsodize. His own imagination took possession of him and led him all around the topic. The more he talked, the more wonderful did he make biography seem, until it seemed the prince of literary forms. Miller's talk was like a dance.

"Biography *can* be fascinating," he said, "—and difficult. It's my one failure, don't you know? I tried to write a book about D.H. Lawrence. I made thousands of notes, and wrote and rewrote, trying to put that book together. But I never could, it always defeated me. Still, I've read hundreds of biographies. At one time, when I studied Rimbaud, everything, even his laundry lists, intrigued me. I read twenty books, by—what was her name?—Enid Starkie and others, on him. He was the greatest sufferer I ever knew of. What a miserable existence! And with many parallels to my own life . . . And Scriabin . . .," Miller made a gesture toward the phonograph, "I *love* Scriabin, did you know that? A young lady came to see me recently and left me those records. Anything I could find out about that master, or about Pablo Casals, would interest me. And of course, the lives of the great sages—like Carlos Suares's book on Krishnamurti, or Rolland's book (did you ever hear of him?) on the Indian prophets, are supreme tales. Yes, the real truth of *anyone's* life, if only it can be told, is always absorbing."

Again, he shifted: "Why not write about yourself?" he inquired. "That's what I always did. Why write about me when you could write autobiography? Don't you know Emerson's comment about autobiographies?—'captivating books,' he calls them. My whole reason for writing, even if I didn't always know it, was to free myself of a demon. I wrote in order to begin to live. My favorites were always men like Keyserling and Strindberg and Nijinsky and that sage, John Cowper Powys, Prester John I call him, who all wrote autobiographies. And Walt Whitman also—his *Song of Myself* had a great influence on me."

I was about to urge that another's life might help illumine one's own, but Miller was improvising and changing direction ahead of me, and I was reduced to nodding in agreement at appropriate intervals. "Of course, I myself have often written about my friends, like Beauford Delaney or Abe Rattner. I wrote a book about a Greek friend named George Katsimbalis, who I dubbed the 'Colossus of Maroussi'. Anaïs Nin: I've frequently written about her. People don't realize just how much of my work is about friends or acquaintances, like the surgeon-painter of Louisiana, Dr. Marion Souchon."

Then Miller moved to more shadowy ground: "There really isn't anything that anyone can say about me. I've written my own biography, you know. Whatever isn't said in my books isn't really important. What good would it do anyone to go around talking to my friends? I see that in your book on West you spoke to everyone who knew him. But that's all useless. Besides, none of my friends knew everything about me: this one knew one part of my life and this one another, but none of them knew it all. Yes, and there are others, like a company detective living in New York still, who wouldn't know me as a writer at all—just a hooligan. Some of my best friends are dead, Joe O'Regan and my great correspondent Emil Schnellock, whom I knew from the time I was ten. No, anyone who tried to write about me would only get one slant. I've written my own truest biography."

I wanted to reply, rather obviously, that he was certainly right. Yet while Miller's autobiographical romances might provide the best possible biography, the biographer's attempt to understand relations which the fictions completely ignored, might also offer something of enormous interest and human value, a sense of the creative process itself, the way that out of an actual life the artist created a life in his fiction. But Miller was already remarking: "Naturally, I haven't told the whole truth in any of my books or even in all of them taken together. Even of my loves—where I've told so much—I haven't by any means told all. I've told many lies to fool my biographers, to lead them off my tracks. There are several affairs of the heart which don't figure at all in my books, and especially one which lasted eight or nine years about which I've never let anything come to light, for the sake of the woman concerned. I've never told anyone why I came to California to stay, and I never will. Much of what I say is my life I've really created, and much of my real life I've left out. No one will ever find this out, but if anyone *could*—!"

"Of course," he said, in an obviously new tack, "I don't give a damn what you write about me. Only an essay by Karl Shapiro and a few essays by French critics have done me justice. About the others I am indifferent. William Gordon, for one, kept insisting that I was influenced by Rank, as if no one else had had a comparable impact upon me. What about Maurice Maeterlinck?—I read more works by him than by any other writer before I went into D.H. Lawrence, as I found out when doing *Books in My Life*. Gordon doesn't even mention him. I tried to put that guy straight, but he'd never listen to me, he had his own ideas, he thought he knew me better than I knew myself."

Though he insisted he was indifferent to criticism, a moment later he snatched a slim volume off a table, a recent critical study of his work. "Look at this! This is by some dame in Massachusetts. I've been looking up the words she uses—I don't understand what she's talking about—thinks I'm a Jungian! Why didn't she ask me? I would have *helped* her!"

"Well, Mr. Martin," Miller sighed. "I'm tired of writing. I like to play now, and I'm going off in a little while after a game of ping pong, to take a nap. I like to play, swim, and paint when I feel like it, and I don't like to get involved in interviews and questions. I couldn't give you much help in your book, you know."

"Anyway," Miller remarked, "I've said the worst things that can be said about myself. You can say whatever the fuck you please about me."

Then he said: "O.K. Let's play ping pong!"

By accident or design, several of Miller's old friends were there that day. Miller's wife Hoki and one of her friends whisked in and were gone as quickly. They all played ping pong or swam and later sat around the kitchen table and talked, downing gin and tonics. Henry's friend, the great pianist Jacob Gimpel, dropped in and played a little. It was a good day, a jolly day.

After a while Miller prepared to go off for a nap. Later, he and the actor Joe Gray were going to dine at a Japanese restaurant, the Yamato, and he gave Gray very explicit instructions on making reservations. "Tell them," he said, "that we want that skinny waitress. You remember, that one you tried to make last time, Joe. She wouldn't give you a tumble, so it's my turn now. Don't forget, tell them the skinny one—the broad with no tits!"

As I left the house, I realized that though on the surface I knew a lot about Henry Miller, I really knew next to nothing. Still, I dreamed of the perfect book. In my ignorance I saw it unfold before me, as if it were on an enormous Chinese screen. Miller once said he wanted to have Rimbaud's remark, "Everything we are taught is false," engraved on his tombstone. Perhaps Rimbaud was right. Still, I dreamed of writing a book that would convey some of the truth of Miller's life.

In the years that followed, I think I never lost that dream entirely. True, when I realized that I would need to read through over a hundred thousand sheets of manuscript materials in more than twenty libraries, I faltered, but I did read them. Interviews with a score of Miller's friends—Man Ray in Paris, George Katsimbalis in Athens, Alfred Perlès in Crete, Renate Gerhardt in Berlin, or Emil White in Big Sur—revived my vision by the sheer beneficence of their human kindness. My tape recorder ran wherever I went, and the hiss of the Mediterranean surf or the street noises around St. Sulpice still sound in the background when I play the tapes or remember those talks.

Certainly I understood that Miller would never believe that anyone could know enough to present his life. Miller once told a friend: "I always seem to object to things (supposedly factual) which others write about me." He told Georges Belmont in 1967 that every book about him was "trivial, superficial, lacking in important details,—based too much upon my books. . . ." And what he had put in his books, he said, was merely "so much skimmed milk." When I at last finished my reading and interviewing and looked at my boxful of notes, I was almost ready to agree with him that to recreate the life I should have dreamed the facts instead of noting them. I felt the sense of helpless defeat which Miller himself once felt as he stared blankly at the vast accumulation of his notes on Lawrence. (I mentioned this to him once: "You refer to my researches on Lawrence," he wrote. "Believe me, it was nothing at all like your present labors.") How could I ever compose a portrait from the innumerable fragments in which his existence had left its record? Perhaps Miller, dubious as ever, was right when he wrote to me: ". . . let me wish you well. If the book turns out the way you wished it to turn out, that is something in itself." That would be something indeed, for I wished to write the book that Miller refused to believe could be written.

The book would be Miller's passion and his passion would be his triumph. When Miller was a child his mother often taunted him by wailing: "He's always dragging behind, like a cow's tail." He *had* dragged behind for a long time, fumbling in action and stumbling in speech. But when at last he found himself in Paris and spread his tail, it was a peacock's. The stains on his soul had turned into star-like gems. His mother had been wrong after all.

That first meeting with Henry Miller began me on my book—unless it had begun years earlier, in Brooklyn. That evening, as I drove toward home, the night came on, and with it the lights of an endless stream of moving cars into which my own path merged. Above me, barely visible, stars and planets whirled. Where was Jupiter? At what point Venus? I wanted to compile an astrology of the constellations of the soul. I knew that the secrets I pondered were not in the stars, or in Special Collections, or even in Miller's books, but in the human heart. This was the truth—wasn't it?—that Miller had tried to tell all these years and that I needed somehow to tell over again, going through all Miller's suffering once more, making his experience part of my own. Quite simply, it was the story of a man, a man who, even though nearly eighty, could look me defiantly in the eye and say: "You can write whatever the fuck you please about me!"

I didn't have a title until the time just before I started to write, when Miller gave me one. In 1972 he wrote a rather sad essay called "On Turning Eighty." I was trying to reflect on his life, as he was doing, and I paid close attention to a passage near the conclusion:

I don't like to end on a sour note. As my readers well know, my motto has always been: "Always merry and bright." Perhaps that is why I never tire of quoting Rabelais: "For all your ills I give you laughter." As I look back on my life, which has been full of tragic moments, I see it more as a comedy than a tragedy. One of those comedies in which while laughing your guts out you feel your heart is breaking. What better comedy could there be?

Miller was absolutely right. His life had been a rich one, good on any terms, tragic or comic. I could think of no life I wanted more to portray with something of the same verve and humanity with which it had been lived. And at the end of the life I can think of no better motto than his own: *Always merry and bright!*

Sequence of Henry in conversation, Big Sur.

As seen by Arnold Newman ca. 1974.

Henry's home in Pacific Palisades

Portrait by Ansel Adams.

Caricature by Brassaï, 1931.

Visiting Synanon, 1961.

Big Sur, ca. 1951.

Big Sur, 1969.

Henry hauling supplies up Partington Ridge,
ca. 1951.

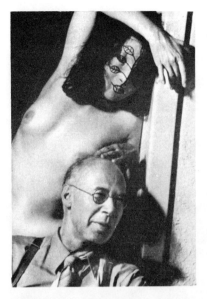

In Man Ray's studio, 1942.

At his watercolor exhibition
in Gallery 667 in 1967.

Bronze portrait by Marino Marini, 1961.

Ca. 1957

Henry improvising on the piano.

Ca. 1942.

1946

Acknowledgments and Notes on Sources

I wish to acknowledge, first of all, Henry Miller's aid in giving me permission to consult restricted manuscript materials.

Second, I am grateful to Lawrence Clark Powell, who first suggested this book; and to those people whom I interviewed or with whom I corresponded meaningfully: Muriel Crowley, Beauford Delaney, Ephraim Doner, Renate Gerhardt, Nikos Ghikas, Charles Halderman, Caryl Hill, George Katsimbalis, Alfred Perlès, Raymond Queneau, Man Ray, Gerald Robitaille, Betty Ryan, Robert Snyder, Emil White, and Noel Young.

For personal encouragement I am deeply grateful to my agent, Owen Laster.

I owe special thanks to those two friends who gave me the most needed support and trust, Noel Young and Peter Davison.

The curators and staffs of the libraries where I worked often spent—and overspent—time and energy carrying manuscript boxes and making Xeroxes for me. These depositories are the following, and it is in these that the manuscripts which form my biography may be found.

Brooklyn Public Library (George W. Wakefield, Assistant Coordinator of Central Service)—36 pages of Miller correspondence.

Columbia University, Butler Library (Kenneth A. Lohf, Librarian for Rare Books and Manuscripts)—33 letters, 2 extensively corrected book manuscripts.

Dartmouth College, Baker Memorial Library. (Walter W. Wright, Chief of Special Collections)—104 letters, 30 manuscripts, 27 Fraenkel letters, miscellaneous material, totalling 600 pages, in the Herbert F. West Collection.

University of California, Los Angeles, Special Collections (Brooke Whiting, Curator). This is the major Henry Miller collection, consisting of over 50,000 pages of manuscripts, documents and other materials. Too extensive to be listed in detail, these materials may be summarized as follows: (1) about 65 boxes of letters written to Miller, with numerous carbon copies of his replies; (2) 32 boxes of literary manuscripts, letters and documents by Miller; (3) 20 boxes of documents, photographs, records, paintings, articles, correspondence, legal briefs, and financial records by Miller.

Library of Congress (Roy P. Basler, Chief (since retired), and John C. Broderick, Acting Chief, Reference Department, Manuscript Division)—13 boxes of legal materials connected with the litigation over the *Tropics* in the Elmer Gertz papers; and 6 boxes of letters and manuscripts in the Huntington Cairns Collection.

The Henry E. Huntington Library—containing 50 letters of Miller and his third wife, Lepska, in the Walker Winslow Collection.

Indiana University (Rebecca Dixon, Head Librarian), Institution for Sex Research—Manuscripts totalling 755 pages; (Elfrieda Lang, Curator of Manuscripts), Lilly Library—paintings and letters.

University of Kansas, Department of Special Collections, Kenneth Spencer Research Library—containing 8 folders of manuscripts and letters.

University of Minnesota (Alan K. Lathrop, Curator of Manuscripts Division)—containing papers of Henry Miller Literary society, legal materials, 290 Miller letters and other manuscripts, totalling approximately six linear feet.

New York Public Library, the Research Library Manuscript Division and Berg Collection (Faye Simkin, Executive Officer)—one book manuscript, other manuscripts, letters, and miscellaneous papers, totalling about 250 pages.

Northwestern University (R. Russell Maylone, Curator) Special Collections, one manuscript, four Anaïs Nin novels, all with corrections and marginalia by Miller, also 20 letters, comprising about 275 pages.

San Francisco Public Library, Special Collections. (John D. Coll, Curator)—126-page unpublished manuscript.

Southern Illinois University, Special Collections—(Kenneth W. Duckett, Curator)—1300 pieces including correspondence with Durrell, Nin and Buñuel, and literary manuscripts.

University of Texas at Austin, Humanities Research Library, (June Moll, Librarian)—an extremely important collection, consisting of 62 manuscripts, 500 letters from Miller to other correspondents, and 500 other items.

University of Virginia, Clifton Waller Barrett Library and Manuscripts Department, Alderman Library, (Mary Faith Pusey, Assistant in Manuscripts)—a very large collection including manuscripts, correspondence, notes, paintings, photographs, and contracts.

Yale University, Beinecke Rare Book and Manuscript Library (Donald Gallup, Curator of American Literature)—manuscripts and correspondence, about 100 pages.

Collections of fewer than 10 unpublished Miller items are located in Bowdoin College, the University of California, Berkeley, Harvard University, the Newberry Library, Ohio State University, Princeton University and the American Academy of Arts and Letters. I have also consulted the complete collection of letters of Henry Miller to Renate Gerhardt, owned by Ms. Gerhardt.

Though my biography is based on unpublished sources I have consulted all of the books, and many articles, written by and about Henry Miller. In the subsequent citations of sources I document only manuscript materials; but here I list, arranged alphabetically by title, the books which I have used.

The Air-Conditioned Nightmare, New York: New Directions, 1945, by Henry Miller.

Aller Retour, New York, Paris: Obelisk Press, 1935, by Henry Miller.

Americans Abroad: An Anthology, The Hague: Servire Press, 1932, by Peter Neagoe.

Art and Outrage: A Correspondence about Henry Miller Between Alfred Perlès and Lawrence Durrell, with Intermissions by Henry Miller, New York: Dutton, 1961.

Big Sur (French translation of *The Stranger*), Preface by Henry Miller, Paris: Denoël, 1948, by Lillian B. Ross.

Big Sur and the Oranges of Hieronymous Bosch, New York: New Directions, 1957, by Henry Miller.

Black Spring, Paris: Obelisk Press, 1938, by Henry Miller,

Books in My Life, Norfolk, Conn.: New Directions, 1952.

The Booster, Nos. 7-10/11, Paris: September, 1937 to Easter, 1939.

Collector's Quest: The Correspondence of Henry Miller and J. Rives Childs, 1947-1965, Edited with an Introduction by Richard Clement Wood, Published for Randolph-Macon College, Ashland, Virginia, Charlottesville: University Press of Virginia, 1968.

The Colossus of Maroussi, San Francisco: Colt Press, 1941, by Henry Miller.

The Cosmological Eye, Norfolk, Conn.: New Directions, 1939, by Henry Miller.

A Devil in Paradise, New York: New American Library, 1956, by Henry Miller.

"The Durrell of the Black Book Days," by Henry Miller, in Harry T. Moore, ed., *The World of Lawrence Durrell,* Carbondale: Southern Illinois University Press, 1962.

First Impressions of Greece, Santa Barbara: Capra press, 1973, by Henry Miller.

Greece, New York: Viking Press, 1964, by Henry Miller.

Hamlet, 2 volumes, Santurce, Puerto Rico: Carrefour Press, 1939-41, by Henry Miller and Michael Fraenkel; also: *Correspondence called Hamlet*, 2 vols. London: Edition du Laurier, Carrefour, 1962.

The Happy Rock: A Book about Henry Miller, Berkeley: Printed for Bern Porter, Packard Press, 1945.

Henry Miller, Minneapolis: University of Minnesota Press, 1966, by George Wickes.

Henry Miller, New York: Twayne Publishers, 1963, by Kingsley Widmer.

Henry Miller, Paris: Editions Universitaries, 1965, by Frederic J. Temple.

"Henry Miller," in *Supertalk,* New York: Doubleday, 1974, by Digby Diehl.

Henry Miller: Between Heaven and Hell, Big Sur: 1961, by Emil White.

Henry Miller: A Chronology and Bibliography, Baltimore: The Waverly Press, 1945, by Bern Porter.

Henry Miller in Selbstzengnissen Bilddokumenten, Reinbek bei Hamburg: Rowohlt, 1961, by Walter Schmiele.

Henry Miller: Expatriate, Pittsburgh: University of Pittsburgh Press, 1961, by Annette Kar Baxter.

Henry Miller: His World of Urania, Foreword by Henry Miller, Preface by James Boyer May, London: Villiers Publishers for 9th House, Hollywood, 1960, by Sydney Omarr.

Henry Miller in Conversation, Trans. by Anthony Macnabb and Harry Scott, Chicago: Quadrangle Books, 1972, by Georges Belmont.

A Henry Miller Miscellanea, San Mateo: Bern Porter, 1945.

The Henry Miller Reader, Edited by Lawrence Durrell, New York: New Directions, 1959.

Henry Miller: Watercolors, Drawings, and His Essay, The Angel is My Watermark, New York: Abrams, 1962.

Henry Miller: Years of Trial and Triumph, 1962–1964: The Correspondence of Henry Miller and Elmer Gertz, ed. Elmer and Gertz and Felice Flanery

Lewis, Carbondale: Southern Illinois University Press, 1978.

Insomnia; Or the Devil At Large, Euclid, Ohio: Loujon Press, 1971, by Henry Miller.

Into The Night Life, Berkeley: 1947, by Henry Miller.

The Intimate Henry Miller, New York: New American Library, 1959.

Just Wild About Harry: A Melo-melo in Seven Scenes, New York: New Directions, 1963.

Knud Merrild: A Holiday in Paint, Waldwick: Bern Porter, 1963, by Henry Miller.

Lawrence Durrell and Henry Miller: A Private Correspondence, Edited by George Wickes, New York: Dutton, 1963.

Letters of Henry Miller and Wallace Fowlie, New York: Grove Press, 1975.

Letters to Anais Nin, with an Introduction by Gunther Stuhlmann, New York: Putnam, 1965, by Henry Miller.

Life Without Principle: Three Essays by Henry David Thoreau, with a Preface by Henry Miller, Stanford University: J.L. Delkin, 1946.

The Literature of Silence: Henry Miller and Samuel Beckett, New York: Knopf, 1967, by Ihab Hassan.

Maurizius Forever, Waco: Motive Press, 1946, and San Francisco: Colt Press, 1946, by Henry Miller.

Max and the White Phagocytes, Paris: Obelisk Press, 1938, by Henry Miller.

The Mind and Art of Henry Miller, Baton Rouge: Louisiana State University Press, 1967, by William A. Gordon.

Mother, China, and the World Beyond, Santa Barbara: Capra Press, 1977, by Henry Miller.

Murder the Murderer: An Excursus on War, Big Sur, 1944, by Henry Miller.

My Bike and Other Friends, Santa Barbara: Capra Press, 1978, by Henry Miller.

My Friend, Henry Miller: An Intimate Biography, with a Preface by Henry Miller, New York: J. Day Co., 1956, by Alfred Perlès.

My Life and Times, Chicago: Playboy Press, 1972, by Henry Miller.

Form and Image in the Fiction of Henry Miller, Detroit: Wayne State University Press, 1970, by Jane A. Nelson.

Nexus, Paris: Correa, 1960, by Henry Miller.

The Nightmare Notebook, New York: New Directions, 1975, by Henry Miller.

Of, By, and About Henry Miller: A Collection of Pieces by Miller and Others, Yonkers: Printed by L. Porgie for the Alicat Bookshop Press, 1947.

On Turning Eighty, Santa Barbara: Capra Press, 1972, by Henry Miller.

Order and Chaos Chez Hans Reichel, with an Introduction by Lawrence

Durrell, Tucson: Loujon Press, 1966, by Henry Miller.

Plexus, Paris: Olympia Press, 1953, by Henry Miller.

The Power Within Us, with a Preface by Henry Miller, London: Drummond, 1946, by Haniel Long.

Quiet Days in Clichy, Paris: Olympia Press, 1956, by Henry Miller.

The Red Notebook, Highlands, N.C.: Jonathan Williams, 1959, by Henry Miller.

Reflections on the Death of Mishima, Santa Barbara: Capra Press, 1972, by Henry Miller.

Remember to Remember, London: Grey Walls Press, 1952, by Henry Miller.

Reunion in Barcelona: A Letter to Alfred Perles, Northwood: Scorpion Press, 1959, by Henry Miller.

Reunion in Big Sur: A Letter to Henry Miller in Reply to His Reunion in Barcelona, Northwood: Scorpion Press, 1959, by Alfred Perlès.

The Rosy Crucifixion, 3 vols., New York: Grove Press, 1965, by Henry Miller.

Scenario (A Film with Sound), Paris: Obelisk Press, 1937, by Henry Miller.

Semblance of a Devoted Past, Berkeley: Bern Porter, 1944, by Henry Miller.

Sexus, 2 vols., Paris: Obelisk Press, 1949, by Henry Miller.

The Smile at the Foot of the Ladder, by Henry Miller; Preface by Edwin Corle, New York: Duell, Sloan and Pearce, 1948.

Stand Still Like the Hummingbird, Norfolk, Conn.: New Directions, 1962, by Henry Miller.

The Sun of Death, with a Preface by Henry Miller, New York: Simon and Schuster, 1964, by P. Prevelakis.

Sunday After the War, Norfolk, Conn.: New Directions, 1944, by Henry Miller.

This Is Henry, Henry Miller from Brooklyn: Conversations with the Author, Los Angeles: Nash Publishing Company, 1974, by Robert Snyder.

The Time of the Assassins: A Study of Rimbaud, Norfolk, Conn.: New Directions, 1956, by Henry Miller.

To Paint Is to Love Again, Alhambra: Cambria Books, 1960, by Henry Miller.

Tropic of Cancer, with a Preface by Anaïs Nin, Paris: Obelisk Press, 1934, by Henry Miller.

Tropic of Capricorn, Paris: Obelisk Press, 1939, by Henry Miller.

Unpublished Selections from The Diary, Athens, Ohio: D. Schneider Press, 1968, by Anaïs Nin.

What Are You Going to Do About Alf?, Paris: Lecram-Servant, 1935, by Henry Miller.

Why Abstract?, New York: G. Wittenborn, 1962 [1946], by Hilaire Hiler, Henry Miller and William Saroyan.

The Wisdom of the Heart, Norfolk, Conn.: New Directions, 1940, by Henry Miller.

The World of Sex, Printed by J[ohn] H[enry] N[ash] for Friends of Henry Miller, 1940; Paris: Olympia Press, 1959, by Henry Miller.

Writer and Critic: A Correspondence with Henry Miller, Baton Rouge: Louisiana State University Press, 1968, by William A. Gordon.

I have also viewed or listened to the following non-print documents:

Henry Miller Asleep and Awake, Los Angeles: 1973, 1 Reel, 16 mm, Color Film, 35 minutes, by Tom Schiller.

Henry Miller Recalls and Reflects, New York: Riverside Records, 1956, a record edited by Ben Grauer.

Henry Miller: Reflections on Writing, Los Angeles: 1971, 1 Reel, 16 mm, Film, 55 minutes, by Robert Snyder.

Interview with Henry Miller, Conducted by George Wickes, London: Sept. 12, 1961, 2 reels, by George Wickes.

The following notes document the manuscript sources for this book. In my citations I have made use of several abbreviations for recurring notes. In all cases I indicate the manuscript depository; when no library is indicated, it should be understood that the manuscript is in the Henry Miller Collection, Special Collections, the University of California, Los Angeles.

The Key to Abbreviations follows:

ACN: The Air-Conditioned Nightmare manuscript

AN: Anaïs Nin

BSN: Black Spring Notes

CCH: The Correspondence Concerning Hamlet [Original Title], by Henry Miller and Michael Fraenkel.

CWBL, UVA: The Clifton Waller Barrett Library, University of Virginia

DC: Dartmouth College Library

ES: Emil Schnellock

HL: Henry E. Huntington Library

HM: Henry Miller

IU: Indiana University Library
LC: The Library of Congress
MM: Miscellaneous Manuscripts
MPM: Miscellaneous Printed Material
MPR: Miscellaneous Prefaces and Reviews
Ms: Manuscript
NU: Northwestern Univeristy Library
NYPL: New York Public Library
PU: Princeton University Library
PN: Paris Notebooks
SFPL: San Francisco Public Library
SIU: Southern Illinois University Library
TC: Tropic of Cancer Manuscripts
T CAP: Tropic of Capricorn Manuscripts
UCLA: Library of the University of California, Los Angeles, Special
      Collections Division
UM: Uncatalogued Manuscripts
UT: University of Texas Library
YU: Yale University Library
WL: The World of Lawrence Manuscripts

The form of the citations is: (1) text page number (2) catch phrase (3) manuscript title (4) date (5) page (6) location of manuscript.

In my book I give the portrait of Henry Miller, individually and in relation to others, that is made possible by the sources available to me. Other people have told somewhat different versions of this story. Any reader who wishes to compare these with mine should consult the following volumes.

Henry Miller's account of his life is given primarily in his "autobiographical romances": *Tropic of Capricorn, Sexus, Plexus,* and *Nexus.* Other volumes touching upon important aspects of his biography include: *Tropic of Cancer, Black Spring, The World of Sex, Quiet Days in Clichy, The Air-Conditioned Nightmare, Big Sur and the Oranges of Hieronymous Bosch,* and *Insomnia.*

Anaïs Nin has treated her relation to Miller in *The Diary of Anais Nin: 1931-1934* Volume 1, ed. Gunther Stuhlmann, New York: The Swallow Press and Harcourt, Brace & World, 1966; *The Diary of Anais Nin, 1939-1944,* Volume 3, ed. Gunther Stuhlmann, New York: Harcourt Brace Jovanovich, 1969, and subsequent volumes of the *Diary.*

Alfred Perlès has written about his relation to Miller in *My Friend Henry Miller*, New York: John Day Co., 1956.

SOURCES

A Programmatic Preface

vii   "we have written": T CAP Ms, 5; adapted by Miller from Miguel de Unamuno's essay "How to write a Novel."

vii   "I see everything": HM to Claude Houghton, April 1942.

viii   "I have by no means": HM to Kurt Kusenberg, 1-28-59.

viii   "know or knew only a fragment": HM to Jay Martin, 9-23-71, Jay Martin Collection.

x   "I am . . . highly suspicious": HM to Jay Martin, 10-17-72, Jay Martin Collection.

x   "I had a thousand faces": HM to Renate Gerhardt, 1-22-62, Gerhardt Collection.

x   "As one who has lived": HM to Neville Armstrong, 6-13-55.

xi   "one author does not even know": "On His Sins of Omission," *New York Times Book Review*, 1-2-72, 10.

xi   "I frankly don't believe": HM to Jay Martin, 10-17-72, Jay Martin Collection.

BOOK ONE

New York

One: Little Henry and His Horse Dexter

3   He was born: HM to Sidney Omarr, n.d. [1962]; HM to Tom Moore 9-21-63, SIU.

3   "I was born happy": HM to Alfred Perlès, in *Art and Outrage*, p. 57

3   paternal grandfather: HM to Eve Miller, [1960]; on other ancestors: PN, II, 153.

4   his own father's house: HM to F.J. Temple, 6-27-65.

5   German atmosphere: HM to Renate Gerhardt, 8-26-66, Gerhardt Collection.

5   Lauretta Anna: Henry Miller Family letters.

5   beloved lilacs [and other details of garden]; "Elemental Events," BSN, 22 ff.

6   tin factory: "Postscriptus" to Dreams of May 30-31, 1933, 15-16.

6   fire: "Astrology," MM, 1.

6   Nieting refused: "Astrology" MM, 1.

6   grandfather worked: BSN, 25.

7   Magic lantern: BSN, 22.

7	well-bred monkey: BSN, 25.
8	a ferryboat captain: *Dreambook* (Commentaries), 18.
7	Eton jacket: *Moloch,* 160-1.
7	wash the windows, *Plexus* Ms, cancelled passage, 779.
8	humiliated terribly: Ms essay, written Christmas, 1965; intended for Franz Schneider Verlag (Munich), "for the benefit of psychically disabled children," 1-3.
8	All the streets, etc.: BSN, 23; *Moloch* Ms., 156-7; T CAP Ms, 93-4.
9	From Fillmore Place: Richard G. Osborn box, folder 2.
9	United States Street: HM to Richard G. Osborn, July 4, [1931], 4.
10	books introduced: BSN, 21.
10	Henty: HM to Norman Holmes Pearson, 9-2-65, Pearson collection; HM to Lawrence Clark Powell, 12-7-60.
10	sister Lauretta: "Astrology," MM, 1.
11	criminal: HM to Renate Gerhardt, 12-22-61, Gerhardt Collection.

Two: The New Neighborhood

12	bought a house: HM to F.J. Temple; BSN, 2.
13	house after house: Henry Miller: Collection of Photographs, UCLA.
14	older boys: Charles Gross to HM, n.d., 2-3.
14	piano lessons: BSN, 13.
14	packages of clothes: BSN, 4.
14	1902: "Astrology," MM, 3.
15	teachers: George Wright to HM, 4-6-51.
15	a prank: "Astrology," MM, 4.
17	"Deep Thinkers": HM to F.J. Temple; *Plexus* Notes, SIU; a Xerxes Society printed New Year's card for 1910 is in UCLA.
17	boys gathered: George Wright to HM, 4-6-51; HM to Renate Gerhardt 12-8-61, Gerhardt Collection; Notes on Dreams, Sept. 1933.
17	". . . merry and bright!" TC Ms, II 1, 70.
18	athletes: HM to F.J. Temple, 1.
18	divided over trifles: *Plexus* Notes, SIU.
18	to snare him: BSN, 5,6.
18	wear himself out: BSN, 5; T CAP Ms, 93-4.
18	disgusted with the curriculum; HM to Huntington Cairns, 7-23-38, Cairns Collection, LC; HM to Henri Fluchère, 7-23-38.
18	Atlas Portland Cement: ACN notes; TC, II, 71.
19	sleepiest clerk: Ray A. Wetzler to HM, 9-2-52.
19	Stanley Borowski: HM to Bern Porter, 5-5-44, 2.
19	*Esoteric Buddhism:* HM to Lawrence Durrell, 11-11-59; HM to Huntington Cairns, 4-30-39, Cairns Collection, LC.
19	Sudermann: HM to John Lane Co., 5-2-51.
20	"Some day": TC Ms, II, 74-5.

Three: *Wine, Women, and Song*

21   experience with sex, etc., BSN, 16, 18.

22   Frances Glanty: PN, II, 142.

22   Miss Green: *Dreambook,* 3-31-33.

23   Edna Booth: *Dreambook,* 2-7-33.

24   appeared radiant: *Moloch* Ms, 95-6.

25   Pauline Chouteau: Materials concerning Miller's relation with her are drawn from: BSN, 5-12; *Moloch* Ms, 99-109; TC Ms, II, 7,8; TC Ms, III, 230; HM to Henri Fluchère, 7-23-38; PN, III, 139; HM to Huntington Cairns, 7-23-38 and 4-30-39, Cairns Collection, LC; HM to AN, May 1932, SIU.

27   cement company dance: PN, III, 119.

27   ditch the old dame: *Moloch* Ms, 102.

27   Dr. Cassius: TC Ms, III, 228-9.

27   to send Henry to Cornell: *Moloch* Ms, 102.

28   Even in his dreams: *Moloch* Ms, 99-102.

29   His mother and father looked ruefully at him: BSN, 5-6.

29   Savage School: BSN, 10.

30   writing letters: BSN, 10.

30   One night: *Moloch* Ms, 107-9.

31   Frances Hunter: *Dreambook,* 9-17-33, 10-14-33.

32   mutilated fetus: TC Ms, II, 77a-78a.

Four: *Slave Days and Schizophrenia*

33   sat on a bench: T CAP Ms, 130-2; HM to Renate Gerhardt, 2-9-62, Gerhardt Collection.

34   cynical perfectionist: William Dewar to HM, 1962.

34   essay on Nietzsche: BSN, 4.

35   Challacombe: T CAP Ms, 133-4; BSN, 13-14.

36   break with Pauline: HM to F.J. Temple, 6-27-65.

36   afraid of the future: *Dreambook,* 42.

37   fit for monsters: HM to Renate Gerhardt 9-23-61, Gerhardt Collection.

37   first job: ACN notebook.

37   lost grip on himself: "What Am I?—Where Am I?—What Am I Doing Here?" Ms, [1968].

37   Bill Parr: PN, III, 118.

38   Goldman: BSN, 9-11.

38   Pauline: HM to F.J. Temple, 6-27-65.

39   theaters: "Preface" to *Ecce Homo* Ms, [1965], 7.

40   Powys confessed: "There is a Tyrant in Every Country" [c. 1947], MPR, 2; Miller also heard Powys lecture on Conrad in 1923: HM to ES, 11-5-23.

40   Persistently he inquired: *Dreambook,* 3-31-33, 5-6; PN, III, 22; *Crazy Cock* Ms, 178.

42   Lou Jacobs: PN, III, 119.

42   elaborate speeches: BSN, 12.

43   his imaginative work: "The Bowery" Ms [c. 1953], 1-3.

43   Harris: "Bezeque" Ms [c. 1933], 2; Elmer Gertz to HM, 1-9-62, Gertz Collection, LC.

43   Boardman Robinson: PN, I, 165.

44   wrote to a California poet: HM to Charles Keeler, 12-9-16, 1-3, HL.

44   two pals: HM to ES, April 1930, 11-12.

Five: The Love Songs of Henry Val Miller

46   Brooklyn pianist: BSN, 11-12; *Moloch* Ms, 143, 154-5, 67.

47   "Miss Wickens and I": HM to Charles Keeler, 12-19-16, 3, HL.

47   War Department: HM to F.J. Temple, 6-27-65.

47   *Washington Post*: HM to Huntington Cairns, 3-6-38, Cairns collection, LC.

47-8   impending marriage: T CAP, Ms 32-3.

48   a shave: *Moloch* Ms, 4.

48   domineering: Barbara Sanford to HM, 2-10-54.

48   being a writer: *Moloch* Ms, 141-2.

48   so many positions: HM to Huntington Cairns, 7-23-38 Cairns Collection, LC.

48   Fifty-third Street: Henry Miller Family Letters, stationery of Henry Miller/Tailor.

48   blackboards: "Rimbaud Opus, Part 2 Ms, cancelled passage, 2.

49   strategic blunder: *Moloch* Ms, 175, 358-61; T CAP Ms, 101; *World of Sex* Ms, 33-15.

50   fought bitterly: *Moloch* Ms, 74-94.

51   Waldo Frank: HM to Richard G. Osborn, n.d.

51   masochistic pleasure: HM to Gerald Robitaille, 3-8-51, SIU.

51   *The Black Cat:* TC Ms, II, 72-4; "The Black Cat Club," *The Black Cat Magazine,* 24 (Jan. 1919), 44-5.

51   first publication: "The Black Cat Club," *The Black Cat Magazine,* 24, #4 (May 1919), 43.

52   He was made: HM to Valentine Miller, 1-22-60; HM to Renate Gerhardt, Gerhardt Collection.

52   dough rolled in: Correspondence from the editor of *The Black Cat Magazine,* H.E.B. to HM, 5-8-19, 6-13-19, 8-5-19, 10-25-19; Miller's essays appeared as follows: 24 #9 (June 1919), 42; 24 #11 (Aug. 1919), 44-5; 24, #13 (Oct. 1919) 44.

53 receivership: HM to Maurice Girodias, 6-24-48.
54 first gift: HM to AN, 5-27-33, 4.

Six: The Cosmodemonic Telegraph Company

55 Western Union: Materials concerning Miller's job include: HM to Harold J. McGrath, 1-9-59; Muriel Cowley to Jay Martin n.d. [December, 1970], and 3-19-71, Jay Martin Collection; *Dreambook,* Sept. 1933; M.J. Rivise to Bern Porter, 7-24-51; *Moloch* Ms, 46-8.
59 grotesque notes: Rosario Dimiceli to HM, 11-30-21.
60 Gupte: TC [First Version] Ms, notes; "Notes on Bizarre Characters" Ms, 1-3 [75 characters are listed and described].
60 Ramakrishna and Tagore: HM Interview with Minoo Javan, Ms [c. 1959]; "Original Unfinished Erotica" Ms in "Material Excluded from the Air-Conditioned Nightmare," 163.
62 he'd grill: *Moloch* Ms, 58-60.
62 boarders: Orvis Ross, "Henry Miller Needs Sympathy," *Minnesota Sunday Tribune,* 1-24-60, 4; Orvis Ross to Tom Moore, 2-27-59, UT; *Moloch* Ms, 77.
63 why didn't Ross: *Moloch* Ms, 76.
64 open misery: T CAP Ms, 36-7; T. Takikana to HM, 9-19-21.
65 Henry was feeling: T CAP Ms, 49-50; *Moloch* Ms, 369-76.
66 One of these victims: William J. Grimmond to HM, 4-8-22.
67 Emil Schnellock: HM to ES, 9-7-33.
68 good for a touch: T CAP Ms, 34.
68 first poem: HM to Lawrence Durrell, 4-29-58.
68 baby butcher: *Moloch* Ms, 260.
69 "I didn't look": HM to ES, n.d. [1924-5].

Seven: Clipped Wings and Other Angels

70 *Twelve Men:* Orvis Ross to Tom Moore, 2-27-59, UT.
71 One luminous evening: "Postscriptus" to Dreams of May 30-31, 1933, 24-5.
71 On March 20: HM to ES, 3-20-22; TC Ms, II, 74.
71 Charles Candles: "Charles Candles—'The Moral Moron,'" in "Messenger Sketch Book," 1-18.
72 woeful glances: TC Ms, II, 75.
72 first day's writing: HM to ES, 4-20-22.
73 other short pieces: "Auctioneer" Ms, 1-4; HM to F. Florian Steiner, 4-8-65; HM to Ingeborg Bertuch, 12-13-57; Mezzotints file; HM to ES, 12-15-23; HM to ES, n.d. [c. 1924]; HM to Bern Porter, written on Ms of *Miscellanea,* n.d.
74 In the kitchen again: mezzotint "The Awakening," MPM.

Eight: June, Julia, Juliette, Henriette, She, Her

76   money in his pocket: T CAP Ms, 19.
77   Central European: HM to Alfred Perlès, 5-21-65, UT.
77   Strindberg: HM to F.J. Temple, 6-27-65.
77   a wall of fog: T CAP Ms, 13-14; Anaïs Nin, "The Labyrinth" Ms, NU; HM to AN, May 1932, SIU.
78   stews of sexual mystery: PN, I, 187; ES, Uncatalogued Papers, n.p.; *Crazy Cock* Ms, 74, 131-2; *Crazy Cock,* 2nd Ms version, 12-13, 55-6; T CAP Ms, 43-7, 92-3.
78   a new life: HM to Claude Houghton, Nov. 1942, 1-5; HM to Eva Sikelianou, 2-7-43.
79   third time he took June out: T CAP Ms, 97.
79   she whispered: *Crazy Cock,* 2nd Ms Version, 175; T CAP Ms, 38.
82   June offered: "Cinema Vanves," Pt. 2, 8.
85   reversed positions: *Crazy Cock* Ms, 131-2.
85   a hotel: T CAP Ms, 100; PN, III, 114.
87   an angry policeman: PN, III (1935), n.p.

Nine: A New Life

89   Bronx: HM to ES, 11-5-23.
89   wept together: *Crazy Cock,* 2nd Ms Version, 146-7.
90   paper and twine: T CAP Ms, 106.
90   *Make it thirty*: HM to ES, 12-15-23.
91   Henry inserted: "Extracts from Letters of Jacobus Hendrik Dun," MM.
91   Willever: *Moloch* Ms, 332.
91   efficiency experts: A.H. Diamond to HM, 10-25-63, 11-26-63.
91   Egyptians: HM to Albert Cossery, 5-2-45; T CAP Ms, 89-90.
91   proper respect: HM to June Mansfield, 9-22-23.
92   name was Smerthe: HM to Renate Gerhardt, 4-17-61, Gerhardt Collection.
94   Nip-and-tuck: HM to ES, n.d. [c. 1924].
95   walked off the job: T CAP Ms, 137-8.

Ten: Candy and Other Rackets

98   hated the sunlight: *Crazy Cock* Ms, 102.
98   as she went from: TC Ms, III, 11-12; TC Ms, IV, 205; *Crazy Cock,* 2nd Ms Version, 89-90; A.K. Baxter to HM, 8-10-57.

99   candy racket: HM to ES, 2-2-25; HM to Richard G. Osborn, 6-8-[33].

100   sumptuous dinners: PN, II, 86 (verso).

101   Whitman's poem: MM.

101   "Mezzotints" MPM; [all extant mezzotints discussed are in UCLA, UT and SIU]; HM to ES, 8-8-24; PN, III, 104 (verso); HM to ES, n.d. [1925].

102   *Pearson's:* Vol. 51, #1 (February 1925).

106   go to Florida: TC Ms, III, 305; HM to Richard Galen Osborn, n.d. [1933].

Eleven: Visions and Revisions

109   she saw no hope: HM to F.J. Temple, 6-27-65.

110   "Diary of a Futurist": T CAP Ms, 140-1.

110   in a joking mood: HM to ES, 11-5-23, 4.

110   Bruce Barton: PN, II, 18.

110   H.L. Mencken: TC Ms, II, n.p.

111   first two tales: HM to Huntington Cairns, 4-30-39, SIU.

Twelve: By the Shores of Junaluska

113   fortune in Asheville: the Asheville adventure is fully recorded in six undated letters from HM to Emil ("Seymour") Cohen (later Conason), written between July and September 1926, addressed by HM from 32 Oakwood Street, West Asheville, N.C.

115   estimation of his work: George Bye to HM, 8-27-26.

116   "We've got to get back": *Crazy Cock,* 2nd MS Version, 42-4.

116   Richmond: HM to ES, 11-15-39.

Thirteen: In the Catacomb

118   Remsen Street, etc.: HM to Richard Galen Osborn n.d. [1933].

118   encyclopedia: HM to Lawrence Clark Powell, 2-15-50; *Crazy Cock,* 2nd Ms Version, 45-89.

119   to sell newspapers: *Crazy Cock* Ms, 250-1.

119   he dreamed: "Novel Based on Dreams," *Dreambook* (1933), 88-9; PN, III, 112.

120   whorehouse routine: PN, I, 163.

120   June had worked out: *Crazy Cock* Ms, 216-7.

120   She used makeup: Muriel Cowley to Jay Martin, 3-19-71.

121   "Like a whore": *Crazy Cock* Ms, 41.

Fourteen: The Fabulous Twins

123   Bodenheim paw June: PN, I, 203.

123   Jean Kronski: materials on the Jean-June-Henry triangle are derived
        chiefly from the several whole or partial versions of the novel *Crazy
        Cock* and Miller's comments, notes and marginalia in the manuscript.
        In addition I use: "Notes for a Novel," 1-23 + 1-7, UT; PN, I,
        156-186; PN, III, 112; TC Ms, III, 224; T CAP Ms, 67; "Brochure"
        (1932-3) marginalia, 224; HM to ES 12-4-33; HM to Renate
        Gerhardt, 9-27-61, Gerhardt Collection.

124   one acquaintance: Alfred Perlès, *The Renegade* (London: George Allen
        & Unwin, 1943), 159-60.

127   "FIVE YEARS": HM to ES, 9-7-33.

129   "The Failure": *Crazy Cock,* 2nd Ms Version, 139.

Fifteen: Legendary Travails

131   a steady job: T CAP Ms, 79.

132   June came to sit: ·T CAP Ms, 80-1.

132   brought presents: HM to AN, May 1932, SIU.

133   Let him live to prove: PN, I, 161.

Sixteen: The Spirit of St. Valentine

135   called his parents: TC Ms, II, 10-13.

136   why not go back: PN, I, 159; *Crazy Cock,* 2nd Ms Version, 90-12,
        117, 149-56.

138   trifling queries: *Dreambook,* May 30-31, 1933, 4.

138   Lindbergh: T CAP Ms, 78-83.

139   set down notes: "Notes for a Novel" ["These notes were originally
        compiled in the space of 24 hours handrunning at the office of the Park
        Commissioner, Queens County, in 1927 while June was in Europe
        with her friend Jean Kronski. Copy of original given to Berthe
        Schrank when in Paris, 1932 or '33."], UT.

Seventeen: The Birth of Dion Moloch

141   baggage with her: TC Ms, III, 6-7.

142   to support her: T CAP Ms, 141-2.

142   "in the Hamsun style": "Capricorn Plan" [Large Sheet].

143   *This Gentile World:* HM to Ralph Lyon, Jr., 11-13-54.

143   told Conason: HM to Emil Cohen [Conason], n.d., 1.
146   Dion Moloch walked: *Moloch* Ms, 10.
146   What the rabble: *Moloch* Ms, 8.
147   "Nothing," he observes: *Moloch* Ms, 6.
147   "All the lies, the counterfeits," *Moloch* Ms, 350.
148   recurring dream: "Dream #4," MM, 2.

Eighteen: The Dream of Europe

149   Henry and June's actual route: manuscript materials relating to the
      European trip include: "Nexus–Vol. 2" Ms, written 10-3-59 [HM
      marginalia: "Interrupted. Never Continued"], 1-3, "Who Am
      I?—Where Am I? What Am I Doing Here?" Ms, in Gerald
      Robitaille, Uncatalogued Papers; HM to Emil Cohen [Conason],
      8-26-28, 1-16; HM to ES, March 1930; "Recollections of Avignon"
      Ms, written 3-17-54, 1-6; HM to Claude Houghton, 5-10-42.
152   Paris was the twin: PN, I, 33,35,43.
158   Monte Carlo: TC Ms, III, 258-9; HM to F.J. Temple, 6-27-65.
158   promissory note: HM to Huntington Cairns, 4-14-39, Cairns Collec-
      tion, LC.
158   night before sailing: TC Ms, 31-4.

Nineteen: The Hand of the Dreamer

160   pimp and whore: "Dialogue with Olle Länsberg" [published in
      Swedish in *Idum Vecko*], MM.
161   the book of his life: *Crazy Cock* Ms; PN, III, 109.
162   first approved version: *Crazy Cock,* 2nd Ms Version, 1.
165   a 1500 word column: HM to Richard G. Osborn, Sunday, Paris, n.d.
      [1933].
165   Henry had to compose: TC Ms, III, 266.
166   "You're my god!" T CAP Ms, 97.
166   his last night: HM to ES, mid October, 1930; PN, I, 27 (verso); PN,
      III, 122 (verso).
168   picked clean: HM to Walker Winslow, 9-23-46, HL.

BOOK TWO

Paris

One: Man of Letters

179   lodgings: HM to Abe Elkus, 2-25-30 [stationery of Melvin Private Hotel], 1-10.

180   "Jesus," he wrote: HM to ES 4-1-30, 5.

181   Return to: for instance, HM to ES, Oct. 1930.

181   Zadkine: TC Ms, I, 4; HM to ES, March 1930 [headed "Spring on the Troittoirs"], 9-10.

182   Hôtel de Paris: for Miller's residences in Paris see PN, II, 5, which lists residences from March 1930 to March 1933, excluding "those places where I 'flopped' for a night."

182   speech broke down: HM to ES, 3-6-30, 5.

183   five stories up: HM to ES, 3-6-30, 1.

183   In his quarter: HM to ES, March 1930, 4.

183-4   In this exhibit: HM to ES, March 1930, 2.

184   his chief guides: PN, I, 70; "Intimate Notes on June" MM.

184   Often lost: PN, I, 29.

185   "even the gendarmes": HM to ES, March 1930, 6.

186   Place d'Italie: HM to ES, April 1930 ["The Romans and the Wops"], 5.

186   Miller's first Sunday: HM to ES, 3-9-30 ["First Sunday in Paris"], 1-5.

188   "So, all in all": HM to ES, 3-6-30, 3-4.

188   Paul Morand: HM to ES, March 1930 ["Apocryphe Hebdomaire"], 7.

189   In the evening: HM to Renate Gerhardt, 11-29-60, Gerhardt Collection.

Two: Paris and Me!

191   "Here are a few": HM to ES, 3-31-30 ["Degringolade"], 8-10.
192   Guy Hickok: HM to ES, 5-10-30, 1; PN, I, 108.
192   letter to Morand: PN, I, 4-1-30, 47.
192   a French title: PN, I, 28.
192   Buñuel to respond: HM to ES, 5-10-30.
192   Dulac's residence: HM to ES, 5-10-30, 7; PN, I, 107.
192-3   Club de L'Ecran: HM to ES, March 1930, 10.
194   It seemed foolish: HM to ES, April 1930 ["Bistre and Pigeon Dung"], 12.
194   Though she had not written: HM to ES, 5-10-30, 11.
194   "Don't let me": HM to ES, April 1930, 16.
196   His specialties: Perlès Scrapbook Articles, UT.
197   case of dysentery: HM to ES, April [21], 1930 ["Degringolade, Tintamarre, Salmongondice, Chinoiserie"], 1.
198   employ a stenographer: HM to ES, April 1930, 15.
198   Henri Müller: HM to ES, 5-10-30; HM to John Slocum, n.d. [June, 1940].
198   "I believe in it": HM to ES, March 1930, 14.

Three: Life Is A Sandwich

199   June only cabled: HM to ES, 6-18-30, 3-4.
200   Champs Élysées: HM to ES, 5-10-30, 6.
202   "rollicking book": HM to ES, 5-10-30, 9.
202   Pension Orfila: T CAP Ms, 164.
203   a bridge along the Seine: "Cinema Vanves" Ms, Pt. 4, 1, UT.
203   gathering material: Jac. H. Dun to HM, 11-9-48; "Cinema Vanves" Ms, Pt. 7, 1-3.
204   Dun had turned: HM to June Mansfield [Miller], 7-4-30, inserted in TC Ms, IV, 1-4.
206   Henry consulted a travel bureau: HM to Emil Conason, 7-18-30.

Four: Cinema Days: June to the Rescue and Other Catastrophes

207   Leçons d'Anglais: PN, I, 106 (and 106 verso).
208   second-hand clothing: HM to Werner Jost, 6-1-48.
208   But staying at the Cinéma Vanves: "Cinema Vanves" Ms, UT; "Cinema Vanves" [c. March 1931]; and "Cinema Vanves," 2nd Ms. Version [c. 1932-3], MM.
210   naughty brothels: "Naughty Joints," PN, I, 21.
210   Nanavati: HM to ES, 8-9-30, 1-4.
211   Lucienne Boyer's: PN, III, 128.

212   June was nowhere in sight: HM to Abe Elkus, 9-29-30.
212   Stepping off the train: TC Ms, III, 257.
213   meet Germaine Dulac: HM to ES, 10-23-30.
213   flimsy evening dresses: HM to Abe Elkus, 10-1-30; HM to ES, 10-30-30.
214   "Seems now": HM to Abe Elkus, 9-29-30, 6.
214   separate paths: TC Ms, II, 106-7; HM to Gunther Stuhlmann, 12-11-64.
214   letters asking Oliver: TC Ms, III, 268.
214   "When I listen": TC, III, 265.
214   two Hindu girls: HM to ES, 10-30-30.
214   English lessons: HM to Joe O'Regan, n.d.[11-3-30].
215   he had succeeded in getting: HM to ES, 10-23-30.

Five: Ballade d'Hiver

216   a chain letter: HM to Abe Elkus, 11-18-30, 1-4.
216   friends couldn't aid: HM to ES, 11-18-30, 1-2.
217   Richard Galen Osborn, Osborn papers, *passim.*
218   "It is just likely": HM to ES, 3-10-31, 4.
218   Germaine Daugeard: HM to ES, 5-10-31, 4-5.
219   Madeline Boyd: TC Ms, IV, 4.
220   he'd shout gleefully: HM to ES, 12-14-31, 4.
220   Cirque Medrano: HM to ES, 3-10-31, 4.
221   On New Year's Eve: HM to ES, 2-16-31, 11.
222   Millard Fillmore Osman: PN, II, 145-8; TC Ms, I, 78; TC Ms, III, 223; *Dreambook* 1-31-33, 5-7.

Six: The Villa Seurat: An Instinctivist Portrait

225   Villa Seurat: HM to ES, 11-[c. 15]-31, 1-4.
225   Beckoning Henry to enter: HM to ES, 5-20-33.
227   under Perlès's name: PN, I, 133; "Miscellaneous Essays on Paris," MPM; HM to ES, 3-10-31, 2.
228   Hôtel Central: TC Ms, I, 82.
228   Hungry, Henry: HM to ES, 3-10-31 and 11-[c. 15]-31; HM to Richard G. Osborn, n.d. [1933]; PN, I, 7-8 [Marginalia].
229   swept off his feet: TC Ms, II, 73; TC Ms, III, 215-6; HM to Renate Gerhardt, 12-8-61, Gerhardt Collection.
231   Fraenkel who declared: HM to Gunther Stuhlmann, 12-11-64.
231   "It's very good": HM to Walker Winslow, 9-23-46, HL.
232   In the early afternoon: HM to ES, begun 8-24-31, completed 9-3-31, 1-19.
233   a wonderful hoax: "The New Instinctivism" Ms, 1-20, CWBL, U VA; HM to ES, 7-12-32.

233   "I never read Rilke": pencilled note on "Rainer Maria Rilke" Ms, MM.

234   conciliatory tone: Samuel Putnam to Alfred Perlès and HM, 8-21-31, UT.

Seven: Happier Days—and Newer Disasters

235   "June Mansfield": PN, I, 59 (and verso).

235   On a Saturday night: TC Ms, "Rejected pages," 99-110, Cairns Collection, LC.

236   Bald came up: TC Ms, II, 104.

237   Hôtel Princesse: HM to AN, May 1932, SIU; TC Ms, II, 105.

237   affair with Bertha: TC Ms, II, 103; PN, III, 129-30.

238   "I am living": "Original Version," TC Ms, I, 1.

239   Anaïs Guiler: Osborn Papers, Folder 2, *passim.*

240   compared her beauty: HM to ES, 9-7-33, 2.

241   any inner passion: HM to Richard G. Osborn, 2-6-33.

242   June soon found Anaïs: Miller's sources of information concerning the relations between June and Anaïs Nin were: (1) conversations with June, Nin, and Perlès; (2) Anaïs Nin's journal and her autobiographical novel in manuscript, "Alraune," which she gave to Miller for comment; thus, what Miller "knew" is highly colored, partly true and partly invented. My sources are: PN, III, 115, 132-33; "Miscellaneous Intimate Notes on June" (1932-3), 1-5; TC Ms, 107-110; Alfred Perlès, "My Friend Henry Miller" Ms, 66-70; Anaïs Nin, "Alraune" Ms, First and Second Versions, with marginalia by HM (1933, 1934), NU; Anaïs Nin, *The Diary of Anaïs Nin: 1931-1934,* Volume I, New York: The Swallow Press and Harcourt, Brace & World, 1966, *passim.* Miller says (HM to ES, 10-14-32) that by 1932 he and AN had exchanged 900 pages of letters.

243   "I'll never marry": PN, III, 113-5.

Eight: Walled In

244   a job in Dijon: HM to Joe O'Regan, 1-25-32; Osborn Papers, Folder 2 [Letters marked "Lycee Carnot/Dijon"]; "Intimate Notes on June," including HM to AN, 1-29-32, MM; HM to AN [Letters from Dijon, 1932, *passim.*], SIU.

248   "le spleen anglais": "Le Cadavre Vivant," [c. 1932], MM.

248   twenty-six articles: List of titles sent to ES, 1932, MM.

248   "It's meant to be": HM to ES, 7-12-32.

248   he went straight: TC Ms, I, 26.

Nine: The Last Book

251   He wrote to Bertha: PN, II, 40 (verso).

251   (a present from Anaïs): HM to AN, 5-27-33.

252   4 Avenue Anatole France: HM to ES, Spring [early March] 1932, 1.

252   lost his job: PN, II, 107; Ralph J. Frantz, Managing Editor, *Chicago Tribune,* to HM, 3-25-37, 2.

252   refused a permit: PN, II, 150 (and verso): a letter of request for working permit.

253   His Teutonic habits: "Work Schedule: Major Program," MM, 1-2; George Wickes, "Conversation with Henry Miller," 6-21-65, Wickes Collection.

257   forgive you for that: TC Ms, II, "Letter from Michael" [Fraenkel], 12-17-31.

257   Osborn actually threatened: Osborn Papers, especially folder 2; HM to Richard G. Osborn, 8-7-32, 1-6; HM to Michael Fraenkel, n.d. [1933], 6.

260   showing it to Lowenfels: Lowenfels's commentary, n.d., 1, CWBL, U VA.

260   calling the novel: various titles proposed in: "Intimate Notes on June," MM; HM to AN, 7-30-32, SIU.

261   *Satyricon:* "Excerpts from 'Satyricon'" MM, 1, underlining with marginalia of quoted passage.

262   "greater than *Ulysses*": TC Ms, IV, 4; HM to ES, 7-12-32, 2-3.

262   Bradley: in Bald, "La Vie Bohème" column of 8-19-31.

262   Bradley answered: PN, II, 70 (verso).

263   first talk: HM to Samuel Putnam, Oct. 1932.

263   "If only June": *Dreambook,* 3-31-33, 4.

263   ranted and raved: HM to Lowenfels, Sept. 1932, 1-6.

263   "I think he's crazy" HM to ES, 10-14-32, 12.

264   Typed on the title page: *Crazy Cock* Ms, II, corrected carbon copy.

264   "fire and dynamite," HM to ES, Tuesday a.m., Oct. 1932.

264   preface: HM to ES, 10-14-32; HM to Luis Buñuel, MM, 3.

264   "by Anonymous": TC Ms, I, Title page.

264   not revise: WL, 4-5.

264   a contract: Henry V. Miller, Esq. of 4, Avenue Anatole France, Clichy (Seine) . . . and the Obelisk Press of 38, Rue Saint-Honore, Paris I.

Ten: She-Who-Must-Be-Obeyed

265   stars ruled: PN, II, 62; HM to ES, 6-12-33.

265   regular contributions: HM to ES, Spring 1932, and 3-16-34.

266   entry in her *Journal:* PN, III, 2.

266   house at Louveciennes: HM to ES, 8-25-34, 8-9; "Written in the Diary of Anaïs Nin," MPM, 2; "Self-Portrait," 4th installment, BSN; Perlès, "My Friend Henry Miller" Ms, 178-9.

267   *"You* have been": HM to AN, in WL [c. Mar. 1, 1933], 9; HM to ES, 10-14-32, 9.

267   Venus: PN, II, "Excerpt from Anaïs' Diary," 62-3; AN to HM, 1933, *passim;* HM to ES, 1-1-33, 6-15-33, 2-15-34; "Notes Written in the Diary of Anaïs Nin, MPM, 1-6; HM to Michael Fraenkel, [1933], 1-7; PN, II, handwritten note AN to HM; Perlès, "My Friend Henry Miller" Ms, 64-7; HM to Huntington Cairns, 5-11-38, Cairns Collection, LC.

267   demanded nothing: AN to Gerald Robitaille, n.d., [Sept. 68].

268   "My next wife": HM to ES, Oct. 1932.

268   Paul Morand: HM to ES, 7-12-32.

268   manuscript of *Tropic of Capricorn:* T CAP Ms, 5; HM to Richard G. Osborn, n.d., Osborn Papers, Folder 2, 10.

268   reappearing in Paris: HM to ES, Oct. 1932.

268   his old manuscripts: HM to ES, 10-23-32, 2.

269   tearing them to bits: *Dreambook,* 10-29-32.

269   June arrived: TC Ms, III, 238-9.

269   The days to come: HM to Richard G. Osborn, 1933, [Café du Depart stationery], 2; PN, I, 166 (verso); Pencilled notes, MM, p. 2.

270   *Scarface:* "Intimate Notes on June," MM, 152.

270   long passages: "Jung (Introduction)," in "Brochure," 64 (verso).

270   creating his own betrayal: PN, III, 110; HM to ES, 10-23-32.

270   He showed Anaïs: Perlès, "My Friend Henry Miller" Ms, 66, 70.

272   "Alraune": PN, III, 132-3; Unpublished Manuscripts in the Nin Collection, NU.

272   For a time Fred: Jay Martin: Interview with Alfred Perlès, Hania, Crete, August 1971.

273   waiting to pounce: "Intimate Notes on June," MM, 1-5; T CAP Ms, 153.

274   a ball of toilet paper: HM to ES, 1-1-33.

274   June unexpectedly arrived: PN, II, 84 (verso); HM to ES, 11-28-32, 1-2; and 1-1-33, 3-5; HM to Richard G. Osborn, 12-6-32, 1-5-33.

277   "Tell Henry": HM to ES, 1-1-33; HM to Richard G. Osborn, 1-5-33.

Eleven: Clichy Days and Nightmare Nights

278   a color wheel: "Color-Form," BSN, 1-9.

279   greatly admired the work of Otto Rank: HM to Richard G. Osborn, 1-5-33, 6-7.

280   keep a dreambook: "To Anaïs Nin, Original M.S. of Dream Book, from Henry Miller" is HM's arrangement into a sequence of what he called the "Old Dream Book" record of his dreams; later he tried to make this into a novella called "At Night All Leaping Fountains Speak With a Louder Tone"; other parts of the dream book are found in "Dream Section" and MM. The dream book has an index arranged

according to "thematic materials," listing nine dreams from the old "copy book record" and describing and analyzing 23 dreams occurring between 9-29-32 and 9-25-33. In discussing Miller's dreams I also use several letters including: HM to Huntington Cairns, 4-30-39, Cairns Collection, LC; and HM to Raymond Queneau, 8-3-50.

Twelve: The Lost Book

285   Covici-Friede: HM to Pascal Covici, 1-3-33.

285   composition of *Tropic of Capricorn:* HM to Richard G. Osborn, 2-23-33, 3-4, and May 1933, 10.

285   a critical work on D.H. Lawrence: in such manuscripts as "Brochure," "The Universe of Death," and "The World of Lawrence"—including two complete drafts, revisions and excerpts of the last. I also refer to HM to ES, 4-11-33, 3; and 9-7-33, 1-3. Of primary importance is the red bound notebook stamped THE WORLD OF LAWRENCE BY HENRY MILLER, "Begun at Clichy as a brochure of 100 pages to precede publication of 'Tropic of Cancer'." At the end of his dream book, HM inscribed: "To Anaïs—who opened up for me the 'world of Lawrence'. Henry V. Miller, Feb. 1934."

285   Kahane had remarked: WL, 1; T CAP Ms, 161.

286   "knocking the shit": HM to Richard G. Osborn, 3-14-33.

286   conception of *Brochure* shifted: the various changes, outlines, plans, revisions, etc., of this work are in: "Themes" of "Brochure," I, 31, 203; "Scheme for Brochure," MM i-iv; "Notes for the Lawrence book, properly or otherwise called 'Brochure' I believe," in HM to Hungtington Cairns; "Contents," in HM to Richard G. Osborn, n.d. [c. May 1933], "The World of Lawrence ('Original Draft')"; "Topical Outline of Brochure," WL, 1-14.

287   this idea to Fraenkel's: HM to ES, 4-11-33, 2.

288   ". . . divorced from names": HM to Richard G. Osborn, n.d. [c. May 1933], 3.

288   "Lawrence . . . has meant": HM to ES, 2-16-31 and 9-7-33; HM to AN, 5-30-33; HM to Frieda Lawrence, 9-8-35.

Thirteen: "All the Loose Ends that Were Flapping About Inside Me"

290   Osborn posted: Richard G. Osborn to HM, 5-1-33.

291   "his junior in years": PN, 141 (verso); HM to Richard G. Osborn, [5-20-33], 1-9.

292   *"Dernières pages":* TC Ms, III, 107-10.

293   "The most difficult": T CAP Ms, 1-2.

293   "Self-Portrait": BSN; HM to Richard G. Osborn, 3-14-33; HM to ES, 4-28-33, 1-2.

294	"Fourteenth Ward": "Postscriptus" to Dreams of May 30 and 31, 1933, *Dreambook*, 12.
294	conversation of Walter Lowenfels: HM to Dante Zaccagnini, 2-8-50.
294	Gottfried Benn: "Soul and Destiny (Gottfried Benn)," "Brochure," II; HM to Eugene Jolas, 7-14-50.
295	lessons from Hilaire Hiler: HM to Hilaire Hiler, n.d. [Fall 1933]; Hiler to HM, 4-20-62.
295	"No. We want": "Self-Portrait (Louveciennes)," BSN, 11-12.
295	The grand insanity": AN, "A Boost for Black Spring" Ms, UT.

Fourteen: Anaïs, Anaïs, Anaïs

297	As early as March: HM to Richard G. Osborn, 3-14-33.
297	"American cunts": HM to ES, 3-2-33.
297	By May: HM to Joe O'Regan, 5-4-33.
297	"I don't believe": HM to ES, 6-12-33.
297	Guiler returned: HM to ES, 6-15-33 and 7-12-33.
298	"Above all," he confided: HM to ES, 12-4-33; HM to Richard G. Osborn, 2-4-34 and March 1934.
299	Anaïs' belief in him: HM to Huntington Cairns, 4-30-39, SIU.
299	to be near her: HM to ES, 2-15-34; "Work Schedule: Major Program, MM, 1-2.
299	(He wrote six pages . . .): "Written in the Diary of Anaïs Nin" 1-1-33; notes begin: "New Year's Day . . . in the quiet of Louveciennes," pages 1-6. These notes are not reprinted in Nin's published *Diary*, a highly condensed version of her *Journal intime*.
299	splendid defense of her work: HM to William A. Bradley, 8-2-33, 1-7.
299	"a work of art": Miller copied several passages from Nin's journal into his notebook—e.g., PN, II, 62-3.
300	considerable feelings of guilt: PN, I, 159 (verso) and 184 (verso).
300	to his dreams: Dreams of 1-25-33, 2-7-33, 2-12-33, 9-19-33, *Dreambook;* PN, II, 136-7.
301	debase their relationship: HM to ES, 6-15-33.
301	a duplicate of June: HM to ES, 6-15-33.
301	angered Perlès: Perlès, "My Friend Henry Miller" Ms, 66.
301	felt guilty toward Hugo: PN, I, 159 (verso); PN, II, 136-7; Dream of 1-25-33; Dream of 2-7-33; Dream of 2-12-33; Dream of 9-19-33, *Dreambook*.
302	Anaïs persuaded Hugo: HM to Richard G. Osborn, n.d. [1933]. Folder 2.
302	Walter agreed: "Henry's Preface (Part I)" ["supposedly by Henry Miller—actually by me, Paris, 1933-34 . . . "] CWBL, UVA 1-3.
302	She moved: HM to ES, [March] 16, 1934, 3.
302	her journal," AN to Gerald Robitaille, Aug. 1971. AN's "Notes on 'Tropic of Cancer'" are in PN, II, 22.

302   Hugo blew up: HM to Richard G. Osborn, July 1934.
303   She herself: HM to ES, 7-21-33; HM corrections on encyclopedia article by Gerald Robitaille, Robitaille Collection.
303   inserted into the contract: contract of 6-18-34, additional clauses # 7, 8.
303   Peter Neagoe's: HM to ES, 5-12-34, 8-25-34 and 8-28-34.
303   Artaud: Raymond Queneau, "Prehistoire de Henry Miller" Ms, Queneau Collection; HM to Paul Jacobs, 9-12-53.
303   Kahane appeared: HM to Alfred Perlès, 4-29-54 and 10-31-54.
303   copy to Bruce Barton: HM to ES, 11-11-34, 3.
303   Osborn wrote: Richard G. Osborn to HM, 10-5-34.
303   Duchamp's wife, Mary Reynolds: HM to Hilaire Hiler, 11-29-34, 8.
304   T.S. Eliot: T.S. Eliot to HM, 4-18-35 and 6-13-35.

Fifteen: Wonders and Portents

305   to set up as an analyst: HM to ES, 8-28-34.
306   Anaïs at his side: HM to ES, 10-25-34.
306   Henry was impulsively: HM to ES, 12-29-34; "Finale," from *Crazy Cock*, UT.
306   Anaïs had to cable: HM to ES, 12-29-34.
307   In bleak letters: HM to Hilaire Hiler 1-5-35, 1-5.
307   Walter Lowenfels patiently: HM to Walter Lowenfels, n.d. [Jan. 1935].
308   he met a few: HM to Hilaire Hiler, n.d., [c. Jan. 20, 1935]; HM to Alfred Perlès, 4-5-35; James T. Farrell to HM, 12-20-43.
308   Nothing in Manhattan: HM to Hilaire Hiler, n.d. [c. Jan 7, 1935].
308   four patients a day: HM to Joe O'Regan, O'Regan papers, n.d. [Feb. 1935]; HM to Walter Lowenfels, 3-14-35.
309   intimacy didn't grow: HM to Renate Gerhardt, 2-29-61, Gerhardt Collection.
309   his final night: HM to ES, Oct. 1935, 3.

Sixteen: "Alone in My Private Glory"

310   "When I read": HM to Alfred Perlès, 4-5-35.
311   self-publicizing campaign: HM to Hilaire Hiler, 10-12-[35]; Jay Martin: Interview with Raymond Queneau, Paris, France, Aug. 1971.
312   explaining to Count Keyserling: HM to Count Herman Keyserling, 2-17-36.
313   "colossal in its pretentiousness": "Rejected Pages," in Huntington Cairns Collection, LC.

313   Fred wrote his first: Alfred Perlès to Michael Fraenkel and HM, 12-2-35 CCH, 2.

313   edit a pamphlet: HM to Walter Lowenfels, 11-13-35.

313   surrealist sketch, HM marginalia on "Portrait of General Grant," MPM.

313   stories of lost souls: HM to Alfred Perlès, 4-5-35; "Agenda," PN, III, 68.

314   frequently pinned notes: Jay Martin: Interview with Betty Ryan, Athens, Greece, July 1971.

314   Twice a day: Jay Martin: Interview with Betty Ryan, Athens, Greece, July 1971.

314   "I have just read": Lawrence Durrell to HM, Aug. 1935, in George Wickes, ed., *Lawrence Durrell and Henry Miller: A Private Correspondence* (New York: E.P. Dutton & Co., Inc., 1963), p. 4.

315   a true sensitive: HM to Conrad Moricand, 7-21-36, UT; "Paradise Lost," Original Version, UT.

315   "a flower-like grace": Richard G. Osborn to HM, 11-28-38.

317   letters he would have *liked* to receive: HM to Richard G. Osborn, n.d. [1935].

317   hoped to illustrate: HM to Richard G. Osborn, n.d. [1935], Osborn Papers, Folder 2.

317   T.S. Eliot: T.S. Eliot to HM, 6-13-35, 8-16-35, 1-1-36.

317   "Opinions": including comments by Paul Rosenfeld, Blaise Cendrars, Raymond Queneau, George Orwell, Edmund Wilson, Aldous Huxley, William Carlos Williams, and Henry L. Mencken.

318   "I am full of Mars": HM to ES, 6-12-33; HM to Richard G. Osborn, 2-6-33.

319   Bijoux: HM to ES, 5-12-34.

319   Jessica Hensley: HM to Sydney Omarr, 7-2-55, 2.

319   T.S. Eliot: T.S. Eliot to HM, 1-1-36.

319   Simon and Schuster: HM to Walter Lowenfels, n.d. [1935], 2, CWBL, UVA.

319   Bennett Cerf: HM to ES, 7-6-36, 4.

320   Alfred Knopf: HM to Francis F. Dobo, 5-10-37; HM to Huntington Cairns, 6-17-37, Cairns Collection, LC; HM to Joe O'Regan, 10-11-37.

320   "Max": Manuel Bickel to HM, 9-5-35; HM to Joe O'Regan, 11-4-37.

320   rejected *Max:* HM to Huntington Cairns, Oct. 1935, Cairns Collection, LC; HM to Abraham Rattner, 11-8-37.

320   inscribed copy: HM to AN, 12-12-36, SIU.

320   Herbert West: HM to Herbert F. West, 6-16-37, West Collection, DC.

320   V.F. Calverton: Huntington Cairns to HM, 2-25-37, Cairns Collection, LC; HM to V.F. Calverton, n.d. [Spring, 1937].

321   Cairns: HM to Huntington Cairns, 6-17-37, Cairns Collection, LC.

Seventeen: Historia Calamitatum

322   He had tried to tell: TC Ms, "Rejected Pages," in HM to Huntington
        Cairns, 6-11-36, Cairns Collection, LC.
322   gave up his notes: PN, II, 64.
323   Keyserling's: HM to Count Herman Keyserling, 8-25-38.
323   Fenollosa's: PN, III, 104.
323   remarks by Ralph Waldo Emerson: TC Ms, 110-1.
323   thematic key: "rejected pages," TC Ms, 1-25.
323   "Gottlieb": "Dream Center," 10-6-32, 12; HM to Count Herman
        Keyserling, 8-25-38; "Original Dream Manuscript" [1932].
324   he told Calverton: HM to V.F. Calverton, n.d. [1938].
324   "Land of Fuck": HM to Huntington Cairns, 3-19-38, Cairns
        Collection, LC.
325   Dante's Beatrice: PN, III, 39.
325   That conclusion: T CAP Ms, Original Conclusion, in HM to ES
        8-25-38, 2-5.
325   "The All-Intelligent": MPM, 1-3.
325   "The Sleeping Sleeper": HM to Jack Kahane, 11-5-38; HM to
        Maurice Girodias; 3-16-46.
326   "Some Pleasant Monsters": HM to Richard G. Osborn,
        10-25-38, 2-5.

Eighteen: The Last of the Best Days

328   "a special begging letter": "Dear Mr. So-and-So's," MPM, 8-5-37;
        "Letter Announcing Booster," 8-19-37, UT.
329   "Villa Seurat Series": "Villa Seurat Series/Editor: Henry Miller,"
        announcement issued by Obelisk Press, 1-4; Jay Martin: Interview
        with Betty Ryan, Athens, Greece, July 1971; HM "Agreement with
        Jack Kahane of Obelisk Press," 12-14-37.
330   such as Esquire: HM to Arnold Gingrich, 8-15-37.
330   numerous American booksellers: for instance, HM to Stanley Rose,
        10-23-37.
330   banned books smuggled: HM to Joe O'Regan, 11-4-37, 4; and
        1-13-38.
330   Anaïs held: HM to ES, 11-11-34.
330   Anaïs aided him: HM to Walter Lowenfels, n.d. [1936],
        CWBL, UVA.
331   "I NEED DOUGH": for instance, HM to John Gawsworth,
        10-7-37, 1-6.
331   literary rarities: HM to "Whom It May Concern," 2-1-38.
331   from his father: in Henry Miller Family Letters, 1937.
332   a phony answer: HM to Lawrence Durrell, Sunday, [Dec.] 1937; HM
        to Henry Miller, Sr., 12-15-37, 1-3.

Nineteen: *Salut au Monde*

334   *Draco and the Ecliptic*: HM to Huntington Cairns, 7-23-38, Cairns Collection, LC; HM to ES, 7-27-38; HM to Richard G. Osborn, n.d. [1938]; "This is My Answer," UT; HM to John Cowper Powys, 5-19-50.

334   "joyous book of the mystic": HM to Count Herman Keyserling, 8-25-38.

335   One English critic: HM to ES, 5-11-38, 2.

335   occult and mystical traditions: HM to Count Herman Keyserling, 6-7-38 and 6-25-38; HM to Sydney Omarr, 7-2-55; HM to Conrad Moricand, 6-3-38, UT; HM to Huntington Cairns 3-28-38, Cairns Collection, LC; HM to ES, 5-11-38 and 8-25-38.

336   But after 1935: HM to ES, 7-6-36 and 11-4-38.

336   told Joe O'Regan: HM to Joe O'Regan, 10-11-37.

337   In August, 1938: HM to Bern Porter, n.d. [1944], in manuscript of "Semblance of a Devoted Past."

337   imprinted "June": HM to Huntington Cairns, 9-25-38, Cairns Collection, LC.

337   In several letters: HM to ES 5-3-39 and 9-27-38; HM to Bessie Breuer, 5-2-39, UT.

339   editor of a Chicago daily: HM to James Taylor Dunn, 6-20-39.

339   "concentration camp": Jay Martin: Interview with Raymond Queneau, Paris, France, Aug. 1971.

BOOK THREE

Passage to America

One: *Journey to an Antique Land*

355   and simply sit: AN to Alfred Perlès, n.d. [1939], UT.

356   "The image": Miller's Horoscope, UT.

358   Old Brazil Coffee House: Jay Martin: Interviews with Charles Halderman and Nikos Gatsos, Hania, Crete; and Athens, Greece, July 1971.

359   Henry simply floated: HM to V.F. Calverton, 7-29-39 and 9-20-39.

360   Katsimbalis: HM to ES, 9-9-39; Jay Martin: Interview with George C. Katsimbalis, Athens, Greece, July 1971.

360   The painter Ghikas: Jay Martin: Interview with Nikos Ghikas, London, England, Aug. 1971.

360   In Hydra, Seferis: George Seferis to HM, 2-5-50.

362   "In Crete": HM to Huntington Cairns, 9-15-39, Cairns Collection, LC.

362   his young son Maurice: HM to Huntington Cairns, 10-15-39, Cairns Collection, LC.

363   pirated letter-press edition: G. Legman to HM, 1-26-40, Cairns
           Collection, LC; G. Legman to Kathryn Mecham, [Aug.] 1940.
363   "Too many times": James Laughlin to HM, 12-30-39.
363   On December 5: HM to ES, 12-5-39.
363   "The Germans": HM to Huntington Cairns, 10-15-39, Cairns
           Collection, LC.
363   his choice was only: HM to ES, 9-20-39.
365   "the world of nature": HM to V.F. Calverton, 9-20-39.
365   he told Osborn: HM to Richard G. Osborn, 2-26-39.

Two: A Man with No Fortune and a Name to Come

367   Anderson was in: HM to Huntington Cairns, 3-12-40, Cairns
           Collection, LC.
367   made his way home: HM to Huntington Cairns, 3-15-40, Cairns
           Collection, LC.
369   "Mara-Marignan": "Mara-Marignan Marinated," Original Ms, 1940;
           HM to ES, 10-19-42; HM to Tullah Hanley, 7-12-56, UT.
369   sheer pornography: "Opus Pistorum," Volumes I, II, Institute for Sex
           Research, IU; also typescript dated: "Carmel 1950, Sunken Eye
           Press"; G. Legman to Bern Porter, 7-27-46 and 10-17-46; HM to
           AN, n.d. [c. May 1941], SIU.
369   "I was cracked": HM to Huntington Cairns, 3-12-40, Cairns
           Collection, LC.
371   the Dalis: HM to John Slocum, n.d. [Aug. 1940].
371   Kahane wrote to promise: Maurice J. Kahane to HM, 3-7-40.
371   Victor Weybright: HM to Victor Weybright, 10-27-48.
371   To John Slocum: "Manuscripts Turned Over to John J. Slocum by
           Henry Miller," 7-3-40; and "Material Turned Over to John J. Slocum
           by Henry Miller," 8-29-40.
371   Slocum couldn't place: John Slocum to HM, 8-16-40.
372   Harold Strauss: Harold Strauss to John Slocum, 7-29-40, NYPL; "An
           Open Letter to Private Alfred Perlès" [cancelled passages], 16.
372   described a book: "America, The Air-Conditioned Nightmare,"
           original outline.
373   Rattner: HM to Herbert F. West, 8-20-40, West Collection, DC.
373   Doubleday: HM to John Slocum, n.d. [Aug. 1940]; HM to Lawrence
           Clark Powell, 3-28-65.
373   I plan to make: HM to Huntington Cairns, Sept. 1940, Cairns
           Collection, LC.
374   Duhamel's: HM to AN, n.d. [c. May 1941], SIU.
374   "to fall in love with the country": HM to Herbert F. West, 8-20-40,
           West Collection, DC.

Three: The Air-Conditioned Nightmare

376   to Allen Tate . . . and to Herbert West: HM to Allen Tate, 9-16-40, Tate Papers, PU; HM to Herbert F. West, 9-14-40, West Collection DC.

377   Rattner accompanied: HM to Huntington Cairns, 5-2-41, Cairns Collection, LC.

377   several great arcs: "Complete Itinerary of Nightmare Trip for J[ames] L[aughlin] ," 1-3; "Itinerary" in "Red Notebook."

377   his father was seriously ill: HM to Knud Merrild, 7-4-44; HM to Syndey Omarr, 10-16-52.

378   "25,000 miles": *The Nightmare Notebook,* New York: New Direction, 1975, unpaged facsimilie. Miller's estimate is, of course, hyperbolic, an expression and symbol of fatigue. This reference and other undocumented references to Miller's trip around America come from Miller's notebook kept for recording this trip. The New Directions edition is a facsimilie of the original notebook in Special Collections at UCLA from which I have taken my references.

379   "both poor": HM to Eva Sikelianou, 2-7-43.

379   South Bunker Hill Avenue: "Bunker Hill" in "Pages Excised from The Air-Conditioned Nightmare," SFPL.

380   Main Street: "Material Excluded from The Air-Conditioned Nightmare," 192; [In *The Last Laugh,* one of Miller's favorite films, Emil Jannings played a lavatory attendant. See Miller's mezzotint, "Christianity at the Sink," MPM.]

381   the script-writer Gordon Kahn: HM to Hilaire Hiler, 7-15-41.

382   Christmas Day, 1941: HM to Huntington Cairns, 12-16-41, Cairns Collection, LC.

382   wrote "Finis": "Original Ending to the Air-Conditioned Nightmare," "Coda," 34-47, CWBL, UVA.

382-3 wrote to his agent Henry Volkening: HM to Henry Volkening, 1-12-42.

Four: Ventilating the Soul

384   he resumed work: HM to Huntington Cairns, Feb. 1942, Cairns Collection, LC, and Huntington Cairns to HM, 10-16-42.

385   ". . . a spiritual corner": HM to Huntington Cairns, 1942, Cairns Collection, LC.

385   The divine Laure: HM to Lawrence Durrell 4-7-44, 2 [excised from published letters]; HM to Sydney Omarr, 10-16-52.

386   lost their "accord": AN to Emil White, n.d., White Collection.

386   "to ventilate my soul,": HM to Herbert F. West, 1-21-42, West Collection, DC.

387   to sign his letters: HM to Lawrence Clark Powell, 12-19-42.

387   slept on a cot: HM to Huntington Cairns, Sept. 1942, Cairns Collec-

tion, LC; HM to Lawrence Durrell, 9-15-42, SIU [passage excised from published letters].

387   "the lowest and craziest": HM to Huntington Cairns [c. Sept. 1942], Cairns Collection, LC.

387   a story idea: "Notes for Imaginary Exotic Film," MM.

388   offered screen work: HM to ES, 11-16-42; Eva Broche de Rothermann to HM, 10-23-42; HM to Herbert F. West, 10-15-42, West Collection, DC.

388   addenda to his synopsis: "Insert (on film itself)," West Collection, DC.

389   superannuated actor: HM to Lawrence Durrell, 9-15-42, SIU [passage excised from published letters].

389   he wrote to Nin: HM to AN, n.d. [1942] , SIU.

390   agent named Donohue: HM to AN, n.d. [Dec. 42] , SIU; HM to Mr. Donohue, 12-12-42, YU; HM to Dudley Nichols, 3-6-43, YU.

390   raise the fare: HM to Huntington Cairns, Nov. 1942; HM to Claude Houghton, Nov. 1942, 5.

390   interviewing ex-convicts: HM to AN, n.d. [1941], SIU.

390   Office of War Information: HM to Leonard Levinson, 12-8-42; HM to Lewis F. Gettler, 4-5-43.

391   "Between you and me": HM to Huntington Cairns, 12-22-42; HM to Cyril Connolly, 1-5-43, UT.

391   sworn never to reach: HM to Christopher Morley, n.d. [1942].

391   books to review: HM to Herbert F. West, 1-4-43, 1-18-43, and 3-6-43, West Collection, DC; HM to Dudley Nichols, 6-11-43, YU.

391   "neurotic cunt": HM to Savington Crampton, 4-14-43 and HM to Crampton, "Friday After Easter" [April, 1943]; HM to Huntington Cairns, 6-12-43.

392   he had finally asked too much of Anaïs: HM, "Notes on Rimbaud" Ms (1945); HM to ES, 6-12-43; HM to LD, 4-7-44; Anaïs Nin, "Diary" Ms. n.d. [Spring 1942], SIU; HM to Sydney Omarr, 10-16-52.

Five: Sevasty-Sevasty

393   "Revered one!": HM to Herbert F. West, 11-3-43, West Collection, DC.

393   Sevasty Koutsaftis: "My Life With Sevasty," 2-3; HM to Dudley Nichols, 6-11-43, YU.

393   soon wrote to Henry: Sevasty Koustaftis to HM, 3-31-43.

394   Lockheed: Sevasty Koutsaftis to HM, 4-7-43.

394   "Anything may happen": HM to ES, 6-12-43.

394   wrote a poem: "O Lake of Light," MPM; HM to Tambimuttu ["Keep title, please! Dedicated to Sevasty Koutsaftis"]; typed manuscript of poem is in HM to Sevasty Koutsaftis, n.d. [Spring 1943].

394   slip it under his pillow: HM to Lawrence Durrell, 4-7-44 [passage

excised from published letters].

395   in June 1943: Sevasty Koutsaftis to HM, 6-11-43.

395   "I know now": HM to Sevasty Koustaftis, n.d. [July 1943].

395   to Eva Sikelianou: HM to Eva Sikelianou, 7-31-43.

396   Pierce Harwell: HM to Savington Crampton, n.d. [March 1943]: Manuscript Notes on Rimbaud Opus"; Pierce Harwell to HM, 6-29-43.

396   "never hurts": HM to Herbert F. West, 8-16-43 and 11-4-43, West Collection, DC.

396   autobiographical book: "My Life With Sevasty."

Six: The Green House Thatched with Women's Hair

397   painting meant almost everything: HM to Alfred Stieglitz, 3-19-43; HM to Syndey Omarr, 10-16-52.

397   strolled by the shop: HM to Herbert F. West, 10-8-43, West Collection, DC.

398   "House of Analysis": "Open Letter to All and Sundry (No. 3)," MM, 1.

398   a little invitational leaflet: the "Open Letter" was printed on both sides of one sheet; "Layout for Printed Notice," in letter of HM to Herbert F. West, 11-4-43, West Collection, DC.

399   Man and Julie Ray: Jay Martin: Interview with Man Ray, Paris France, August 1971; HM to George Metzger, 9-14-48.

399   "air of authenticity": HM to Herbert F. West, 11-4-43, West Collection, DC.

399   "Well, Emil ol' top": HM to ES, 1-3-43, 2.

400   "Open Letter to All and Sundry": HM to Herbert F. West, 4-10-43 and 11-22-43; Henry Morton Robinson to HM, 7-16-43; HM to Huntington Cairns, 10-3-43; HM to Abraham Rattner, 11-8-43.

400   James T. Farrell to HM, 12-4-43.

400   screenwriting contract: HM to ES, 11-3-43.

400   admirers appeared: Paul Weiss to HM, 5-7-43.

401   touchingly to Abe Rattner: HM to Abraham Rattner 11-8-43, 5.

Seven: A Paradise for the Artist

402   in Mexico: HM to Bern Porter, 1-18-44.

402     $50 for fifty weeks: HM to "Dear Friends" [twenty friends received copies], Easter Sunday [1944].

403   from Henry Volkening: Henry Volkening to HM, 4-24-44.

403   His nearest revelation: Anonymous Patron to HM, 6-29-44.

404   Henry sent $100: HM to Bern Porter, 5-4-44; HM to Huntington Cairns, 5-5-44 and 5-31-44, Cairns Collection, LC; HM to Bern Porter, 7-7-44.

404   "I think you know": HM to Huntington Cairns, 5-5-44, 3, Cairns
           Collection, LC.
404   "a 3-ring circus": HM to Knud Merrild, 2-28-44.
405   "nearest to Tibet": HM to George Dibbern, 4-17-45.
405   "No monkey business": HM to Herbert F. West, 3-13-44, West
           Collection, DC.
405   ten dollars a month: HM to F.J. Temple, 6-27-65.
405   "doing my utmost": HM to Knud Merrild, 4-20-44.
405   to Osbert Sitwell: HM to Osbert Sitwell, 4-9-44.
406   dressed in a long robe: UCLA Photograph Collection, HM's annota-
           tion: "Photo of HM during early Partington Ridge days when he
           aspired to be a monk."
406   said his morning prayers: Bern Porter, "Notes," UM, 1944.
405   told Bern Porter: HM to Bern Porter, n.d. [Feb. 1944].
407   "I get so many letters": HM to Knud Merrild, 4-20-44.
408   *The Rosy Crucifixion:* HM to Frederic Carter, 4-14-44; HM to Cyril
           Connolly, 1-9-43, UT.
408   Now at Big Sur: Interviews with Emil White, Ephraim Doner, and
           Noel Young, in Big Sur, 1977.

Eight: Other Bright Messengers

410   "All I need": HM to Bern Porter, [March] 12, 1944.
410   June Lancaster: the following account is drawn from: Harry
           Herschkowitz, undated letters to HM, from February to May 1944;
           June Lancaster to HM, 2-15-44, 2-17- to 2-21-44, 3-4-44, 3-17-44,
           3-20-44, 4-11-44 [telegram], 5-8-44, 5-11-44 [telegram], 5-19-44
           [telegram]; June Lancaster, "Notes on Henry Miller" [1944]; HM to
           June Lancaster, Feb. 1944, 4-30-44, 5-5-44; HM to Lawrence Dur-
           rell, 5-5-44; HM to Knud Merrild, 5-19-44 and 5-31-44; HM to
           Bern Porter, 6-20-44.
412   mother was gravely ill: HM to Huntington Cairns, n.d. [early Oct.
           1944], Cairns Collection, LC.
413   "Dresden figurine": Walker Winslow to HM, n.d., HL.
413   subversive and a traitor: HM to Herbert F. West, 1-26-45 and
           5-12-45, West Collection, DC; HM to Huntington Cairns, 6-6-45,
           Cairns Collection, LC.
414   Henry and Lepska were married: HM to Herbert F. West, 12-18-44,
           West Collection, DC; HM to Knud Merrild, 12-20-44; HM to
           Maurice Girodias, 6-20-45.
415   the "incest-motive": WL, 7-8.
416   "It's a girl": HM to Huntington Cairns, 11-20-45, Cairns Collection,
           LC.

Nine: Money and How It Came His Way

419   *Into the Night Life:* HM to Herbert F. West, 4-4-46 and 3-13-47, West Collection, DC; Bezalel Schatz, "The Story of the Making of the Book [*Into the Night Life*]"; HM, "Text for Circular on *Into the Night Life*" [1947].

420   "I can bide": HM to Bezalel Schatz, 4-30-47.

421   Jack Kahane's son: Maurice Girodias to HM, 10-2-44; HM to Dane Rudhyar, 10-20-55.

421   prohibited the exportation: Maurice Girodias to HM, 1-3-46 and 3-15-46; Michael A. Hoffman to HM, 9-19-46.

422   half of the royalties: HM to Patience Ross, 9-25-45.

422   Agence Hoffman: Michael A. Hoffman to Patience Ross, 9-18-45; Michael A. Hoffman to HM, 5-23-47.

423   "Little hope": HM to Huntington Cairns, 6-4-47.

423   "Come the worst" HM to Maurice Girodias, 7-10-46.

424   "I am sorry": HM to Maurice Nadeau, 2-1-49.

425   "Where Henry Miller is specially great": John Cowper Powys to Dante Zaccagnini, 8-17-50.

Ten: Devils In Paradise

427   a plea from Conrad Moricand: HM to Conrad Moricand, 10-6-46, UT.

427   1947 he cabled: HM to Conrad Moricand, UT; HM to Maurice Girodias, 7-10-47.

428   Caresse, he remarked: HM to Maurice Girodias, 8-9-47.

428   hardly had Moricand arrived: HM to ES, 2-12-48; Huntington Cairns to HM, 2-20-48.

429   at his wit's end: the Moricand affair is best summarized in HM to Conrad Moricand 4-29-48; HM to Werner Jost, 5-25-48 and 6-1-48; and HM to Sydney Omarr, 7-2-55.

429   *Chronicle:* July 8, 1948.

430   March of 1946: "The Miller Affair," 1-2; HM to Herbert F. West, 3-16-46, West Collection, DC.

430   Girodias gleefully: Maurice Girodias to HM, 9-14-46.

431   Girodias brought suit: HM to Herbert F. West, 9-30-47, West Collection, DC.

431   in the United States: Lepska Miller to Walker Winslow, n.d. [April 1947], HL.

431   Miller was counterattacking: HM to Maurice Girodias, 6-20-45, 8-20-45, 12-18-47.

431   "As you know": HM to Maurice Girodias, 9-30-48.

431   "In the autobiographical": HM to Maurice Nadeau, 12-15-49.

431   shrug off criticism": HM to Pierre Lesdain, 10-15-49; HM to Eugene Jolas, 10-8-50.

432   "Received Sexus from Paris": LD to HM, 9-5-49, in *Lawrence Durrell and Henry Miller: A Private Correspondence,* pp. 264-5.
432   "This time": HM to Pierre Lesdain, 10-15-49.
432   "What I want to tell you is this": HM to LD, 9-28-49, in *Lawrence Durrell and Henry Miller: A Private Correspondence,* pp. 267-269.
433   in late 1949: HM to ES, 12-29-49.
433   making wall charts: "Plexus Notes and Charts," SIU.

Eleven: Life's Traces

434   Instead of continuing: HM to Lawrence Clark Powell, 1-16-50.
434   it would "supplement": HM to "Dear Friends" [form letter] 2-4-50.
434-5   D.H. Lawrence and Maurice Maeterlinck: HM to Helene le Boterf, 4-25-51.
435   a moralizing book: "Preface," *The World of Books,* 2nd Version, 2; HM to Dante Zaccagnini, 2-27-50, UT; HM to Lawrence Clark Powell, 2-3-50.
435   "The Quick and the Dead": HM to Robert Vosper, 12-8-50.
436   Lepska's kindness: HM to Renate Gerhardt, 2-11-64, Gerhardt Collection.
436   Walker Winslow interceded: Walker Winslow to HM, 8-12-56, HL.
438   In her first letter: Eve McClure to HM, 11-20-51.
438   love notes: HM to Andrew Horn, 4-16-52; Eve McClure to Andrew Horn, 9-21-52.
438   She "reminds me": HM to Lawrence Durrell, 4-27-52 [passage excised from published letters].
438   a printed advertisement: HM to "Dear Friends," n.d. [Spring 1952].
439   needed all the dough: HM to Lawrence Clark Powell, 6-23-51, 7-4-51, 11-14-51.
439   New Year's Eve: "Mejores no Hay!", 1-19, CWBL, UVA.
440   famous as a movie star's: HM to Lawrence Clark Powell, 3-10-53.
441   "What is 'paradise' ": Eve Miller to Emil White, 2-11-53, White Collection.
441   George Katsimbalis: HM to Pére Raymond Leopold Bruckberger, 6-23-54.
441   to "reach the girl": HM to Richard G. Osborn, 11-1-34.
441   Around 1940 he had enlisted: HM to Joe O'Regan, 10-11-37, 11-4-37, 1-8-38, 2-15-38; John Slocum to Barbara Sandford, 8-21-40; John Slocum to HM, 8-21-40; HM to John Slocum, n.d. [late August 1940]; Barbara Berch to Barbara Sandford, n.d. [c. 1944].
441   the postman delivered: Barbara Sandford to HM, 2-10-54.
442   Barbara and Val together: Barbara Sandford to HM, 6-21-54.
442   "Lauretta tried": Alfred Perlès to HM, 1-2-55.

Twelve: A Womb in Which the Sun Is Bursting

443   "Now is the time": "Peace and Solitude: A Free Fantasia" [cancelled]; "A Potpourri," Original Version, including "Contents," UT.

443   "It flows": HM to Neville Armstrong, 6-13-55; HM to Michael A. Hoffman, 6-15-55; HM to Lawrence Clark Powell, n.d. [c. July 1955]; HM to Sydney Omarr, 7-2-55.

443   told his agent: HM to Michael A. Hoffman, 6-3-56.

443   "I nailed him": HM to Bezalel Schatz, 10-5-55.

443   theme of a Paradise Lost: Walker Winslow to HM, 8-12-56, HL; HM to Thomas Parkinson, 7-30-58.

444   his relationship to her: HM to Sydney Omarr, 8-14-55.

444   An old dream: "Dream Center," 47; T CAP Ms, Original Version, 25-6.

444   "When she dies": HM to Renate Gerhardt, 9-29-61, Gerhardt Collection.

445   "Christ!" Eve wrote: Eve Miller to Emil White, 2-25-56, White Collection.

445   Once, toward the end: Jay Martin: Interview with Renate Gerhardt, Berlin, Germany, August 1971; Jay Martin: Interview with Gerald Robitaille, Bourg-la-Reine and Paris, France, July and August 1971.

445   "A new life": HM to Paul Jacobs, 4-5-56.

445   getting Lauretta settled: HM to Lawrence Clark Powell, 4-6-56.

445   to sue him: Barbara Sandford to HM and Eve Miller, 6-8-57.

446   National Institute: Malcolm Cowley to HM, 2-13-57.

446   two tales written in 1940: HM to Ben Grauer, 5-31-56; "Quiet Days in Clichy," Three Revisions of Two Short Stories, UT; HM to Maurice Girodias, 2-15-57.

446   Henry had a vision: HM to Sydney Omarr, 12-18-58.

447   "Reichel . . . ": HM to Dante Zaccagnini, 1-3-59.

447   Working for a few months: HM to Lawrence Durrell, 4-25-58 [HM marginalia]; Eve Miller to Jean Bagby, 5-15-58; HM to Alfred Perlès, 1-14-59; Eve Miller to Lawrence Durrell and Claude Durrell, 3-18-59.

Thirteen: We Who Make Life Unliveable

449   Rosset mentioned: HM to Barney Rosset, n.d. [c. June 17, 1959], SIU.

450   Miller explained: K.S. Giniger to HM, 4-9-51.

450   Penguin books: HM to Victor Weybright, 10-27-48.

450   George Oldhausen: HM to George Oldhausen, 6-26-50.

450   When two film makers: James B. Harris and Stanley Kubrick to HM, 6-10-58; HM to James B. Harris and Stanley Kubrick, 6-20-58.

450   her life was sterile: HM to Renate Gerhardt, 7-24-60, Gerhardt Collection.

451   Eve shared the blame: Jay Martin: Interviews with Emil White, October 1977.

451   Her name was Caryl Hill: Jay Martin: Interview with Caryl Hill, January 1978.

451   "I know you and Henry": Eve Miller to Lawrence and Claude Durrell, 11-7-59 and 12-6-59; Emil White to Lawrence Clark Powell, 12-2-59.

452   Before the . . . Festival started: "Itinerary of Henry Miller and Vincent Birge," 9-24-60 to 6-17-61 and "Note to Itinerary."

452   Rowohlt's assistant: HM to Eve Miller, 4-23-60; Jay Martin: Interview with Renate Gerhardt, Berlin, Germany, August 1971.

453   the Italian actress Falconetti: HM to Eve Miller, 11-29-60.

453   she decided to act: Eve Miller to Lepska Verzeano, 5-17-60.

453   time to get a divorce: Eve Miller to HM, 5-17-60.

454   "I think all you say": HM to Eve Miller, 5-22-60.

454   Caryl, he remarked: HM to Renate Gerhardt, 7-5-60, Gerhardt Collection.

454   "on—like some wandering ghost": HM to Renate Gerhardt, 7-24-60, Gerhardt Collection.

454   "Deep down": HM to Renate Gerhardt, 8-8-60, Gerhardt Collection.

454   "St. Valentine": HM to Renate Gerhardt, 7-24-61, Gerhardt Collection.

454   "Gottlieb": HM to Renate Gerhardt, 11-28-60, Gerhardt Collection.

454   "It's such a wonderful": HM to Renate Gerhardt, 11-28-60, Gerhardt Collection.

454   "Love me": HM to Renate Gerhardt, 11-8-60, Gerhardt Collection.

454   "a new life and love": Ben Grauer to HM, 12-9-60; HM to Gerald Robitaille, 12-13-60, SIU.

454   news of his divorce: HM to Eve Miller, 12-12-60.

455   "More and more": HM to Renate Gerhardt, 11-17-60, Gerhardt Collection.

455   on Christmas day 1960: HM to Eve Miller, 12-28-60.

456   Germany was depressing: HM to Renate Gerhardt, 11-7-60, Gerhardt Collection; HM to Eve Miller, 3-18-61.

456   "I seem to have gone": HM to Eve Miller, 6-3-61.

456   sensed Renate's disappointment: HM to Renate Gerhardt, 6-3-61 and 7-9-61, Gerhardt Collection.

Fourteen: Over the Equator

458   She had married: Richard G. Osborn to HM, n.d. [Jan. 1945]; Janice Pelham to HM, n.d. [1945]; HM to Robert W. Hill, 11-5-55; A.K. Baxter to HM, 11-3-56.

458   "I have not the courage": HM to Mr. Oldfield [Claude Houghton], 1-31-42.

458   June cried for help: June E. Corbett to HM, 12-25-56.

459   a single room in a bad area: June E. Corbett to HM, 1-24-59.

459   "wonderfully well": June E. Corbett to HM, 10-7-61.

459   become furious when she learned: HM to AN, 5-7-55; Alfred Perlès to AN, 5-9-55.

459   gave her an idea: HM to Eve Miller, 5-26-62.

460   "still the same": HM to Eve Miller, 7-31-62.

460   "bright angelic smile": HM to Eve Miller, 10-14-62.

460   Rosset . . . proposed: Barney Rosset to Michael A. Hoffman, 4-2-59.

460   Rosset next offered: Barney Rosset to Michael A. Hoffman, 6-23-59; HM to Barney Rosset, 8-5-59; HM to Lawrence Clark Powell, 2-5-60.

461   "We all need money": HM to Maurice Girodias, 1-28-60.

461   "hit like a bomb": HM to Jean Fanchette, 2-15-60.

461   "drastic changes": HM to Barney Rosset, 1-20-60.

462   "I have been waging": HM to Barney Rosset, 7-14-60.

464   took up his pen and signed: HM to Eve Miller, 2-20-61.

464   troubles started immediately: voluminous legal documents in the Elmer Gertz Collection, LC, were consulted in full.

Fifteen: A New Life Revisited, and Other Burlesques

466   he took a furnished room: HM to Lawrence Clark Powell, 9-27-61; HM to Eve Miller, 9-25-61; HM to Renate Gerhardt, 9-24-61, Gerhardt Collection.

467   not known to the manager: HM to Renate Gerhardt, 9-29-61, Gerhardt Collection.

467   tried to work on . . . *Nexus*: HM to Renate Gerhardt, 2-1-62, Gerhardt Collection.

467   the money disappeared so rapidly: HM to Renate Gerhardt, 1-6-63, 7-9-63, 7-18-63, 8-21-63, 8-27-63, 9-3-63, 9-15-63, 10-5-64, 11-25-64, Gerhardt Collection; HM to Margaret Mondragon, 12-5-64.

468   Tony wrote plaintively: Tony Miller to HM, 10-18-62.

468   Henry told Renate: HM to Renate Gerhardt, 12-15-62, Gerhardt Collection.

468   Henry liked the idea: HM to Eve Miller, n.d. [Nov. 1962]; HM to Renate Gerhardt, 2-7-62, 11-16-62, 12-15-62, Gerhardt Collection.

468   divorce from Eve: HM to Eve Miller, 4-26-61.

468   In February of 1963: HM to Lawrence Clark Powell, 2-25-63.

468   "As I arrrived": George Wickes to Lawrence Durrell, 2-27-62.

Sixteen: Cancer, Schmanser What's the Difference
so Long as You're Healthy

470   reached Alfred Perlès: Alfred Perlès to HM, 8-31-62; Elmer Gertz to
           HM, 3-29-63.
470   It was alleged that: HM to Renate Gerhardt, Feb. 1964, Gerhardt
           Collection; HM to Eve Miller, 3-1-64 and 3-6-64.
471   he began a one-act burlesque: HM to Renate Gerhardt, 9-15-63,
           Gerhardt Collection.
471   part owner of the film: HM to Renate Gerhardt, 6-27-64, Gerhardt
           Collection.
471   Then Perlès complicated: HM to Alfred Perlès, 5-25-64 and 6-22-64.
472   Ziva Rodam: HM to Eve Miller, Oct. 1963.
472   "as easily and as frequently": HM to Nicholas Nabokov, 4-21-63; HM
           to Renate Gerhardt, 1-30-64, Gerhardt Collection.
472   Someone was always hounding him: HM to Alfred Perlès, 7-5-64,
           UT.
472   Rellim Productions: HM to Harry Millard, 7-5-63.
473   To Renate Gerhardt alone: HM to Renate Gerhardt, 7-9-63, 7-18-63,
           8-21-63, 8-29-63, 10-5-64, and *passim.*, Gerhardt Collection.
473   as he lay awake at night: HM to Alfred Perlès, 5-25-64, UT.

Seventeen: Another Goethe

474   a "whacking" bill: HM to Renate Gerhardt, 8-8-64, Gerhardt
           Collection.
474   a string of young women: HM to Tullah Hanley, 7-21-63, UT; HM to
           Eve Miller, 4-15-64 and 4-23-64; HM to Alfred Perlès, 5-25-64, UT.
474   Tony . . . and Val: HM to Alfred Perlès, 9-17-64.
474   American publication of *Sexus*: George Wickes, "Conversation with
           Henry Miller, 6-21-65," Wickes Collection.
474   Henry admitted: "For the Minister of the Interior," 1-2.
475   He told Maxwell Geismar: HM to Maxwell Geismar, 1-10-66; HM to
           Renate Gerhardt, 6-18-63, Gerhardt Collection.
476   one photograph album: HM to Monsieur Fresnay, 6-16-65.
476   What did it matter: HM to Alfred Perlès, 5-21-65, UT.
476   She wrote to Henry in 1962: HM to Eve Miller, 4-4-62.
477   He fell in love: HM to Gerald Robitaille, 8-9-66, SIU.
477   Prevalakis's novel: HM to Alfred Perlès, 5-21-65, UT.
481   Hiroko Tokuda: HM to Bezalel Schatz, 6-4-67; HM to Rokuro
           Tokuda, 9-9-67; Rokuro Tokuda to HM, 9-11-67 and 3-2-68; HM to
           A.S. Neill, 10-14-68; Jay Martin: Interviews with Gerald Robitaille,
           Bourg-la-Reine and Paris, July and August, 1971.
481   told Theodore Schroeder: HM to Theodore Schroeder, 3-9-42.
482   To an interviewer who was praising him in 1976: Jonathan Kirsch,

"Henry Miller at 84: The Prisoner of Pacific Palisades," *Los Angeles Free Press,* July 30–August 5, 1976, 1, 6-7. In this section I also use: Ben Reuven, "Miller Recollects in Tranquility," *Los Angeles Times Book Review,* April 4, 1976, p. 3; and Jonathan Cott, "Reflections of a Cosmic Tourist," *Rolling Stone,* February 27, 1975, pp 35-46, 57.

483   "die at the typewriter": HM to Ron Phelps, 2-17-63.

485   "If I could go backwards": HM to Gerald Robitaille, 11-13-53.

Epilogue: The Final Dissolving

488   "I never read a thing Norman Mailer": quoted in Jonathan Kirsch, "Henry Miller at 84: The Prisoner of Pacific Palisades," *Los Angeles Free Press,* July 30–August 5, 1976, 1, 7.

493   "You refer to my researches": HM to Jay Martin, 10-17-72, Jay Martin Collection.

Index

547